Democracy in India

This volume situates Indian democracy in the context of the basic principles of democratic theory and discusses its relationship with civil society, cultural diversity, and development. The essayists explore a variety of themes, including the colonial lineage of democracy in independent India and its inherited contradictions; the complex relationship between the state and democracy and whether democratic politics has undermined the state's capability to govern; the relationship between democracy and development; and the impact of caste and religious identities on India's democracy. The volume also assesses India's unique experience of negotiating cultural diversity through democratic institutional mechanisms.

While identifying tensions between political democracy and economic development, it looks at how democracy is experienced at the local level, especially through institutions of local self-government. It also examines the future of Indian democracy as a variety of political discourses—from Dalit political mobilization to Hindutva—seek to redefine it.

The *Themes in Politics* series presents essays on important issues in the study of political science and Indian politics. Each volume in the series brings together the most significant articles and debates on an issue, and contains a substantive introduction and bibliography.

OTHER BOOKS IN THE SERIES

The Indian Public Sphere
Readings in Media History
Arvind Rajagopal (ed.)

Language and Politics in India
Asha Sarangi (ed.)

Globalization and Politics in India
Baldev Raj Nayar (ed.)

Hindu Nationalism and Governance
John McGuire and Ian Copland (eds)
(Oxford India Paperbacks)

Civil Society and Democracy
A Reader
Carolyn M. Elliott (ed.)
(Oxford India Paperbacks)

Parties and Party Politics in India
Zoya Hasan (ed.)
(Oxford India Paperbacks)

Democracy in India
Niraja Gopal Jayal (ed.)
(Oxford India Paperbacks)

Gender and Politics in India
Nivedita Menon (ed.)
(Oxford India Paperbacks)

Secularism and its Critics
Rajeev Bhargava (ed.)
(Oxford India Paperbacks)

State and Politics in India
Partha Chatterjee (ed.)
(Oxford India Paperbacks)

Democracy in India

edited by

Niraja Gopal Jayal

Oxford University Press is a department of the University of Oxford. It furthers the University's objective of excellence in research, scholarship, and education by publishing worldwide. Oxford is a registered trademark of Oxford University Press in the UK and in certain other countries

Published in India by
Oxford University Press
22 Workspace, 2nd Floor, 1/22 Asaf Ali Road, New Delhi 110 002

First Edition published in 2001
Oxford India Paperbacks 2007
27th impression 2025

ISBN-13: 978-0-19-569157-3
ISBN-10: 0-19-569157-1

Typeset by Excellent Laser Typesetters, Delhi 110 034
Printed in India by Manipal Technologies Limited, Manipal

for

Sujata Mehta
in friendship

and

Geeta Vohra Ramadhyani
in fond memory

Acknowledgements to Publishers

The publishers wish to thank the following for permission to include the articles/extracts in this volume:

Frank Cass & Company Limited for James Chiriyankandath, ‘“Democracy” Under the Raj: Elections and Separate Representation in British India’, *Journal of Commonwealth and Comparative Politics*, vol. 30, no. 1, pp. 39–64 and Subrata Mitra, ‘Ballot Box and Local Power: Electoral Politics in an Indian Village’, *Journal of Commonwealth and Comparative Politics*, vol. 17, no. 3. Reprinted with permission from *Journal of Commonwealth and Comparative Politics*, published by Frank Cass & Company Limited, 900 Eastern Avenue, Essex, England. Copyright Frank Cass and Company Limited.

Cassell and Company for Rajni Kothari, ‘The Crisis of the Moderate State and the Decline of Democracy’ in Peter Lyon and James Manor (eds) *Transfer and Transformation: Political Institutions in the New Commonwealth*, Leicester University Press, Leicester, UK, 1983.

Cambridge University Press for Atul Kohli, ‘Political Change in a Democratic Developing Country’ in Kohli, *Democracy and Discontent: India's Growing Crisis of Governability*, 1990 and for Richard C. Crook and James Manor ‘India (Karnataka)’ (abridged) in Crook and Manor, *Democracy and Decentralisation in South Asia and West Africa*, 1988.

University of Chicago Press, Llyod I. Rudolph and Susanne Hoeber Rudolph for Rudolphs' abridged and merged versions of Chapters 7 and 8 from *In Pursuit of Lakshmi: The Political Economy of the Indian State*, 1987.

Basil Blackwell Limited, Oxford and UNESCO for Pramod Parajuli, 'Power and Knowledge in Development Discourse: New Social Movements and the State in India', *International Social Science Journal*, 127, 1991, pp. 173–90.

University of California Press, Berkeley, for Walter Hauser and Wendy Singer, 'The Democratic Rite: Celebration and Participation in the Indian Elections,' *Asian Survey*, vol. XXVI, no. 9, 1986.

American Political Science Review and Arend Lijphart, for Arend Lijphart, 'The Puzzle of Indian Democracy: A Consociational Interpretation', 90(2), 1996.

Economic and Political Weekly for Deepak Nayyar, 'Economic Development and Political Democracy: Interaction of Economics and Politics in Independent India', *EPW*, 5 December 1998.

Editor's Acknowledgements

My special thanks to Partha Chatterjee for his unfailingly prompt and helpful advice on a variety of issues relating to the volume. At the Oxford University Press, this book moved from the efficient custodianship of Nitasha Devasar to the unobtrusive but competent and amiable editorship of Gaurav Ghose. I thank them both.

I am grateful to James Chiriyankandath, James Manor, Subrata Mitra, Deepak Nayyar, and Susanne and Lloyd Rudolph, for their help in obtaining permissions. I thank Neera Chandhoke for her cheerful forbearance in serving as a sounding board for even quarterbaked ideas, and Zoya Hasan for bringing to my notice one of the articles included in this volume.

The Introduction to this volume has been written keeping in mind an essentially student readership. I would like to thank all my students, past and present, for their invisible, but not intangible, contribution to this effort, and hope that they will find this collection useful.

Contents

Tables

Figures

Contributors

PRANAB BARDHAN is Professor of Economics, University of California at Berkeley, and was the Chief Editor of the *Journal of Development Economics* from 1985–2003. He has many books and articles in the areas of political economy, agrarian institutions, rural poverty, and international trade, including *The Political Economy of Development; Development and Change*; *Development Microeconomics*; and *Scarcity, Conflicts and Cooperation*.

JAMES CHIRIYANKANDATH is Senior Lecturer in the Department of Politics and Modern History, London Metropolitan University. Awarded his doctorate by the School of Oriental and African Studies, University of London, he has been a British Academy Postdoctoral Fellow at the University of Hull. He has published widely on the politics and contemporary history of South Asia and the Middle East and has a particular interest in the politics of religion and nationalism.

RICHARD C. CROOK is Fellow in Governance at the Institute of Development Studies, University of Sussex. He has researched and published extensively in the areas of decentralization and local politics, elections, public administration and organizational performance. He has co-authored *Democracy and Decentralisation in South Asia and West Africa: Participation, Accountability and Performance.*

JEAN DRÈZE is Honorary Professor at the Delhi School of Economics, Delhi. His books include *Hunger and Public Action; India: Economic Development and Social Opportunity; Indian Development: Selected Regional Perspectives* and *The Dam and the Nation: Displacement and Resettlement in the Narmada Valley* (all as co-author or co-editor).

WALTER HAUSER is Professor Emeritus of History at the University of Virginia, Charlottesville, USA. His publications include an edited translation of Swami Sahajanand's *Jharkhand ke Kisan*, in *Swami Sahajanand and the Peasants of Jharkhand: A View from 1941.*

CHRISTOPHE JAFFRELOT is Director of CERI (Centre d'Etudes et de Recherches Internationales) at Sciences Po (Paris), and Research Director at the CNRS (Centre National de la Recherche Scientifique). He teaches South Asian politics to doctoral students at Sciences Po. He is the Director of the quarterly journal *Critique Internationale.* His recent publications are *The Hindu Nationalist Movement and Indian Politics, 1925 to 1990s*; *India's Silent Revolution: The Rise of the Lower Castes in North India;* and *Dr Ambedkar and Untouchability: Analysing and Fighting Caste.* He is also co-editor (with T.B. Hansen) of *The BJP and the Compulsions of Politics in India.*

NIRAJA GOPAL JAYAL is Professor of Political Science at the Centre for the Study of Law and Governance, Jawaharlal Nehru University, New Delhi. She has published articles on political theory and Indian political processes in learned journals, and her books include *Sidney and Beatrice Webb: Indian Diary; Drought, Policy and Politics in India*; *Democracy and the State: Welfare, Secularism and Development in Contemporary India*; and *Representing India: Ethnic Diversity and the Governance of Public Institutions.*

SUDIPTA KAVIRAJ is Professor of Indian Politics and Intellectual History, Columbia University. He has earlier taught Politics in the School of Oriental and African Studies, London, Jawaharlal Nehru University, New Delhi, and University of Burdwan, West Bengal. He is the author of *The Unhappy Consciousness: Bamkimchandra Chattopadhyay and the Formation of Nationalist Discourse in India*, and has edited *Politics in India* and co-edited *Civil Society: History and Possibilities.*

ATUL KOHLI is David K. E. Bruce Professor of Politics and International Affairs at Princeton University, Princeton, USA. He is a scholar of comparative political economy of development with a strong interest in India. He is the author and editor of nine books including a volume titled *The Success of India's Democracy*, and has also published some fifty essays. He is Chief Editor of the journal *World Politics.*

RAJNI KOTHARI, former Director of the Centre for the Study of Developing Societies, is a political scientist based in New Delhi,

India. He is the author of numerous books including *Politics in India; Politics and the People; State Against Democracy: In Search of Humane Governance*; and *Growing Amnesia: An Essay on Poverty and Human Consciousness.*

AREND LIJPHART is Research Professor Emeritus of Political Science, University of California, San Diego, USA. He is the author of many books, which includes *Patterns of Democracy: Government Forms and Performance in Thirty Six Countries*; India is one of the countries included in this comparative study. He served as President of the American Political Science Association in 1995–6.

JAMES MANOR is Emeka Anyaoku Professor at the Institute of Commonwealth Studies, University of London, and the V.K.R.V. Rao, Professor at the Institute for Social and Economic Change, Bangalore. His books include *Democracy and Decentralisation in South Asia and West Africa: Participation, Accountability and Performance* (co-author) and *Nehru to the Nineties: The Changing Office of Prime Minister in India.*

SUBRATA K. MITRA is Professor and Head of the Department of Political Science, South Asia Institute, University of Heidelberg and Visiting Fellow at the Centre for the Study of Developing Societies, Delhi. He has earlier served as Head, Department of Research and Development and Data Analysis, French Institute for Public Opinion, Paris; and Director, Centre for Indian Studies, School of Social and Political Science, University of Hull. He has authored and edited a number of books, which include *The Puzzle of India's Governance: Culture, Context and Comparative Theory; Legitimacy and Conflict in South Asia*; *Subnational Movements in South Asia*; and *Power, Protest and Participation: Local Elites and Development in India.*

DEEPAK NAYYAR is Professor of Economics, Jawaharlal Nehru University, New Delhi. He was Vice-Chancellor of the University of Delhi. He has also taught economics at the Indian Institute of Management Calcutta and the University of Sussex. His books include *India's Exports and Export Policies; Migration, Remittances and Capital Flows*; and *The Intelligent Person's Guide to Liberalization* (co-author). He has also edited *Economic Relations between Socialist Countries and the Third World; Industrial Growth and*

Stagnation: The Debate in India; Trade and Liberalization; and *Economics as Ideology.*

GAIL OMVEDT is a citizen of India with a permanent home in Kasegaon, Maharashtra, where she writes, teaches, and works with social movements. She is the author of several books, including *We Shall Smash This Prison: Indian Women in Struggle; Reinventing Revolution: India's New Social Movements; Dalit Visions*; and *Dalits and the Democratic Revolution.* A translation of a Marathi Dalit autobiography by Vasant Moon, *Growing up Untouchable in India: A Dalit Autobiography.*

PRAMOD PARAJULI is Co-Founder, Executive Director and Core Faculty, Portland State University's Portland International Initiative for Leadership in Ecology, Portland, USA; He teaches anthropology, ecology, and social movements at Syracuse University, New York. His research interests lie at the intersection of social movements, ecology, and traditions of knowledge among ecological ethnicities—peasants, indigenous peoples, rural peasants, fisherfolks, etc. He is actively involved in various ethno-ecological movements and movements for sustainable livelihoods in Nepal and India. His works include *Tortured Bodies and Altered Earth: Ecological Ethnicities in the Regime of Globalization.*

LLOYD I. RUDOLPH and SUSANNE HOEBER RUDOLPH are Professors Emeriti of Political Science at the University of Chicago, USA and frequent visitors to India. Their books include *Postmodern Gandhi and Other Essays: Gandhi in the World and at Home, The Modernity of Tradition; In Pursuit of Lakshmi: The Political Economy of the Indian State;* and *Reversing the Gaze: Amar Singh's Diary, A Colonial Subject's Narrative of Imperial India* (co-authors).

AMARTYA SEN is Lamont University Professor and Professor of Economics and Philosophy at Harvard University and was until recently the Master of Trinity College, Cambridge. He is the author of several books including *Collective Choice and Social Welfare; Poverty and Famines: An Essay on Entitlement and Deprivation; Inequality Re-examined;* and *Development as Freedom.* He was awarded the Nobel Prize for Economic Sciences in 1998.

WENDY SINGER is Associate Professor, South Asian History, Kenyon College, Ohio, USA. She is the author of *Creating Histories:*

Oral Narratives and the Politics of History-making and a monograph on the history of elections, '*A Constituency Suitable for Ladies*'.

DAVID WASHBROOK is Reader in Modern South Asian History and Professorial Fellow of St Antony's College, University of Oxford. He has taught at Cambridge and Warwick Universities in the UK and the University of Pennsylvania and Harvard University in the US. He has written extensively on the history of south India in the early modern and modern periods including *The Emergence of Provincial Politics: The Madras Presidency, 1870–1920.*

Preface to the Paperback Edition

The Introduction to the first edition of this book (2001) identified some trends in Indian democracy—such as the politics of inclusion and the vibrancy of civil society—that have been consolidated in subsequent years. Among those identified as challenges to India's democracy, the politics of Hindutva acquired their most malevolent expression just a year after its publication, though they appear less threatening at present. But unquestionably, the most visible change that has occurred is in the external perception of Indian democracy and the veritable globalization of appreciation for it. Western proselytizers and would-be exporters of democracy, possibly threatened by the towering economic presence of China, have of late been eagerly handing out testimonials to India's democracy, which has therefore become an important element of India's new and self-confident image as an economic player of consequence in a globalized world.

This global appreciation has begotten a local complacence, and with it an unwillingness to ask or confront inconvenient questions about the substantive quality of Indian democracy, or indeed its possibilities and limits. This preface to the paperback edition of *Democracy in India* identifies three dogmas of Indian democracy and suggests, in response to these, some reasons why Indian democracy-watchers should be willing to entertain a sense of disquiet.

The first dogma is that democracy is chiefly, if not exclusively, about representation; indeed, that the test of democracy is the extent to which it succeeds in representing various groups, especially those that have historically suffered from disadvantage and exclusion. The success or otherwise of democracy is adjudged by the extent to which political mobilization and electoral processes generate a microcosmic representation of the diverse ascriptively defined groups within Indian society. Pared to its essentials, this approach commands us to carve up society into its multiple ethnic, religious, and caste groupings (and sub-groupings), count the numbers, and check these against their percentage representation in the institutions of governance: the legislature, the civil service, and the judiciary.

No democrat could ever dispute the proposition that exclusion is a denial of democracy, and that disadvantaged groups must be properly and effectively represented. But, equally, no democrat should be naïve enough to suspend disbelief once such representation has been achieved—whether through reserved quotas or party political mobilization—and not ask the further question as to whether the interests of these disadvantaged and excluded groups are in fact being appropriately and robustly reflected in public policy.

Representation is a mechanism that can facilitate participation and hopefully trigger policy impact. But to treat representation as the *sine qua non* of democracy, its desired end-state, is to be insufficiently demanding of democracy. For, there is danger in presuming that the tasks of democracy are complete once proper representation has been achieved, and that policies that reflect everyone's preferences automatically flow from this. This fetishization of representation serves only to detract attention from its limits in terms of both policy outcomes and the actual welfare of the groups in question.

There is, in India, a frequent convergence between cultural and material inequalities; between, on the one hand, the inherited symbolic or cultural disadvantages of caste or religious identity and, on the other, of economic disadvantage. Low caste status is often accompanied by deprivation, and traditional and historical forms of social inequality co-exist with, and are reinforced by, inequalities arising out of the sphere of production and economic activity. Data on human development indicators and poverty amongst various social groups clearly show that levels of deprivation are highest for the Scheduled Castes (SCs), followed by the Scheduled Tribes (STs), with Muslims being just slightly better-off than the other two groups.[1] The economic impoverishment of these groups thus mirrors their social marginalization. Of course,

[1] Abusaleh Shariff, *India: Human Development Report: A Profile of Indian States in the 1990s* (Delhi: National Council for Applied Economic Research [NCAER] and Oxford University Press, 1999).

it is obviously not the case that *all* members of these groups are poor, or that there is no poverty among other groups, but only that there is a high degree of overlap between being poor and belonging to these groups.

Some of these groups have had access to quotas guaranteeing their presence in public institutions. However, studies have shown that the entire panoply of institutional quotas has failed to generate policies that substantively address the disadvantages that mark the condition of the vast majority of these groups. The explanations offered for this gap range from accusations about elites within these groups cornering the benefits and reproducing them intergenerationally, to more radical arguments about the difficulty of dislodging entrenched social hierarchies that maintain the stranglehold of the upper castes and upper classes on Indian society. Whatever the factors that explain this phenomenon, it is clear that representation is only a necessary, but by no means sufficient, condition of democracy. As such, the assumption that the project of democracy begins with seeking, and ends with achieving, representation is profoundly inadequate.

The second dogma is to be found in conviction that political mobilization of backward castes is adequate proof of the deepening of democracy, which started its career on Indian soil as an elite affair, but is now more widespread. Even scholars who have strenuously argued this point now acknowledge that this process has reached a plateau, with the virtual freezing of group identities and their political alignments. There is no question that the Fourteenth Lok Sabha, elected in 2004, is a much more representative body than the First Lok Sabha elected in 1952, in which the backward castes were represented to the tune of barely five per cent, as contrasted to twenty-five per cent today. The jubilation about democracy having been deepened by the political and electoral processes that have brought about this transformation is, however, a trifle premature. To begin with, it fails to observe some disturbing elements of the Indian political process that can only be described as Schumpeterian.

Schumpeter's 'realist' definition of democracy saw it not as a form of government designed to express the will of the sovereign people, but rather as a form of elite competition in which seeking popular vote was only a means to acquire power. Scholars of Indian democracy have on the whole preferred to romanticize democracy.

They ignore evidence of the resemblance between Schumpeterian realism and the way in which parties—including those that claim to represent the poorest and most backward groups in Indian society—are organized, their lack of internal democracy, and their functioning as family-owned firms. It is perhaps time we asked ourselves if the project of deepening democracy is compatible with parties created and run as personalized individual fiefdoms, with no accountability whatever; with outrageously corrupt leaderships; with exclusively symbolic responses to the claims of social justice, but little by way of material improvements in the quality of people's lives.

On the other hand, the more heartening recent accomplishments of our democracy include the now decade old constitutional initiative in the sphere of local democracy and the very recent national legislation guaranteeing the Right to Information. The first has had its teething troubles and obstructionists, and so undoubtedly will the second. But there is no doubt that the new *panchayats* have created public spaces where citizens—especially women, dalits, and adivasis—can meet with those who have traditionally oppressed and exploited them, on relatively equal terms. Likewise, the achievement of the Right to Information is a measure of the success of Indian democracy in creating radical possibilities for civil society to make claims that will hopefully enable citizens to recover a core component of the democratic ideal, namely, accountability. From decentralization to the right to information, from the right to education to the campaign for a right to food, it is these initiatives that represent the more substantive ways of deepening democracy.

This brings us to the third dogma, that of treating democracy as a shibboleth, and as self-referential. In theory, of course, democracy has a fundamental intrinsic value, so that we value it because it is a good in itself, and not only because it is an instrument to some other good. The instrumental value of democracy lies in making possible—through the apparatus of rights and freedom—collective action for greater justice and even redistribution. However, the enabling conditions for such public action are not always present in a society. In situations like these, the attachment to democracy *qua* democracy can sometimes cloud our judgement and prevent us from seeing that there may be problems in our society and polity for which democracy does not hold the magic key.

In general, making democracy a holy cow—'if it's democratic, it must be fine'—can be a sticky business. In political practice, the grossest violations of public morality have been justified in its name: we are all familiar with the phenomenon of politicians contesting elections from jail or claiming that a favourable verdict in the people's court outweighs any conviction by a court of law. In scholarship, the fetishization of elections means that election analyses tend to become state-of-the-democracy reports. In fact, the character of a democracy can only partially be inferred from its elections. The electoral verdict by itself is not very helpful because it explicates the merits of rival electoral arithmetics and strategies rather than advancing our understanding of the subterranean as well as manifest political tendencies and processes at work. Elections are surely important moments in political life which—as they capture a slice of time when political temperatures are at their highest—are possibly the most striking in symbolic and ritualistic terms, but they are far from being either the exclusive or the most accurate barometer of a democracy.

This reduction of the democratic idea to elections is of course a global trend, as the evangelists of democracy have taken it upon themselves to spread democracy across the world. The world has witnessed many (and not always altruistic) attempts at creating or propping up or bankrolling political parties, at encouraging and organizing 'free and fair elections', and so forth. The project of democracy promotion is deeply flawed, both morally and politically. The moral argument against it is simple: surely it is profoundly undemocratic to swear by democracy and at the same time deny others—whether individuals or nations—the basic democratic right to determine for themselves the design of society and polity that they want. Can people be forced to be democratic any more than they could be forced, *pace* Rousseau, to be free? Ultimately, howsoever strongly and deeply we are convinced of the goodness and value of our way of life, we do not have the right to impose it on others.

The political argument about democracy promotion is about practicability and feasibility, about the conditions under which democracy can actually be introduced from the outside. Does democracy require what has been called a 'cultural and civic infrastructure'? India, it was long assumed, lacked a cultural predisposition to democracy, on account of its hierarchical and inegalitarian social structure. But, today, democracy has a striking hold on the popular political imagination, and this is only partly the result of a process realized over time through participation and engagement in political activity from the national movement onwards. Such a culture may be central to the democratic way of life, but it must evolve and grow organically from within a society. Setting up the institutions—the architecture or infrastructure—of democracy may provide only a shell rather than the real thing. It may, therefore, be time to think afresh about democracy, not in a formulaic manner, but through exploring ways of pluralizing democratic conceptions. Must democracy necessarily be the same for all societies and all peoples?

In sum, a strong commitment to democratic principles should not restrain us from making more exacting demands on our democracy, which treating democracy as a shibboleth does. Likewise, the cause of inclusion and the representation of diversity are not well served by making a holy cow of representation while ignoring the importance of welfare and redistribution for the disadvantaged. Finally, a commitment to the goal of deepening democracy calls for setting more stringent criteria by which to judge this deepening, and for more substantive content to the idea of social justice than that commonly encountered in our contemporary political discourse.

Introduction: Situating Indian Democracy

I

For anything that has ever been said about Indian democracy, there is a good chance that its opposite has also been asserted. If some have described democracy in India as an anomaly, others have seen it as an ideal case for testing democratic theory. If there are those who marvel at its resilience and endurance, there are also those who see it as hopelessly fragile. If some are impressed by the multiple levels and forms of participation, others regard this as a mask that conceals the reality of unequal access. Indeed, if there is, in the study of Indian politics, any single issue that remains unvaryingly contentious, and on which there are as many verdicts as there are scholars, it is surely the complex trajectory of India's fifty-year experiment with this unique political form.

For the rest, everything about Indian democracy that appears unfamiliar or inexplicable in terms of western democracies, has been flung into the basket of Indian exceptionalism. That basket is now bulging at the seams, and even overflowing as almost everything that is central to India's democratic experience now lies in it, and the lid no longer fits. In the pages that follow, we shall attempt to not merely evaluate the strengths and weaknesses of India's democracy, but also reflect upon the bewildering variety of the descriptions, interpretations, and explanations of it, some of which are reproduced in this volume.

The diverse and conflicting verdicts—ranging from unqualified success to unmitigated failure—suggest that even as scholars differ about the promise and the performance of India's democracy, they appeal to some mental construct of what democracy is or should be. It is their different definitions of what constitutes the core or essence of democracy that yields the many different yardsticks—for measuring its extent, describing its nature, and explaining its performance—that underpin these evaluations. Though many, if not all, subscribe to democracy as a desideratum, it is not always clear which of the different normative justifications that can be offered for the democratic ideal is being invoked. For there is more than one reason why democracy may be considered a goal worth cherishing and a project worth advancing. The common assumption that democracy is self-evidently a good thing, has tended to direct scholarly attention to devising the best methods by which to measure and explain it, and so to decide whether a particular democracy is good, bad, or indifferent. And this is precisely the point at which the underlying normative principles become important, for it is our expectations from democracy as a political ideal that tend to determine our evaluations of particular democracies.

As a way of arriving at decisions among a group of persons, whether organized as a polity or as a neighbourhood association, the essential value of democracy is presumed to lie in its moral superiority over any other way of arriving at decisions which take everybody's interests into account, and are equally binding on everyone. If we were to identify a common minimum set of principles that underpin and justify democracy, they would be premised on the idea of individual autonomy, according to which individuals are autonomous beings, capable of rational thought and, therefore, of determining what is good for them. Democracy, however, does not follow unless there is the further presumption of equality. This requires that all individuals should have an equal say in the determination of collective decisions which affect all of them equally, and so provides the fundamental rationale for government by the people.

However, even if they agree on the purposes of their collective endeavour, human beings will surely disagree about the methods of achieving it, and so unanimity is generally impossible. The most plausible procedure for arriving at a commonly agreed upon result, therefore, is the principle of majority rule. Though democracy is often equated with the principle of majority rule, it is important to keep in mind that majority rule represents only the most practical and morally acceptable procedure for arriving at decisions when people disagree. The inspiration for democracy continues to rest with the ideas of equality and the common pursuit of the general interest. However, since in large and complex societies, it is not always possible for people to gather together to make decisions on every issue (as they may have done in the direct democracy of ancient Athens, for instance), modern democracy is generally given effect through representative institutions. Through these, people elect their representatives to a legislative body which is mandated to take decisions on their behalf. However, in keeping with the spirit of democracy, ultimate sovereignty rests with the people, and their representatives are merely meant to carry out their will. Democracy now transmutes into a set of procedures and institutions by which people can elect their representatives and hold them periodically accountable. We shall return to the theoretical aspects of these questions in the next section, but let us now see how an emphasis on some of these principles may influence our assessment of Indian democracy.

Those who view democracy purely as a set of institutions—encompassing free and fair elections, legislative assemblies, and constitutional governments arising out of these—tend to be sanguine about India as the world's largest democracy (because electorate) which has successfully voted out corrupt or repressive regimes. But to those whose mental construct of a democracy is a society peopled by truly equal citizens, who are politically engaged, tolerant of different opinions and ways of life, and have an equal voice in choosing their rulers and holding them accountable, Indian democracy appears to be a poor candidate. In political theory, these two contrasting models of democracy are referred to as procedural (or formal) and substantive democracy respectively.

The scholars who subscribe to the limited, proceduralist view of democracy, are generally buoyant about Indian democracy—its past as well as its future. In support of their optimism, they cite chiefly election data about participation—voter turnouts of between 50 and 60 per cent—and the frequency with which elections have been held in recent years. However, because their definition of democracy is restricted to election data, they tend to slip into what has been called the fallacy of electoralism. Thus, their analyses emphatically exclude the many social and economic inequalities that make it difficult for even formal participation to be effective. There are many formidable obstacles that prevent voters from doing even the few simple things that they—as the political sovereign—may reasonably expect to do. The free exercise of the franchise, for example, may require freedom from caste superiors, from dominant landlords, or, in the case of women, from male heads of household. It may be curtailed when people do not have the power of independent decision-making; when they have inadequate access to relevant information; when they are helpless in holding their representatives accountable; and, above all, when their exercise of the franchise fails to yield a responsive administration. Further, in societies like India where there are significant minorities—based on religion, language, and ethnicity—majoritarian democracy tends to be unfair, because the aspirations of permanent minorities are either ignored, or else systematically outvoted. Such minorities thus never have a real, let alone equal, opportunity to influence the overall outcome of the decision-making process. Given these constraints, to raise a cheer for Indian democracy purely on the basis of voter participation may be somewhat rash.

This is why the proponents of a substantive definition of democracy argue that the democratic project is incomplete until the meaningful exercise of the equal rights of citizenship have been guaranteed to all. On this account, free and fair elections, freedom of speech and expression, and the rule of law and its equal protection to all, are the necessary, but by no means sufficient conditions for a democracy to be meaningful. The project of democracy is not accomplished by merely securing legal and political equality, it may be severely compromised by inequalities of wealth, power, and social status, which deny many from having a truly equal opportunity to influence governmental decisions. Democracy, therefore, should not be seen as confined to the sphere of state and government, but also as the principle governing collective life in society. This 'social agenda of democratization' (Beetham 1993: 66) has been invoked by socialists who argue that capitalism undermines democratization because it facilitates the use of private wealth as a political resource and lever of political influence. It has also been invoked by feminists who believe that gender inequality negates democracy, and that the family and gender relations constitute an important site of democratization.

In similar vein, inequalities of race and ethnicity in western societies, and of caste in India, are seen to undermine democracy. It has even been argued that among the serious inequalities that endanger democracy are those stemming from the concentration of expert knowledge, symbolized by the influence of public policy specialists over government policy and public opinion (Dahl 1991: 333–5). As policy increasingly becomes the preserve of the expert, popular control over it is necessarily diminished. In the Indian context, Atul Kohli has shown how economic policy-making, especially on liberalization, has been a closed-door exercise in technical efficiency, conducted by experts and altogether insulated from democratic pressures (Kohli 1993).

It may, of course, be argued that to insist on the criterion of substantiveness for a democracy is an unfair, even impossible, test that no existing democracy in the world would pass. There are poor and homeless people even in the affluent societies of the western world, just as there are also racial minorities, indigenous people, and other victims of prejudice. It may be true that a perfectly substantive democracy is to be found nowhere outside Utopia, but is there another conception of democracy that enables us to consider inequalities of class, race, and gender as issues that are relevant to the functioning of democracy, and therefore imperative for democratic theory to address? The substantive conception of democracy is required to redress the failure of the procedural definition in providing space for the recognition that social and economic inequalities seriously undermine democracy.

The following pages will draw attention to many other paradoxes of democracy, its procedures, and its relationship to other social and economic goals that societies adopt. As we have already noted, the institutions of representative democracy (based on the principles of majority rule and one person-one vote) generate dilemmas in multicultural societies, where minorities based on race or religion may be systematically disprivileged on account of their small numbers, and therefore unlikely to ever have their will prevail. In the context of post-colonial societies, the assumption that democracy slows down and even hinders development (defined purely in terms of economic growth), resulted in a debate about whether democracy and development are compatible. There are also disagreements about the nitty-gritty of electoral, political, and governing institutions in a democracy: is the parliamentary system more intrinsically democratic than the presidential? Is a competitive two-party system essential for a functioning democracy? Do more political parties mean more democracy? Is the election of candidates who enjoy the support of only a minority of votes in the first-past-the-post system of election less democratic than one based on proportional representation, and so on. In the next section, we examine the contours of some important and relevant debates in democratic theory, as a backdrop to problematizing some important issues in the practice of Indian democracy.

II

Democracy: A Theoretical Excursus

In this section, we shall essay a barebones biography of the idea of democracy, with a view to recapitulating some of the key ideas in democratic theory. Our point of departure is a brief historical survey, from which we proceed, in the second sub-section, to examine some important justifications for democracy, famously described by Winston Churchill as the worst form of government except for all the rest. The third sub-section is about the process of democratization, and its relationship to capitalist development, while the last sub-section discusses some of the problems encountered by those who have sought to measure democracy and rank existing democracies on the basis of these measures.

A Short History of a 'Generally Acknowledged Folly'

In 1992, 2500 years of democracy were enthusiastically celebrated across the world. While it is usual for the birthdays of great leaders and the anniversaries of nations and revolutions to be commemorated in this manner, no other political ideal has ever been celebrated in this way. This should not, however, lead us to believe that democracy was always the object of universal approbation. Both democratic institutions, as well as the word that describes them—*demokratia*, meaning the rule of the people[1]—are of ancient

[1] To the ancient Greeks, democracy signified rule by the many or rule by the people, which was another way of saying rule by the ignorant or dominance by the poor over the rich. This is why democracy was not the subject of general approval, with the historian Thucydides, the philosophers Plato and Aristotle, and the playwright Aristophanes being equally, if subtly, disparaging of it. (Cf. Arblaster 1987: 16.)

Greek origin. But even in Athens, believed to be the historical progenitor of democracy, the achievement was not as impressive as it may appear. The virtues of direct and participatory democracy were here offset not only by the power of generals and demagogues, but more significantly by a citizenship so restrictively defined as to give it a wholly unrepresentative character. This is how, in 415 BC, the arrogant young Athenian aristocrat, Alcibiades, could describe democracy as 'a generally acknowledged folly' and demand a high office of state on the grounds that his racehorses had won a spectacular victory in the recent Olympic Games! (Hornblower 1986: 141)

In what is arguably the longest single *karmic* cycle, the 'generally acknowledged folly' was reborn as the younger sibling of liberalism two millennia later. It was, of course, resisted by the privileged social classes of the time, which correctly feared that their monopoly over wealth and the 'civilized' life would be threatened by the enfranchisement of the lower classes. If political struggle was the means of making democracy more inclusive, the struggle for social rights made it possible, by the mid-twentieth century, to sever the historical link between democracy and capitalism, as the spirit of social democracy found institutional embodiment in the welfare state.

The twentieth century saw an unparalleled extension of democracy in terms of both its *inclusiveness* as well as its *spatial expansion.* Beginning with the extension of the suffrage to women in the older western democracies, and ending with the dismantling of apartheid in South Africa, democracy in the twentieth century undoubtedly became more inclusive. Today, we even have a robustly argued case for the extension of rights to nature, including plant species and wilderness areas.[2] Secondly, the provenance of democracy also increased in spatial terms, as—following decolonization in the 1950s and 1960s—it was eagerly adopted across much of the globe. In Asia and Africa, the process of decolonization provided democracy with new environments and unusual laboratories, as many newly independent nations assumed democratic purposes as naturally—and despite the contradiction—as they inherited colonial

[2] It has been suggested that nature is 'just the latest minority deserving a place in the sun of the American liberal tradition' (Roderick Nash, cited in Eckersley 1996: 77).

structures of governance. More recently, the post-Communist states of Eastern Europe have joined the ranks of those queuing up outside democracy's door.

It is however curious to note that the unfinished tasks of democracy in the contemporary world are precisely those that have conventionally been deemed to be the flaws of Athenian democracy. In the city-state of ancient Athens, the exclusion of three categories of persons—the slaves, the *metics* (or foreigners), and women—from citizenship has long been regarded as the chief deficiency of Athenian democracy. The lower classes and immigrants in modern societies may be viewed as the contemporary equivalent of slaves and *metics*, respectively. In modern democracies, despite their formal enfranchisement and inclusion, it is precisely these groups—women, immigrants, and the poor and the lower classes—that continue to symbolize the unfinished project of democracy, and so draw our attention to a striking parallel between ancient Athens and the modern world.

That the twentieth century represents the triumph of democracy has nevertheless become one of the most tried clichés of our time. Certainly, it is the twentieth century, more than any other, that shows us the most varied and diverse appropriations of the label, and encourages us to recognize what C. B. Macpherson called the 'genuine confusion' (1978: 1) surrounding the term democracy. It is now a commonplace that democracy has different meanings not only for different individuals, but also for different societies and peoples. The eagerness with which the title is claimed, however, points to the unparalleled legitimacy that this form of government has come to enjoy in our times. As democracy was rapidly adopted in the countries of the developing world, and translated into myriad local political vernaculars, the borrowing invited both repudiation and endorsement. Could every self-styled democracy legitimately be called one? Some were manifestly reluctant to accept every claim as valid, doubting as to whether so unresembling a cousin could indeed be treated as family. Others argued that if democracy is not necessarily equated with liberal-democracy, then the claims of the developing countries to the title are valid. Socialists likewise insisted that liberal-democracy was incomplete, and only social democracy could legitimately claim to be democratic.

Both these claims highlighted what is probably the most striking fact about democracy in the twentieth century, viz. that there is a perhaps irreconcilable tension between liberalism and democracy.[3] The philosophical issues in this debate have been addressed by Bhikhu Parekh, who argues that liberal-democracy is a historically specific form of democracy, based on a culturally specific theory of individuation. It combines liberalism as a theory of the state, and democracy as its form of government. Given that many societies attach greater significance to the community than the individual, the democratic part of liberal democracy (such as free elections and free speech) is more universalizable than the liberal component (Parekh 1993: 172). Today, the tensions between liberalism and democracy have come to be accepted as unresolvable, and democracy and difference have come to be seen as important dimensions of each other. It has thus become possible to speak not only of different paths to democracy, but also of different ways of being democratic or even being 'differently democratic' (Schmitter and Karl 1991: 77).[4]

It is nevertheless true that the chief normative justifications for democracy are to be found within the tradition of liberal political theory which frequently provides the criteria by which the success or failure of particular democracies is judged. It is therefore to these that we now turn our attention.

3 For a lucid exposition of these tensions, cf. David Beetham (1993).

4 Not all, however, are so tolerant of difference. From squarely within the parameters of a proceduralist definition, Fareed Zakaria proposes a distinction between liberal and illiberal democracies. Illiberal democracies, which account for half of the 118 countries deemed to be democracies today, are those in which governments are chosen through competitive, multi-party elections, but in which constitutional liberalism—the tradition of protecting individual autonomy, liberty, and rights against coercion, regardless of whether that coercion emanates from state, society, or church—is absent. Democracy without constitutional liberalism is, he argues, not merely inadequate, but also dangerous. Nevertheless, standing by a minimalist definition of democracy, Zakaria rejects the idea of substantive democracy, because to imbue democracy with normative connotations such as 'good government', or to allow only such countries to be called democratic as guarantee a wide range of social, political, economic, and religious rights, is to turn the word democracy into 'a badge of honour rather than a descriptive category', and so to render it 'analytically useless' (Zakaria 1997: 25).

Justifying Democracy: The Worst Form of Government Except for All the Rest?

The phrase 'rule of the people' may define democracy, but it does not tell us why it is better that people, rather than kings, should rule. We still need principles which tell us why democracy is a goal worth striving for and cherishing, or why democracy should be valued for its own sake, rather than because it fulfils other desirable ends. The principles justifying democracy are best viewed as a mosaic, the elements of which, by themselves, or in a variety of combinations with each other, generate different models of democracy. The model of democracy, in each case, depends upon which principles are combined and, among them, which are privileged. Thus if *freedom* and *equality* are identified as the central justificatory principles of democracy, and *autonomy* as the principle underpinning both, it is particular combinations of all (or some) of them, and the dominant role played by any one in this combination, which contribute to the construction of a particular model of democracy.

The basic idea underlying the principle of *autonomy* is an extension of the value we attach to possessing control over our own persons, decisions, and life-choices. For we are not only individuals acting for ourselves, but also members of collectives like society and the polity, and because decisions taken in these arenas determine the common good and affect our lives, our participation in and control over those decisions is as much an exercise in self-determination as the decisions we make in our private lives about what to wear, whom to marry, and so forth.

Historically, in alliance with the idea of freedom, the principle of autonomy leads us in the direction of *popular government*, in which the people rule themselves as free and equal beings. The cornerstone of this alliance between autonomy and freedom is the emphasis placed on the personal liberty of the individual. At least part of the task of government—following John Locke's formulation of early liberalism—is the protection of the individual's life, liberty, and property equally from the depredations of a potentially tyrannical state and from other individuals. The most familiar institutional form that the idea of popular government takes is, of course, the classical model of *representative democracy.* Here, formal political equality—in the form of universal adult franchise, free and fair elections, freedom of speech and expression, the rule of law, and inclusive citizenship—provide the contours of a democracy which at least supports prospective equality.[5] The commonest form of representative democracy in the twentieth century is the liberal pluralist model, in which democratic politics are seen as the only authentic way of representing the multiple interests in society, as articulated by political parties and pressure groups, and the state is viewed as a neutral arbiter.

As argued earlier, different normative premises yield different conceptions of democracy and correspondingly of politics and the state. Privileging the principle of freedom, we are led to a view of democracy that has a strong affinity with the politics of the New Right in Europe and the United States in the early 1980s. This libertarian view accords the highest importance to the rights and personal freedoms of the individual, and so mandates a limited state whose intervention in society is minimal. The state must be neutral rather than perfectionist, that is it must not attempt to regulate politics, society, or the economy in accordance with any particular notion of the good life. On this account, any programme of redistributive justice undertaken by the state is illegitimate, because it violates individual rights (Nozick 1974). Democracy is merely an instrument by which the highest political end of liberty may be achieved.

If, however, we approach the democratic ideal privileging the idea of equality, we find ourselves in the company of theorists such as C. B. MacPherson and Carole Pateman, who remind us that equality before the law is of limited use, if individuals do not possess the capacities by which they can truly determine their life-plans. Hence, if we wish to extend the control people have over their own lives, we have to first remove the disadvantages that

5 *Prospective equality* obtains when, in a decision that is about to be made, no persons or groups suffer particular disabilities which prevent them from determining that decision, and so every citizen starts off with an equal chance of influencing the outcome of the democratic process. *Retrospective equality* is achieved if, in a decision already taken, we can say that everyone equally determined that decision. Since only a unanimous decision could guarantee retrospective equality, decision by majority is the only procedure which guarantees prospective equality and is also most conducive to retrospective political equality, because it may be said that more people favoured the winning alternative over all others (Lively 1975).

accrue from their social subordination or economic deprivation. In an early though somewhat limited form, this view found expression in the classical model of *Athenian democracy* which—despite a rather exclusive definition of citizenship—guaranteed equality and liberty to all citizens, and encouraged civic virtue by providing every citizen with the opportunity to rule as well as to be ruled. The maximal preoccupation with equality is found in the model of *social democracy*, which is concerned with ways of reducing the concentration of not merely political power—as liberal democracy seeks to do—but social and economic power as well. Social democrats emphasize the importance of redressing the social, economic, and gender inequalities that originate in the concentration of economic power and the dominance of patriarchy within the family.[6] Unlike the libertarians, they believe in redistributive policies, the welfare state of the mid-twentieth century being the earliest institutional embodiment, however imperfect, of this impulse.

The principle of autonomy, in alliance with that of equality, supports the model of *participatory democracy*, which emphasizes community rather more than it does liberty. The value of participation has historically been defended in many different ways, two of the most influential accounts of it being those found in the writings of Jean-Jacques Rousseau and John Stuart Mill. For Rousseau, participation is predicated upon the equality of citizens, and so ensures that political equality is truly effective in decision-making. But it is also valuable because it has a positive psychological impact on the participants, as it educates them to be responsible citizens engaging in responsible social and political action. Mill recognized the virtue of both representative democracy as well as participatory democracy: the first for the mundane business aspects of government; and the second for its educative value, as it enabled the moral and intellectual self-development of the citizen. At the same time, recalling old fears of democracy, in terms of the ignorant and mediocre masses storming the protected bastions of the civilized elites, he proposed multiple votes for the educated, to ensure that participation did not lead to the 'tyranny of the majority', and that leadership remained with the custodians of excellence and talent.

6 Beyond this, only Marxism is uncompromisingly committed to the ideal of complete equality, regarding anything less as bourgeois democracy.

Like Mill, contemporary theorists also believe that the equal opportunities of self-development can only be achieved in a truly participatory society (Pateman 1970; Barber 1984). Whether in the workplace or in local self-government, participation enhances political efficacy, evokes in citizens a concern for matters of common interest, and helps to create aware and knowledgeable citizens who can contribute constructively to the process of governance. Theorists of participatory democracy question the worth of the formal rights of participation which, on account of inequalities of gender, ethnicity, race, and class, are denied to large numbers of people.

Participatory democracy thus rejects the liberal pluralist model in which democratic politics are a way of reconciling the conflicting interests of individuals and groups. It is also unequivocally opposed to the *'realist'* model that we encounter in the writings of theorists like Max Weber, Robert Michels, and, above all, Joseph Schumpeter. Schumpeter challenged the classical eighteenth century model of democracy, the primary purpose of which was to vest the power of political decision-making in the people, who would (and this was the secondary purpose) elect rulers to carry out their common will. For Schumpeter, it was more realistic to posit the primary purpose as the secondary, and vice versa. The common good and the will of the people were to him equally mythical, and democracy was no more than an institutional arrangement for arriving at political decisions, by giving the power to decide to those individuals who were successful in getting themselves elected through a competitive struggle for the people's vote. Democracy, in this conception, was reduced to nothing more than a method for selecting a skilled political elite (Schumpeter [1943] 1979: 250–83). In the model of participatory democracy, thus democracy is normatively superior to any other mode of collective organization, and has as intrinsic value, which issues in human results. In the realist model, by contrast, democracy is shorn of all normativity, and has at best an instrumental value as a convenient method of choosing a leadership that enjoys legitimacy. If participatory democracy ties together the principles of autonomy, equality, and community, the realist model rejects all these.

Finally, the model of *deliberative democracy* privileges the principle of autonomy, in alliance with the principles of freedom and equality, in its interpretation of popular rule as a means of encouraging free and open public deliberation on issues of common concern. The most justifiable public policies are seen to emerge as autonomous persons enter the public sphere and engage with each other through reasoned argument and persuasion (Gutmann 1993: 417–18).

The various models of democracy identified above thus incorporate the basic principles of democracy (such as liberty and equality) in different ways, usually privileging one or the other of these. Further, any assessment of the actual functioning of a democracy uses certain criteria, the choice of which is inevitably influenced by the particular model of democracy we have in mind as we set out to evaluate it, and therefore of the underlying principles that we implicitly consider to be important.

Democratization: The End of History?

In the previous sub-section, we saw how political theorists approach the idea of democracy, and the principles they invoke to justify it. In this section, we discuss some approaches to the study of actually existing democracies, which compare democracies in different parts of the world, and explicate the relationship between democracy and capitalism, as well as—which is not necessarily identical with it—democracy and development.

What explains the diverse processes of democratization? The evolution of modern democracy through the nineteeth century in Europe and the United States has been treated as the exemplar of democratization. But it is post-colonial democratization in Latin America and Asia, and the recent post-Communist democratization in Eastern Europe, that have provoked a vast range of scholarship on questions such as: why do democratic institutions take root in some countries and not in others? what are the social, economic, and political conditions most conducive to democratization? In the 1960s, it was customary to emphasize the indices of modernization and development as necessary conditions for the successful pursuit of the democratic path. Subsequently, political processes driven by elite initiatives and choices were identified as being crucial to facilitating the move from authoritarian rule to liberal democracy. More recently, it has been the structural approach, with its emphasis on the long-term processes of historical change, that has held sway (Moore 1977; Rueschemeyer, Stephens and Stephens 1992).[7]

In one of the earliest studies of the social origin of democracy on a world canvas, Barrington Moore, Jr ([1966] 1977) examined the political role played by landed classes and the peasantry in the transformation of agrarian societies into modern industrial ones, and in the emergence of, variously, democracy, fascism, and communism. He found it difficult to fit the Indian case into any theoretical scheme that could be constructed for the other countries, despite the fact that classes and class alignments in India historically developed so as to give rise to the structural conditions necessary for the eventual establishment of parliamentary democracy. However, democracy could not take deep roots, because the actions of the very same people who—profoundly influenced by the British traditions of liberal democracy—brought democratic institutions to India, were circumscribed by class structures.

In similar vein, Rueschemeyer, Stephens, and Stephens (1992) have examined the evidence from Europe, Latin America, Central America, and the Caribbean islands in a historical and comparative framework, to argue that processes of democratization are powerfully shaped by *class power, state power,* and *transnational power.* Though capitalism presupposes class inequality, the contradictions of capitalism have advanced the cause of political equality, by changing the balance of class power in favour of subordinate classes. Democracy, in turn, has been a means of transforming capitalism, and further moves in the direction of substantive democracy will require further transformations in the nature of capitalism and the structure of power in society. The key to the fulfillment of the substantive democratic promise thus lies with democratic socialism.

The debate on democracy and development shifts the focus from the social underpinnings of democracy—and hence class and other social forces as constraints on it—to democracy as a regime type. Nevertheless, there is a continuity with the earlier debate, in that while the former links the history of capitalist accumulation with the history of social classes and democracy, the latter examines—in the context of the developing nations—how conducive democracy is to capitalist development. An early survey of the comparative evidence on this issue concluded that democracy

7 For a lucid and detailed account of these approaches, see David Potter 'Explaining Democratization', in Potter *et al.* (eds) (1997).

was not necessarily bad for development because, though the state-dominated democracies of the Third World were largely an elite affair, they were nevertheless capable of (a) generating and sustaining moderate but satisfactory growth rates; (b) stabilizing income distribution; (c) managing external debt effectively; and (d) holding out the promise of modifying inherited inequalities through the use of democratic state power (Kohli 1986).

The contention that democracy is inimical to economic growth was based on the argument that democracy is unable to reduce consumption in favour of investment. It is insufficiently insulated from particularistic pressures, from ethnic groups as well as large corporations and unions, making concerted action by the weakened state institutions difficult. In response to such pressures, democratic regimes also succumb to populist welfare programmes, at the expense of long-term growth and development. Conversely, the example of the developmental states[8] of East Asia was taken to suggest that state autonomy from such pressures holds the key to the superior performance of these states and their ability to force savings and launch economic growth. However, comparative studies have been inconclusive, showing that there is no necessary or inevitable relationship between democracy and development (Przeworski and Limongi 1993).[9] The weak patrimonial and undemocratic states of Africa were developmentally ineffective, while the equally undemocratic 'soft authoritarian' states of East Asia were highly effective in bringing about economic development. Likewise, the developmental success of East Asia's non-democratic regimes may be contrasted with the impressive growth record of Botswana's democracy.

Ultimately, it is probably plausible to say that while politics do matter, regime types by themselves may not hold the key to the

8 Adrian Leftwich has defined the developmental state in terms of a set of attributes that include the following: determined developmental elites committed to economic growth; the relative autonomy of the elites and the state institutions which they command; powerful and insulated bureaucracies with the authority to direct and manage economic development; a weak civil society with a poor human rights record; a mixture of state repression and often widespread legitimacy due to an effective distribution of economic growth in terms of schools, health care, housing, and roads (Leftwich 1995: 285–9).

9 For a lucid survey of the democracy–development debate, see Georg Sorensen (1993).

explanation. As Pranab Bardhan has argued, even state ability, which is arguably an important factor for the successful pursuit of long-term developmental goals, may be only partially determined by the democratic or non-democratic nature of the regime. Other factors, such as the social homogeneity of the population (for example, in Japan and South Korea, as opposed to India); an initially more egalitarian wealth distribution (in South Korea and Taiwan, as opposed to, say, Latin America); and dense networks of connections between public officials and private capitalism (for which Japan and South Korea are well known), are among the important determinants of state ability to accomplish economic development (Bardhan 1993: 46–7).

Perhaps the most significant chapter in the history of democracy in the twentieth century began to be written after the collapse of communism in Europe. This event came to be interpreted as the 'third wave' of democracy (Huntington 1991) and even celebrated as 'the end of history' (Fukuyama 1992), because it ostensibly signalled the triumph of capitalism and liberal-democracy all over the world. Despite the rather egregious complacency of this description, the transition, both economic and political, currently underway in the post-Soviet societies of Eastern Europe, has engaged the attention of scholars. A blueprint for sustainable democracy for countries of the South and East (by a scholars' collective called the Group on East–South Systems Transformations) argued that there can be no democracy without an effective state, and warned against the weakening of state institutions, which are needed to provide the conditions for an effective exercise of citizenship. Further, because transitions to democracy often coincide with economic crisis and entail reforms, the report was emphatic on the point that these required continued state intervention, especially for the provision of social services, public expenditure, and income maintenance. Thus, 'without an effective state, there can be no democracy and no markets'. (Przeworski *et al.* 1995: 11).

The East European experience also effected a shift from the study of democracy and economic growth as cause or consequence of each other, to a new emphasis on the cultural conditions for democratization. It foretold the resurrection, in democratic theory, of a concept long buried in its annals. This was the idea of 'civil society' which, in the East European context, was treated as synonymous with, and even a precondition for, democratization. Its revival effected a shift from the study of the state to the study of processes of democratization in society, through the practices of social movements and other forms of associational life. While some argued that democracy and freedom are necessary for a vibrant civil society, others claimed that a vibrant civil society is itself an essential condition for consolidating democracy. A significant variant of this concern is the revival of the idea of 'civic culture' in the work of Robert Putnam (1993), whose study of democracy in northern and southern Italy concluded that relations of civic engagement and networks of trust and solidarity among citizens make democracy work better.

Measuring Democracy

Despite definitional differences, the assessment of actually existing democracies generally invokes a combination of the ideas presented in the foregoing pages. Some of these assessments have taken the form of statistically measuring democracy and, on the basis of these measures, ranking particular democracies according to their scores (cf. Hadenius 1992: 61–2). One of the earliest attempts at measuring democracy was that of Robert Dahl, who proposed two indicators: ***public contestation*** (or the extent of public opposition and political competition) and the ***right of participation*** (in the system of public contestation, through the right to vote, contest for office, etc.) (1971: 4). Since it is possible to have one without the other, Dahl insisted that both these elements must be present before we can speak of democratization. Another set of indices, proposed by David Beetham, emphasizes the principles of ***popular control*** and ***political equality***. Popular control has several dimensions, including the popular election of the legislature and head of government; the political, legal, and financial accountability of government; civil and political rights and liberties; and civil society as a necessary condition for democracy. These dimensions were disaggregated into a set of thirty indices, to develop a 'democratic audit' for the United Kingdom (Beetham 1994).

Most attempts at measuring democracy begin with measuring participation, though the complexity of this phenomenon is today widely recognized. To assess levels of participation, it has long been customary to look beyond figures of voter turnouts, because voting per se does not indicate a deep commitment to democracy or tell us very much about reality of democratic citizenship in a country. Voter turnouts were deceptively high (upto 99 per cent) in the erstwhile Soviet Union, mainly because of the unspoken threat of coercion. On the other hand, the democracies of western countries do not record particularly impressive voter turnouts, staying at around 50 per cent in the United States of America. This is why students of participation explore other aspect of participation, such as taking part in political protest, signing petitions, fund-raising or canvassing in party campaigns, or even organizing people on civic issues, and contacting elected representatives.

However, even these apparently comprehensive measures of participation are found to be wanting, when we consider that different interests in society frequently do not find equal opportunities to represent their interests, or that social and political structures place constraints upon their effective representation. Indeed, a group that claims to represent a particular community or interest may not even be particularly democratic in its internal structure. Research into the question of how participation, and its effectiveness, varies in relation to wealth and education has revealed that, even in many western countries, those who are disadvantaged tend to under-participate and do not succeed in 'compensating for their weak economic position by raising their political voices' (Parry and Moyser 1994: 54).

III

Indian Democracy Prefigured

While the age of democracy in India can be said to have been properly inaugurated only in 1950, when India's republican Constitution came into effect, representative institutions had been slowly evolving over the past half-century and more of colonial rule. The demand for more representative councils (with elected Indian members and with real control over financial resources) ran parallel to, and was even anticipated by, the demand for freedom of expression, which found early articulation in the speeches and writings of Raja Rammohun Roy. The principle of elected representation was first introduced at the level of municipal councils and rural bodies through Lord Ripon's resolution of 1882.

Historians have argued that these meagre reforms were actually motivated by the need to levy new taxes for local requirements which would appear more legitimate if these bodies had elected Indian members (Sarkar 1983: 19). Unsurprisingly, the reforms met with resistance from the bureaucracy, which implemented them very slowly. In any case, these bodies had very little power or financial resources.

Between 1862 and 1892, the Governor-General's Executive Council had only forty-five Indians nominated to it, who were mainly rulers of princely states, or wealthy *zamindars* and merchants, or retired government officials. Many took positions opposed to those of the nationalists, while some did not even speak a word of English (Chandra *et al.* 1988: 114). Meanwhile, the formation of the Indian National Congress, and its pressure for constitutional reform, led to further changes in the composition of the Legislative Councils, beginning with the Indian Councils Act of 1892, which was partially intended to contain the Congress agitation and co-opt the moderates within it. However, the continued official majority on councils, and the denial of the right to vote on budgetary matters, led nationalists to express their dissatisfaction with this legislation. The Congress now raised the slogan of eighteenth-century England, viz. 'No taxation without representation', and also demanded self-government within the British Empire, on the Canadian and Australian model.

Ironically, any democratic potential in the subsequent reforms of the Government of India Act 1909 was emphatically disowned by their joint author, Lord Morley, thus:

> If it could be said that this chapter of reforms led directly or indirectly to the establishment of a parliamentary system in India, I, for one, would have nothing at all to do with it. [Quoted in Chiriyankandath 1992: 41]

The gradual spread of democratic ideas is signalled by not only the demand for greater representation and powers in the provincial and central legislative councils, but also in the demand for civil liberties and the right to free speech. Indian political opinion had accepted the constraints on free speech imposed during the first World War, but when the Rowlatt Bill of 1919, proposing the same in peacetime, was introduced in the central legislature, it was strongly resisted. The commitment to democratic values thus paralleled the demand for more representative councils.

The Government of India Act of 1919 (also known as the Montagu–Chelmsford reforms) introduced direct elections for all levels from local bodies to the national legislature. Though Indian ministers at the provincial level were now allowed charge of 'transferred' subjects, the coercive and extractive functions of government remained with the provincial governors and their nominees. Seventy per cent of the members in the provincial and legislative councils now came to be elected by less than 3 per cent of the Indian population, comprising mainly propertied males who paid income-tax, or land revenue, rents, and local rates. Thus, between 80 and 90 per cent of those elected to the provincial council of the United Provinces in 1926 were lawyers and landowners. Women and the so-called 'depressed' classes were clearly disadvantaged in the matter of representation.[10] (Chiriyankandath 1992: 44–8)

The Congress contested the elections of 1937, even as its election manifesto rejected totally the provisions of the 1935 Act. Jawaharlal Nehru's campaign was energetic: he travelled 80,000 kilometres and addressed 10 million voters, carrying the message of the Congress. By 1946, even limited democracy in India, as it stood at the threshold of independence, included 40 million voters, the second largest electorate in the non-communist world (ibid.: 58). In July 1937, Congress formed ministries in six provinces, and subsequently in another two. In its twenty-eight month rule, it restored civil liberties, released political prisoners, and even attempted agrarian reform in favour of the peasantry. Jawaharlal Nehru captured the spirit of the time, saying that it was as if an electric current had run through the countryside, and an oppressive weight had lifted from the people, releasing a suppressed mass energy:

> The fear of the police and secret service vanished for a while at least and even the poorest peasant added to his feeling of self-respect and self-reliance. For the first time he felt that he counted and could not be ignored. Government was no longer an unknown and intangible monster, separated from him by innumerable layers of officials, whom

10 The Government of India Act, 1935 liberalized somewhat the property qualification, and introduced literacy as a criterion for granting the vote, which therefore enfranchised literate women as well. However, in some states, like Bombay and Bengal, only matriculates could vote.

he could not easily approach and much less influence, and who were bent on extracting as much out of him as possible. The seats of the mighty were now occupied by men he had often seen and heard and talked to; sometimes they had been in prison together and there was a feeling of comradeship between them.

At the headquarters of the provincial governments, in the very citadels of the old bureaucracy, many a symbolic scene was witnessed... suddenly, hordes of people, from the city and the village, entered these sacred precincts and roamed about almost at will. They were interested in everything; they went into the Assembly Chamber, where the sessions used to be held; they even peeped into the Ministers' rooms. It was difficult to stop them for they no longer felt as outsiders; they had a sense of ownership in all this, although it was all very complicated for them and difficult to understand. [Nehru (1946) 1989: 369–70)]

The Indian National Congress had been demanding adult suffrage since the 1920s but, as we have seen, the franchise was very gradually extended to cover only 11.9 per cent of the population. The promise of universal adult suffrage was finally realized only in the Indian Constitution.[11] By almost unanimously opting for universal adult suffrage and direct election to the legislatures, the framers of the Constitution endorsed the path of modernity for the Indian nation-state, in contrast to the alternative Gandhian vision of decentralized village-level democracy, with indirect elections. Adult suffrage was perceived as the only way of giving voice, and thereby power, to the aspirations of the people who had long been denied any representation of their interests. Likewise, the virtue of direct elections was seen to lie in the fact that they made possible the creation of a new national identity superseding the parochial and caste identities of people (Austin [1966] 1999: 46–9).

The same unanimity did not, however, obtain in the matter of cabinet government, in which the ministry would be directly elected, and the head of state indirectly elected. Religious

11 Even before the drafting of the Constitution began, the Sapru Committee (1945) pointed to the educative effect of the 1937 elections, arguing that adult franchise was the only way of preventing the concentration of power in the hands of a few, even if the average voter's 'judgement may be faulty, his reasoning inaccurate, and his support of a candidate not infrequently determined by considerations removed from a high sense of democracy.' Cf. Austin [1966] (1999: 147).

minorities like the Sikhs and Muslims, for instance, supported the system of an indirectly elected ministry, with a directly elected head of state.[12] Arguing that political parties in India represented religious and other communities rather than ideology, they proposed the introduction of a Swiss-style system, based on proportional representation, in which representatives of every party in the legislature would be part of the ministry. These proposals were strongly resisted by Nehru and others who were convinced that this would only further entrench communal loyalties and inhibit the creation of a modern national identity.

IV

Fifty Years of Indian Democracy: A Stock-taking

The history of the working of India's republican Constitution is, in a sense, the history of India's democracy. Any chronicle of political events, and any narrative of public debate since 1952 (the year of the first parliamentary election), would say something of consequence about India's democracy. In this section, therefore, assuming a basic familiarity with the broad contours of Indian politics in the last half-century, we shall desist from attempting such a factual narrative and turn our attention instead to broad trends in the history of India's democracy, and the way in which scholars have understood and explained these.

On the occasion of the adoption of the Constitution on 25 November 1949, Dr Ambedkar warned against being content with mere political democracy, which could not last unless social democracy lay at its base. Two things, he argued, were missing in Indian society: one was the principle of equality, and the other that of fraternity.

12 Cf. Farzana Shaikh's thesis that the liberal theory of representation was alien to Indian Muslims, because it assumed individuals, rather than communities of race, religion, or language, to be the fundamental units of society. Political action likewise was not perceived as a sphere autonomous of religious values, but rather a sphere in which people gave expression to their religious obligations (1991: ch. 3).

On the 26th of January 1950, we are going to enter into a life of contradictions. In politics we will have equality and in social and economic life we will have inequality. In politics we will be recognizing the principle of one man one vote and one vote one value. In our social and economic life, we shall, by reason of our social and economic structure, continue to deny the principle of one man one value... . How long shall we continue to deny equality in our social and economic life? If we continue to deny it for long, we will do so only by putting our politcal democracy in peril. [Ambedkar (1949) 1968: 944]

If fraternity, he argued further, implied being one people, it was clear that a people divided into thousands of castes could not constitute a nation. Similarly, the monopolizing of power by a few had to end by accommodating the aspirations of the down-trodden for self-realization and participation in governance (ibid.: 945–6).

Embodied in the principle of universal adult suffrage, and given effect through popularly elected representative institutions, democracy was thus a revolutionary principle for a society marked by multiple hierarchies, and entailing modes of oppression entrenched over centuries. The major challenges were caste dominance (often congruent with economic dominance in the structures of land ownership), patriarchal domination over women, and vast economic disparities, with a large population whose life conditions were marked by poverty and deprivation. In a predominantly agrarian—often feudal—society, the iniquities of the caste system, and its linkages with ownership and control over land, was the most striking manifestation of social inequality. The introduction of political equality in such a society should have been explosive but Ambedkar had correctly foreseen the resilience of entrenched structures.

The superimposition of democracy on these structures was expected to dissolve older ascriptive identities, and create in their stead the new overarching identity of the Indian citizen, equal before the law and equal in political voice. The presumption that political modernity would naturally come to supplant tradition was however belied, as the vote of the subordinate castes was easily assimilated into existing patron–client relationships. The place of caste in modern democratic politics now became the object of fascination for political scientists in the 1960s and 1970s. Arguing that modernity and tradition are not radically contradictory, Lloyd and Susanne Rudolph noted that Indians seemed to be forming 'their notions of common citizenship and common humanity by expanding rather than destroying the natural associations of birth and locality'(Rudolph and Rudolph 1967: 111–12). Caste itself, Rajni Kothari argued, was transformed in the process of its appropriation by modern democratic politics. The real challenge therefore lay not in the destruction of tradition, but in the traditionalization of modernity itself, as the secular dimensions imparted by modern democratic politics became an enduring part of India's tradition (Kothari 1970: 23).

Participation, Mobilization, and Contestation

In the period immediately after independence, political participation was largely restricted to elections, but it was not long before other forms of political mobilization began to emerge. Presaging later forms of identity politics were movements based on language (the anti-Hindi agitation in Tamil Nadu and the conflicts between the Assamese and the Bengalis in Assam), religion (as in the demand for a Punjabi *Suba*), or region (as in the 'sons of the soil' movement in Maharashtra). Later identity-based mobilizations took various forms: movements for greater autonomy or statehood; mobilization by the backward classes (for example in Gujarat in the mid-1980s and in Uttar Pradesh and Bihar in the 1990s); and movements related to tribal identity (such as the autonomy movements in North-East India, and also the Jharkhand and Chhatisgarh movements). Ethnic conflict in Punjab and Assam was at the forefront of Indian politics in the 1980s, while the North-East and Jammu and Kashmir have remained more continuously troubled. Interest-based political mobilization initially took the form of struggles of the peasantry and agricultural labour in the Naxalbari and Telengana movements. In the mid-1980s, it was the turn of the middle-caste farmers of north India to organize themselves politically in formations like the Bharatiya Kisan Union. Atul Kohli has intepreted the proliferation of political mobilization as too much of the wrong kind of democracy, and not enough of the right kind (1990: x). India's democracy, he argues, has encouraged unprincipled mobilization and overpoliticization, leading to ever-increasing demands on the state, seen as the controller of scarce national resources, both material and symbolic. The weakening of state institutions, unable to accommodate and manage these conflicting demands, has led to a 'crisis of governability' (ibid.: 20).

Political participation measured by voter turnout has been continuously increasing. In the first two general elections, it was just under 50 per cent, but in all the landmark elections[13] such as those of 1977, 1984, 1989, and 1998, it has stood at over 60 per cent, which compares favourably with voter turnouts in the western democracies. It has also been observed that voter apathy is largely confined to the affluent, while the underprivileged sections of society come out to vote in larger numbers. Moreover, an *adivasi* is almost as likely to vote as an upper caste or Other Backward Class (OBC) Hindu, while in a state like Uttar Pradesh, the odds that a *dalit* will cast his vote are substantially higher than that for the upper castes (Yadav 2000: 122–34). Despite the encouraging signs that they portend, there is reason to be cautious in not inferring from these facts more than they can tell us about the health of a democracy. Nevertheless, these facts have laid to rest many assumptions that, on the basis of the experience of the world's older democracies, are taken to be axiomatically true of democracy per se. The assumption that educational and economic advancement hold the key to higher participation is one of these.

Recent years have witnessed the emergence of two trends which are quite unparalleled in their attempt to extend the frontiers of Indian democracy. These are the multitude of social movements (sometimes also called grassroots politics) and the political assertions of the historically disadvantaged lower castes, primarily the *dalit*s and the castes officially designated as the Other Backward Classes. The newer social movements emerged as a response to, among other things, the violations of civil liberties and human rights, the subordinate position of women in Indian society, the degradation of the environment, the population displacement caused by development projects, and the destruction of tribal cultures. These have often been referred to as 'new social movements', because of an apparent similarity with contemporary social movements in Western Europe, such as the women's, peace, and environmental movements. A more cautious approach to labelling would probably be more prudent, for the European counterparts

13 The 1977 election, held after the Emergency, was the election that brought the first non-Congress government to power at the Centre; the 1984 election, in the wake of Mrs Gandhi's assassination, gave the Congress under Rajiv Gandhi its biggest majority ever; the 1989 election brought the Janata Dal to power on the issue of the Bofors scandal.

of the so-called new social movements in India were all essentially post-industrial, post-materialist movements, led by the middle-classes, arising out of the disillusionment with institutional state-sponsored politics, and seeking alternative political spaces through the reconstitution of civil society (Offe 1985). Social movements in India have had a rather different character. They are not post-industrial movements (in many cases, they are pre-industrial), and while several are active in the arena of extra-parliamentary politics, their claims are perforce addressed to the state. Ecological conflicts in India, for example, have not been movements of middle-class urban environmentalism, but rather livelihood struggles for people whose lives depend on natural resources such as forests and the sea (Gadgil and Guha 1994). Thus, whether it is the struggle against felling trees in the forests of Garhwal and Kumaon, or that against bauxite mining in the largely tribal belt of the Gandhamardan hills in Orissa, or even that against commercial fishing trawlers off the coast of Kerala, these are clearly quite distinct from the environmental movements in the western hemisphere.

What is new about these social movements from the mid-1980s onward is that they are not linked to any revolutionary programme (as, for instance, the earlier peasant movements were), or to party politics, and rarely even to each other. Thus, for instance, movements defending human rights and civil liberties have worked independently of the women's movement, and both these separately from the environmental movement. Indeed, it has been argued that their fragmentation and ad hocism is the chief malady of these movements, as it prevents them from providing an alternative agenda for radical social change (Kothari 1997: 448). Nevertheless, these movements can be said to have expanded the frontiers of conventional politics quite considerably and, even from their distinct vantage point of extra-parliamentary protest, added to the vocabulary of Indian democracy.

The political assertions of the historically disadvantaged castes in the 1990s have, at least partly, been linked to the implementation of the Mandal Commission Report (submitted in 1980, but implemented only two years later by the V.P. Singh government), guaranteeing reserved quotas for members of these castes. 'Compensatory discrimination' (Galanter 1984) had already been provided for in the Constitution, through reservation in parliament as well as the state legislatures, public employment, and education for the Scheduled Castes and Scheduled Tribes, approximately in accordance with their proportion in the population. Almost contemporaneously with the acceptance of the Mandal Commission's recommendations, recent years have seen the emergence of a politcal alliance of the *dalit–bahujan* castes, often seeking also to encompass the Muslim minority in its fold. The political parties representing these social groups are conventionally identified as the Bahujan Samaj Party (BSP), the Samajwadi Party, and sections of the Janata Dal. Their geographical concentration has been mainly in the plains of north India, especially in Bihar and Uttar Pradesh, and their ideological programme has also been somewhat limited; that of the BSP, for example, has remained largely restricted to the 'capture' of political power which it sees as the first essential step to its transformation of Hindu society. Being largely devoid of an economic or even larger politcal programme has meant that the BSP is content to play the politics of the moment, instead of articulating a comprehensive programme of long-term social change. Its role in truly democratizing Indian society and polity will therefore depend upon its ability to forge not just political alliances, but also ideological alliances with a multitude of oppressed groups sharing a more integrated vision for the future. The larger trend signified by these developments is the 'ethnification' of the party system, such that we find all the major political parties openly grounding their political appeal in ethnic identity. Kanchan Chandra has argued that even as we take cognizance of the fact that previously marginalized groups are entering the political arena in larger numbers than ever before, we need also to remember the terms on which they are being inducted (Chandra 1999).

What have these recent assertions meant for the process of democratization in India? Many scholars have observed that these developments have contributed to the deepening of Indian democracy. It might, however, be more accurate to say that they have contributed to making Indian democracy more inclusive, by extending its range rather than deepening it. The first view, of a more inclusive democracy, involves a picture of Indian society exclusively in terms of its caste-based social stratification, with democracy steadily chipping away at the hierarchy and moving downwards. The project of deepening democracy, on the other hand, invokes a picture of greater complexity in which caste is not the singular axis of social stratification, and inequalities of, say, class and gender also count, as do the handicaps stemming from belonging to a particular religious or ethnic group. On this latter view, then, the deepening of democracy is contingent upon the most deprived and oppressed—in terms of caste *as well as* other criteria of stratification and social difference—being rendered more equal. As presently constituted, however, the idea of 'social justice' in *dalit–bahujan* political discourse has bestowed an altogether different meaning on the conception of social justice associated with the radical programme of the left. This new conception of social justice does not seek to transform the entire social order, or even to impart a more equitable meaning to the universalist idea of citizenship, but rather to create special categories of citizenship in relation to certain social goods, mainly education and public employment, and latterly, political power. Consequently, class differences are pushed into the background and those inequalities which happen not to be congruent with caste tend to get ignored. It is sometimes argued that even as policies are devised to compensate for historical wrongs and over time cause the abominable caste system to disappear, such processes may actually result in the greater entrenchment of caste identity and the consolidation of caste consciousness.

Democratic Challenges to Centralization

Even as participation in 'normal' politics expanded, and political mobilization of various types intensified, there was simultaneously taking place a greater concentration and centralization of political authority, reaching its acme in the National Emergency, declared by Prime Minister Indira Gandhi, between 1975 and 1977. With this, came a decline in the legitimacy of the main institutions of governance and democracy (including Parliament, the judiciary, and the free press), as also the greater visibility of political violence and corruption in public life. The centralized control of its leadership over the Congress party in the years of its unchallenged supremacy gradually extended to centralization in administration, as well as centralization at the level of the Union government vis-à-vis the states. Centralization was also inherent in the logic of the development strategy chosen at independence. A command economy, with centralized planning and centrally administered resources, could not but constrain severely the formal federal structure of governance.

In recent years, the logic of democratization has, along with other factors, provided some counterweights to the centralization of power. At least three such counterweights can be readily identified. The first of these is the federalization of the polity, consequent upon the gradual erosion of what Rajni Kothari called 'the Congress system' and the emergence of regional parties as strong forces to be reckoned with in their own right. In 1987, the Sarkaria Commission on Centre–State Relations had made a series of wide-ranging recommendations for putting the Indian federation on a firmer footing. Its recommendations were never officially implemented, but in recent years, the patterns of voting in the general elections suggest that a federalization of the polity is willy-nilly taking place at the behest of the voter, rather than that of any government. Political parties which are regional in provenance, have acquired greater importance, as no government at the Centre has, since 1996, managed to sustain itself without the critical support of such political parties. By participating in government, or lending critical political support, these parties have drawn attention to the regional imbalances engendered by the centralized model of development planning. They have also come to enjoy a greater clout in their demands for resources than regional parties did when the distribution of development funds was decided by the Congress dispensation at the Centre, on the basis of the political complexion of the regime in a particular state. The manifest weakness of the Centre in recent years has, in any case, rendered it increasingly incapable of denying or discriminating against any state government, in the way in which stronger governments in the past were wont to do.

A second democratizing factor has been the revival, by the 73rd and 74th Constitutional Amendments, of the Panchayati Raj system. The idea of local democracy is generally justified by two kinds of arguments. The first, instrumental justification, suggests that decentralized decision-making is better than centralized decision-making because the latter can only provide inappropriately uniform solutions to diverse local problems. On the other hand, decentralized decision-making ensures that decisions are collectively arrived at, with the participation of all those who are likely to be affected by them. The second, and stronger, defence of local democracy is found in the view that the quality of political participation, and therefore of public life, will be positively transformed only when people gather together to collectively debate and deliberate on issues of common concern, and are provided with decision-making powers to give effect to their shared concerns.[14] Since the constitutional amendments came into effect in 1993, most states, barring a few, have held elections to the new *panchayats* and despite mixed results, the overall experience bodes well. Voter turnout in *panchayat* elections is generally higher than for assembly or parliamentary elections, there is more energetic participation in activities like campaigning, and people are on the whole more involved in the election at a level which is more proximate to them. The provisions for reservation of one-third seats for women in *panchayats* at every level, and for reservation for *dalits* and *adivasis* in accordance with their proportion in the population, have given a new impetus to local democracy. Stories abound of the constraints under which dalit, adivasi, and women representatives function or are not allowed to do so. No-confidence motions are passed to remove them from office, in order to subvert the intent of the Amendment. Dominant and powerful upper-caste groups often effectively control the elected representatives, whose subordinate social status prevents them from asserting themselves. Similarly, elected women *sarpanches* are often replaced by proxies—usually their husbands—who virtually run the *panchayats*. There are, however, heartening stories also of how several individuals elected against such reserved seats resist being removed or co-opted. Some even managed to prevent the appropriation of development funds by dominant groups, and impart transparency and a new direction to local development works, such that these are sensitive to the needs of the poorer sections of local society. Above all, there is a new consciousness of the empowerment opportunities provided by these local institutions, and with it a greater political awareness as well as the desire to acquire education and the skills needed to participate.

A third factor has been the emergence of environmental and other movements, protesting against the dominant strategy of development. Through such movements, people have begun to demand a voice in the choice and location of development projects,

14 Democracy, writes Benjamin Barber, is not representative government or majority rule, but citizen self-government. 'It makes citizenship not a condition of participation but one of participation's richest fruits' (Barber 1984: 212).

based upon the consequences these projects are likely to have for local society. The movement against the construction of the Sardar Sarovar dam in the Narmada Valley is only the most well-known example of these. Planning has, since independence, been a rather closed-door affair dominated by economists and scientists, rarely allowing local voices to intrude upon, let alone inform, their deliberations. This model of development planning has been challenged not only by movements such as those mentioned above, but also by alternative and more sustainable models of development that have emerged through practice. The mobilization of the village community of Ralegaon Shindi by Annasaheb Hazare is one such example of how community effort transformed the life of a village which could produce barely 30 per cent of its food requirement. Galvanized into action by Hazare, the people built storage ponds and embankments to collect rainwater, eventually leading to the recharge of the groundwater table and increased crop productivity. Both the Narmada Bachao Andolan and the Ralegaon Shindi experiment not only convey a message in favour of sustainable and decentralized development but are also underpinned by a belief in participatory democracy.

On the whole, therefore, it is apparent that there has been a tremendous increase in political participation and contestation, measured not only by voter turnout and formal political competition but also by the various social movements that have drawn in large numbers of the dispossessed and marginalized social groups. Democracy has firmly taken hold of the political imagination. It is another matter that these groups are yet to acquire an effective voice in the political process of the country, and until that is achieved, the promise of Indian democracy will remain unrealized.

Judging Indian Democracy

How then do we judge the record of Indian democracy over the last fifty-odd years? One plausible way of attempting this is to invoke the distinction, posited at the beginning of this chapter, between procedural and substantive democracy, and evaluate the performance of India's democracy on the major indices that each of these encompass. Doing so might help us to appreciate why Indian democracy is neither an unqualified success nor an unmitigated failure. It has undoubtedly scored some remarkable successes, but it continues also to be trapped within the confines of oppressive social structures and economic inequalities that prevent its full potential from being realized.

Two of the most commonly used indices of a procedurally adequate democracy are those already discussed at some length above, viz. political participation and contestation. But a closer examination of the Indian record on procedural democracy would appear to warrant an assessment of some of the basic principles of democracy to which the Indian Constitution was committed. These included universal adult suffrage, one person–one vote, equality before the law and equal protection of the law, and an array of personal freedoms and civil liberties. Further, political accountability and governmental responsiveness were implicit attributes of the parliamentary system in which voters could influence policy through their representatives and punish non-performing governments at the hustings. While Indian democracy has acquitted itself passably on most of these counts, there have nevertheless been strains which cannot be altogether ignored.

Surveys have repeatedly shown that the poor and unschooled have regularly exercised their franchise, whereas it is the more educated and affluent classes that tend to be apathetic. The most striking, and oft-cited, validation of universal suffrage in a society marked by poverty and illiteracy is the 1977 election in which the authoritarian Emergency regime was decisively defeated. The principle of one person–one vote, however, can and sometimes does tend to work against religious minorities and other disadvantaged groups. In relatively homogeneous societies, the principle of rule by the majority is, in technical terms, simply the best procedure for decision making, because it is the only plausible choice between two extremes. The first of these—which requires unanimity in decision making—is clearly unrealistic while the second—decision making by the minority—is obviously unacceptable. In such societies, further, the composition of majorities and minorities would differ from one political issue to another. The same people who are of one view on Policy A may be of completely opposed views on Policy B. Enlarging this picture to a large and complex polity, it is apparent that majorities and minorities are relatively fluid entities in homogenous societies.

In heterogenous societies, by contrast, majorities and minorities defined in terms of religion or race have relatively fixed identities, and their proportions do not vary significantly. This implies that just as a majority is more or less permanently so, a minority is equally permanently a minority. In such societies, then, the operation of the principle of majority rule is bound to prejudice the interests of minorities, by constantly privileging the aspirations of the majority. This presupposes, of course, that all the issues that are being decided upon are of a non-secular nature, or that on every policy issue there will be a majority and a minority perspective which will differ in every particular. This is obviously not true. Nevertheless, important questions such as the rights of minorities to their own way of life, and guarantees against discrimination, are necessarily rendered vulnerable if they depend upon the pleasure of a majority which owes allegiance to a completely contrary and even hostile world-view. This is why democracies in heterogeneous societies are faced with the difficult task of negotiating a tricky balance between, on the one hand, the imperative of providing adequate safeguards for minorities and, on the other, the necessary pursuit of a universalistic ethic of citizenship which draws the citizens of the polity together as the joint authors of common purposes.

The makers of India's Constitution were firm in their rejection of systems of proportional representation, because they believed that the creation of Indian nationhood would be inhibited by such a system. However, the insistence of some members of religious minorities on proportional representation appears to have had some basis if we consider the facts regarding the representation of religious minorities. Muslims, for instance, have been consistently under-represented in Parliament. Though they constitute approximately 12 per cent of India's population, Muslim representation in Parliament currently stands at 4.6 per cent (in the 13th Lok Sabha). It averaged 6 per cent in all the Lok Sabha elections from 1952 to 1998, and has registered a consistent decline since 1980 (Bhambhri 2000: xiii). Women's representation in the Lok Sabha, between 1952 and 1996, also averages only 6 per cent, with the highest ever proportion of women members in the lower house being 8.1 per cent (in 1984) (Parmar 1997: 51). This is part of the reason why the Women's Reservation Bill (pending before the Lok Sabha for the last two years) has acquired so much significance.

As the foundational moral principle underlying the idea of democracy, equality was enshrined in the Indian Constitution in two basic forms: equality before the law and equal protection of the law. The Constitution (Article 15) prohibited discrimination on grounds of religion, race, caste, sex, or place of birth, but qualified this by providing that the state could nevertheless make special provision for the advancement of any socially and educationally backward classes of citizens and for the Scheduled Castes and Scheduled Tribes. The equal protection of the law implies the protection of the citizen from coercion by other citizens as well as by the state itself. It is, however, not uncommon to encounter instances where state personnel, such as the police, not only fail to protect citizens for violence perpetrated by other (usually more powerful) citizens, but also themselves engage in the violation of citizens' rights. The rule of law may formally obtain, but autonomous spheres of power may and do emerge, inflicting injustices on subordinate social groups. The frequent episodes of caste massacres perpetrated by the Ranvir Sena against *dalits* in Bihar in recent years are only one example. Equality before the law is also severely compromised for those who lack the wherewithal to approach courts for the violation of their rights. Above all, social prejudice and discrimination remain impervious to legislative fiat.

The guarantees of freedom, especially civil liberties such as free speech and the freedom to dissent, have generally been sustained, except of course during the Emergency. Often, when challenges have arisen to these, the courts have stepped in to redress the balance (as the Supreme Court did in the famous *Crossroads* case in 1950).[15] The Emergency gave an impetus to the civil liberties movement, making citizens more vigilant about the protection of their rights. However, the pages of any newspaper will testify to the fact that, though civil liberties and personal freedom are formally recognized, gross violations of basic rights and freedoms continue to occur on a routine, almost daily basis. These include detention without trial; rape and other types of abuse and violence against women; forced evictions from dam sites, as well as the location of mines and other development projects; bonded labour; the forced confinement of labour or of the mentally ill, and many others. Nevertheless, Jean Drèze and Amartya Sen have argued (see chapter 10) that India has been more successful than China in preventing large-scale famine, primarily due to the existence of institutionalized adversarial politics and a free press which act as

15 See Granville Austin (1999: 40–2)

warning triggers, enabling a quick response from the government's crisis-management mechanisms.

Despite the fact that elections have been regularly held, and have for the most part been free and fair, it is on the twin dimensions of accountability and responsiveness that democracy in India, judged even on limited procedural criteria, has proved inadequate. Voters have periodically voted out non-performing or corrupt or repressive regimes, but the structures of governance—never particularly transparent—have tended to be largely inaccessible to the ordinary citizen. Recent years have witnessed the voicing of popular demand for a right to information, and some legislative initiatives in that direction. For instance, members of the Mazdoor Kisan Shakti Sangathan in Rajasthan have organized *jan sunwai*s, in which elected *panchayat* leaders are questioned about their use of development funds. The works actually undertaken and the accounts pertaining to them are cross-checked in the presence of administrative officials, and the occasional *sarpanch* guilty of misappropriation of funds has even been shamed into returning these. Bringing about greater accountability at every level of the political system remains an important challenge to Indian democracy.

The democratic process also mediates the responsiveness of the administration to the needs of the people, insofar as it is through elected representatives that the people's needs and aspirations are communicated to policy-making institutions. The record of Indian democracy on this score is also fairly weak, as contending viewpoints and interests rarely inform the process of policy-making. Indeed, it is even believed to be a virtue of such institutions that they are largely insulated from popular pressure! The only exceptions to this may occasionally be found at the *panchayat* level in some states where the *panchayati raj* experiment has been reasonably successful. One such success is reported in the study by Richard Crook and James Manor of *panchayat*s in Karnataka (see chapter 15). Using survey methodology along with other measures, the respondents were asked about the extent to which popular preferences—in order of perceived importance—were fulfilled by official policies, as also about their satisfaction with particular projects. They found that because citizens were familiar with the business of representing their concerns to their elected representatives and constantly put pressure on them, the policy response was reasonably satisfactory, though to a lesser degree for women and *dalit*s.

A definition of democracy limited to its formal institutional aspects thus yields a reasonably comforting picture of Indian democracy. However, even by these purely procedural criteria, there are, as we have seen, inadequacies that should inhibit any observer from claiming more than partial success. On a substantive definition of democracy, however, a different and somewhat more sobering picture of Indian democracy emerges. The substantive conception of democracy encourages us to consider how political equality is compromised and even undermined by inequalities in the distribution of resources and power in a society, and how the concentration of economic and social power is a factor that limits democracy. Thus, for instance, social relations of domination and subordination ensure that, despite formal political equality, the interests of the powerless in society are largely ignored, while those of the powerful are not merely expressed, but often also embodied in policy. Clearly, the basic conditions for effective political participation require more than merely the guarantee of equal political rights and a vote that is formally weighed as equal to every other. The rights of equal citizenship are, in and of themselves, necessary conditions for democracy, but the sufficient conditions require that the meaningful exercise of these citizenship rights be assured to all.[16]

In India, the obstacles to such a meaningful exercise of the equal rights of citizenship are formidable. Patriarchal domination, caste hierarchy, and the vulnerability of *adivasis* and minorities are among the most visible symbols of these. These are often congruent or overlaid with economic and social deprivation. In a complex society, where such forms of oppression have been entrenched across centuries, there are also multiple identities yielding as many oppressions: a *dalit* woman who also happens to be a landless labourer, for example, is simultaneously subject to subordination in the caste hierachy, patriarchal subjugation, and class exploitation. What, in real terms, are her chances of enjoying the constitutional rights of equal citizenship? And what, further, are the possibilities of her being able to meaningfully participate in a democratic polity, as someone capable of exercising her political rights in an enlightened manner, or in calling her democratically elected government to account.

16 See Jayal (1999), excerpted in chapter 6 of this volume.

Indian Democracy: A Test Case for Democratic Theory?

It was in recognition of the formidable obstacles to democracy in India that the country was described as 'an ideal case for testing democratic theories' (Weiner 1983: 51). According to the standard Western understanding of democracy, the conditions that are hospitable to democratic institutionalization include a homogeneous society and reasonable social and economic equality. India, being a highly diverse, multicultural, and hierarchical society, with a predominantly agrarian (often feudal) economy, was assumed to lack a cultural predisposition to democracy. However, the experience of the last two decades in particular has shown that 'the idea of democracy has...irreversibly entered the Indian political imagination' (Khilnani 1997: 60), substantively transforming the principle of political authority in Indian society. We may, of course, qualify this assertion by recognizing that this phenomenon also places a greater strain on democratic structures, understood in terms of Western institutions (Kaviraj 1991: 93).

The Indian experience interrogates the received wisdom of democratic theory, and qualifies some of its usually uncontested assumptions. One explanation of the success of India's democratic institutions suggested that British colonialism was unique in providing opportunities of political participation to the nationalist elites, which equipped them with the requisite skills and so laid the foundation for democratization after independence (Weiner 1989). This can form but a small part of a more complex explanation which takes into account the rich legacy of the nationalist movement itself, despite the derivative nature of its discourses (Chatterjee 1986). Independent India's experiment with democracy also presents a contrast to the troubled political history of India's neighbours in the subcontinent in which, despite the same historical legacy, military regimes have been the rule and democratic regimes the exception. Despite the many and manifest inadequacies of Indian democracy, there is little basis for the argument that the main prop of India's formally democratic structure has been 'a creeping if mainly covert authoritarianism' (Jalal 1995: 251).

The practice of democracy in India speaks to at least three important debates in democratic theory. These are the debates on democracy and diversity; democracy and development; and democracy and civil society.

DEMOCRACY AND DIVERSITY

Classical liberal theory was, till the middle of the twentieth century, rather ambivalent on the question of cultural diversity. The civil rights movement in the United States was arguably the first significant challenge of pluralism in a liberal polity. In later decades, the demands for cultural recognition and rights articulated by immigrant populations in Europe and by indigenous people in Australia, Canada, and the United States brought liberal theory to a turning point in its history. Its individualistic premises came to be interrogated, especially by communitarian philosophers who insisted that a liberal polity that claims to be committed to individual equality but is blind to diversity is bound to be insufficiently respectful of cultural plurality. This is so because the presumption of equality precludes a special sensitivity to those groups which, by virtue of their distinctive cultural identity, are rendered socially unequal. How liberal societies negotiate the balance between recognizing plurality and endorsing equality remains the unresolved problem to which communitarian theorists have alerted us. What can the Indian experience contribute to this debate?

The Indian experience anticipated this debate, in the sense that the discussion on community and nation in the freedom movement, as also the deliberations of the Constituent Assembly, resulted in a constitutional document that was more sensitive to the needs of a plural society than any other constitution till that time. The Indian Constitution was unique in providing for rights for cultural collectivities, at a time when the debate in political theory—on the question of whether only individuals are plausible bearers of rights, or whether groups can have rights, too—was still thirty years away. Even as the Constitution enunciated the quintessentially liberal principle of state neutrality between religions, it provided for freedom of religion, and the protection of the cultural and educational rights of religious minorities. For social groups disadvantaged by histories of oppressive social practices, the Constitution made special provision for compensatory discrimination, through reservations in representative institutions, public employment, and education. Setting apart the Indian state's role in effectively fomenting and ineffectually managing ethnic conflict, the history of the last fifty years has nuanced the debate on democracy and diversity considerably. The Shah Bano case (and the subsequent enactment of the Muslim Women [Protection of Rights in Divorce] Act, 1986), for instance, showed how the commitment to cultural rights for minority communities can sometimes endorse practices that violate the principles of gender justice, as also the constitutionally guaranteed rights of equal citizenship. Should states endeavour merely to provide for formal equality between diverse communities in a society, regardless of inequalities of voice within the community? Should there be a set of core individual rights which can, under no circumstances, be trumped by the cultural rights of the community? What are the limits of cultural rights and how should they be determined—by constitution-makers, the state, the community, or affected sections of the community?[17]

DEMOCRACY AND DEVELOPMENT

The second debate to which the Indian experience is germane is, of course, the debate on democracy and development. Does the existence of democratic institutions make the task of development more difficult by allowing the unrestricted expression of diverse interests and claims on scarce national resources? This argument was offered as crisis-management analysis by American social scientists in the 1960s and 1970s,[18] and was also offered as an explanation for the troubled career of Indian democracy by scholars in the 1980s. As we saw in an earlier section, the comparative evidence on whether development and democracy inhibit or encourage each other remains inconclusive. What does the Indian experience suggest?

Without doubt, both development and democracy were integral to the modernizing project of the Indian state at independence. It was widely assumed that development—as the imitative traversing of a path rehearsed and charted elsewhere in the world—would

17 Cf. Jayal (1998).

18 For a comprehensive treatment and critique of the political development school and its pessimism about the prospects for democracy in the Third World, see Paul Cammack (1997).

inform the transition to an industrial economy, lend a helping hand to the project of social transformation, and work in tandem with political democratization. Imitatively conceived, 'development' was naturally defined in fairly conventional terms, viz. as economic growth. By this definition, the Indian economy has not performed spectacularly well, and certainly not in any way comparable to the economic performance of the so-called Asian Tigers. Of course, the East Asian miracle ceased to be the exemplar of development after the recent financial crisis in these economies, which has even been linked with the absence of democracy, as it prevented public participation and transparency in business (Sen 2000: 185).

Unlike the East Asian economies, India—which adopted the strategy of industrialization led by the public sector and based on import-substitution, rather than an export-led model—maintained a very modest but consistent rate of growth. Its major failure has been the inability to distribute the benefits of growth, as evidenced in the area of human development; on these indicators India's performance has been dismal, comparable with that of sub-Saharan Africa.[19] This is why it has become imperative to reconsider the model of development and focus on its human dimensions, especially the enlargement of what Jean Drèze and Amartya Sen have called human capabilities (1996: 10–13).

The Indian experience suggests, firstly, that the debate on democracy and development, both empirically and normatively, is somewhat misconceived. It assumes three things that may be contested: that these are contradictory rather than compatible goals; that societies are not historically constrained in choosing the one or the other as from a restaurant menu; and that trade-offs can be made between them. By positing democracy and development as mutually exclusive alternatives, it ignores the fact that possession of equal democratic rights can be a powerful weapon against poverty and deprivation, insofar as it makes it possible for people to make claims upon the state, and insist that it respond

19 Drèze and Sen have noted that, despite India's relative political stability and democratic record, economic and social inequalities, including gender inequality, are more acute in India than in sub-Saharan Africa. The similarities include their performance on adult literacy and infant mortality (Drèze and Sen 1996: 30–2).

to their needs. Democratic states are, despite all their flaws, somewhat more likely to be responsive to people's needs than undemocratic ones. The enthusiastic participation of India's poor in elections certainly suggests that the poor are not indifferent to the importance of their civil and political rights. However, the lack of success that has undoubtedly attended the efforts of the poor to give voice to their basic needs cannot be blamed on democracy per se, but should be attributed to the concentration of economic and social power that predisposes the state to act in ways that are biased in favour of the 'dominant coalition' (Bardhan 1984) rather than the underprivileged. In any event, if we value democracy for its own sake rather than for any instrumental purposes that it might serve, we would attach greater importance to democracy and try to calibrate our other social and economic goals to the limitations imposed by it.[20]

Secondly, and consistently with the first caveat, the Indian experience also suggests the importance of interrogating the received notion of development in terms of economic growth. By privileging the dimension of human development instead, it draws attention to the importance of providing people with what Amartya Sen has called economic entitlements and social opportunity structures, as a way of enlarging the capabilities of human beings, and their ability to determine their own life plans. This expanded notion translates development into terms that are more immediately human, instead of the complex statistical data which, whether they report growth rates that are dismally low or excitingly high, make sense chiefly to economists, and are otherwise far removed from the real lives and experiences of ordinary people. It is this sense of development that is most compatible with democracy, as both are informed by the like objective of making people participants in a common endeavour. So defined, development makes political participation more meaningful, just as democracy in the best sense makes it possible for people to press their claims for development (as they define it) upon the state.

[20] If, for instance, it were analogously argued that democracy encourages caste politics, and therefore a caste-neutral dictatorship is preferable, our anterior commitment to the value of democracy would generally predispose us to tolerate caste politics, little though we may like it.

DEMOCRACY, STATE, AND CIVIL SOCIETY

The idea of 'civil society' took an East European detour to return to Western political theory after a long period of virtual oblivion. In most current usages, the concept carries with it the burden of normativity, as it is seen as a category of approval, a valuable goal, and a desideratum. In descriptive terms, civil society is frequently conceptualized as a space or an arena which stands in necessary opposition to the state, its other, that which it is defined in terms of and against. Indeed, following Hegel, it is often defined as the realm of social interaction that falls between the family, on the one hand, and the state, on the other. A more robust notion of civil society, tracing its ancestry to Tocqueville, sees civil society as a check upon the potentially arbitrary and even tyrannical tendencies of the state. This implies that civil society must be independent of the state, in principle accessible to all citizens, and a genuinely participatory arena of free civic engagement, deliberation, discussion, and dialogue (Chandhoke 1998: 162ff).

In the different conceptions of civil society on offer, there is some equivocation on the role of the state, which may be the target of civil vigilance but also, if necessary, of attack by civil society. The state, it is believed, should play a positive role in the promotion of civil society, by providing the institutional framework within which civil society can prosper and flourish. Thus, to the extent that it guarantees (or not) freedom, rights, and equality for its citizens, it can encourage or inhibit civil society. There is a clear presumption of democracy here, not only because civil society has the potential to ensure political accountability, but also because it is a genuinely participatory sphere, open to all. To this meaning of civil society, the existence of many voluntary associations and institutions such as a free press, is crucial.

Recent Indian experience cautions us against ignoring the difference between the descriptive and prescriptive aspects of civil society, because these aspects do not always converge, and because not all groups that inhabit the space we call civil society are animated by democratic ideals and purposes. Indeed, it is easy to think of many associations which are manifestly undemocratic, intolerant of plurality, and even advocates of incivility. This is why we should consider, as part of civil society, only those associations which affirm openness of entry and exit, and stand by universalist criteria of citizenship. As such, any association which excludes persons on the basis of ethnicity, class, or religious persuasion is clearly not a part of civil society. But civil society remains an important site of ideological contestation, where battles such as those between liberal secularism and religious majoritarianism, or between liberalization and welfare, are joined.

The importance of civil society in India is intimately linked to the future of democracy. One of the most important tasks of civil society in India is arguably to effect a bridging of the gap between democracy in the formal structures of governance, on the one hand, and the absence of the necessary conditions for the realization of democracy, on the other. Further, the future of neither civil society nor democracy can be delinked from the role of the state, despite the gradual erosion of its pre-eminence in contemporary India. Democracy requires the state, because the state alone can create conditions for the effective exercise of citizenship, provide and sustain the framework within which the rights and obligations of citizens can be respected and guaranteed, and arbitrate and resolve disputes about these. But precisely because states are notoriously prone to undermining, and even destroying, democratic institutions, a strong civil society is needed as a bulwark against these authoritarian tendencies.

While Indian democracy today is, in institutional terms, fairly well secured, it remains embattled by forces both external and internal. Internally, the most important challenge is the project of Hindutva, which has gained ideological ground in the recent past, seeking to redefine democracy in emphatically majoritarian terms and exposing the tenuous character of Indian pluralism. Internally, it also continues to be faced by the enduring challenge of creating a more equal society, and reducing the vast economic disparities that are being accentuated by the process of globalization. That process, of course, represents the major external challenge, seeking to legislate global regimes in such matters as trade, environmental regulation, and intellectual property. Accompanying these are the attempts to lay down global standards for 'good governance', and to forge networks between non-governmental organizations for the creation of a 'transnational' civil society. In all of these, there is little space for democratic politics as self-determination.

The project of democracy in India today is thus both fragile and beleaguered. Though it is commonly believed that the greatest signifier of its success is the fact of its having survived and endured, that is to make a virtue of necessity. It might be more accurate to say that, despite all its alarming deficiencies, the singular merit of Indian democracy lies in its success in providing a space for political contestation and an opportunity for the articulation of a variety of claims.

References

Ambedkar, B.R. [1949], (1968), 'Speech on the Adoption of the Constitution' in B. Shiva Rao (ed.), *The Framing of India's Constitution: Select Documents*, vol. IV. New Delhi: Indian Institute of Public Adminstration.

Arblaster, Anthony (1987), *Democracy*. Milton Keynes: Open University Press.

Austin, Granville [1966], (1999), *The Indian Constitution: Cornerstone of a Nation*. Delhi: Oxford University Press.

———— (2000), *Working a Democratic Constitution: The Indian Experience*. New Delhi: Oxford University Press.

Barber, Benjamin R. (1984), *Strong Democracy: Participatory Politics for a New Age*. Berkeley: University of California Press.

Bardhan, Pranab (1984), *The Political Economy of Development in India*. Delhi: Oxford University Press.

———— (1993), 'Symposium on Democracy and Development', *Journal of Economic Perspectives*, vol. 7, no. 3.

Beetham, David, (1993) 'Liberal Democracy and the Limits of Democratization' in David Held (ed.), *Prospects for Democracy*. Oxford: Polity Press.

———— (1994), 'Key Principles and Indices for a Democratic Audit' in David Beetham (ed.), *Defining and Measuring Democracy*. London: Sage Publications.

Bhambhri, C.P. (2000), *The Indian State After Independence*. New Delhi: Shipra Publications.

Cammack, Paul (1997), *Capitalism and Democracy in the Third World: The Doctrine for Political Development*. London: Leicester University Press.

Chandhoke, Neera (1998), *The State and Civil Society: Explorations in Political Theory*. New Delhi: Sage Publications.

Chandra, Bipan *et al.* (1988), *India's Struggle for Independence 1857–1947*. New Delhi: Penguin Books.

Chandra, Kanchan (1999), 'Post-Congress Politics in Uttar Pradesh: The Ethnification of the Party System and Its Consequences' in

Ramashray Roy and Paul Wallace (eds), *Indian Politics and the 1998 Election: Regionalism Hindutva and State Politics.* New Delhi: Sage Publications.

Chatterjee, Partha (1986), *Nationalist Thought and the Colonial World: A Derivative Discourse.* Delhi: Oxford University Press.

Chiriyankandath, James (1992), '"Democracy" Under the Raj: Elections and Separate Representation in British India', *Journal of Commonwealth and Comparative Politics*, vol. 30, no. 1.

Dahl, Robert (1971), *Polyarchy: Participation and Opposition.* New Haven: Yale University Press.

——— (1991), *Democracy and Its Critics.* New Delhi: Orient Longman Ltd.

Drèze, Jean and Amartya Sen (1996), *India: Economic Development and Social Opportunity.* New Delhi: Oxford University Press.

Eckersley, Robyn (1996), 'Liberal Democracy and the Right of Nature: The Struggle for Inclusion' in Freya Mathews (ed.), *Ecology and Democracy.* London: Frank Class.

Fukuyama, Francis (1992), *The End of History and the Last Man.* New York: Free Press.

Gadgil, Madhav and Ramachandra Guha (1994), 'Ecological Conflicts and the Environmental Movement in India', *Development and Change*, vol. 25, no. 1.

Galanter, Marc (1984), *Competing Equalities: Law and the Backward Classes in India.* Delhi: Oxford University Press.

Gutmann, Amy (1993), 'Democracy' in Robert E. Goodin and Philip Pettit (eds), *A Companion to Contemporary Political Philosophy.* Oxford: Blackwell.

Hadenius, Axel (1992), *Democracy and Development.* Cambridge: Cambridge University Press.

Held, David (1987), *Models of Democracy.* Oxford: Polity Press.

Hornblower, Simon (1986), 'Greece: The History of the Classical Period' in John Boardman, Jasper Griffin and Oswyn Murray (eds), *The Oxford History of the Classical World.* Oxford: Oxford University Press.

Huntington, Samuel (1991), *The Third Wave: Democratization in the Late Twentieth Century.* Oklahoma: University of Oklahoma Press.

Jalal, Ayesha (1995), *Democracy and Authoritarianism in South Asia.* Cambridge: Cambridge Univesity Press.

Jayal, Niraja Gopal (1998), 'Secularism, Identities and Representative Democracy' in Mushirul Hasan (ed.), *Islam, Communities and the*

Nation: Muslim Identities in South Asia and Beyond. New Delhi: Manohar Publishers.

———— (1999), *Democracy and the State: Welfare, Secularism and Development in Contemporary India.* Delhi: Oxford University Press.

Kaviraj, Sudipta (1991), 'On State, Society and Discourse in India' in James Manor (ed.), *Rethinking Third World Politics.* London: Longman.

Khilnani, Sunil (1997), *The Idea of India.* London: Hamish Hamilton.

Kohli, Atul (1986), 'Democracy and Development' in John Lewis and V. Kallab (eds), *Development Strategies Reconsidered.* Transaction Books.

———— (1990), *Democracy and Discontent: India's Growing Crisis of Governability.* Cambridge: Cambridge University Press.

———— (1993), 'Democracy Amid Economic Orthodoxy: Trends in Developing Countries', *Third World Quarterly,* vol. 14, no. 4.

Kothari, Rajni (1970), 'Introduction' in Kothari (ed.), *Caste in Indian Politics.* New Delhi: Orient Longman.

———— (1997), 'Rise of the Dalits and the Renewed Debate on Caste' in Partha Chatterjee (ed.), *State and Politics in India.* Delhi: Oxford University Press.

Leftwich, Adrian (1995), 'Two Cheers for Democracy? Democracy and the Developmental State' in Leftwich (ed.), *Democracy and Development.* Cambridge: Polity Press.

Lively, Jack (1975), *Democracy.* Oxford: Blackwell Books.

Macpherson, C.B. (1978), *The Real World of Democracy.* Oxford: Oxford University Press.

Moore Jr, Barrington [1966] (1977), *Social Origins of Dictatorship and Democracy.* Harmondsworth: Penguin Books.

Nehru, Jawaharlal, [1946] (1989), *The Discovery of India.* Delhi: Oxford University Press.

Nozick, Robert (1974), *Anarchy, State and Utopia.* New York: Basic Books.

Offe, Claus (1985), 'New Social Movements: Challenging the Boundaries of Institutional Politics', *Social Research,* vol. 52, no. 4.

Parekh, Bhikhu (1993), 'The Cultural Particularity of Liberal Democracy' in David Held (ed.), *Prospects for Democracy.* Oxford: Polity Press.

Parmar, Chandrika (1997), 'Factfile 1952–1997', *Seminar,* no. 457, *Empowering Women,* September.

Parry, Geraint and George Moyser (1994), 'More Participation, More Democracy?' in David Beetham (ed.), *Defining and Measuring Democracy*. London: Sage Publications.

Pateman, Carole (1970), *Participation and Democratic Theory*. Cambridge: Cambridge University Press.

Potter, David, David Goldblatt, Margaret Kiloh and Paul Lewis (eds) (1977), *Democratization*. Cambridge: Polity Press in association with The Open University.

Przeworski, Adam *et al.* (1995), *Sustainable Democracy*. Cambridge: Cambridge University Press.

Przeworski, Adam and Fernando Limongi (1993), 'Political Regimes and Economic growth', *Journal of Economic Perspectives*, vol. 7, no. 3.

Putnam, Robert (1993), *Making Democracy Work: Civic Traditions in Modern Italy*. New Jersey: Princeton University Press.

Rudolph, Lloyd I. and Susanne H. Rudolph (1967), *The Modernity of Tradition: Political Development in India*. Chicago: Univesity of Chicago Press.

Rueschemeyer, Dietrich, Evelyn Huber Stephens and John D. Stephens (1992), *Capitalist Development and Democracy*. Cambridge: Cambridge University Press.

Sarkar, Sumit (1983), *Modern India: 1885–1947*. New Delhi: Macmillan India.

Schmitter, Philippe C. and Terry L. Karl (1991), 'What Democracy is...And is Not', *The Journal of Democracy*, vol. 2, no. 3.

Schumpeter, Joseph [1943] (1979), *Capitalism, Socialism and Democracy*. London: George Allen and Unwin.

Sen, Amartya (2000), *Development as Freedom*. New Delhi: Oxford University Press.

Shaikh, Farzana (1991), *Community and Consensus in Islam: Muslim Representation in Colonial India, 1860–1947*. Bombay: Orient Longman.

Sorensen, Georg (1993), *Democracy and Democratization: Processes and Prospects in a Changing World Boulder*. Colorado: Westview Press.

Weiner, Myron (1983), 'The Wounded Tiger: Maintaining India's Democratic Institutions' in Peter Lyon and James Manor (eds), *Transfer and Transformation: Political Institutions in the New Commonwealth*. Leicester: Leicester University Press.

——— (1989), 'Institution Building in India' in Myron Weiner and

Ashutosh Varshney (eds), *The Indian Paradox*. New Delhi: Sage Publications.

Yadav, Yogendra (2000), 'Understanding the Second Democratic Upsurge: Trends of Bahujan participation in electoral politics in the 1990s' in Francine Frankel, Zoya Hasan, Rajeev Bhargava and Balveer Arora (eds), *Transforming India: Social and Political Dynamics of Democracy*. Delhi: Oxford University Press.

Zakaria, Fareed (1997), 'The Rise of Illiberal Democracy', *Foreign Affairs*, November–December.

I

Indian Democracy Prefigured

The experience of representative institutions in colonial India, for the six decades preceding independence, has received little scholarly attention. Though these were patently institutions of limited democracy, the fact that they were extracted, inch by inch, from a reluctant colonial authority, makes them legitimate precursors of the democratic institutions that were established after independence. James Chiriyankandath's article in this section shows how elected institutions evolved under colonial rule, and were—along with participation in the national movement—a major channel of political socialization. Though the electorate was extremely restrictively defined, India's electorate in 1946 comprised 40 million voters, and electoral democracy became a familiar reality at least for some sections of the Indian population. The most important continuity between the pre- and post-independence periods, noted by Chiriyankandath, is that elections based on separate electorates made it virtually inevitable that political parties would—even after the abolition of separate electorates in independent India—appeal to caste, religious community, and regional loyalties. Indeed, he traces the controversies over the Mandal report, the Shah Bano case, and Sikh separatism directly to the legacy of separate representation and the recognition, by the state, of social groups on the basis of caste and religion.

David Washbrook's article sees the contradictions of both democracy and development in contemporary India as rooted in the historical legacies of the late colonial era. He points out that democratization in late colonial India was effected in a way that was compatible with colonial rule, and was mediated by a state apparatus that was heavily influenced by British political culture. In this culture, democracy was thought of rather instrumentally, and was generally accompanied by the expansion of state authority. Washbrook identifies two colonial legacies related to the idea of representation that continued to inform the practice of Indian democracy after independence. These are, firstly, the idea that the real function of representation is 'advisory', while the task of policy formulation is best left to the bureaucracy and the judiciary. The second is the question of who could properly represent whom, which laid the foundations for separate representation. In the political ideas of the ruling British elites, it was almost definitionally assumed that members of civil society could only represent sectional interests, and the state alone could represent the whole of society. The way in which the post-colonial state seeks legitimacy, Washbrook argues, shares an affinity with this view, and helps us to understand better the phenomenon of communal strife in contemporary India. Washbrook also provides a trenchant critique of the Government of India Act 1935 and the implications of the 1937 elections, both of which left a lasting imprint on the Indian constitution and polity, respectively. It is in the failure to interrogate the colonial inheritance that Washbrook also locates India's problems of development, and the bias of India's state-oriented development strategy towards the preservation of elite privileges.

1

'Democracy' Under the Raj: Elections and Separate Representation in British India+

*James Chiriyankandath**

Introduction: The Significance of Elections

You can no more expect representative institutions in their proper form to flourish in India than you can expect hot-house flowers to blossom in the icy cold of the North.[1]

Such were the unambiguous terms in which A.K. Fazl-ul-Huq, a minister in the Bengal government and former president of the Muslim League, damned the experiment in limited democracy five years into the working of the dyarchal constitution introduced by the 1919 Government of India Act. Forty-four years after independence, the survival of representative democratic institutions in the Republic of India appears to belie his dire prognosis. This paper is concerned with how elected institutions developed and democratic politics spread in the sixty years before independence.

+ *Journal of Commonwealth and Comparative Politics*, vol. 30, no. 1, 1992, pp. 39–64.

* I would like to thank Subrata Mitra and David Potter, for their helpful comments on the first draft of this article, and Susan Wiles, for painstakingly typing the tables.

1 Note by A.K. Fazl-ul-Huq, 'Reports of the Local Government on the Working of the Reformed Constitution, 1924', Cmd. 2362, *GB Parliamentary Papers 1924–25*, vol. 10, 5 July 1924, pp. 150–1.

The significance of the institutional framework in shaping politics has been an aspect emphasized in the recent historiography of the subcontinent. Some of the pioneering work in analysing the dynamics of elections in British India has come from scholars such as Chris Baker and Chris Bayly; but there is still a paucity of studies on the subject despite valuable contributions by Peter Reeves (on the United Provinces), Ian Talbot (on Punjab), and B.R. Tomlinson (on the Indian National Congress and elections in the 1930s).[2] There is still no published work devoted exclusively to one or more of the six sets of national and provincial elections that took place between 1920 and 1946. Nationalist historians have understandably tended to focus upon the role of Congress as an anti-colonial movement[3] while their Marxist and, more recently, 'subaltern, studies' counterparts have sought to emphasize economic and social changes.[4]

My hypothesis is that elections and the electoral framework help to determine the formation of mobilizable political categories within society. Harold Gould, writing about pre-independence Faizabad, remarks at 'how spontaneously...the ethnic dimensions of caste and religion came to the forefront once democratically

2 C. Baker, 'The Congress at the 1937 Elections in Madras', *Modern Asian Studies*, vol. 10, no. 4, 1976; C.A. Bayly, *The Local Roots of Indian Politics: Allahabad 1880–1920* (Oxford 1975); P. Reeves, *A Handbook to Elections in Uttar Pradesh, 1920–1951* (Delhi: 1975); I.A. Talbot, 'Muslim Political Mobilisation in Rural Punjab 1937–46', in P. Robb (ed.), *Rural India, Land, Power and Society under British Rule* (Delhi: 1986); B.R. Tomlinson, *The Indian National Congress and the Raj. 1929–42: The Penultimate Phase* (London: 1976). The significance of electoral politics in an Indian princely state is considered in my '"Communities at the Polls": Electoral Politics and the Mobilization of Communal Groups in Travancore', vol. 27, no. 3, 1993, pp. 643–65. *Modern Asian Studies.*

3 R.C. Majumdar, *History of the Freedom Movement* (Calcutta: 1962–3).

4 For instance, Sumit Sarkar argues, 'the massive anti-imperialist upsurge of 1919–22 is surely much too big a thing to be explained by a paltry extension of voting rights to at most between one and three per cent of the adult population. Far more significant were the economic and social consequences of the First World War, bringing to the surface and sharpening the numerous contradictions between Indian and British interests...' (S. Sarkar, *Modern India, 1885–1947* (London: 1989), p. 168). In point of fact about five per cent of adults were enfranchised (2.7 per cent of the total population).

constituted political arenas had been established'.[5] The form the new representative institutions took had far-reaching repercussions for the course of Indian politics. For Francis Robinson 'The character of the political arena and the outcome of struggles for political power between competing elites within it may determine whether a communal group is mobilized for political action or not.'[6]

Electoral politics, along with the politics of movement, whether nationalist, separatist, or 'subaltern' in scope, was an important channel of political socialization. The electoral arena and representative bodies acted as an intensive training ground for politicians in the art of successfully adapting the exogenous forms of competitive democratic politics to indigenous modes of political discourse and patterns of social organization. Furthermore, even if it did not necessarily politically educate a widening electorate in the manner envisaged by British Indian policy-makers, regular elections ensured that an alien form of political expression became accepted as a familiar reality by a significant section of the Indian population even before independence.

While we are primarily concerned with the establishment of democratic institutions in South Asia, the study of India's colonial experience of representative politics is also instructive from the broader perspective of the colonial impact on Afro-Asian political development. In the subcontinent, as in Africa, the British bequeathed a state that was an amalgam of authoritarian and statist, as well as democratic, aspects. Allowing for the very different setting, the principal distinguishing factor in India was the length of the process of colonial 'state formation': for instance, representative institutions were introduced in India almost six decades before independence, in contrast to a decade or two prior to the establishment of full self-government in Nigeria. Nevertheless, British rule reinforced ethnic division in both these plural societies with incremental devolutionary administrative policies.

5 H. Gould, 'The Emergence of Modern Indian Politics: Political Development in Faizabad. Part 2: 1935–1947', *The Journal of Commonwealth and Comparative Politics*, vol. 12, no. 2, 1974, p. 180.

6 F.C.R. Robinson, 'Nation Formation: The Brass Thesis and Muslim Separatism', *The Journal of Commonwealth and Comparative Politics*, vol. 15, no. 3, 1977, p. 216.

These were underpinned by a perception of ethnic and religious distinctness that placed the colonial state in the role of an indispensable 'neutral', essentially autocratic, alien arbiter.[7]

Post-independence India and Nigeria, both ethnically complex societies, have undergone traumatic experiences as a result of the politicization of religious divisions (Hindu versus Muslim in India, and, more obliquely, Muslim versus Christian in Nigeria). While, unlike India, the principle of communal representation was never enshrined in the Nigerian electoral system, the colonial administrative divisions that formed the basis of the country's federal system conflated regions with ethnic and, to a lesser extent, religious groups. This ensured that when full-scale electoral politics were launched in 1951 'it was virtually inevitable that these first elections would see the organization of political parties along ethnic and regional lines'.[8]

Indirect Franchise and the Introduction of Separate Electorates

Nationalist politicians and scholars have sought to trace the roots of India's democratic system back to antiquity—to the *sabhas* and *samiti*s referred to in the *Rig-Veda* in the second millenium BC.[9] However, while this ancient legacy has been utilized to impart an indigenous legitimacy to the representative institutions of modern India, the more tangible legacy has been the colonial one. In the inimitable words of Morris-Jones:

> it is of inestimable value that at least some of the leading men of the [nationalist] movement acquired a skill and affection for parliamentary institutions.... This went far towards avoiding a groping in the dark when it came to constitution-making; they knew what they were accustomed

7 L. Diamond, 'Nigeria: Pluralism, Statism and the Struggle for Democracy' in L. Diamond, J.J. Linz, and S.M. Lipset (eds), *Democracy in Developing Countries. Vol. 2: Africa* (London: 1988), pp. 33–92. For a discussion of colonial perceptions of Indian society see P. Robb, 'Muslim Identity and Separatism in India: The Significance of M.A. Ansari', *Bulletin of the School of Oriental and African Studies*, vol. LIV, no. 1, 1991, pp. 104–25.

8 Diamond, 'Nigeria', op. cit., p. 37.

9 S.C. Kashyap, *Our Parliament* (Delhi: 1989), p. 1.

to and they found it good. It also ensured that left to themselves they would in fact be able to work such institutions and communicate the spirit of the rules to a younger generation.[10]

Judith Brown evokes much the same sense of continuity but expressed in more accurately functional terms in speaking of how 'Congress lowered foreign imports on to an indigenous social structure.'[11]

The principle of elected representation was first introduced at the level of municipal councils and rural boards. Envisaged as 'an instrument of political and popular education', Lord Ripon's 1882 Resolution on Local Self-Government recognized that 'as education advances, there is rapidly growing up all over the country an intelligent class of public spirited men whom it is not only bad policy, but sheer waste of power to fail to utilize'.[12] Given such a rationale, the parochial electoral politics brought into being by the reforms were inevitably limited to a very few. For instance, Chris Bayly found that in Allahabad the municipal board electorate was confined to a small number of house proprietors, mainly professional men, and traders—less than one in fifty of the city's population of 150,000.[13]

At the provincial and national level, the elective principle was introduced in a convoluted manner, perhaps so as to dispel any notion that these were steps towards representative self-government on the English parliamentary model. The 1892 Indian Councils Act allowed for a minority of the seats, both on the provincial councils and in the Indian legislature presided over by the Governor-General, to be filled by nominations on the recommendation of certain bodies. In the case of the provincial councils, the bodies were mainly municipal and district boards, while for the Indian Legislative Council, members were recommended by non-official members of each of the provincial councils.[14]

10 W.H. Morris-Jones, *The Government and Politics of India* (Huntingdon: 1987), p. 41.

11 J.M. Brown, *Modern India, The Origins of an Asian Democracy* (Oxford: 1985), p. 344.

12 HMG, *Report of the Indian Statutory Commission*, 1 (London: 1930), pp. 299–300.

13 Bayly, *Indian Politics*, op. cit., p. 100.

14 HMG, *Report of the Indian Statutory Commission*, 1, op. cit., p. 116.

In some respects the Morley–Minto reforms of 1909 were a logical elaboration of the changes set in motion in 1892. Certainly, that represented the spirit in which they were instituted. In an oft-quoted passage, Lord Morley declared in the House of Lords: 'If it could be said that this chapter of reforms led directly or indirectly to the establishment of a parliamentary system in India, I, for one, would have nothing at all to do with it.'[15] Under the reforms the official majority in the provincial councils was abandoned and the elective principle made explicit with the majority of the non-officials elected either indirectly, by local authorities, trade associations or universities, or directly, by separate electorates of large landholders and Muslims chosen on a very restricted property franchise. The Indian Legislative Council was expanded on a similar basis.[16]

The most momentous feature of the Morley–Minto package was clearly the provision for separate electorates. Ostensibly a concession made in response to the demands of elite Muslims articulated through the newly established All-India Muslim League, the consequence was to accentuate fissiparous tendencies in the nascent Indian body politic. Rajat Kanta Ray, writing on Bengali politics in this period, has little doubt that the main significance of the constitutional arrangements lay in that they 'brought into sharper focus the emergence of the Hindus and the Muslims as distinct supra-local political communities.'[17] From a rather different perspective, Bayly, inclined to emphasize the primacy of interests, also recognizes the importance of the change in his study of Allahabad:

> Men who were Muslims or who paid large sums of government land revenue had previously found no reason to organize *qua* Muslims or *qua* landlords because their interests could be met in other personas or at lower levels of interaction with government. Now they received a fiat. Soon other opposing interests began to be organized as 'cultivator' associations or as Hindu associations, and political groups were encouraged to project their more sharply defined identities back into the wards and, ultimately, into the villages.[18]

15 Ibid., pp. 118–19.

16 Ibid., pp. 117–18.

17 R.K. Ray, *Social Conflict and Political Unrest in Bengal, 1875–1927* (Delhi: 1984), p. 198.

18 Bayly, *Indian Politics*, op. cit., p. 204

'Dyarchy' and the Expansion of Electoral Politics

Such repercussions were acknowledged by Morley and Minto's successors—Edwin Montagu and Viscount Chelmsford—when they came to consider the next instalment of reform. Their 1918 Report admitted that 'The communal system stereotypes existing relations' and '...teaches men to think as partisans and not as citizens.'[19] In justifying the retention of separate electorates despite such obvious shortcomings, Montagu and Chelmsford cited both their predecessors' pledge to the Muslims and the acceptance of special electorates in the reform scheme which had been jointly adopted by Congress and the Muslim League at Lucknow in 1916.[20]

As regards the franchise, the principal thrust of the Montagu–Chelmsford Report was the need to abandon the system of indirect elections under which, except in the cases of the landholders and the Muslims, there was 'absolutely no connexion between the supposed primary voter and the man who sat as his representative on the legislative council.'[21] The report also criticized the very restricted voting qualifications—the largest constituency returning a member to the Indian Legislative Council did not exceed 650 persons.[22] Even the primary electorates were miniscule. For instance, voters for the district boards in the United Provinces represented just one in every 2000 inhabitants of the province.[23]

The 1919 Government of India Act, the outcome of the Montagu–Chelmsford Report, marked a significant watershed in the evolution of representative politics. For the first time the principle of direct elections was accepted as the norm at all levels of politics, from local boards to the provincial and national legislatures. In addition, at the provincial level, Indian ministers, chosen from among the legislators, were allowed charge

19 HMG, *Report on Indian Constitutional Reform* (London: 1918), pp. 187–8.

20 Under the 'Lucknow Pact' Muslim special electorates were to be under-represented on the provincial legislative councils in the provinces in which Muslims were in a majority (50 per cent in Punjab, 40 per cent in Bengal) and over-represented where they were in the minority (33 per cent in Bombay, 30 per cent in United Provinces). No Muslim was to stand for a general seat. L. Curtis, *Dyarchy* (Oxford: 1920), Appendix, pp. 90–5.

21 HMG, *Constitutional Reform*, op. cit., p. 71.

22 Ibid., p. 70.

23 Curtis, *Dyarchy*, op. cit., p. 367.

of 'transferred' subjects involving 'nation-building' activities such as local self-government, education, industry, agriculture, and public works. However, the chief repositories of coercive and extractive power—police, justice, prisons, and land revenue—remained in the hands of the provincial governor and his appointed executive councillors.[24] And at the national level, the Viceroy's government remained essentially irresponsible, as far as the Indian electorate was concerned, until independence.[25]

Both the constitution of the legislatures and the franchise were considerably liberalized. The 1919 Act stipulated that at least 70 per cent of the members of the provincial councils and the Central Legislative Assembly were to be elected, as was a bare majority of the central Council of State (see Table 1.1). Under the Act just below three per cent of the population (see Table 1.2), including one in ten Indian men and one in 200 Indian women over age 21 years could vote in the provincial elections.[26] At the top of the electoral edifice barely one in 10,000 were entitled to vote for the Council of State.[27]

Separate electorates were retained for Muslims throughout India on the basis of the 1916 Lucknow Pact,[28] and extended to Sikhs in Punjab, Indian Christians in Madras, Anglo-Indians in Madras and Bengal, and Europeans in five provinces (see Table 1.1). In addition, a number of seats were reserved for non-Brahmins in Madras and Marathas in Bombay, both 'majority communities, who were thought likely to be under the dominance of a strongly entrenched [Brahmin] minority.'[29] Special constituencies were also maintained for large landholders, commercial and industrial interests, and universities. The overall effect was to direct electoral and legislative politics into, primarily, communal and, more tangentially, class channels. This was at a time when the impact of mass politics was making itself felt across the subcontinent with the non-cooperation campaign of 1920–2 and the transformation

24 HMG, *Statutory Commission*, 1, op. cit., pp. 148–52.

25 Ibid., pp. 126–7.

26 Ibid., p. 191.

27 In 1930 the electorate for the Council was just 40,515 (out of a British Indian population of 257 million in 1931) ('Return Showing the Results of Elections in India, 1929–30', Cmd. 3922, *GB Parliamentary Papers 1930–31*, 24, 10).

28 Compare the proportions given in fn. 20 with Table 1.1.

29 HMG, *Statutory Commission*, 1, op. cit., p. 138.

Table 1.1: The Composition of the Provincial and Central Legislatures under the 1919 Act

Members	Council of State	Central Assembly	Madras	Bombay	Bengal	UP	Punjab	Bihar & Orissa	CP	Assam
Nominated	(27)	(41)	(34)	(28)	(26)	(23)	(23)	(27)	(18)	(14)
Officials	17	26	23	20	22	20	18	18	11	12
Depressed classes	–	1	10	2	1	1	–	2	4	–
Anglo-Indians	–	1	–	1	–	1	1	1	1	–
Indian Christians	–	1	–	1	1	1	1	1	–	–
Labour	–	1	–	3	2	–	1	1	1	1
Others	10	11	1	1	–	–	2	4	1	1
General	(30)	(93)	(85)	(75)	(92)	(90)	(64)	(67)	(48)	(33)
Non-Muslim	16	47	65	46	46	60	20	48	41	20
Muslim	11	30	13	27	39	29	32	18	7	12
Sikhs	1	2	–	–	–	–	12	–	–	–
Indian Christians	–	–	5	–	–	–	–	–	–	–
Anglo-Indians	–	–	1	–	2	–	–	–	–	–
Europeans	–	9	1	2	5	1	–	1	–	–
Non-communal	2	5	–	–	–	–	–	–	–	1
Special	(3)	(11)	(13)	(11)	(22)	(10)	(7)	(9)	(7)	(6)
Landholders	–	7	6	3	5	6	4	5	3	–
University	–	–	1	1	2	1	1	1	1	–
Commerce	3	4	6	7	15	3	2	3	3	6
Total	60	145	132	114	140	123	94	103	73	53

Note: Twenty-eight of the 'General Non-Muslim' seats in Madras were reserved for non-Brahmins as were seven for Marathas in Bombay. The only provincial constituency in the country where elections were held on a non-communal basis was Shillong in Assam.

Source: HMG, *Report of the Indian Statutory Commission*, 1 (London, 1930), pp. 144–5 and 167–8.

Table 1.2: The Franchise and Electoral Turnout for the Legislatures Established under the 1919 Act

(per cent)

Legislature	Franchise	Electoral Turnout					
		1920	1923	1926	1929–30	1934	1945
Council of State	0.01	55.6	–	34.0 (in 1925)	33.4	–	–
Central Assembly	0.5	25.2	41.9	48.1	26.1	53.5	52.2
Madras	3.0	25.0	36.3	48.3	43.1	–	–
Bombay	4.1	34.9	48.2	40.6	16.5	–	–
Bengal	2.4	33.4	39.0	39.3	26.1	–	–
UP	3.5	33.0	42.2	50.2	24.6	–	–
Punjab	3.2	32.2	49.3	51.4	38.5	–	-
Bihar and Orissa	1.1	39.7	52.2	60.5	33.2	–	–
CP	1.3	22.5	57.7	61.9	33.3	–	–
Assam	2.9	24.2	42.1	44.2	28.3	–	–
Provincial Total	2.7	29.0	39.9	42.6	Not known	–	–

Note: The percentage enfranchised (column 2) is calculated on the basis of the 1929/30 election and the 1931 census returns.

Source: *Census of India, 1931* 1, pt 1, 35;
Cmd. 1261, *GB Parliamentary Papers 1921*, 26, 11;
Cmd. 2154, *GB Parliamentary Papers 1924*, 18, 497;
Cmd. 2393, *GB Parliamentary Papers 1927*, 18, 393;
Cmd. 3922, *GB Parliamentary Papers 1930–31*, 24, 363;
Cmd. 4939, *GB Parliamentary Papers 1934–35*, 16, 1073;
Government of India, *Return Showing the Results of Elections to the Central Legislative Assembly and the Provincial Legislatures in 1945–46* (Delhi: 1948), p. 6.

of Congress under Gandhi from an elite pressure group into a popular movement.

The historian Sumit Sarkar argues that:

> So far as divisions among politicians and educated people are concerned, the crucial factor behind the growth of communalism in the 1920s lay in the very logic of participation in the post-1919 political structure. The Montford reforms had broadened the franchise, but preserved and even extended separate electorates; there was, therefore, a built-in temptation for politicians working within the system to use sectional slogans and gather a following by distributing favours to their own religious, regional or caste group.[30]

Who were the electors under dyarchy? The franchise rule varied considerably from province to province, being most liberal in scope in Bombay and least so in Bihar and Orissa (see Table 1.2). The 1930 Indian Statutory Commission Report summarized the main features:

> ...residence within the constituency, coupled with the payment of a small amount in land revenue, rent, or local rates in rural areas, and of municipal rates in urban areas. All payers of income tax, and all retired, pensioned or discharged officers or men of the regular forces are also enfranchised.[31]

Though initially women were not granted the vote, legislatures were empowered to remove the sex barrier themselves and by 1930 all but the Council of State had done so. Yet, owing to the reliance upon a property qualification, only one in 30 electors for the provincial councils were women.[32] For the same reason, members of the depressed classes were also placed at a disadvantage. For instance, in Bombay with eight per cent of the population they formed only two per cent of the electorate, while in the Central Provinces a Brahmin was 100 times more likely to possess the vote than a Mahar.[33] Others placed in an unfavourable position included the landless, rural tenants in certain areas like Punjab, and factory and plantation labour. In sum, therefore, the great majority of electors were relatively prosperous caste Hindu or Muslim males.

Despite the fact that the literacy rate exceeded the franchise rate, large numbers of voters were illiterate. Indeed, in the United

30 Sarkar, *Modern India*, op. cit., p. 234.

31 HMG, *Statutory Commission*, 1, op. cit., p. 134.

32 'Results of Elections, 1929–30', op. cit.

33 HMG, *Statutory Commission*, 1, op. cit., p. 191.

Provinces the great majority (70–90 per cent in most areas) were illiterate and had their ballot papers marked by polling officers in the presence of the candidate's agent[34]—a practice that made no pretence at preserving the secrecy of the ballot and greatly strengthened the hand of entrenched local interests. A similar system was followed in Punjab and Madras while in Bombay readily recognizable pictorial symbols were shown by candidates' names on the ballot paper. Elsewhere such symbols were placed on the ballot boxes, or a system was followed by which candidates were assigned boxes of different colours.[35]

From the often jaundiced perspective of the provincial governments, the electoral experiment was not generally regarded as a success, either in terms of attracting public interest or of political education. In 1923 the Bihar and Orissa government reported that '...fully 95 per cent of the electors neither know nor desire to know what is going on.'[36] This poor impression can partly be explained by an ingrained scepticism, and partly by a lack of familiarity with the political processes that were at work. One major difficulty was how to understand and explain elections in the absence of the familiar characteristics of a functioning party system. In the 1920 elections, boycotted by Congressmen, the only contending bodies in any way analogous to political parties were the non-Brahmin Justice Party in Madras and the Unionist Party, representing cross-communal rural landowning interests in Punjab. Both these groups possessed an extra-legislative existence, however amorphous, and, more importantly, had a regional *raison d'etre* which enabled them to enter government and effectively utilize the powers of patronage.

The only body that claimed a national existence was the National Liberal Federation that had been set up by erstwhile Congress 'Moderates'. Essentially a coalition of leaders with few followers it possessed an electoral organization only in theory and

34 United Provinces Government, *Report on the Working of the System of Government, United Provinces of Agra and Oudh, 1921–1928* (Allahabad: 1930), p. 174.

35 'Report of the Committee on the Delimitation of Constituencies and Connected Matters', 1, Cmd. 5099, *GB Parliamentary Papers 1935–36*, 9, p. 265.

36 'View of Local Governments on the Working of the Reformed Constitution, 1923', Cmd. 2361, *GB Parliamentary Papers 1924–25*, 10, p. 205.

the Liberal Leagues in the provinces showed little activity.[37] Nevertheless, outside Punjab and Madras the majority of individuals appointed ministers in 1921 claimed the Liberal badge.[38]

A report by the United Provinces government gives an insight into the conduct of elections in this period. Many of the prominent aspects of electioneering in the west—holding public meetings, issuing addresses, and so on—were little used. Though canvassers were employed and leaflets, posters, and satirical poems were widely distributed in some places, what was most important for a candidate, especially in rural constituencies, was to gain the support of landowners and other influential local persons.[39] Access to funds was also important, with the quite considerable total of Rs 565,000 spent by the 211 candidates who contested eighty-three United Provinces council seats in 1926 (an average of Rs 2677 per candidate).[40] Candidates and their associates were ordinarily expected to provide transport and refreshments for voters who were brought to the polls in large batches, generally by village but sometimes by caste. The voters were usually organized by friends of the candidates, retainers of important local landlords, activists belonging to communal organizations such as the Hindu Sabha or Arya Samaj, and, where a member of a rural board was standing, employees of that board.[41]

In some urban areas there was more of a public campaign but, overall, the assessment of the 1920 election given by one successful candidate in Madras rings true:

> The general politics of press and platform hardly affect the voting. The landlord, the merchant, and the lawyer have their clientele, and every man has his tribe, clan or creed behind him who follow with sheepish fidelity. In this medievalism, political conviction counts for little.[42]

Under the circumstances it was no surprise that landholders and lawyers predominated among the successful candidates; 80–90 per cent of the members of the United Provinces council in the

37 Ibid., p. 143.

38 B.D. Shukla, *A History of the Indian Liberal Party* (Allahabad: 1959), chapter VII.

39 UP Government, *Report 1921–28*, op. cit., p. 172.

40 Ibid., p. 175.

41 Ibid., p. 172.

42 C. Baker, The *Politics of South India, 1920–1937* (Cambridge, 1976), p. 35.

1920s belonged to these two occupational categories. In terms of caste, upper-caste Brahmins, Thakurs, Vaishyas, and Kayasths, who formed just over a fifth of the Hindu population in the United Provinces, provided 93 per cent of the MLCs.[43] A similar pattern could be discerned in the Central Provinces, where N.K. Kelkar, a Maratha Brahmin who served as a minister from 1921 to 1924, in demanding that members' qualifications be made much higher, argued:

> We cannot reasonably expect to have responsible government if we make it possible for any one deliberately to return to the Councils illiterate, ignorant and inexperienced Darjis, Chamars and Bhadbhunjas or persons who have got no political or administrative experience.[44]

Kelkar was referring to the return in the 1920 elections of 'some members of low social status, such as a tailor, vegetable seller and petty shopkeeper.'[45] The view of the local government was that this was the consequence of the Congress boycott having deterred many men better fitted for the council from standing. Many Congressmen had only accepted Gandhi's call to abstain from the legislatures reluctantly. Before the 1923 elections C.R. Das and Motilal Nehru formed the Swaraj Party in order to allow Congressmen to participate, though the party's manifesto stated that legislators elected on its ticket would resort to a policy of obstruction until the government conceded the right of self-government to India.[46]

The results of the 1923 and 1926 elections proved that a candidate's personal influence and the successful aggregation of local interests did not, in themselves, afford a sufficient explanation of electoral politics under dyarchy. In the 1923 poll the Swarajists won 27 per cent of the provincial council seats, emerging as the largest party in Bombay and Bengal and winning an outright majority in the Central Provinces. Except in Madras and Punjab, where the Justicites and the Unionists continued to hold sway, the Swarajists' Moderate and Liberal opponents, suffering from

43 UP Government, *Report 1921–28*, op. cit., p. 560.

44 Note by N.K. Kelkar, 'Reports of Local Government 1924', 31 May 1924, p. 326.

45 Ibid., p. 309.

46 B.B. Misra, *The Indian Political Parties. An Historical Analysis of Political Behaviour up to 1947* (Delhi: 1976), p. 219.

their lack of organization and their association with the colonial government, lost ground everywhere.[47] In some cases, as the Chief Secretary of Bihar and Orissa grudgingly had to concede:

> ...the supporters of the other side could only canvass the amiable personality of their candidate. Thus callow youths, in themselves insignificant, could secure election because they stood for a party and a policy, while their opponents stood for nothing but themselves.[48]

While the Swarajists' 1923 success highlighted the mobilizing force of nationalism and the importance of party organization, the 1926 poll demonstrated the limitations of uncompromising nationalists politics in the electoral arena. Even before the election the Swarajists suffered splits. A Responsive Co-operation Party was launched by mostly Maharashtrian Congressmen favouring the acceptance of ministerial office, and a Nationalist party, including the Responsivists, was formed under the leadership of Madan Mohan Malaviya. This marriage of political moderation and Hindu nationalism attracted the support of the Hindu Mahasabha and powerful religious figures such as Swami Shraddhananda, the principal promoter of the *shuddhi* (purification or reconversion) and *sangathan* (consolidation) movements that had greatly contributed to the heightening of Hindu–Muslim tensions in north India.[49]

The impact of these developments was especially felt in the United Provinces where the appeal of 'Hind–Hindi–Hindu' held a particular resonance. There the Sawarajists' rump suffered a serious setback. Elsewhere, most significantly, the late C.R. Das's achievement in constructing an inter-communal nationalist party in Bengal was utterly negated in the aftermath of the Calcutta riots of 1926 and the new Swarajist leadership's coalition with the militantly anti-Muslim Karmi Sangh. While the Swarajists won 35 of the 46 non-Muslim seats (compared to 26 in 1923), they retained only one of the 21 (out of 39) Muslim seats they had held.[50] Only in Madras, in the guise of a loose coalition of nationalists and

47 Ibid., p. 220.

48 'Reports of Local Governments 1924', op. cit., p. 253.

49 J.T.F. Jordens, *Swami Shraddhananda. His Life and Causes* (Delhi: 1981), pp. 164–6. Instrumental in getting the reluctant Swami to lend his active support was the businessman G.D. Birla, who stood successfully for the Central Legislative Assembly from Benaras.

50 Ray, *Social Conflict*, op. cit., pp. 363–4.

out-of-office malcontents, did the Swarajists achieve a temporary success, enabling a non-Justice Party ministry to be formed in 1927.[51]

The last provincial elections under dyarchy, held in 1929–30, were not seriously contested as they took place in most provinces six months after the Civil Disobedience movement launched by Gandhi in March 1930. Almost half the seats were filled without a contest and the turnout was often derisory—as low as six and eight per cent respectively in non-Muslim urban constituencies in the United Provinces and Bombay[52] (see Table 1.2). Significantly, however, in the Muslim constituencies where polling took place, the turnout was considerably higher—about double the percentage in non-Muslim seats in Bombay, the United Provinces, Bihar and Orissa, and the Central Provinces. This disparity reflected the growing alienation from the nationalist movement felt by the majority of the Muslim political elite after the mid-1920s.

The 1935 Act and the Emergence of Separatist Politics

The communal divergence was accentuated by the discussions that marked the prelude to the last major step in pre-independence India's constitutional development—the 1935 Government of India Act. The wholly British Indian Statutory Commission, headed by Sir John Simon and boycotted by most established Indian political groups, submitted its report in May 1930, recommending the end of dyarchy and the introduction of unitary responsible government in the provinces.[53] Partly owing to the failure of the representatives of Hindu and Muslim communal organizations to arrive at a consensus at the Round Table Conferences that followed, the deepening communal divide in national politics remained unbridged, and Prime Minister Ramsay MacDonald's 1932 Communal Award generally followed the pattern set by the 1919 Act but for two significant departures. First, the Muslim majority in Bengal and Punjab, and the Sikh minority in Punjab, benefited disproportionately from the removal of the fifth of the seats that had been allocated to unelected officials and nominated

51 Baker, *Politics of South India*, op. cit., p. 163.

52 'Results of Elections 1929–30', op. cit.

53 HMG, *Statutory Commission*, 2, op. cit., p. 33.

non-officials in the dyarchal legislatures. And second, the general (that is, Hindu) representation was further reduced to allow for separate representation for the depressed classes.[54] The latter provision was later amended at Gandhi's behest in the Poona Pact, by which the seats reserved for the depressed classes were more than doubled on the basis that they would forego separate electorates,[55] already extended by the Award to Indian Christians, Anglo-Indians, and Europeans throughout India (see Table 1.3).

One of the primary justifications for separate representation and separate electorates was the limited franchise which, for instance, had the effect of translating the narrow Muslim popular majority in Bengal and Punjab into a minority of electors.[56] This was recognized by the principal Indian attempt at constitution-making—the August 1928 report of the All-Parties Conference Committee chaired by Motilal Nehru. It demanded an end to separate electorates and the adoption of universal adult franchise, but was rejected by the Muslim League because the political structure it suggested was more unitary than federal and provided for reserved seats for Muslims only at the centre and in provinces where they were in a minority.[57]

Among the Indians who co-operated with the Simon Commission, the depressed classes leader, Dr B.R. Ambedkar, was alone in advocating universal adult franchise. In an impassioned plea, he asserted that as 'associated life is shared by every individual and as every individual is affected by its consequences, every individual must have the right to settle its terms.'[58] He also rejected the connection drawn between literacy and enfranchisement, pointing out that illiteracy was not the fault of the illiterate and did not

54 'Communal Decision'. Cmd. 4147, *GB Parliamentary Papers 1931–32*, 18,965.

55 The total number of non-reserved 'General' seats in the provinces was reduced from 746 (of 1548) in the Communal Award to 666 (of 1581), or 42 per cent.

56 In Bengal in 1926, Muslims represented 54 per cent of the population but were only 45 per cent of the electorate, and in Punjab the respective figures were 55 and 44. HMG, *Statutory Commission*, 1, op. cit., pp. 146–7.

57 R. Coupland, *The Constitutional Problem in India* (London: 1944), Pt. 1, pp. 88–96.

58 Report by Dr B.R. Ambedkar (Appendix D to Report of the Bombay Committee) in HMG, *Statutory Commission*, 3, op. cit., p. 105.

Table 1.3: The Composition of the Provincial Legislative Assemblies under the 1935 Act

Constituency	Madras	Bombay	Bengal	UP	Punjab	Bihar	CP	Assam	NWFP	Orissa	Sind	Total
General	146 (30)	115 (15)	78 (30)	140 (20)	42 (8)	93 (15)	84 (20)	47 (7)	9 (–)	45 (6)	18 (–)	817 (151)
Muslim	28	29	117	64	84	39	14	34	36	4	33	482
Sikh	–	–	–	–	31	–	–	–	3	–	–	34
European	3	3	11	2	1	2	1	1	–	–	2	26
Indian Christian	8	3	2	2	2	1	–	1	–	1	–	20
Anglo-Indian	2	2	4	1	1	1	1	–	–	–	–	12
Backward Areas and Tribes	1	–	–	–	–	–	1	9	–	–	–	11
Women	8	5	2	6	1	3	3	1	–	2	1	32
Muslim Women	–	1	2	–	2	1	–	–	–	–	1	7
Sikh Women	–	–	–	–	1	–	–	–	–	–	–	1
Commerce	6	7	19	3	1	4	2	11	–	1	2	56
Labour	6	7	8	3	3	3	2	4	–	1	1	38
Landholders	6	2	5	6	4	4	3	–	2	2	2	36
Tumandars	–	–	–	–	1	–	–	–	–	–	–	1
University	1	1	2	1	1	1	1	–	–	–	–	8
Total	215	175	250	228	175	152	112	108	50	56	60	1581

Note: The numbers of general seats reserved for the Scheduled Castes are shown in brackets. An additional four members were nominated to represent backward tribes in Orissa.

Source: HMG, *Return Showing the Results of Elections in India 1937* (London: 1937).

disable him from 'understanding broad issues and of choosing the candidate who in his opinion will serve him best.'[59]

In spite of such arguments, the 1935 Act reflected the views of the Simon Commission, the Franchise Subcommittee of the Round Table Conference, and the 1932 Indian Franchise Committee. It limited the expansion of the provincial electorate to a total of 30.1 million, a more than fourfold increase on the dyarchal electorate but still only representing a tenth of the population (see Table 1.4). This figure included about a fifth of the adult population—between a third and two-fifths of males and around one in 15 Indian women[60] (the proportion of women electors ranged from a quarter in Madras to one in 50 in the North West Frontier Province and 14 per cent overall).[61] Outside Madras, where by 1930 the franchise for local boards had been lowered to include rural smallholders,[62] even the qualification to vote in local elections in the other provinces exceeded those set by the 1935 Act for the provincial assemblies. So, for many the 1937 elections represented their introduction to electoral politics.

Apart from a liberalization of the property franchise, the major innovations were the extension of the vote to all literate women, and to women whose husbands were either serving or retired militarymen or held enhanced property qualifications, (for example, in Bombay those paying twice as much rent or four times as much land revenue as the ordinary voter).[63] In addition, ignoring Ambedkar's argument, for the first time literacy qualifications were introduced which varied from giving all literates the vote in Madras to only matriculates in Bombay and Bengal.[64]

However, the most significant aspect of the 1935 Act was not the change in the franchise but the fact that for the first time Indian politicians had the opportunity of winning real power at the provincial level, even though it was power circumscribed by the

59 Ibid., p. 112.

60 HMG, *Return Showing the Results of Elections in India 1937* (London: 1937), pp. 5 and 14.

61 F.O. Bell, 'Parliamentary Elections in Indian Provinces', *Parliamentary Affairs*, vol. 1, no. 2, 1948.

62 Baker, '1937 Elections', op. cit., p. 558.

63 'Government of India Bill (as amended in Committee and on Report)', *GB Parliamentary Papers 1934–35*, vol. 2, pp. 336–7.

64 Ibid., pp. 327–75.

Table 1.4: Franchise, Turnout, and Party Share of the Vote in the 1946 Provincial Elections

Province	Franchise	Turnout	INC	ML	Com.	HM	Unionist	Akali/ Panthic	Other
Madras	13.8	46.8	68.3	9.6	11.6	0.1	–	–	10.4
Bombay	(14.8)	47.8	78.9	5.3	1.3	2.7	–	–	11.8
Bengal	13.4	51.1	45.3	37.2	2.8	1.4	–	–	13.3
UP	11.0	44.4	69.6	24.1	0.9	0.5	–	–	4.9
Punjab	11.4	60.4	23.1	32.8	1.9	–	20.2	7.8	1.9
Bihar	(7.8)	53.9	74.8	13.7	0.4	0.8	–	–	10.3
CP	11.2	41.3	72.5	5.3	0.2	2.3	–	–	19.7
Assam	9.5	50.3	54.2	25.3	2.5	0.7	–	–	17.3
NWFP	10.2	66.7	42.5	38.9	–	0.0	–	1.8	16.7
Orissa	–	36.7	76.8	5.3	2.7	–	–	–	15.2
Sind	–	51.5	20.8	46.3	0.1	3.2	–	–	29.6
National Total	11.9	49.8	59.0	21.3	3.2	1.3	2.0	0.8	12.4

Abbreviations
INC: Indian National Congress
ML: Muslim League
Com.: Communists
HM: Hindu Mahasabha

Note: The percentage enfranchised is calculated on the basis of the 1937 election and 1931 census returns. The franchise figures for Bombay and Bihar include the new provinces of Sind and Orissa.

Source: 1. *Census of India, 1931*, 1, Pt. 1, op. cit., p. 35.
2. Government of India, *Return Showing the Results of Elections in India in 1945–46* (Delhi: 1948), pp. 58–79.

discretionary and emergency provisions that, ultimately, allowed a governor to take over and indefinitely run the administration of a province. While the federal section of the Act, which envisaged a form of dyarchy at the centre, was never implemented,[65] the provincial part of the scheme came into force when elections to the new provincial legislatures were held at the beginning of 1937.

The Congress election manifesto, drafted by Jawaharlal Nehru, left open the question of accepting office,[66] and for Nehru himself the elections were not so much about winning limited power as a golden opportunity to propagandize and assert the Congress popular credentials. In his presidential address to the Lucknow Congress in April 1936, he declared:

> One of the principal reasons for our seeking election will be to carry the message of the Congress to the millions of voters and to the scores of millions of the disfranchised, to acquaint them with our future programme and policy, to make the masses realise that we not only stand for them but that we are of them and seek to cooperate with them in removing their social and economic burdens.[67]

He was faithful to his word—during the election campaign Nehru covered more than 50,000 miles, mainly by road and rail. He said of the experience:

> Most of the touring was done in rural areas and apart from the meetings which had been arranged, there were innumerable impromptu gatherings by the roadside. During a day as many as a dozen meetings might be held, some of them having audiences of thirty thousand or more. Some mammoth gatherings approached a hundred thousand.... On a rough and conservative estimate, it can be said that ten million persons actually attended the meetings I addressed, and probably several million more were brought into some kind of touch with me during my journeying.[68]

The perspective of the provincial Congressman was somewhat different. Lord Erskine, the Governor of Madras, described local Congress leaders as 'panting for office.'[69] More than had been the

65 The federal section was aborted by the failure of a majority of the princely states to accede to it before the outbreak of World War II.

66 S. Gopal (ed.), *Selected Works of Jawaharlal Nehru* (Delhi: 1975), vol. 7, pp. 459–64.

67 Ibid., pp. 184–5.

68 S. Gopal (ed.), *Selected Works of Jawaharlal Nehru* (Delhi: 1975), vol. 8, p. 43.

69 Baker, *Politics of South India*, op. cit., p. 296.

case with the Swarajists in the 1920s, participation in the elections had a definite impact on the ways in which the party operated. Two of the three principal criteria set by the Congress Central Parliamentary Board for choosing candidates was that they should be men adjudged capable of winning and of financing themselves. This naturally favoured the influential and wealthy, and not necessarily the faithful.[70] In Madras almost a third of the successful Congress candidates were recent converts to the cause, many of them ex-Justicites, and, as in the dyarchal councils, large landowners, businessmen, and lawyers predominated in the new legislature.[71] B.R. Tomlinson sums up the processes set in motion within the Congress Party nationwide in these terms:

> As factions within the district Congress organizations fought for dominance, their political horizons were forced outwards. They forged alliances with local magnates and local agitators and so, by internal factional struggle, brought a large slice of the local polity into the confines of the Congress movement.[72]

Tomlinson concludes that by forming the government in seven of the eleven British Indian provinces in 1937, 'Congress became more than a nationalist movement or a political party, it became the whole provincial political environment.' However, while this 'proto-Congress System'[73] formulation may have broadly reflected the trend in the six provinces in which Congress won, or came close to winning, a majority (see Table 1.5), elsewhere the pattern was more variegated. Congress contested only 58 of the 482 general Muslim seats[74] and the electoral failure of the Muslim League in the Muslim-majority provinces left the picture in these areas confused. In Punjab the cross-communal coalition of rural interests

70 Judith Brown estimates that Congress candidates spent an average of Rs 4000 per contested seat (Brown, *Asian Democracy*, p. 292).

71 Baker, '1937 Elections', op. cit., pp. 584–7.

72 Tomlinson, *Congress and the Raj*, op. cit., p. 78.

73 Ibid., p. 85. The phrase the 'Congress System' was coined by Rajni Kothari to describe the phenomenon of one-party dominance within a competitive multi-party setting in the first two decades of independent India ('The Congress "System" in India', *Asian Survey*, vol. 4, no. 12, 1964).

74 S.R. Mehrotra, 'Congress and the Partition of India', in C.H. Phillips and M.D. Wainwright (eds), *The Partition of India, Policies and Perspectives 1935–1947* (Cambridge, Mass.: 1970), p. 190.

Table 1.5: A Comparision of Party Performance in the 1937 and 1946 Provincial Assembly Elections

Party	Madras	Bombay	Bengal	UP	Punjab	Bihar	CP	Assam	NWFP	Orissa	Sind	Total
INC	159/165	85/125	52/83	134/152	19/51	92/98	70/92	33/58	19/30	36/47	6/22	705/923
AIML	9/29	18/32	39/114	26/54	1/73	–/35	5/14	10/31	–/17	–/4	–/27	108/430
Communist	–/2	1/2	–/3	–/–	–/–	–/–	–/–	–/–	–/–	–/1	–/–	1/8
Unionist	–	–	–	–	91/21	–	–	–	–	–	–	91/21
HM	–/–	–/1	2/1	–/–	–/–	–/–	1/1	-/-	–/–	–/–	–/–	3/3
Sikh Parties	–	–	–	–	24/20	–	–	–	–/1	–	–	24/21
Praja	–	–	36/4	–	–	–	–	–	–	–	–	36/4
Justice	21/-	–	–	–	–	–	–	–	–	–	–	21/–
NAP	–	–	–	22/-	–	–	–	–	–	–	–	22/–
ILP/SCF	–	13/–	–/1	–	–	–	1/1	–	–	–	–	14/2
Minor Muslim Parties	1/–	–/–	5/–	–/8	4/–	3/4	8/–	24/3	–/2	–/–	34/3	79/20
Minor Hindu Parties	–/1	–	3/1	–	11/–	–	–	–	7/–	–	12/–	33/1
Others	25/18	58/15	113/44	46/14	25/10	57/15	27/4	41/16	24/–	20/4	8/8	444/148
Total	215	175	250	228	175	152	112	108	50	56	60	1581

Abbreviations:

INC: Indian National Congress; HM: Hindu Mahasabha; ILP: Indian Labour Party;
AIML: All Indian Muslim League; NAP: National Agriculturist Party; SCF: Schedule Caste Federation.

Note: The Congress totals included 26 out of 58 Muslim seats contested in 1937 (15-NWFP, four each in Madras and Bihar, 2-Punjab, 1-UP) and 22 out of 89 contested in 1946 (18-NWFP, 3-UP, 1-Bihar), as well as five Sikh seats in 1937 and ten in 1946. In 1946 Nationalist Muslims and the anti-partition Jamiat al-ulama i-Hind contested 97 seats, winning 13 (seven Nationalists in UP, six Jamiat in Assam (3), NWFP (2) and Sind (1)).

Sources: HMG, *Return Showing the Results of Elections in India 1937* (London: 1937); Government of India, *Return Showing the Results of Elections in 1945–46* (Delhi: 1948).

represented by the Unionists defeated both Congress and the League, adding enough general seats to its sweeping victory in Muslim constituencies to attain an overall majority.[75]

The standard contemporary official British explanation for the Congress success emphasized, as in the case of the Swarajist a decade before, the party's organization and its effective use of potent nationalist symbols. The Governor of the United Provinces wrote of the Congress campaign there:

> As the time for the election approached, they developed their activities, not spasmodically but continously, through their resident workers in every village. Meetings and processions, slogans and flags, the exploitation of grievances, promises which held out the vision of a new heaven and a new earth, stirred the countryside into a ferment such as it had never before experienced.[76]

In Madras Lord Erskine too observed how 'The slogan "vote for Gandhi and the yellow box" carried all before it.'[77]

Such explanations, lending greater weight to broadly ideological appeals and popular feeling, do not negate Tomlinson and Baker's more functionalist perspective but rather serve to balance and complement it. Local elites—the socially privileged and economically powerful—may not have gravitated to Congress primarily because they were caught up in a wave of popular excitement, but the latter phenomenon cannot but have been an important factor in determining political orientations. The provincial elections formed part of a process of mobilization of support that had already been seen at the district and local level. For instance, in Madras the Civil Disobedience movement in the early 1930s had recruited to the Congress a large number of young men from notable families and the elections to local government boards in 1935 had shown how older politicians were also prepared to 'marry their local assets to the provincial and national prestige of the Congress.'[78]

The most important shift in electoral fortunes that occurred between the 1937 and 1946 provincial elections was in the four Muslim-majority provinces, where from winning just 40 of the 275 Muslim seats, all but one of them in Bengal, the Muslim League

75 HMG, *Results of Elections 1937*, op. cit., pp. 73–81.
76 Coupland, *Constitutional Problem*, Pt. 2, op. cit., p. 15.
77 Ibid., p. 16.
78 Baker, '1937 Elections', op. cit., p. 565.

advanced to taking 226 seats. At the same time Congress, too, increased its tally nationwide by over 200 seats, winning a two-thirds majority or better in six provinces and a simple majority in two more (see Table 1.5). Unlike 1937, when regional and sectional interests like the Unionists in Punjab, the National Agriculturist Party in the United Provinces and Dr Ambedkar's Independent Labour Party in Bombay could offer some competition, in 1946 local interests and rivalries were subsumed by the issue of Pakistan and the partition of the subcontinent. In over a quarter of the seats, twice as many as in 1937, there were unopposed returns, and the percentage of candidates forfeiting their deposits doubled to 36.[79] The position was polarized between, on the one hand, Congress which declared 'in this election petty issues do not count nor do individuals, nor sectarian cries—only one thing counts; the freedom and independence of our Motherland',[80] and on the other, the Quaid-e-Azam, Jinnah, crying 'If the Muslim verdict is against Pakistan, I will stand down.'[81]

Peter Hardy characterizes the Muslim League that emerged victorious in the winter of 1945–6 as more a chiliastic movement than a political party.[82] While this may contain a measure of truth, the League had built the basis for its success, both in the Muslim-majority provinces and in the United Provinces, the historic heartland of Muslim India, using tactics not dissimilar to those that had reaped Congress such rewards in the Hindu-majority provinces. In the United Provinces a third of the League's successful rural candidates in 1946 had stood in 1937, most of them successfully, either as independents or members of the landlord National Agriculturist Party. They represented a clear accession of strength to the League, both in terms of regional influence and credibility with the Muslim electorate.[83] Similarly, Ian Talbot

79 Government of India, *Return Showing the Results of Elections to the Central Legislative Assembly and the Provincial Legislatures in 1945–46* (Delhi: 1948), p. 54; HMG, *Results of Elections 1937*, op. cit., pp. 5–13.

80 Maulana A.K. Azad, *India Wins Freedom* (Madras: 1988), p. 132.

81 Z.H. Zaidi, 'Aspects of the Development of Muslim League Policy, 1935–47', in Philips and Wainwright, *Partition of India*, op. cit., p. 272.

82 P. Hardy, *The Muslims of British India* (Cambridge: 1972), p. 239.

83 P. Reeves, 'Changing Patterns of Political Alignment in the General Elections to the United Provinces Legislative Assembly, 1937 and 1946', *Modern Asian Studies*, vol. 5, no. 2, 1971, p. 142.

ascribes the League's remarkable triumph in Punjab to the support of a large section of the Muslim rural economic and religious elite, large landlords, and *pirs*, who deserted the Unionists in 1944 and 1945 as it seemed to them that its loyalist non-communal approach had lost its *raison d'être*.[84]

Conclusion: The Legacy of Empire

By 1946 limited democracy in India had expanded to involve over 40 million voters—the second largest electorate in the non-communist world. From their modest beginnings with Lord Ripon's attempt to win the co-operation of the emerging class of English-educated professionals by introducing the equivalent of parish pump politics to India, elective institutions had acquired a mass character. Their evolution paralleled the transformation of the nationalist movement from the preserve of a small, largely Anglicized, minority pursuing the politics of mendicancy, to a powerful force capable of a sustained challenge to the Raj. These related processes of change, one institutional, the other popular, laid the foundations of post-independence Indian democracy.

The character of the representative institutions introduced by the Raj helped to determine the channels into which the emerging politics flowed. The introduction of separate electorates in the 1909 Morley–Minto reforms set the pattern for subsequent development. It legitimized the language of communal and interest group politics by acknowledging its primacy and according it institutional recognition. This made it much harder, perhaps impossible, for even professedly secular Indian politicians not, at least tacitly, to do the same.

The trend was reinforced as the scope of both institutional and movement politics expanded in the 1920s and 1930s to draw in people for whom the language of liberal democracy conveyed little. The 1937 elections saw the entry into the legislatures of a new breed of Congressmen, less cosmopolitan, more representative of rural and small-town India, and more comfortable with the language of community and caste.[85] The transformation by 1946

84 Talbot, 'Muslim Political Mobilisation', op. cit.

85 S.A. Kochanek, *The Congress Party of India: The Dynamics of One-Party Democracy* (Princeton: 1968), pp. 370–404.

of the Muslim League into a party which could also claim demonstrable mass support, albeit only that of four and a half million Muslim voters out of a British Indian Muslim population in excess of 80 million,[86] provided further proof of how expanding electorates based on communal categories served to strengthen the appeal of communalism. Separate electorates had given communalism an institutional utility for politicians seeking election. It was therefore logical for the Constituent Assemblies of the new Dominions of India and Pakistan not to be elected through the exercise of non-discriminatory universal franchise—a long standing Congress demand—but to be chosen on a communal basis by the provincial legislatures elected in 1946.

Politics and elections in contemporary India, as in the India of the 1930s and 1940s, continue to be shaped by community and faction to a much greater degree than in any other country sustaining liberal democratic institutions on the Western model. Even institutionally the legacy of a democracy created to reflect perceived group interest rather than individual judgement remains in the reserved Schedule Castes and Tribes seats in the central Parliament and state assemblies. Reginald Coupland, reviewing the position in 1944, speculated how:

> Conceivably, if the system of representation had been wholly non-communal, a beginning at least might have been made of inter-communal cooperation for political purposes. But representation of communities... undermined the foundations of parliamentary government of the British type.... The result was a steady growth of communal self-consciousness in politics as in everything else.[87]

Today Indian politicians and voters—as forward, Backward Class, and Scheduled Caste Hindus, as Muslims, as Sikhs—continue to have to come to grips with the consequences.

We began by referring to the colonial legacy as a mixture of the authoritarian, statist, and democratic. In building upon that legacy, the successor states of British India have emphasized different aspects of it. Myron Weiner has contrasted India's faithfulness to the competitive representative institutions 'that the British either nurtured or tolerated' to the tendency of the

86 Government of India, *Results of Elections 1945–46*, op. cit., p. 55.
87 Coupland, *Constitutional Problem*, Pt. 3, op. cit., p. 17.

rulers of Pakistan and Bangladesh to rely 'on those institutions that sustained the imperial state'[88] (that is, the army and the tradition of viceregal autocracy). One explanation for this variance lies in the invidious position that the Muslim League found itself in Pakistan after 1947. Unlike their Congress counterparts across the border, many of whom had gained invaluable governmental experience at the provincial level in 1937–9, the bulk of the leadership of the League was made up of *mohajirs* (Muslim refugees from north India) who had little or no governmental experience in the five provinces (East Bengal, West Punjab, Sind, the North West Frontier, and Baluchistan) that constituted the new Muslim state.

However, while the administrative versus representative contradictions of the imperial legacy were felt most intensely in Pakistan, in India too they have persisted. Successive governments have utilized authoritarian colonial institutions and precedents, especially in crisis situations. Most prominently, Prime Minister Indira Gandhi's declaration of emergency rule in 1975 was accompanied by the large-scale detention of political opponents under the Defence of India Rules and the Maintenance of Internal Security Act, both modelled on colonial measures.

In terms of the legacy of separate representation and the recognition by the state of distinct social groups on the basis of caste and religion, the past lives on to deleterious effect. Most recently this has been seen in the controversies over the Mandal Report, the Shah Bano case, and the continuing separatist movement in Punjab. With reference to the last, it is significant that the Sikhs of Punjab were, apart from the Muslims in the four provinces where they were granted an electoral plurality, the only instance where separate representation coincided with territorial concentration (see Table 1.3). In both 1937 and 1946 the majority of Sikh seats were won by Sikh parties and not by Congress (see Table 1.5).

Though separate representation has thrown up unique problems for the maintenance of liberal democratic institutions in South Asia, it has been argued that ethnic cleavages can serve

88 Myron Weiner, 'Institution Building in South Asia', in R.A. Scalapino, S. Sato, and J. Wanandi (eds), *Asian Political Institutionalization* (Berkeley: 1986), p. 290.

as 'a basis of social pluralism and political competitiveness'[89] where a plurality of ethnic, religious, regional, and linguistic cleavages exist. In such a situation social divisions do not cumulate, as happened in Sri Lanka in the 1980s, to end in separatism and civil war. The system of communal representation adopted in British India failed in this respect. Superficially pluralistic in scope, it reflected a primarily two-fold division of the subcontinental electorate. The linguistic post-independence reorganization of the Indian states has, arguably, made it easier for New Delhi to decentralize conflict and, with varying degrees of success, to insulate the politics of the periphery from those of the centre.

89 L. Diamond, 'Introduction: Roots of Failure, Seeds of Hope', in Diamond, Linz, and Lipset, *Democracy*, op. cit., p. 12.

2

The Rhetoric of Democracy and Development in Late Colonial India[+]

David Washbrook

At first sight, the reasons for discussing democracy and development in the context of the late colonial Indian state may seem very curious. Not only did the latter do very little to advance the causes of either, but, being a 'British' colonial state, it also held only the most limited understanding of them. The concepts of democracy and development are not the first to come to mind when considering the history of even the domestic British state during this, the inter-war period.

Yet, from another angle, India's experiences in this era of democracy and development, and of the relationship between them, may have been extremely important in setting the agendas of the future. For, try as it might, the British colonial state could not shut out the insistent demands on its policies and practices made in the name of these core values of the twentieth century. A rising nationalist movement at home and deepening struggles with Fascism and Bolshevism abroad forced it to revive Britain's formal credentials as a liberal power; while depression, war, and a rapidly changing structure of the international economy wrecked the old colonial system and obliged consideration of how India might be 'developed' within the framework of a new one. The

[+] Sugata Bose and Ayesha Jalal (eds), *Nationalism, Development and Democracy: State and Politics in India* (Delhi: Oxford University Press, 1998), chapter 3, pp. 36–49.

epoch witnessed a broadening of 'representative', if not particularly democratic, forms of government in the economy.

If, however, the colonial state had to accommodate these pressures from the beginning of the twentieth century on and could not, as it undoubtedly would have liked, preserve indefinitely that combination of bureaucratic despotism and free market economics that had characterized the nineteenth-century, it was not without means of containing them. Institutionally, it retained a firm grip over the apparatuses of governance and, ideologically, it possessed far more experience than any of its opponents, at least inside India, at redefining the terms 'democracy' and 'development', those most flexible of concepts, to make them compatible with continuing authoritarian rule and the privileging of narrow vested interests. It conceived a series of strategies, symbolized perhaps by the amazing 1935 Government of India Act, designed to extend representation and promote economic growth without, apparently, changing any of the basic relations of power and wealth constructed under its long period of rule. Democracy and development here were meant to be imprisoned within the structures of the colonial past.

At one level, at least, the strategies plainly failed: in 1947 India acquired freedom with a commitment to universal democracy and to planned national development, which went far beyond anything evolved under the late colonial state and, indeed, represented policies deliberately conceived in opposition to its highly constraining influences. In many ways, the stroke of midnight on 15 August 1947 shattered the links between the colonial past and the national future. But at other levels these conservative strategies were extremely successful and may be seen to have come down to independent India, patterning some of her own responses to the problems of later years. The success derived from the extent to which the strategies became embedded in institutional practices and professional ideologies taken over wholesale by the newly independent state and exercising subtle, often unseen, restraints on the imagined freedoms which India's politicians thought they had won.

There is perhaps no clearer indicator of this subtle post-colonial influence than the ultimate fate of the 1935 Government of India Act, originally designed to undermine the national integrating functions of the Congress, to submerge the voices of *demos* beneath those of executive authority and aristocratic privilege, and to keep India tied to the apron-strings of Westminster. The Act did not entirely die with the rule of the King-Emperor: when India wrote 'her own' constitution in 1950, she took more than 250 of its clauses straight out of the relevant Parliamentary publication. Included among those clauses were the ones which Mrs Gandhi later would use 'constitutionally' to suspend the constitution and to revive a form of President/Viceroy's rule first seen in 1939.

The Rhetoric of Democracy

Extensive though the contributions of British scholars to political theory may be, they have rarely offered much elucidation of the concept of 'democracy'. Even the most celebrated essay on the subject in the English language preferred the title 'On Representative Government' and though regarded as radical in its mid-Victorian day, can scarcely escape the charge of elitism brought against it latterly by Maurice Cowling, among many others.[1] Over the course of the nineteenth century, the dominant British liberal tradition succeeded in appropriating the term 'democracy' from eighteenth century popular radicalism and giving it a quite different set of meanings. 'Democratization' now came to refer to that slow process whereby ruling elites co-opted into the functioning of the state successive layers of 'sub-elites' who were to prove their 'responsibility' by providing consensual support for the judgements of their masters. And a very slow process it was too: Britain, 'the mother of liberty', achieved full adult suffrage only in 1928, scarcely a generation before India and many generations after the majority of societies in Western Europe and North America. Moreover, what relationship this suffrage has to organization and exercise of state power, and whether it is meaningful to conceive of the existence of democratic 'rights', as opposed to 'concessionary privileges', remain open questions. Britain possesses no written constitution and, in the light of several legal judgements of recent years, it is arguable whether 'subjects' possess any rights at all, even of interrogation, against the executive authority of the state.

Conceptually, the dominant British political tradition has always been inclined to conceive of the state as prior to the interest of any of its constituent members. As a result, arguments about the virtues and vices of democracy (even, for that matter,

1 See Maurice Cowling, *Mill and Liberalism* (Cambridge: Cambridge University Press, 1963).

Mill's) have tended to be couched in terms, not of inalienable human rights, but of what would better facilitate the functioning of the state and the maintenance of social order. This has had several serious consequences for the nature of British political structure.

First, it has meant that the symbolic and the executive elements in the state have taken precedence over the representational and the legislative. The former (the monarchy, bureaucracy, law, and armed forces) stand for continuity, order, and guardianship over 'the whole of society'. The latter are merely transient and particularistic which, if not watched carefully, will bring about disruption (that is, change) and chaos (that is, a realignment of the social order). This position has two corollaries: first, of course, it imputes a demeaned function to 'politics', including democratic/representational politics. These last are held to reflect only sectional, if not individual, sets of interests, to be potentially corrupt and to threaten the workings of 'good' government. In the British state tradition, being 'above politics' (as the monarchy, the civil service, etc.) represents a higher, more legitimate, condition than being 'in' them; and the final accolade sought by every major politician is to be regarded as 'a statesman' who has risen out of the day-to-day, hurly-burly of the political process to join the other metaphysical beings protecting the continuity of 'the state'. The second corollary is that, in the British tradition, representational/democratic politics take place inside a highly conservative institutional and ideological straitjacket designed to constrain most of their urgings. The tightness and strength of the straitjacket may be judged from the extent to which it has enabled an extremely narrow 'gentry' stratum of society to repel, or accommodate, the challenges of industrialization, urbanization, and 'mass' society until very recently, without losing its cultural hegemony.

A further consequence for British political culture has been the tendency to conceive of democracy instrumentally, in terms of the ends which it will achieve rather than the rights which it reflects. Most usually, those ends have been concerned with deepening state power and control over areas of society inaccessible to it before. The co-option of sub-elites and their incorporation into state processes as 'representatives' for wider constituencies has been particularly efficacious in this regard. While, at one level, modern British history may be a history of progressive democratization, at another it is also a history of expanding state authority and coercion. In a large number of cases, ranging from local government to school boards to police committees, the two have been but opposite sides of the same coin.

These rather lengthy remarks about the meanings of democracy in British ruling culture may seem out of place in a paper supposedly dealing with India. But they gain their relevance from the extent to which the pressures and strains pushing late colonial India towards democratization were mediated by a state apparatus heavily influenced by this culture. In India, no less than (indeed somewhat more than) in Britain, the executive elites sought to deflect demands for democracy into recipes for representation and to preserve the supposed autonomy and integrity of 'the state' from the insistent importunings of mass politics. As in Britain too, one part of the tragedy of modernity may be the remarkable extent to which they succeeded.

Institutionally, India's pathway to democracy could hardly have been less promising. The first representative institutions were introduced to strengthen the colonial state after the shocks caused by the Mutiny. Most famously, they consisted of Governors' Councils where prominent notables were invited to offer advice to the Indian Civil Service (ICS) so that the latter could keep in touch with 'native opinion'. The notion that the real function of representation was advisory, while 'policy' was made by the bureaucracy, remained basic to British schemes of democratization right up to the Montagu–Chelmsford reforms of 1919, if not indeed the Government of India Act of 1935. It was, of course, later challenged and in large part overturned by the very different conception of representative democracy held by the national movement. However, at least two legacies of this initial ideology of representation were bequeathed to India even beyond 1947.

It was over the question of who had the right to represent whom that the issue of 'communalism' first entered the structure of the state. Familiarly, the introduction of principles of separate representation for 'Hindus', 'Muslims', landholders, etc., has been seen as a peculiarly colonial device constructed by the British for the purposes of 'divide-and-rule'. From a broader angle, however, it may be seen, more simply, to reflect British ruling elite ideas about the nature of representation itself. By definition, members of civil society could only represent specific and sectional interests since it was axiomatic that societal integration took place only through the state and thus the state executive alone could represent the 'whole' society. To conceive of the possibility that any member of civil society, 'Indian' or other, could represent his 'whole' society would have been to undermine the functions and legitimacy of the entire British ruling tradition. It was, and remains, a crucial strategy of this kind of state, to preserve its authority, that civil society be seen as 'naturally' divided. When independent India inherited a large part of the ideology and apparatus of the late colonial state, it also inherited this necessary strategy. In seeking to understand the post-colonial intensification of 'communal' strife, it may be important to consider not only developments in civil society but also the sources wherein the post-colonial state tries to ground its legitimacy.

The second and related legacy was the inflated role accorded to itself by the bureaucracy (and judiciary) as the proper makers of policy and the guardians of society. Although, from the time of Cornwallis, bureaucrats and judges had tried to give themselves this status, their success had been limited by the fact that they were, technically, the employees of a joint stock Company whose primary function was to make money. This situation changed with the abolition of the Company and with the introduction of representative institutions against whose implications the bureaucracy now had to define its own place. (It also changed, it might be added, at this time with the rise to power over Oxford schools of Jowett and the beginnings of a 'service' ideology for the British civil 'service' itself.) The later Victorian ICS, as also the whole of the British 'establishment', developed a high-flown rhetoric of impartiality and guardianship, which served to protect its moral authority, and quasi-hereditary elite status, from the challenges of rising democracy. To a degree, that rhetoric, and the ideology behind it, continued into the post-colonial era where it was used to delegitimate programmes of radical change in everything from the law to the linguistic bases of the state. Indeed, once the Indian National Congress became the state, the pretence of being 'above politics' plainly passed into its own ideology of leadership.

Yet perhaps the most significant paths towards Indian democracy (as opposed to democracy in India) were laid by post-Mutiny developments in much humbler areas. The Mutiny created not only a moral and political crisis in the colonial state but also a financial and economic crisis. The new Crown state was saddled with burgeoning debts but had to be cautious in increasing taxation lest it foment further revolt. It also had to abandon the highly extractive fiscal policies of the Company era, which had brought several parts of the Indian economy to ruin, and to find ways of reviving and stimulating an economic growth without which India would have been a very poor imperial asset. To help it out of these problems, the colonial state turned to 'democracy', or rather to representation, at the local level—thereby initiating a series of strategies which continue to affect the Indian polity.

The task here was to extend and off-load many of the petty functions—for roads, sanitation, primary schools—onto locally elected and co-opted 'native' boards and municipalities. Once these were in place, taxation could be increased by means which made it appear that Indian society was taxing itself; and much time-consuming local administration could be passed to unpaid 'politicians'. That the extension of these responsibilities should not involve any meaningful shift in power, however, was guaranteed by a complex system of controls, which kept budgets and administration under central surveillance and dependent upon handouts of official patronage; and by a construction of local political structures, which kept them parochial, divided, and distant from the real centres of power.

As early as the 1860s, the British began to discover forms of representative government, which were largely compatible with their continuing overrule and which, over the next several generations, they steadily expanded, in part to meet cheaply the many new tasks being asked of government but also in part as a response to oppositional demands for the widening of democracy. The hope was that India's democratic urges could be contained and ensnared in these institutions, which serviced the colonial state's needs; that they were incapable (except in a few cases, such as Calcutta[2]) of providing launching pads for a broader oppositional politics and were controllable through networks of resource distribution. In the later colonial period, whenever the national movement asked for 'democracy', the British replied by offering 'devolution' and their model, conceived after World War One, for their progressive 'withdrawal' from India was based upon steadily expanding the

2 C.R. Das and his followers were successful to an extent in the 1920s in subverting the institutions of local and municipal governments to achieve their own nationalist ends.

principles of so-called local self-government from the bottom of the Indian political pyramid upwards.

As a strategy for preserving British authority to the last possible minute, for undermining the functioning of any meaningful 'national' politics, and for creating a context of relations in which the jibes of bureaucrats at the corruption and particularism of politicians became almost self-fulfilling prophecies, it needs to be said that these ploys were only too successful. In 1937, the Indian National Congress, albeit against the advice of its 'high command', voted to buy the British conception of democracy as devolution and 'entered' the institutions of 'representative' local and provincial self-government. The result was a very sorry period in the history of the national movement. The concern to offer consistent and united opposition to the British disappeared amidst unseemly scrambles for patronage, bitter factional feuds over the status and fruits of office, and sharpening communal antagonisms. Gandhi's call in 1939 for 'the resignation of the Ministries' came not a moment too soon to rescue the Congress from itself and to restore the ideals of the freedom struggle. However, the political model had been established and, after 1947, it was clearly used by the new Congress state to develop 'the machine' system of politics, based upon patronage links between central and local government, which sustained its power until the 1960s.

A further corollary to these politics was the elaboration of a highly problematic system of pseudo-federalism. Faced with the uncomfortable prospect, after World War One, of having to concede broader rights of representation, the colonial state developed a strategy of 'retreating to the centre'. It seemed to concede the principles of democratic right by establishing franchises, legislatures, and ministries in the various provinces and, after 1937, even handing over powers of what it called 'self-government' to them. This gave the emergent Indian constitution the appearance of a kind of federalism. But it was a very peculiar kind for, of course, all the most important powers of government (fiscal, military, foreign policy, etc.) were held 'reserved' at a centre which, itself, was virtually outside any democratic control. The system was actually more dualistic than federal; it passed administrative responsibility, and little else, to democracy in the provinces, while keeping real power firmly in the hands of the bureaucracy (and, it was hoped, aristocracy) at the centre.

The implications of 1937 for the development of an Indian politics were very serious. Democratic aspirations were fanned in provincial legislatures with promises of meaningful self-government. Yet the provincial legislatures, which were designed to divert attention away from the centre more than anything else, had not the means of meeting these aspirations. They were also designed to offset demands for a national polity by promoting divisive regionalist sentiments. What the would-be 1935 constitution offered was a recipe for expanding internal political conflict between the centre and provinces over their respective roles, between executives and legislatures over their respective powers, and between democracy and oligarchy over their respective principles. It represented the last-ditch stand of a waning colonial state trying, against reason and history, to define some continuing place for itself.

The events of 1947 finally aborted the 1935 proposals but, problematically, those of 1950 brought more than a fair share of them back again. As noted before, the authors of the Indian Constitution put an extraordinary degree of faith in the political wisdom of the British and drew heavily on the 1935 Act. By so doing, they thus drew quintessentially 'colonial' forms of political relationship into the core of their emergent national democratic state. That issues concerning the design of provincial states and their relationship to the centre, concerning the uneasy relations between executive and legislature, and concerning the provenance of democratic authority should subsequently have bedevilled the history of the Indian nation cannot be regarded as wholly surprising. They came as part of a colonial inheritance which was all too readily accepted.

The Rhetoric of Development

In many ways, several of India's major problems of development also can be seen to derive from a failure to question seriously enough the colonial inheritance. Although inclined to pose as a *laissez-faire* state for much of the later nineteenth century, and to allow Britain's industrial monopoly to bring its own rewards through the market-place, the British Raj also possessed a strongly interventionist side. The eagerness of the Company to lay claim to all possible sources of land revenue meant that, from an early date, its government found itself simultaneously charged with responsibility for providing irrigation and various support services to agriculture. The needs of the military and of emergent plantation economies required large-scale involvement in a variety of labour and factor markets. India's massive railway building programme was also closely directed by the state. It is arguable, however, whether the nineteenth century colonial state thought of any of these activities immediately in terms of their implications for socio-economic 'development': they were conducted, and costed, much more for reasons of 'state' profit and power. Indeed, even the elaboration of the famine code was promoted as much by concern for the losses of revenue, which famine brought, as for the loss of life.

The First World War dramatically changed both the political context within which issues of economic growth and social welfare were considered and the economic context within which they had to be resolved. On the one hand, a nascent domestic public opinion and a rising national movement demanded greater accountability and policies geared more obviously to India's rather than Britain's interests. On the other, the decline of the colonial staples and a shift in India's relations with the rest of the world economy necessitated a radical restructuring of her system of production and trade. At one level, the colonial state responded to these changes purposefully. It progressively abandoned its (albeit selective) stance on non-interference in markets; it instituted wide-ranging inquiries into areas of the economy about which it had previously been in blissful ignorance; it drew up plans and recruited experts and technicians; most noticeably, it even found itself defining and defending a notionally 'Indian' national economy, replete with its own tariff barriers, Reserve Bank, and industrialization strategies. Many of the instruments and controls with which independent India was to try to 'manage' her own economy were forged in the last years of the British Raj, particularly in the 1930s and 1940s under the successive strains of depression and war.

At the same time, however, and perhaps obviously, these instruments and controls were never designed simply to promote India's economic welfare and the development of her 'national' economy. They also served a variety of other purposes: in part, to keep going for as long as possible the residual benefits of the colonial system and to slough off the additional costs which it now was incurring; in part, to safeguard the authority of the bureaucracy itself; in part, to secure the social bases of privilege on which the Raj was founded. Although the cause of Indian development was enthusiastically embraced by the late colonial state, amidst a paper shower of committees and reports, plans and promises, the rhetoric was often meant to mislead or to disguise the extent to which the embrace encircled India's throat. What was achieved was less the provision for India of a new economic dawn than the prolongation of a long post- or neo-colonial night.

In the first place, the inter-war era of emergent planned development was marked by a spectacular decline in levels of state, and state-supported, investment in the economy. Major programmes of railway building came to an end; changing military priorities reduced the need for investment in support structures for the army; perhaps most significantly of all, with the completion of the major riverine irrigation projects, capital investment in agriculture dried up. By the early 1930s, Sir George Schuster could proudly proclaim the state's capital expenditure commitments cut to a mere Rs 6 crores from an average of Rs 24 crores in the 1920s and, in real terms, many time more than that in the later nineteenth century. This was to be an era of planned development without money.

Given both the unstable international financial climate and the prospect of foreseeable British 'withdrawal', the reasons for the colonial state's parsimony in capital investment seem clear enough. More interesting, perhaps, is how in the context of nationalist opinion, the state was able to get away with it. In part, this seems to have been due to conceptual illusions created by the invention of new categories: with planning and development spawning their own rhetoric, departments, and bureaucracies, sight seems to have been lost of the many implications for development of other forms of government activity. 'Specialization' here produced tunnel vision. In part, however, the colonial state was able to 'get away with it' because of severe limitations in the conceptual apparatus of its principal political opponent, the Indian National Congress. The economic thinking of the Congress remained locked into the nineteenth century, viewing India's problems primarily in terms of distributional relations with Britain and within Indian society itself. Its own programme centred on forcing industrialization behind protection and on promoting land reform. It failed to see that the economic cheese of capital investment, particularly in agriculture, was being stolen from under its nose. This blindness continued into the 1950s, creating a situation in which an agriculture, starved of capital investment for, by then, a generation, threatened to creak to a halt.

With the thorny issue of agricultural productivity, in an epoch of declining prices and dwindling markets, removed, apparently by mutual agreement, from the agenda of development, the colonial state could look much more happily on the problems of planning. Its concession of the case for selective tariff reform (by then, hardly the issue in British politics which once it had been, save in the Labour Party which had been taken over by J. Hobson's anachronistic free trade ideals) opened opportunities for protecting colonial markets, for promoting new styles of imperialism, and for forging new relations of mutual support with India's rising industrial capitalists. The tariff policies which emerged in the 1920s and 1930s were aimed primarily at keeping the Japanese, and other 'foreign' competitors, out of Indian markets while judiciously dividing the remaining cake between British and indigenous interests. The resulting tariff barriers provided as much cosy protection for British, as for Indian, industrial capital to find safe profits for itself. Indeed, so safe that as A.K. Bagchi has seen, many new Indian industries rapidly reached positions of overcapitalization as resources flooded in to take advantage of the artificial security.[3]

This situation was no doubt ironic for a capital-short economy like India's but it was one whose lesson was only partially learned after 1947 by a post-colonial state which continued to confuse state-sponsored industrialization with state-protected profitability. The results were to provide very expensive and very lopsided trajectories of development for India and ones whose political implications went a long way towards altering the social complexion of the state. The conduct of the economy during World War Two made plain how close the relationship had become between the interests of private industrial capital and the public policies of the late colonial state. After independence, this relationship carried on and, indeed, was greatly strengthened. It was no accident that

3 A.K. Bagchi, *Private Investment in India 1900–39* (Cambridge: Cambridge University Press, 1973).

the very first bill introduced into independent India's new legislature should have been one to emasculate free trades unionism nor that the 'socialist' industrialization policies of the early five-year plans should have spawned some of the largest privately owned industrial conglomerates in the non-Western world.

At least, however, the development strategies of the late colonial state produced some industrial benefits, if at considerable political price. Why this is remarkable is that, for the most part, these strategies were aimed at not producing or changing anything at all. The greater part of the state's interventions in the market place had as their objective the keeping of things going, which otherwise would have fallen down. The successive shocks of depression and war destabilized a wide variety of commodity, credit, and food markets threatening to wreak havoc not only with the economic relations which they expressed, but also with the social relations. The inter-war years saw deepening tensions marked by conflict and riot, between groups at every level of the social system. To preserve order, as much to prevent breakdowns in the economy, the bureaucracy found itself having to intervene and coming, whether it liked it or not, to take over the regulation of large areas of India's complex and multiple systems of exchange.

Arguably, the underlying causes of these breakdowns went deeper than the international events which were often the occasions of them and reflected changes in structural conditions. On the land, population growth in the context of technological stagnation was altering the balance between capital and labour, pressing down the latter's share of the social product. In commodity markets, new monopsonistic conditions of demand, both at home and overseas, were eating into producers' returns. If these problems were satisfactorily to be resolved, at least to the point at which the market could be 'restored' and buyers and sellers command sufficient returns to reproduce both themselves and their material production, a radical social restructuring of the distribution of resources and labour power was necessary.

Such a radical restructuring, however, was practically impossible for the late colonial state, whose bases of social power lay with groups privileged by the present distribution, even to consider. Three corollaries flowed from this: first, having initially intervened in various markets as a short-term expedient, the state found it impossible ever to get out again. It was obliged to take an ever-widening responsibility for the regulation of exchange, spawning an ever more elaborate system of controls and licenses. Second, to explain its activities, it began to generate an anti-market ideology which put the blame for its predicament on the greed of, particularly, petty merchants rather than the structural conditions under which they had to work. In a curious elision of apparently opposite philosophies, for example, the highly conservative late colonial state of the 1930s began to propagate Fabian socialist ideas about the irrationalities of the market-place and the evils of 'the middle-man'.

And third, it hid its essentially political purposes behind a rhetoric of development aimed at helping the already-privileged groups, whose support it courted, rather than those most desperately in need. These last consisted principally of what it called 'the peasantry' and which, by European social reference, were supposed to represent the bottom of the social heap. But, of course, by Indian reference, landholding 'peasants' were the elite groups of village society with whom the colonial state, abandoning its erstwhile affection for rentier landlords, had been seeking a closer alliance since the later nineteenth century. Policies of aid, subvention, and development aimed at 'the peasantry' helped further to support those groups who had done best out of the colonial economy but ignored the landless masses beneath, whose plight progressively worsened.

Once more these 'interventionist' instruments and ideologies, originally designed to serve the specific needs of the colonial state and to arrest decay in the socio-economic structures on which it was founded, seem to have had a long after-life beyond 1947. Of course, the post-colonial state came into existence with a mandate to effect a far more radical redistribution of social resources than its predecessor had dared consider. But the terms of the mandate were at least confused by the degree to which the nation's new leaders subscribed to the colonial myth that rural India was at base a 'peasant' society. Extra resources (taken principally from a landlord class whose significance had long dwindled) were thus given to those groups in rural society who, arguably, needed them least and the structural problems, which has necessitated state intervention on the first place, went unresolved. In these circumstances, the new state no more than the old could withdraw from the market-place and it found itself having to take yet greater responsibility for holding the exchange system together as imbalances in the relative market positions of different economic groups deteriorated further. Moreover, it also adopted that curious ideological mixture of Fabianism and conservatism to legitimize its actions and for a long time, set out to hunt down the middle-man and the entrepreneur as the principal enemy of 'the people'. The new state, like the old, devoted a disproportionate share of its 'developmental' energies to keeping things going and ameliorating the consequences of change rather than leading it in more novel and constructive directions.

Conclusion

Democracy and development, which ought to be mutually supportive, stand today in sharp and antagonistic juxtaposition. Given their respective histories, of interpretation and institutionalization, in the colonial state, this situation can hardly be deemed surprising. Democracy was 'conceded' in ways meant to separate power from responsibility, to diffuse opposition, and to protect elite authority. Development was a synonym for conservation, for interposing state power to protect privileges and relations of erstwhile dominance, which changing conditions in the marketplace were undermining. A starting point for a redefinition of these concepts would be to emancipate them from the historical legacies of the late colonial era.

II

Democracy and the State

The relationship between democracy and the state has been theorized in many ways. For some, the substance of democracy will vary depending upon the nature of the social formation, and the economic organization of society, which determines the class character of the state. For others, democracy is inextricably linked to liberalism, without which it is unthinkable and even a sham. It makes sense to see the relationship between democracy and the state as one of mutuality, such that (a) without an effective state to underwrite democratic arrangements, there can be no democracy, and (b) a strong civil society is necessary to protect citizens from the potential tyrannies of the state precisely because states are notoriously prone to undermining democracy.

The first article in this section is by Rajni Kothari who catalogues the main challenges facing democracy in plural societies, and argues that the twin impacts of welfarism and developmentalism have everywhere effected a decline of the moderate state. The moderate state is a state which, despite the powerful modernist tendency towards centralization and homogenization, acts as an instrument of social justice and human freedom. The Indian state, between 1947 and 1967 (and partly even up to 1975) was just such a state and it is the reasons for the decline of 'moderate statehood' in India that Kothari explores in this article. The greatest achievement of Indian democracy in this phase was to build a unity which derived its strength from diversity, rather than from the steamrollering of differences, and the politics of accommodation and consensus followed by the Congress party ensured this in great measure. However, though traditionally deprived communities were empowered by a new consciousness of their rights, their demands for economic redistribution were not met, and indeed could not be met, given the model of development pursued by the Indian state. The response of the state to the problems of poverty, unemployment, and vast disparities of wealth, and to pressures for an all-providing state, took the form of populist politics. Institutions declined, the polity became increasingly centralized, and even personalized. A crisis of values, including the dissociation of the state from its moral imperatives, ensued.

The weakening of state institutions in the face of multiplying demands is also the subject of Atul Kohli's piece. His attempt to explain the 'crisis of governability' in India relies upon political rather than social and economic factors as independent variables in the explanation of political change. He shows, firstly, how political leadership—at both the national and regional levels—has played a deinstitutionalizing role. At the local level, secondly, the decline of the Congress party, and the weakness of other political parties, has created an authority vacuum, which is responsible for many of the problems of governability: the emergence of demagogic leaders and of hoodlums as local power brokers, corruption, instability, and violence as a mode of settling political conflicts. Thirdly, the logic of democracy has allowed the unchecked political mobilization of various caste, ethnic and religious groups; and, finally, the conflicts between the haves and the have-nots in civil society have manifestly increased. Somewhat like Kothari, Kohli too blames the absence of development on the centralizing nature of state power and the role of personalistic and populist leadership.

Susanne and Lloyd Rudolph theorize the political economy of the Indian state, and its relationship to democratic processes, through an analysis of the interaction between rising levels of political mobilization and changing state capability. This is done through the two models of a demand polity (in which decisions reflect the preferences of sovereign citizens) and a command polity (in which states, rather than citizens, are sovereign). There is, however, no necessary correlation between the type of polity (demand/command) and regime type (that is, democratic or authoritarian government). The relationship of economic performance to (a) types of politics (command or demand polity) and (b) types of regime (democratic or authoritarian) is analysed by dividing the period 1952–86 into four phases. These political variables are related to economic performance, measured in terms of public investment, agricultural and industrial production, and inflation. On the basis of wide-ranging statistical data, the authors argue that though demand and command polities are more strongly associated with economic performance than regime types, the relationship between type of regime and type of politics, on the one hand, and economic performance, on the other, is on the whole indeterminate.

The last essay in this section views democratic institutions and processes as mediations between state and society. The conception of democracy adopted here invokes not merely its formal-procedural aspects but encompasses also the substantive aspect of democracy, which implies that the effective and meaningful exercise of the rights of citizenship is achieved and guaranteed to all. Thus attempting to bridge the gap between political theory and empirical political analysis, the author explores the careers of three goals which were pre-eminent on the state's agenda at the time of independence. Each of these goals—welfare, secularism, and development—is illuminated through a case-study to which the challenges of democracy and citizenship are central. The constraints on the effective exercise of citizenship rights in each case are seen to place constraints on the realization of democracy itself.

Page 100 Blank

3

The Crisis of the Moderate State and the Decline of Democracy[+]

Rajni Kothari

The liberal conception of democracy contained in it a certain view of the relationship between state power and society. It was a view based on moderation and restraint in the use and abuse of power, its wide diffusion across various segments and 'interests', and its balancing through negotiated settlement of conflicts and cleavages. Though in its pristine formulation (never fully realized in practice) this took the form of a competitive interplay of interests in a free 'market', as the liberal polity was consolidated it was through a set of institutions that its operating culture was crystallized. And it was through the formulation of a set of legal and political norms and conventions, and 'rules of the game' in regard to their application, that the institutional framework was legitimized. As a result of this legitimacy and authority of the institutions the play of power was brought about and its excesses and concentration checked.

Such an institutionalized pattern of political behaviour proved crucial in containing and channelling the other major consolidation during the same period of history—the modern national state conceived as a social institution.[1] The very processes that put an

+ Peter Lyon and James Manor (eds), *Transfer and Transformation: Political Institutions in the New Commonwealth* (Leicester, UK: Leicester University Press, 1983), pp. 29–47.

1 In writing this paper I have tried to bring together my work on Indian politics from the early positive analysis of the operating culture of the 'system' to the more critical questioning of recent vintage, arising out of some basic questions

end to the *ancien régime* in various regions of the world also gave rise to a new conception of the state as a social institution. Among these were: the expansion of the base of political participation, extension of the reach of the state to cover economic tasks that were hitherto performed by diverse 'estates', the emergence of the state as a mediator, indeed an arbiter, in conflicts arising out of divisions based on class, and on ethnic and nationality factors.

Underlying this new conception of the state have been three critical shifts in the structure of the relationship between power and society in the modern age. First, there emerged a territorial 'centre' in each major juridical–political entity around which identities were built, with which political affiliations (of various 'peripheries' and 'sub-centres') were structured, and which became the primary source of legitimacy. Second, the new state centre became the spokesman of the emergent political form everywhere, namely the nation, defining both its internal and its external boundaries. Third, as the state centre began to extend towards

---

about the whole Indian model of political development and the theoretical postulates on which it was based (including some of my own postulates). It was in the fitness of things that a piece written for a *festschrift* for a person (W.H. Morris-Jones) whose work strode along the panorama of interaction between institutional resources and social reality should encompass such a comprehension of a dynamic reality. In the main, I have used and dwelt further on some of my own recent work, mainly on a paper for the Indo-British Exchange III held in British in June 1980 on the subject of the rise of populism, but also on a few others.

Rightly or wrongly, I have written the paper mainly with a foreign academic audience in mind who, again rightly or wrongly, I believe to be at a much further remove from Indian reality than used to be the case. If in the process I have drawn heavily from my own evolving analysis, I offer no apology for the same, partly because it was necessaty to document the sources of this analysis and partly because most foreign writing on India, with some exceptions (the most outstanding exception being Morris-Jones himself), has remained insensitive to Indian thinking and writing on India. This is partly because foreign area specialists tend to draw on each other's writings and often act like a ghetto of Indian studies—especially in the US—but partly also perhaps because Indian thinking is increasingly expressed in media that are not strictly academic and not always in English. On the whole, I have, for the last few years, not written for foreign journals and books. If I have to make an exception, as I must in a *festschrift* to Morris-Jones, it is as well that I state candidly what I am about.

the peripheries and the lives of the people in its attempt to deal with economic and social affairs and to 'manage' diverse forms of conflict, there emerged the phenomenon of mass society with its inherent tendency towards homogenization and standardization. In turn this led to a continuing expansion in the functions of the state and paved the way for its increasingly managerial and bureaucratic as well as mercantilist[2] and welfare orientations.

Reinforcing and in some ways greatly accentuating these three basic tendencies—of centralization, of nationalization, and of the straitjacketing of social differentiations into a mass society—has been the external role of the national state. This has forced the state to close ranks, to become the only legitimate spokesman of each nation in a world of nations, and with this aim to build itself up into a national security state in order to defend the integrity of its borders, its economy, and its culture. The greater the perceived threat to this security, the greater the reliance on force and military strength, with a potential hardening of state arteries and a closing-in of the open spaces between the state and the citizenry.

It is largely through the consolidation of democratic institutions in crucial countries, and generally the power of the democratic impulse everywhere, that the convergence of all these factors into the all-encompassing impact of the modern state has been held in check. It is still, and perhaps increasingly, a difficult task given the power of technocratic and corporate structures everywhere and given the pressures generated by the age of mass politics, now a global phenomenon. It is not surprising that in large parts of the world, liberal democracy, faced by internal turmoil and external challenge, or simply through the opportunism, ficklemindedness, or vainglory of leaders, has been overwhelmed. Indeed, what is surprising is that despite such a confluence of historical forces,

2 It is true that the physical—and, to an extent, juridical—consolidation of the state took place through the *ancien régime.* But this was more in the nature of a territorial unit and, in the case of the maritime powers, a mercantile power. Internationally, the Treaty of Westphalia (1648) legitimized the modern nation-state. However, the role of the state as an entity that intervened in settling rival claims to authority as between different classes or estates—first between the bourgeoisie and the aristocracy and later between the proletariat and the bourgeoisie—is largely a development after the French revolution on the one hand and the industrial revolution on the other, and the worldwide expansion of European power and ideology.

liberal democracy continues to survive both as a form of human governance and—even more—as a value system that continues to remain steadfast for millions of people. In fact it continues to gain new adherents in all parts of the world, including those who, at an earlier period, have categorically rejected it.

The imminent struggle of the whole period since the rise of the modern national state is between the totalitarian tendencies inherent in the statist thrust of a mass-based democracy and the libertarian spirit inherent in the same democratic ideology. It is a struggle that is now entering its most critical period with the elites of most democratic societies losing their original impulse towards moderation in the use and dispersal of power and, faced by the challenge of unprecedented politicization of the masses, succumbing to the temptation of using populist postures as a means of political survival.

These issues become all the more pronounced and intensified, as well as highly complicated, in the case of culturally plural societies.[3] It is to this specific configuration of the problem stated above that this chapter is devoted. I shall first consider the *problematique* in the form of a set of questions and then deal with them with particular reference to India.

'Development' and Democracy in Plural Societies

There is as yet no adequate theory on the growth and decline of democracy in multicultural societies. The closer democracy gets to the roots of such societies, the more pulverized it becomes and the more alienated the operating elite becomes, as well as less able to deal with multiple polarities and increased demands from the grassroots. Ironically, the more the socio-economic assumptions of democracy become realizable the less the system is able to 'aggregate' demands in a meaningful manner, leading it to a politics of postures instead of a politics of performance—in reality, a politics

[3] Again, many of the builders of the *ancien régime* pursue either mercantilist or bureaucratic conceptions of the state: the maritime powers in the first case and Germany and Russia in the second. What is distinctive of the modern nation-state is its adoption of these roles as integral to the very conception of the state, as a generalized doctrine and not a result of some ambitious or imaginative ruler (Frederick the Great in Germany, Catherine the Great in Russia, emperors of the Thang dynasty in China).

of deceit—forcing it to take recourse to authoritarian shortcuts and when this does not work, to the sheer politics of survival.

A whole series of issues demand close and serious probing.

1. Is it inevitable that in multi-ethnic and plural societies the effective political community is restricted to the dominant structures of both class and ethnic type, virtually treating the peripheries as subject populations and colonies? Examples are: Athenian democracy; modern Western democracies, as they become multi-ethnic as in the USA, or as their politics become effectively multi-ethnic as in the UK; above all, India.

2. How far is it possible to respond to the demands of the lower classes in a liberal polity that has no access to external colonies—is 'internal colonialism' a substitute for external colonialism?

3. How does the class factor operate in a multi-ethnic society?

4. Then there is the question of poverty and economic development. According to the received wisdom of development theory based on liberal internationalism, a cushion is provided for poor societies which lack adequate generation of surplus from within, by mobilizing external resources through aid, preferential trade, and transfer of technology. (The liberal polities of the West also had access to external resources but that was through a long stretch of colonialism and its in-built transfers.) But has it not transpired that these transfers of resources have only exacerbated the problem of internal disparities and inequities, and of internal colonialism with respect to regional, ethnic, and class peripheries?

5. There is, further, the whole issue of ethnicity and class. Cultural and ethnic pluralism is not a serious problem for liberal democracy so long as the political community is limited to upper and middle strata and so long as democracy means a politics of accommodation and co-optation. It is only when politics moves into a mass age, when, in short, ethnic differences take on a class or neo-class character, that the problem becomes serious. It is against this background that the phenomena of radicalization at bottom and authoritarianism at the top, with the left and 'radical' parties either disappearing or becoming part of the dominant structure, have to be perceived.

6. The transition from an inter-elite political community (that is restricted largely to upper and middle strata) to a mass society

also highlights the changing nature of caste. Democratic politics becomes the great catalyst in a transformation from a rigid caste hierarchy to a competitive structure of rival coalitions, politicizing large parts of the social system and rendering it capable of a whole series of accommodations and, on that basis, of an expansion of the base of the political system. If this process politicizes the lower strata without in fact providing institutional channels for challenging elite hegemonies—through, for instance, a massive process of compensatory legislation and redistributive politics on the basis of caste[4]—conflicts rooted in caste and communal identities begin to operate outside the institutional space and become unmediated, direct, and violent.

7. The same is true of regional disparities. Since these are generally uninstitutionalized, there is little hope of correcting them. The net result is a colonial relationship, as can be seen in 'backward' regions in large parts of the Third World.

8. Faced by these myriad cultural expressions of the political process, the political elite resorts to populist and plebiscitary politics and a gradual undermining of both institutional intermediates and (in many larger polities) the federal structure of governance and communication. After that all that remains is charisma and its direct appeal to the masses. With this, mass society becomes the purveyor of an authoritarian polity and a captive state structure. Such a resort to populist politics and commensurate operating style of the top elite (and their local dependents) also escalates tensions in other fields—in minority politics especially but also in areas, such as the politics of language and regionalism. The temptation to play loyalty games with these most sensitive of all 'peripheries' (social more than economic) grows and this disrupts the long-term process of working out a multi-religious and multi-racial polity through the normal expansion of opportunities and resources. It also exacerbates local community tensions and undermines those factors which work for cohesion and integration.

9. In time, all of these processes of tension-generation and the decline in the mediating role of politics sow seeds of disaffection, parochial separatism, and ultimate disintegration. This can only be halted by resort to more and more repression, by

4 This should be distinguished from the conception of political pluralism as found in the analysis of Western democracies.

transforming issues of social management into problems of law and order and 'security', and by increasing the incidence of violence, both horizontally (inter-community) and vertically (between the state and the people). Yet all of this occurs against the background of the heightened consciousness and politicization of lower strata and peripheral communities.

10. Such a politics of populist pretence also destroys inter-elite consensus and the political process based on certain minimum rules of the game. No society can survive without an authoritative elite that shares such minimum values and goals. Populism destroys both the role of the people and the role of the elite.

11. The point is that distributive justice also has to be institutionalized, just as are liberal freedoms and concepts such as equality before law. There is no automaticity about either the institutions of parliamentary democracy or economic growth leading to distributive justice. It has to be deliberately built into the design for national development, and into the nature of the state sturcture.[5] Failing this, liberal freedoms too would go under, at any rate for large sections of the people. 'Equality' then becomes an empty slogan which is used to take away the freedoms that exist, instead of providing economic benefits to the poor, raising their hopes and, on that basis, gaining their loyalty and their votes.

12. On the other hand, such a system, based as it is on an ideology of justices without its institutionalization, generates pressures from the educated and semi-educated classes and relatives of various influential people. These pressures strain the state apparatus well beyond normal bounds of efficiency, and draw into it a large lumpen element that then becomes a drag on the exchequer. Thus arises the parasitism of the urban middle classes.

13. In Western democracies the limitations of a liberal polity have been overcome by building a welfare state and a democratic version of corporatism through the public sector. This has inherent difficulties in a nascent state structure that is lacking in a well-

5 The most outstanding case of correcting historical injustices on ethnic lines is that of the *bhoomiputra* movement in Malaysia. In India such a politics was successfully conceived by Devaraj Urs, the erstwhile chief minister of Karnataka. For a detailed documentation of this, see James Manor, 'Pragmatic Progressives in Regional Politics: the Case of Devaraj Urs', *Economic and Political Weekly*, annual number, 1980.

grounded institutional apparatus and traditions that safeguard it against private encroachments and corrupt practices. Here both welfarism and developmentalism become instruments of a burgeoning state for the benefit of the prosperous and powerful. Planned development too, in such a state, reinforces existing disparities and injustices. Education, health, the co-operative sector, all become arenas of malpractice, deprivation, and destitution, while the state apparatus goes on getting bigger and bigger.

14. The same applies to forms of struggle and conflict from below which have elsewhere resulted in powerful movements of deprived people, the working class, the peasantry, and so on. In the West, this has induced in the democratic process a strong social and economic content—all the way from the base of society and the floor of the economy up to the national level, in course of time transforming the nature of the state and the structure and composition of the elite. In large parts of the developing world this process is far more difficult—to integrate a far-flung polity that also happens to be divided by barriers of language, ethnicity, religion, and caste. All of these things prevent the 'state' from really becoming a 'nation'. Instead, it becomes identified with government and the ruling group. Fundamental rethinking is called for in respect of the very structure and constitution of the state in such multi-cultural, multi-lingual, and virtually multi-national societies. Equally radical thinking is called for in respect of the proper territorial framework within which the struggle for justice, democracy, and social transformation is to be waged.

15. Important global tendencies have reinforced this decline in the liberal state and democratic values in the developing countries. There is taking place a strange convergence of local elite aspirations in the Third World and international efforts at co-opting sources of challenge to domination and exploitation. One of the most important vehicles of this convergence has been militarization of Third World societies. Meanwhile, many of the slogans which originated in the Third World have also been adopted as part of an international strategy. Examples include 'basic needs', 'self-reliance', 'alternative strategies of development', indeed even the slogans of the new international economic order. This is being done to co-opt the developing countries into following a path of development that is less demanding of world

resources and therefore less disruptive of the prevailing international structure.

16. Alongside the militarization and the new doctrine of international development strategy,[6] there has of late emerged a new doctrine of containment, arising out of the view that the standards and the lifestyle that have been achieved by the developed countries must be protected from any threat from the Third World, if need be by physical intervention in Third World regions. This new doctrine of containment ranges over a variety of strategies, from the co-opting of new centres of power in the world, to a strident 'resource diplomacy', to new doctrines of military preparedness against real or potential challenge from the Third World.[7] All of these developments pose a serious challenge to both liberal and egalitarian movements in the developing countries with the result that the prospects for human freedom and dignity there seem more remote than ever before.

17. Finally, there is a growing sense of threat to cultural identity and civilizational values in Asia, in Africa and, though in a slightly different and tortuous way, in Latin America, so that even the traditional defences of poor societies seem to be crumbling before their eyes. Their technological know-how is being eroded, their traditional lifestyles and their sense of a shared heritage are being undermined, their religious and cosmological springs of survival and changes are being destroyed. The political challenge involved in such a cultural encounter is therefore total. It calls for a comprehensive corrective to the ideological framework that is based on the doctrines of progress, modernization, and statism which originated in the West long ago and whose latest incarnation is in the theory of development for developing countries.[8]

18. In institutional terms, this theory of development has given rise to a growing faith in centralized institutions. Subtly,

6 See José A. Silva Michelena, 'Issues in Comparative Analysis of Development and Underdevelopment', in Rajni Kothari (ed.), *State and Nation Building: A Third World Perspective* (New Delhi: 1976).

7 For a critical posture on international development strategy, see my Report of the UN Symposium on a New International Development Strategy, held at Scheveningen (the Netherlands), July 1979. UN Document.

8 See the report by the Rand Corporation prepared for the United States Air Force, *Military Implications of a Possible World Order Crisis in the 1960s: A Project* AIR FORCE *Report* (Santa Monica: 1977).

both the liberal doctrine of a free society and the communist doctrine of a classless society have endorsed the role of a centralized bureaucracy for achieving social ends. During the very decades when participation has become the dominant value with people everywhere, in actual practice it has not meant much. The capacity of citizens to participate in the social process in the more developed nations has become severely limited because of the high degree of centralization of most institutions resulting from the growth of a technocratic state. In this there is not much difference between formally democratic countries (at least most of them) and countries that avowedly believe in 'democratic centralism'. As for the countries of the Third World, most of them have been subjected to authoritarian tendencies, in both domestic and international arenas, much of this in the name of development. It has been a period in which developmentalism has emerged as perhaps the most important reason of state.

The sum up, the sources of the decline of the moderate state are to be found in this transformation in the nature of the modern state under the impact of welfarism on the one hand and developmentalism on the other. To be sure, it would be a serious mistake to take a rigidly negative view of the state as an instrument of human will. The profound perception of all great thinkers that the state is a necessary condition of good life has been lost sight of in an age dominated by the positivist thrusts of modern technology and the dogmas of development. That nations are historical and cultural entities with long traditions of their own, that they transcend great internal diversity (as in India) as well as state boundaries imposed by colonial regime (as in Africa, the Arab world, and Latin America), that state power is crucial to the realization of social goals, and that the political process geared to the acquisition of state power acquires a dynamic of its own which is autonomous of social and economic factors—all this needs to be affirmed. The post-1945 era of nation-building in diverse historical contexts, based on a common struggle for political autonomy and human dignity encompassing vast regions of the world, represents a major turning point in human history.[9] What

9 'Development and Political Systems'. Introductory paper for the Asian Conference on Development and Political Systems 1980, mimeographed, available at the Centre for the Study of Developing Societies, Delhi or the Centre for Policy Research, New Delhi.

is threatening such a creative orientation of the state is the progressivist creed and its attempt to make the state into an economic instrument, as an agency for exploitation, control, and subjugation—nationally and internationally. The crisis of the liberal state arises from this totalistic vision of state power which is undermining its role as a civilizational process and as an instrument of human values. In this also lies the intellectual and political challenge of our time.

The Case of India

There are in the whole world only a few societies in which, despite the powerful centralizing and homogenizing thrusts of the modern age, the state has been made into an instrument of human freedom and social justice. While each of these societies faces new threats to democratic survival, it is also true that in each of them there have been distinguishing and special reasons why it has been possible to moderate totalistic tendencies of the modern state.

In the developing world without doubt the leading example of such moderate statehood is that of India. There is no space to go into the full genesis of the Indian case, much less into the basic cultural mores that have sustained such an evolution.[10] Instead what I propose to do is to examine the special case of India as a moderate state and a democratic polity as it operated from 1947 till about 1967 (and in an attenuated form till 1975), to discuss the reasons for its decline, and to relate these to the challenges posed by the growing demands of a conscious electorate for structural change in the institutional set-up which India's Westernized elite appears incapable of bringing about.

The Indian Model

In order to make a realistic assessment we need to bear two things in mind. First, when India came of age as a nation, it was heir to powerful humanistic traditions emanating from a dynamic interaction between the Western world and a reawakened Orient in response to the Western challenge. Dominant among the values that were imbibed as a result of this interaction were those

10 The issue was dealt with at length in my 'State and Nation Building in the Third World', in Kothari, *State and Nation Building*. See also the contributions of Satish K. Arora and D.L. Sheth in the same volume.

of freedom and democracy, of national self-determination and self-reliance, of equality and social justice, of 'service' to the poor and to society at large—together synthesized in the Gandhian concept of *swarajya.*

Second, as a matter of choice and volition the Indian leadership undertook to follow a specific course of development for realizing these values without necessarily bearing in mind the full implications thereof. In a sense this was just as well, for had the leadership anticipated all the consequences of its choices, it would not have dared to undertake the bold and historic journey that it did. Some of the more seminal developments in human history have taken place because the catalysts and initiators of change did not anticipate the full consequences of their actions. This has also been the case with contemporary India. It is also true that in the course of time the model that was adopted gave rise to deeper mutations, uncovered issues that had not been fully apprehended, and brought forth a dialectic with which the 'system' cannot now cope.

But it is better to move along and intervene in the process of history and face new challenges as they arise than to be too circumspect and steer one's course too timidly.[11]

That the steps taken by the first generation leadership were not timid or even circumspect is clear to anyone who takes cognizance of the distinctiveness of the Indian model of development. It was a model based on the simultaneous pursuit of four basic goals: (i) national integration of an enormously intricate and diverse social structure; (ii) economic development for raising the standard of living of a people whose income levels had remained stagnant or had declined for over a century; (iii) social equality in a society that for centuries had been based on the principle of inequality; and (iv) political democracy in a culture that had valued authority based on status, hierarchy, and concentration of power in the hands of a small elite. Nothing like this had ever been undertaken anywhere on such a large scale. What is more, it was a design that went against India's own heritage of an apolitical, parochially-structured, hierarchically-oriented, and essentially inequitable social order.

India not only undertook to pursue all these tasks simultaneously, which itself was unprecedented, but also decided to

[11] See my *Politics in India* (New Delhi and Boston: 1970), esp. the chapter on 'Political Culture'.

make the democratic political process central to the whole enterprise and made the other major processes—of nation-building, of economic development, and of achieving an egalitarian social order—contingent upon the democratic process. By shifting the basis of right from inherited status to numerical preponderance, by raising the consciousness of the large and hitherto subject castes against the small and traditionally entrenched upper castes, by giving primacy to the secular element in caste and community relations as against ritualistic and segmental divisions and thus by unsettling the antecedent structures of local tutelage and power, the democratic principle sought to transform a social structure which over the centuries had become rigid and ossified and had lost its inner vitality.

It was these values, the institutions they nurtured, and the pragmatic political forms through which they were played out that provided the sinews of integration to a highly diverse, in many ways divided, and inherently plural and segmented social fabric. This was the greatest achievement of democracy in India, of building a unity which derived its strength from infinite diversity and differentiation and did not need to steamroller the country into some dead uniformity under a leader or a party or an idea. Indeed, by now the experience that India has had (including periods when it has strayed away from the basic model) is significant enough to suggest that only in this way could national integration be achieved and that crucial to this mode of integrating India's vast diversity has been the democratic political system. In what follows we examine the structural characteristics and operating culture of the Indian system.

The Congress System

The Indian system crystallized around two seemingly opposite political and psychological pulls. On the one hand the need for consensus and co-operation was affirmed by all. A nation-building ethos emphasized the need for integration, especially with the forceful reminder of a long history of political fragmentation and disunity. At the same time, the uninhibited development of competitive party politics and its penetration at so many levels of the social and administrative hierarchy gave rise to a differentiated, highly varied structure of competition and dissent, which has since expressed itself in ever new forms by a large spectrum of social and political groups in opposition to the ruling groups. All of this results in a unique style of nation-building—a constant search for unanimity amid a shifting structure of factions—which is in many ways a continuation of the long Indian tradition of unity in diversity.

It was from a very small and homogeneous (upper-class, English-educated) elite that the ruling class of India was formed, and it was from this ruling class that oppositional elements emerged. This situation was perpetuated by (a) the length of dominance of the Congress party and the fact that the more effective opposition was carried out *within* the fold of the Congress and of the governmental and patronage structure to which it gave rise, (b) the process of selective assimilation in the Congress, through which leaders from other social groups were co-opted into the framework of dominance, and (c) the socialization within the Congress of the men who challenged its dominance.

There was a marked tendency towards accommodation by agglomerating various groups and sub-groups into a loose and amorphous organizational structure, reflecting the cultural style of traditional Indian society. The result was a fragmented and amorphous structure of authority that bred even more fragmented oppositions, which were often hard to distinguish from the coalitions in power. This made it difficult to identify positions and demarcations; all entities seemed to dissolve into 'the ruling class'.[12]

At the same time it should be remembered that the Opposition was given an importance which was out of proportion to its size.[13] This, in turn, helped sustain the morale and activity of the opposition in spite of there being a slender chance of its coming to power. Also, certain prominent leaders of the opposition were given considerable personal importance by the ruling group in the Congress (especially by Nehru), thus preventing frustration and bitterness from taking undesirable forms. This in turn created a wide gap between the leadership and the rank and file in the opposition, shielding and protecting the former from the radicalism of the latter.

12 These and the following points were developed in my 'India: An Assessment', Vikram Sarabhai Memorial Lecture, Indian Institute of Management (Ahmedabad: 1980, mimeographed).

13 These points were first developed in 'Oppositions in India' in Robert A. Dahl (ed.), *Regimes and Oppositions* (New Haven: 1972).

All this ensured the democratic and competitive character of the intellectual climate in which the party system developed in India, again setting it apart from the 'one-party' models of many other countries. The model of a one-party state was anathema to the Congress from the beginning. While continued dominance and a nationwide spread led to an impressive consolidation of power in the hands of the Congress, this did not lead to authoritarianism because of the free working of the electoral process, the crystallization of a factional structure within the party of consensus, the continuous pressure exercised by the opposition, and the general tendency of the leadership to preserve democratic forms, to respect the rule of law, to avoid undue strife, and to hold various elements together in some sort of a balance of interests. In the development and consolidation of the Congress as a party of consensus, the role of dissent, of movements of protest, and even of a wide variety of agitational politics was preserved, and any suggestion of imposing an authoritarian model of the party system in order to avoid dissidence and preserve unity was categorically rejected. The 'one party dominance' as found in India was based on consensual authority and not simply on civil or military power.[14]

Legacy from the Pre-modern Period

Such a relationship between power and plurality, between dominance and dissent, has drawn upon basic traits in India's history and culture. The striking thing about India's historical culture is the great variety and heterogeneity that it has encompassed and preserved. This is owing to many reasons—the diversity of ethnic and religious groups that have come in succession and settled down; the eclectic, rather than proselytizing style of spiritual integration characteristic of Hinduism; the absence of either a unifying theology or a unifying and continuous secular tradition; and above all, a highly differentiated social system that has brought functional hierarchies, spatial distinctions, and ritual distances into a manifold frame of identifications and interdependence. The result of all this has been a continuous pattern of coexistence between diverse systems and lifestyles; persistence

14 Morris-Jones was the first to draw attention to this fact. See his *Parliament in India* (1975).

of local subcultures and primary loyalties; and an intermittent, unstable, and discontinuous political centre.

Many of these patterns are, of course, new and have been crystallized through various political structures in India's modern constitution: the party and electoral system, the federal system of politics and administration (down to the districts, blocks, and villages), the legislative forums, and the caste and communal configurations underlying politics. But, although these forms arose relatively recently in India, the fact that they were so quickly legitimized and in some measure institutionalized can be explained only by reference to its long tradition of diversity and dissent, adaptation in the face of challenge, and continuity through change.

Responding to such a crystallization, there emerged a very large number of social and political organizations at all levels, pressing the government and the dominant party for participation, resources, and recognition, as well as for specific policy changes and administrative actions. The chief vehicle for the exercise of such pressures was the party system, either through the factional network within the Congress party or through pressures from outside, exerted individually or through other political parties. Furthermore, as the elaborate group structure of the Congress party reflected almost all shades of opinion and interest, there quickly developed a series of structural relationships between oppositional groups outside the party and corresponding factions within it.[15]

This role of the opposition in structuring the internal operation of the ruling party was a peculiar feature of the Indian system for a long time. It enabled the Congress to remain in power because the party was periodically undergoing change and alternation in parliamentary and governmental personnel. It also led to a sense of efficacy among opposition parties, despite their thin chances of assuming governmental power for almost 20 years. At the same time, dissidence within the dominant party continued and often found easy outlets because of the multi-party nature of the opposition outside the Congress. It was the availability of

15 The full model of this party system was developed in two stages: R. Kothari, 'Party System', *Economic Weekly*, vol. 13, 3 June 1961, and 'The Congress "System" in India', *Asian Survey*, vol. 4, no. 12, December 1964. For a schematic presentation, see W.H. Morris-Jones, 'Dominance and Dissent', *Government and Opposition*, vol. 1, no. 4, August 1969.

such dissidence that ultimately caused anti-Congress coalitions to crystallize in various states after the fourth general elections held in February 1967 and, at the centre of the polity, after the Emergency.

Such a model of horizontal aggregation was, in turn, based on a deliberate strategy of vertical *disaggregation.* By this is meant the role of intermediate elites in settling disputes and generally deciding most issues at lower levels, not permitting these to aggregate upwards and thus shielding the Centre from parochial pressures and social conflicts. This was the most important aspect of the evolution of a moderate centre in India.[16]

Through all of this the party system contained and modified the centralizing tendencies inherent in planned development and in the bureaucratic consequences of the Westminster model of government. The Congress made mobilization of the public in economic and nation-building tasks a function of political participation rather than of bureaucratic control and ideological rigour. With the passage of time this model opened up, brought new groups and parties into positions of power, led to a widening of the national consensus and a chastening of doctrinaire and volatile sections within all parties, and made power the great moderator in politics. It is this system that operated in India, despite periodical strains, for two decades and more.

Erosion and Decline

Such a model of democratic nation-building was bound to produce contradictions in the very process of working itself out, slowly generating major mutations in the social fabric.

It was in the social arena that these mutations primarily took place, essentially because of the continuous operation of an open political process, giving to the traditionally deprived communities a sense of power and a consciousness of their rights under the system, and leading to a gradual challenge to traditional privileges and hegemonies. The content of such striving was not just political; it entailed first, the demand for economic restructuring and redistribution of resources and opportunities. Second, it also entailed a redefinition of social status and a challenge not just

16 Kothari, 'Party system', op. cit.; Morris-Jones, 'Dominance and Dissent', op. cit.

to the power of the economically rich and privileged and the traditional caste hierarchy, which were no doubt the most important. It further entailed a challenge to the overarching bureaucratic–managerial apparatus that obtained at higher levels, the elite that controlled the various sectors of the establishment, especially in the administration, higher education, the judiciary, and the law and order machinery.

Challenge from the Bottom

Now such a challenge to established privilege was only to be expected in a model of development that was based on the politicization of social diversity as an inherent feature of its dynamic thrust.[17] Unfortunately, while this was accepted as inherent in India's approach to nation-building, the leadership failed to relate institutional and programmatic means to this eventuality, with the result that before long the institutions and programmes became static and vacuous and failed to restructure social reality. As this happened, they became instruments of privilege and the concentration of power rather than of equity and broad-based participation.

Thus the means adopted by the leadership for the basic task at hand—namely the removal of poverty, unemployment, and disparities in levels of living—tended to concentrate attention on achieving overall growth rates through the laying out of a considerable infrastructure for development and the building of a modern sector. The leadership hoped that as all this spread and seeped downwards, everyone, including those in the lowest place, would be able to participate in the national endeavour and benefit from it. *No systematic effort was made to ensure that this would in fact happen.* Distributive justice was not built into the nation-building design and the development model.[18]

Such a model of economic development was persuasive for groups that stood to benefit from it and identified national

[17] This theme was first developed at length in *Politics in India,* op. cit.

[18] This point has been forcefully presented in R. Kothari, *An Agenda for India* (Delhi: 1980, third edition, available from the Centre for the Study of Developing Societies) by characterizing the crisis that India faces as essentially a 'crisis of change'. The term was first mooted by Bashiruddin Ahmed. See his 'The Crisis of Change', *Seminar,* vol. 242, October 1979.

prosperity with their own. These groups included not only the commercial, industrial, financial, and managerial segments of the capitalist structure and the upper peasantry in the rural areas but also a very wide spectrum of lower middle classes which was accommodated through a vast expansion of the middle and lower rungs of the state apparatus. It is this latter, on the whole unproductive and *lumpen* class of people, who have become a continuous drag on the national exchequer and have greatly contributed to the inefficiency of the governmental process and hence of the economy. A model of development that failed to give productive employment to the educated classes ended up by making parasites of them.

Response from the Top

In this lies the root of the politics of populism and of the pressures for an all-providing state. A framework of economic development which fails to provide consciously for a steady, even if modest, expansion of opportunities for all results in reinforcing the demand component of the political process and gradually discounting its affiliative component. And in the hands of a leadership that is unable to disaggregate demands through a diffuse and decentralized framework of governance (as was the case under the Congress system) this leads to a politics of premature promises as a device to deal with basic inadequacies in policies and a steady decline in the performance of the system. Such a method of misleading and disorienting a public that has come to expect results soon begins to be looked upon as an exercise in deceit and leads to a fast deterioration in the legitimacy of the system. In turn the managers at the centre of the system seek to deal with restlessness and alienation of the public by recourse to increased coercion and repression. This is exactly what has happened in India over the last decade or so.

Centralization, which may have been once thought of as an instrument of purposive interventions by a cohesive and disciplined elite, soon turns out to be a strategy of mere survival based on a deliberate withdrawal from lower levels of the system, and leads to a breakdown of the party system and the federal structure and of wider affiliations that were built through them. It also produces a growing load on the centre and expectations from it precisely when it has lost the capacity to make the diverse elements in the system deliver the goods.

Failure to deliver the goods in a period of growing expectations points to a need for basic structural changes in the system but instead produces a politics of postures, a purposely diffuse populist rhetoric aimed at the poor and the dispossessed, dramatic overtures to socialism (which boil down to nationalization and state ownership) and an avid assertion of developmentalism as the principal *raison d'être*—in short, a new genre of statism according to which the fate of the socially deprived and the destitute rests securely in the hands of the state and a strong central authority. This leads to a political style that seeks to establish a direct link with the masses and evokes symbols of solidarity and blind trust in charismatic leaders and in turn underrates the importance of intermediate institutions and mediating structures.

In the year following the Congress split in 1969 the new operators all but dismantled these mediating structures and greatly weakened the intermediate buffers between the Centre and the various peripheries. As the political system failed to stand the test of performance that the new leadership had itself invoked, it ended up in directing pubic discontent more and more upward—from party and other functional agencies to the government, and ultimately from a large spectrum of national and regional elites to the Prime Minister. The result was that when the end came in March 1977 there was little to fall back on by way of a framework of power linking various levels of institutions.

The Janata Party, itself put together almost overnight, stepped into this massive vacuum. It did little to fill it, of course, and in fact wasted a unique opportunity to build a truly federal and decentralized structure of power and authority, bolstered by necessary policy correctives to fulfil people's expectations and channelize them towards a new pattern of development. What it sought was to adopt a series of measures aimed at economic decentralization. In the absence of a commensurate political structure that could implement these measures, such an approach boomeranged as it provoked a counter-offensive on the part of established interests—which succeeded in defeating the new politics and destabilizing the regime.

In fact the years of Janata, as of Mrs Gandhi's Congress before and since (which too has from time to time resorted to economic palliatives), have all painfully exposed the dangers of a centralized polity seeking to control a political process that had produced a restless and impatient electorate, given rise to wide-ranging social conflict, and made the performance of the government the principal basis for legitimacy. A centralized polity is inherently incapable of dealing with such challenges; what it does is to aggregate discontent and direct it all to the central apparatus of power instead of dealing with it at various levels and in a disaggregated and decentralized manner. It is equally unable to deal with the backlash from established interests in the form of atrocities against the poor and the weak and resort to settling conflicts outside the institutional framework, by the use of money power on the one hand and muscle power on the other. A centralized polity is also ill-equipped to deal with centrifugal and divisive forces and leads to a sense of alienation among the 'peripheries'. Under the circumstances, resort to force is the only means left to deal with strife and challenge which are inherent in a democratic polity. Nearly all the theoretical issues that were posed in the preceeding section hold true in the Indian case.

Oppositionalism

Contributing further to the culture of populism and an exaggerated emphasis on the centre of the system has been the political stance of the opposition in India. There has been an increase in the tendency of the opposition to subordinate other goals to the simple aim of displacing those who happen to be in power. As a result, while there is considerable consensus on fundamentals, there is great structural and organizational fluidity, with a consequent erosion of political authority and a decline of its 'majesty'. The ambiguous concept of democracy lends justification to a shifting structure of loyalties and the recurring phenomenon of defection from parties and coalitions on grounds of presumed injustice. The same grounds provide the rationale for directing agitations to the simple aim of removing those who happen to be in power.[19] As

[19] On this whole issue, see my 'Integration and Performance: Two Pivots of India's Model of Nation-building', in Rajni Kothari (ed.), *State and Nation Building*, op. cit. For an early critique, see Francine Frankel, 'Democracy and Political Development: Perspectives from the Indian Experience', *World Politics*, vol. 21, no. 3, April 1969.

democracy entails both representative and plebiscitary connotations, it lends justification to populist strands (including mob actions) and weakens the authority of constitutional means in the expression of protest.

A Crisis of Institutions

Such a process of decline and erosion of institutions places too great an emphasis on personalities, their sense of personal security and their attempt to use the public realm as an arena for resolving personal crises. In India the last several years have witnessed precisely this. It has been a period of rapid erosion of institutions. There has been too much stress on leadership, too little on institutions and their integrity and autonomy. This has not only led to a sharp erosion of both effectiveness and morale in crucial segments of the state apparatus—the party system, the Parliament, the bureaucracy and law and order machinery, the judiciary—and a corresponding increase in arbitrariness and in highly partisan and reckless interventions by political upstarts. Much worse, it has led to a systematic neglect of the public realm and a tendency to treat power as a means of personal aggrandizement and the state as an instrument of patronage and profit.[20] Once this happens, the whole fabric of the polity becomes petrified, any claim to the loyalty and commitment of vital segments arouses indignation and the deeper springs of nationhood begin to dissipate. Eventually this leads to a breakdown of authority.

This is the basic crisis facing India—institutional erosion in the face of massive change. The distinctiveness of the Indian model of nation-building, which had set it apart for most other Third World societies, lay in its ability to build a powerful institutional structure which ordered and moderated individual drives and ambitions—a unique party system, a rule-bound administrative and judicial structure, the planning machinery, a large network of autonomous

20 These remaks are not limited to non-Congress parties. It applies equally to the Congress. Indeed, the extent to which Mr Sanjay Gandhi used agitational methods, including use of violence and gangsterism, in embarrassing the administration, the courts, and Janata leaders beat all records of opposition tactics in a Indian politics. At the state level the Congress in opposition resorts to all manner of coercive tactics, often with the tacit approval of Mrs Gandhi.

institutions and voluntary bodies operating at various levels, and a plural basis of informed criticism and debate. Culturally and historically too, Indians have shown a remarkable capacity to order their plural identities and their considerable ideological ambiguity by resort to a well-laid-out operating hierarchy based on formalized rules and conventions. The Indian secular tradition has permitted considerable ideological fluidity but it had always laid emphasis on an ordering mechanism. This was carried over into the modern period by conceiving the national state as such an ordering mechanism, a new all-India cultural tradition based on the ideas and the ideals of the new intelligentsia on which the Indian National Congress and the new state were based. The orderly growth of the first two decades owes itself to this institutional factor.

This has since been dissipated. In a way this was inherent in the process of change. A particular institutional apparatus in course of time proves to be a drag and an obstacle to social change. It needs to be overhauled and changed. By the late 1960s the Congress system, the colonial bureaucracy, the rule-enforcing and adjudicating machinery, and planning apparatus had all become too rigid and too conservative to permit new social formations to emerge and produce a just and humane society in the face of massive demographic, social, and psychocultural shifts. It called for a change in the operating framework.

In a sense Mrs Gandhi's struggle with the 'Syndicate' and the 'Grand Alliance' at the turn of the 1960s signified this tension in India's historical process. Unfortunately she did not follow up her decisive victory in this struggle by a new institutional strategy. Disruption of a given institutional framework may be necessary for building a new polity; it cannot be an end in itself. One must come forward with a new institutional model. Lenin, Gandhi, and Mao did precisely this. In a way Nehru did the same, building partly on Gandhi's legacy and partly on new thinking based on his own reading of the role of the Indian state in the modern world. This cannot be said of most other Third World leaders.

This then is the central issue that faces India in working out a transition to the next phase of nation-building. In seeking to absorb the dynamics generated by social change engendered by the democratic political process, the new Congress leadership under Mrs Gandhi adopted a style that threw the old institutional order out of gear but was unable to replace it by a new structure.

It has instead been replaced by an increasingly personalized and plebiscitary politics on the one hand, with a tendency to overlook and in effect undermine institutions and traditions, and parochialized politics on the other, with a tendency to negotiate political and economic issues with local potentates rather than an all-India elite.

The basic thrust of the Indian model was to create a unified system that was, however, sensitive to the social reality of a highly dispersed and decentralized society and which permitted quite a large role to voluntary effort outside the state sector. It was a model for building unity by drawing on India's innate diversity, something that emerged out of a given population and land mass with a highly voluntaristic ethos. This was possible largely because of the continuous presence of a unique party system, which ensured that the centralizing thrust of both the ideology of development and the bureaucratic apotheosis inherent in the Westminster model[21] were moderated by pressures from below and imbued by a culture of accommodation and consensus. With the decline of party as the basic institution of the system and its displacement by the bureaucracy on the one hand and personal charisma on the other, the system has entered a period of crisis.

A Crisis of Values

This was one aspect. No less important was the nature of leadership and its capacity to instil in the system a set of values, norms of behaviour, and rules of the game. The role of Gandhi in providing pace-setting personal example and diffusing moral standards based on indigenous symbols and identities is well known. This was followed by Nehru who personally shaped the post-independence political system, provided it with a set of basic norms and values which he constantly reiterated in his role as the nation's schoolmaster, and enabled the system to bear the loads of an expanding framework of political participation, economic and social mobilization, and open competition and criticism.

But Gandhi also created dozens of smaller Gandhis and although Nehru lacked Gandhi's talent of self-reproduction and freedom

21 See my 'The Failure of a System: Politics as Private Enterprise', *The Times of India*, 10 April 1975. For a fuller statement of the diagnosis presented here, see my *Democratic Polity and Social Change in India: Crisis and Opportunity* (New Delhi: 1976).

from any sense of insecurity, and Patel did not live long enough, several Nehrus and Patels came into being under the system of which Jawaharlal was only the chief operator. All over the country outstanding individuals came to the fore and provided a dominant style of leadership for a considerable length of time. Their word was law, they consolidated political machines encompassing large territories on the basis of support networks they built, penetrated into a wide array of both traditional and developmental institutions, and constantly mediated in disputes and differences. But above all they imbued politics with an ethical code and imparted to it the concept of 'service', of duty, of the Gandhian emphasis on *dharma*. Central to the moderation of state power is this insistence on a larger ethical code without which politics is bound to degenerate into a cold and cynical exercise in control and manipulation and ultimately its takeover by musclemen and mafias. This is what has happened over the last few years.[22]

In the ultimate analysis Gandhi was right that politics and religion are closely intertwined. Either the state is an instrument of morality or it is made into an instrument of some positivist force, be it progress or national glory or the glory of a person who is supposed to personify the destiny of the whole people. Whenever the state is shorn of the moral imperative and the nuances and controls that go with it, it becomes totalitarian—no matter what its legal constitution be.

The Moral Dimension

There is need to return to some of these larger issues. For they are among the central questions of our time. They were very much part of intellectual reflection, study, and discourse a few decades ago. This has since been discounted in the preoccupation with the so-called 'scientific' study of politics—at a time when in fact the ground has been slipping from under most societies, the traditional sanctions against the exercise of power are disappearing, and cultural and ethnic identities are being rapidly eroded.

22 Morris-Jones happens to disagree with me on my view about the Westminster model. My own critique is developed in my *Democratic Polity and Social Change in India*, op. cit. Morris-Jones's dissent from my position was expressed in the first Indo-British meeting held in Delhi in 1978 and published in *Future of Democracy* (New Delhi: 1978).

It is therefore not surprising if in large parts of the world there is a revival of interest in religious identities, and often a religious revolt against the modern state. In many ways this is a reflection of the growth in consciousness of the masses and their search for a more authentic identity than is provided by the modernizing-bureaucratic state. At the same time, unless this search for authenticity is transformed and institutionalized in the framework of a new political and economic order, it may not be possible to avoid the fanaticism and dogmatism that usually accompanies religious revivals, and this will only increase the power of state oligarchies and military juntas, or simply the terror of rootless youth masquerading as spiritual disciples of some great messiah. This is precisely the problem posed by the Islamic resurgence from Morocco to Indonesia, the incipience of religious militancy in other regions, and the nativistic revulsions to modernization found in several Third World countries.

Here perhaps lies India's distinctive role in working out a transition towards its own version of a post-modern, post-secular society. Steeped in the tradition of social pluralism discussed in this paper (as distinct from the mere political pluralism as found in Western democracies) and in a conception of unity based on dispersed identities and shared values, endowed with a non-theological religious pedigree without a fixed doctrine or an official clergy, and given its high tolerance of ambiguity and a deeply ingrained tradition of scepticism, India may be better placed than most societies to carve out a niche for itself in a world undergoing great transformations. Its real test will lie in its capacity to contain the centralizing impacts of the modern positivist age and especially moderate these impacts in the political sphere where the spectre of populism threatens the very survival of institutions and values.

There are many indications that out of the present struggle between a centralized and increasingly repressive state and various movements of protest and defiance based on local organizations of the poor and ethnic minorities, peasants' movements, and movements for regional autonomy and decentralization of power may emerge as an alternative formation that will prove more sensitive to India's indigenous cultures, its great diversity, and essentially decentralized character, its being a predominantly rural society with great reserves and tenacity against the homogenizing thrust of both modern statehood and the modern economy, as well as its penchant for a larger ethical code that restrains and moderates the exercise of power.[23]

This confrontation between centralizing and decentralizing thrusts, which is being waged in various regions as well as nationally (and, in respect of the larger forces at work, internationally) is, at the moment of writing, producing a massive backlash from powerful interests, both in the economy and the polity, both in the countryside and the metropolitan areas, against the forces of change and reconstruction of the polity. But it appears that the issue has been joined and, though things are likely to get worse before they get better, the ground forces at work cannot be put down for long. Much will depend on how effectively those among the middle classes—the bourgeoisie—who feel committed to the values of a liberal democracy and a just social order will throw their weight behind the forces struggling for an alternative political order and in the process save the country from both internal atrophy and eventual disintegration. This has been the main proposition of the liberal intellectual tradition of India—a convergence of interests between a liberal elite and a democratic mass, each moderating the other and the two together ensuring the broadest possible consensus for democratic nation-building.[24]

23 I have candidly laid out what has happened in a recent article. See 'Where are We heading?' *Indian Express*, 29 November 1981.

24 For a comprehensive documentation on the grassroots movements and the debate among them on an alternative polity, see the literature coming out of the project 'Lokayan' of the Centre for the Study of Developing Societies.

4

Political Change in a Democratic Developing Country[+]

Atul Kohli

This study seeks to describe and explain India's growing crisis of governability. Important political institutions in India have been weakened, and power conflicts have multiplied. The result is that national leaders find it increasingly difficult to put together durable coalitions, to undertake major policy initiatives, and to settle political conflicts without violence. Although the explanation developed here for India's growing turmoil is multicausal, political variables are emphasized. Empirical materials suggest that India's political structures and the choices made by its national leaders have played central roles in moulding political changes in India. With that as a general theme, this discussion summarizes the empirical materials, reviews the analytical argument, and attempts to tease out some comparative implications of this study.

The Empirical Study

It is important to begin by stating the sense in which the terms 'crisis' and 'governability' are used in this chapter. The topic of Indian government tends to attract doomsayers. Therefore, it is especially important to reiterate that this characterization of contemporary Indian politics as being in crisis does not predict imminent breakdown of the democratic political order. Rather,

[+] *Democracy and Discontent: India's Growing Crisis of Governability* (Cambridge, UK: Cambridge University Press, 1990), chapter 13, pp. 383–403.

the word 'crisis' is used to draw attention to certain tendencies toward steady deterioration within the Indian polity. The 'system' in India can continue to function but if it does so without major changes, its level of performance will remain quite low and will probably decline even further.

The concept of governability draws attention to the tasks a government can be expected to perform. For a democratic developing country like India, governability has been defined here as the capacity of the rulers to do three things: maintain coalitional support, initiate solutions to problems perceived to be important, and resolve political conflicts without force and violence. Thus, a democratic developing country is well governed if its government can simultaneously sustain legitimacy, promote socio-economic development, and maintain order without coercion. The growing incapacity in India to perform these tasks is what has been conceptualized in this study as a manifestation of a crisis of governability.

Problems of governability are common to much of the developing world. India once was considered an exception. Scholars of Indian politics had long recognized the exceptional nature of India's stable and effective democracy within the developing world. Because specialists can easily be guilty of admiring too much the subjects they study, it is important to recall that those concerned with broader issues of comparative development also used to describe Indian politics as uniquely 'modern' and well 'developed'.[1] Unfortunately for India, its problems of governability have grown considerably more acute over the past two decades; India is fast catching up with the rest of the Third World. Instead of a strengthening of India's democratic base, we see a steadily widening gap between institutional capacities and socio-economic problems. This pattern of political change raises crucial questions for analysis: What happened? Was this outcome inevitable? If so, why? If not, who or what should be held responsible? More generally, what forces can help explain India's growing crisis of governability?

To help provide some answers to these complex questions, a study of five districts, four states, and economic and political

1 See, for example, Samuel Huntington, *Political Order in Changing Societies* (New Haven: Yale University Press, 1968), pp. 84–5; Barrington Moore, Jr, *Social Origins of Dictatorship and Democracy: Lord and Peasant in the Making of the Modern World* (Boston: Beacon Press, 1966), p. 314.

decision-making at the national level was undertaken by this author.[2] The study serves several purposes. First, it generates what can loosely be called a 'thick description' of Indian politics. Second, it helps explain patterns of political change at various levels of the polity. Taken together, these three parts of the study also help address a single theme of Indian politics: the causes and the consequences of the growing gap between institutional capacities and problems requiring political solutions.

A detailed study of the same five districts conducted by Myron Weiner twenty-five years ago is helpful in describing and explaining broad changes in the governing of India's vast political periphery. The picture that emerges is that of an increasing authority vacuum. The organizational ability of the Congress party has declined, and popular new parties have failed to fill the organizational vacuum. In addition, traditional authority patterns in the social structure have been weakened; the capacity of the dominant castes and of other 'big men' to influence the political behaviour of those below them in the social hierarchy has diminished. These two trends—the growing democratization of traditional power relations in the civil society, and the failure to create a rational basis for generating new leadership through formal political institutions—are at the heart of the increasing authority vacuum in Indian politics. That vacuum, in turn, contributes to many of the problems of governability: coalitional instability, the emergence of low-quality leaders with demagogic rather than programmatic appeal, the growing significance of toughs and hoodlums as de facto brokers of local power, ineffective and corrupt local governments, and the increasing tendency to resort to violence to 'settle' political conflicts.

A complex array of forces has produced the authority vacuum in the periphery. The socio-economic forces at work are well understood by development scholars and require only brief reiteration. Economic development has generated new patterns of division of labour that have undermined traditional caste authority. The spread of commerce has similarly replaced seemingly reciprocal patterns of exchange with the impersonal medium of money, again undermining the traditional bonds of 'solidarity' between social 'superiors' and 'inferiors'. Unequal economic gains

2 Atul Kohli, *Democracy and Discontent: India's Growing Crisis of Governability* (Cambridge: Cambridge University Press, 1980).

have also generated new types of tensions that increasingly resemble class conflict.

What looms even larger than these socio-economic forces is a series of political variables. The spread of democratic values and practices has hastened the decline of traditional authority. The deinstitutionalizing role of national leaders has thwarted the possibility of developing a new and stable set of political norms. Finally, weak political institutions have encouraged undisciplined political competition, and that has politicized all types of social divisions, including caste, class, and ethnic cleavages. Numerous strategies, including the use of violence, have been used to gain access to the state's resources, thus adding to the growing political chaos.

A comparative analysis of three states can help refine the themes concerning the causes and the consequences of deinstitutionalization. Clearly, the crisis conditions are most severe in the state of Bihar. There is a qualitatively different, sporadic pattern of turmoil in Gujarat. In contrast to both of those cases, political order has been restored in West Bengal after a period of considerable turmoil. How does one explain this regional diversity?

Our comparative analysis suggests that these regional political variations are not products of economic changes. Both Gujarat and Bihar, which respectively are better developed and less well developed economically, have experienced considerable political turmoil. Although unique conditions are operative in each state, the common issues appear to be political. Governments across Indian regions control large blocks of resources. The spread of democracy has mobilized a diversity of new groups. As a result, power conflicts aimed at gaining access to the state's resources have proliferated. That is the common theme running through the discussion of Bihar, Gujarat, and West Bengal.

In addition, the cohesiveness of any regional government is itself a major variable that is best understood as a product of the nature of the ruling party. Fragmented ruling parties in both Bihar and Gujarat have not only made it difficult for governments to act effectively but have also encouraged intra-elite conflicts and thus elite-led movements and countermovements. By contrast, a cohesive party in power in West Bengal has generated moderately effective government. It has accommodated new power challenges by a combination of reformism and organizational cohesion.

Finally, an analysis of national policy making has helped focus attention on the implications of deinstitutionalization at the centre of the Indian polity. Organizational weakness in the Congress party, in conjunction with failure to provide for systematic incorporation of the bottom half of the population into the political process, has put a high premium on personal appeal, populism, and mobilization of 'primordial' loyalties as strategies for gaining and maintaining power. Those strategies enabled India's ruling dynasty to legitimize its hold on power through democratic means until the end of 1989. That personalistic and populist ruling style, however, has become a major impediment to the use of state power to solve the nation's problems.

An analysis of the attempts by Rajiv Gandhi to liberalize India's economy, rebuild the Congress party, and resolve the fratricidal conflict within Punjab provides support for this broad contention. Policy failures in each of those areas can be traced back to the desire of Rajiv Gandhi to maintain both personal power vis-à-vis other elites and a broad base of mass support. The national political situation in India has thus begun a vicious cycle. It is increasingly difficult to translate personalistic and populist support into the political ability to accomplish policy goals. Policy failures, in turn, tend to undermine popular support. The strategies for winning power thus come to be even further removed from developmental problems. At the heart of this growing rift between the state's representative and developmental functions in Indian politics lies the absence of coherent parties and programmes.

This political analysis of select local, state, and national materials helps chart out the dimensions of India's growing crisis of governability. It is important to state that this study does not anticipate an immediate disintegration of India's democratic political order. There are many positive attributes in India's political economy that need to be stressed. Indians continue to enjoy more civil liberties than most populations in the Third World. The calibre of Indian civil servants as problem-solvers remains relatively high. India's macroeconomic performance in the 1980s was respectable by international standards. India, therefore, is not about to 'fall apart.' Nevertheless, it is also the case that India's political problems are increasing. Power challenges are multiplying, and the institutional capacity for systematic accommodation of such challenges is not keeping pace. If these trends continue, they are likely to chip away at India's democracy. No problem in contemporary India is likely to prove more serious than the disintegration of its major problem-solving institution: the democratic state.

The Analytical Argument

This analysis of Indian's governability crisis has focused attention on the growing disjuncture between weakening institutions and multiplying demands. That manner of conceptualizing the problem tends mainly to identify the components of the larger problem. Clearly, that is not unimportant. The real explanatory issues, however, have to do with why institutions have weakened and how and why various groups have been mobilized at the rate and in the manner that they have. The explanation developed for those processes by our analysis is multi-causal with several independent variables. It is important to distinguish the argument presented here from other arguments in the literature and to delineate some of the distinctive implications of this study.

The foregoing empirical analysis has suggested that four major factors have influenced the nature of political change in India: (1) the deinstitutionalizing role of national and regional leaders; (2) the impact of weak political parties; (3) the undisciplined political mobilization of various caste, ethnic, religious, and other types of groups; and (4) the increasing conflicts between the haves and have-nots in the civil society.

It is important to understand the sense in which these four variables are considered in this study to be independent variables. First, they are independent only insofar as they are not fully reducible to one another. For example, whereas the actions of national leaders may be important factors contributing to the weakness of political parties, that weakness is not solely a function of leadership actions. Low levels of economic development and cultural diversity are other important variables that have made it difficult to create well-organized, cohesive national parties in India. Similarly, the patterns of political mobilization may in part reflect the weakness of parties, but they also reflect the highly fragmented nature of India's pre-modern society.

A second caveat concerning the independent variables is that they are treated as independent only by analytical choice. If the object of this study were different, they could be considered dependent variables and thus objects for detailed analysis. The chain of causation in social life can be pushed ever further, until sometimes it even comes back to the phenomenon under investigation, thus completing a circle. The definitions of dependent and independent variables in any analysis, therefore, reflect choices concerning what is being studied and why.

These four significant independent variables can be readily collapsed into larger analytical categories. Three of the four variables—the role of leaders, the impact of weak parties, and the phenomenon of undisciplined political mobilization—are all political variables in the sense that they concern issues of power distribution and conflicts over access to the state's resources. Only one of the four variables, the increasing dissension between the haves and the have-nots, primarily reflects changing values and the distribution of economic resources in the civil society. I have attempted to be consistent in resisting the tendency toward a priori exclusion of significant explanatory variables, and the empirical findings have clarified that not only socio-economic variables but also political variables are important for an analysis of political change in contemporary India.

Before discussing why that is so and the implications of this argument, it may be useful to distinguish briefly the political explanation developed here from its alternatives. The major alternative to the state-oriented argument presented here would be an explanation stressing socio-economic or market variables. A developmental explanation, for example, would analyse India's growing governability crisis as an inevitable by-product of modernization in general and economic development in particular. A related neo-Marxist argument could stress the growing conflicts over economic distribution as the root cause of India's political problems. Neither of those explanations would be 'wrong'. It is rather a matter of sifting through numerous causes and assigning them weights. Our analysis finds the market-related economic forces to be far from insignificant. On their own, however, they have not proved to be the most important factors. While taking them into account, the empirical materials that were analysed moved the focus away from the market and toward the state.

The state and the market compete for space in all societies. Industrial transformation and the related developmental changes in nineteenth-century Europe were, on balance, propelled by market forces. It is not surprising, therefore, that major theories of development, modernization and Marxist alike, tend to focus on market processes—division of labour or class relation—as determinants of politico-economic change. Those nineteenth-century ideas have continued to influence (and, one is tempted to add, distort) how we think about contemporary developmental experiments.

The relative roles and significance of the state and the market in economic change have been altered in the twentieth century. For the most part, major developmental transformations in this century, communist and capitalist alike, have been state-propelled. Our inductive social theories—and most development theories are inductive—are only slowly beginning to comprehend the distinctiveness of state-led development. The analysis of political change in one important state-led capitalist experiment of the late twentieth century forms a small part of this large intellectual puzzle.[3]

Many of the reasons that political variables have played such important roles in moulding patterns of political change in India can be traced back to the state's crucial role in India's political economy. The state is not only an agent of political order in India; it is also responsible for promoting socio-economic development. Those dual responsibilities have led to a highly interventionist Indian state. Because that interventionist state is organized as a democracy, politics and political competition tend to permeate much of social life. Thus, the nature of India's political structure and the roles played by India's political leaders have been major determinants of political and social changes in India.

What aspects of India's political structure have made that country increasingly difficult to govern? The 'deeper structures' are often in the background in a process-oriented analysis. Without reference to them, however, important questions remain unanswered. Why should the Indian state attract so much attention from social groups? What enables a leader to play such a profound role in the Indian polity? Why should political mobilization result not in new organized political initiatives but in chaos? It is now important to move one level of causation deeper and focus

3 A broader research agenda of this type was laid out by a group of distinguished scholars: Peter Evans, Dietrich Rueschemeyer, and Theda Skocpol (eds), *Bringing the State Back In* (Cambridge: Cambridge University Press, 1985), passim, but especially chapters 1 and 11.

sharply on the political structures that have conditioned political change in India.

The Indian state is highly interventionist, and whether one approves of this or deplores it, it is an important organizational feature in contemporary India that is not likely to change soon. An interventionist state at low levels of economic development, moreover, is a feature that India shares with many Third World countries, but it contrasts with past experiments in capitalist economic development, especially those in the Anglo-American context. Two political implications of that state–society macro-characteristic are evident in our analysis, but have not always been recognized in the literature.

First, an interventionist state in the early stages of development has difficulty establishing a separation between the public and private spheres in social life. That has many consequences. The most important from the standpoint of a study of governability is that an interventionist state cannot claim that distributive problems are social and not political problems. The coexistence of political equality with considerable economic inequality facilitated the establishment of proto-democracies in parts of nineteenth-century Europe. The interventionist welfare state developed only under resource-abundant, mature capitalism. In an Indian type of situation, however, a highly interventionist state is inherent to the overall design of state-led development. That tends to politicize all forms of societal cleavages—old versus new, social, and economic. Thus, the accumulating distributive claims on the state partly reflect the state's attempt to penetrate and reorganize socio-economic life.

Second, an interventionist developing state typically controls a substantial proportion of a poor economy. Thus, many of the society's free-floating economic resources are controlled by politicians and bureaucrats. Who should have access to those resources? Unlike situations involving the products of private endeavour, the legitimacy of claims on public resources is not easy to establish. Given the scarcities in a poor economy, moreover, the competitive energies of the many individuals and groups seeking economic improvements tend to get focused on the state. Thus, competition over the state's resources often results in intense conflict, contributing to the problems of governability.

Another major characteristic of India's political structure is India's democracy. On balance, periodic elections and the existence of basic civil liberties are among India's most prized political possessions. Certain specific features of Indian democracy, however, have also contributed to India's growing problems of governability. India's democracy has been democracy from above. For most of its existence, it has been more of a gift from the elite to the masses than something the masses have secured for themselves. There is no doubt that the longer democracy is practised, the more difficult it becomes for the elite to take away basic democratic rights. Nevertheless, a tremendous concentration of power in the hands of a few leaders is an undeniable feature of India's democracy. Leaders may not be able to turn democracy on and off, but Indira Gandhi came close.

That concentration of power cannot simply be wished away. It is part of the overall design by which the leaders have made democracy a gift to the society. One recurring consequence of that design is that whenever the ruling elite are threatened, further centralization of power is a readily available alternative. Because centralization of power in individuals nearly always emasculates fragile institutions—strong institutions do constrain the power of individuals—there is a built-in incentive in India for leaders to undertake periodic deinstitutionalization. As long as a democracy remains more a gift that a society's leaders give to its people and less an established framework that dwarfs the leaders, only exceptional leaders are likely to resist the tendency to maintain personal power at the expense of institutional development.

An elite-dominated democracy has also structured the patterns of political mobilization. Leaders have mobilized socio-economic groups more as power resources in intra-elite struggles and less to satisfy group aspirations. That pattern of elite-led mobilization is distinguishable from the more conventional concept of social mobilization that supposedly accompanies industrialization, urbanization, literacy, and so forth. Whereas social mobilization is generally produced by economic development and 'modernization', elite-led mobilization often reflects patterns of intra-elite conflict. Thus, Indira Gandhi discovered India's poor when she was pressed politically by other members of the Congress elite. Devraj Urs and Karpoori Thakur similarly discovered the backward castes when they desperately needed to establish new ruling coalitions.

The Akalis began stressing issues of Sikh nationalism only when thrown out of power. The suggestion here is not that such patterns of mobilization are bad or wrong; they are the stuff of democracy. What is wrong here is the disregard for the consequences of such mobilizations.

The primary goal of elite-led mobilization in India has been power for the elite. The issue of whether or not the aspirations of the mobilized groups can be satisfied has always been secondary in the minds of the mobilizers. Indira Gandhi basically ignored the poor. Both Devraj Urs and Karpoori Thakur offered little more than tokens to the backward castes. The Akalis have been willing periodically to sell their nationalistic claims for state power. That is 'normal' politics, but what has not always been appreciated is that mobilized but unorganized groups that are ignored by politicians once they have served their political purposes add considerable volatility to the polity. When 'real groups' with 'real interests' such as labour, are mobilized, there is a realistic chance that the mobilization will be accompanied by organization and that group demands can be accommodated after negotiations. By contrast, mobilization from above often attracts demagogues. Because it remains unorganized and really does not have concrete, even if incremental, gains for the mobilized groups as its priority, such mobilization periodically tends to generate political turmoil.

This focus on elite-led mobilization should not detract attention from the fact of real distributional conflicts. The developmental model that India has pursued has exacerbated existing inequalities along regional, rural-versus-urban, ethnic, class, and caste lines. The resulting dissatisfaction provides the raw material for elite-led movements. The point, however, is that dissatisfied groups have only rarely produced their own leaders and sustained oppositional movements on their own. The pattern, instead, has been one in which professional but opportunistic politicians have sensed some dissatisfaction and have mobilized it almost to the point of frenzy. Such mobilization, in turn, brings short-term partisan benefits at the expense of the political health of the whole.

Finally, the last important characteristic of India's political structure that needs to be noted is the weakness of India's political parties. The organizational viability of Congress has declined. Most other parties have failed to fill the organizational vacuum. Because party organization has been treated as an intermediate variable in this study, both the cause and the consequences of organizational weakness need to be spelled out briefly in general terms.

The diversity of India's social structure naturally militates against the development of cohesive national parties. Because regional parties have not done much better, however, one suspects that factors other than cultural diversity are also at work. One hypothesis that fits the Indian materials is that strong parties—parties with well-developed political identification, programmatic goals, and organization—develop mainly as vehicles for gaining power. Conversely, leaders who acquire power because of personal appeal have little incentive to encourage the development of parties from above; on the contrary, parties as institutions often constrain the individual discretion and personalistic power of charismatic leaders. Thus, well-developed parties often emerge from below rather than from above.

That hypothesis fits broadly the development of the pre-independence Congress party, as well as the later growth of the Jana Sangh (now the Bharatiya Janata Party), the Communist Party of India, and the DMK in Tamil Nadu. Conversely, we also know that many of India's popular leaders not only have not helped the development of parties, but have even sought to destroy the existing institutional constraints. That was as true of national leaders like Indira and Rajiv Gandhi as it was of non-Congress regional leaders like M.G. Ramachandran in Tamil Nadu and N.T. Rama Rao in Andhra Pradesh.

As to the consequences of party organization, well-organized parties can perform several important political tasks. To repeat, they can help train and socialize new leaders, minimize factional conflict among existing leaders, and clarify lines of authority. Mobilization undertaken by parties, rather than by individuals, is also more likely to be accompanied by organization. Not only are new participants brought into the political arena, but their political energies are simultaneously harnessed to accomplish specific goals. Most important, well-organized parties tend to have long-term programmes and a stable core of membership to support those programmes. When such parties come to power, they help narrow the gap between the state's representative and developmental goals. The coalition that such a party brings to power is likely to favour the policies that the new government wishes to pursue.

The logic of why weak parties are major sources of governability problems in a democratic developing country is not difficult to explicate. Ample empirical evidence supporting this claim has been provided. Not only has the presence of weak parties been systematically related to governability problems, but the opposite, namely, the positive contributions of well-organized parties, has also been demonstrated. Thus, it is not unreasonable to conclude that the organizational vacuum in Indian politics is a root cause of the growing gap in the country between how power is won and how power is used, or between personalization of power, on the one hand, and the inability to use that power to solve pressing problems, on the other.

To sum up, the study has developed a multi-causal explanation of India's growing crisis of governability. The attempt to distinguish the more important causes from the less important has led to an emphasis on variables that can best be described collectively as political variables. It has been proposed further that the reason political factors play such an important role in India is traceable back to the relative balance between the state and the market in India's political economy. Given the state's pervasive presence, specific aspects of India's political structure have considerable bearing on patterns of political change. A highly interventionist state, the peculiarities of democracy bestowed from above, and the weakness of political parties have encouraged a number of trends: rapid political mobilization of diverse groups, a deinstitutionalizing role of leaders, and, more broadly, a situation in which institutions fail to keep pace with growing demands. The result has been a growing crisis of governability that has manifested itself in unstable political coalitions, governmental policy ineffectiveness, and, most important, the increasing use of force and violence in politics.

Finally, then, what are the implications of this argument for India? Three issues can be addressed: Was this pattern of political change inevitable? What is the appropriate frame of reference for the study of political change in India? What, if anything, can be done to reverse the growing crisis?

As for the complex issue of inevitability, the unhappy conclusion is that, on balance, a fair amount of what happened had to happen. Although the specific rates and patterns of changes obviously could have been different, given the emphasis on the political structures in the argument it is difficult to imagine a scenario in which India's political institutions would not have been weakened and power conflicts would not have multiplied.

India was much easier to govern when the nationalist legacy was alive, when the ruling elite were a relatively narrow and cohesive group, and when most of India's masses remained pre-political and deeply entrenched in a traditional caste hierarchy. Over time, many of those traits had to change. Nationalism had to decline. Given a highly interventionist state and electoral competition, both intra-elite struggles for power and struggles involving groups contending for access to the state's resources were bound to grow. Furthermore, the spread of commerce and egalitarian values had to undermine traditional patterns of domination, leading to growing conflicts within the civil society. Given the intra-elite struggles and conflicts among competing groups, it is also difficult to imagine how a 'consensual' party like Congress could have continued as before. Such patterns of decline of major institutions and increasing power conflicts spell political trouble in most polities. How could India have been any different?

This emphasis on inevitability needs two important qualifications. First, at some deep level of causation, as long as human beings make decisions, nothing in political change is ever inevitable. At some point, all paths involve choices. However, over time, the choices that are made become structures that mould future patterns of change. India's state, therefore, did not have to be as highly interventionist as it was. Once the decisions on patterns of state intervention were made, however, they were not easy to reverse. Numerous unanticipated consequences, some beneficial and some not so beneficial, followed. Similarly, there clearly was room for choice on distributive issues. Land reforms could have been implemented. A more benign pattern of stratification might well have created fewer problems of political accommodation. Once distributive issues were ignored, however, numerous 'inevitabilities' followed. For example, populism as a leadership strategy became one of the few alternatives for winning support among the lower strata. Populism, in turn, is inherently deinstitutionalizing.

The foregoing emphasis on inevitability, therefore, assumes many of the important structural decisions as given. Those decisions reflected many constraints that were operating when they were taken. Of course, if those major decisions had been different, the nature of political change in India could also have been different.

A second qualification concerns choices made by leaders that were distinctly less 'structural' in nature, but still had important and harmful consequences for the quality of government in India. Indira Gandhi, for example, came to preside over a Congress party in the 1960s that was already deeply factionalized at the top and rapidly losing its old coalitional base at the bottom. There is no reason to assume that the only way to reverse that situation was to split the Congress party, let the old Congress organization die, fail to rebuild any new organization, and revert to a highly deinstitutionalizing form of populism. It is possible to imagine the same rhetoric of populism that Indira adopted, combined with the old Congress organization, leading to a marginally different political outcome. Other examples can be presented to make the same point. Sanjay's goons and Rajiv's incompetence were hardly sociological necessities. At numerous points, therefore, different decisions could have led to a somewhat different outcome. The balanced conclusion on the issue of inevitability is that whereas the general trend of political change in India over the past two decades had to be toward a more turbulent polity, the specific rate and pattern could have been somewhat different.

This study also has an analytical message for those investigating political change in India, easily derived from the foregoing discussion. There are many schools of thought among observers of Indian politics. This study speaks directly to two of the more popular ones. One approach to Indian politics tends to focus on the role of leaders. For example, an inordinate amount of intellectual energy has been devoted to denouncing the deinstitutionalizing role of Indira Gandhi in Indian politics. Similarly, scholars often attribute great promise to preferred new leaders as soon as they appear on the political horizon. A second school of thought continues to view politics in terms of its underlying socioeconomic determinants. Whereas there are fewer and fewer scholars who view Indian politics through the old 'modernization' eyeglasses, there are many who still opt for the Marxist lens.

Those who emphasize the role of leaders are not necessarily wrong. They do, however, tend to underestimate the deeper determinants of Indian politics. Our findings suggest that even without Indira Gandhi, many features of Indian politics would still be the same.[4] This is not to deny that Indira Gandhi made some of the most important decisions involved in producing the political change one sees in India today. However, the most important question remains: Would a different leader have done things very differently? Indira Gandhi operated under constraints. Different leaders might have made some different decisions, but they also would have had to cope with the broader political pressures. In general, leaders always make a difference, sometimes even a very important difference, but there are always important structural forces at work that mould patterns of political change.

Marxist scholars are more acutely sensitive to this issue of choice versus structure, but as far as India is concerned, they often are too focused on the wrong set of structures. Issues of class relations, conceived narrowly, or of economic distribution, conceived more broadly, are far from inconsequential for an analysis of Indian politics.[5] Given the disproportionately large role of the state in moulding market relations in India, however, the role of political structures loom larger than those of social classes. If this contention seems a bit exaggerated, a modified position might be acceptable even to some Marxist scholars. No analysis of political change in India can be complete without taking into account the significance of such political variables as electoral competition, the weakness of political parties, the roles of leaders, and the virulent competition over state-controlled economic resources.

A third implication concerns the future. It is suggested that if current trends continue unchecked, India's political crisis is likely to get worse. Given the emphasis on the structural origins of the crisis, the kinds of leadership actions that could halt or reverse India's erosion of authority would have to involve major changes. Such changes would not be easy to initiate or to implement. Two policy prescriptions emerge: the need to strengthen

4 For an intelligent argument that stresses the role of leadership, see Paul R. Brass, *The Politics of India Since Independence. The New Cambridge History of India,* IV. 1 (Cambridge: Cambridge University Press, 1990).

5 One important collection (mostly non-Marxist) traces the roots of political disorder in contemporary India to issues of both class and caste distributions: Francine Frankel and M.S.A. Rao (eds), *Dominance and State Power in Modern India: Decline of a Social Order,* 2 vols (Delhi: Oxford University Press, 1989–90); see especially the contributions by Frankel.

the organizations of the major parties, and the need to narrow the gap between the state's commitments and capacities.

The need for better-organized parties has been emphasized, as have the many obstacles that stand in the way of such a development. The agents most likely to be able to initiate such major changes would be India's prominent leaders. Given the current circumstances, however, such leaders have little incentive to strengthen party organizations, for that would tend to check their personal power. What conceivable kinds of developments, if any, could help break that vicious circle?

A party with a clear programme is more likely to develop a stable membership, a core of active workers, and clear lines of authority and functions. The development of such programmatic national parties would be more likely in India if Congress were to cease being the centrist, populist majority party; all major parties compete for the central political space that Congress occupies. The most likely way for that to happen, at present, would be through the rise of an alternative leader with personal appeal who could outdo Congress's populism. That mode of political competition clearly is not helpful for organizational development. If, by chance or necessity, Congress should move to the left or the right, that could encourage the emergence of other programmatic national parties. Such a move probably would be destabilizing over the short run, as a vacuum of sorts would be created in the middle. Over the longer run, however, such a development could strengthen both Congress and the competing national parties, especially in the organizational dimension, thus adding a measure of coherence to India's turbulent polity. The debate between a democratic left and right, in turn, could help introduce real issues into what at present is largely mere populist posturing that scorns political problems. Such a debate could also cut across the caste, religious, and ethnic divisions that have become major sources of political turmoil. Our findings indicate that India has little to fear from the emergence of class politics; rather, centrism and populism are the primary sources of the problems in Indian politics.[6]

6 There is a study that conceives of continued 'centrism' as a source of stability in Indian politics: Lloyd and Susanne Rudolph, *In Pursuit of Lakshmi: The Political Economy of the Indian State* (Chicago: University of Chicago Press, 1987).

A prescription of this type is not the same as a prediction. Over the short run, neither Congressites nor the motley opposition groups are likely to abandon their centrist and populist postures. If one had to predict, it would seem that the most likely outcome over the next decade would be more of the same: policy ineffectiveness and continuing turmoil, encouraging further centralization and the use of force, punctuated by occasional bursts of hope created by elections and electoral gimmicks. How long such a process can go on within the framework of a democracy is difficult to predict. One prescription that emerges is that if one were to set out to alter the current political trends, then strengthening the party organizations would be an important area for action.

There is a related area in which there is a need for major action: narrowing the gap between the Indian state's commitments and its capacities. That could be done by reducing its commitments, by increasing its capacities, or more likely by some combination of the two. Non-partisan scholarship cannot suggest which alternative would be better. Those are major political issues that should be debated and settled by compromise among the contending political actors themselves. What scholarship can emphasize, however, is that the ongoing populist posturing of India's political parties, without the capacity to deliver on promises, has become a serious political problem. That pattern of rule raises aspirations without satisfying or harnessing them, thus continually contributing to the growing problems of governability.

Comparative Implications of Indian Materials

Finally, some comparative implications of this study of India can be suggested. Three issues, however, two substantial and one methodological, appear to be especially relevant. The substantial issues concern how and why centralization in developing countries creates powerlessness, and why attempts to institutionalize democracy in such settings will remain an uphill battle. The methodological issue concerns how best to study the problem of political disorder in developing countries.

Centralization and Powerlessness

Two types of power resources should be distinguished analytically: the power of leaders to control the state's decisions and exercise negative sanctions, especially coercion—let us label it 'centralizing power'—and 'real power', that is, power to bring about socio-economic development, however, development is defined—let us label it 'developmental power'. There is no necessary link between centralizing power and developmental power. On the contrary, whereas attempts at further centralization may have helped leaders preserve their personal power, they also have enfeebled the state in terms of accomplishing socio-economic goals. Thus, in India, centralization and powerlessness have turned out to be simultaneous tendencies.

The distinction between centralizing power and developmental power, and the related attempts to understand the conditions under which growing centralization may facilitate or undermine a state's developmental efficacy, opens up a range of comparative questions for future research. For example, we do not completely understand why authoritarianism in many African countries has failed to create developmental dynamism, whereas the results of authoritarianism in East Asian countries like South Korea have been nearly the opposite. Why are some centralized and authoritarian regimes efficacious in terms of accomplishing developmental goals, whereas others are not? This line of questioning suggests that a state's capacity to foster development is not likely to vary in a simple, linear way along the one-dimensional continuum from democracy to authoritarianism. The paramount question has to do with the conditions under which a democratic or an authoritarian government can facilitate socio-economic change from above—an issue that is as important as it is poorly understood.[7]

Although the findings in this study of India can help focus attention on such puzzles, they, of course, cannot come close to resolving them; that must be the function of multi-country research endeavours. One broad line of thinking, however, that emerges from the foregoing analysis may be of some utility. A state's capacity to facilitate development is primarily a function of how the state and the society relate to each other, and only secondarily a function of the characteristics of the state or the

7 A wide-ranging study that addresses this question is by Joel S. Migdal, *Strong Societies and Weak States: State–Society Relations and State Capabilities in the Third World* (Princeton, NJ: Princeton University Press, 1988). My major quarrel with that insightful book is its tendency to view power distribution as a zero-sum game between the state and society.

society alone.[8] More specifically, institutionalized patterns of authority that link (or do not link) the state and society are likely to be major determinants of the state's developmental efficacy. For example, leaders who preside over states that tend to exclude most social groups from both political participation and systematic economic benefits are likely to be deemed devoid of legitimacy, so that—barring extreme uses of coercion—they will be incapable of pursuing state-led development. Conversely, states that attempt to satisfy many social groups simultaneously may be deemed more legitimate over the short run, but again may not be all that efficacious, because of the problems inherent in attempting too many things at once. That is why the most efficacious states are likely to be those that selectively and systematically incorporate some social groups in a ruling alliance while using coercion to deal with the excluded groups. Both communist experiments and successful state-led capitalist experiments in the Third World have authority organized along these principles—at least over the medium term, beyond which the solution of new or neglected problems forces reform. The implication for effective democratic governance is the utility of well-organized competing parties that can incorporate selected social groups and yet create a coherent centre of national power.

Representation versus Development

A second general implication of the preceding empirical analysis concerns a possible explanation of why attempts to institutionalize democracy will remain uphill battles in the developing world. Democracy in the Third World has had many false starts, a pattern that is not likely to change soon. Many countries have attempted to 'democratize', but it has been a rare developing country in which stable and effective democratic government has taken root. Why is that so? A detailed study of political change in India suggests that democracy's fragility may reflect a persistent tension between the state's representative and developmental functions in the Third World.

8 Peter Evans, for example, emphasizes bureaucratic competence and the presence or absence of landed oligarchies as important determinants of a state's capacity to facilitate industrialization. See his 'Predatory, Developmental and Other Apparatuses: A Comparative Political Economy Perspective on the Third World State', *Sociological Forum*, vol. 4, no. 4, Fall 1989, pp. 561–87.

The state in much of the developing world is not only an agent of political order; it is also responsible for socio-economic development. The findings in India emphasize that the attempts of leaders to promote democratic political order often conflict with efforts to steer development from above. For example, if national leaders choose to build a popular base of support, that often inclines them to appeal to as many groups as possible. There are, however, few established traditions of inter-group collaboration in such settings. Therefore, a systematic ruling coalition often is difficult to sustain. The more the state internalizes the socio-economic conflicts of the civil society, the more difficult it becomes to establish a coherent political centre. Because a state without a coherent political centre is really no state, there is a recurring tendency in democratic Third World states to resort to leaders with personal and populist appeal as a short-term solution to the problem of political order.

Personalistic and populist leaders are, in turn, seldom effective at building institutions or at promoting economic development. Unless leaders are exceptionally committed to the public good, the logic of their political positions militates against stimulating the development of new ruling institutions. Such institutions can develop only if rules are put above personal discretion and if authority is systematically delegated to second, third, and even lower strata in the political hierarchy. Such a policy often means putting limits on personal power. Few leaders deliberately undertake actions that will eventually undermine their own power.

Populist leaders also find it difficult to promote economic efficiency. Nationalistic and redistributive themes often are central to a populist discourse; nationalistic and redistributive economic rhetoric helps legitimize fragile democratic rule. This does not mean that redistribution is effective. Rather, it means that leaders presiding over such arrangements often are reluctant to make the difficult economic decisions. Moreover, there is a recurring tendency to use the state's resources not to promote economic development but to buy political support. That tendency exists in a wide variety of regimes, but it is especially difficult to counter in the interventionist Third World democracies.

Democracy in a Third World context has a tendency to evolve toward a populist ruling arrangement, and populism as a ruling strategy has not been notably effective either for building institutions or for promoting economic development. It is that tendency that introduces into Third World democracies the recurring tension between their representative and developmental functions. Lest one conclude that this is an argument for authoritarianism, I must state that only some types of authoritarian regimes are effective at promoting economic development, and even they do not offer long-term political alternatives. Their failure to represent diverse interests leads periodically to power challenges, again creating considerable tension that is likely to be resolved only by movement toward a more open and legitimate polity.

A way out of the ubiquitous tension between the state's representative and developmental functions in Third World democracies is suggested by our findings for India. Well-organized political parties can help narrow that gap. Such parties can build stable coalitions around coherent programmes. Coalitions and policy priorities that have been tested in electoral competition, in turn, can help reduce the tension between the state's needs to represent diverse interests and simultaneously to promote socio-economic change from above. If democracy is an important goal in the Third World, then the development of well-organized parties will be a crucial factor in reaching that long-term goal.

The Study of Political Disorder

The last general theme that this empirical study can help to address is how best to study political disorder in developing countries. It must be clear to theoretically inclined readers that the approach informing this study is built on some prevailing ideas and departs from others. This study, while taking both developmental and class variables into account, emphasizes the political origin of political disorder. If labels are called for, the approach adopted here can best be described as a state–society approach.

This study shares with the works of Samuel Huntington, among others, the notion that the study of political order in developing countries is important. The virtual ideological disdain in some quarters concerning issues of order is short-sighted. The problem of political disorder ought to be of analytical and normative concern to diverse groups of scholars, whether they be on the left, on the right, or somewhere in between. The real debate should be about how best to explain the conditions that lead to order and disorder, and about the prescriptions that may flow from such analyses.

The study, further, shares the commonly held view that issues of order and disorder are best viewed in terms of a balance between institutional capacities to absorb societal demands and the nature and quality of the demands themselves. The basic formulation of 'institutions versus demands', 'integration versus differentiation', or 'hegemony versus class conflict' is common to both developmental and Marxist lines of analysis, the convergence being most evident in the works of such 'political development' scholars as Samuel Huntington and Guillermo O'Donnell. The main debate, once again, should be about the forces that propel group demands and, even more important, the conditions under which adequately institutionalized, non-coercive polities become established.

There are several important points, however, on which this study departs from 'developmental' formulations. First, the study of political order in a specific developmental setting is inseparable from the study of a state's ability to facilitate socio-conomic development. This view emerges from an understanding of the Third World state as an agent not only of order but also of development. Thus, a 'crisis of governability' is understood in this study to be manifest not only in growing political violence but also in the state's developmental incapacity. This modified focus, in turn, leads to a view in which order is not always to be preferred to disorder; an orderly state that fails to facilitate balanced development is hardly an effective and desirable state.

On more analytical grounds as well, this examination of how demands are mobilized and how institutions become weakened (or fail to develop) departs from some of the prevailing ideas. India's growing demands are not mainly a function of rapid socio-economic modernization. Instead, the spread of competitive politics in a setting in which the state has disproportionate control over societal resources provides the broad context for over-politicization. This modified perspective aids our understanding of the high degrees of politicization in low-income settings. More important, when state-controlled resources become objects of virulent competition, some of the conventional distinctions concerning whether conflict is over politics, status, or economic resources get blurred. For example, old group identities based on caste, language, or religion, or new identities based on occupation or class, can be used as a foundation for mobilization by competing groups of the political elite seeking a greater share of state-controlled economic resources. Is modal conflict of this nature ethnic, economic, or political? Because it is a bit of each, the dynamics and the consequences of such group mobilizations in state-dominated contexts require wider attention in comparative studies.[9]

This analysis of Indian materials also generates an insight concerning the dynamics of institutional development that may be of some general interest. Powerful leaders in India often have proved to be enemies of institutions such as political parties. Because institutions tend to constrain personal power, those who attain positions of power because of personalistic traits usually show little interest in institutional development or, worse, actively seek to weaken existing institutions. A similar

[9] Some analysts, working in contexts other than India, have already noted the significance of this link between extensive state intervention and rapid politicization. For example, Claude Ake has this to say about Nigeria: 'The crux of the problem of Nigeria today is the over-politicization of social life.... We are intoxicated with politics; the premium on political power is so high that we are prone to take the most extreme measures to win and to maintain political power.... As things stand now, the Nigerian state appears to intervene everywhere and to own virtually everything including access to status and wealth. Inevitably a desperate struggle to win control of state power ensues.' From Claude Ake, 'Presidential Address to the Nigerian Political Science Association', *West Africa*, 25 May 1981, pp. 1162–3. Other analysts of Nigeria have adopted a similar standpoint to explain why political breakdown is less a 'tribal' and more a state-generated phenomenon in that country. See Larry Diamond, *Class, Ethnicity and Democracy in Nigeria: The Failure of the First Republic* (Syracuse, NY: Syracuse University Press, 1988), especially pp. 297–300. In the Latin American context, where class ideologies often dominate the political discourse, discerning analysts have pointed out that the pattern of recurring shifts in regime types are rooted less in class conflict and more in the nature of the 'politicized state', in which institutions are weak and 'everything is possible'. The process of politicization is, moreover, 'reinforced' by a 'central role of the state in Latin American society.... The control and manipulation of the state apparatus are therefore a major element in the political struggle'. See Douglas A. Chalmers, 'The Politicized State in Latin America', in James M. Malloy (ed.), *Authoritarianism and Corporatism in Latin America* (Pittsburg: University of Pittsburgh Press, 1977), pp. 26, 30, 31.

deinstitutionalizing tendency on the part of personalistic leaders has been widely noted in the African context.[10] It is arguable that even in a somewhat different non-personalistic context, like that of Brazil, the legacy of highly bureaucratized authoritarian rule has hardly been strong democratic parties.[11] Such recurring failures of rulers to initiate the rebuilding and maintenance of institutions clearly have general relevance.

One is led to conclude that political disorder results not only from the demands of newly mobilized groups but also from the institution-destroying proclivities of a powerful state elite. That, in turn, suggests that it is misleading to assume that highly mobilized social groups are the main enemies of public order and that the state is the most likely guarantor of public good. We encountered case after case in which the state elite had proved to be a crucial part of the problem of political disorder. Clearly, in our analyses of political disorder in developing countries, the conservative bias that often is suspicious of mobilization from below while tolerant of power abuses by authorities, in the belief that the state is the ultimate provider of the public good, needs to be rethought, if not expunged.

The main prescriptive implication of this analysis is that there are no shortcuts to the establishment of non-coercive political order. Heavy-handed rule cannot be justified on the ground that it can help generate consensus-building institutions such as parties; neither logic nor evidence supports that contention. Instead, power conflicts must be negotiated and worked out. The development of integrative institutions at the interstices of the state and society, especially parties, will remain crucial for moderating these conflicts. Such developments, however, are more likely in cases in which power conflicts are worked out from below; they are less likely to result from social engineering from above.

10 See, for example, Robert H. Jackson and Carl G. Rosberg, *Personal Rule in Black Africa: Prince, Autocrat, Prophet, Tyrant* (Berkeley, CA: University of California Press, 1982); Richard Sandbrook, *The Politics of Africa's Economic Stagnation* (Cambridge: Cambridge University Press, 1985).

11 See the detailed account in Thomas E. Skidmore, *The Politics of Military Rule in Brazil, 1964–85* (New York: Oxford University Press, 1988).

5

Demand Polity and Command Polity[+]

Lloyd I. Rudolph and Susanne Hoeber Rudolph

We address the relationship between polity and economy in independent India by using contrasting models: demand polity and command polity. These models allow us to raise questions about the tension between conflicting requirements of state sovereignty and popular sovereignty, which determines the degree of state autonomy on the one hand and state responsiveness on the other. We use this tension to illuminate the relationships between governability and mobilization, between saving and consumption, and between investment in future benefits and expenditures on welfare now.

The play of contesting sovereignties, the state versus the people, in the tension between command and demand polities helps us to explain India's political economy by tracing the interaction since independence between rising levels of political mobilization and the changing capabilities of the 'state'. The use of competing sovereignties in the form of command and demand polities avoids conventional but increasingly unproductive arguments about whether 'capitalism' or 'socialism' is better for prosperity, freedom, or equality. For example, both models allow, *inter alia*, for planned or corporatist capitalism or market socialism under conditions of more or less equality and freedom.

[+] Abridged versions from chapters of *In Pursuit of Lakshmi: The Political Economy of the Indian State* (Chicago: University of Chicago Press, 1987), pp. 211–19, 220, 222–44.

Demand and Command Polities

In our model of a demand polity, voter citizens are sovereign. Extractive and allocative decisions reflect citizens' preferences as they are expressed through party competition in elections and through representation by interests, classes, communities, and movements. In the theory of voter sovereignty, voters are said to be analogous to sovereign consumers in a competitive market economy, insofar as consumers' preferences and choices in markets, like those of voters' in elections, are not 'distorted' by widely asymmetrical distributions of wealth, power, and information.[1]

In our model of a command polity, 'autonomous' states are sovereign. Extractive and allocative decisions reflect the preferences of the elected and appointed officials who choose and implement policies. They favour, repress, license, or co-opt classes, interests, communities, and elites. Using the economic analogy again, the role of the state is like that of monopolistic or oligopolistic producers who can determine what and how much is produced because they control investment and product choice and shape consumer preferences accordingly.

The demand polity is oriented toward short-term goals; toward competitive processes for determining policies and the public interest (for example, voting, deliberation, and bargaining); and toward the provision of private goods. It is constrained and directed by the imperatives of electoral victory and by pluralist and class influence on public choice. It is also oriented toward the

[1] For theoretical treatments of related issues see Anthony Downs, *An Economic Theory of Democracy* (New York: Harper and Row, 1965), and Donald Wittman's critique showing how producer rather than consumer or voter sovereignty can govern market and electoral outcomes, 'Parties as Utility Maximizers', *American Political Science Review*, vol. 67, no. 2, June 1973. We distinguish our models from Charles E. Lindblom's by integrating his two domains of 'politics' (that is, public authority and markets) into state and popular sovereignty, with the latter expressed in the collective and individual action of citizens as voters, producers, or consumers. See Lindblom's *Politics and Markets: The World's Political Economic Systems Compared* (New York: Basic Books, 1977). We do not treat market relationships in demand and command politics as a necessarily autonomous domain because we take the existence, viability, and quality of markets to be dependent on state decisions and policies that, in a circular fashion, depend on the 'balance' of command and demand politics in particular contexts.

'rationality' of incremental policy choice,[2] because the next step from a known position is better than a leap in the dark. The command polity is oriented toward state-determined long-term goals and formulations of the public interest and the provision of collective goods. Rationality in command polities derives from comprehensive and detailed calculations that relate social objectives to available resources.[3] A necessary condition for the command polity's ability to formulate goals, strategies, and policies is the state's ability to free itself from the constraints of societal demands through leadership, persuasion, or coercion.

Legitimacy, support, and producer commitment in both command and demand polities require equity in the allocation of benefits and sacrifice. Demand polities tend to maximize legitimacy, support, and producer commitment by stressing equity with respect to benefits; command polities, by stressing equity with respect to sacrifice.

Because demand and command polities are heuristic constructs and appear in the real world in mixed forms to varying degrees, we use the terms command and demand *politics* to signal their empirical referents. Democratic or authoritarian regimes sometimes express elements of demand and command polities, respectively, but there is no necessary congruence between regime and polity. For example, strong and skillful institutional or personal leadership in democratic regimes can practise command politics that favour long-run objectives and collective goods by appealing to national pride and social justice and by manipulating incentives and sanctions to achieve the desired goals. Democratic regimes, in arguing the trade-offs between investment in future benefits and expenditure on present consumption and welfare, can and do advance the former. Jawaharlal Nehru's Congress governments exemplified the possibility of combining command politics with a democratic regime. On the other hand, leaders of authoritarian regimes can distort or subvert the command polity commitment to future benefits and collective goods. Beset by the exigencies of the political struggle and the immediate needs of political survival,

2 Charles E. Lindblom, 'The Science of Muddling Through', *Public Administration Review*, vol. 19, Spring 1959, pp. 79–88.

3 See Lindblom's *Politics and Markets*, where he contrasts incremental and synoptic rationality.

they may attempt to maintain themselves in power by claiming that their self-interested repression of current demands serves long-term goals and the public good.

Legitimacy in demand politics depends on the state's capacity to provide short-run equitable treatment of citizens' demands. Legitimacy in command politics depends on the credibility of the state's call for equitable sacrifice to achieve future benefits and avoid social costs. Short-term demands articulated by interest groups, elites, or classes need not be perceived as partial or unjust by large portions of society. For example, the Polish workers' demands in 1980 for cheaper food and the right to independent representation were widely supported. But short-term demands can be perceived as partial and unjust. Such was the case in India when the highly advantaged Life Insurance Corporation employees and Air India pilots struck for higher wages and other benefits in the early 1970s. The efforts of Indira Gandhi's emergency regime to stop hoarding and black marketeering by punishing violators won wide support because they seemed to promote equity of sacrifice. On the other hand, the regime's vasectomy programme was perceived by poor Muslims and untouchables as illegitimate, not only because it involved coercion and the violation of personal liberty but also because its implementation discriminated against them. An authoritarian regime can, up to a point, manufacture positive perceptions of its goals and performance, but it too is subject to tests of legitimacy. Ultimately, an authoritarian regime's legitimacy may hinge as much on its recognition of the demand for independent representation as on its performance with respect to its professed goals.

Economic and Political Correlates of Demand and Command Politics

Our models of demand and command polity include both political and economic characteristics. The demand polity is characterized politically by voter sovereignty and the societal direction of the state; the command polity, by state sovereignty and state hegemony (domination or control) over policy and politics. The economic characteristics of the demand model feature shorter-term market or state consumption and welfare expenditure; those of the command model, longer-term investment expenditure in public goods and future benefits.[4]

The Nehru years, 1950–64, represent a command politics under democratic auspices. Over the course of those years, the central government was able to increase the proportion of its annual budget allocated to investment (capital formation) from 30 to 50 per cent (see Fig. 5.2). With the onset in 1966 of the first period of demand politics (1966–75), the proportion declined rapidly. By 1969, it had returned to nearly where it began in 1951, about 32 per cent. Central government investment continued at a low level until 1974, when many of the economic policies later pursued under the emergency regime were initiated. During the authoritarian regime (1975–7), the share of the central government's budget allocated to investment increased further. But when the Janata government restored a democratic regime in 1977, investment allocations did not decline. Instead, they remained at or above the levels reached under the authoritarian regime. Nevertheless, the investment levels reached in the mid-1970s and maintained through the mid-1980s remained below the level of the peak year, 1965–6. More seriously, central government investment expenditure during this period was increasingly negated by a rising capital–output ratio, an increase driven primarily by poor performance in the public sector.

The high levels of government investment attained under the Nehru and Shastri governments cannot be attributed exclusively to successful democratic leadership. International and domestic determinants beyond the reach of government policy made important contributions too. Cheap oil, for example, contributed to low levels of inflation and positive foreign exchange balances. High commodity prices during the Korean War boom helped. So too did the low defence expenditures that prevailed prior to the China

4 'It may be necessary', Jon Elster writes of the dichotomous view of investment and consumption, 'at some point to take one step backwards in order to be able later on to take two steps forwards. An instance of this pattern is investment—consuming less now in order to be able to consume more later on.' An 'intentional agent' must be able to say 'yes to unfavourable options now in order to say yes to very, very favourable ones in the future...the suboptimal action only makes sense in view of future gains that it makes possible'. [Jon Elster, *Making Sense of Marx* (Cambridge: Cambridge University Press, 1985), pp. 108–9].

and Pakistan wars in 1962 and 1965. Equally important, during the Nehru era the relatively low levels of political mobilization paralleled and reinforced the helpful effects of international determinants.

India's dominant elites and policy intellectuals since independence have tended to favour command politics as a faster and surer means of creating a self-reliant economy and a powerful state. However, the practice of political economy in the post-independence era has strongly indicated not only that demand politics is compatible with economic growth and governability but also that it may promote them. The consumption and welfare expenditures that demand politics generates can improve the productivity of human capital and enhance legitimacy; the voter sovereignty that demand politics expresses can promote governability by enhancing the legitimacy and efficiency enabled by citizen and producer commitment.

The command polity's investment orientation has also raised questions about the extent to which, after a self-reliant industrial economy has been established, continuing to invest in basic and heavy industry will promote growth and employment or help alleviate poverty.

The links between command and demand politics and economic policy and performance have to be understood in the context of changing conceptions and the goals for development and the ways to achieve them. The future-oriented promise of command politics implied the postponement of immediate gratification in the interest of accumulating and investing capital to obtain future benefits. This was a social version of the this-worldly asceticism that Weber associated with the Protestant ethic and the rise of capitalism in the West. The scientific asceticism of socialist regimes collectivized the Protestant ethic when it called for postponement of current consumption in order to extract the surplus for state investment. For almost three decades, this psychology and morality of postponed gratification animated Indian planners and their economic policies. The short-run orientation of demand politics is associated more with the quality of life as it is lived now and less with the uncertain promise of future growth and its benefits. For supporters of future-oriented development theory, the current consumption they associated with demand politics ate up the income and assets needed to insure future benefits. Expenditure on current consumption reflected the spendthrift propensity of irresponsible politicians seeking quick fixes to obtain political support and cope with economic crisis.

More recently, postponement theories that call for sacrificing the present for the future have lost ground to development theories that identify goals other than growth in the Gross National Product (GNP) and different means to reach them. Postponement theories have been impugned because of the high cost to current generations of a future orientation. In India, postponement development theory was translated into import-substitution and basic industry strategies that bore fruit in a relatively self-reliant economy. Once self-reliance and growth in GNP had been achieved, it became clear that these goals did not address the distribution and character of benefits. Nor was it clear where to go next—what investment goals to address or how to address them.

New goals emerged from the realization that the poor were neither benefiting from nor contributing to development. Indeed, it became clear that they were the primary victims of postponement theories of development. Forty to fifty per cent remained below the poverty line, under- and unemployment rates grew, and the poor lacked the skills, assets, and health to contribute to economic growth. Development that addressed 'basic human needs' and unemployment became the established view of most multilateral agencies after the World Bank gave it its imprimatur.[5] The physical quality of life index (PQLI), a measure of development that combines literacy, life expectancy, and infant mortality, was devised as an alternative to measures based on growth in per capita GNP.[6] The PQLI gave a different meaning to the goals of development. Measures of per capita GNP do not address the distribution or character of benefits but the PQLI does.

The political characteristics of demand and command politics raise questions other than those raised by their economic characteristics. Demand politics threatens governability when mobilizations overrun established channels. It jeopardizes regulated conflict and the representational infrastructure, and it undermines a government of laws. Even so, mobilization that articulates

5 See Hollis Chenery *et al.*, *Redistribution with Growth* (Oxford: Oxford University Press, 1977).

6 See Morris David Morris, *Measuring the Condition of the World's Poor: The Physical Quality of Life Index* (New York: Pergamon, 1979).

perceived needs and inequities can contribute to governability by making the state respond in ways that foster support and legitimacy. Command politics holds out the potential for governability and discipline but can be a rationalization for authoritarian suppression of demands that jeopardizes legitimacy, support, and labour commitment.

These ambiguous potentialities are exacerbated by the conditions of modern Indian politics. In the second half of the twentieth century, the political context for capital accumulation is dramatically different from that in the eighteenth century, during the first industrial revolution, or from the political context that affected the Soviet Union's industrialization in the 1920s and 1930s. Radical asymmetries in economic and political power enabled England to build an industrial economy on considerable mass suffering. A repressive regime that sacrificed millions enabled the Soviet Union to extract, from the countryside and elsewhere, the surplus required for industrialization.

Capital accumulation in England and the Soviet Union occurred under political conditions very different from those in independent India which, *ab initio*, adopted universal suffrage and responsible government. India's attempt to create a political context for rapid industrialization comparable to that in England and the Soviet Union, the emergency regime of 1975–7, revealed that the 'discipline' that accompanied the initial stage of authoritarian rule was ephemeral, more a question of bottling up political opposition and economic demands than of transforming consciousness, institutions and commitments.

If demand politics features voter sovereignty and societal direction of the state, what have been the consequences in practice? An implication of the centrality of voter sovereignty in demand politics is that the many who are poor will benefit more than the few who are rich. However, in India as elsewhere, political participation in the context of interest group and social pluralism has favoured the better organized and more affluent, who not only have been more influential in shaping the policy agenda than the unorganized or underorganized poor but also have often appropriated the benefits of state-inspired pro-poor policies. Bank employees, doctors, airline pilots, office workers, professionals, and the labour aristocracy—all located for the most part in the public sector of the organized economy—have benefited more from demand politics than have landless labourers, marginal cultivators, and workers in craft and small-scale industries in the private sector and unorganized economy. Industrial workers and agricultural producers with more organization and assets have gained more from demand politics than those with less, an outcome not inconsistent with what critics of interest group pluralism have found in other industrial democracies.[7]

One reading of demand politics holds that the poor are unable to represent themselves. Such a reading led some Indian political leaders and intellectuals to hold the view that an authoritarian version of command politics was preferable to demand politics because it could enable the state to act as the friend, benefactor, and protector of the poor.

The disenchantment with authoritarian rule in 1975–7 revived the belief that voter sovereignty in the form of demand politics can contribute to both social justice and development, that is, that it does not necessarily serve only the well organized and prosperous. Without being able to mobilize on their own behalf, the poor are voiceless and defenceless. Demand politics gives the many poor an opportunity to represent themselves, to assert and protect their rights and interests, to protest and, sometimes, to limit the diversion by vested interest of the benefits of pro-poor policies.

Amartya Sen has drawn attention to the contrast between the People's Republic of China, where famine did occur, and independent India, where it did not. Sen attributes this difference to the presence in India of channels of political communication and representation that draw attention to dramatic deprivations and to the absence of such channels in China. He adds, however, that these channels 'easily allow the quiet continuation of an astonishing set of persistent injustices [such as] endemic malnutrition and hunger that is not acute, so long as they happen quietly'.[8]

[7] See Lloyd I. Rudolph and Susanne Hoeber Rudolph, *In Pursuit of Lakshmi: The Political Economy of the Indian State* (New Delhi: Orient Longman, 1987), chapters 10, 13.

[8] For Sen's argument, see 'How is India Doing', *New York Review of Books*, 16 December 1982. This article and a similar one in *Mainstream* spawned a lively debate. See Sen, 'Conflicts in Access to Food'; K.N. Raj, 'Chinese Data and Amartya Sen', *Mainstream*, 15 January 1983; Sen and Raj, 'Amartya Sen vs. K.N. Raj on Chinese Data', *Mainstream*, 12 February 1983; and Sen, 'Reply to K.N. Raj', *Mainstream*, 19 February 1983. See also Ranjit Sau, 'Growth,

Mobilization of the poor via demand politics depends on their being organized and connected to political processes, including policy choice and implementation. The deinstitutionalization of the Congress party and the rise of plebiscitary politics associated with Indira Gandhi's national leadership substituted a leader–mass following relationship for the organizational infrastructure of the institutionalized party that connected the poor, among others, to political and policy processes. In plebiscitary politics, the leader gains and holds support by appealing directly to voters. Such appeals short-circuit the mediating role of a representational infrastructure summed and integrated by the competition among parties. Party competition encouraged the Congress party to extend its support base to previously unrepresented constituencies as well as to hold old constituencies and attract those of rivals. As demonstrated by the parties of Chief Ministers Devraj Urs in Karnataka, Karpoori Thakur in Bihar, and Sharad Pawar in Maharashtra and the CPI(M) in Kerala and Bengal, parties often were mechanisms for disestablishing old political elites, widening participation, and representing new constituencies. The absence of agreed procedures for making demands and for bargaining and deliberating about them tends to radicalize demands. Deinstitutionalization not only reduced the likelihood that the poor and other constituencies would be represented but also weakened the capacity of the state to contain and redirect demands that could not or should not be accommodated. Without an open and effective representational infrastructure that mediates between demand politics and the state, the bargaining and deliberation that compromise interests and articulate common purposes will atrophy.

Types of Politics and Economic Performance

The relationship between politics and economics is one that continues to perplex politicians, policy intellectuals, and social

---

Stagnation and Fluctuation in Indian Economy', and Sen, 'India: The Doing and the Undoing', *Economic and Political Weekly*, 12 February 1983. We have profited from Barnett Rubin's argument for a connection between the alleviation of poverty and participatory democracy in his 'Private Power and Public Investment in India: A Study in the Political Economy of Development' (Ph.D. dissertation, University of Chicago, 1982).

theorists. Does poverty in developing countries lead to revolution or fatalistic apathy? Does economic growth yield frustrated rising expectations or contented cooperation?[9] Too often, the answers to such questions have been ad hoc and a prioristic deductions or inferences from theory, occasionally buttressed by examples. We examine below the association in India since independence between types of politics and types of regimes and economic performance.

The Relationship between Politics and Economics

In this chapter, 'politics' becomes two qualitative variables—type of regime and type of politics—and four quantitative mobilization variables—voter turnout, riots, workdays lost, and student indiscipline—that operationalize important aspects of demand politics. The intervening variables are politically determined levels of investment and consumption expenditure. The question we address is, how have variations over time in our qualitative and quantitative political variables affected economic performance, defined primarily as growth but operationalized in the four variables of public investment, agricultural and industrial production, and inflation?

[9] Alexis de Tocqueville may have been the first modern social theorist to address the generic problem of the relationship between improving economic and status conditions of the many and collective action directed at regime change. In his *Old Regime and the French Revolution*, (Garden City, N.Y. Doubleday Anchor, 1955), he pointed out that France's peasants under improving economic circumstances became increasingly discontent with residual 'feudal' exactions (e.g., corvee, market controls and costs, hunting privileges), while Prussia's oppressed and exploited serfs remained docile and obedient. A century later in his study of Prussian landworkers, Max Weber argued that most preferred insecurity with freedom to security with domination (*Schriften des Vereins für Sozialpolitik*, vol. 60, *Die Verhältnisse der Landarbeiter im Oestelbischen Deutschland* (Berlin: Duncker and Humbolt, 1892). Charles Tilly's recent study, *From Mobilization to Revolution* (Reading, Mass.: Addison-Wesley, 1978), provides a 'partial synthesis' between causal and purposive explanation of collective action that leads to revolution and rebellion. Our 'Determinants and Varieties of Agrarian Mobilization', in Meghnad Desai, Susanne Hoeber Rudolph, and Ashok Rudra, *Agrarian Power and Agricultural Productivity in South Asia* (Berkeley and Los Angles: University of California Press and New Delhi: Oxford University Press, 1989) gives equal attention to why radical collective action does not and does occur.

Prime Minister Indira Gandhi and many of those in India who supported the 1975–7 emergency shared the view that in developing countries there is a positive relationship between authoritarian regimes and economic performance. So too did significant segments of the world press and financial opinion that looked favourably on India's emergency regime. India seemed to be adopting the then-fashionable authoritarianism-cum-growth model, a model that seemed to be entailed, if not necessarily intended, in International Monetary Fund (IMF) conditionality. According to the model, authoritarian regimes are better able to keep wages down, cut or eliminate subsidies and transfer payments, foster savings as opposed to consumption, and, by virtue of their putative political stability and alignment, attract foreign aid, loans, and investment. Consent, representation, and human rights might have to wait; they were a luxury for poor peoples not accustomed to freedom.

Prime Minister Indira Gandhi justified the emergency by arguing that selfish, antisocial, and politically destabilizing activity had to be checked and replaced by state-imposed 'discipline'. Authoritarian, repressive rule won tacit approval abroad, particularly in banking and financial circles. Robert McNamara, president of the World Bank, and H.J. Witteveen, director of the IMF, praised the economic performance of the emergency regime. Their assessment supported Gunnar Myrdal's earlier diagnosis: India's inability to develop rapidly was attributable to its 'soft state'.[10]

The belief that an excess of democracy constrains economic growth and jeopardizes governability had a certain currency in developed countries too. By the mid-1970s, when Mrs Gandhi was promoting authoritarian rule in India, the democratic 'excesses' of the late 1960s had begun to influence social theory and policy prescription in the West.[11] Excessive and unruly demand led not only to 'ungovernability' but also to expansive welfare states that diverted increasing proportions of GNP from investment in growth to 'unproductive' expenditures on entitlements and social

10 Gunnar Myrdal, *Asian Drama: An Inquiry into the Poverty of Nations* (New York: Twentieth Century Fund, 1968).

11 See Albert O. Hirschman, *Shifting Involvements* (Princeton: Princeton University Press, 1982), chapter 5, where he criticizes Mancur Olson's theories of collective action as reflecting concern about the effects of 1960s-like mobilizations.

rights.[12] Stagflation accompanied by costly new demands and escalating established benefits put welfare states, themselves products of democratic politics, at risk and revealed cultural as well as political and economic contradictions.[13] Theories of the 'overloaded state' and proposals for how to insulate government from democratic politics multiplied.[14]

In the developing world, the rise in the 1970s of newly industrialized countries (such as South Korea, Taiwan, Hong Kong, Singapore, and Brazil) suggested that the future lay with authoritarian regimes and export-led growth in an expanding world economy based on free trade and easy access to commercial bank credit.

However, in the 1980s, the authoritarian-cum-growth model began to unravel parallel with a rash of restorations of democracy. World recession, debt, worsening terms of trade for primary products (including the collapse of oil prices), and creeping protectionism seemed to show that it was the buoyant world economy of the 1970s, not authoritarian regimes, that accounted for economic growth.

Our analysis in this chapter suggests that in India there are discernible but indeterminant relationships between political variables and measures of economic performance. Under an authoritarian British Raj, per capita income had remained stagnant between 1901 and 1946, the last forty-five years of colonial rule. Raj authoritarianism did make the trains run on time but did not make the economy grow.[15] Independent India under Jawaharlal Nehru's leadership proposed to do better. Over four decades of

12 For a summary and critique of 'overloaded government', see Colin Crouch, 'The State Capital and Liberal Democracy' in *State and Economy in Contemporary Capitalism* (New Delhi: St Martin's, 1979).

13 See Claus Offe, *Contradictions of the Welfare State* (Cambridge: MIT Press, 1984), particularly chapter 2, 'Ungovernability: The Renaissance of Conservative Theories of Crisis', pp. 65–87.

14 See Michel Crozier, Samuel P. Huntington, and Joy L. Watanuki, *The Crisis of Democracy: Report on the Governability of Democracy for the Tri-lateral Commission* (New York: New York University Press, 1975) and Samuel P. Huntington and Joan M. Nelson, *No Easy Choice: Political Participation in Developing Countries* (Cambridge: Harvard University Press, 1976).

15 'In the years since independence, Indian economic growth has been much faster than in the colonial period. From 1948 to 1969, real national income rose by 3.3 per cent per year...acceptable estimates for 1900–1946...show a

mostly democratic rule, per capita income increased by at least 1.3 per cent per year.[16] India's economy has not grown as fast as those of post-war pacesetters among industrialized societies, such as Japan and Germany, or leaders among developing societies, such as South Korea and Taiwan. Until the 1980s, it seemed to be locked into what the late Raj Krishna identified as the 'Hindu rate of growth', 3.5 per cent of GNP. In the 1980s, when other Third World economies were faltering, the Indian economy seemed to have broken with the Hindu rate of growth by reaching a long-term annual rate of 5 per cent.

Our findings in this chapter suggest that authoritarianism was not an important determinant of India's modest but significant economic growth and that it is not likely to become one. The notion that authoritarian rule in India has been positively associated with economic growth and that democracy has not is more contradicted than supported by the available evidence. Both good and bad economic performance occurred under both authoritarian and democratic regimes.

Authoritarianism in India lacks legitimacy. It is likely to have a short half-life without a Stalinist-type regime, which India seems reluctant to mount. Authoritarianism in India faces not only a legitimacy constraint but also a productivity constraint; that is, authoritarian rule can coerce workers in the short run, but in the long run the productivity of human capital depends on willing commitment. It also faces an investment constraint. As the decline in public investment during the emergency suggests, the regime used consumption expenditure to gain or hold support, in a sense substituting consumption expenditure for coercion. Finally, authoritarianism in India faces an efficiency constraint. As practised in India (and the Philippines under Marcos), it

---

compound growth rate of real national income amounting to 0.7 per cent a year from 1900 to 1946 and rose to 2.4 per cent a year in 1948–1969. Therefore, *per capita* income has grown by 0.9 per cent per year since independence, compared with a more or less stagnant level from 1900 to 1946' [Angus Maddison, *Class Structure and Economic Growth: India and Pakistan since the Moghuls* (New York: Norton, 1971), p. 76]. Calculations based on table A-2 (p. 165) and B-1 (p. 167) show that per capita income between 1900 and 1936 increased from Rs 71 to Rs 78.

16 World Bank, *World Development Report, 1984* (New York: Oxford University Press, 1984), Table 1, pp. 218–19.

exaggerated the already patrimonial and personalistic features that characterized democratic rule under Mrs Gandhi's leadership. The quality of investment, commercial and professional activity, and public authority and the productivity of physical capital deteriorated as favourites and courtiers enlarged their ability to influence decisions and to extract rents and profits.

Over the four decades since independence, state capacity and autonomy declined. The decline encompassed both authoritarian and democratic regimes. The long-run deterioration in state capacity and autonomy was associated with the deinstitutionalization of both political parties and state institutions. There has been a secular decline in the authority and capacity of state agencies and political parties to articulate a public philosophy and to respond to and broker political demands within the framework of that philosophy.

In examining the association between politics (operationalized as type of politics and regime type) and growth, we focus on the rising levels of participation and mobilization that characterized the years after 1965. While authoritarianism was instituted in order to counter the pressure of such mobilization and while it did temporarily limit it, rising and persistent demand pressures have affected Indian politics and policy regardless of the type of regime or type of politics.

We approach the relationship between politics and growth by distinguishing four periods since Indian independence. Each manifests a different combination of regime type (democratic or authoritarian) and type of politics (demand or command). Next we relate the four periods to various measures of economic performance and to indicators of demand politics. We conclude that demand and command politics are more associated with economic performance than are regime types per se but that neither association is very compelling. Politics seems not to matter as much for economic performance as politicians and political scientists would like to think. We also note that the higher mobilization of the post-Nehru era both narrowed and lowered the range within which economic performance varies.

In addressing the question of the association between demand and command politics and economic performance, we use a different mix of evidence for economic performance than we do for type of politics. The evidence for economic performance is mostly quantitative, while that for type of politics is more qualitative. Where available, we have also used quantitative evidence to make the case for the existence of demand and command politics. At the same time, we have resisted the temptation to pursue an attractive but spurious symmetry of quantitative measures for economic performance and type of politics and to attempt the statistical manipulations that then become possible. Not only is accurate medium- to long-term quantitative evidence for type of politics scarce, but also—and more important—the available qualitative evidence is more valid and reliable. Our explanatory project encounters the phenomenon of circular causation. While we are primarily interested in analysing the effect of type of politics and regime on economic performance, we recognize that economic performance also affects the type of politics and regime. Problems about causal direction are inherent in analysis. The relationship is mutually determined.

The era of 1952–86 included four distinct periods for types of regime and types of politics. Our periodization starts with the period covering the first three five-year plans, when India embarked on a strategy of limited autarky based on investment in heavy and basic industry and import substitution: (1) 1952–3 to 1963–4: democratic regime/command politics I (mainly Nehru); (2) 1964–5 to 1974–5: democratic regime/demand politics I (mainly Indira Gandhi); (3) 1975–6 to 1976–7: authoritarian regime/command politics II (emergency); and (4) 1977–8 to 1985–6: democratic regime/demand politics II (Janata/Congress).[17]

1952–3 to 1963–4: Democratic Regime/ Command Politics I

The Nehru era was characterized by a democratic regime and non-authoritarian command politics. Nehru-led Congress governments

[17] The calibration and synchronization of political periods (regime types and type of politics) with our measures of demand politics and of economic performance are complicated by the facts that demand politics and economic performance data are sometimes given on the basis of calendar year (1 January–31 December) and sometimes on the basis of financial year (1 April–31 March), that political events occur stochastically, and that five-year plan periods (starting in 1951) have been modified by a plan 'holiday' (or annual plans) (1966–7 through 1968–9) and by a one-year reduction in the fifth plan (from 1974–9 to 1974–8).

were able to invest in the future because they could rely on Nehru's persuasive leadership, the effectiveness of the Congress party's organizational wing at the centre and in the states, and autonomous and authoritative state institutions. They benefited from the residual consensus of the nationalist era and a less mobilized, more dependent society and electorate. Quantitative indicators of demand politics—such as voter turnouts, workdays lost due to strikes, incidents of student 'indiscipline', and number of riots—remained low (see Fig. 5.1 and Table 5.1). The Congress party exercised firm control, winning two-thirds or more of parliamentary seats and three-fifths or more of assembly seats in the 1952, 1957, and 1962 general elections.[18] Economic performance was good to outstanding.

Table 5.1: Indicators of Demand Politics

Year	Riots (Thousands)	Student Indiscipline: Reported Incidents	Workdays Lost (Millions)	Voter Turnout (%)
1.	2.	3.	4.	5.
	Democratic Regime/Command Politics I (Nehru)			
1952	–	–	3.3	45.7
1953	21	–	3.4	–
1954	23	–	3.4	–
1955	24	–	5.7	–
1956	25	–	7.0	–
1957	24	–	6.4	47.8
1958	25	93	7.8	–
1959	27	120	5.6	–
1960	27	80	6.5	–
1961	27	172	5.0	–
1962	29	97	6.1	55.4
1963	28	109	3.3	–
	Democratic Regime/Demand Politics I			
1964 } Shastri	33	395	7.7	–
1965 } Shastri	33	271	6.5	–

Contd.

[18] See, for example, Myron Weiner, *India at the Polls: The Parliamentary Elections of 1977*. (Washington, D.C.: American Enterprise Institute, 1978), p. 68, and Robert L. Hardgrave, Jr, *India: Government and Politics in a Developing Nation*, 3rd edition (New York: Harcourt Brace Jovanovich, 1980).

Table 5.1 (contd.)

1.		2.	3.	4.	5.
1966	I. Gandhi	35	607	13.8	–
1967		42	–	17.1	61.3
1968		45	2665	17.2	–
1969		56	3064	19.0	–
1970		68	3861	20.6	–
1971		64	4380	16.5	55.3
1972		–	6365	20.5	–
1973		–	5551	20.6	–
1974		81	11,540	40.3	–
		Authoritarian Regime/Command Politics II (I. Gandhi)			
1975		67	3847	21.9	–
1976		63	1190	12.8	–
		Democratic Regime/Demand Politics II			
1977	Desai	80	7520	25.3	60.4
1978		–	9174	29.7	–
1979		–	9203	29.8	–
1980	I. Gandhi	–	10,600	29.6	–
1981		–	7740	29.2	56.9
1982		–	5200	33.2	–
1983		–	7188	38.3[a]	–
1984		–	–	49.4[a]	64.0
1985	R. Gandhi	–	–	–	–

[a] Provisional, and excludes Bombay textile strike.

Sources: Riots: Baldev Raj Nayar, *Violence and Crime in India* (Delhi: Macmillan, 1975); Government of India, Ministry of Home Affairs, Bureau of Police Research and Development, *Crime in India* (annual); student indiscipline: Government of India, Ministry of Home Affairs, 'Student Indiscipline' (1967, Mimeograph), *Report* (annual), and *Third Report of the National Police Commission, 1980* (Delhi, 1980); and *Data India*, 18–24 September 1978, p. 594; workdays lost: Government of India, Ministry of Labour, Labour Bureau, *Indian Labour Statistics* (Chandigarh and Simla, annual), and *Indian Labour Yearbook* (Chandigarh and Simla, annual); and Government of India, Ministry of Finance, *Economic Survey* (Delhi, annual) (the figures in *Economic Survey* are for fiscal years; e.g., 1978–9 corresponds to 1978 in the table).

Notes: Data on riots and 'student indiscipline' were not available after 1977 and 1982, respectively. As a result, our figures do not account for what may have been extraordinary increases in both. In the 1980s, riots and student indiscipline may have merged when highly mobilized student-led regional movements in Assam and Punjab engaged in (Punjab) or triggered (Assam) violence.

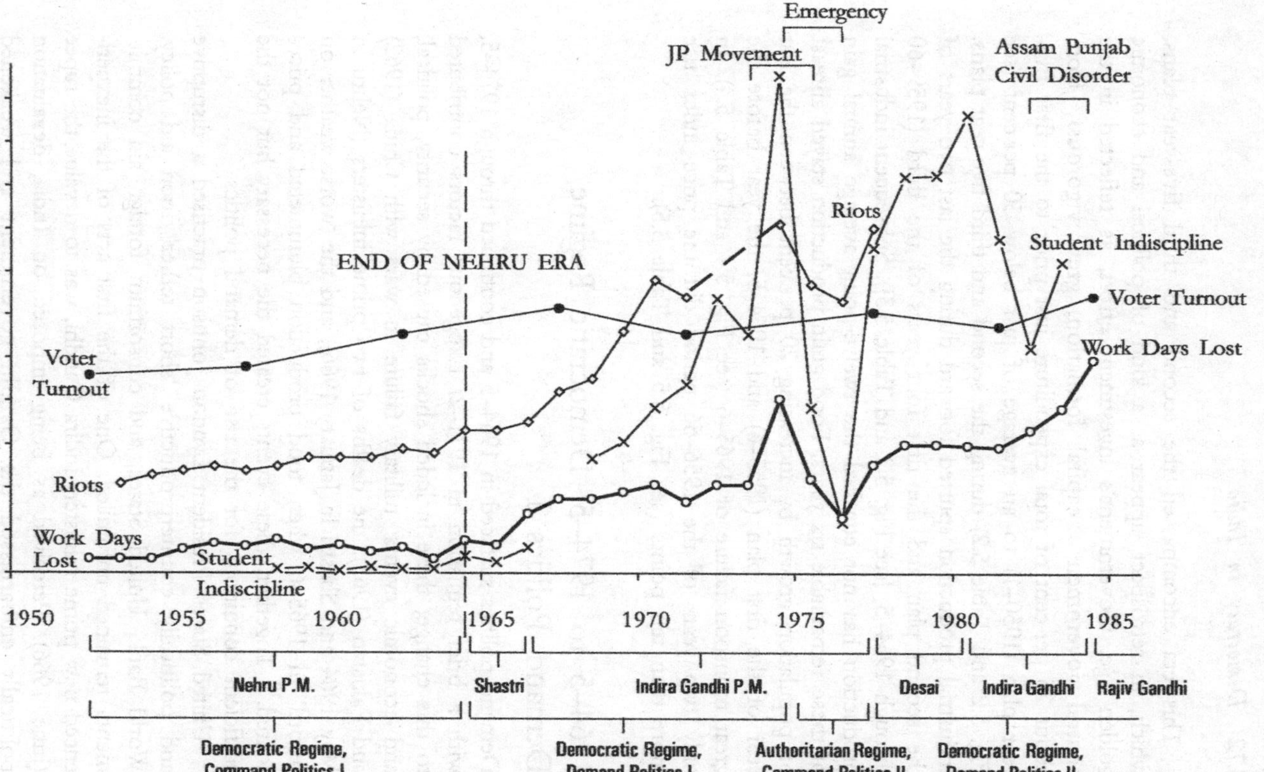

Fig. 5.1: Indicators of Demand Politics: Voter Turnout, Riots, Workdays Lost, and Student 'Indiscipline'.

This era encompassed the second and third five-year plans, which, in retrospect, appear as a kind of political and economic golden age. Government's investment effort, as reflected in the central government's capital formation, grew vigorously from about 25 per cent of total expenditure just prior to the first five-year plan (1950–1) to an average of just below 50 per cent (see Fig. 5.2 and Table 5.2) during the second and third five-year plans. Industrial production spurted forward during the last two years of the second plan and the first four years of the third (1959–60 through 1964–5, [see Fig. 5.3 and Table 5.3]). Subsequent industrial production has not equalled the twelve-point average annual gain of these remarkable six years. Food grain production stayed abreast of population growth by increasing 20 per cent between the last year of the first plan (1955–6) and 1964–5, the year before the great monsoon failure of 1965–6 (see Fig. 5.4 and Table 5.4). In only two years of the 1956–66 period did the price index rise more than ten points (see Fig. 5.5 and Table 5.5).

1964–5 to 1974–5: Democratic Regime/ Demand Politics I

Demand politics surfaced in 1964–5 and continued through 1974–5, with a brief remission in 1971–2. Exogenous factors contributed to this change; these included shocks caused by security, political, and economic events: military failure in wars with China (1962) and Pakistan (1965); the deaths of two prime ministers (Nehru in May 1964 and Shastri in January 1966); and the 'worst weather on record' in 1965–6 when food production plummeted and prices soared.[19] Together, these events created the necessary but not the sufficient conditions for the rise of demand politics.

United States President Lyndon Johnson practised a disruptive and politically counterproductive 'short tether' food aid policy. World Bank, United States, and consortium foreign aid commitments remained unfulfilled. One of the first acts of the inexperienced new prime minister, Indira Gandhi, was to devalue the rupee (June 1966). Perceived as being imposed on India, devaluation politically embarrassed the Gandhi government and weakened

[19] John Mellor, *Developing Rural India* (Ithaca, NY: Cornell University Press, 1968), p. 87.

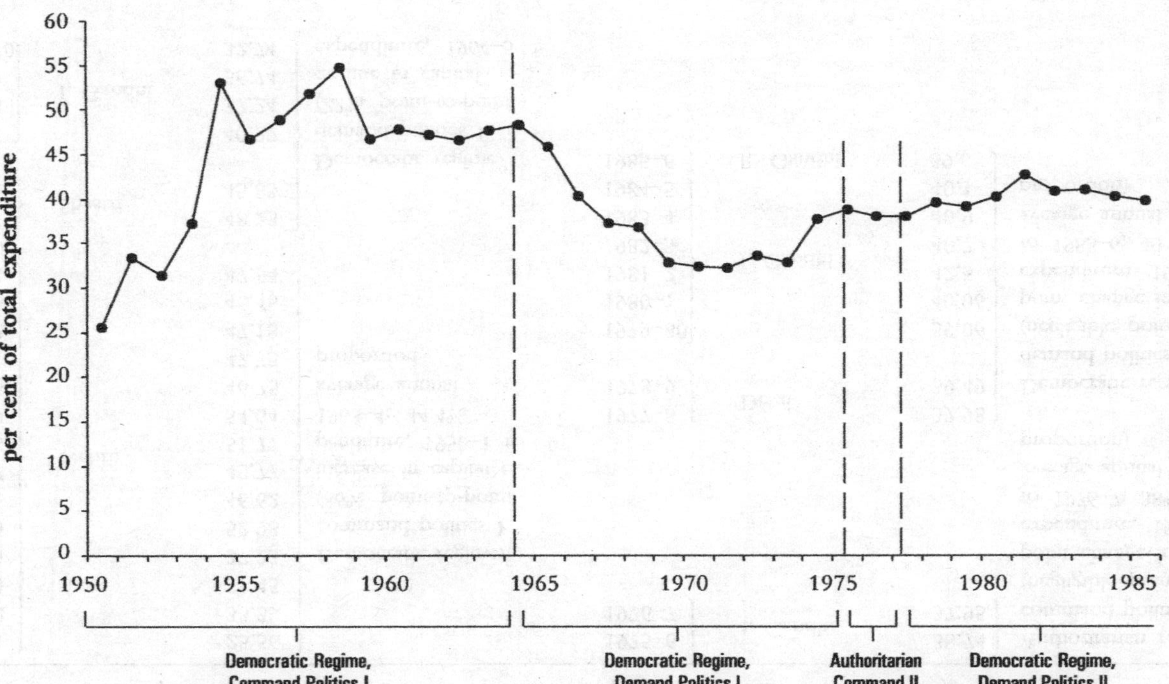

Fig. 5.2: Central Government Capital Formation as a Percentage of Total Expenditure (in Current Prices), According to Regime Type and Politics Type.

Table 5.2: Central Government's Capital Expenditure as a Percentage of Total Expenditure (in Current Prices)

Year		%		Year		%	
1950–1	Nehru	25.56	Democratic regime/ command politics I (86% point-to-point increase in capital expenditure, 1950–1 to 1963–4; 44.4% average annual proportion	1975–6	I. Gandhi	38.74	Authoritarian regime/ command politics II (negligible point-to-point change in capital expenditure, 1975–6 to 1976–7; 38% average annual proportion)
1951–2		33.39		1976–7		37.95	
1952–3		31.45					
1953–4		37.23					
1954–5		52.98					
1955–6		46.62					
1956–7		48.77					
1957–8		51.77					
1958–9		54.64		1977–8	Desai	37.98	Democratic regime/ demand politics II (negligible point-to-point change in capital expenditure, 1977–8 to 1985–6; 40% average annual proportion)
1959–60		46.75		1978–9		39.49	
1960–1		47.73					
1961–2		47.18		1979–80	I. Gandhi	39.06	
1962–3		46.46		1980–1		40.06	
1963–4		47.54		1981–2		42.5	
				1982–3		40.7	
1964–5	Shastri	48.23	Democratic regime/ demand politics I (22% point-to-point decline in capital expenditure, 1964–5	1983–4		40.9	
1965–6		45.83		1984–5		40.1	
				1985–6	R. Gandhi	39.6[a]	
1966–7	I. Gandhi	40.22					
1967–8		37.24					
1968–9		36.74					
1969–70		32.74					

1970–1		32.37	
1971–2		32.20	to 1974–5; 37%
1972–3	I. Gandhi	33.48	average annual
1973–4		32.77	proportion)
1974–5		37.58	

[a] Budget estimate

Source: Barnett Rubin, 'Private Power and Public Investment in India: A Study in the Political Economy of Development', Ph.D. dissertation, University of Chicago, 1982, Table 9. Rubin's sources include, Government of India, Ministry of Finance, *An Economic and Functional Classification of the Central Government Budget* (Delhi, annual) and *Economic Survey*.

Table 5.3: Annual Variation in Industrial Production

Year		% Variation		Year		% Variation	
1952		10.0		1975	I. Gandhi	3.9	Authoritarian
1953		4.9		1976		9.8	regime/command
1954		7.0					politics II
1955		8.1					(6.85% average
1956	Nehru	8.6	Democratic				annual increase)
1957		3.5	regime/command				
1958		1.7	politics I				
1959		8.9	(7.5% average	1977		5.3	
1960		11.6	annual increase)	1978	Desai	6.9	
1961		7.0		1979		1.2	Democratic
1962		9.6		1980		4.0	regime/demand
1963		8.4		1981		8.6	politics II
				1982	I. Gandhi	3.9	(5.5% average
				1983		5.4	annual increase)
				1984		5.8	
1964	Shastri	8.6					
1965		9.1					
1966		–0.8					
1967	I. Gandhi	–0.7	Democratic				
1968		6.4	regime/				
1969		7.1	demand				

1970		4.8	politics I
1971		2.9	(3.7% average
1972	I. Gandhi	7.1	annual
1973		–1.4	increase)
1974		2.2	

Note: The index was set at 100 in 1951 and again in 1960 and 1970.

Source: Reserve Bank of India, *Report on Currency and Finance* (Bombay, annual).

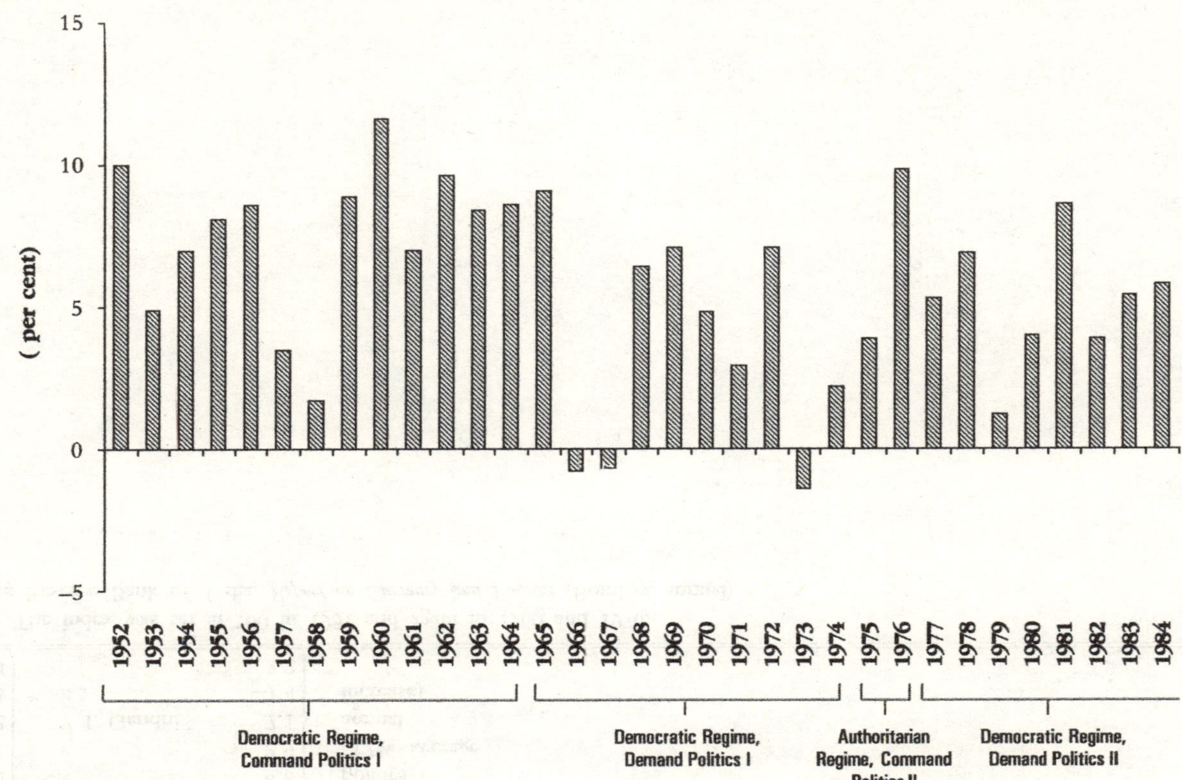

Fig. 5.3: Annual Variation in Industrial Production According to Regime Type and Politics Type.

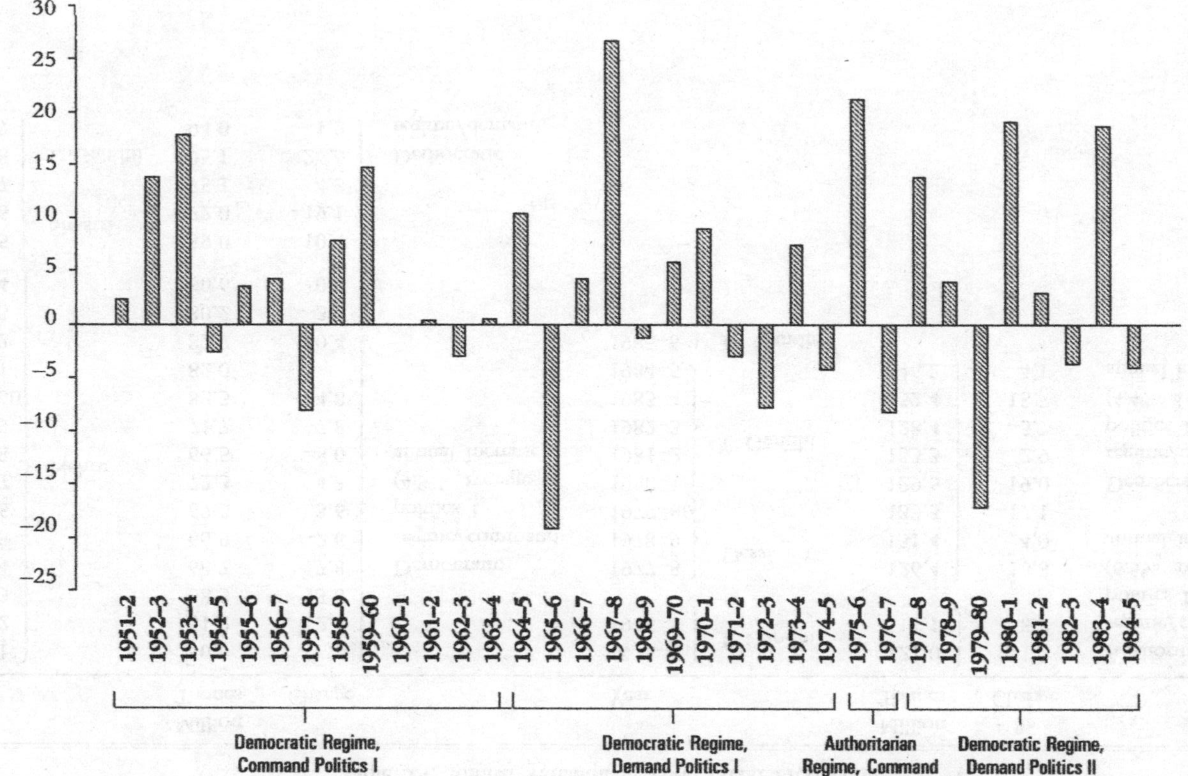

Fig. 5.4: Annual Variation in Food Grain Production According to Regime Type and Politics Type.

Table 5.4: Annual Variation in Food Grain Production

Year		Million Tonnes	% Change		Year		Million Tonnes	% Change	
1950–1		50.0	–		1975–6	I. Gandhi	121.0	21.2	Authoritarian
1951–2		51.2	2.4		1976–7		111.1	–8.2	regime/command
1952–3		58.3	13.8						politics II
1953–4		68.7	17.8	Democratic	1977–8	Desai	126.4	13.8	(6.5% average
1954–5		66.9	–2.6	regime/command	1978–9		131.4	4.0	annual increase)
1955–6		69.3	3.6	politics I	1979–80		133.3	–17.1	
1956–7	Nehru	72.3	4.3	(4.3% average	1980–1		129.6	19.0	Democratic
1957–8		66.5	–8.0	annual increase)	1981–2		133.3	2.9	regime/demand
1958–9		71.7	7.8		1982–3	I. Gandhi	128.4	–3.7	politics II
1959–60		82.3	14.8		1983–4		152.4	18.7	(4.4% average
1960–1		82.0			1984–5		146.2	–4.1	annual increase
1961–2		82.7	0.4		1985–6	R. Gandhi			
1962–3		80.2	–3.0						
1963–4		80.6	0.5						
1964–5	Shastri	89.0	10.4						
1965–6		72.0	–19.1						
1966–7		75.1	4.3						
1967–8	I. Gandhi	95.1	26.6	Democratic					
1968–9		94.0	–1.2	regime/demand					

1969–70	I. Gandhi	99.5	5.8	politics I (2.6% average annual increase)
1970–1		108.4	8.9	
1971–2		105.2	– 3.0	
1972–3		97.0	– 7.8	
1973–4		104.2	7.4	
1974–5		99.8	– 4.2	

Source: Ministry of Finance, *Economic Survey*.

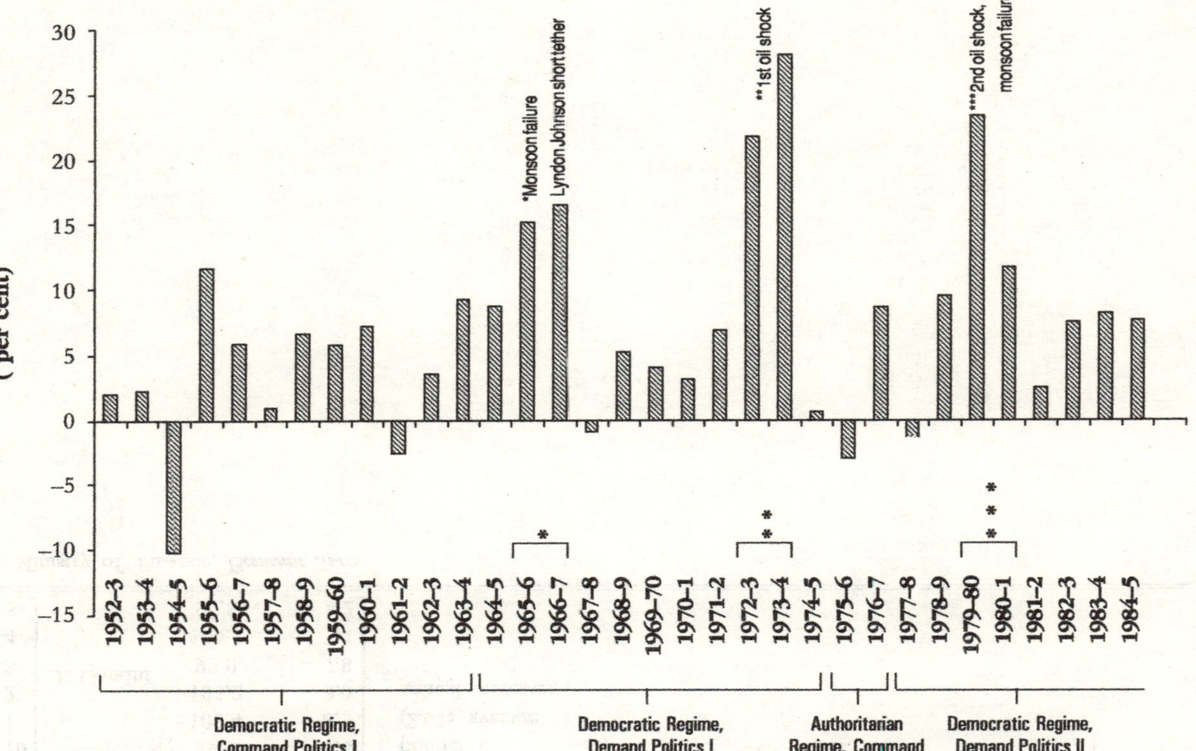

Fig. 5.5: Annual Variation in Wholesale Prices According to Regime Type and Politics Type.

Table 5.5: Annual Variation in Wholesale Prices, All Commodities (Point to Point)

Year		% Variation		Year		% Variation	
1952–3	Nehru	2.0	Democratic regime/ command politics I (3.5% average annual increase)	1975–6	I. Gandhi	–3.0	Authoritarian regime/ command politics II (2.8% average annual increase)
1953–4		2.3		1976–7		8.6	
1954–5		–10.2		1977–8	Desai	–1.3	Democratic regime/ demand politics II (8.6% average annual increase)
1955–6		11.6		1978–9		9.5	
1956–7		5.9		1979–80	I. Gandhi	23.2	
1957–8		1.0		1980–1		11.7	
1958–9		6.6		1981–2		2.5	
1959–60		5.8		1982–3		7.5	
1960–1		7.2		1983–4		8.2	
1961–2		–2.6		1984–5		7.6	
1962–3		3.6		1985–6	R. Gandhi		
1963–4		9.3					
1964–5	Shastri	8.7	Democratic regime/ demand politics I (10% average annual increase)				
1965–6		15.2					
1966–7	I. Gandhi	16.5					
1967–8		–0.9					
1968–9		5.2					
1969–70		4.0					
1970–1		3.1					
1971–2		6.8					
1972–3		21.7					
1973–4		27.9					
1974–5		0.6					

Source: Reserve Bank of India, *Report on Currency and Finance*.

its standing and authority.[20] Poor economic performance both reflected and compounded the effects of exogenous shocks on the rise of demand politics. Economic indicators for the fifth year of the third plan (1965–6) turned sharply downward. Industrial as well as agricultural production declined; plan investment, already adversely affected by the doubling of defence spending after the China war (October 1962) (see Fig. 5.2), slumped further; and prices shot up.

The fourth general election (February–March 1967) illustrates the mutually determinative relationship between type of regime and of politics on the one hand and economic performance on the other. Voters turned out in unprecedented numbers (see Fig. 5.1 and Table 5.1) to protest poor economic performance and to vote against government's domestic and foreign economic policy failures. The result was virtual repudiation of Congress, the party of nationalism and independence. Between the third general election in 1962 and the fourth in 1967, Congress's share of parliamentary votes and seats dropped from 46 to 40 per cent and from 73 to 54 per cent, respectively; its share of state assembly votes and seats, from 44 to 40 per cent and from 60 to 49 per cent respectively,[21] and its control of sixteen state governments from fourteen to eight as regional parties or opposition party coalitions formed governments in half. In circular fashion, the electoral outcome fostered demand politics, as narrow and uncertain Congress majorities at the centre and unstable and warring opposition coalitions in the states rendered governmental authority more suspect and vulnerable.

The election results weakened public authority. At the centre, Congress government was inhibited by a razor-thin majority. After Congress split in November 1969, its minority government remained in power until the 1971 parliamentary election, with the

20 See James Warner Bjorkman, 'Public Law 480 and the Policies of Self-Help and Short-Tether: Indo-American Relations, 1965–8', in Lloyd I. Rudolph and Susanne Hoeber Rudolph (eds), *The Regional Imperative: The Administration of U.S. Foreign Policy Towards South Asian States Under Presidents Johnson and Nixon* (New Delhi: Concept, 1980; Atlantic Highlands, NJ: Humanities Press, 1981).

21 For an interpretation of the election, see our 'New Era for India', in S.P. Varma and Iqbal Narain (eds), *Fourth General Election in India* (Hyderabad: Orient Longman, 1970), pp. 1–17.

support of the CPI and DMK. With eight opposition-governed states, it lost some of its capacity to initiate and coordinate policy between the centre and the state governments. At the state level, party parochialism and rivalry in coalition governments fragmented and discredited authority. With the writ of government enfeebled, it became much more difficult to combine a democratic regime with command politics.

Quantitative and historical evidence for the rise of demand politics after 1965 include increases in electoral participation (turnout), riots, strikes, student 'indiscipline' (see Fig. 5.1), and agrarian unrest. Baldev Raj Nayar has shown that the ratio of riots to population was relatively stable for the decade from 1954–5 to 1963–4, slowly accelerated between 1964–5 and 1966–7, and then rose dramatically from 1967.[22] Between April and August 1966, when food shortages were acute, there were widespread *bandhs* (suspension of business) and demonstrations demanding food rationing and protesting price rises, tax increases, hoarding, and profiteering.[23] Industrial unrest, as indicated by workdays lost, more than doubled between 1965 and 1966, rose about 25 per cent the following year, and continued to rise through 1970 (see Fig. 5.2 and Table 5.2). Incidents of student 'indiscipline', an administrative euphemism for goals as various as postponing examinations and 'total revolution', increased dramatically from 271 to 607 between 1965 and 1966, increased more dramatically to 2665 by 1968, and continued steadily upward through the early 1970s (see Fig. 5.1 and Table 5.1).[24] Participation in the 1967 election

22 Baldev Raj Nayar, *Violence and Crime in India: A Quantitative Study* (New Delhi: Macmillan India, 1975), p. 24. For a study covering earlier years, see David H. Bayley, 'Violent Public Protest in India: 1900–1960', '*Indian Journal of Political Science*, vol. XXIV, 1963. The treatment of political riots and deaths in G. Bingham Powell, Jr.'s more recent *Contemporary Democracies: Participation, Stability, and Violence* (Cambridge: Harvard University Press, 1982) is unsatisfactory for our purposes, because Powell 'simply' adds up events and divides by a number of years to arrive at measures of political riots and deaths, does not control for population (i.e., uses absolute rather than per capita figures in making comparisons among states), and makes no attempt to deal with contextual time-bound relationships between political and economic conditions and levels of political riots and deaths. (See his Tables 2.3 [p. 22], [p. 232]).

23 *Keesing's Contemporary Archives,* 19–26 November 1966, pp. 217–24.

24 Lloyd I. Rudolph, Susanne Hoeber Rudolph, and Karuna Ahmed, 'Student Politics and National Politics in India', *Economic and Political Weekly*, July

increased 11.7 per cent over the 49.6 per cent average of the first three general elections (see Fig. 5.1 and Table 5.1).

An agrarian version of demand politics began with alarming intensity after the defeated Congress government of West Bengal was replaced in February 1967 by a United Front government that included the CPI(M). Taking their name from Naxalbari, a village in the narrow neck of Darjeeling district that precariously connects Bengal to Assam, the Naxalite rebellions by tribal landless labourers spread west to Bihar and south along the tribal belt of the Eastern Ghats to Andhra Pradesh and Kerala.[25] By 1970, the state's use of force had crushed them. Naxalite rebellion was followed by a new version of agrarian protest, the land grab movement. Led by leftist parties (CPI, Samyukta Socialist party, and Praja Socialist party)[26] landless labourers engaged in symbolic occupation or harvesting of land large landowners should have given up under the land ceilings legislation. A Home Ministry study reflected the national alarm. In language uncharacteristic of Indian bureaucratic speech, it observed that 'an explosive situation' existed and attributed it to the state governments' failure to carry out the necessary land reforms. The patience of the cultivating classes was 'on the verge of boiling over', and the resulting explosion 'could rock India'.[27]

The events of 1969 through 1972 suggested that under Mrs Gandhi's leadership Congress could restore the party's credibility

---

1971 (Special no.). We have put quotation marks around 'indiscipline' to mitigate a necessarily negative implication. The various causes, reasons, forms, and levels of student 'indiscipline' can both promote and undermine representational processes and policy dialogue.

25 There is an extensive literature on the Naxalbari rebellion, the Naxalite movement and violence, and Naxalism. Naxalbari village has in fact supplied Indian English with terms for agrarian radicalism and rebellion. Among the leading works on Naxalite politics are Marcus F. Franda, *Radical Politics in West Bengal* (Cambridge: MIT Press, 1971); Mohan Ram, *Maoism in India* (New Delhi: Vikas, 1971); Bhabani Sen Gupta, *Communism in Indian Politics* (New York: Columbia University Press, 1972); Biplab Dasgupta, *The Naxalite Movement* (Bombay: Allied, 1974); J.C. Johri, *Naxalite Politics in India* (Delhi: Institute of Constitutional and Parliamentary Studies, 1972); and Sohail Jawaid, *The Naxalite Movement in India* (New Delhi: Associated Publishing House, 1979).

26 *Keesing's Contemporary Archives*, 28 November–5 December 1970, p. 24319.

27 Ibid., pp. 24319–20. See also sources for Table 5.1).

and government's authority and perhaps return to the democratic regime/command politics of her father's time. In 1969, she split the party, purged the old guard state bosses, and began to advocate progressive and populist measures, such as the nationalization of the fourteen largest commercial banks, and, in 1971, the eradication of poverty (*garibi hatao*). Her leadership for a time restored Congress's élan and support. In 1967, the electorate had voted against bad government by repudiating Congress. In 1971, the electorate voted against bad government again by using the 'delinked' parliamentary election to signal its repudiation of coalition governments in the large North Indian states and in West Bengal. In a 1972 khaki election for state assemblies held soon after India's military victory over Pakistan in December 1971, the electorate not only confirmed its 1971 judgement but also rewarded Mrs Gandhi's conduct of the war by returning Congress majorities in most states. Formal indicators of demand politics receded: the number of workdays lost declined in 1971, and the Home Ministry reported a respite in challenges to law and order.[28]

However, the party credibility and governmental authority gained in these elections were soon dissipated. Instead of using her mandate and the enhanced legitimacy and effectiveness of the party and the government to implement progressive measures at the centre and in the states, Mrs Gandhi began the process of deinstitutionalization that substituted centralized personal rule for party and state governance.[29] By 1974, it was abundantly apparent that the opportunity offered by the 1971 and 1972 elections to combine, as in the Nehru era, a democratic regime with command politics had been lost.

The intense pressure on government that had characterized the 1965–70 period quickly resumed (Fig. 5.1). It was exacerbated by new exogenous shocks that lowered production and raised prices: the first oil price rise (1973) and a series of poor monsoons. The deterioration of party credibility and governmental authority quickened. All indications of unrest and discontent accelerated exponentially. The number of workdays lost jumped from sixteen

28 Government of India, Ministry of Home Affairs, *Report, 1971–72* (Delhi, 1972).

29 Stanley A. Kochanek, 'Mrs Gandhi's Pyramid: The New Congress' in Henry Hart (ed.) *Indira Gandhi's India: A Political System Reappraised* (Boulder, CO: Westview Press, 1976).

to twenty million between 1971 and 1972 and reached an unprecedented forty million in 1974, the year of a national railway strike that challenged Mrs Gandhi's government (see Fig. 5.1 and Table 5.1). Incidents of student indiscipline grew phenomenally after 1965, increasing from 271 in 1965 to 11,500 in 1974;[30] the number of riots more than doubled, from 33,000 in 1965 to 80,000 in 1974. These indicators represent economic and political discontent, including a response to the extraordinary thirty-five-point price rise in 1974–5 following the oil shock, and student participation in the mobilization of protest by Jayaprakash Narayan that eventuated in the emergency proclamation. The JP movement for 'total revolution' (that is, fundamental transformation of Indian society) was most active in Bihar and Gujarat, where students were an essential component.[31] On 26 June 1975, Mrs Gandhi imposed an emergency regime on the country.

1975–6 to 1976–7: Authoritarian Regime/ Command Politics II

Mrs Gandhi's authoritarian and corporatist version of command politics ended the 1965–75 period of demand politics by banning strikes and demonstrations, arresting opposition leaders, censoring the press, and depriving citizens of their civil and political rights. The declared purpose of the emergency regime was to restore civil order and economic discipline. Reported incidents of student indiscipline declined dramatically in 1976 (from 11,540 in 1974 to 1190 in 1976) as did the number of workdays lost due to strikes (from forty to thirteen million) (see Fig. 5.1).

While the period of authoritarian rule may be too brief to support reliable findings, economic indicators suggested some

30 'Demonstrations, strikes, bandhs, etc. imposed unusual strains on the law and order machinery....Student unrest...has been a cause for serious concern' [Government of India, Ministry of Home Affairs, *Report, 1973–74* (Delhi: 1974), p. 1]

31 See Ghanshyam Shah, *Protest Movements in Two Indian States* (New Delhi: Ajanta, 1977); John R. Wood, 'Extra-Parliamentary Opposition in India: An Analysis of Populist Agitators in Gujarat and Bihar', *Pacific Affairs*, vol. XLVIII, Fall 1975, pp. 313–34; and Dawn E. Jones and Rodney W. Jones, 'Urban Upheaval in India: The Nav Nirman Riots in Gujarat', *Asian Survey*, vol. 16, no. 11, November 1976, pp. 1012–23.

positive performance. Food production increased, with help from a favourable monsoon. So too did industrial production (see Fig. 5.3 and Table 5.3). Stimulated in part by gains in the industrial sector, the increase was associated with a lower level of workdays lost through industrial disputes, a result that, at least in the short run, supports one of the claims of the authoritarian growth model. However, as Table 5.2 shows, the authoritarian regime, despite a price decline, was not able over two budgets to increase the proportion of total expenditure devoted to capital formation; proportionately, public saving declined and consumption expenditure increased.

1977–8 to 1984–5: Democratic Regime/ Demand Politics II

The Janata party's unexpected election victory in March 1977 abruptly ended authoritarian rule. When its government restored constitutional government, a liberal state, and democratic political processes, quantitative and qualitative evidence indicated a resurgence of demand politics, which persisted after a Gandhi Congress government returned to power in 1980. Rates of student indiscipline in 1980 and workdays lost from 1979 to 1984 surpassed those of the 1960s. Student indiscipline rates approached figures for the most extreme prior year, 1974, and workdays lost by strikes exceeded them. The Home Ministry reported serious law and order problems for 1978–9, 1979–80, and again after 1982. It especially noted the appearance in 1980–1 of farmers' agitations for remunerative prices, a development that signalled the emergence of a new constituency for demand politics.[32] In 1984, labour unrest reached unprecedented levels.

The restoration in 1977 of a democratic regime and the consequent release of pent-up demands was not accompanied, as some had expected, with declines in economic performance. To the contrary, economic performance under democratic rule was equal to or markedly better than it had been under authoritarian rule. Both the Janata government and the Congress governments that preceded and followed it presided over substantial increases in agricultural production as well as the declines that accompanied poor monsoons in 1979 and 1982 (see Table 5.4). Industrial

32 See our 'Determinants and Varieties of Agrarian Mobilization', op. cit.

production accelerated slowly in the late 1970s but rapidly in the 1980s, apparently breaking through the 'slow industrialization' of the 1960s and 1970s.[33] Contrary to what might be expected, gains in the rate of industrial growth were paralleled by marked increases in workdays lost. The proportion of central government expenditure on capital formation increased slightly over emergency levels, a gain that many regarded as futile given an apparent marked increase in the capital–output ratio.

In the accompanying figures, we plot regime types and then types of politics against measures of economic performance in order to judge whether they are correlated. Our project is limited and contingent, well short of causal statements but designed to examine the proposition that regime types and/or types of politics may be associated with variations in economic performance. To anticipate our findings, the emergency regime that institutionalized the authoritarian growth model did make some difference for economic performance, but not as much as Mrs Gandhi's rhetoric claimed or as was anticipated in the IMF–World Bank conditionality era. Industrial production increased, and strikes, student indiscipline, and prices declined, but on the crucial performance variable of public savings for investment, the authoritarian regime faltered; that is, the level was below those that immediatel preceded and followed the emergency years. By contrast, under the democratic politics of the Nehru era, when inflation was kept low, proportions of central government capital expenditures reached levels never attained subsequently. At the same time, the type of regime does not seem to have made much difference for annual differences in the growth of industrial and agricultural production, which reached points as high after as during the emergency.

After 1965–6, there is a striking association between declining levels of economic performance, as measured by our four indicators, and increases in our four measures of demand politics (riots, student indiscipline, strikes, and voter participation). Higher plateaus in measures of demand politics indicate a qualitative change in the conditions under which politics influences economic performance. Regardless of regime type or type of politics, state actors after 1965–6 faced a differently constituted political universe that

33 Isher Judge Ahluwalia, ***Industrial Growth in India: Stagnation since the Mid-Sixties*** (New Delhi: Oxford University Press, 1985).

seemed to make outstanding economic performance more difficult. Yet the 1980s seemed to belie the inverse relationship between demand politics and improved levels of economic performance. As industrial production spurted upward, so too did mobilization indicators. The limited time frame calls for caution but such figures seriously compromise the proposition that high levels of mobilization necessarily impede economic growth.

In Tables 5.1–5.5 and Figs 5.2–5.5, we have plotted democratic and authoritarian regimes against four economic indicators: government capital formation, industrial production, food grain production, and wholesale prices. Wide variation in all four measures were apparent during the democratic regime of 1952–75 (Nehru–Gandhi). During the authoritarian regime, performance varied narrowly within plateaus reached just prior to its imposition. Under the democratic regimes of Janata and Congress (1977–86), investment showed slight and industrial production marked gains while food grain production and prices, except during the 'second oil shock', performed well. Overall, there is no consistent time-bound association between the type of regime and economic performance, and the view that economies perform better under authoritarian than under democratic regimes is thus disconfirmed.

We have also plotted types of politics against the same four measures of economic performance. The most striking contrast is that between command politics I (1952–3 through 1963–4 [Nehru]) and demand politics I (1964–5 through 1974–5 [Gandhi]). Economic performance was better during the earlier period on all indicators except food grain production. However, there was little difference between economic performance under command politics II (1975–6 through 1976–7 [emergency]) and under demand politics II (1977–8 through 1985–6). Capital formation did slightly better and growth in industrial production about the same under demand politics II, while prices did slightly better under command politics II (the emergency). Overall, the relationship between type of politics and economic performance is slightly more discernible than that between regime type and economic performance.

We conclude that there is an indeterminate relationship between type of regime and politics on the one hand and economic performance on the other. The indeterminant relationship holds in both the pre- and post-Nehru political universes. The success of authoritarian rule under the emergency in achieving state objectives—control of hoarding, recouping of black money, better attendance in government offices, compulsory deposits, more stringent tax collection, decline in prices, a wage freeze—lent some credence to the view that command features of an authoritarian regime provide short-term gains by repressing mobilization and participation. Yet during the Nehru era and under the Janata, Indira Gandhi, and Rajiv Gandhi governments, democratic regimes were associated with good economic performance.

The view that there is a positive relationship between authoritarian regimes and economic performance and the view that state sovereignty is necessarily better for economic growth in developing economies than popular sovereignty is not supported by our analysis of the Indian evidence. A second finding concerns the association between economic performance and indicators of demand politics: riots, student indiscipline, workdays lost, and voter participation. There was a striking association after 1965–6 between declining levels of economic performance and increases in demand politics indicators (see Fig. 5.1). These quantitative changes suggest a qualitative transformation of mobilization and participation that affected subsequent economic performance and growth regardless of regime or polity type. In the post-Nehru era, state actors faced a differently constituted political universe that seemed to jeopardize growth. Yet events in the 1980s suggest otherwise. As industrial production spurted upward, so did the indicators of mobilization.

Mrs Gandhi's effort from 1970 to free herself from the pressures of demand politics had a profound effect on Indian political institutions and conduct. Her strategy was to deinstitutionalize party, Parliament, public services, and the federal system. It was a strategy aimed at narrowing or eliminating the channels through which demands might be articulated. Instead of engaging discontented or disgruntled constituencies and responding to or brokering their demands, Mrs Gandhi sought to escape them. This strategy ultimately failed when demand groups, deprived of regular channels for expression, voiced their claims in the streets, that is, outside legal and conventional channels. The agitational politics of opinion 'out of doors' developed highly elaborated political art forms to persuade or coerce public opinion and elected and appointed state officials.

6

The State and Democracy in India or What Happened to Welfare, Secularism, and Development[+]

Niraja Gopal Jayal

I

Fifty years after independence, many of the foundational principles of the Indian nation-state have been called into question, not least the very project of the nation itself. Among the goals of social transformation prioritized on the state's agenda at independence, at least three—welfare, secularism, and development—remain issues of central importance today, and inform what are arguably the most significant contemporary debates in the country. The project of the welfare-state has been gradually undermined and discredited in the wake of the ideological struggle between the state and market and the shifts in economic policy entailed by the processes of globalization. The project of secularism has increasingly been under threat as communal ideology and political forces have come to enjoy greater purchase in society and the polity. And, finally, the project of development has come to be decisively questioned by the advocates of sustainable

[+] This paper is substantially based on my book *Democracy and the State: Welfare, Secularism and Development in Contemporary India* (Delhi: Oxford University Press, 1999). This version was presented at the India 50 Conference at the University of Sussex in September 1997, and also appears in Vinita Damodaran and Maya Unnithan (eds), *Post-colonial India: History, Politics, and Culture* (Delhi: Manohar, forthcoming).

development strategies as well as by movements questioning the rationale of projects which cause the large-scale displacement of tribal people and threaten their survival.

Though these projects of social transformation arose out of a deliberative–legislative, rather than participative–democratic, process, they were unquestionably the product of a consensus negotiated and evolved in the course of the movement for freedom. They were also quite unambiguously expected to be realized within the framework of a democratic polity, an aspiration that appeared at the time to be as non-negotiable as the agenda of social transformation itself. Clearly, the democratic project was expected to inform, inspire, and cohere with the state's initiatives in the areas of welfare, secularism, and development.

While the mutuality of the state and democracy is widely accepted,[1] the relationship between them is often conceptualized in extreme ways. In what we might call the pessimistic view of Indian democracy, the inability of the state to effect its declared agenda is frequently attributed to the logic of democracy which, by enhancing participation, leads to greater contestation and the multiplication of demands on the state, whether for scarce resources or for the recognition of identity-based claims. Indeed, many scholars believe the travails of the Indian polity to be directly traceable to 'too much' democracy. In this view, the state, as the owner and dispenser of vast economic resources, has become the object of political competition that it is frequently unable to manage and contain.[2]

1 There are broadly two types of arguments that theorize the necessity of a link between the state and democracy. The first is the argument that without an effective state, there can be no democracy, because the state alone can provide and sustain the necessary institutional framework for it (Przeworski *et al.* 1995). The second argument, premised on the belief that it is states, and not societies, which generally destroy democratic institutions (Weiner 1983: 55), suggests that a vibrant civil society and democracy are needed as a bulwark against the potentially authoritarian tendencies of the state.

2 This is the view of Atul Kohli (1990) who sees increased democratic mobilization and the expansion of political participation as factors impeding stable governance. Similarly, Lloyd and Susanne Rudolph (1987) have shown how pressures from a variety of demand groups have diminished the autonomy of the state and rendered it 'weak–strong'. Pranab Bardhan (1993) has argued that democracy engenders parochial conflict and constrains economic

On the other hand, what we might (admittedly at the risk of some oversimplification) call the optimistic view of Indian democracy draws our attention to the widening, in recent years, of the social base of power.[3] It suggests that the state's inability to effect its own agenda was, in no small measure, due to the monopolizing of all resources (natural, social, economic, and political) by the modernizing, developmental, but irredeemably upper-caste and upper-class elites, from whose hands the initiative is now finally being wrested. In this perspective, the increase in political assertions by previously marginalized groups—such as the historically disadvantaged backward castes—and a variety of social movements is a positive sign that democracy is proving to be an empowering and successful experiment in India.

> I consider the new turmoil in the Indian masses and the new forms of protest and struggle waged by a new set of actors as part of the continuing commitment to democracy, indeed a still further deepening and broadening of its base.... They need to be seen as expressions of new stirrings of consciousness engulfing large masses of the people, a new conception of rights and responsibilities, an urge to find new creative spaces in what is fundamentally a conflict-ridden social situation in which avenues of participation have been cornered by a few, producing for many a sheer struggle for survival in an increasingly inequitous world. [Kothari 1998: pp. 100–1.]

It is arguable that the excessively institutional focus of the first, pessimistic, view causes it to lose sight of the sorts of successes underscored by the optimistic view. Conversely, it is all too easy for partisans of the optimistic view to forget that the particularistic assertions of recent years are still fairly limited to groups which have learnt the political uses of numerical preponderance only after decades of experience with the politics of accommodation as

---

development. Moreover, the problems of conflict management by the state have been compounded now that the conflict is no longer between members of the dominant proprietary coalition, but includes also 'turmoil from below' in an open polity (Bardhan 1984: 82).

[3] We shall not here be considering that other—largely popular—variant of the optimistic view which sees in the regularity of elections in the 'world's largest democracy', definitive evidence of the success of democracy. The excessive reliance of this view on institutional aspects, and especially on elections as the defining criterion of democracy, is disconcerting.

practised by the Congress party.[4] One impact of these assertions on the polity is the fragmentation of the public sphere, as they seek to create categories of citizenship in relation to particular social goods and, in doing so, seek to fragment and reserve, rather than universalize, rights. Another, more serious, is that the exclusionary politics of such groups are imitative of the politics practised by erstwhile upper-caste elites, the political equivalent of Sanskritization.[5] As such, they may and do leave several, more disprivileged and thus far unmobilized, groups on the margins, to await a fresh spate of assertions.[6] Consequently, not only does the search for *social justice* come to be defined euphemistically, in rather partial and exclusivist terms, it also displaces altogether from any foreseeable political agenda the programme of *distributive* justice.

Even the social movements, in whose existence the optimistic view rejoices, have been largely ineffectual in making claims on the state and have been forced to carve out a political space outside the party political system and state institutions. Thus, the two kinds of assertions—of groups defined by their particularistic character and of social movements of various kinds—have remained largely segregated. There has been no dialogue between

4 Following Manor (1990), it could be argued that the politics of accommodation institutionalized by the Congress have ensured that the conception of democracy that prevails is delinked from its historical association with liberalism, and therefore from the commitment to rights and state neutrality that this usually entails.

5 It is now widely accepted that many of the so-called backward castes are actually those that benefited from the land reforms process, when their tenant status was legally converted into ownership. In Uttar Pradesh alone, 84 per cent of the area transferred benefited the backward castes (Patnaik and Hasan 1995: 286). This fact goes hand in hand with that of the out-migration of upper castes from rural areas, and is politically underscored by the perception of rural *dalit* groups of the backward castes as their new oppressors (cf. Omvedt 1996: 342). Meanwhile, even among the *dalits*, dominant groups tend to monopolize state resources allocated for *dalit* welfare, giving rise to resentment within the caste (Pinto 1997: 1876).

6 In western Uttar Pradesh, for instance, scholars have noted the emerging conflict between the *dalits* and the Most Backward Castes, the lowest in the caste hierarchy among the backwards, who are yet to evolve a distinct collective identity. These castes perceived themselves to be excluded by OBC mobilizations and being disprivileged even when the state government was controlled by the Bahujan Samaj Party (Pai and Singh 1997: 1356).

them as the former are exclusively concerned with power-sharing while the latter are inspired by visions of improving the quality of life (in terms variously of habitat, environment, and only indirectly, structures of domination) but without striving for political power as an instrument of achieving this.

There is a case for avoiding equally the twin extremes of unremitting gloom and unqualified jubilation about India's democratic career. To evaluate the relative degree of success or failure of any democracy, we need to specify the criteria by which we propose to do this. Invoking the distinction between procedural and substantive conceptions of democracy, it may be argued that while procedural–institutional aspects are undoubtedly important, institutions are necessary, but not sufficient, conditions of a flourishing democracy. The project of democracy in the substantive sense cannot be said to have been accomplished till such time as the effective exercise of the rights of citizenship is achieved and guaranteed to all. This is a combined function of (a) the enforceability of constitutionally guaranteed equal rights within a universalist legal system and (b) the social conditions which make their effective exercise possible. Such a conception of citizenship, it is argued, should form the cornerstone of our definition of democracy, and any and every claim about democracy in the Indian context must be tested against it. The conception of democracy that results will necessarily—and, one might argue, desirably—encompass both the procedural and substantive aspects of democracy. It will perceive the democratic project as a task of democratizing not only the structures of the state, but also society and social relations.[7]

Applying this test, it becomes manifestly clear that the truth about Indian democracy lies somewhere in the grey area between the pessimistic and the optimistic view, drawing upon but

[7] It is important to underscore the point that an effective democracy is virtually unrealizable outside of suitable institutional arrangements. However, institutions cannot exclusively and by themselves ensure democratic performance in the actual functioning of a polity, and are substantially limited by the social and cultural context within which they subsist. Thus, it is not unusual for multicultural societies to witness conflicts over institutions themselves, because institutions have distributional consequences, and groups claiming to represent ethnic, religious, linguistic, or caste groupings often compete with each other for control over these (cf. Przeworski *et al.* 1995: 49).

transcending both. Thus, the anxiety about institutional capacity and governability that marks the pessimistic view fails to take note of and interpret the wide variety of political assertions that have been made possible by democratic spaces, some given and others prised open. Conversely, many of the apparent triumphs of democracy prove, on closer examination, to possess profoundly undemocratic features. In the next three sections, I propose to illustrate this latter point by the use of three recent examples, one each from the spheres of welfare, secularism, and development which were pre-eminent on the state's agenda at independence. Each of these examples can be and has been interpreted, though in widely differing ways and from quite distinct perspectives, as a democratic success. I would like to point to some undemocratic outcomes in each case, and to suggest that these are explicable in terms of the twin processes of state action and social and economic inequalities which render largely fictional the idea of citizenship.

II

Welfare

At independence, the imperative for welfarism was obvious: widespread poverty, including food insecurity, especially in the rural areas. Fifty years on, with 39 per cent of the Indian population officially subsisting below a rather sparely defined poverty line, incidents of acute food insecurity continue to occur. In policy terms, the challenge of food insecurity was to be met by the strategy of increasing agricultural production, combined with a public distribution system which would subsidize the poor. If the first was a vital component of the modernization project of the Indian state (resonant with the anti-imperialistic slogans of self-sufficiency and self-reliance), the second was quite unambiguously a part of its welfarist orientation.[8] It is a commonplace today that, in concentrating on bringing Green Revolution technology to the

8 I have argued elsewhere that the Indian state may be appropriately characterized as an interventionist, rather than a welfare state. This interventionism did subsume a welfarist orientation, but its primary purpose was developmentalist. The developmental initiatives of the state, however, were largely directed to the modern industrial sector, while welfarist initiatives were directed substantially towards the redressal of poverty stemming from

irrigated areas, the planning process in India has seriously neglected the problems of rainfed agriculture, which accounts for 70 per cent of the land under cultivation in the country, but contributes a disproportionately small part of value added in the agricultural sector. These areas are more vulnerable to ecological degradation, and when deviations occur in their normal rainfall patterns, drought results, compounding the problems of low productivity, fragile ecology, and poverty. It is not surprising that the concentration of population below the poverty line is higher in regions of rainfed agriculture. Kalahandi district in the state of Orissa is just such a region.

Since 1985, Kalahandi has been more or less uninterruptedly suffering food crises of alarming dimensions, officially and disarmingly described as drought, but unofficially, by critics, as famine. The politics of nomenclature apart, Kalahandi has become a metaphor for hunger in several other districts in the more backward hill areas of south-western Orissa, largely populated by tribals, especially Bolangir, Koraput, and Nuapada (till 1993 a part of Kalahandi). It is possible to see this as a good example of the public action model, which posits a link between the existence of a free press and adversarial politics, one the one hand, and more effective state intervention in preventing famine, on the other (Drèze and Sen 1989). The model has indeed been applied to the Kalahandi situation, and endorsed (Currie 1996, 1997). It is true that the first accounts of widespread hunger and starvation in Kalahandi in 1985 were reported by the local press and then were taken up in the legislative assembly. If we add to this the exemplary role of the state judiciary in responding to two public interest litigations, we have the perfect copybook example of democratic initiatives spurring state intervention. But if we also observe the fact that Kalahandi, despite being a food surplus district throughout this period,[9] has continued to suffer from food insecurity almost

---

inequalities in the ownership and use of land, without however disturbing the rural power structure (Jayal 1994: 20).

[9] Kalahandi's per capita food grain production in 1989–90 was 331.86 kg, which compares very favourably with the Orissa average of 253.03 kg and the India average of 203.13 kg (Pradhan 1993: 1085). However, only 25 per cent of Kalahandi's food grain output is consumed within the district, the remainder goes out of the region through networks of merchants and moneylenders (Sainath 1996: 335).

without respite for the last decade, even in years of near-normal precipitation,[10] and as recently as 1996–7,[11] we need to ask what quality of state intervention was actually requisitioned by these ostensibly democratic initiatives.

It was the Baidyanath Mishra Commission Report (1991) that officially established the occurrence of starvation deaths in Kalahandi. It documented the terrible conditions of poverty and unemployment in the district, the absence of health care, and the distress sale of assets. It authenticated the fact of migration (surreptitiously organized by labour contractors) in search of wages and food and, above all, it recorded high levels of indebtedness and the exploitation of the rural, especially tribal, poor. Several cases of land-grabbing, encroachment, and the illegal and *benami* transfer of tribal lands were recorded by the commission in an indictment of the administration's failure to implement various legislations pertaining to land reform, moneylending, and bonded labour. In fact, the district administration was charged with apathy, and accused of collusion with moneylenders who exploited the illiterate tribal labourers whose lands they would mortgage in exchange for loans, refusing to return these even after the loans had been paid back with interest.

On investigating the performance of development programmes in the district, the Mishra Commission insinuated that corruption, fraud, and leakages were taking place in addition to the usual non-use and misuse, wastefulness, and mismanagement of development funds. It is true that even though Kalahandi has been among the

10 Kalahandi has had an average annual rainfall of over 1250 mm, which is higher than what some districts get in 'normal' years. Its lowest rainfall in the last twenty years was 978 mm, higher than the minimum 800 mm that is believed to be sufficient to get by (Pradhan 1993: 1084).

11 In February 1998, the National Human Rights Commission published its report investigating complaints of starvation deaths in Kalahandi, Nuapada, and Bolangir. Commenting on the high levels of deprivation in the area, and especially on inadequate income levels and the insufficient outreach of relief measures, it stated that 'the possibility of deaths having occurred owing to prolonged malnutrition and hunger, compounded by diseases, could not be ruled out (1998: 8). These conclusions were endorsed by a report of the Rajya Sabha's Committee on Petitions, which suggested that nearly 90 per cent of the population of the KBK (Kalahandi, Bolangir, and Koraput) districts live below the poverty line (1998: 6).

more generously provisioned districts of Orissa (in terms of the Jawahar Rozgar Yojana and other development programmes) its percentage utilization of these funds has also been substantially lower than that of other districts.[12] On the other hand, it has shown an almost limitless capacity to absorb calamity relief expenditure which is, by definition, more easily diverted and appropriated than regular development funds.[13] Neither the massive funding for emergency feeding and gratuitous relief, nor the somewhat lower levels of development funds, have however reduced the vulnerability of the poor to hunger, or rendered them capable of independent means of suvival. Resources have flowed into Kalahandi, but have generally come in late, misutilized, misadministered, and possibly even misappropriated on their way to those for whom they were intended.

Official study teams of the central government have repeatedly underlined that at the root of Kalahandi's 'distress' (the genteel official euphemism for widespread hunger) lies abject poverty. One such report argued that while the proximate causes of 'starvation' deaths may have been food poisoning, gastroenteritis, or meningitis, it was malnutrition, ignorance, and ill-health which rendered the largely tribal population vulnerable to these. Such was the magnitude of their insecurity that food aid provided by voluntary groups was being hoarded for times when even mango stones and tamarind seeds would not be available (Government of India 1992). Another report documented heavy outmigration, underemployment, malnourishment, bonded labour, the sale of children, the sale of young girls into prostitution in neighbouring Andhra Pradesh and in Bombay, and a high incidence of diseases like tuberculosis, polio, and scabies (Government of India 1993).

The overlap between particular social groups (namely, the *dalits* and tribals) and the category of landless agricultural labour is too

12 Only 39.21 per cent of Jawahar Rozgar Yojana funds were utilized in Kalahandi in 1992–3, while even other predominantly tribal districts, like Keonjhar and Koraput, reported between 50 and 75 per cent utilization (calculations based on statistics in Government of Orissa 1993).

13 In 1992–3, Kalahandi received Rs 132.39 lakhs towards drought relief, out of the Calamity Relief Fund. This was the highest allocation for any district in Orissa, and more than double of that received by every other district, with the exception of Bolangir.

striking to escape notice. Together, the Scheduled Castes and Tribes account for 84 per cent of the agricultural labour force of the district. Viewing the abysmally low literacy rates of these groups (15.58 per cent for the Scheduled Castes and 10.10 for the Scheduled Tribes) in conjunction with this occupational profile, it hardly needs underscoring that the conditions for effective citizenship are absent. Their formal enfranchisement is contained within a public sphere they are effectively unable to enter. The interpenetration between tribal identity, poverty, and structural backwardness is expressed in a disturbing overlap between class and ethnicity. The structural causes of Kalahandi's poverty and backwardness have however gone unattended. The reform of an inequitous landowning structure remains unattempted, as do the problems of bonded labour and high levels of indebtedness. It is not therefore surprising that the feeble economy of Kalahandi reports starvation even when the monsoon is timely and adequately precipitative.

The landless tribal poor are implicitly governed as subjects rather than citizens. The conception of welfare that informs state response is one of institutionalized charity and, as such, disables them as citizens. Lacking effective citizenship, they also lack rights. Lacking information—and the means or opportunity to acquire it—they lack also the wherewithal to access democratic institutions and processes through which to articulate their demands. It is no accident that even the Mishra Commission suggested that the social welfare functionaries of the government should educate people on how to assert their legal and constitutional rights, and that their rehabilitation should not begin and end with giving government subsidies as largesse (Baidyanathan Mishra Commission Report 1991: 64).

Thus, the story of Kalahandi is only superficially a vindication of the success of adversarial representative democracy. It is important not to lose sight of the fact that none of the public pressure—whether in the press or in the legislature—was authentically representative. It was the voicing of protest on behalf of, rather than by, the affected people, which may well account for the persistence of hunger. The dehumanization of the people of Kalahandi bears embarassing testimony to the absence of democracy from the lived experiences of ordinary citizens and underlines their threefold exclusion: from the economy, as landless and sometimes bonded labour; from society, as mostly Scheduled Castes and Tribes; and from the polity, as participation even in the minimal political act of voting without knowledge and information is meaningless.

A necessary preliminary to understanding the role of the state in Kalahandi is the disaggregation of three levels: the local state, the national state, and a crucial intermediary level, the regional state. The local state—as the Mishra Commission showed—has been indifferent and apathetic, often making common cause with local elites, rich farmers, moneylenders, and contractors. Influential politicians are often also large landowners, having links with *gountia*[14] families, with whom they share a common interest in promoting large projects likely to benefit the already prosperous. Evidence abounds of bank officials who routinely appropriate a large portion of the loans they grant; of profiteering by middlemen in the administration of employment programmes; of the intimidation of the poor by family planning officials; of the bribery and corruption rampant even in the Welfare Extension Office; and of the illegal 'selling' and transfers of vast amounts of tribal land. The other face of this supremely exploitable backwardness has been its unattractiveness to government officials who regard it as a punishment posting which they actively work to avoid. Thus, about one-third of the total official positions, especially those in educational and medical institutions, where opportunities for profiteering are limited, generally remain unfilled.

The role of the intermediate level of the state government is burdened with a contradiction. It responds to democratic pressures by, on the one hand, firmly denying the occurrence of starvation deaths and, on the other, petitioning the Centre for money, thereby signalling an abdication of responsibility. Vis-à-vis the central government, it plays a basically mendicant role, seeking funds and relief assistance. Within the state, however, it is the whipping-boy of adversarial politics, which puts it on the defen-

14 The *gountia* system in Orissa prevailed in the *khalsa* areas (state controlled land, as opposed to *zamindaris*). The gountia, mostly *brahmin* or *kulta* by caste, was designated by the ruler as the tax collector and usually also the headman of the village. In return, he received land—sometimes whole villages—for his own cultivation, and this was generally also the most fertile land.

sive, and renders it accountable for the hardship. One way of reducing accountability is to essentialize the problem in terms of its factual existence, of whether it occurred at all or not. Thus, the Orissa government resolutely denied throughout that widespread hunger leading to starvation deaths had occurred, and firmly stood by its official—and politically much less threatening—diagnosis of drought. The criterion for officially declaring an area drought-affected is crop loss of 50 per cent or more on account of a shortage in rainfall, and the state government accordingly highlighted the correlation between crop loss and the absence of adequate rainfall ('a natural calamity'), on the basis of which it could claim both moral absolution and relief funds from the Centre.

Finally, the national state, at farthest remove from local society, assumes an attitude of paternalistic benevolence, expressed through its role as chief fund-giver. However, once the relief money is sanctioned, the central government loses interest in it and surrenders control over it. Far from attempting to monitor the expenditure, the Government of India does not even maintain data regarding the district-wise or sectoral allocations made by the state government.[15] The more visible, though less meaningful, aspect of the Centre's involvement has taken the form of prime ministerial visits, to announce largesse in the form of grants of relief funds, in consonance with the philosophy of welfare as philanthrophy. These tokens of modern political ritualism are naturally expected to fructify in terms of enhanced legitimacy and votes.

The example of Kalahandi is instructive to the extent that it cautions us against reposing excessive faith in what appear to be encouraging examples of democratic performance. The fact that Kalahandi continues, despite the evidence of 'public action', to suffer hunger almost uninterruptedly is not the only pointer to the limitations of a textbook approach to the problem of democracy. The more disturbing pointer is the fact that the people of Kalahandi have never participated in raising their own voices, or even using their vote, to protest. Citizenship has clearly not yet been experienced in Kalahandi.

15 This observation is based on interviews with senior officials in the Natural Disaster Management Division of the Union Ministry of Agriculture, as also in the Union Ministry for Rural Development.

III
Secularism

Another kind of disfranchisement is highlighted by our second case, which illustrates the overlap between religion and gender, pointing to a category of citizens who are disprivileged as a result of both their minority status and their gender identity. The Shah Bano case (1985) and the subsequent enactment of the Muslim Women (Protection of Rights on Divorce) Act, 1986 may be seen not only as a tragic metaphor for the fate of the secular project in independent India, but also as an example of the consequences, for democracy, of competing constructions of identity. Situations in which it is possible to construct more than one identity on behalf of the same 'community' sometimes necessitate a choice of which identity is to be politically privileged as the critical criterion of collective self-definition. The project of democracy is thus confronted by at least two kinds of problems: first, making democracy receptive to the claims of communities in a plural society, and preventing it from degenerating into majoritarianism in a way that consistently disprivileges minorities; and second, searching for ways of rendering compatible conflicting identities, without the effacement of either and in a manner that safeguards the equal rights of citizenship. The Shah Bano case and its aftermath are adequately illustrative of both these problems.[16]

16 The case of Shah Bano vs. Mohammed Ahmed Khan (Criminal Appeal No. 103 of 1981) was decided by the Supreme Court in a landmark judgement delivered in April 1985. The case pertained to the claim for maintenance of a seventy-three year old divorcee, Shah Bano. Her husband, Ahmed Khan had moved the Supreme Court in appeal against a High Court judgement making the payment of a small maintenance allowance incumbent upon him. Ahmed Khan argued that since he had fulfilled his obligations under Muslim Personal Law by paying her an allowance for the three months of the *iddat* period, and paid her *mehr* as well, he was not bound to do more. The Supreme Court was thus implicitly asked to pronounce on the relationship between religious personal law and some provisions of the Criminal Procedure Code of 1973, which relate to destitution and vagrancy, and were being regularly invoked for maintenance petitions by abandoned wives. The Court upheld the High Court judgement, ruling that the criminal law of the country overrides all personal laws, and is uniformly applicable to all, including Muslim women. This judgement sparked off a political storm in which guarantees were

Majoritarian democracy, almost everywhere, has shown itself to be less than capable of handling the problems of multicultural heterogeneous societies. Institutions of representative democracy—designed for more or less homogeneous societies—have therefore been modified to allow for special provisions of a protective nature for minorities, and to rule out what Dworkin has called 'double counting'.[17] In practice, however, these institutions remain open to the charge that they function in ways that give majorities greater purchase in the polity, and also undermine the constitutional guarantees of equal citizenship enjoyed by individuals belonging to minority social groups, however defined. The charge of majoritarianism as an institutional bias is manifestly not mitigated by the state's formal adoption of secularism as a goal, and the legislation that was enacted to counteract the effects of the Supreme Court's judgement in the Shah Bano case was ostensibly intended to provide additional safeguards for minority rights. It failed, however, to secure the rights of Muslim women divorcees, against the conservative and patriarchal construction of the community's right to protection for its culture that would indefatigably prevail.

The enactment of the Muslim Women (Protection of Rights on Divorce) Act, 1986 was a source of some comfort to the liberal secular conscience, as it showed that even a minority community could use the parliamentary and para-parliamentary avenues of the democratic process to formally secure its right to determine its personal law without interference by a majoritarian society and state. It is not a little ironical that, even as the discourse of protection for *minority rights* hung heavy over the parliamentary debate on the Bill, at least five distinct arguments offered by the

---

demanded for safeguarding personal law, grounded in the claim of rights to cultural community. In deference to the opinion of the politically influential community leadership, the Rajiv Gandhi government hastily drafted a legislation which explicitly excluded Muslim women from the purview of the criminal law, to which all citizens otherwise have recourse.

17 The idea of double counting is premised upon the distinction between personal preferences (for one's own enjoyment of some goods and opportunities) and external preferences (for the assignment of goods and opportunities to others). Given that external preferences, political or moral, are generally not independent of personal preferences, but grafted on to the personal preferences they reinforce, counting them as if they were independent has grave consequences for equality, e.g., racism (cf. Dworkin 1977: 235–6).

government in its defence were justified by reference to the democratic principle of *majority rule*. Of these, the first two pertained exclusively to procedural–institutional aspects : the first argued the superior competence of parliament as an elected body to represent and legislate, over the judiciary which represents nobody and should remain confined to the enforcement of law; the second was an argument of vulgar majoritarianism, as—in an unmistakable reference to the Congress party's majority in parliament—it invoked the notion of majority rule as the only legitimate procedure for decision-making *within* the legislature. A third argument drew upon the identification between the state and the majority community, and prescribed legislative restraint in the matter of the personal law of minorities. The insecurity and alienation of the minority community, and its perception of threat to its religious and cultural identity, were emphasized with the government seeking to project itself as the protector of Muslim minority rights, even as it implicitly identified itself with the majority community.

I think we have to be sensitive to the fact that since *they* are in a minority *we* have all to be very careful that this House does not steamroller.... (emphasis added). [Lok Sabha Debates, 5 May 1986: 389–90]

The conception of secularism implied here is clearly one that presupposes that the majority is doing the legislating, while the minority is in a position of being legislated for, or even possibly against.

The fourth argument centred around the wishes of the majority *within* the minority community. Many Congressmen, including several ministers, repeatedly sought to establish the legitimacy of the Bill by citing the percentage of Muslims who, in their estimation, supported it. This majority of the minority—which varied from 80 to 99 per cent depending largely on personal whimsy—was held up as the acid test of the Bill's acceptability. In the Rajya Sabha, Home Minister Narasimha Rao stated:

We happen to be in charge of the Government. We happen to be the body which has to make an assessment of the situation. We have made it. You have every right to differ. You may say 90 per cent of the Muslims don't want this Bill, but only 5 per cent want it. Whether it is 95 per cent or 5 per cent it is up to you.... There is no question of your arithmetic changing ours. [Rajya Sabha Debates, 8 May 1986: 420–1]

Finally, the opinion of those—Muslim women divorcees—who would be directly affected by the legislation was barely mentioned, except by the Opposition. Clearly, if the government was seized of the question of minority rights, it was concerned exclusively to protect male minority rights. As one sympathizer of the Bill said, a minority of a minority in the polity as a whole was too miniscule to be entitled to a solicitation of its opinion by the government, but the press and public opinion had become so 'obsessed' with this issue that

> one would think that India's population consists mainly of Muslim women.... that too divorced women and that India had no greater problem to solve than this. Sir, as a matter of fact, the Muslim population is 12 per cent. Of them, children and adolescents form 6 per cent. Then males are 3 per cent and females another 3 per cent. Among them married women will be 1 per cent and the divorced will be .001 per cent, a miniscule minority within the minority.... [ibid.: 329]

These five versions of the majoritarian principle served to underwrite its validity both as a procedural rule for decision-making and as a normative principle, justifying at once the overriding of minorities (such as Muslim women) if they are numerically insignificant or powerless, and their 'protection'.[18] What is quite unmistakable is the overwhelming understanding of the democratic ideal in majoritarian terms. Democratic theory has for long recognized that the majoritarian principle as a decision-making procedure is only the best of all practicable alternatives, and far from being an ideal solution to the problem of a dissenting minority, even if it is a minority of one. It is, moreover, addressed to the specifically procedural and institutional aspects of democratic practice, and has little to contribute to the substance of the democratic ideal, which it could even be said to sometimes undermine. In this debate, the least attractive, make-do aspect of the theory of democracy is sanctified as its hallowed moral core, to justify the passage of a Bill which had more to do with the

[18] There is a strange convergence between the discourse of protection for minorities and for women. An alliance is forged between protector and protected which conceals the heirarchical opposition 'that assigns higher value to the first term: strong/weak, man/woman, majority/minority, state/individual' (Pathak and Sunder Rajan 1989: 566).

political exigencies of winning elections than any genuine concern for the cultural rights of communities.

This legislation was nevertheless defended as a success for Indian democracy and the secular state, as it made possible—in response to the demands of the ecclesiastical leadership of several theological schools of Islam in India—the provision of additional safeguards for the protection of minority rights, overriding not only judicial injunction, but also constitutional provisions regarding the uniform applicability of the criminal law to all citizens. This interpretation deserves interrogation not merely from the standpoint of gender justice, but more broadly, from that of the rights of equal citizenship. As the Muslim woman's community identity is privileged over her identity as a citizen, a filter of community control is introduced through which alone she has access to the state, and that access is further restricted by the state's self-limiting assumption of the role of a mere arbiter in determining who shall be responsible, and in what measure, for the care of a divorced Muslim woman.[19] In the absence of a reformed divorce law, women are unequal vis-à-vis men and vulnerable to unilateral divorce; they are also now rendered unequal vis-à-vis other women who continue to enjoy recourse to the law in respect of maintenance. Through this legislation, the primacy of cultural/community rights over political/citizenship rights is endorsed and the state willingly circumscribes its own domain by editing even its criminal legislation so as to exclude some citizens from the purview of rights uniformly available to others. It withdraws its telluric laws to make way for those of ecclesiastical origin, unmindful of the danger of providing precedents liable to misuse by the majority community.

The Muslim woman emerges as a doubly disadvantaged citizen. She is disadvantaged both as a member of a minority community and as a woman. The sources of her oppression—material as well as ideological—may on occasion be mutually reinforcing as when the state and patriarchy act in tandem. Her membership of a

19 The 1986 Act provides that in cases where a divorced Muslim woman is unable to maintain herself after the *iddat* period, the Magistrate can order such of her relatives to maintain her as are entitled to inherit her property, and in the proportion to which they would so inherit it in accordance with Islamic law. If the woman has no such relatives, or they do not possess the means to maintain her, or default in doing so, the Magistrate would ask the State Waqf Board to pay the maintenance.

religious minority renders her simultaneously vulnerable as a Muslim (vis-à-vis a predominantly Hindu society as well as the state) and as a woman (vis-à-vis the state and Muslim men). Ironically, it is the realization of the community's project of obtaining recognition for its cultural rights and the securing of legal safeguards for these, that compounds her vulnerability.

The secular project of the Indian state has run into heavy weather before, and heavier weather since, the Shah Bano case. It is now obvious that it cannot be merely a negative project of state abstinence or of multi-theocratic secularism. It must also necessarily be a project of equal rights and uniform conditions of citizenship, of democratic citizenship that (a) ensures that minority rights are safeguarded against the possibility of majoritarian democratic procedures working consistently to the disadvantage of minorities; (b) provides sufficient space for the articulation of more than one identity (for example, gender or religious identity) without securing one at the expense of the other; and (c) ensures that the expression and recognition of neither identity is subversive of the principles of equality and justice.

IV

Development

Finally, we turn to our last example, from the sphere of development, using the example of what is unquestionably the most powerful and visible social movement of the last decade, the movement against the construction of the Narmada Valley Projects, and the Sardar Sarovar Dam in particular. Unlike the Kalahandi case which exemplifies a quintessentially parliamentary mode of democratic protest, and the campaign against the Shah Bano judgement which was parliamentary and para-parliamentary, the movement against the Narmada Valley Projects has been almost entirely extra-parliamentary, eschewing the institutions of formal democracy and even, on occasion, engaging in the boycott of these, such as elections. This example is also concerned with a category of citizens who are doubly disadvantaged: as in Kalahandi, they are mostly tribal, landless labourers, but they are also additionally victims of involuntary displacement and even sometimes of forced eviction. Again, as in Kalahandi, this example underscores the importance of mediations and mediators in Indian democracy.

The Sardar Sarovar Dam, which has been at the centre stage of this controversy, is only the first of the works collectively described as the Narmada Valley Projects, comprising 30 major, 130 medium, and over 3000 minor dams. These have been represented as development projects justified by the requirements of economic growth, on the one hand, and the socially useful purpose of providing drinking water to chronically drought-affected regions, on the other. The powerful projection of the Sardar Sarovar Project (SSP) as 'the lifeline of Gujarat' by successive governments in that state has given added strength to the latter claim. The substance of this claim has however been repeatedly called into question. Its critics have pointed to the unavailability, even up to the present, of any official plans for the pipelines to be laid to send water to Kutch and Saurashtra, with three out of the six districts of Saurashtra (viz., Jamnagar, Junagadh, and Amreli) not even figuring in the Project Command.[20] In any event, the Sardar Sarovar Nigam Limited authorities have always projected the drinking water benefits to these areas as the longer-term, and therefore most distant, goals of the project, to be accomplished not earlier than 2020. In the meantime, there is considerable evidence that the major beneficiary districts will be those which are already the most prosperous and developed, viz., Baroda, Ahmedabad, Kheda, Gandhinagar, and Surendranagar.[21] Of the 70 talukas in the SSP command area, only 20 fall in the desert or drought-prone region. Thus, 72 per cent of the command area is in the rich, central plains which already have plenty of water (Paranjype 1990: 143). In fact, in the early reaches of the command area, in Kheda and Baroda districts, several new sugar factories are planned or under construction, with the big landowning farmers of the region

20 The Gujarat government has now tacitly admitted that the Sardar Sarovar Project will not benefit Kutch and Saurashtra, and is considering reviving another scheme for this purpose, for which the pre-feasibility reports have been commissioned (cf. Prajapati 1997: 694).

21 Data on the output growth rates of major crops in these districts shows that while Baroda and Surendranagar improved their performance substantially between the 1960s and the early 1980s, Ahmedabad and Kheda remained constant. By contrast, the output growth rates in Kutch fell over the same period (Bhalla and Tyagi 1989: 127–30).

waiting for the dam waters to irrigate their sugarcane crops.[22] Further only 6.5 per cent of the irrigation benefits are designed to accrue to the tribal areas, many of them benefiting only in a small way (to the extent of between 5 and 20 per cent), belying the Planning Commission's confidence that the project would have a positive impact on tribal poverty.

Activists of the anti-dam movement have consistently argued that the model of development adopted by the Indian state at independence—of which such projects are an example—is economically inequitable, environmentally unsustainable, and politically less than democratic in its denial of the rights of equal citizenship. Given that the computation of costs and benefits undertaken by planners is purely technical and economic in nature, it ignores the question of who (in terms of social groups or classes) the beneficiaries of the project are, and which social groups are bearing its costs. In the official justification of the project as being in the common good or the national interest, the movement sees sinister shades of the national security argument. Thus, detractors of the project are made to appear as anti-national, seditious, and even akin to terrorists,[23] while the displaced are projected as those who have to make sacrifices for the public good.

The movement against the dam has also questioned the project on the basis of its environmental impact, and the large-scale displacement—199,500 Project Affected Persons along with an

22 It is not surprising that the enormous pro-dam mobilizations that have been sponsored by the Government of Gujarat, have received considerable financial support from the Gujarat Chamber of Commerce and Industry.

23 Basic civil liberties have been denied and systematically violated in the Narmada Valley. Since 1988, the Official Secrets Act has been imposed at the dam site. Human rights violations in the area include the arrest of activists, often without information as to the charges or the bailability of the offence; their repeated detention on exaggerated charges; denial of the rights of access to family and legal counsel in preventive detention; and abuses in custody (Asia Watch 1992). In Gujarat, the emotional charge this project has come to possess has created a strange politics of 'democratic' unaninimity, and dissenters have had to pay a heavy price for voicing their opinions. In 1988, for example, Mrinalini Sarabhai was dubbed an enemy of Gujarat and unceremoniously removed from the chairmanship of the Gujarat Handlooms and Handicrafts Development Corporation for affixing her signature to a memorandum to the Prime Minister, asking for a reappraisal of the project.

additional 140,000 Canal Affected Persons, who remain outside the purview of official compensation—it has necessitated. The rehabilitation and resettlement (R&R) efforts of the concerned governments have been characterized as inadequate by the Narmada Bachao Andolan (NBA), though some non-governmental organizations, such as the Arch Vahini, have been working in cooperation with the Gujarat Government to improve the R&R implementation. This has been anathema to the NBA, which has adopted a position of truculent opposition to the construction of the dam, and has been unwilling either to negotiate a reduction in its height to lessen the area of submergence or to cooperate in improving R&R.

It is true that the resettlement and rehabilitation policy has been far from adequate, but only a part of this inadequacy stems from the shortage of good land to make a viable land-for-land policy of compensation possible. The inadequacies of the policy package have been rendered more acute by failures of implementation, not excluding fraudulent and corrupt practices. Most importantly, resettlement policy has been insensitive to the special needs of tribal communities. Ninety per cent of those displaced in Gujarat, 95 per cent in Maharashtra, and 49 per cent in Madhya Pradesh, are tribals. The policy, including the Award of the Narmada Water Disputes Tribunal (NWDT), ignores the fact that these communities do not recognize individual rights to property in land, and have no legal title to land (in the form of revenue records) that could entitle them to compensation. Policy-makers have firmly refused to recognize as worthy of consideration the traditional rights of these tribals, including the customary rights of usufruct; their traditional self-governing institutions; their dependence on the forest for subsistence, including all their needs of food, clothing, shelter, and medicine; and their desire to be relocated as communities rather than as individuals or families. The Indian state has been sensitive to the demands of communities defined by religion and caste, as they have made claims to special needs such as the protection of culture or affirmative action in public employment and education. It has arguably been much less receptive to the claims made by tribal communities, and considerably more invasive and predatory in its relationship towards them.

On the face of it, the movement against the dam has been a resounding success. It has succeeded in frequently mobilizing tens of thousands of people (most notably in the Harsud rally in September 1989 and in the Sangharsh Yatra at Ferkuwa on the Gujarat–Madhya Pradesh border in 1990–1). Its leaders' deposition before the Independent Review instituted by the World Bank was among the factors that influenced the Bank in 1992 to suspend funding and withdraw from the project. Its protest has rendered the future of the project uncertain, with Madhya Pradesh now persuaded to accept fewer benefits as the price of less submergence and the Supreme Court having stayed construction since May 1995. Above all, it has been instrumental in most powerfully articulating the challenge of alternative, sustainable strategies of development. Despite repression (by the state, aided by the commercial interests involved in the construction of the SSP), the movement has followed chiefly Gandhian methods of protest. These include fasting, long marches, the boycott of state institutions and personnel (for example, the census, elections, and government officials of any description), and the threat to submerge themselves in mass suicide when the waters rise to engulf their villages.[24] There is little doubt that if there is any one movement which has placed issues of the environment and development on the national agenda, it is this.

The movement against the dam asserts a participatory conception of democracy, but the right to information—a necessary preliminary for such a consultative process of decision-making—is unavailable. Even though the NWDT Award required that oustees be informed about submergence at least one year in advance, and be resettled at least six months prior to actual submergence, these minimal conditions have not been observed. Instead, a conspiracy of silence has prevailed, with development activities—from banks to schools—quietly drying up in areas expected to be submerged (MARG 1986–8). Even the rights of association, including the right to unionize, have been undermined by a variety of means, ranging from discouragement and intimidation to outright harassment and police action, and most of all by the imposition of the Official Secrets Act.

Meanwhile, the idea of democracy has proved to be extremely serviceable to a variety of interests. The state has marshalled at

[24] The slogans of the movement express some of these ideas: *doobenge, par hatenge nahin* (we will drown, but we will not shift); *amra gaon, amra raj* (our village, our rule).

leasts three types of ostensibly democratic arguments in defence of the project. The first of these is the political argument of majoritarianism, which chooses as the test of democracy, the numbers of people affected positively and negatively by the project, and weighs these numbers against each other. Thus, the putatively beneficiary population of Kutch and Saurashtra (as at present, rather than a projection for 2020, the earliest that the water might reach these regions) is traded off against the number of displaced persons, its needs—drinking water—shown to be more basic and vital, and the project found to be entirely justifiable. The second argument is overtly developmentalist and appeals to the idea of 'public purpose', which enables the state to ask sections of its citizenry to sacrifice some of their rights in order that the nation as a whole may benefit.[25] Finally, there is a cultural argument which appeals to the notion of a 'national mainstream', claiming that critics of the project are conspiring to keep the tribals out of the mainstream (cultural and economic), and thus preventing them from enjoying the fruits of development.[26]

Unlike the quiescent tribals of Kalahandi, the displaced tribals of the Narmada Valley have been mobilized and have actively participated in the agitation against the dam. However, the core leadership of the movement has remained entirely in the hands of urban, educated activists from middle-class backgrounds who lead the Andolan and formulate its strategies. Despite the patent sincerity of their social commitment, many have questioned their role and, by extension, the authenticity of the voice in which the tribal speaks.[27] Is he constituted by this middle-class leadership, or

25 The argument of public purpose is best illustrated by quoting from a letter written by Indira Gandhi in 1983 to Baba Amte, a social worker who has also been involved in the agitation against this dam. She wrote: 'I am most unhappy that development projects displace tribal people from their habitat.... But sometimes there is no alternative and we have to go ahead in the larger interest....' (Colchester 1984: 253).

26 Veena Das has made a case for diachronic comparison to compare the pre-settlement status of communities with the post-settlement scenarios. This could have important policy implications, for while some communities may show a reasonable degree of well-being before resettlement, others may score poorly on basic indicators (Das 1996: 1513).

27 In 1991, Amita Baviskar argued that 'adivasis (as well as non-adivasis from the Valley) do not initiate any programmes of Andolan action. Strategic

does he present himself authentically? Are his slogans his own, or given by others? Are his politics the product of his own (and his community's) authentic and original understanding of their world? This search for the 'authentic' is part not only of the carping critic's baggage, but also of the activist's intellectual equipment. The stereotypes that are invoked by the activist in representing tribal identity, as well as the cynicism of those who believe that outside leadership can only contaminate authentic political struggle, are equally questionable. Medha Patkar sees the role of the activist as that of a facilitator rather than a leader and, in her perception, this is part of a democratic learning process:

> They felt it was unjust, and that their way of life would be snatched away from them. Such feelings and opinions were expressed in the meetings. But they never saw it clearly as a fight to stop the Sardar Sarovar Project....
>
> Once the local representative group was formed, after detailed organizational work with even a hamlet as a unit, the representatives always came out of the community, many of them who had not even seen the *tehsil* ever before. Once they went through this process and had a kind of dialogue with the government, they understood the reality themselves. [Patkar, 1992: 276–7]

Critics of the movement have also recently begun to articulate concerns relating to the support base of the NBA. Given the hysterical regional frenzy whipped up in Gujarat over the last decade in support of the project, the NBA has built up greater support in Madhya Pradesh. This is unsurprising when we consider that Madhya Pradesh is, under the original award of the NWDT, paying a higher price in terms of the extent of the area of submergence and resettlement costs. In recent years, the Madhya Pradesh Government has begun supporting a reduction in the height of the dam—which is unacceptable to Gujarat—in order to reduce its area of submergence. It is notable that the area which

---

and tactical decisions are taken by activists; the people of the Valley only have the power to veto what is proposed....By and large, people do not raise questions about proposed programmes; they agree with what the Andolan does on their behalf.... So the structure of the Andolan is pyramidal' (1991: 96). Anil Patel of Arch Vahini has made even sharper accusations against the NBA, of disinformation and the manipulation of tribal aspirations (1997: 86).

would come under submergence, were the dam to be built to its originally intended height (of 460 feet) would be the extremely fertile Nimar valley. This valley also happens to be home to a class of upper-caste landowners called the Patidars, who belong to the middle and rich peasantry that has become politically powerful in recent years. While they have funded and supported the NBA, it is unlikely that they subscribe to its alternative development strategy. The NBA, for its part, has underplayed the Patidars' role in the movement, and showcased that of the tribals (Baviskar 1995: 217–21). It would be uncharitable to the NBA leadership to suggest that the movement has a hidden agenda of promoting the interests of this class of landowners, but that this group would nevertheless profit from a reduction in the height of the dam is also true. However, the NBA continues to staunchly maintain a no-dam position, and a mere reduction in the height of the dam is unlikely to satisfy it, regardless of the immediate human costs entailed.

Despite these reservations about the authenticity of the protest, the mediatory role of outside activists and the social groups that would benefit from a possible reduction in the height of the dam, it is unquestionable that the movement against the dam has been infinitely more successful than any other comparable struggle. It has displayed staying power, its members have withstood state repression and the self-imposed hardships of struggle alike, and it has squarely placed on the national agenda the debate between development and the environment in an accessible, even if over-simplified, form.

However, the claims to recognition of tribal communities have been ignored. If the project is eventually allowed to proceed, displacement and forced eviction will continue apace and these claims will equally certainly continue to remain unheard. In the alternative scenario, if a reduction in the height of the dam is politically negotiated and accomplished, its beneficiaries will also be a vastly more privileged group of big landowners in the Nimar region, rather than the disadvantaged tribal citizen. In either case, authenticity will be an irrelevant issue. If, finally, the construction of the dam is indefinitely stayed, the situation of those already displaced will not improve, nor their rights be further safeguarded.

Thus, the displaced tribal emerges as a disadvantaged citizen, whose physical displacement entails cultural displacement, and more. From a position of marginality in the Indian social structure of stratification by caste, these tribals are now dragged to the bottom of the class structure, as labourers in agriculture, mines, and factories. Together, their location in the social and economic structure render almost inevitable their position in the structure of power, as citizens who—despite political mobilization—have little voice in the polity to ensure for themselves even better rehabilitation prospects, much less social justice.

V

What emerges from our discussion of these examples, *contra* the pessimistic view, is not a problem of institutional overload limiting the state's capacity to give effect to its self-ordained agenda of social transformation. Equally, the optimistic view of democratic processes contributing to the empowerment of the marginalized, appears to be a somewhat premature hurrah. In agreement with the optimistic view, we recognize with satisfaction that democracy in India has provided a space and an opportunity for the articulation of a variety of claims. However, we recognize also that democracy remains, after fifty years, still a substantially unrealized project. There are formidable difficulties in the way of accomplishing it, and our examples serve to illustrate some of the social conditions which inhibit its realization, as the constraints on the effective exercise of citizenship rights translate with alarming swiftness into constraints on the realization of democracy itself.

The expression of economic and social inequalities—frequently overlapping—in distortions of democratic practice, is rooted in the failure to address the social requirements of citizenship, in addition to the purely legal ones. Citizenship may be undermined in at least two ways, the first of which is the absence of public enforcement of a universalistic legal order. This mode of undermining citizenship can take several forms: the state may fail to ensure the enforceability of the constitutionally guaranteed rights of citizenship; state personnel such as the police force may fail to protect citizens from privately perpetrated violence; or they may themselves engage in the violation of citizens' rights. Different sections of the citizenry may be differentially protected by the state, the rule of law may apply to some but not to all, autonomous spheres of power may emerge which inflict injustices on weaker groups in society, and so on. While many of these can be easily illustrated with Indian examples, our cases exemplify more sharply the second way in which equal citizenship is undermined. This relates to the absence of the social conditions which make possible the effective exercise of citizenship. If effective public policy is seen as a function of public action, then these may validly be considered the enabling conditions of public action, if not its prerequisites.

The limits on effective democracy, then, stem chiefly from inequalities in social relations and only secondarily from the logic of democracy itself. As we know quite well, the concentration of social power is as undesirable as, and not reducible to, the concentration of economic power, though they do coalesce with extraordinary regularity. Social relations of domination and subordination also tend, with disturbing frequency, to find political resonance such that the voice of the powerful gets expressed while the powerless go largely unrepresented, except in the formal and ineffectual sense of periodically participating in elections.[28]

These distortions arguably influence the state's capacity to effect (or not) its goals of social transformation. Democratic institutions play the role of filters, providing restricted access to the state. This is almost an auxiliary and adjunctive role, for it is the salience of the groups in question that is expressed through the democratic process which proves to be extremely serviceable for some interests, but closed to others. Often, organized interests find voice, while the politically unorganized poor have to be mobilized to extra-institutional protest (as in the Narmada Valley), or else do not protest at all (as in Kalahandi).

28 That democracies are highly sensitive to income inequalities is of course widely accepted. Economic resources are prone to translate into political resources, but while greater individual resources (of wealth or education) do not necessarily translate into higher participation, those who are disadvantaged underparticipate, and do not succeed 'in compensating for their weak economic positions by raising their political voices' (Parry and Moyser 1994: 54). In recent years, studies have also related social and economic inequalities to *attitudes* about democratic politics, with surveys showing that more educated people in Spain, Brazil, Hungary, and Poland believe that democracy is better than dictatorship (Przeworski *et al.* 1995: 37).

There is, thus, paralleling the unorganized sector in the economy[29] what may be described as an unorganized sector in the Indian polity. Many organized interests, even of the disadvantaged, enjoy some voice, even if only at election time when they are assiduously courted as convenient pre-aggregated stocks of valuable political currency (or 'vote banks' in everyday parlance). On the other hand, groups such as the tribals of Kalahandi, have largely subsisted on the margins of the polity, and have not forged a political identity in the same way. Women, particularly those belonging to the poorer classes or ethnic minorities, are victims of similar political disablement. Despite its size, this unorganized sector of the polity is exceedingly vulnerable.

A fundamental shortcoming of Indian democracy is its inauthenticity and unrepresentativeness. Despite the clamour of celebration that attends every election ritual, and the tributes paid to the vibrancy and resilience of Indian democracy, there is cause for concern in that intermediaries are crucial to this democracy, not just as brokers of votes, but also to represent the needs of the vulnerable. That the hungry of Kalahandi or Muslim women divorcees did not represent their own cases is not accidental. That it took a group of middle-class activists to energize the movement against the SSP is also not surprising. Conditions for democracy—even of the formal, procedural kind—have not been consolidated, facilitating the state's unchallenged deviation from its own avowed purposes and projects. It thus becomes possible for the state to pay only token attention to the demands of welfare; to compromise secular principles and deny its Muslim female citizens equal rights; and to answer challenges to its development strategy by resorting to arrogant technocratic arguments.

The ambivalent and even contradictory responses of the state to these claims suggests that it is not one or another form of democratic articulation that predisposes the state to act or respond in a particular, predictable manner. The conventional exercise of assessing the efficacy of democratic processes from state response is clearly an inappropriate, and even sterile, way of approaching the question. For it is the substantive content of the challenge—

29 It has been suggested that the unorganized sector of the economy accounts for 90 per cent of the workforce, which suffers from welfare and employment insecurity (Rudolph and Rudolph 1987: 21, 370).

in terms of which specific interests it threatens, not excluding reasons of state—that prejudices state policy. Of the three examples discussed here, two represent demands to give effect to the state's agenda of welfare and secularism. The third example, from the Narmada Valley, questions the state's agenda by interrogating the content of its project of development. In the first two cases, the state's agenda has not been effected, chiefly because the state enjoys manifest autonomy from the large, legally enfranchised but politically marginal, mass of affected citizens. In the third case, the anti-development mobilization is ineffectual in obtaining state recognition for its demands, in the face of formidable state and commercial interests.

Clearly, the state's own project of social transformation, as expressed through its developmentalist or welfarist goals, is not above bargaining and compromise. It is closed only to democratic negotiation by vulnerable categories of citizens. In its attentiveness to some interests, the public agenda is permissively open and vastly inclusionary, while towards other less influential ones it remains severely exclusionary. The core projects of the state are rendered differentially open to negotiation. As with almost any other resource, therefore, this is not a problem of too little or too much democracy, but of its selective availability.

The ultimate test of a successful democracy should surely be its ability to determine or at least influence the agenda of the state. Disputation about the ends and goals of a society is an intrinsic part of the democratic project. To accord sacrosanctity to the agenda adopted by the state at a given moment in its history is to Leviathanize democracy. As in Hobbes, this anoints the principle of consent, only to withdraw it after its first exercise (authorizing the sovereign to act on behalf of the subjects) is completed. If electoral politics are an inadequate guarantee of continuous consent, and the public agenda of a society cannot be perennially open to negotiation, is there any pragmatic centre to be found between these two extremes of democratic practice? When the formal conditions provided for participation by citizens in a democratic polity are precluded from being realized—as they manifestly are in all our cases—that agenda must be reopened to take account of the legitimate needs of the socially vulnerable and politically marginalized. The needs invoked in all three cases are fundamental: they call for security and basic sustenance, for life itself. Expressed as rights, they represent variously the right to food, the right to a way of life of one's choice, and the right not to be rendered destitute. Other forms of rights-claims by groups, such as the demand for caste-based affirmative action or self-determination on the basis of religion, speak to the state from a position of strength. Couched as threats, they compel the state to garner its energies to address these demands. The rights-claims articulated in our examples, however, present no serious threat to the state. They point, rather, to the failed promise of 1947, to the violation and compromising of the rights guaranteed in 1950 in order to evade those promises, and to the lack of voice in the continuously profluent refashioning of the state's agenda.

References

Asia Watch (1992), *Before the Deluge: Human Rights Abuses at India's Narmada Dam*, vol. 4, no. 15. New York.

Baidyanath Mishra Commission Report (1991), 'Inquiry into Original Jurisdiction Cases No. 3517 of 1988 and No. 525 of 1989'. Cuttack: High Court of Orissa.

Bardhan, Pranab (1984), *The Political Economy of Development in India.* Delhi: Oxford University Press.

——— (1993), 'Symposium on Democracy and Development', *Journal of Economic Perspectives*, vol. 7, no. 3, Summer.

Baviskar, Amita (1991), 'The Researcher as Pilgrim', *Lokayan Bulletin*, vol. 9, nos 3–4, May–August.

——— (1995), *In the Belly of the River: Tribal Conflicts over Development in the Narmada Valley*. Delhi: Oxford University Press.

Bhalla, G.S. and D.S. Tyagi (1989), *Patterns in Indian Agricultural Development: A District Level Study*. New Delhi: Institute for Studies in Industrial Development.

Colchester, Marcus (1984), 'An End to Laughter? The Bhopalpatnam and the Godavari Projects' in E. Goldsmith and N. Hildyard (eds), *The Social and Environmental Effects of Large Dams. Vol. 2: Case Studies.* UK: Wadebridge Ecological Centre.

Currie, Bob (1996), 'Laws for the Rich and Flaws for the Poor? Legal Action and Food Insecurity in the Kalahandi Case' in John Toye and H. O'Neill (eds), *A World Without Famine.* London: Macmillan.

——— (1997), 'Power, Legitimacy and Hunger: Re-examing the Link between Democratic Governance and Food Security'. Paper presented to the ECPR Joint Sessions of Workshops, Bern. February–March.

Das, Veena (1996), 'Dislocation and Rehabilitation: Defining a Field', *Economic and Political Weekly*, vol. 31, no. 24, June.

Drèze, Jean and Amartya Sen (1989), *Hunger and Public Action*. Delhi: Oxford University Press.

Dworkin, Ronald (1977), *Taking Rights Seriously*. London: Duckworth.

Government of India (1992), *Report of the Central Study Team on Koraput and Kalahandi*. Ministry of Agriculture, September.

——— (1993), *Tour Report of Bolangir and Kalahandi Districts, Orissa*. Ministry of Rural Development, 6–10 March.

Government of Orissa (1993), *White Paper on Drought Situation in Orissa, 1992–93*. Revenue Department.

Jayal, Niraja Gopal (1994), 'The Gentle Leviathan: Welfare and the Indian State', *Social Scientist*, vol. 22, nos 9–12, September–December.

Kohli, Atul (1990), *Democracy and Discontent: India's Growing Crisis of Governability*. Cambridge: Cambridge University Press.

Kothari, Rajni (1998), 'Pluralist Politics in India—Cultural Roots, Recent Erosions' in D.D. Khanna, L.L. Mehrotra and Gert W. Kueck (eds), *Democracy Diversity Stability: 50 Years of Indian Independence*. Delhi: Macmillan India Ltd.

Lok Sabha Debates, 1986.

Manor, James (1990), 'How and Why Liberal and Representative Politics Emerged in India', *Political Studies*, vol. 38.

MARG (1986–8), *Sardar Sarovar Oustees in Madhya Pradesh: What do They know?* Vols I–V. New Delhi.

National Human Rights Commission Proceedings (1998), Case No. 37/3/97-LD, Chaturanan Mishra, Union Minister of Agriculture (Complainant). New Delhi.

Omvedt, Gail (1996), 'The Anti-Caste Movement and the Discourse of Power' in T.V. Sathyamurthy (ed.), *Region, Religion, Caste, Gender and Culture in Contemporary India*. Delhi: Oxford University Press.

Pai, Sudha and Jagpal Singh (1997), 'Politicisation of Dalits and Most Backward Caste', *Economic and Political Weekly*, vol. 32, no. 23, 7–13 June.

Paranjype, Vijay (1990), *High Dams on the Narmada: A Holistic Analysis of the River Valley Projects*. New Delhi: INTACH.

Parry, Geraint and George Moyser (1994), 'More Participation, More Democracy?' in David Beetham (ed.), *Defining and Measuring Democracy*. London: Sage Publications.

Patel, Anil (1997), 'Resettlement Policies and Tribal Interests' in Jean Drèze, Meera Samson and Satyajit Singh (eds), *The Dam and the Nation: Displacement and Resettlement in the Narmada Valley*. Delhi: Oxford University Press.

Pathak, Zakia and Rajeswari Sunder Rajan (1989), 'Shahbano', *Signs*, vol. 14, no. 3.

Patkar, Medha (1992), 'The Strength of a People's Movement'. Interview with Dunu Roy and Geeti Sen, *India International Centre Quarterly*, vol. 19, nos 1 and 2.

Patnaik, Utsa and Zoya Hasan (1995), 'Aspects of the Farmers' Movement in Uttar Pradesh in the Context of Uneven Capitalist Development in Indian Agriculture' in T.V. Sathyamurthy (ed.), *Industry and Agriculture in India since Independence*. Delhi: Oxford University Press.

Pinto, Ambrose (1997), 'Emerging Social Tensions among Dalits', *Economic and Political Weekly*, vol. 32, no. 30, 26 July.

Pradhan, Jagadish (1993), 'Drought in Kalahandi: The Real Story', *Economic and Political Weekly*, vol. 28, no. 22, 29 May.

Prajapati, Rohit (1997), 'Narmada, the Judiciary and Parliament', *Economic and Political Weekly*, vol. 32, no. 14, 5 April.

Przeworski, Adam (1995) *et al.*, *Sustainable Democracy*. Cambridge: Cambridge University Press.

Rajya Sabha Debates, 1986.

Rajya Sabha Committee on Petitions (1988), 106th Report on the Petition signed by Shri Chittaranjan Mandal of Orissa pertaining to improper use of funds meant for poverty alleviation programmes leading to starvation deaths in undivided districts of Kalahandi, Bolangir and Koraput in Orissa.

Rudolph L.I. and Susanne H. Rudolph (1987), *In Pursuit of Lakshmi: The Political Economy of the Indian State*. Bombay: Orient Longman.

Sainath, P. (1996), *Everybody Loves a Good Drought*. New Delhi: Penguin India Ltd.

Weiner, Myron (1983), 'The Wounded Tiger: Maintaining India's Democratic Institutions in Peter Lyon and James Manor (eds), *Transfer and Transformation: Political Institutions in the New Commonwealth*. Leicester: Leicester University Press.

III

Democracy and Civil Society

It is arguable that the most important task of civil society in India is to effect a bridging of the gap between democracy in the formal structures of governance, on the one hand, and the absence of the necessary conditions for the realization of democracy, on the other. The intensity of civil society activity in India since the late 1970s is manifestly a response to the centralizing tendencies of state structures, as well as to the inadequacy of state policies and their implementation, especially in the sphere of development. It is in the twin contexts of broadening and deepening democracy, and fostering a sustainable pattern of development, that civil society in India has acquired salience.

Pramod Parajuli discusses the challenges posed by the new social movements to statist discourses on development. The state's subordination of women, *dalit*s, tribals, and minorities are being challenged by feminist, ecological, and indigenous people's movements. In particular, Parajuli focuses on the alternative forms of governance being articulated by the women's movement, forest struggles, and the movements against big dams. Not only are the new social movements redefining and transforming the nature of politics through a revival of civil society, they are also, he argues, regenerating subaltern knowledge that has been subordinated and suppressed by dominant forms of knowledge. By demystifying development, further, these movements are also redefining democracy as a consultative and participatory social relation.

A less radical form of protest, but one which has potential to influence governmental policy, is illustrated in the excerpt from Jean Drèze and Amartya Sen, which demonstrates the importance of public action, both collaborative and adversarial, in preventing famine. Drèze and Sen contrast the occurrence of mass-scale famines in modern China with the Indian experience where, despite endemic hunger and malnutrition, there has been no large-scale famine. This contrast is attributed to the existence of a free press and adversarial politics, which make it impossible for governments to conceal the occurrence of mass starvation and also help to render them accountable.

Democracy is, however, more than just an arena of struggle or a space where citizens collectively mount pressure on the state. Grounded in the principle of equality, it is also a principle that challenges inherited hierarchies and, capturing the popular imagination, predisposes people to think in egalitarian ways. This is the subject of Sudipta Kaviraj's paper, which argues that democracy is central to the understanding of culture as it undermines traditional cognitive processes, and privileges new ones. Through a song in a popular film of the 1950s, he shows how the Hindi cinema has been the carrier of the Nehruvian ideal of nationalism and the principles of social and political equality in which democracy is based. As the barriers of traditional society have broken down, democracy has provided ordinary people with the language to reject social subordination, even if insubordination cannot, in material terms, achieve very much for the poor. The article by Walter Hauser and Wendy Singer presents a somewhat different account of the culture of democracy. Here, elections are viewed as a political festival, drawing upon elements of secular and religious rituals, and marked by the ceremonies of nominations for tickets, the campaign, the polling, and the counting, all these culminating in the victory processions after the results have been announced. Through this democratic rite, voters not merely endorse particular candidates, they also redefine political hierarchy and create new sets of individual and collective relationships in the polity.

Finally, there remains the question of how democracy can help us to negotiate the diversity of cultures within the Indian nation-state, such that majoritarianism is kept at bay and the rights of minorities are adequately respected. In the Introduction, we saw how institutions of representative democracy create dilemmas in multicultural societies, where minorities based on religion or ethnicity may, by virtue of their small numbers, be systematically disprivileged in processes of decision-making. Arend Lijphart examines India's experience with democracy with reference to his theory of consociationalism (or power-sharing). The consociational model claims that democracy is possible in multiethnic societies only if four conditions obtain. These are: (1) government by grand coalition in which all ethnic groups are represented; (2) cultural autonomy for such groups; (3) proportional representation in politics and the civil service; and (4) minority vetoes on issues concerning minority rights and autonomy. The Indian experience is then tested against these elements of the consociational model, to conclude that India is 'an impressive confirming case' for consociational theory. There could, of course, be disagreements about the extent to which these elements are actually found in Indian political experience. Firstly, the absence of any formal requirement for the representation of all minority groups in government has resulted in, at best, tokenism, and the claim that the Congress system (because of its umbrella nature) has provided the foundation for a consociational grand coalition is contestable. Secondly, Lijphart interprets India's federal polity, along with special provisions for religious minorities, as signs of cultural autonomy, but these remain highly contentious issues, as minorities have—despite constitutional guarantees—remained vulnerable to a variety of threats, including violence. Thirdly, and once again formally, the Indian political system is based on the Westminster parliamentary model rather than on proportional representation. Protective discrimination, in the form of special constitutional provisions for the scheduled castes and tribes, can hardly be considered synonymous with proportional representation. Finally, the minority veto remains a political rather than constitutional, instrument, dependent upon the efficacy of minorities in mobilizing themselves to protest.

7

The Culture of Representative Democracy[+]

Sudipta Kaviraj

I

An anniversary[1] is a time for self-congratulation. Particularly when it is an anniversary of a nation, the line of congratulatory discourse turns decidedly towards the self; it is a time of reflexive congratulation. Many guilty upper-class liberals would undoubtedly say that there is nothing to celebrate in these fifty years. Our principal task is to mourn the death of our dreams. I do not wish to spoil the atmosphere of this happy occasion. It is true that as a society we have failed to make a lot of our cherished principles work. We have not been very good, collectively, at either socialism, federalism, secularism, or even, if we look closely at our tendency to search for close substitutes for royalty, at republicanism. And essays can be written about these failures. I feel, however, that we have been very good at one particular thing. While we failed to enact a version of a Marxian revolution, we have collectively succeeded in ushering in one expected by de Tocqueville. This is true in every sense, on all sides. No one complains, except for a fringe of the upper middle classes, about an excess of democracy. No party starting from the Congress to the formally Stalinist CPI(M) to the communal BJP has a serious open programme against democracy. Political democracy, if we

+ Partha Chatterjee (ed.), *Wages of Freedom: Fifty Years of Indian Nation-State* (Delhi: Oxford University Press, 1998), pp. 147–75.

1 Fiftieth anniversary of India's independence.

distinguish it from its more problematic social and economic extensions, appears to have been an unqualified historical success. I shall take up for consideration the process by which this has happened, and its consequences for culture. As a result, in this search, it is most appropriate to follow de Tocqueville in his picture of a democratic revolution in society.

Democracy is based, even in its most limited, formal, political sense, on a principle of equality. But this principle of equality is abstract, and is capable of several subsidiary forms, depending on which particular sphere of social life it is being applied. Accordingly, it can have distinctive forms as political, social, or economic equality: these principles are not the same, and the historical and moral consequences of their application to a hierarchical society are bound to be significantly different. Although these are distinct, they tend to be interconnected. Its application in one field usually generates a demand for its extension to another. De Tocqueville thought there is an innate tendency of this principle to spread from the political public sphere, where it was first devised, to all others, leading to far-reaching consequences for social stratification and cultural practices. And since these things affect the general performance of a society in a world which was becoming increasingly interdependent, this affected the larger global performance of the society as a whole. Is democracy then a good thing or a bad thing? By 'the coming of a democratic society', de Tocqueville meant precisely the gathering together of the historical consequences following from an extension of the logic of democratic equality to what early sociologists called 'the society'—the customs, habits, and practices that infuse and structure our everyday life. Democracy is after all a way of imagining the world, and is powerfully affected by movements of the aesthetic imagination too, especially, I shall argue, in its popular forms.

We are, however, concerned here with the problem of culture in a very specific sense. In talking about democracy and culture, I shall leave aside the spheres of artistic and intellectual activity usually associated with the restrictive sense of that term. I have a special interest in particularly one segment of culture which deals with knowledge of society. It covers education in the formal sense, but its centre lies in those often unstructured processes of social instruction through which agents form a grasp of their own social identity, the opportunities that exist for themselves (of the kind that an uneducated but sharp shopkeeper has of the price movements of commodities), and also of the possible opportunities in the political universe in which he lives. Modernity seems to be essentially concerned with a society's learning processes, with knowledges. These are not knowledges in the Western philosophical sense of production of truth and reliable pictures of the world, but in the indigenous meaning of producing *vidyā*, skill through which we produce all things, cognitive and otherwise. Modern times introduce an immense imagination of self-conceived and self-directed change in its plastic world, and living in this world constantly emphasizes the significance of learning. Keeping the world stable is a cognitive enterprise and has to be learnt, just as much as making it different, because revolution, as Marx noted, also has an irreducible cognitive dimension. Democracy, both as a deliberative system which affects collective reflexive action, and as an indirect process that undermines the claims of traditional cognitive procedures, makes the cognitive process central to the problem of culture in modern times. I shall take up four cultural themes in succession: democracy and insubordination, democracy and distinction, democracy and disorder, and finally, what happened to our vaunted claim that democracy enables us, collectively, to live a special life of our choice. It is a life that we have not merely made ourselves, but also chosen and consequently understand. Culture is concerned with images and texts, in stories, poetry, and music. Let me first take a text, a suitably degraded, lowbrow text, from the middle levels of culture of the 1950s to make our entry into this world.

II

Democracy in the decades after independence was not merely a political principle; it also had a clearly marked space of residence. It was universally known to live in the city. The city—Calcutta and Bombay par excellence—had that mysterious quality, liberating and contaminating at the same time. It regularly broke hearts and conceptual structures. Well-intentioned young men from the traditional countryside, Bengali novels always showed, never came back with their innocence unimpaired. The city liberated them by corruption, and corrupted them by freedoms denied in the idyllic countryside which appeared breathtaking in technicolour because its social relations could not be seen. If we analyse why the city was such a seat of enjoyable corruption in the eyes of traditional society, we detect the effectiveness of the Tocqueville argument. The city was a realm in which, in contrast to the villages, two forms of the principle of equality reigned. In the city, caste segregation broke down with alarming ease, leading to dangerous miscegenation between upper and lower castes. In traditional eyes, this was assisted by the deplorable dominance of modern ideals of romantic love. Caste and the claustrophobic lives of women in love were not captured in colour landscapes. Heroes of novels often made the unintelligible decision to live in grubby rented rooms in the city, spurning the village greens. It was a journey that film heroes, from Pramathesh Barua in early Bengali cinema to Raj Kapoor in the popular Bombay movies of the 1950s, made with consummate pathos endless times in their lives, so meaningful precisely because it was being enacted countless times in ordinary lives in that small stretch of history.

Of the various contending forms of Indian nationalism, a certain Nehruvian ideal—secular, reformist, mildly egalitarian, cosmopolitan[2]—acquired historical dominance. Nehru and the elite surrounding him have been criticized, rightly in my view, for neglecting to foster this form of nationalism. They did nothing to produce a continuous dialogue in which this ideal could constantly, unfailingly provide justification for itself in the everyday market-place of ideas and ideals. It neglected the ordinary schools. It did not devise other arenas of constant everyday ideological discourse. Parliamentary debate in which this ideal was constantly debated and justified was too distant for ordinary citizens to follow or its arcane legalisms to understand. But this argument usually forgets one ideological force which came to spread and constantly represent the Nehruvian ideal of nationalism and its interpretation of the meaning of democracy in the Indian context. This was the vast imaginative universe of the Hindi film: an enormous aesthetic structure which connected a number of significant poles of Indian cultural life. In its contents, it usually drew upon the vast repertoire of stories from diverse sources: from the historical past (films like *Mughal-e-Azam*), mythologies and folklore, straightforward

[2] In their search for lyrics these films rummaged through the classical modern repertoire like Iqbal (*chino arab hamara/hindustan hamara*), but also invented a kind of joyous form of homelessness reflected in songs like *mera joota hai japani/yeh patloon inglistani/sir pe lal topi russi/phir bhi dil hai hindustani.*

nationalist narratives (*Mother India*), and the inexhaustible resources of modern Indian literature. These were supplemented by the considerable inventiveness of radical writers many of whom were once active in the Communist-influenced Indian People's Theatre Association (IPTA), but were rendered unemployed by the Party's indifference towards serious art and decided preference for cheap propagandistic material. On another side, it continued, if Mukund Lath is right, an immemorably ancient tradition of mixed entertainment coming down from the *Nāṭyaśāstra*, and put to use a varied repertoire of musical forms, exploiting the established popularity of both folk and semi-classical forms for its own commercial purposes. The film, thus, like all other forms of India's aesthetic modernity, drew upon and reinterpreted elements from its traditional repertoire, to produce cultural forms and objects which were attractive and intelligible. I wish to suggest that it was the Bombay film which carried on the function of ideological persuasion for the Nehruvian nationalist ideal. Both its narrative and its musical repertories were interpreted to give a primarily Nehruvian construction: a typically democratic view of social reality. A central ideological strand of these popular films was the deployment through stories of the twin principles of political and social equality that we have associated with democracy.

A song in a popular Hindi film captured this mood with great aesthetic accuracy, and associated it with the city. Incidentally, in a purely textual sense too this was quite defensible. Nehru himself, and the modernist sensibility he represented, tended to see the line of division between city and country as coinciding with the one between progressive culture and backwardness. Not merely for Bombay and Calcutta films, but for serious interpreters of Indian modernity too, the city, however squalid, was the realm of freedom. The song conveyed, through this undistinguished jingle, the amazed entrant's sense of the city and its unaccustomed democratic culture.

Ye dil hai mushkil jeena yahan
zara hathke zara bachke ye hai Bombay meri jaan.
Kahin building, kahin tram-en, kahin motor, kahin mill,
milta hai yahan sab kuchh ek milta nahin dil
insan ka nahin kahin nam-o-nishan
zara hathke zara bachke ye hai Bombay meri jaan.

The song advised the entrant to be wary, to twist, turn, and dodge at every step, because it was Bombay, *meri jaan*, where you had to constantly save yourself, move off, step aside from the path of the advancing traffic, which is also the path of the early expansive capitalism. After all, the song portrayed Bombay, the commercial metropolis of modern India. But, from the other side of the world, for those who did not have the implements of commerce on their side, it was not a place of expansion at all. Its evident modernity was inimical to equality. It was a place where it was difficult to live—using wonderfully the deep ambiguities of that democratic verb *jeena* (to live). To exist, to live, was, if there was anything, an absolutely minimal demand of all human beings; *jeena*, to merely exist, must be the most effortless activity. But in Bombay even that was hard. If we read Bombay not as the immediate signifier of the city, but in a broader sense, as a sign of modernity itself, this line of thought immediately reveals subtle connections with a radical, preferably Marxist, wonder at the divorce of means of production from the labouring poor. It was amazing that mere living could become so difficult an accomplishment anywhere; a truth said in a rueful repetitiveness to one's own self, because the city was not a place of dialogue, but of soliloquy—the place of ultimate loneliness.

In the 1950s, the cultured lower middle-class Indian still looked at the proposals for living proferred by capitalist modernity with some amazement, and considered this loneliness, which was the price of individuation, with sadness and disquiet. Yet the attractiveness of the song came from its strange contradiction. Against the sadness of its wording played the liveliness of its staccato tune. It was a tune that sought to copy the rhythms of the city crowds and clatter of traffic in something akin to ironic joyousness. It suggested, underneath, that for those who were corrupted and liberated by its deeply Baudelairian atmosphere, Bombay was a place of strange, mysterious, degraded joys. The song had found a new rhythm, part of a new aesthetic which the Hindi films of the 1950s broadly reflected. An army of gifted left-wing writers, made redundant by the Communist party's cultural sectarianism, infiltrated the world of popular Bombay films and composed wonderfully knowing, sceptical, and complex lyrics for surprisingly sentimental and simplistic films. But the sense of the city captured by the song is endemic of the better Hindi cinema of the

1950s. This sense of a squalid address of freedom, the loneliness of the modern individual, his or her search for a refuge against the heartlessness of the city in romantic love, is evoked by the endless walks on rainy nights taken by couples in Bombay's popular films. They wandered through streets whose lack of an ontological hospitality was symbolized by high, tightly shut iron gates which barred their access, behind which, the spectators knew, the new bourgeoisie lived lives of morally tainted opulence. Still, the city was in a Baudelairian way, beautiful—degrading, freeing, mysterious, corrupting rustics by its freedom.[3]

The city was both joyous and fearsome precisely because of the logic of democracy—of a mixing, of a levelling of a certain kind. I have already mentioned the urban knowingness of the words: words crafted sometimes by gifted middle-class poets, not mercenary versifiers. They sought to impart an element of their genuine sense of bitterness and irony, about the cities that had loved and betrayed them, into their inconsequential film songs. They often carry within them a fugitive signature of a radical rejection of the city's incipient capitalist culture; but this radicalism had to remain indistinct, smuggled into vehicles of cheap commercial success. The petty bourgeois poets often produce a discourse of those marginalized in the city, like the clear case of this song; but this discourse and its implicit political stance might give us a clue to a larger problem of what democracy has done to culture. If we take a sample of such lyrics, they would form quite an impressive literary genre, with sharply observed facts, considerable narrative wit, and often high skill in execution. But in a sense that cluster of attributes was what made them unreal. They *represented* a lower-class optics or vision of the city in a manner which makes some analysis of the process of representation necessary. I am sure the real people of Bombay—of course, a real space and a sign—did not speak with that kind of cultural cunning, wit, and artifice of

3 I had direct experience of this dual attraction of the city when my grandfather accompanied me to Presidency College in Calcutta on the first day of enrolment. When going out of the gates into College Street, he cast a withering glance at the Coffee House across the street, and warned me, on pain of some mysterious punishment, not to go in that direction. As it happened, I obeyed him strictly, and avoided the great talking shop of Calcutta, though on grounds not of moral but noise pollution. I discovered that in that wonderful place of exchange of ideas, it was literally impossible to converse.

self-interpretation. That is how they *would have* spoken if they had the gift of a language of poetry, if they knew the appropriate speech and knew how to translate their resentment into educated words. If they had to express their sense of resentment, they would have spoken differently.

I grew up in a small religious town, Nabadwip, still misty with the sentimentality of living *vaishnava* culture in the 1950s. I must say a bit more about the context in which I listened to this song. At dawn, the town rang with the gentle pastoral tone of the tunes by which good Vaishnavas were supposed to acknowledge the gift of a new day. At eight in the morning, however, several shops on its main street would suddenly start blaring out these new ditties of a clattering urbanism. Not only were the tunes of these genres different; in the latter, the sound of the city street and the deft movements of the urban man moving through dense and lawless traffic could be distinctly heard. The two songs met every day in a strange ritual of noise, based on two utterly different 'structures of feeling'. One was gentle, peaceful, worshipful; the other quick-witted, alert, ironic about the world and the self, rapid, and constantly interrupted. Yet there was no denying the tunefulness, the expressiveness, and the musicality of this new music originating not in the sacred domain of religion, but the especially degraded one of films. People felt that there was a structure of urban experience, the life-world of the city, which deserved a music of its own. It must be an easy, popular, untechnical, in other words, *democratic* music. Curiously, even in our childhood, we sensed the attractiveness of this music—precisely because of its strangely fascinating invitation of liberation and the subtle, enticing corruption of disobedience. The song had many other sides within its short structure. The main singer, the utterer of this slightly bemused picture of the city, which felt to him like a violation of every natural thing, was a man. But it also had, briefly cutting into it, a frivolous, female voice, and the way it spoke about the mysteries of Bombay showed clearly that it had a greater awareness of city life. She seemed more at home in artificiality and degradation, a curious inversion of the roles of men and women. Listening to these songs were considered a degrading influence by the older generation. This naturally heightened their popularity and attractiveness among the young by the unmistakable proof of their subversiveness in the disapproving annoyance of elders.

III

The city was unmistakably more democratic, but there were, on careful observation, real internal limits to this aesthetic of defiance. The song wonderfully evokes the culture of the first historical stage of modern Indian democracy precisely because of the implicit social geography it contains. Culturally, all this was a house quarrel among the culturally articulate and privileged, and did not involve the bystanders. Even the radicalism and insubordination was signed by the unmistakable mark of *representativity*. Representative democracy is a surprisingly non-innocuous phase. It can change its meaning astonishingly with a shift in emphasis. I do not wish to stress the constitutional fact that we had a representative *democracy*; but that our democracy was deeply *representative*. In Western political theory, this alienating, emptying aspect of representativity was best theorized by Rousseau, almost in a manner anticipating Gramsci's later insights into the constant wars of position. Democracy and privilege were usually locked in an endless and ever-renewed contest over the control of the plastic world of the modern, constantly playing moves and countermoves. It is to some of these moves and countermoves in our cultural world that I wish to turn.

The point of using the film song was not just my love of the frivolous. It showed in a wonderfully graphic way the *representativeness* of the Nehruvian democratic experiment. Similar trends had emerged in the history of Europe and America as well, at certain points of the history of modern democracy. Students of formal political theory would remember that the debate about 'delegates' and 'representatives' was not, as it now appears, politically pointless. After democratic arrangements of government, especially elections, were reluctantly conceded to the lower classes, the social elites in Western societies increasingly resorted to 'representative' rather than 'delegate' arrangements as a device for reducing the effects of direct popular power by using representation as a class filter. The working classes could cast votes, but evidently, because of their cultural deficiencies, could not represent themselves effectively in a highly discursive form of political exchange. To pursue their collective interests effectively under the given institutional arrangements, they needed to send to legislatures representatives who had the requisite skills. It was not surprising therefore that often the electoral representatives of the working class were reformist individuals from the elites. It followed that the lower classes could thus determine who could go into Parliament, but not enter it themselves. In principle, relations of basic political life could be shaped by their deliberate actions, but the instruments by the use of which this shaping action could be performed required a skill they had in very short supply. Thus, their relation to the historical world of social plasticity had also to be mediated, or represented. They had to act upon the historical world through the intricate, over-elaborate, labyrinthine, and mysteriously legalistic procedures of parliaments, the central site of the deliberative processes of modernity, only through their representatives.

This historical peculiarity was evidently influenced by the gradualist way in which the European poor gained their entry into the deliberative processes of democratic politics. They did not crowd into the House of Parliament destroying manners and sweeping everything before them in a wave of fury and resentment. John Reed graphically describes the entry of the revolutionary crowd into the Winter Palace during the Russian revolution. They took particular pleasure in the destruction and defilement of the objects of refinement and luxury that fell their way. The entry of the lower classes into parliaments could also take that destructive, radical character. But in Western Europe, by and large, it happened very differently. The democratic historical process operated more like a sluice-gate, allowing entry to a comparatively small bloc out of the overwhelming majority of capitalism's dispossessed, who were waiting impatiently outside. The effect of this was what Benedict Anderson has called a process of 'pacification'. Not merely did it quieten the clamour for electoral power, at least for a time. This had a wonderfully disorienting effect on the few who gained entry at each stage. Outside, they were part of a huge, overwhelming majority, and savoured the savage power of the crowd. Once inside, they were isolated and encircled, insecure because of their cultural difference and their lack of knowledge of the rules and etiquettes of the game. They had to learn the forms, manners, and techniques of parliamentary politics, and were domesticated in the process. The great majority of the poor entered democratic constitutionalist politics in instalments, fragments, small groups, always as insecure of resentful minorities within the parliamentary precincts. Consequently, they got disciplined and domesticated by parliamentary conventions. Within the august halls of parliament, they constituted a timid, insecure, surprised, diffident, unconfident minority. They were thus immediately culturally remodelled by their entry—not wholly, of course, but partially. Often, this set in motion a process of unmistakable bourgeoisfication that Tocqueville describes in his accounts of radical politicians in the French legislatures. At least sufficiently significantly to make the term 'participation' a realistic name for what they had wanted, and were going through. Participation, strictly, is a process in which there is a set of standing institutions whose internal rules are widely regarded as legitimate in society, but people who are outside these institutions protest their exclusion. They wish to enter, not shake the structures into dust. This is due to a historical fact generally neglected by political scientists. This is all happening at a time of the most extraordinary spread of 'low' literacy in Europe and the creation of the structures and process of the Habermasian 'public sphere'. It was the discursive structures of the public sphere—the intricate and elaborate network of places of talk and quarrels in coffee-houses, meetings, demonstrations, journals, reviews, conversations—which connected those who were enfranchised with those who were not, the inside and the outside of formal power. Above all, it turned the state into a common, public object of concern, a *res publica.* One of the principal conditions for such a common discursive relation about the state was the rise of literacy and social information.

In the West, democracy was an autochthonous development. That is not necessarily a complaint, and it need not lead by implication to an argument of despair. From that, it no way follows that democracy cannot be successfully practised elsewhere, but it does imply that a simple imitative effort would be bound to run into trouble. To be successful, the political principles that constitute democracy should be disentangled from the specific forms of political institutions in which these were born. After all, what we call the West in the singular is a complex unity of several national trajectories of political evolution. Elements of liberal democracy emerged historically in various political traditions: renaissance Italy, seventeenth-century England, eighteenth-century France and America. Although eventually, a number of countries of the West came to develop a recognizably similar type of political arrangement, their historical sequences and trajectories of development were quite different. If we look at the legal–constitutional arrangements more closely, so were the resulting political forms. My argument is that we should not simply extend to the cultures outside the West a similar possibility of historical differentiation. Most processes of modernity, not only political ones, demonstrate a similar trend towards universality and differentiation at the same time. The processes are universal in the sense that they successfully reach all other social forms across the entire world; but since the historical and cultural conditions under which these processes unfold themselves are often strikingly different, the actual historical phenomenal forms that they assume become inevitably differentiated. The fact that the historical provenance and trajectory of democracy was different in India does not mean it is bound to fail, unless we define democracy so narrowly as to imply that any failure to produce exact copies of Western institutional models would by definition be classified as a 'failure' of democracy. It still remains true, however, that the historical emergence of democracy was radically different in India. In the West, it was a result of elite and popular experimentation with common life in the state. Bringing the society under the state's sovereign control, the literal meaning of sovereignty, was in fact prior to the democratization of this central, concentrated power. In India, at least initially, it was a matter of pure intellectual initiative and conviction, marked, to use Partha Chatterjee's memorable phrase, by an unmistakable derivativeness. We should not, however, fall into the inexpensive temptation of a patronizing rejection of the Nehruvian elite, since all the alternatives suggested are either unworkable or thinly veiled restatements of the Nehruvian liberal project. When they wrote the legal principles of political egalitarianism into the new Constitution, they were moved partly by genuine liberal conviction, partly by moral cunning. Certainly, a section of the reformers of traditional Indian society saw a wonderful opportunity of combining material and moral advantage at the same time. The projected constitutional reforms were meant to destroy caste and feudal privilege, but they often show a sharply contrasting gentleness towards class and capitalist inequality. The Nehruvian elite therefore had the moral satisfaction of reforming society and the material satisfaction of not falling victim to their introduction of social equality.

But plasticity of the social universe does not imply untroubled symmetry of projects and performance. Widespread perception of social plasticity invites large collective action by groups in the hope of using this quality for their own benefit, but these actions can rarely be contained and controlled by those who initiate them. This is why modernity is the age of revolutions. Revolutions are the greatest signs not merely of the world's plasticity, but of the fact that most people act on that knowledge. But revolutions are merely the evidence of the possibility of large actions, not the exercise of perfect control over their course. Democracy, even in the limited, indirect, representative form, threatened a frightening levelling of privilege, however distant. It threatened the élite, even by its rhetoric of political equality, with an utterly unfamiliar process of sharing the world with their habitual inferiors. It threatened them with prospects of crowded streets, genteel middle-class localities run over by lower-class shanties, buses full of shirtless fellow citizens, refuse spilling on to pavements, and of course the slow wrenching of public spaces from the control of well-bred elites by the simple, strategic, and unanswerable use of filth. The constitutional invitation to equality, though heard unbelievingly by the poor and the lower caste, was sufficient incitement to gingerly testing the improvising capacities of the downtrodden, and when it succeeded, to be more widely used. Its effects in political terms were apparent quite early in the life of the republic, through the creation of new, untraditional self-descriptions of castes. Social reform movements of the nineteenth century too sometimes worked energetically for the abolition of untouchability. But these were movements of the upper groups directed at improving conditions of untouchables who remained trapped in the segmentary structures of the traditional caste system. Constitutional provisions provided a novel caste identity: the concept of Scheduled Castes was initially a highly artificial legal construct, which did not come from the traditional grammar of caste practices. But instead of remaining a legal fiction, like many other things, they are turned into a socially real entity by the quotidian pressures of electoral practice. It is this, rather than any principled high-mindedness which made politicians like Jagjivan Ram indispensable to Congress political strategies. However, caste prejudice was sufficiently strong to deny him even the post of a chief minister throughout his career, not to speak of the premiership which could have been his in 1977.

But Jagjivan Ram was a cultural mutant, like Ambedkar before him, trained into the norms of refinement of the upper classes of Indian society, and entirely inappropriate as a symbol of the cultural self-assertion of the unreconstructed low-caste poor man. They had come through the sluices of democracy, not bursting the dams. Indeed, from this point of view, the growing status of Ambedkar as a symbol of low-caste mobility is somewhat puzzling.

Often political analysis of social conflict mistakenly construes the struggle between groups as a static and finite process. Social inequality and political conflicts about them are not static. It is not as if there is a single field of social inequality in which there is going to be a conflict between the major contenders, as happens in the case of caste conflict for recognition or prestige, or class struggles over assets or incomes. One of the most significant features of the historical conflict between dominant and underprivileged classes is that the ruling groups have the capacity to alter the nature of the struggle by translating their advantage into a different key. The conflict is a strategic system in which precisely one of the greatest strategic advantages of the dominant groups is to change the terms of the strategic action.

Even the slow-acting, sluice-gate democracy of the first two decades was vaguely threatening to the dominant classes whose pre-eminence was a straightforward combination of caste and class advantages. Concession to the basic democratic principles of the constitutional settlement undermined open and explicit forms of privilege. But this did not imply that social privilege was seriously reduced; it was merely forced to change its form. The Indian elites did not await their historical destruction by the processes of constitutional democracy: they used the technique of dominant classes to refashion and reconstruct structures of inequality. Presiding over the new inequalities of capitalist development, they produced enormously effective countermoves. Political uncertainty at the time of independence contributed to a situation that worked to their advantage. An utterly nervous Congress elite, worried at the disorder of partition, decided to preserve the main pillars of the colonial system—its police, its bureaucracy, and its educational system. In these historical circumstances, both the coercive and administrative apparatuses of the colonial state remained largely unchanged, with education, the main avenue of approach to the conventional bastions of professional power, remaining firmly wedded to the structures of colonial culture. Under colonial rule, the major cultural distinction between the privileged and the masses was the former's control over the English language. However much the Nehruvian elite professed democratic principles, and they were probably quite sincere in their professions, they were products of this cultural process, and did not know how to work in any other. Nehru's government initially understood the democratic necessity to undermine the privilege of the English-speaking, and adumbrated an energetic policy for propagation of Hindi as the official language. The official theory was that gradually Hindi would take over from English as the principal language of communication between diverse vernacular groups. This policy had to face several obstacles. First, the argument from a majority principle did not suit the case for Hindi. It was the language of the largest segment of the Indian people certainly; but equally a majority of Indians did *not* speak Hindi. Second, Hindi itself was a somewhat recent construct, and suffered from internal resentment from dialects which felt they were unjustly suppressed in the process of creation of an 'official' Hindi. At times, as with Maithili, they wanted to secede from Hindi and declare independence as a separate language, weakening Hindi's claim to a majority even further.

Despite the considerable initatives of Nehruvian reform, which should never be confused with socialism, social inequality assumed an increasingly complex form in independent India. The institutional system clearly discouraged forms of inequality the elite considered 'backward', primarily the practice of caste in the public domains. The ideological system of official pronouncements was reconstructed and spoke in terms of a discourse of radical equality. Yet it was quite clear that the system encouraged, at least treated with uncharacteristic gentleness, new forms of inequality based on capitalist development. The environment of government protectionism fostered Indian capitalism in the half century of freedom and, despite conventional liberal wisdom, so has the state as an economic and administrative structure. Although state and market structures may have deep-lying contradictions of economic interest, they have colluded in the making of a world of modernity which sits with ever greater weight on the pre-modern economy and patterns of traditional livelihood. Both the state and capitalist industry require a national labour market, which capitalism creates and the state administers; a recognizable grid of education whose certification can be trusted within the domain of the modern economy, and which controls entry into its professions. And this economy, by its constant expansion, has become a large enough independent life-world within which the species of beings known as 'Indians' live in happiness and prosperity.

Formerly, the cultural organization of the life-world was quite mixed and complex, and it was impossible to speak one's way in English through the diverse demands of everyday life—from the chatter within the family, nursery, school, college, workplace, retirement, friends, taxi drivers, and vegetable sellers. Now, within the life-world of the middle class, it is eminently possible to linguistically live in English. Some crummy vernacular is required to carry on broken conversation with the shadowy world of servants that surrounds comfortable middle-class lives. Since its common sense speaks, thinks, sees, conforms, and even defies in English, its natural connections often stretch towards the West outside, rather than inside with the vernacular world which, because of the high artificial illumination of the modern sector, appears increasingly dark. Formerly, modern individuals lived lives that were sites of transaction between the modern and the traditional, English and the vernacular. Modern Bengali novels often provide graphic accounts of these interactions, through which the undertaking of a modern life had to pick its way. In contemporary English writing by Indian authors, there is often a parodic evocation of such encounters, but the vernacular and its foibles are seen with a kind of pitying witticism, from the unstated *normalcy* of a standard Western point of view, speaking a standard internationally intelligible literary language. In earlier literature, the non-English vernacular world was an unforgettable, enveloping presence. Now it is possible to meet metropolitan Indians whose only relation to this world is as landscape, as earth, not as world. Yet this increasing mental distance is in direct contrast to a greater nearness in material terms. Formerly, the lifestyle of the really opulent remained enclosed within the privacy of their mansion, or the stricter privacy of clubs, expensive restaurants, or the unreality of films—into which others were denied access. Till the 1960s, this was in part due to the traditional culture of conspicuous frugality of the merchant castes. The rise of more serious and widespread capitalist enterprise made this culture increasingly untenable, by adding to the list of the commercially wealthy entirely new groups of people untrained in the traditional caste practices of restraint. Traditional business families went by these rules until their younger sons returned with quite other ideas from shallow training in American business schools. Conspicuous consumption became the norm with a new class of people, wrongly called 'businessmen', who thrived on government contracts secured not by any known rules of competitiveness, but plain patronage of politicians. From the late 1970s, a new middle class introduced into the society a culture of consumer competitiveness. Now, the television, particularly the intensity of advertisement which makes a visual spectacle of this 'high' living, ends the comparative reticence, bringing it out into the open, turning it into an endless exhibition of the enchantment of material goods. Ordinary Indians do not have to go seeking for these images; they come at them. Capitalism does not liberate agency; it liberates desires. Competitiveness in middle-class lives also introduces a particularly cruel form of well-being, where the enjoyment of pleasure or of affluence lies precisely in the spectacle and the enjoyment of its denial to others. Capitalist commerce introduced an essential economic ingredient to the modern city—the glass shop-window—the most massive and insidious form of invitation and denial. Advertisement and television intensifies and generalizes this process to an unprecedented extent.

In some ways, the Nehruvian elite acted on a script of history based very clearly on the narratives of European nation-states, and in that drama homogenizing education played an essential part. Educational structures supplied the sovereign absolutist state subsequently with the cultural ingredients of modern nationalism. Education was a central element of the nationalist project in India too; equally essential for general economic development and the specific design of Nehruvian industrialization. Evidently, spread of education in the real sense is also essential if democracy is to take its benign, and not destructive cultural trajectory. In India, this would have meant not merely greater access to education for all, but, crucially, to the *same* education as the middle classes received. However consistent this might be for the theory of Nehruvian democracy, the middle classes in India did not resign themselves to these fables of equality of opportunity. Whenever such historical transformations threaten, the middle-class elites usually fashion counter-strategies to counteract their long-term effect and the decline of their privileges. The interesting feature of capitalist modernity is that liberal ideology prevents the reaction of formal rules of discrimination. The strategies of the elite thus have to operate through social processes, without explicit legal restrictions imposed on others. Two effective counter-strategies were eventually collectively improvised by the Indian elite against the dangers of a democratic wave sweeping away their privileges. The first was the creation of two different layers of Indianness and turning English, ironically, into a mark of being a 'true' Indian as opposed to a mere Tamil or Bengali or even a Hindustani. The second was a massive deception in the name of education in which the Nehru government happily colluded—fobbing off the poor by an inferior substitute for education, which could be passed off as the real thing simply because their objects lacked the cultural skill to judge its quality.

I have argued elsewhere that our nationalism was based on an essentially bilingual cultural form, made of a particular way of mixing the usage of vernacular and English. English was used as a mode of communication not only with the rest of the world but also with other parts of the country speaking different vernaculars. Typically, that form of Indian nationalism considered it impossible to be an Indian without simultaneously being a Bengali, or Oriya, or Tamil. Even Jawaharlal Nehru, who seems an unlikely candidate for such nationalism today, began the narrative of this self by the assertion of being Kashmiri. Without that more fundamental level of identity, no one could reach the secondary identity of an Indian. Through the negligence of the well-intentioned and active stratagems of the devious sections of our élite, that essential diglossia is now falling apart. It is replaced primarily by two unilingual groups fighting for supremacy. The English-speaking are distanced from our material and cultural world by the infinite distance of language. There are referential forms and shapes contained in a language; in the case of English, these referential forms distance and alienate them from Indian social reality. A description that would fit with a predetermined snugness, something in the Indian social world must be approached through a concept which has at best an approximate fit. It is not surprising that poetry written in English, though often of considerable skill and nuance, fails to turn nature into a poetic residence. But actually the range of usages this English can perform is, usually, barring spectacular individual exceptions, very narrow. Usually, the English of this new elite is a purely functional language, definitionally impoverished; unable, in Tagore's words, 'to dance'. It marks the decided victory of Khushwant Singh over Rabindranath Tagore. What I find surprising and difficult to explain is the opposite side of this divide. It probably shows the depth and ineradicability of the tragedy of subalternity. In large parts of the country, there is either an assertion of a blind plebianism expressed in the vernacular, which accepts and enacts the contemptible image that English-speakers have of the vernacular world, or a sullen inertness which does not attempt to question the privilege of the English-speaking vulgarity in a language of vernacular refinement. The idea of a vernacular refinement or cosmopolitanism has become increasingly difficult to conceive and defend.

In the context of the rise of democracy in nineteenth-century France, de Tocqueville feared that one possible trend of a democratic society might spell the end of cultural distinction; and in that sense, he was the first theorist who anticipated the rise of Western mass culture. The idea of a mass society has, of course, to be used in the context of contemporary India with great care. In one sense, in any society, effective democracy would generate pressure towards the dominance of a 'mass' culture. However, what this mass culture is in real terms depends crucially on historical circumstances. Establishment of a culture of cheap books and printed material, and the parallel development of mass literacy, gave this process in the West its peculiar and specific form. In India, low levels of literacy, lack of general education, and lack of a widespread print culture has often turned it in a different direction. A wide print culture helps diffusion of opinion across a national political domain. Its want in India has tended to segment the culture of political ideas and produced distinctive political-cultural 'forms' specific to different regions, in which regional or local intellectuals and politicians can mobilize opinion and actions without much critical response. I wish now to briefly explore the Tocquevillean theme of democracy and distinction in our context.

IV

Democracy introduces pressures towards equality and homogeneity in culture. But since that starts in a situation marked originally by great cultural inequality, this pressure can have two different results. The culture of a society, under the pressure of democratic power, can go towards an *upward* equality through the spread of cultivation, or at least access to it, or towards a *downward* equality of common plebianization. This is, of course, an analytical model. In historical fact, a society is rarely subjected to a purely upward or downward motion, particularly because the logic of democracy affects individual social practices and their domains in different ways, and often its impact on different fields is diverse. What has happened in Indian society is a complex picture made up of both trends in different social fields, and there can be further doubt about whether we can culturally speak of India as a single unit at all. Some trends in cultural life can however be identified fairly clearly, and some of these can certainly be attributed to the causal influences of democracy.[4]

Over the past fifty years, it is possible to see evidence of such complex mixes of upward and downward egalitarian effects in different aspects of Indian social life. To take social life in West Bengal, it is easy to point to undeniable upward equality in at least two things: codes of dress and the Bengali spoken language. In the 1950s, the map of West Bengal was far more linguistically diverse, with a majority of small townspeople speaking spontaneously in a pronounced regional dialect. Even the city of Calcutta was a richly polyglot society in terms of the accents of spoken Bengali. Formal middle-class Bengali was sharply different from the lower-class Bengali spoken in the bazaars by shopkeepers or fishmongers, who were far less concerned about their linguistic self-presentation. The joint efforts of the radio and the popular films, and the unseen efficacy of social emulation, has levelled up spoken Bengali to an astonishing degree and consequently homogenized it.

[4] One of the major problems with de Tocqueville's analysis of American and French democracy is precisely its monocausal intensity. He is undoubtedly a great observer of social change, and even the minutest shifts do not escape him. The problem, however, is his readiness to attribute all these transformations to the single causal line of democracy, rather than capitalism, or industrialization, or spread of modern science. Even when such causal forces are acknowledged, exactly like the more sophisticated forms of Marxism, these are further attributed to a deeper causality of democracy. Democracy is thus given a primacy very similar to the status enjoyed by production in Marx's theory, as the cause of causes.

In the Calcutta bazaar in the late 1990s, there is little noticeable difference between the language of the buyer and lower-class sellers. Pavement hawkers, especially of the younger generation, in the Gariahat shacks, standardly speak a Bengali popularized by the film idol Uttam Kumar and the radio newscaster Debdulal Bandyopadhyay. That does not mean that the world of the spoken language has become one of equality. Upper-class people obviously look for new markers of difference, so that following the utterance of the first spoken sentence, they are not confused with common Bengalis. This is accomplished by either switching entirely to English, affecting a lack of fluency in Bengali, a cultivated English accent that conveys to their listeners of the English standing close, if inarticulate, behind their Bengali. Even the deep baritone which is now mandatory for speeches on dialectical materialism or such other aspects of the serious mysteries of the universe, or the conspiracy of the central government against the imminent prosperity of West Bengal, has radiated from these models of universal cultural emulation.

The second example, again, taken from Calcutta's cultural history can be generalized more easily across the whole of India. Again, in the 1950s, there was a clear distinction in the dress worn by people from various social strata. The Bengali office-going dress of either the expensive dhoti and *punjabi*, or shirt and trousers, was strictly limited to middle-class professionals. All the rest wore either coarser dhotis with upper vests, or some other combination which set off their difference from the middle-class élite; and in the second class coaches of Calcutta trams, one would often meet people wearing a *ganji*, or entirely without an upper garment, which was the national uniform of the peasantry. By the 1980s, these dress differentials had been almost entirely erased in favour of the universal synthetic shirts and trousers, worn of course with the usual class differentials of style and cleanliness. It is difficult, at least in urban India today, to make class distinctions in terms of the dress worn outside the home.

At the same time, there are other strands that go in the opposite direction. All societies would require some types of functions to be performed with effectiveness. It is essential, if this is true, to distinguish between various levels of excellence in performing social functions or basic social practices. If practising medicine is considered significant for the society, it is essential to first recognize and then reward excellence in this field—to recognize distinction. This cannot be accomplished without some differentiation of performance. Tocqueville makes a powerful case that under conditions of political democracy, when this is translated into a *social* principle, it might become impossible to defend this necessity of recognizing distinction. Rhetorically, distinction is immediately assailed as unfair discrimination, and equality of treatment mistakenly extended to block any process that discriminates between excellence and mediocrity as discrimination on grounds of untenable social prejudice. Interestingly, under some circumstances, certain types of arguments of modern social science might reinforce such trends. It might be pointed out, for instance, that social institutions are constructed and socially produced conventions. Distinctions in particular practices are therefore merely constructs, usually serving to maintain the dominance of ruling social groups. Therefore, a defence of 'excellence' is a fraud calculated to maintain social dominance. In India, such arguments are insistently pressed with regard to educational practices, and efforts to raise standards beaten down by arguments of 'democracy'. In West Bengal, one of the most interesting instances is the constant undermining of an educational institution like Presidency College on the basis of a confusion that automatically equates distinction with privilege. It is dedicated to the destruction of a centre of intellectual excellence under the mistaken belief that it is a bastion of upper-class predominance.

Let me now state my cultural argument succinctly. I think democracy has brought in an enormous change in the language, culture, and semiotics of the dislike that ordinary people feel for their social superiors. They have come out of the cultural structure of *representativity* reflected in the songs I mentioned at the start. The poor and the disprivileged have rejected the restraints and alienation imposed by that representativity. Due to the sheer expansion of capitalism, the number of the professional middle-class elite has grown massively, and also the illusion that it is a world unto itself, and consequently its display and arrogance has also increased prodigiously. Life inside that world of high capitalism is not, of course, ideal and has its own predicaments, despairs, and indignities, but through the peculiar transparency of wordless images, these social relations are somehow filtered out and suppressed, creating our own Indian version of the material enchantment of capitalism. The restraints of traditional society have broken down on both sides of the barrier of classes—both for the poor and the wealthy. Conventional Hindu society, of course, cultivated in the poor the most abject gestures of supplication, deference, and self-abjection. One of its rare attractions was, however, that it bound the comparatively wealthy by parallel ties of restraint. All this has changed irreversibly. Modern consumerist capitalism has destroyed the restraints associated with wealth.

On the other side too, cultural changes have been no less remarkable. Conventional restraints on poverty have broken down, but that has not been replaced, as in some Western cultures, by a culture of social egalitarianism. Increasingly, the docility fostered by the caste system is being replaced by a tendency on the part of the poor and oppressed to assert themselves, giving rise to a culture of insubordination. I think the trend in the recent decades of the popular Hindi movies reflects this culture of insubordination, making a constantly repeated spectacle of narrative humiliation of the affluent. The enormous popularity such films enjoy must, at least in part, be due to this taste for social defiance. They offer a dream, not of rags to riches like American romances, but the bitter dream of the poor of an entirely symbolic retribution for their lifelong ignominy in a single great act of retributive humiliation. This logic is not limited to the collective fantasy of the cinema hall where real social relations are suspended for two hours; the real world is obscured into non-existence and the audience can enjoy the pleasures of inversion; where the lonely man can fight a gangster machine to death, the wronged mother's son bring eventual retribution, powerful criminals and their politician accomplices brought to divine, usually not constitutional, justice, and the poor can draw revenge for the insults of the rich. Indocility spills over into reality in the gratuitous, often spectacular, rudeness to social superiors, especially if there is an audience around, in a fight unto death for recognition on city streets. This is done by the annoyance caused by microphones directed strategically and aggressively at the quiet privacy of the middle-class high-rise flats, by the wilful desecration of legal or parliamentary procedural symbolism in our political institutions. All around us in Indian society of today, there are signs of this rising insubordination.

There are serious limits, however, to what such insubordination can achieve. The elite does not take these developments supinely, with an air of resignation. They conceive of strategic countermoves through a restructuring of inequalities, selecting a terrain on which the assertive lower groups would suffer a disadvantage, through disingenuousness or coercion, usually an improvised combination of both. To understand the reasons for their persistent advantage despite democratic advances by the poor, it is important to differentiate between the material and intellectual sides of culture. Social elites not merely have greater control of economic assets, but also of cultural capital. For advancing groups and individuals from the lower classes, once they achieve some economic improvement of their condition, it is easy to acquire the material culture of modern life. Access to intellectual culture is much more difficult. Also, usually, upward class or power mobility is achieved by a small number of individuals from these social groups which are among the most numerous. Achievement of political pre-eminence by a few among them cannot solve the real problems of the majority of these groups. Politicians are thus tempted to large symbolic solutions. These might take the form of purely symbolic acts of a positive or a negative kind, exaltation of Dalit symbols, or relegation of upper-caste icons to a relatively modest place, or relatively inexpensive reallocation of government benefits like reservation of jobs. Insubordination can produce cathartic climaxes in cinema halls, precisely because these stories have ends; but they are far less decisive in the unendingness of everyday life. When the battle between domination and insubordination resumes in the daylight of social reality, it turns into a matter of economic and cultural capital, not just single-handed daring against upper-class condescension. Despite its hallowed, now mummified source, the statement that 'if injustice is the order of the day, disorder is the beginning of justice' is a misleadingly one-sided and over-optimistic idea. It does not take into serious account as a historical possibility the indefinite attrition we find in different parts of the world today. Gramsci's view is, to my mind, more historically responsible: equating revolution with a moral and imaginative project, along with the practical capacity of subaltern classes to create a 'new order'. Insubordination will not disappear because, though episodic, indecisive, it is immensely satisfying, particularly when people have no other means of expressing their sense of injustice.

In a society with a deep memory of caste, it is an act of protest against a social order that has lost its moral legitimacy. Despite the immense satisfaction of the occasional act of defiance, it leaves the world as it found it. It creates a sharp, shocking, spectacular occasion of inverted inequality, but has no means of creating an equal status. It is not surprising that the discourse of the lower castes and Dalit activism largely remains within this form of symbolic insubordination, without more serious reflection on the means by which society can achieve principles of equality. We must beware, however, of an excessive and unthinking materialism which finds this snatching of prestige entirely unreal. I wish to supplement my Marx with my Tocqueville precisely because I believe modernity sets in motion two processes of redistribution—not only of assets, but also of the intangible good of prestige.

How does democracy affect distinction, turning back to Tocqueville's great anxiety. It is essential, I think, to make a further distinction between distinction in the narrower sense and privilege, to understand the problem seriously, and to go beyond Tocqueville's despairing answer. Though we must acknowledge the historical connection between social privilege and cultural refinement, I am suspicious of a peculiarly undiscerning radicalism which thinks all claims to distinction are a conspiracy of the propertied. Although this argument originates from Dalit and lower caste groups, its consequences for the reproduction of social skills can be fatal. It is understandable that there is a subtle and despairing perception of the truth of the case I have been making in this claim. When subaltern groups realize the tenacity of cultural privilege, the intractability of these to state actions, and the capacity of the ruling classes to rewrite the rules of the game when they seem to be losing the present one, there can be an understandable urge to question all cultural and cognitive distinction as being socially constructed cultural capital. But this argument is dangerous, because its implication is the most widespread levelling down of culture, a trend clearly discernible in the politics of Indian education. For any society to flourish, to improve the base and the high points of the skills on which its reproduction depends, it is essential to draw a distinction between a high and a mediocre performance in a necessary function, and separate them from those that are poor. Not merely in intellectual fields like science and the arts, but in the useful arts as well, it is possible to establish claims of distinction. Unfortunately, such distinction is rarely a result of pure talent. The development and flourishing of talent requires social conditions of support which the privileged either exclusively enjoy, or enjoy in a disproportionately greater degree. It is hardly a matter of surprise that in the city of Calcutta, there are more numerous poets among the petty bourgeoisie than among tram drivers. This argument should not, however, be confused with a sociological fact. If tram drivers could be provided with equality of conditions for becoming poets, there would still be the need to distinguish between the excellent poets and the rest. In other words, I do not subscribe to the view which would maintain that the eminence of Tagore in modern Bengali poetry is essentially a matter of upper-class conventions. Given different conventions, someone else, from a suitably plebian origin, could be held to be the great poet of modern Bengali. It is precisely the analytic distinction of excellence from mediocrity and the social conditions required for the cultivation of excellence which makes this problem so difficult to handle.

Clearly, there can be two lines of reasoning which can flow out of this problem. The first would be to argue that since there is a connection between cultural excellence and social privilege, the project of rewarding excellence itself should be abandoned as undemocratic. This would lead to the Tocquevillean scenario of levelling down; but in actual fact, no society can afford to do this in a literal sense. The practical consequence of this is usually some mechanism by which majoritarian politics in some form, usually through the instrumentality of an elected government, gains the right to confer fraudulent eminence on people of its choice. Indira Gandhi's regime followed this practice singlemindedly, with seriously negative consequences for the fields of education and culture. But other governments have often followed the same line of action to the great detriment of regional cultures.

Distinction, if we accept that it exists and is not a socially maintained illusion, is threatened simultaneously by privilege and plebian power. Both types of actual privilege in Indian society—the market-based privilege of money and the state-based one of political power—wish to purchase, entice, corrupt, or overpower various forms of cultural excellence. Conversely, there is sometimes pressure from subaltern groups, particularly their politicians, to suffocate distinction in quest for a means of eradicating privilege. Precisely because democracy is such a strongly legitimate principle, it creates a temptation among people to apply it to all circumstances. It is appropriate to some types of decision-making, but it tends to spread to others, and if misapplied to other spheres, like education, it produces a typical situation where distinction, as much as individuality, becomes immensely vulnerable. It is always possible to encircle excellence and bring it down by the 'legitimate' power of numbers. In our society, I see this in the excessive and inappropriate 'politicization' of all kinds of practices—from the educational to the artistic. In this regard, European societies of early modernity followed a substantially different trajectory.

In early modern Europe, most social groups regarded the absolutist state as both an indispensable necessity and a potential danger. It provided the fundamental political order and civil peace which was a precondition for all 'civilized' pursuits, particularly of commerce. But social groups were at once apprehensive about the state's power—the merchants of its ability to tax them to ruin, the peasantry of its tendency to extract excessive rent, ordinary citizens of its readiness to send them to their deaths in useless wars, the intellectuals of its capacity to stifle them in the name of high principles. This deep mistrust of the state, out of their historical experience, led to the origin of two different strategies. One was to alter the nature of the state by imposing accountability on its use of power by devising institutions and rules of constitutionalism, *rechtstaat*, and later representative democracy. There was also an additional safeguard through the implicit distinction between the spheres of the state and civil society that jealously reserved certain social practices and their typical domains from the interference of the state—from the functioning of commercial firms, to the self-regulation of the universities, etc. A whole range of institutions housing useful practices were kept away from the control of the state in the name of a principle of autonomy of civil society. The state responds to requests of regulation, but usually these are recognized to have a character that is public, but not state–political. Developed liberal societies are, of course, not entirely free from state interference, and in certain historical phases, as in the Thatcherite and Reaganite era, such autonomy of civil society institutions was seriously eroded, ironically in the name of a free market society. But Western societies have political resources that enable them to fight back in the name of liberalism and the value of the pursuit of excellence in different fields of intellectual or artistic creation.

In our case, without a historical tradition that produced such entrenched jealousies of a civil society, other practices are peculiarly powerless against the interference of a democratic state. This happens on two counts—because it is the state, and secondly, because it is democratic. What I mean by this is that arguments against state interference, while occasionally conceded, are then outflanked by the different one that this state is democratic; and therefore what Laloo Prasad Yadav or Jayalalitha wish to be done about educational appointments is in effect part of the process of the reflexivity of what that particular society itself wants to do to. Consequently, there is an emerging idea of publicity, or what is public, but this lacks internal differentiation, that is, different types of publicity which have to be treated quite differently, and in particular subjected to different types of deliberative processes. There is only one form of the public, and that is legitimately the sphere of the state, not to control through the mediated form of regulation, but by straight direction. It takes only a small step in this slippery slope to say that by a natural extension of the elective principle, these spheres must become provinces of influence of the majority party. Thus, the historical situation in terms of practical concepts of political life is strangely paradoxical. There is an over-extension of the public sphere and an under-differentiation of the forms of publicity. The natural consequence of this is a rapid encirclement of excellence and its razing by the weight of numbers.[5]

But what, finally, about a more radical argument which suggests that these trappings of culture are not indispensable? Do we really need education? Or is it merely a conspiracy of the adventitiously

[5] I know of a university where a Scheduled Caste professor said he rejected the idea of a distinction between mediocrity and excellence. It was basically a conspiracy of the upper castes: the basic difference was between those who spoke English and those who did not. This is an interesting point. Undoubtedly, in many Indian universities, including the one in question, fluency in English passed off as thoughtfulness, causing enormous harm to academic practice. It is, however, a typical conflation of two distinctions to say that due to this, distinction is largely an upper caste/class conspiracy to keep the lower orders out of jobs.

educated to create an illusion of their own indispensability? I think it is a bit of both. Every society requires reproduction of skills to carry on the basic business of civilized living—but of course skills are learned, not always attained, through education. The idea that people learn everything through a formal, institutionalized education process is a typical educated prejudice. Modernity intensifies the process of integration of the world, and societies are placed in relations of potential generalized competitiveness and exploitation by this narrowing of the world. Marx's accent on structures and logics underlying the flow of events needs, as he clearly saw, cognitive strategies for understanding and charting them. Educative systems, particularly social theory, is an essential part of this cognitive and deliberative equipment of societies to cope with modernity's peculiar plasticity. The general accent on plasticity also requires theoretical and cognitive vigilance, to sense, anticipate, understand, and use the direction in which this plastic might suddenly collapse and reform. A degradation of the deliberative process in a society would reduce its ability to deal with history. We must not allow these deliberative processes and the capacity to produce original, distinctive, acute pictures of the present as history to decline, if we are not to slide into an extreme form of disjunction between making and choosing. In the present world, it is easy to fall into a state when we 'make' our own history, not as we but others please.

8

Power and Knowledge in Development Discourse: New Social Movements and the State in India[+][*]

Pramod Parajuli

Development as Discourse

The time is ripe to undertake a critical analysis of relations between new social movements in India, the role of the state, and the discourse on development. Conventional assumptions about development have reached an impasse. New social movements of women, indigenous people, and the rural poor are challenging statist indicators of growth and asserting livability, sustainability, and equality as new parameters of development. This new discourse has important implications for the development paradigm and the knowledge claims of the state, for the new social movements express a sustained critique of the ideology of

[+] *International Social Science Journal*, no. 127, 1991, pp. 173–90.

[*] This analysis evolved out of my two years of travelling (1987–8) and participating in various grassroots movements in India and Nepal. I wish to acknowledge the insights I have derived from various ecological groups in the Jharkhand region in India and my mother and her friends in my own village in Gunjanagar, Chitwan, Nepal. At Stanford, I have benefited from interaction with Elizabeth Enslin and Richard Haavisto at various stages of this text. I am especially grateful to Akhil Gupta and Pradeep Dhillon for pointing me to the complexities of the Indian political economy. I am, however, solely responsible for any shortcomings.

development. In addition, they are challenging the role of the nation-state as the guardian of the subaltern groups. Finally, they are regenerating and rearticulating the existing knowledge of the subaltern groups as a valid system of thought, to contest the basic idea of what we mean by knowledge and who the knowers are.

The emergence of new social movements coincides with the declining hegemony of the development discourse both in the 'First World' (Sutton 1989; Nerfin 1986; Friberg and Hettne 1988) and in the 'Third World' (Addo 1988; Kothari 1988; Nandy 1987; Shiva 1988; Chatterjee 1986). Following Paulo Freire, I refer to the First and Third Worlds not as geographic divisions but sectors of populations divided by the equation of power. I argue that the Third World is a political concept symbolizing a world of silence, of oppression, of dependence, of exploitation, of violence exercised by the ruling classes over the oppressed (Parajuli 1986). In this sense, the so-called First World has its own Third World, and the Third World also has its own First World. While in the First World the critique of development is focused on maldevelopment and overdevelopment, in the Third World, it is the crisis of survival and identity which informs the growing discontent with development.

I will analyse this contestation between the development discourse and the new social movements by using Gramsci's notion of 'hegemony' (Gramsci 1971, 1985)[1] and Foucault's notion of 'discourse' (Foucault 1980, 1988)[2] to demonstrate that hegemony is constructed within the field of discourse.

The contestation between the new social movements and the state are discourses because they are relations that are not fixed

1 There is a rich literature on the Gramscian notion of hegemony. Hegemony in Gramscian terms is a predominance obtained by consent rather than by force of one class or group over other classes through myriad ways in which institutions of civil society diffuse and popularize the world-views of the ruling classes to such an extent that the subaltern classes perceive and evaluate social reality in that context. In other words, it is the orchestration of the will of the subordinates into harmony with the established order of power (Gramsci 1971; Carnoy 1984; Sasson 1986).

2 Foucault suggests that the field of discourse is primarily constituted by relations of power while the primary effect of knowledge is the exercise of these relations. Discourse is a field of strategies and tactics that create differentiations, by posing limits on what can be stated and by whom.

once and forever. They are hegemonic relations in which the meaning of each element in the relationship is contestable. Foucault (1980) suggests that power has no centre, it is dispersed throughout the social formation in various sites of power. Each site of power expresses a relation of exploitation and subordination. If exploitative relations separate direct producers from what they produce dominative relations differentiate in terms of ethnic, social, and religious forms.

Gramsci's notion of hegemony is important to analyse this contestation as well. Although Gramsci considered the class conflicts as the central relations in history, he broadened it to an 'ensemble of relations' to cover a broad terrain of struggle spanning from politics and economics to philosophy, culture, and ideology (Carnoy 1984). He argued that hegemony is not a political process played out between the polar opposites of an imposing 'dominant' culture and the 'weak' subordinate culture but between two contending ideologies. That is why the culture of the subordinate groups never confronts the dominant culture in either a completely supine or totally resistant fashion. In the struggle to open their own spaces for resistance and affirmation, subordinate cultures have to negotiate and compromise around both those elements they surrender to dominant culture and those they keep as representative of their own interests and desires (Bennett 1987). Ranajit Guha, the subalternist historian, has captured this dialectic succinctly:

> ...hegemony stands for a condition of dominance (D) such that, in the organic composition of the latter, Persuasion (P) outweighs Coercion (C). Defined in these terms hegemony operates as a dynamic concept and keeps even the most persuasive structure of Dominance always and necessarily open to Resistance. [Guha 1989: 231]

Today, the development discourse articulates a relation of domination–subordination between the First World and the Third World. In this imperialist scheme of development, the Third World is peripheralized in theory as well as in concrete relations. Theoretically, the First World subjugates the Third World in many ways, such as 'exclusion', 'discrimination', and 'recognition'.[3] Through exclusion, the First World renders the Third World

[3] These apt terminologies are from Franco (1988) who uses them to analyse the subordination of Latin American literature by the North American and European ones.

irrelevant in the formulation of development theory. The First World also discriminates against the Third World's knowledge, degrading it as irrational and inferior to Western rationality. Even when the Third World is recognized, the First World portrays it as a region of the unconscious and a source of fantasy (Franco 1988; Nandy 1989).

As a hegemonic discourse, development works at various levels. First, it links nation-states with the global circulation of capital by fostering a world culture based on modern technology and a pervasive communications and information order (Kothari 1988; Abdel-Malek 1981). It tries to homogenize not only economic but secular and temporal space as well. As Mouffe (1988: 92) argues, 'capitalist relations have penetrated most aspects of our lives: culture, leisure, death, sex—everything is now a field of profit for capital'. The logic of the capital accumulation process subordinates the Third World to the First World, both by destroying its environment and by transforming everyone into a consumer.

The nation-state in the Third World is a problematic concept. The modern state did not evolve in the Third World in a natural way. Its structure was imposed by Europe and promoted as the engine of the post-colonial ideology of development and progress. Recognized by the international order as the only legitimate agent of social change, development was to be carried out only by modern state apparatuses, not by traditional ones. As Sheth (1989: 619) has accurately observed, those in the Third World have to live either as people without a state or in a state which is not theirs. The expansion of the European model of the state to the rest of the world was advantageous to the European core. It became easier for the European nation-states to co-operate with one another and retain their own sovereignty while establishing hegemony over the new nation-states.

At the same time, states in developing societies mediate between the 'universal consciousness of capital' and population sectors marginalized by it, such as women, indigenous people, and the rural poor. The state subjugates these groups to the dominant discourse of national elites. In the discourse of development, the state is mandated to unify the national economy, to establish a common national market, and to impose linguistic and cultural norms. The Indian state has mediated class, ethnic, gender, and caste conflicts through the medium of secularism, political democracy, and the capitalist economic system. Although couched in a vocabulary of 'protection and development', the development discourse of the Indian state subordinates women, *dalits*, tribals, and minority populations. Under the guise of a welfare state, national elites have transformed caste, gender, and ethnicity from relations of difference into relations of domination. Each social entity is both defined by the state and ordered in relation to the state. As the official guardian and development of these groups, the state denies them any creative alternative.

New social movements challenge, to borrow Octavio Paz's phrase, 'the philanthropic ogre' of the modern nation-state which aspires to be a dominating force with totalitarian ambitions and at the same time claims to be guardian of its citizens. It tries to regulate both 'accumulation' and 'legitimation', 'capitalism', and 'democracy'. As representatives of 'people-nations' new social movements challenge the state's authority and its claim to represent the people. By affirming the local, the regional, and the ethnic, actors of new social movements are attempting to overcome both the economic exploitation and politico-cultural subordination by the state. While the Indian state tries to integrate everybody as a citizen (through democratic electoral processes) and as a consumer (through the free market), the actors of social movements seek autonomous social governance (Sheth 1989). Although the basis of social governance may have been destroyed to a great extent by state and development-induced changes, some of the movements are in the process of regenerating. Certain alternatives are represented in Mahatma Gandhi's version of 'village republics' (Chatterjee 1986: ch. 4; Parekh 1989: ch. 5) as well as the notion of a 'civil state' (Sheth 1989: 626). Other possible forms are likely to emerge as the feminist, ecological, and indigenous people's movements articulate alternative forms of governance.

New social movements are distinct from traditional anti-systemic movements such as oppositional parties in two ways. First, the focus of these movements is not to capture state power through elections or a violent revolution but rather to transform the nature of politics itself. Second, new social movements in India and elsewhere dispel the myth of a vanguard. In these movements, antagonisms are expressed not only through class but through multiple 'sites of power' such as gender, ethnicity, caste, and regional identity.

Partiality of Counterhegemonic Movements

This tension between the developmentalist state and new social movements can best be characterized as a struggle for hegemony. Hegemonic relations, by their very nature, are neither unidirectional nor monolithic. They are fraught with resistances and breaks. Both hegemonic and counterhegemonic movements interact with each other in the field of power through idioms of consent as well as contestation. If the Indian state uses both coercion and persuasion to generate consent for development, the counter-hegemonic movements of the marginalized use the dual strategy of 'collaboration' and 'resistance'. This is why we find tensions within the dominant development discourse as well as within the new social movements.

I extend Guha's (1989) exposition of the idioms of domination and subordination in pre-colonial and colonial India to analyse contemporary development discourse. I argue that the Indian state's development metaphor projects as protector/benefactor of the underprivileged. There is a continuity of metaphors through pre-colonial, colonial, and post-colonial India. Development is a contemporary substitute of the ideology of *dharma* in pre-colonial India and 'improvement' in colonial India (Guha 1989).

Constituent elements	Pre-colonial[4]	Colonial	Post-colonial
Coercion	*Danda*	Order	Law and order
Persuasion	*Dharma*	Improvement	Development/ protection
Collaboration	*Bhakti*	Obedience	Participation in development
Resistance	*Dharmic* dissent	Rightful dissent	New social movements

[4] The pre-colonial configuration of domination and subordination was guided by the supreme concepts not only of the prerogatives of coercion (*Danda*) but also an obligation to protect, foster, support, and promote the subordinate (*Dharma*). *Dharma* also implies on the part of the subordinates conforming to one's place in the hierarchy of caste, class, age, and gender. The subordinates, on the other hand, simultaneously used the complete servility to the deity as if self-induced and voluntary (*Bhakti*) and moral opposition to the king's authority if it fails to protect the subordinate (Guha 1989: 239–71).

A full explanation of the above formulation goes beyond the scope of this article. My purpose in juxtaposing the discourse of development in the historical context of domination and subordination within Indian polity here is to show how development is contested by the subaltern groups. I argue that contemporary debates on Indian development exemplify the dialectics between persuasion and collaboration, coercion and resistance. On the one hand, India's durable democratic tradition has created the political space in which new social movements have emerged. On the other, increasing bureaucratization and political centralization in the 1970s and 1980s have repressed local struggles for autonomy. While new social movements have sometimes benefited from state-sponsored developmental and welfare programmes, even these serve as avenues of contestation with the state.

In the cause of development, the state generates one programme after another in order to co-opt people's initiatives. For example, after a decade of grassroots struggles by women, indigenous people, and the rural poor, the recent strategy of the Indian state has been to co-opt their issues as if the problem of ecological deterioration and subordination of women could be solved within the dominant development paradigm. However, as the state is committing itself more and more to these issues, the contradictions between capitalist accumulation and democracy are becoming clearer, which has revealed not only the contradiction between capital and labour but also the contradiction arising from breaking up the natural circulation of matter between humans and the earth. The state's ability to mobilize both ideological and material resources for development programmes is facing an acute crisis.

New social movements use multiple strategies to counteract state power by applying their own indicators to assess the desirability of development. The issue, they argue, is not merely to integrate women into development or to 'catch up with men', it is to seek identity and autonomy for those peripheralized by the state's development policies. New social movements like *dharmic* dissent in pre-colonial India and rightful dissent in colonial India represent the resistance of subalterns.

As carriers of emerging hegemony, new social movements are neither uniform nor devoid of tensions. The debates and tensions within the women's, indigenous peoples', and ecological movements in India are by no means resolved. They do not have a uniform code of do's and don'ts, neither are they imprisoned by universal categories or predetermined visions. More significantly, at the core of these movements there is a self-critical spirit and a sustained inner struggle. In each struggle, there is an internal tension between grasping available opportunity and claiming identity, between participating in the existing politico-economic space and seeking autonomy. A new culture is emerging from social conflicts that appear within this process of transformation (Touraine 1988).

In the following sections the tension between the Indian state and the popular classes in women's movements, forest movements, and anti-dam movements is delineated.

Women's Movements

Contemporary women's movements in India are the most visible and assertive in challenging the established political, economic, and cultural order. They may potentially offer an alternative framework not only for relations between men and women, but also for relations between humans and their environment, knowledge and power, the state and civil society.

Women's movements in India are neither homogenous in composition nor uniform in orientation. I identify three distinct trends: 'developmentalist', 'socialist-feminist', and 'eco-feminist'.[5] Working under the theoretical umbrella of 'Women in development' the developmentalist orientation has attempted with considerable success to obtain state patronage for the economic benefit of women. The liberal Indian state has made a commitment to uplift and integrate women into its development programmes following the Women's Decade (1975–85).

The eco-feminist and socialist-feminist orientations have also utilized the liberal developmentalist ideology of the Indian state as well as the positive atmosphere brought about by the Women's

[5] These categories are not fixed and by no means perfect. Nor do the women of India or even activists in the movements categorize themselves in these terms. On the contrary, a given women's group could be categorized as 'developmentalist' on one occasion, 'socialist-feminist' on another, and eco-feminist' on yet another issue. However in regional and national affiliations and networkings, such orientations are becoming distinct.

Decade to focus public attention on the oppression of women in the domestic and public spheres. In the domestic sphere, they have raised issues surrounding dowry deaths, male violence against women, and problems of inheritance. Women's movements in rural India have also taken up issues of equal pay for women, and struggled to implement employment guarantee schemes and minimum wage laws. Rural women have struggled to protect the ecological niches which guaranteed bio-mass availability for agriculture, animal husbandry, food, water, and fresh air.

Women have become increasingly aware, in their campaigns against the dowry and other social ills, that they are only attacking the symptoms, not the disease itself (Omvedt 1989). They have come to the conclusion that they should be fighting for inheritance rights, land, and property. They have begun to show that state-induced development subordinated women. They argue that the patriarchal state and its capitalist model of development is a major factor in the subordination of women. Modern technology and the Green Revolution in rural India have displaced and subordinated female labour to male labour. The decline in female labour is highest (approximating 90 per cent) in Punjab—the heartland of the Green Revolution—followed by Tamil Nadu, West Bengal, and Maharashtra, three states where capitalist relations of production in the agricultural sector are most visible (Kelkar 1981).

Studies have shown that while women's work increases, its value decreases because it produces for family consumption and not for the market. For example, Srilata Batliwala's study shows that the contribution of women, men, and children in rural India is 53, 31, and 16 per cent (of total work hours per household per day), respectively (as cited in Shiva 1988: 118). Nonetheless, women are paid less and fed less. Their prestige and status with respect to the cultivation of cash crops for the market decreases because they lose decision-making power regarding the requirements of grain at home or in the pricing and income of grain.

Women's increasing ecological concerns cannot be overestimated. To an alarming extent, the reduction in soil fertility is due to the reductionist methods of scientific agriculture, forestry policies, and big dams. According to one estimate, India is losing at least 2.5 million hectares of land every year. As a result, the amount of cultivable land *per capita* has decreased from 0.48 hectares in 1951 to 0.26 in 1981 (Chowdhary 1989: 141). The capital-intensive agriculture introduced by the Green Revolution destroys soil fertility by depleting soil nutrients (Shiva 1988: 143). In addition, such agriculture demands too much water but conserves less.

Rural Indian women see the interdependence of soil fertility and the sustenance of life resources. Whether it is an attempt to stop bauxite mining in Gandhamardan, Orissa, limestone mining in the Doon Valley, or uranium mining in Singhbhum, Jharkhand, these women express a world view which understands the interdependence of water, soil, forest, and agriculture. It is ironic that the Indian state has failed either to protect or to develop these peasant economies. As a result, a critique of the state has become a central focus in feminist movements.

These ecological and agrarian issues have widened the differences between those women's groups seeking state patronage and those seeking autonomy from the state. If developmentalists accuse autonomists of becoming too political, anti-state, and anti-male, the autonomists accuse developmentalists of merely integrating women into patriarchal maldevelopment. The differences within the eco-feminist and socialist-feminist orientations are worth considering. Although both are anti-patriarchal, and anti-capitalist, the eco-feminist critique is focused against the homogenizing project of technological and capitalist development (Shiva 1988), while the socialist-feminist critique is focused on women's oppression under semi-feudal relations of production (Omvedt 1987). These debates should not be seen as dividing lines but as a positive process in cultural development and self-criticism. Only through such debates will a feminist theory of the state and development emerge.

Feminist challenges to the hegemony of the Indian state have begun to emerge both on academic and activist fronts. While recent analysis of Indian nationalism has demonstrated the subordination of gender to patriarchal high-caste values (Chatterjee 1989; Chakravarti 1989), women's activist groups have shown that the state not only uses its own violence but also is one of the sources of violence against women in the family, workplace, or neighbourhood. Women's groups are establishing the linkages between state, capitalism, and patriarchy (Kothari 1986; Shiva 1988). Such views dispel the myth of the state as guardian and protector of women.

Forest Struggles

Many communities are also active in a struggle to save and regain local control over forest resources. Tribals, women, and hill people have begun to contest the developmentalist policies of the social forestry programmes promoted by the Indian state and the World Bank. These groups have realized that these programmes promote single, fast-growing species of trees such as eucalyptus and teak to meet the needs of a market economy (Fernandes 1988; Kulkarni 1987). Although teak has higher market value and matures in 40 years as opposed to 60 years, the tribals of Jharkhand and elsewhere have argued that the *saal* (shorea robusta) provides better biomass productivity. People use its seed for oil, its branches for fodder, its leaves and bark for medicine, and its wood for housing. Jharkhandi festivals, such as *Sohrae Karam*, resemble the life cycle of *saal* trees. In hilly and forest economies these trees also act as insurance against famine (Fernandes 1988).

As a result, grassroots movements are pulling out teak and eucalyptus saplings (Omvedt 1987). Small farmers in the Tumkur district of Karnataka pulled out eucalyptus saplings and replaced them with tamarind and mango trees in 1983. Similarly, in 1980, the tribals of Jharkhand pulled out teak saplings and replanted with *saal* saplings.

Only about 10 per cent of India's land was still forested in 1985.[6] Hence, local or state management of the country's remaining forest resources is a critically important issue. Should the state or the people who are directly dependent upon them control these resources? Rural women and indigenous people argue that it is in their vested interest to save trees. For they still retain the *aranya sanskriti* (forest culture) which is based on the 'creative interdependence between human evolution and the protection of forests'.

6 While the Indian government's goal is to retain 33 per cent forest cover and has been able to enclose 22 per cent of land into Forest Department control, recent aerial surveys have shown that only 8–10 per cent is actually under closed forest (Omvedt 1987). According to one estimate, India is losing 1.5 million hectares of forest cover every year (Chowdhary 1989).

Forests are not viewed as a resource in the sense of quantifiable commodity but as the source of light and air, food and water, fertility and sustenance (Bahuguna 1988). The sanctity of trees is preserved by religious and ritual associations such as the *sarna* (sacred grove)[7] among tribals and *tapovan* among the Hindus. For tribals and Hindus alike forests symbolize an inexhaustible source of cosmic fertility (Shiva 1988).

In Jharkhand, I found that tribals had imposed social sanctions on the felling of trees in various ways. For example, tree felling was restricted to certain seasons, as well as to certain stages of the trees' growth. In addition, sacred species of trees or those within the *sarna* complex could never be felled. No one was allowed to cut more trees down than was necessary to meet domestic needs. Forests were treated as an integral part of a life support system that has to be preserved. Furthermore, forest resources were linked to the continuity of the tribe through the creation myths and rituals. Speaking about the native American Indian's ways of knowing, Pam Colorado (1988: 50) shows the intrinsic value of a tree in their consciousness:

> Native science, often understood through the imagery of the tree, is holistic. Through spiritual processes, it synthesizes information from the mental, physical and cultural/historical realms. Like a tree, the roots of native science go deep into the history, body and blood of the land.

The Chipko movement primarily led by women in the foothills of the Himalayas, provides yet another example.[8] Here the issue is to plant ecologically appropriate fodder, fruit, and firewood trees which will sustain the region's water sources and vegetation.

[7] *Sarna* is a cluster of original forest protected since the first settlement of each community. Among Santhals, Undas, and Hos, Sarna is the home of deities and a public space where the community decisions are made and where sacred and the profane meet.

[8] In the 1980s, the Chipko movement had become a household word in ecological consciousness in India. So far the Chipko movement has spread to 300 villages in the northern districts of Uttar Pradesh. Similar movements are spreading in the western Ghats of southern India and the hills of middle India. The Chipko movement was also successful in getting legislative sanction from the Indian state in 1981. The government decree now prohibits felling of trees above 1000 metres all over the country and specifically in areas of 40,000 sq kilometres surrounding Tehri Garhwal district in Uttar Pradesh (Bahuguna 1988).

Chipko's ecological policy is fourfold. Its primary goal is to preserve natural forests. Chipko declares water (besides oxygen and soil) to be the main product of forests. The movement is converting monoculture forests into mixed forests while giving priority to those trees which promote community self-sufficiency in basic needs. Chipko also advocates local community power over forest management (Bahuguna 1988: 9).

Whose Water? The Anti-Big Dam Movements

Big dams are another contested terrain. While the World Bank proposes a water-intensive, technology-intensive, mono-crop agriculture, the Santal, Mundas, and Hos Adivasis of Jharkhand advocate agricultural and water management systems based on prudent water use and locally manageable ponds and tanks. While the construction of large dams takes water from the rural agricultural sector to meet urban and industrial needs, the local technology of building *ahars* (rain water collection systems), ponds, and tanks tries to get optimal use of available water for local agrarian purposes. The popular movement to stop the Subarnarekha Multipurpose Dam Project,[9] for example, has been successful not only in postponing the construction of the dam but also in regenerating indigenous irrigation schemes as an alternative to big dams.

Such grassroots efforts to solve water problems are urgent in a period when India is simultaneously facing acute problems of drought, desertification, and flood. These problems are caused by a model of development which tries to solve the water problem by submerging forests and mountains, diverting rivers, erecting dams, and building canals (Singh 1990).[10] Forest and rivers are

[9] Subarnarekha Multi-Purpose Dam Project is one of the bigger dams to be built in the Jharkhand region. At an estimated cost of $ 127 million, the project promises to irrigate 255,000 hectares of land, provide water for industrial and municipal use, reduce flood damage and generate 10 MW of hydro-electricity. It includes two large dams, one in Chandil on the Subarnarekha river and another in Icha, on the Kharkai river, including two barrages and seven long irrigation canals.

[10] India is the biggest dam builder in the world. More than 1554 dams have been built in India during the last three decades. Among them fifty are major

treated, in the developmentalist vocabulary, in a linear rather than cyclical fashion. Rivers are seen as wild beasts to be tamed, managed, and controlled. As an advertisement for cement in India reads, 'the river is furious, but the dam will hold'.

The anti-dam struggles of marginalized people, on the contrary, have shown that 'damming a river is damning the people'. It is in essence stopping the life cycle. Big dams have resulted in heavy externalities such as low water availability, heavy silting, and waterlogging. Big dams are not the temples that Nehru, the late Indian prime minister, promised but 'burning *ghaats*' (the cremation ground) for the adivasis. Adivasis have paid their own survival and identity as a price for the big dams. Thousands of them have been displaced by these monumental projects. As expressed in the local memory of Santal peasants displaced by the Damodar Valley Corporation (DVC), development resulted in nothing other than their own cremation grounds.[11] The evicted Santals expressed this alienating enterprise in the following manner:

which company came to my land to open a *karkhana*[12]
it awakened its name in the rivers and the ponds calling itself the DVC?
it throws earth, dug by a machine, into the river
it has cut the mountain and made a bridge the water runs beneath
roads are coming, they are giving us electricity
having opened the *karkhana* the *praja*[13] all question them
then ask what his name belongs to
when evening comes they give paper notes as pay
where will I keep these paper notes?
they dissolve in the water.
In every house there is a well which gives water
for brinjal (egg plant) and cabbage
every house is bounded by walls which makes it look like a palace
This santal tongue of ours has been destroyed in the district
You came and made this a bloody burning *ghaat*, calling yourself a DVC.
[as quoted in Shiva 1988: 190]

---

irrigation projects with a command area of over 10,000 hectares each and 517 are medium projects (Omvedt 1987; Singh 1990).

11 Modelled after Tennessee Valley Authority in USA, Damodar Valley Corporation was one of the first river valley projects in India.

12 *Karkhana* means industry with the use of tools and machines.

13 *Praja* is the subject of a ruler, the Raja. Praja here symbolizes the situation of powerlessness.

These lines capture the deep-rooted resistance of indigenous peoples against big dam projects. Development projects have everywhere been intolerant to the voices of tribals, women, and low castes. The scientific, modernized state has a mandate to destroy their ecological niches (Viswanathan 1987). By the logic of development, marginalized people must either acculturate or disappear.

Development, Endogeneity and the Critique of Growth

Development is no longer a sacred cow or an unquestionable truth. The questions that ecological, women's, and indigenous people's movements have posed raise important issues concerning the relation between ecology and economy. How should environmental resources such as forest, water, and minerals be used? For whose benefit? For short-range profit or long-range sustenance of the 'five Fs' fodder, fuel, food, fertilizer, and fibre? Should irrigation and dams be capital-intensive, requiring external technology, and resources, or rely on indigenous technologies?

These movements have demonstrated the two fallacies of development. The first fallacy is that development promotes internal equality. The second fallacy is that development fosters economic growth enabling the underdeveloped to 'catch up' with the developed countries. But it is now evident that what the developing countries followed was the objective of 'catching up' and not that of equality. The cruel irony is that they neither caught up nor achieved equality. Development has neither achieved equality via growth nor will it deliver growth through equality.

The metaphor of growth is now attacked from both grounds, its epistemological premise as well as the possibility of achieving its claims. Epistemologically, growth is not necessarily good and more growth is not always better. Actors of new social movements espouse the ethics of 'survival–sustenance–coexistence and open-endedness' instead of the irreversible process of 'domination–expansion–growth–efficiency', as embedded in developmentalist ideology (Friberg and Hettne 1988). Practically speaking, development is not a matter of scientific knowledge concerned with the achievement of progress but a product of particular historical configurations between the so-called 'First' and 'Third' World.

Yet advocates of the development discourse present these new social movements as groups seeking larger shares in the economic pie. Such a view is the result of a reductionist view of politics and economics. It epitomizes the popular Nepali saying 'money can talk but cannot listen'. These movements are not traditional pressure groups lobbying for their share of the rewards awarded by the development process. They are seeking to redefine the entire matrix of development and progress, survival and identity, body and health, food and nutrition, time and space, nature and humans, men and women. They envision different ways of achieving equality and democracy, autonomy and identity.

In India, as in Europe, a critique of growth is increasingly linked with the criterion of livability (Habermas 1981: 35). The organic foundation of human existence is in crisis. The ecological deterioration has impaired soil fertility, productivity, and, concomitantly, our health. In both places, it is realized that the process of maldevelopment has robbed not only the labourer but the soil as well.

However, there is a difference between the recent interpretations of European movements and those of India. Some (Habermas 1981; Fuentes and Frank 1989; Boggs 1986) argue that the new politics in Europe are concerned primarily with a crisis in the quality of life. They are less concerned with the distribution of economic benefits and services. Unlike those of Europe, the basic thrust of India's ecological and women's movements is to stop the monopolistic control of the rich over their natural resources (Agarwal 1988; Kothari 1988; Omvedt 1987). The conflicts within ecological movements in India are not about 'productive' versus 'protective' uses of the environment; they are about alternative 'productive' uses (Guha 1988). Ecological crisis is caused largely by uneven distribution of resources among different strata of population in a given ecological niche. That is why ecological movements in South Asia propose correctives to the uneven and maldevelopment patterns which created a dual society: the Indian island of consumerism surrounded by the Bharatiya ocean of poverty.[14] While the island of prosperity is inhabited by the 'iron triangle' of the politicians, urban industrialists, rich farmers and bureaucrats,[15] the masses (the tribals, the nomads, the rural artisans, the landless, agricultural labourers, the small and marginalized farmers, and the urban slum-dwellers) live in the ocean of poverty (Gadgil 1990; Kothari 1988). That is why ecological movements in South Asia are at the same time peasant movements, women's movements, and poor peoples' movements.

The beauty of these movements, however, is that the struggle for survival has grown into a struggle for regional autonomy as well as for the formation of ethnic and gender identities. While the struggles found their initial impetus in the concrete problems of diminishing livelihood, they have evolved into a serious questioning of the whole matrix of growth and development.

The Politics of Social Movements: State Power or People's Power?

The political significance of these struggles is that they challenge the notion of the integrationist and developmentalist Indian state. Moreover, there is the recognition that the ruling elite has articulated its class interest as the common interest of the whole nation. The domain of the subalterns, however, could not be incorporated into the ruling class ideology during the struggle for independence nor after independence. While fighting against British rule, nationalist elites subordinated the issues of women, lower castes, and indigenous ethnicities to the hegemonic project of national independence. The tenets of Indian nationalism were based on patriarchal attitudes towards women as well as patronizing attitudes towards *dalits* and tribals. After achieving for

14 This apt phrase of 'India', meaning the modernized sector and 'Bharat', the rural sector is taken from a personal interview with peasant leader, Sharad Joshi in Pune, February 1987.

15 The 'iron triangle' according to the Indian environmentalist, Madhav Gadgil, is composed of three actors, those who enjoy state subsidies (the urban industrialists and the rich farmers), those who decide on subsidies (the politicians), and those who administer subsidies (the bureaucracy).

themselves the power to define and articulate the issues of India's women and minorities, nationalist elites resubordinated them in the name of the greater cause of *swadeshi* (Chatterjee 1989). Portrayed as goddess and mother vis-à-vis the colonial ideology, Indian women were advised to remain inside the patriarchal ethos of Aryan culture. Similarly, *dalit*s and adivasis were put under a strict moral code of caste hierarchy.

The state faces yet another constraint which it derives from the legacy of its linkages with the metropolitan core. The 'universal consciousness of capital' seeks the participation of nation-states as juridical actors irrespective of whether they represent or are supported by the people (Sheth 1989). Chatterjee (1986: 168) accurately captures this paradox of Third World states:

> Conservatory of the passive revolution, the nationalist state now proceeds to find for 'the nation' a place in global order of capital, while striving to keep the contradictions between capital and the people in perpetual suspension.... The state now acts as the rational allocator and arbitrator for the nation. Any movement which questions this presumed identity between the people-nation and the state-representing-the-nation is denied the status of legitimate politics.

The contradictions and limitations of the special tribal and women's development schemes of the Indian state emanate from this historical caveat. The elitist historiography and analysis of the Indian state (Frankel 1978; Rudolph and Rudolph 1987), however, sees politics as the contest between dominant castes and/or geographic regions for power and privilege. It argues that local, provincial, and caste elites compete for their share of the development pie (Guha 1989; Gupta 1989). A much-needed improvement of these analyses is offered by Bardhan (1984) who identifies three dominant proprietary classes: the landed interest, the industrial elites, and the bureaucracy as contesting elements in the Indian state. Although such an analysis shows the relative autonomy of the Indian state over the sections of the ruling elites, it does not explain how the basic legitimacy of the state is contested by the new social movements.

Such analyses do not explicate the inherent contradictions in state development policies: they do not analyse the manner in which states seek legitimacy through various reforms and/or concessions to contending groups (Gupta 1989). The theatre of the state seems like a passive monologue of competing elites without voices of dissent or contestation by the oppressed majority.

Analyses of the state in Europe and the United States have not resulted in a satisfactory view of new social movements either. This gap is felt in both traditions of developmentalist diffusionist approaches (see Kazancigil 1986: 123–5) and neo-Marxist approaches (Carnoy 1984; Therborn 1986). While the former is concerned with developing the state as a vehicle for capitalist/socialist development, the latter is preoccupied with social classes as the central category and does not seriously take into account the agency of women, ethnic groups, and other minorities.

The peripheral state is not only theoretically impoverished; its base is also fragile. It is constrained in its ability to represent 'people-nation' because it emerged by neglecting the indigenous social fabric of institutions, social movements, brotherhoods, and networks of communitarian solidarity which made up civil society in pre-state societies. Kazancigil (1986: 138) has described this poverty of peripheral states succinctly:

> The peripheral state, completely absorbed in the task of constituting itself, building up the apparatus and integrating segmented communities into a nation, has ignored or often seen them only as obstacles to be overcome. Because of this, popular movements and networks of institutions and solidarities, some of which could have been transformed and mobilised into societal resources for the formation of the modern nation state in the periphery, have functioned as counter-powers and centres of resistance against a state that excluded them.

The actors of new social movements are trying to reclaim their lost territory from a developmentalist–integrationist state. They use both offensive and defensive strategies against a shared moral sense of injustice (Fuentes and Frank 1989: 181). In India, such parameters are *dharma* (righteousness) and *nyaya* (justice) (Guha 1989). As Offe (1985) argues, in the context of the new European social movements, the alternative politics of these groups is in dismantling the 'private versus public' paradigm of old politics. By bringing 'private' and the 'domestic' into a legitimate public discourse, new social movements transcend (to borrow his phrase) 'the institutional boundaries of old politics'. Therein lies the hope of transcending the focus from capturing state power to transforming the nature of politics itself.

In India too, the modern parameters of nationhood, citizenship, and democracy are changing, while the identity and autonomy of subalterns are becoming an assertive element rather than an appendage in the nationalist discourse. The new politics as envisioned in these movements integrates both state and civil society in a manner that allows for a dynamic relationship between 'political' and 'social' relations, parties, and movements (Boggs 1986: 19). When civil society becomes autonomous the state will cease to rule over it but become an element within it (Laclau and Mouffe 1985). At the same time there will be no privileged historical political subject; instead, each socio-cultural subject will be endowed with its own symbolic productivity.

Knowledge as a Contested Terrain

New social movements are also sites of creating and regenerating subjugated knowledge. Through these movements, indigenous people, women, and other marginalized groups have reasserted their own knowledge which reflects their autonomy and identity. This knowledge is built on local memories of resistance and struggle in their everyday lives: in other words, a history of struggle informs their system of thought. Resurrection of subjugated knowledge takes place in two ways. First, the movements regenerate subjugated knowledge rendered obsolete by the dominant knowledge. At the same time, they modify it through self-criticism and make that knowledge relevant in the contemporary struggle for their identity and autonomy.

There is a vast difference of meaning between the way the development discourse defines the tenets of underdevelopment and the way the subalterns see it themselves. According to Gustavo Esteva, a deprofessionalized Mexican intellectual, while the former is infused with modern specialization, the latter represents 'plural' and autonomous community values (Esteva 1987). But it is not merely a juxtaposition of 'tradition' versus 'modernity', or 'rural' versus 'urban', or even 'core' versus 'periphery' as found in the development literature. The choice is not between traditional knowledge and modern knowledge; it is between different traditions of knowledge (Nandy 1987). The emergence of subaltern knowledge is an attempt to change the power relations between these traditions. This is not a struggle over mere semantics. The emerging consciousness expresses the subalterns' desire to conquer not only political and economic autonomy but also the power to define themselves, their aspirations, and the development process.

Let us take as an example the power of concepts such as 'underdeveloped', 'backward', 'malnourished', 'slum dweller', 'subsistence farmer' as used in the development discourse. Nobody denies that life at the periphery is extremely difficult. But it is another thing to define it as 'underdeveloped' and argue that this deficiency can only be overcome through foreign aid, industrialization, and the growth of a free market. In these formulations so-called 'Third World' people are treated as patients who need constant medication, advice, and expertise from the 'First World'. There is only one diagnosis—underdevelopment—and only one treatment—the injection of aid (Rahnema 1988). The most dangerous implication of this reductionist view is that developed countries have claimed hegemony not only over the definition of the problem but also its solution.

It is true that during the last forty years the validity of developmentalist concepts has been almost universally accepted in all societies which has turned yesterday's dissent into today's establishment (Nandy 1989: 270). Not surprisingly, much of the discourse in new social movements is also caught up in these categories. However, there is hope. In my own village, in the Himalayan foothills of Nepal, peasants and women understand the environment as an equilibrium of social space, religious merit, and community well-being. For them ecological well-being is embedded in the spiritual act of building *chaupaaris*, planting banyan, pipal, and swami trees around water sources, in village commons, and on pathways. *Chaupaaris* reflect not an isolated knowledge but a knowledge intrinsic to existence. First, *chaupaaris* encourage the planting of trees. Second, they provide a social space around which neighbourhood meetings, village festivities, and religious–cultural discourses occur. Moreover, a *chaupaari* is a marker of social responsibility in that it provides shade and fresh air to weary travellers, cowherds, and goatherds. An ecological movement built on these knowledge systems could also regenerate women's social spaces (Parajuli and Enslin 1990).

Subalterns create social spaces at least partially by referring to symbolic and ritual values bestowed in the past. In Nepal, women have used the socially sanctioned ritual spaces such as *teej*[16] to criticize injustice in patriarchal society. Women in the Sistrens Collective in Jamaica also use the 'tale-telling' tradition as a repository of knowledge in their struggle against a racist and sexist society:

> The tale-telling tradition contains what is most poetically true about our struggles. The tales are one of the places where the most subversive elements of our history can be safely lodged, for over the years tale tellers convert fact into images which are funny, vulgar, amazing and magically real. These tales encode what is overtly threatening to the powerful into covert images of resistance so that they can live on in times when overt struggles are impossible or build courage in moments when it is. [Sistrens Collective 1987: 3.]

Nepalese women's *teej* poems or Jamaican women's tales combine aesthetic imagination with the process of empowerment. Their knowledge is embedded within the ways in which they contest meanings, identities, and knowledge about development in such areas as agriculture, forestry, and water or soil conservation. Although such poems and tales may not be liberating in a clear-cut fashion and although they may be partial and contradictory, they concern the most intimate and long-lasting logic of social struggles.

In Mexico, a Consortium of Analysis, Development and Self-Management (ANADEGES) is involved in regenerating the community strength of the urban barrios of Tepito (only eight blocks from Mexico City's main square). It is promoting what it calls *vision indigena* (indigenous vision) as against *vision colonial* (colonial vision). According to this group native concepts such as *comida* (food and nourishment), *salud* (health, well-being), *morada* (dwelling space: intimacy and society), and *cultura* (human

16 *Teej* is an annual festival exclusively of and for women where they communally bathe in sacred rivers, fast, sing, and dance in order to purify themselves and receive powers of fertility and personality from the Hindu God Shiva (Parajuli and Enslin 1990: 55).

culture) have much deeper and culturally relevant meanings than those preached by the development discourse which has replaced these notions with food provisioning, medical services, housing, and transport as well as educational services (Redclift 1987: 167–70; Esteva 1987). In the context of agricultural communities in the United States, Wendell Berry (1988: 50) makes similar comments:

> People are joined to the land by work. Land, work, people and community are comprehended in the idea of culture.... To presume to describe land, work, people and community by information, by quantities, seems invariably to throw them into competition with one another. Work is then understood to exploit the land, the people to exploit their work, the community to exploit its people. And then instead of land, work, people and community, we have the industrial categories of resources, labor, management, consumers and government.

The rationale behind defining the problem in such quantifiable and observable forms as does the developmentalist discourse is understandable. Such notions give a uniform view of the Third World's problems as well as a uniform solution which is handy to implement and evaluate. But what is lost in this translation is the Nepali peasant's, Jamaican women's, and Mexican slum-dweller's ways of defining the problems and their ways of solving them. The historical agency of those in whose name the project of development is being carried out is subjugated in the process of development.

In doing so, the dominant development discourse subjugates the subaltern's knowledge by perpetuating two assumptions. The first assumption is that subalterns identify with the dominant values and cannot validly interpret their own oppression. The second assumption is that they are cognitively unable to articulate their own standpoint. On the contrary, I find that these subalterns are capable of not only resisting the dominant knowledge but also of articulating their own world views. Their autonomous knowledge in many respects opposes the dominant developmentalist knowledge. For example, while developmentalist rationality equates nature as a resource to be tapped for productivity and profit (WCED 1987), women and tribals in South Asia are showing that nature is the very basis and matrix of economic life (Shiva 1988: 224). For them the elements of nature that the dominant view has treated as 'waste' are the basis of sustainability and wealth.

Many argue that such examples are too local, limited, and contextual to be considered a valid knowledge. This criticism is well taken. For subalterns do not claim universality for their knowledge, as do the hegemonic groups. Haraway's (1988) assertion that feminist knowledge is a 'situated knowledge' applies to the knowledge of other subaltern groups as well. Situated knowledge is neither objective nor relativistic in the old sense of the term. Situated knowledge is a knowledge that is accountable to the knower. It is a knowledge that acknowledges being located in time and space; it is always a marked knowledge. Unlike modern science, it claims no universality and hence no accountability. As Haraway (1988: 583) says about feminist knowledge, only partial perspective promises objective vision:

> All western cultural narratives about objectivity are allegories of the ideologies governing the relations of what we call mind and body, distance and responsibility. Feminist objectivity is about limited location and situated knowledge, not about transcendence and splitting of subject and object. It allows us to become answerable for what we learn and how we see.

Situated knowledge should not be confused with relativism. Situated knowledge negates relativism as much as scientific objectivity. For both do not locate, embody, and accept partiality of knowledge. Both do not take risk and thus make it impossible to see well (Haraway 1988: 584). On the contrary, situated knowledge is intrinsically participatory. As Shiva (1988: 38–41) observes about the ecological knowledge of women in India:

> Ecological ways of knowing nature are necessarily participatory. Nature herself is the experiment and women as sylviculturalist, agriculturalist and water resource managers, the traditional scientists. Their knowledge is ecological and plural, reflecting both the diversity of natural ecosystems and the diversity in cultures that nature-based living gives rise to.

Because it is participatory in process and answerable to the knower, situated knowledge is intentionally political. It echoes the yearning for identity and survival of those who are the victims of exploitation and subordination. However, situated knowledge does not have an essential character. For subalterns know that essentializing is a tool of oppressors, not of the oppressed. If it is in the interest of the oppressor to create unmarked, disembodied, unmediated, transcendent knowledge, it is in the interest of the marginalized to create knowledge that is locatable in time and space, embodied in struggle, and participatory in process. For only such knowledge promises more adequate, sustained, objective, and transforming accounts of the world.

Conclusion: Whither New Social Movements?

Several questions emerge out of the above discussion. How will the politics of new social movements take shape? Will the various movements continue to operate separately or will they find a common ground to form a 'popular-national-will'? How will the knowledge base of these identities be articulated? What will emerge out of these multiple micro-experiments is open to the future. We need to suspend judgement in terms of existing theoretical lenses. What I propose to do is to speculate on the possible future directions.

The new social movements in India provide a counter-discourse to the 'universal consciousness of capital' trying to colonize the precapitalist territory of women, tribals, and rural peasants. As a counter-discourse, new social movements seek and promote personal and collective identity. That is why high value is placed on the particular, small social spaces, decentralized forms of interaction, and non-differentiated public spheres. To borrow Habermas' (1981: 39) phrase, these are in the 'seam between system and life-world'. They are a reaction to the 'colonization' of the life-world by economic and politico-administrative systems. New social movements do not have faith in 'equality via growth'. The aim is not equality or democracy but both.

These movements have also shifted their emphasis away from the capture of state power to reactivating civil society and constructing social movements able to transform their worlds. The crucial question is: how will this reactivated civil society interact with the Indian state and its political parties? The promise of new social movements lies in the fact that the benevolent image of the state in independent India and elsewhere is outdated. More and more, it has become an appendage to market forces and the international economic order. Traditional political parties have also lost the vigour and credibility to provide alternatives.

New social movements in India and elsewhere, however, would be ineffective without global linkages and solidarity. Building multiple movements and linking them worldwide has three fundamental functions. The first function is to demystify development as an inevitable goal for every country. People have become tired of testing one development alternative (such as integrated-development, eco-development, sustainable development) after another. For they find, as Nandy (1989: 270) accurately argues 'most of the efforts are also products of the same world view which has produced the mainstream concept of science, liberation, and development. Now they are seeking an alternative to development itself'. The need of the hour is to give up in Majid Rahnema's (1988) words, development as a 'Frankenstein-type dream' which has damaged, perhaps irreparably in many cases, the inbuilt immune systems of local cultures and subsistence economies. It has become urgent to regenerate these immune systems.

A second task is to seek solidarity among new social movements worldwide by redefining political and economic democracy. Democracy should be defined not only as representative democracy but as a social relation which is consultative and participatory. New social movements have a potential to initiate this participatory process. Participatory democracy necessitates a change in the prevailing notion of power itself. We should begin to recognize that power is not necessarily exercised through the apparatuses of government or political parties but is manifested in every sphere of our lives through cultural, communicative, and ethical forms as well. Thus, the question is not to integrate the new social movements into the nation-states; it is to restructure the state so that it can be accommodated within civil society.

The third task is to evolve a distinctive knowledge system which can represent the experiences of the subaltern groups by using alternative ways of producing and validating knowledge. I am not proposing that women's, *dalit*'s, and indigenous people's knowledge be integrated into a ready-made body of dominant development discourse. For developmentalist knowledge is in many ways antithetical to the best interest of these groups. What I am proposing is a twofold task for the new social movements. First, the folkloric, commonsensical knowledge of these people must be regenerated and made relevant to the contemporary struggles. Second, the language of the dominant development discourse must be reconstructed in appreciation of these knowledge claims from the bottom.

References

Abdel-Malek (1981), A., *Nation and Revolution*, Vol. 2 of *Social Dialectics*. Albany: State University of New York Press.

Addo, H. (1988), 'Beyond Eurocentricity: Transformation and Transformational Responsibility', in H. Addo (ed.), *Development as Social Transformation*, pp. 12–47. Tokyo: United Nations University.

Agarwal, A. (1988), 'Ecological Destruction and the Emerging Patterns of Poverty and People's Protests in India', *Social Action*, vol. 35, 1985, pp. 55–80.

Bahuguna, S. (1988), 'Chipko: The People's Movement with a Hope for the Survival of Mankind', *IFDA Dossier*, no. 63, pp. 3–14.

Bandhopadhyay, J. and V. Shiva (1988), 'Political Economy of Ecology Movements', *Economic and Political Weekly*, 11 June, pp. 1223–32.

Bardhan, P. (1984), *The Political Economy of Development in India*. New York: Blackwell.

Bello, W. (1989). *Brave New Third World? Strategies for Survival in the Global Economy*. San Francisco: The Institute for Food and Development Policy.

Bennett, T. (1987). *Culture, Ideology and Social Process*. Milton Keynes: Open University Press.

Berry, W. (1988), 'People, Land and Community', in R. Simonson and W. Walker (eds), *Multi-Cultural Literary*. Saint Paul, Minn: Graywolf Press, pp. 41–56.

Boggs, C. (1986), *Social Movements and Political Power*. Philadelphia: Temple University Press.

Carnoy, M. (1984). *The State and the Political Theory*. Princeton, NJ: Princeton University Press.

Chakravarti, U. (1989), 'Whatever Happened to the Vedic Dasi? Orientalism, Nationalism and a Script of the Past', in K. Sangari and S. Vaid (eds), *Recasting Women: Essays in Colonial History*. New Delhi: Kali for Women, pp. 22–87.

Chatterjee, P. (1986), *Nationalist Thought and the Colonial World: A Derivative Discourse*. London: Zed.

———— (1989), 'Nationalist Resolution of Women's Question', in K. Sangari and S. Vaid (eds), *Recasting Women: Essays in Colonial History*. New Delhi: Kali For Women, pp. 233–53.

Chowdhary, K. (1989), 'Poverty, Environment, Development', *Daedalus*, Winter, pp. 141–58.

Colorado, P. (1988), 'Bridging Native and Western Science', *Convergence*, vol. 21, no. 2/3, pp. 49–72.

Escobar, A. (1985), 'Discourse and Power in Development: Michel Foucault and the Relevance of His Work to the Third World', *Alternatives*, vol. 10, pp. 377–400.

Esteva, G. (1987), 'Regenerating People's Space', *Alternatives XII*, vol. 1, pp. 125–52.

Fals-Borda, O. (1985), *Knowledge and Peoples' Power*. New Delhi: Indian Social Institute.

Fernandes, W. (1988), *Forest, Environment and Tribal Economy*. New Delhi: Indian Social Institute.

Foucault, M. (1980), *Power/Knowledge: Selected Interviews and Other Writings* (1972–1977). New York: Pantheon.

———— (1988), *Politics, Philosophy, Culture, Interviews and Other Writings 1977–1984*. London: Methuen.

Franco, J. (1988), 'Beyond Ethnocentrism: Gender, Power and the Third World Intelligentsia'. in C. Nelson and L. Grossberg (eds), *Marxism and the Interpretation of Culture*. Houndmills: Macmillan Education, pp. 503–18.

Frankel, F. (1978), *India's Political Economy 1947–1977: The Gradual Revolution*. Princeton, NJ: Princeton University Press.

Friberg, M. and B. Hettne (1988), 'Local Mobilization and World Systems Politics', *International Social Science Journal*, no. 117, pp. 341–60.

Fuentes, M. and A. Frank (1989), 'Ten Theses on Social Movements', *World Development*, vol. 17, no. 2, pp. 179–91.

Gadgil, M. (1990), 'Population, Resources and Environment', *Seminar*, no. 365, pp. 52–6.

Gramsci, A. (1971), *Selections from Prison Notebooks*. New York: International Publications.

———— (1985), *Antonio Gramsci: Selections from Cultural Writings*,

Trans. William Boelhower. Cambridge, Mass.: Harvard University Press.

Guha, Ramachandra (1988), 'Ecological Trends in Indian Environmentalism, *Economic and Political Weekly*, 3 December, pp. 2578–81.

Guha, Ranajit (1989), 'Dominance Without Hegemony and Its Historigraphy', in Ranajit Guha (ed.), *Subaltern Studies*, vol. VI. New Delhi: Oxford University Press, pp. 210–309.

Gupta, A. (1989), 'The Political Economy of Post-Independence India: A Review Article'. *Journal of Asian Studies*, vol. 48, no. 4, pp. 787–97.

Habermas, J. (1981), 'New Social Movements'. *Telos*, vol. 49, pp. 32–40.

Haraway, D.S. (1988), 'Situated Knowledges: the Science Question in Feminism and the Privilege of Partial Perspective'. *Feminist Studies*, vol. 14, no. 3, pp. 575–99.

Kazancigil, A. (1986), 'Paradigms of Modern State Formation in the Periphery' in A. Kazancigil (ed.), *The State in Global Perspective*. Paris: Gower/UNESCO, pp. 119–42.

Kelkar, G. (1981), *The Impact of Green Revolution in Women's Work Participation and Sex Roles*. Geneva: ILO.

Kothari, R. (1986), 'State, Classes and Masses', *Alternatives XI*, pp. 167–83.

———— (1988), *Transformation and Survival: In Search of Humane Governance*. New Delhi: Ajanta.

Kulkarni, S. (1987), 'Forest Legislation and Tribals: Comments on Forest Policy Resolution', *Economic and Political Weekly*, 12 December, pp. 2143–8.

Laclau, E. and C. Mouffe (1985), *Hegemony and Socialist Strategy*. London: Verso.

Mouffe, C. (1988), 'Hegemony and New Political Subjects: Toward a New Concept of Democracy' in C. Nelson and L. Grossberg (eds), op. cit., pp. 89–104.

Nandy, A. (1987), *Traditions, Tyranny and Utopia*. New Delhi: Oxford University Press.

———— (1989), 'Shamans, Savages and the Wilderness: on the Audibility of Dissent and the Future of Civilizations', *Alternatives*, vol. 14, pp. 263–77.

Nerfin, M. (1986), 'Neither Prince nor Merchant: Citizen: an Introduction to the Third System', *IFDA Dossier*, no. 6, pp. 3–20.

Offe, C. (1984), *Contradictions of the Welfare State*. Cambridge, Mass.: MIT Press.

———— (1985), 'New Social Movements: Challenging the Boundaries of Institutional Politics', *Social Research*, vol. 52, no. 4, pp. 817–68.

Omvedt, G. (1987), 'India's Green Movements', *Race and Class*, vol. 18, no. 4, pp. 29–38.

———— (1989), 'Rural Women Fight for Independence', *Economic and Political Weekly*, 29 April, pp. 910–13.

Parajuli, P. (1986), 'Grassroots Movements, Development Discourse and Popular Education', *Convergence*, vol. 19, no. 2, pp. 29–40.

Parajuli, P. and E. Enslin (1990), 'From Learning Literacy to Regenerating Women's Space: a Story of Women's Empowerment in Nepal', *Convergence*, vol. 23, no. 1, pp. 44–56.

Parekh, B. (1989), *Gandhi's Political Philosophy*. London: Macmillan.

Rahnema, M. (1988), 'A New Variety of AIDS and Its Pathogens: Homo Economicus, Development and Aid', *International Social Science Journal*, vol. 40, pp. 117–36.

Redclift, M. (1987), *Sustainable Development Exploring the Contradictions*. New York: Methuen.

Rudolph, L. and S. Rudolph (1987), *In Pursuit of Lakshmi: the Political Economy of Indian State*. Chicago: University of Chicago Press.

Sasson, A. (1986), 'The People, Intellectual and Specialized Knowledge', *Boundary* 2, vol. XIV, no. 3, pp. 122–36.

Sheth, D.L. (1989), 'State, Nation and Ethnicity: Experience of Third World Countries', *Economic and Political Weekly*, 25 March, pp. 619–26.

Shiva, V. (1988), *Staying Alive: Women, Ecology and Development*. London: Zed.

Singh, S.K. (1990), 'Evaluating Large Dams in India', *Economic and Political Weekly*, 17 March, pp. 561–74.

Sistrens Collective (1987), *Lionheart Gal. Life Stories of Jamaican Women*. Toronto: Sister Vision.

Sutton, F.X. (1989), 'Development Ideology: Its Emergence and Decline', *Daedalus*, Winter, pp. 35–58.

Therborn, G. (1986), 'Neo-Marxist, Pluralist, Corporatist, Statist Theories and the Welfare State', in A. Kazancigil (ed.), op. cit. pp. 204–232.

Touraine, A. (1985), 'An Introduction to the Study of Social Movements', *Social Research*, vol. 52, no. 4, pp. 749–87.

——— (1988), *Return of the Actor: Social Theory in Post-industrial Society*. Minneapolis: University of Minnesota Press.

Viswanathan. S. (1987), 'From the Annals of a Laboratory State', *Alternatives*, vol. XII, pp. 37–60.

World Commission on Environment and Development (WCED) (1987), *Our Common Future*. Oxford: Oxford University Press.

9

The Democratic Rite: Celebration and Participation in the Indian Elections[+][*]

Walter Hauser and Wendy Singer

The courtyard hums with the chatter of party workers and constituents waiting to honour the winning candidate. D.P. Yadav arrives in his white Ambassador sedan, which is decorated with marigolds and orange streamers. As he presses through the crowd assembled at the Election Commission office, enthusiastic campaign workers, their faces coated in bright pinks and reds, sprinkle powdered colours of victory on him as well. At the rear of the crowd supporters begin to chant, 'D.P. Yadav Zindabad!' [Hail to D.P. Yadav!] and 'Congress Party Zindabad!'. The candidate nods and beams with pride as he ducks into the government building to reappear momentarily on a high balcony.

Here, overlooking the courtyard, which is teeming with participants of the month-long campaign, the District Magistrate delivers a certificate of victory to the re-elected Member of Parliament (MP).

+ *Asian Survey*, vol. XXVI, no. 9, 1986, pp. 941–58.

* Funding for the research on which this essay is based was provided by the Office of Fellowships and Grants of the Smithsonian Institution. For being both critic and friend, the authors are indebted to Kailash Chandra Jha. Other critics, too numerous to mention, will recognize their positive influences as well. The largest contribution to this essay, however, is that of the election officials, candidates, and voters, whether in New Delhi, Monghyr, Patna, or Lakhisarai. Of course, the responsibility for what the authors have ultimately written is theirs.

The crowd below, engrossed in its own revelry, takes little notice of the official event. Meanwhile, a truck and other vehicles elaborately trimmed with posters, flyers, and banners, ragged from the campaign, gather beyond the square. They stand poised for the victory procession. A small band wearing crisp, clean uniforms heralds the march with the sound of a trumpet and the loud beat of drums. The MP, now surrounded by his supporters, is swept onto the truck bed. Finally, the leader of the procession, a ten-foot elephant, begins the parade through Monghyr town.

This ceremony marks the final hours of India's elaborate rite of democracy. Through its performance Indians reaffirm the unity of the nation and the investment of power in the rulers by the ruled. The central importance of this rite to the political system is obvious even in a superficial view of the election that shows only the massive level of participation by candidates, party workers, voters, and the non-voting population. In this respect the election is a political festival incorporating the elements of planning, pilgrimage, procession, and other collective experiences that characterize both secular and religious rituals in the subcontinent. Accordingly, it is not enough to understand an election merely in terms of who won, by how many votes, and with the support of which constituents; such information tells us something about the candidate, less about the voter, and very little about the process by which the results were achieved. In a democratic experience of this magnitude it is centrally important to know what that vote means to the individuals who cast it and to the society that organizes its political culture around it. Based largely on observations of the 1984 parliamentary elections and 1985 state assembly elections, and using the metaphor of ritual, this essay begins to explore some of these meanings.

The significance of the electoral process in Indian politics is often illustrated by the 1977 election, which after twenty-one months of Emergency rule reaffirmed the country's commitment to democratic government. As Myron Weiner has suggested:

> An authoritarian government that appeared to be well entrenched called a genuinely free election, permitted political parties to openly seek electoral support, ended press restrictions, released the bulk of political prisoners from jail, and politically neutralized the police and civil administration. Not only that, but when it lost the election, the government quickly stepped down.... If, instead of elections, a violent upheaval

had marked this turning point, we might be writing about India's 'democratic revolution'.[1]

Thus, this election served as a dramatic demonstration of the ritual function of elections in India—namely, through the choices made at the ballot box, to affirm the people's confidence in a government and its policies, or if not, to replace it. Mrs Gandhi sought to confirm that her government had this implied approval and hence called for elections in March 1977. In the circumstances, the electorate and Mrs Gandhi's government together demonstrated a strong commitment to the democratic process in the Indian political experience.

In the election ritual, approval is given both individually by voters as each personally selects a candidate for office, and collectively as voters go to the polls and through their ritual action bring a party into or out of power. Ultimately, the process affirms societal norms concerning the roles that leaders can and cannot play in the social system, and the forms of power that will be allotted to them in that society. From the perspective of Victor Turner's elaboration on the meanings of ritual generally, the election sets up 'a symbiotic interpenetration of individual and society' by reinforcing the symbolic association between individual needs and societal needs.[2] As ritual, the election defines and redefines political hierarchy both literally and symbolically by formalizing the roles that individuals and groups will play during the ritual and 'causing real transformations of character and social relationships' after the ritual.[3] Candidates win and candidates lose, and in this displacement new sets of individual and collective relationships in the body politic are created and old ones are redefined. Most important, throughout this process, society asserts its belief in its own changing political and social culture by the actual performance of the ritual itself. The national election is performed cyclically every five years, as prescribed by the constitution. The many ceremonies that define the election,

1 Myron Weiner, *India at the Polls: The Parliamentary Elections of 1977* (Washington, DC: American Enterprise Institute for Public Policy Research, 1978), p. 1.

2 Victor Turner, *Dramas, Fields, and Metaphors: Symbolic Action in Human Society* (Ithaca: Cornell University Press, 1974), p. 56.

3 Ibid.

and in fact become the election, carry on for five weeks from the constituting of party tickets to the celebration of the winning candidates' victories.[4] For this period the participants—the entire society—move in and out of ritual time. They continue to fulfil their normal daily duties *and* to celebrate the political festival happening around them. The rhythm of that festival increases and decreases, but reaches its most intense level on the day of polling.

It is in the rite of casting the ballot and doing so in massive numbers that Indian citizens collectively ratify the norms of their political system. On 24 and 27 December 1984, more than 238 million people participated directly in this rite by voting: official statistics show that 64 per cent of India's eligible voters cast their ballots. Although this turnout was the largest in the history of Indian elections, it followed the pattern set in the first general elections of 1952. In 1977, 62 per cent of the people voted; in 1980, the figure was 56 per cent.

Still, the extent and nature of participation must be gauged in other terms than the large number of voters. The number of parties, party candidates, independent candidates, and political workers also characterize the quality of democratic participation. In fact 5241 candidates contested 508 parliamentary seats in 1984—that is, about ten candidates per seat. While many of these candidates were affiliated with national or regional parties, 3696 ran as independents. Equally remarkable was the number of officials required to organize and carry out an election of this scale.

In an effort to reach as many potential voters as possible, the Election Commission located polling booths widely across each of the parliamentary constituencies, in most cases no more than a two-kilometre walk for any voter. In Bihar, each of the fifty-four parliamentary constituencies consisted of approximately 1200 polling places, and each polling place served no more than 1000 voters. In the rural countryside, polling booths were most often situated in schoolhouses, while in the cities other public buildings were also used. A polling party of three government workers

4 On 13 November 1984, Rajiv Gandhi announced that the elections for the Eighth Lok Sabha would be held in the last week of December. Accordingly, the entire campaign took place over a period of forty days. Counting was done on 28 December, the day following the second day of polling.

managed each booth on election day to assure that the voting was carried out efficiently and fairly. These civil servants were recruited by the district-level election officer from their regular duties as teachers, engineers, and administrators. They were modestly paid for their work, but saw the job primarily as an extension of their official responsibilities as government servants.

The central duty of the polling party in managing a local booth was to protect the ritual artifacts of the election, most notably the official ballot and the rubber stamp used to mark it. Voters and, significantly, the non-voting population, recognized the ballot and stamp as representing the collective political will of the Indian people. To the candidates, the expression of popular will as it was re-enacted through the ritual of marking the ballot gave them power both literally and symbolically. By their participation in that ritual they reaffirmed the faith of their constituents and renewed their store of political energy. Indeed, the election conveyed to them the actual political power of office.

Democracy is government fuelled by the political will of the people. In India, that will is officially articulated by the voters who mark the ballot, but it is as legitimately expressed by non-voters and children who join in the other ceremonies of the election. Collectively they create change, and in so doing both reinforce and redefine elements of the political system.

That system has its own internal logic that may or may not look like the politics of other democracies. For example, de Tocqueville, commenting on his observations of democracy in America, claims that democracy increases individualism, especially following a democratic revolution. He argues that a democratic system detaches individuals from their ancestors, companions, and children by allowing them all to make their own way and satisfy their own needs. 'They owe nothing to any man, they expect nothing from any man; they acquire the habit of always considering themselves as standing alone.'[5]

In India, perhaps because democratic ritual grew out of ancient Indian political philosophy and culture, preceding 'democratic' philosophy (as it is known in the West), individualism is not the core of that experience. Rather, it might be argued that the

5 Alexis de Tocqueville, *Democracy in America*, vol. II (New York: Alfred A. Knopf, 1945), p. 99.

collective expression of political will forms the basis of the democratic system in this cultural environment. Similarly, fundamental political change, such as the one that brought India independence in 1947, has come about by massive peaceful demonstrations of the public will. The election of 1977, which ended the authoritarian rule of the emergency, was certainly also a collective demonstration of the public will.

To define these cultural qualities of Indian democracy, it is important to view the ritual of the election process through four consecutive ceremonies. The first takes place before the campaign proper, when candidates receive party endorsement (a ticket) from the major political parties. The second ceremony, perhaps the most extensive, is the actual campaign, which involves candidates, workers, voters, and everyone else as both player and audience. The third ceremony—in fact, the central performance—is the day of polling. Finally, the closing ceremonies of the election rite follow a secluded counting ritual in which the winners are determined for public announcement. These final ceremonies culminate the election festival with victory marches and parades that display the new legislators and their supporters to all of the participants in the ritual experience—the citizens of the constituency and the nation.

Getting a Ticket

In the Eighth Parliamentary Elections in December 1984, 1545 potential candidates received the endorsement of particular political parties for their candidature. 'Getting the ticket' to run under a party banner requires a prescribed performance that takes place in state capitals and in New Delhi rather than in the constituency. It is a ritual of preparation, a preliminary necessary for the ultimate democratic rite. The political actors begin to experience the hectic schedules of a campaign, both competing with and assisting one another in party activities. The most stylized of these ticket ceremonies occurs in the Congress-I party, the oldest, largest, and most successful of India's political parties.

In this process, long before the actual polling, influential local figures create and reinforce the political alliances that they eventually play out on the election platform. Once the elections have been called, potential candidates activate their political connections in the party and lobby for support. Important state leaders seek tickets for their closest associates and make lists of possible candidates. They meet with the party high command and negotiate their lists of candidates.

Thus, while local candidates vie for endorsements, state politicians affirm their respective positions of power in the party hierarchy. A politician measures his political prowess by the number of party tickets he gains for his followers. The press recognizes this ritual as significant by following closely the movements of state leaders in and out of Delhi. For example, the Bihar Chief Minister, Chandra Shekar Singh, and the former chief minister, Jagannath Mishra, express their political rivalry in the battle for control of Congress party tickets for the Bihar parliamentary constituencies. State and national newspapers pick up on this pre-election campaign, speculating on the possible decisions of the prime minister and national party officers. But the hopefuls do not leave their political fates solely in the hands of these two powerful leaders: they flock to Delhi, crowding the grounds and parlours of Bihar Bhavan, the building reserved for state officials when they visit the capital.

The atmosphere of Bihar Bhavan during the week of ticket selections is festive; the chatter on the grounds includes personal gossip and political speculation.[6] The potential candidates sit in clusters, sometimes moving from one group to another to learn the latest political news. Enterprising vendors of spicy snacks, ice cream, tea, and Campa Cola line the street as they do near the grounds of any festival.

At three o'clock Chandra Shekar Singh's Ambassador sedan pulls into the front driveway. As he and two associates climb out of the car, dozens of celebrants leave their picnic-style groups and gather around. Eagerly they listen for the latest news about party meetings. The chief minister greets the party workers, expressing his gratitude for their support and the large turnout,

[6] The final list of candidates to run on Congress-I tickets was released on 27 November 1984. Consequently, the most intensive week of ticket lobbying was 20–27 November. Candidates nominated by the Congress-I then began campaigning in their constituencies on 28 November and continued until 22 December, set by the Election Commission as the last day for pre-election campaign activity.

but provides no new information. One hopeful interrupts, 'I'm Rajinder Sharma from Begusarai. An article in today's *Hindustan Times* says that the opposition is fielding common candidates in all twenty-six seats in Gujarat'.[7] The chief minister nods as he moves away and slips into the building. Sharma, having failed to get his attention, retreats to the lawn.

More important to this ticket-getting ceremony than the gathering, the discussions, and even receiving the updated news, is the constant attempt among the hopefuls to 'show face'. Many of the young Congress party members such as Rajinder Sharma are seated on the lawn merely to be seen by the Chief Minister or Dr Mishra or other important leaders of the national party. With this gesture they hope to demonstrate their commitment and loyalty to the Congress-I.

Of course, the actual distribution of tickets is also based on other considerations. The character of the constituency, the quality of the incumbent, and his or her party affiliation are all taken into account. In some cases the decision has already been made before the 'face-showers' reach the political verandas of Delhi. Still, the ceremony is a characteristic feature of elections, and its real and symbolic importance as part of the larger process cannot be ignored. Most of the hopefuls remain in their parties even after they are denied tickets and often try again at the next election. But others join the long list of independent candidates and launch campaigns of their own.

The Campaign

The four-week campaign that follows the nominating process is the dramatic pilgrimage of the election. Candidates return to their political base and follow the same paths traversed by other politicians—even freedom fighters—before them. In the marches and rallies of the campaign, the political leaders meet their followers on equal or subservient terms. This inversion of power from the hands of the politicians back to the hands of the voters,

[7] 'Hectic Talks on for Final Adjustments', *Hindustan Times*, 25 November 1984. Several leading opposition parties in the state of Gujarat agreed to field a single candidate for each of the twenty-six Lok Sabha seats. In doing so, they increased their chances of defeating the Congress-I candidates in that state.

an essential theme of the election, begins in this intensive and spectacular rite.[8]

This rite touches the entire nation; candidates and their supporters canvass for votes even in the most remote villages. Villagers in turn erect welcome arches out of bamboo poles and cover them with streamers, political posters, flags, and banners. The candidates and party workers traverse rural roads on foot and bicycles, and in three-wheeled motor scooters, cars, and rugged trekkers (a large jeep-like vehicle). A government minister's speech or the visit of a well-known politician speaking for local candidates attracts voters and their children from far-off villages. And not surprisingly, one such event spawns another—one party's 'party' sparks its opposition to stage a more elaborate spectacle. The competition over issues and political strength extends to the competition over political display. A massive example of this display transforms a field near the small town of Bikramganj, in Rohtas District of Bihar, into a well-designed arena for 200,000 people waiting to catch a glimpse of their Prime Minister. It is 18 December 1984, just six days before the election.

After completing morning chores and following a long walk from neighbouring villages, the crowd has begun to gather not long before Rajiv Gandhi's 10.00 a.m. arrival. Party buses speed down the state road carrying people from more distant villages. Amid a thick cloud of dust, Rajiv arrives in a helicopter to make brief comments on the merits of the local Congress-I ticket holder. Women, who make up more than a third of the growing crowd, fill a reserved section closest to the platform. Sitting among them playing hand-games are their small children. Other children carry banners and flags and wear buttons as signs of their political participation—a few collect the buttons of several parties. Since Tuesday is a school day some girls in the crowd are dressed in pale blue and white school uniforms.

[8] The definition of pilgrimage used here is that of a ritual with specific rules and norms that involve processions toward a common goal. In such a ritual the collective experience provides an elimination of hierarchy or even a role reversal for the duration of the ritual. See Victor and Edith Turner, *Image and Pilgrimage in Christian Culture* (New York: Columbia University Press, 1978), especially chapter one. In this case the object or shrine of the pilgrimage is a rally or political meeting in the constituency or some other central place where the candidate meets the voters and the voters meet the candidate.

This particular election festival is, of course, sponsored by the Congress party, but other parties celebrate as well. At the approaches to the crowded field, members of the Dalit Mazdoor Kisan Party raise their green party flags, and the red flags of the Communist Party of India flap nearby in the cool December breeze. These rival campaign workers use the gathered crowd as an opportunity to express their own political messages. Indeed, the audience has come to see the Prime Minister rather than necessarily to support the Congress-I party.

At the conclusion of the short campaign speech, Rajiv Gandhi, standing with the Bikramganj candidate, urges the crowd to proclaim their support, '*Hath chap ko vote deejiyay*' [Vote the Congress party], he calls, raising his right hand in the sign of the Congress.[9] Most of the people in the crowd respond in unison, their arms held high demonstrating their support for Congress (or at least this moment's enthusiasm). Equally striking are the members of the audience who stand in loud silence with hands at their sides.

Campaign rallies such as this not only provide a forum for political rhetoric and help educate the voters, but also serve as social functions for the participants. Voters come to meet neighbours and relatives, to celebrate an outing, to see an important political leader, and to demonstrate the popular strength of their constituency. As a voter reported in a similar political rally for Tarkeshwari Sinha in Vaishali constituency, 'I have come to do darshan'.[10] Seeing a political leader and particularly the 'First among Ministers,' is in itself a powerful experience that evokes the vision of the divine kings of ancient India.

9 'Hath chap ko vote deejiyay', literally urges voters to give their vote to the Congress by stamping the hand symbol of that party. The symbol appears on the ballot next to the name of the candidate. A voter wishing to select the Congress candidate in the Bikramganj Parliamentary constituency, for example, would mark the ballot by stamping an X with the official rubber marker either on the candidate's name, in this case the incumbent, Tapeshwar Singh, or on the image of the hand.

10 *Darshan* means to see the divine, and to benefit from the experience of being in the presence of the divine, or, in this case, in the presence of a great person. Tarkeshwari Sinha has been a prominent political figure in Bihar since the early 1950s. She was a member of the Lok Sabha from 1952 to 1971 and in 1984, running on the Dalit Mazdoor Kisan Party ticket, lost narrowly to the Congress-I candidate, and incumbent, Kishori Sinha.

Much of the overt support at rallies reflects political courtesy. A voter in another Bihar village explained that many candidates came through to canvass for support. When asked about a particular incumbent candidate, she responded, 'We showed him respect and came to see him, putting up banners of welcome, but most of us are not going to support him'. Such politeness represents a part of the ritualized function of the elections. Participation in these rituals does not necessarily correlate with the decision the voters will express at the ballot box.

On a clear, warm day in March 1985, Ashwani Kumar Sharma prepares for a pilgrimage into the heart of his Legislative Assembly constituency in Bihar.[11] Walking with his Congress party campaign organizer through the central bazaar of the town of Lakhisarai, he oversees the arrangements for two drummers and two crowd leaders to accompany him to nineteen remote villages, the last in the constituency he has not yet visited as the campaign draws to a close.

At eleven o'clock in the morning he meets the drummers, party workers, and two visitors who have come to study the elections. Together the seven set out along the dusty road. The drummers and campaign workers—an advance party—run ahead to announce the candidate's arrival at the first village, Kurauta. When Ashwani approaches, children run out to greet him. Laughing and joking with them, the candidate strides down the road that he has built for his constituents. 'This road is my caste!' he explains proudly to one of the visitors.[12] 'I built it for these villagers who never had a road before.'

11 Lakhisarai is one of 324 Legislative Assembly constituencies in Bihar and is part of the Begusarai Parliamentary Constituency. The assembly elections were held on 2 March and 5 March 1985. In Lakhisarai voters went to the polls on 5 March.

12 For Ashwani Kumar Sharma the road, the creation of his political labour, is in the sense of caste the very essence of his being. With this comment, he also pokes fun at the assumption that people in Bihar vote primarily by caste. He is a Bhat Brahman, and his family are the only members of that caste in his constituency. He was elected to the Legislative Assembly in 1980 on a platform of rural development, and the road and an electrification project stand as monuments to his success. In 1985 he is campaigning on these issues, which he places above any specific caste allegiance.

As he enters Kurauta, a young man places a bright flower garland around Sharma's neck, but he removes it, gesturing a respectful 'namaste' to the crowd. By this time the musicians are circling the meeting place at the centre of the village, drumming—dancing—competing sharply with their rhythms. The young organizer raises his hands, stepping side to side with the drumbeats, calling out, 'Indira Gandhi amar hai', 'Rajiv Gandhi Zindabad!' [Indira is immortal, long live Rajiv!]. The crowd picks up immediately on this powerful rhythmic chant, and continues in counterpoint with the caller, 'Congress Party Zindabad', 'Hey, Ashwani Zindabad!' Then, in culmination, the caller shouts, 'Ashwani Sharma ko vote do! vote do'! [Vote for Ashwani Kumar Sharma!] The children too, respond in kind, louder and always more emphatically. Men and women in separate groups move closer to Ashwani. An old man breaks through the loose audience, moving with difficulty toward the legislator. He lifts his hands over the politician's head: 'May Ishwar protect you and make your campaign successful.' With his head bowed to receive the blessing, the candidate leans forward in deference to touch the old man's feet.

After the encounter at Kurauta, Sharma continues his pilgrimage through the Lakhisarai constituency. He passes through eighteen more villages before the end of the day speaking to small or large groups at each stop. And from one village to the next he has more and more followers accompanying him on his path—their road.

The road and his pilgrimage ends at Belauri, six kilometers from any nearby market and connected to the outside world only by this road. The sun is beginning to set and the figures make silhouettes against the twilight. Ashwani and his companions—now twenty in all gathered from the stops along the way—will take food with the people of Belauri, the largest of the interior villages. First, he visits every tola or neighbourhood of the village discussing problems of old-age pensions, more water for irrigation and better water for drinking, schools, and the politics of Rajiv Gandhi's election victory and his mother Indiraji's assassination. Finally, after circling the village twice paying homage at every corner, he sits down with his hosts to eat an elegant village meal of chicken, dal, rice, and chapatis.

The Central Ritual: Marking the Ballot

The ritual of marking the ballot is so fundamental to the democratic process that an Indian court ruled—in response to a proposition that the government institute voting machines—that the physical act of stamping the ballot by hand is a right guaranteed by the constitution. To exercise that right, voters in great numbers go to the polling booths to vote. The booths are systematically distributed throughout the constituency and are managed by a presiding officer and two assistants appointed by the District Magistrate, who is also the election Returning Officer for those parliamentary constituencies falling within his district.

The role of the presiding officer and his assistants is defined by law and custom. In this labour-intensive environment they spend much of their time checking and balancing the jobs of their colleagues and trying to prevent inevitable human error. In fact, the elaborate ritual of voting reflects, specifically, the need for checks and double checks that assure the integrity of each vote, each booth, and each election.[13]

The voting ritual is both private and public at the same time. Voters with individual ballots make individual decisions throughout India in secret ballot rooms. In a very real sense, the voters themselves stand guard by the boxes that hold their ballots to assure that they remain sealed; citizens defend this right to secrecy vehemently in the courts and legislatures. The public nature of the ritual is displayed in the fine attire of the voters who celebrate with their neighbours at the polls. They become united by their participation in the common act of voting and literally united as well in the ink mark placed on their left forefingers to show they have voted.

The sun is barely rising and the fog not yet burned away when workers begin to set up tables in the Kishanpur schoolhouse early on 24 December. By 8.00 a.m. the polling officers, with ballots, ballot boxes, voters lists, and official rubber stamps

13 In this essay we give a few examples of these 'rituals of security' that assure secret ballots and seek to prevent possible fraud. For obvious reasons we have limited the detail of the description and omitted important procedures. Also, in certain examples we have not used the real names of voters and polling officers to respect their right to privacy.

have turned the schoolhouse into polling booth 125. Party workers and early morning voters, wrapped in *chaddars* (shawls) against the cold, linger by the roadside waiting for the voting to begin.[14]

On the veranda of the school-transformed polling booth, the election personnel arrange two tables adjacent to the door of the classroom. Polling assistants sit behind the tables arranging the election materials. A ballot box stands prominently at the front of each table defining the boundary between the polling workers and the voters. Additional ballots and boxes lie in neat rows on the floor between the two officers.[15]

The presiding officer at the booth, Satish Prasad, has ultimate responsibility for the voting arrangements. He spends most of his time checking the handiwork of the polling assistants and assuring that the whole process runs smoothly. Satish is a veteran of the voting system; this is his third election as a poll worker. Ordinarily he works for the government as an engineer in Ranchi, but for the training of new presiding officers and polling assistants he has been away from home for fifteen days. In fact he has not only trained the young men who are assisting him at booth 125, but most of the other new polling assistants in the constituency as well. For each presiding officer, the goal is to have an uneventful polling day, for all the votes to tally properly at the end of the day, and for the flow of voters to remain steady and orderly.

Anand Singh, a representative of the Janata candidate, approaches the table to ask for admission to the voting area as a poll watcher. He carries his own voters list meticulously marked with the names of voters favourable to the Janata party. Satish examines his official certificate and ushers him to one of the

[14] An essential prop for the election is the voters list, which contains the names of all eligible voters in the area around the polling booth as determined by a survey completed several months before. Voters are listed by name and household; each entry also indicates the voter's age, gender, and father's, mother's, or husband's name. The 408 names on the Kishanpur voters list identifies this as a relatively small booth.

[15] Kishanpur No. 125 is one of 180 polling booths in the Surajgarha assembly segment of the Monghyr Parliamentary Constituency. In Bihar, each of the 54 parliamentary constituences is made up of six state legislative assembly constituencies, or segments.

vacant chairs near the election table. Anand Singh will spend the day observing the election to assure its legitimacy for the Janata candidate.[16]

The first voters in booth 125 are two young men, Lakhan and Rajendra, who wait near the school for the polls to open at 8.00 o'clock. They are Communist Party of India (CPI) workers who will set up 'a booth' of their own in a vacant shed next to the voting station; their booth will be an ad hoc election office for the local Communist candidate. From this outpost they do last minute campaigning, assist those who come to the poll, and keep track of those among their supporters who have not yet voted. The shed is decorated with red CPI posters and flags and contains a table at which Rajendra sits with his own copy of the village voters list, some sample ballots to show his supporters, and a stack of *parchas* (small paper slips) that he will use to record the voter's name and voting number.[17]

Just after 8.00 a.m., the presiding officer motions to the young men that he is ready. Quickly they walk to the veranda forming a line of two. Lakhan tells the polling officer that his voter number is 24, and promptly the officer marks off his name from the list. The stub, or counterfoil, of the first ballot displays the serial number 01 in the top right corner. Lakhan shows it to his friend noting that he is indeed the first voter. He signs the counterfoil with a sweeping stroke of the pen; the polling assistant then detaches the ballot from the signed counterfoil.[18] Next, the

16 The job of the poll watcher is to observe the voters as they come to the polls and to challenge the identity or age of anyone about whom he has a question. This process is designed to assure a fair election and allows the various parties to monitor the voting procedure and to guard against people voting twice, voting in the wrong booth under a fictitious name, or voting before the franchise age of twenty-one. In this rural setting the party agents in fact know the names of the voters and their families and the possibility of outsiders attempting to vote is slim.

17 Such parchas enable the voter to have a personal record of his voting number. At the polling booth, the voter presents this number so that the officer can more easily find his name on the nonalphabetized voters list.

18 The Election Commission takes many precautions to assure the integrity of the Indian elections. Ballots are bound in stacks of fifty and consist of a numbered counterfoil, and in Monghyr, a nine-by-eleven inch ballot that lists the fifteen candidates and their parties. The polling officer is responsible for returning all the counterfoils to the district election officer. Voters sign the

assistant marks Lakhan's left forefinger with purple ink and hands him the ballot and official election stamp. Lakhan hesitates for a moment—deciding whether or not the option for secrecy is necessary for a well-known Communist party supporter—then slips into the classroom and stamps the symbol of the sickle and sheaf of grain that represents his party. He folds the ballot twice into a small square and inserts it into the empty ballot box. Once back on the veranda he waits for Rajendra to complete his vote and together they return to the party shed.

After thirty minutes of polling and shuffling CPI supporters in and out of the shed with the parchas, an older party member approaches the 'office'. 'A floating party of security personnel is coming down the road. You should move this party station farther away from the poll', he advises.[19] He is concerned that the close proximity of the shed to the polling site might create a conflict with the roving security because official regulations require party workers to remain one hundred metres from the booth. Taking his advice the younger workers move the makeshift office to another spot a little farther down the road.

Later that morning in the inner part of Rampur village, east of Kishanpur, another voter, Veena, is finishing her morning cleaning, having cooked breakfast for her family. About 10.30 a.m. she puts on her nicest sari, bangles, and silver earrings, preparing to go to the voting place. Above her small village house is a flag of the Congress-I party—a statement of her father-in-law that he strongly backs the Congress candidate. Veena meets three other young women of her tola and they set out down the main village road to the local school. She carries her smallest child on her hip. When they reach the school the women go to the Congress-I party 'office' that consists of a small, low table placed next to a tree. The Congress worker, a short, fat man, sits on the table with his list and parchas, gossiping with a circle of cronies. Veena and her friends each receive a white slip marked with their voter numbers

---

counterfoil to indicate that it has been used. Then the officer tears off the lower part—the actual ballot—which is unsigned and not designated with a serial number, so the voter knows that his vote will remain secret.

19 Security parties travel throughout the constituency all day checking the booths and assuring that the presiding officers do not require assistance in controlling crowds of voters or dealing with other untoward incidents.

and their husband's names as recorded on the voters list. Parchas in hand, they proceed to the booth.

The lines at this time of the day are long and the polling officer tries to expedite things by establishing separate queues for women and men. Many other people cluster around the polling booth, having just voted, waiting to vote, or simply enjoying the chatter. Veena and her friends discuss their children, the crowd, and the events of the day as they approach the head of the line. At the voting table Veena tells the officer her name and hands him the slip of paper. He crosses her off the list and puts an ink mark on her left index finger.

Then she takes her ballot and disappears into the classroom-cum-voting booth. She examines the names of the fifteen candidates that appear on the ballot. Some of them have never campaigned in her village and she does not even know who they are. Next to each candidate is the symbol of his party, or in the case of independents, an approved symbol. Finally, forced to make the decision she has thought about all week, Veena passes over the hand symbol of the Congress party that her father-in-law supports, and with a gesture of self-confidence stamps the name of the Janata party candidate.

By noon the polling officers are thinking about lunch. Each polling party is accompanied by someone who cooks for the election personnel since they clearly cannot leave their posts. Vegetables and *dal* simmer in pots on a platform built near the polling space while the cook slaps *chapatis* and puffs them on the open fire. He prepares enough food for the polling officers as well as the armed security personnel who guard the booth. Some party observers leave and eat at home.

Several teenagers spend the day trying to get into the polls. In one village along the main road, Gopal, a boy about sixteen, follows his older friend in line at the polls. He has obtained a parcha containing his father's name and voting number knowing that his father will not come to vote. Gopal's friend, who is also underage, has been working for the Janata party, and the two boys have decided to vote for the Janata candidate. As they approach the door both boys shift their weight back and forth and giggle nervously. As Gopal sees the official inside the polling place, he suddenly wants to run away, but his friend eggs him on, telling him to go first. At the door, Gopal presents his father's voting number and when asked his father's name, he gives the name of his grandfather. Once inside, his finger is marked and he receives a ballot. Just then one election officer mumbles something to another and finally one of them questions out loud, 'Does anyone know this boy? Is he really twenty-one?' The election officer pulls Gopal aside and makes him sit down and wait while he decides what to do. Seeing this, Gopal's friend slips out of line and runs away, leaving Gopal alone inside the polling booth with the election officer, who only wishes he didn't have to deal with this kind of trouble. Gopal cowers in the corner almost in tears. Finally, after minutes that seem like hours, the polling official sends Gopal home with a verbal rebuke.

As the day comes to a close, the election workers are all tired. In booth No. 54, at a remote school set back a mile from the road, the line is as long as it has been all day. At four o'clock the polling officers have to break the line and turn away eager voters. It will not be long before trucks with armed police come to carry away the sealed ballot boxes, and between now and then there is still much to do. Sealing the boxes is the important concluding ceremony of the day. Each of the five boxes used in this booth has to be appropriately closed and sealed with wax. All the election workers and the party observers participate.

The voters, now finished with their performance, still linger at the booth, having tea and waiting to see their ballots carried away. Unlike the official guards who protect the ballots as part of their formal duties, villagers have protected the ballots because they represent their political voices. Children press their noses to the shutters of the school trying to see what secret tasks the election officers are performing.

Inside, the metal ballot boxes lie stacked against the wall. The presiding officer meticulously counts and records the number of signed ballot stubs while one of his workers goes through the voters list, first counting the number of voters whose names have been marked off and then tallying how many were men and how many were women; this information is kept for Election Commission records. Once the counting is complete, the two poll workers compare the number of ballot stubs to the number of marked-off voters. The figures in the first count are nearly lost in the noise of the children from outside and do not coincide, so the presiding officer begins again. Finally, in the second try, the numbers tally and the presiding officer records them on appropriate Election Commission forms.

When the counting is complete the officers seal the ballot boxes. The boxes are equipped with special fasteners that are secured with wire twist ties. Once the fasteners are secured, the metal boxes are placed in a white cotton sack drawn up and tied with string. The string is then pressed against the sack and sealed with hot wax. The presiding officer stamps the wax with the insignia of the district election commissioner. The other bags are similarly sealed with this official mark. Each observer, from the Congress-I party, the Janata party, the Communist Party of India, and the Bharatiya Janata Party takes his turn inspecting the secured boxes and pressing his party seal into the strategically positioned lump of wax.

By 5.30 or 6.00 p.m. security vehicles arrive to collect the boxes, and other transportation is provided to pick up the election workers. As the validated ballots—the votes of the people—go to the district capital, the dwindling crowd finally disperses. Then, with the departure of the last polling officer, the election is done.

History as Epilogue

The election ritual as it was performed in India in 1984 and 1985 defined political culture in a general sense but also in very specific local terms. The participants functioned simultaneously in political and ritual arenas. In this essay we have dealt primarily with the ritual arena; the local realities of winning and losing, however, are equally relevant. It is significant therefore that the candidates depicted here as examples, both winners and losers, are culled from different parties. Although certain parties with substantial resources and more supporters may have had political advantages in the election, all had equal access to cultural symbols and ritual practice.

Perhaps the most interesting campaign, in this sense, was that of Fazal Ahmad, a former Inspector General of Police (IG) for the state of Bihar and a respected local figure. Fazal Sahab was a novice in the art of campaigning but performed his role as well as many veterans. His oratorical skills and physical vigour rivalled those of any candidate in the country, and his pilgrimage into the constituency provided a grand spectacle of decorated trucks, honking horns, and festive processions. Still, despite his articulate platform and lavish execution of ritual practice, he lost his bid for the Monghyr parliamentary seat.

Fazal Sahab was born in Urain village of Monghyr District and received strong electoral support from the area surrounding his home. He ran on the Janata party ticket with modest campaign funding and logistical support from the state and national parties. With these limited resources, added to his own, he managed to print fliers and buttons and provide party workers to most of the polls on election day. To stay within his budget, however, he used only national Janata party posters and produced no posters or banners of his own. Fazal Ahmad's campaign emphasized his service to the state and his family's role in the development of the local area. Yet, despite his effective campaigning, he was unable to overcome the organizational efficiency of the Communist Party candidate, nor was he able to displace the popular Congress-I incumbent, D.P. Yadav, whose resource base was more substantial, and who ran on his successful record and promoted his role in the Indira and Rajiv governments.

Still, it is not accurate to assume that Congress party influence alone made or broke campaigns. Other examples in the district of Monghyr illustrate that opposition parties and even independents could experience success. During the 1985 Legislative Assembly campaign, Rajo Singh, a dissident Congress-I politician running as an independent won a seat from the Sheikhpura constituency in the western part of the district by a massive majority. Similarly, in the hotly contested race for the assembly seat of Lakhisarai constituency, the Janata candidate overwhelmed the CPI candidate and surpassed the Congress-I incumbent, Ashwani Kumar Sharma, in an impressive victory.

As the March sun warms the roof of the local jail near the small town of Lakhisarai, inside the building officials are establishing the edifice as a counting arena for the Legislative Assembly election. There are no prisoners in the jail and its secure location makes it ideal for the tightly controlled counting process. The guarded entrance is restricted to counting officers and party observers who verify the validity of the process. From 7.00 a.m. these select individuals have been working intently to bring the 1985 election to a close. Periodically, food is ferried into the counting officers by other government workers; candidates or their agents bring breakfast and a few hours later lunch to their workers as well. Between these short breaks the officers open the sealed ballot boxes and count the votes for each candidate.

Outside, voters and supporters, and the vendors who follow such crowds, wait for the results of this secluded ceremony. Finally at 6.00 p.m. after hours of waiting, the crowd, having grown to 1000, gathers at a platform set up in a tent near the gate. Here the subdivisional officer, who is the presiding official in this election, announces the awaited results. 'By 10,813 votes', he says, 'Krishna Chandra Prasad Singh of the Janata Party has been elected to the Bihar State Legislative Assembly'. He goes on to list the other candidates and their support, but a hum rises in the crowd. Disappointed supporters of the Congress party candidate, Ashwani Kumar Sharma, gradually fade from the gathering, followed by the supporters of other candidates, until the mass of people consists only of the supporters—and momentary converts—of the new legislator.

The cheering and shouting crowd forms an impromptu parade toward the candidate's campaign truck. Two senior campaign organizers rally this spontaneous celebration into a victory march. Someone unfurls the large orange and emerald-green flag of the Janata Party as young party workers file onto the raised bed of the brightly coloured truck. 'Krishna Chandra Prasad Zindabad!' 'Janata Shakti Zindabad!' [Long live the power of the Janata Party, the powers of the janata! (the people)]. On the cabin of the truck beneath two delicately painted eyes, the engine grate grins a smile of victory. Just ahead six drummers lead the victory march, hammering out unison beats to correspond with the rhythm of the Hindi cheers.

As the truck enters Lakhisarai town, the traffic on the narrow road is stalled behind it. More cheering supporters, laughing and waving their arms, join the final victory procession along this main street to the central bazaar. From shop fronts other revelers throw pink, red, and blue powder onto the truck, the drummers, and hangers-on. Others splash coloured water on the pavement and the parade.

Winding up the steep hill to the railroad station at the centre of the market, the truck honks its loud horn and attention turns to the rear of the crowd. Lifted on the shoulders of Janata supporters, the new member of the Legislative Assembly is slowly pushed through the crowd to the front of the procession. With cheers behind him, he leads the people—the celebrants of his victory—in the final steps of the democratic rite.

10

Hunger and Public Action+

Jean Drèze and Amartya Sen

Hunger is not a new affliction. Recurrent famines as well as endemic undernourishment have been persistent features of history. Life has been short and hard in much of the world, most of the time. Deprivation of food and other necessities of living has consistently been among the causal antecedents of the brutishness and brevity of human life.

Hunger is however, intolerable in the modern world in a way it could not have been in the past. This is not so much because it is more intense, but because widespread hunger is so unnecessary and unwarranted in the modern world. The enormous expansion of productive power that has taken place over the last few centuries has made it, perhaps for the first time, possible to guarantee adequate food for all, and it is in this context that the persistence of chronic hunger and the recurrence of virulent famines must be seen as being morally outrageous and politically unacceptable. If politics is 'the art of the possible', then conquering world hunger has become a political issue in a way it could not have been in the past.

Public Action for Social Security

It would be hard to deny that there is a straightforward public-interest issue involved in the elimination of starvation and of nutritional deprivation. The challenge of confronting in an effective manner the scourge that chastises and haunts a substantial part of humanity inescapably calls for diverse forms of public

+ Excerpts from *Hunger and Public Action* (Delhi: Oxford University Press, 1989), pp. 3, 4, 17–19, 210–14, 257, and 259.

action. The provision of social security cannot exclusively rely either on the operation of market forces, or on some paternalistic initiative on the part of the state, or on some other social institution such as the family.

The *need* for public action does not, however, in itself point to the *nature* of the action to be undertaken. There are different areas of action, different strategies to pursue, different agents for undertaking action. The decision problems implicit in the choices involved are both complex and momentous. The issues include political and social phenomena as well as economic ones. The strategy of public action can be as difficult as it is urgent.

There are various facets of the challenge of public action for the elimination of famines and endemic hunger, but a few elementary considerations deserve immediate mention. First, the orientation of public action must clearly depend on the feasibilities of different courses of action. These feasibilities relate not merely to the causal factors that lead to deprivation and hunger, but also to the nature and power of the agencies involved. In particular, the character of the state, and the nature of the government undertaking state actions, can be crucial. The questions raised include not merely the administrative capabilities of governments, but also the political commitments and loyalties as well as the power bases of the holders of political power.

The countries with which we shall be concerned in this chapter have enormously divergent political systems and social balances of power, and the forms that public action can take will undoubtedly depend on these political and social parameters. For example, whether the Chinese success in subduing chronic hunger can be repeated, say, in India, or whether Indian achievements in the elimination of famines can be emulated in sub-Saharan Africa, or whether the sub-Saharan African record of lower gender inequalities in nutritional well-being can be duplicated in India or China or the Middle East are all important and complex questions that call for careful scrutiny of the backgrounds against which these experiences have taken place.

Second, the public is not a homogeneous entity, and there are divisions related to class, ownership, occupation, and also gender, community, and culture. While public action for social security is in some sense beneficial for all groups, the division of the benefits involved cannot escape differential pulls coming from divergent interest groups. The art of public action has to take note of these cooperative conflicts. To think of public action as action for the benefit of a homogeneous public is to miss a crucial aspect of the challenge.

Third, state action for the elimination of hunger can take enormously divergent forms. It need not involve only food production or food distribution. It can take the form of income or employment creation on a regular basis to combat endemic undernourishment. It can also involve famine relief operations in the form of employment for wages in cash or in kind to regenerate the purchasing power of hard-hit occupation groups. It can include the provision of health care and epidemic control, which may be important not merely as basic ingredients of the general well-being of the population, but also in preventing undernourishment, which is often associated with parasitic ailments and other forms of morbidity. State action can also take the form of enhancing economic development, in general, and the growth of incomes and other means of subsistence, in particular, through the expansion of productive activities. The discipline of public action may be widely different in these various fields, and the strategy of public action for social security has to be alive to the respective issues involved. The complementarities and trade-offs between different avenues of action also have to be firmly faced in developing an overall effective public programme for eliminating hunger in all its forms.

Fourth, some public institutions, in particular the market, have often been seen as being an alternative to state action. To some extent this is right, since market mechanisms determine certain allocations and distributions, and state actions can alter or even take over many of these functions. While the conflicts between the reliance on markets and that on state action have to be fully acknowledged, it is also important not to see these two avenues as being in constant combat with each other. A purist philosophy can be awfully short of logistic means.[1]

1 The either-this-or-that 'exclusive' view often attributed to leaders of classical political economy was by no means universally endorsed. The effectiveness of the market mechanism in achieving certain types of efficiency was clearly seen by that great critic of capitalism, Karl Marx, and the fact that 'want, famine and mortality' can arise from unemployment in a market economy was explicitly noted by that great defender of the efficiency of markets, Adam Smith.

The need to consider a plurality of levers and a heterogeneity of mechanisms is hard to escape in the strategy of public action for social security. The internal diversities involved in an effective public action programme can be quite extensive. For example, several countries have achieved some success in preventing famines by combining cash transfers to vulnerable groups in the form of wages for public employment with reliance on the private sector for moving food to affected regions, along with public participation in food distribution to prevent the emergence of collusive manipulations by private traders. These combined strategies illustrate the fruitfulness of taking an integrated and pluralist view of public action.

Fifth, public action should not be confused with state action only. Various social and political organizations have typically played a part in actions that go beyond atomistic individual initiatives, and the domain of public action does include many non-state activities. Indeed, in many traditional societies, individual security has tended to depend greatly on support from groups such as the extended family or the community.[2] The active role of the state in the modern world should not be seen as replacement of what these non-governmental groups and institutions can achieve.

Finally, even as far as state action is concerned, there is a close relationship between public understanding and awareness, on the one hand, and the nature, forms, and vigour of state action in pursuit of public goals, on the other. Political pressure plays a major part in determining actions undertaken by governments, and even fairly authoritarian political leaders have, to a great extent, to accept the discipline of public criticism and social opposition. Public enlightenment may, thus, have the role both of drawing attention to problems that may otherwise be neglected, and of precipitating remedial action on the part of governments faced with critical pressure. For example, the role of newspapers and public discussions, which can be extremely crucial in identifying famine threats (an energetic press may be the best 'early

2 The profound concern of traditional societies for social security, and the variety of institutions they have evolved in pursuit of that objective, have been explored by Jean-Philippe Platteau (1988). See also Drèze and Sen (1989), chapter 5.

warning system' for famine that a country can devise), can also help to keep the government on its toes so that famine relief and preventive measures take place rapidly and effectively.

The question of public enlightenment and awareness involves both institutional features and the nature of social and political movements in the country. Since these are not immutable factors, the role of public action must be examined not merely in terms of consolidation of past achievements, but also with a view to possible departures in new directions. It is important to see the public as an agent and not merely as a passive patient.

The Chinese Famine and the Indian Contrast

The Chinese famine of 1958–61 followed the debacle of the so-called Great Leap Forward that was tried out from late 1957 onwards.[3] While the failure of the Great Leap Forward came to be widely recognized after the initial euphoria, the existence of the famine oddly escaped open scrutiny and even public recognition, until very recently.[4] This is particularly interesting given the monumental scale of the famine—arguably the largest in terms of total excess mortality in recorded history.

Comparing actual mortality with pre-famine mortality yields remarkably high figures of extra deaths in this famine. Estimates of extra mortality vary from 16.5 million to 29.5 million.[5] These figures are extraordinarily large. For example, the excess mortality in the last Indian famine, viz. the so-called Great Bengal famine of 1943 (occurring four years before independence), is estimated to

3 Various regions of China also suffered from adverse weather conditions during 1959–61, involving drought and flooding in different parts of the country. These conditions certainly contributed to the production problems, but it is hard to escape the conclusion that the bulk of the problem was caused by the failure of the policy changes initiated by the Great Leap Forward. In fact, the adverse climatic conditions were particularly important in making it harder to identify precisely how fully the 'Leap' had failed.

4 On this see Sen (1982, 1983), Bernstein (1983), Riskin (1986, 1987).

5 See Coale (1981), Aird (1982), Ashton *et al.* (1984), Peng (1987). The largest estimate of 29.5 million (Ashton *et al.* 1984) attempts to take full note of unreported deaths. Peng's (1987) estimation based on provincial demographic data suggests a figure of 23 million.

be about 3 million.[6] In the scale of 'extra deaths' the Chinese famine was, thus, about five to ten times as large as the largest famine in India in this century.[7]

Many things are still uncertain about the causation of the famine, but it is clear that there was an enormous collapse of agricultural output and income. Food availability decline certainly played an important part in the genesis of hunger that gripped China for three years. Taking the average national grain output per capita of 308 kg in 1956 and 1957 as the point of reference, the 1959 output was 17 per cent below this and by 1960 the per capita grain output was as much as 30 per cent down. Even in 1961, the shortfall vis-à-vis the 1956–7 average was 28 per cent, and the pre-famine figure was not reattained until the latter half of the 1960s.[8]

Further, some regions suffered particularly serious declines and the sharp differences between food availability in the different regions continued through the period of distress.[9] For example, in 1960, while the provinces of Heilongjiang and Yunnan had respectively 229 and 209 kg of grains per head for their rural population, the corresponding figures for Henan, Sichuan, and Hebei were respectively 143, 137, and 122 kg. The contrast between the rural and urban areas was also striking (for example, between 288 kg in urban Hebei as against 122 kg in the rural areas of that province).[10]

Public distribution at the local level was comprehensively disrupted. The problem for the rural areas was made much worse

6 That figure was obtained also by using the same method of comparing actual mortality with pre-famine mortality, and making allowances for unreported deaths (Sen 1981: Appendix D). The official estimate of excess mortality was 1.5 million, but that involved an undercounting due to incomplete temporal coverage.

7 It must, however, be remembered that since the Chinese mortality rates had come down sharply already *prior* to the famine, the 'extra death' estimates based on pre-famine mortality rates are in comparison with a pre-famine death rate lower than that of most poor countries in the world. But even if considerably higher pre-famine mortality rates are used, the excess mortality in China still amounts to astonishingly high figures.

8 See Peng (1987: pp. 653–5, esp. Table 3).

9 See Riskin (1986, 1987) and Peng (1987).

10 The data are taken from Peng (1987).

by the sharp increase in state procurement of food grains, and the rural communes were in many cases desperately short of food. In addition to that, there were also remarkable inequalities in the distribution of whatever food was available. This applied not only between the regions and between urban and rural areas, but even within a given rural region. Some provinces evidently suffered from much sharper *intra*regional inequalities than others did, with correspondingly higher mortality. For instance, rural Sichuan and Henan suffered from much greater death rates than rural Hebei which did not have, on the average, any more food. Particularly, there was a great deal of wastage and excess consumption in particular 'commune mess halls'.[11]

The Chinese famine of 1958–61 was closely linked with policy failures—first in the debacle of the Great Leap Forward, then in the delay in rectifying the harm done, and along with that in accentuating distributional inequalities through enhanced procurement and uneven sharing. The remarkable aspect of the famine is its continuation over a number of years without an adequate recognition of the nature of the crisis (and without leading to the necessary changes in public policy).

This is one respect in which India's record since independence must be seen to be very much superior. The fact that there has been no large-scale famine in India since independence is a positive contrast with the Chinese experience. The contrast is particularly interesting when account is taken of the fact that there have been several alarming dips in food output and availability in India over the same period (the latest being in the drought of 1987), and that on many occasions the entitlements of large parts of the population have been severely threatened both directly and indirectly (particularly through employment declines associated with droughts or floods).

There are two different features involved in the Indian system of famine prevention. One is a worked-out procedure for entitlement protection through employment creation (usually paying the wages in cash), supplemented by direct transfers to the 'unemployable'. The origins of this procedure go back to the

[11] On this see Peng (1987). 'Ironically', notes Peng, 'almost all the provinces that were praised by a *People's Daily* article for their 'good performance' in establishing rural mess halls experienced severe excess mortality' (p. 664).

1880s and the Famine Codes of the late nineteenth century, though a number of important developments (including the use of the public distribution system to stabilize food prices) have taken place since independence. The other part is a political 'triggering mechanism' which brings the protection system into play and indeed which keeps the public support system in a state of preparedness. It was this triggering mechanism that was lacking in the famine prevention system of British India after the Famine Codes were set up. In the Bengal famine of 1943, not only were the Famine Codes not invoked, that was indeed a deliberate decision of the government.[12]

On the other hand, given the political system of post-independence India, it is extremely hard for any government in office—whether at the state level or at the centre—to get away with neglecting prompt and extensive anti-famine measures at the first signs of a famine. And these signs are themselves more easily transmitted given India's relatively free media and newspapers, and the active and investigative role that journalists as well as opposition politicians can and do play in this field. The adversarial participation of newspapers and opposition leaders is, as we have discussed earlier, an important part of the Indian famine prevention system. It yields a rapid triggering mechanism and encourages preparedness for entitlement protection.

The contrast with China is striking primarily in the second respect. Given its system of public distribution, China did not lack a delivery and redistribution mechanism to deal with food shortages as the famine threatened in 1958 and later. Despite the size of the decline of food output and the loss of entitlement of large sections of the population, China could have done a much better job of protecting the vulnerable by sharing the shortage in a bearable way.

What was lacking when the famine threatened China was a political system of adversarial journalism and opposition.[13] The Chinese famine raged on for three years without it being even

[12] The Governor of Bengal, Sir T. Rutherford, wrote to the Viceroy of India explaining that a famine had not been declared to avoid the obligation to undertake the relief measures mandated by the Famine Codes. See Mansergh (1973: 363, Document No. 158).

[13] The reasons for this diagnosis and the empirical evidence for this view are discussed in Sen (1982, 1983).

admitted in public that such a thing was occurring, and without there being an adequate policy response to the threat. Not only was the world ignorant of the terrible state of affairs in China, even the population itself did not know about the extent of the national calamity and the extensive nature of the problems being faced in different parts of the country.

Indeed, the lack of adversarial journalism and politics hit even the government, reinforcing the ignorance of local conditions because of politically motivated exaggeration of the crop size during the Great Leap Forward and the fear of local leaders about communicating their own problems. The pretence that everything was going all right in Chinese agriculture and rural economy to a great extent fooled the national leaders themselves. 'Leaders believed in 1959–60', as Bernstein puts it, 'that they had 100 MMT more grain than they actually did.'[14] This misconception was crucial in keeping down Chinese imports of food grains, which fell to virtually nothing in 1959 (about two thousand tons compared with 223 thousand tons in 1958), and stayed incredibly low in 1961 (66 thousand tons), before jumping to 5.8 million tons in 1961 as the fact of the famine and the agricultural debacle became at long last clear. Chinese exports of food grains, similarly, peaked in 1959, and stayed high in 1960, before beginning to come down in 1961. The Chinese net exports of cereals rose from 1.9 million tons in 1957, to 2.7 in 1958, 4.2 in 1959, and 2.7 in 1960—as the famine devastated the lives of tens of millions of people across the country.[15]

The misinformation and misreading also led to a sharp *increase* in the extent of food procurement from the rural areas. The percentage net procurement out of total output went up from 15 and 17 per cent in 1956 and 1957 to 21 per cent in 1958 and 28 per cent in 1959.[16] The rural Chinese—hit by a production decline—were hit again by having to part with a larger proportion of the reduced output as procurement by the state.

The misinformation also contributed to the non-revision of production and distribution policies and to the absence of any

14 Bernstein (1984: 13).

15 The figures are from the *Statistical Yearbook of China 1981*. See also Riskin (1986, 1987) and Jowett (1988).

16 Riskin (1987), Table 6.5. See also Bernstein (1984) and Peng (1987).

emergency entitlement-protection programme.[17] Aside from the government's informational inadequacy, which made its own assessment of the situation disastrously wrong, the absence of an adversarial system of politics and journalism also meant that there was little political pressure on the government from any opposition group and from informed public opinion to take adequate anti-famine measures rapidly.

We end this section with three interpretative remarks. First, famine prevention is an important achievement of India, and there is something to learn from that experience in this famine-ridden world. The fact that even post-revolutionary China, with its outstanding record of entitlement promotion and enhancement of living conditions, could fall prey to a gigantic famine indicates that the lesson may be far from negligible. In fact, the precise feature of the absence of adversarial politics and open journalism that may have contributed to the occurrence, magnitude, and duration of the Chinese famines of 1958–61 are also present in most sub-Saharan African countries today. While the political systems are quite different, this feature of absence of political opposition and free journalism in African politics is a cause of famine vulnerability in Africa as it was in China at the time it had its own disaster. Also, greater tolerance of criticism and more open journalism in China would have a positive effect on helping to make China secure against the kind of political and economic crisis that ushered in the famines of 1958–61. But unfortunately political democratization in China has not really kept pace with the speed of economic liberalization.

[17] In 1962, shortly after the famine, when the recent experiences were being reviewed, Mao Zedong noted the problem of informational failure for planning in the absence of local democracy: 'If there is no democracy and ideas are not coming from the masses, it is impossible to establish a good line, good general and specific policies and methods.... Without democracy you have no understanding of what is happening down below; the situation will be unclear; you will be unable to collect sufficient opinions from all sides; there can be no communication between top and bottom; top-level organs of leadership will depend on one-sided and incorrect material to decide issues, thus you will find it difficult to avoid being subjectivist; it will be impossible to achieve unity of understanding and unity of action, and impossible to achieve true centralism' (Mao Zedong 1974: 164). On this pronouncement and its context and relevance, see Sen (1983, 1984).

Second, as India's experience shows, open journalism and adversarial politics provide much less protection against endemic undernutrition than they do against a dramatic famine. Starvation deaths and extreme deprivation are newsworthy in a way the quiet persistence of regular hunger and non-extreme deprivation are not. Endemic hunger may increase the morbidity rate and add to the mortality rate (in these respects India's performance continues to be quite awful), but that is primarily a statistical picture rather than being immediately palpable and—no less importantly—being 'big news'. To bring endemic deprivation into the fold of news reporting and to make it a major focus of political confrontation are inherently more difficult tasks, and seem to have been largely beyond the normal activities of journalists and politicians in India.[18] That situation could change (there are some signs of that already), and this is clearly a field in which there is scope for the public to play a very creative role in India. But as things stand, the Chinese political commitment—not unrelated to the ideological predispositions of the Chinese political system—seems to have served the country well for combating endemic deprivation, despite its failure as a defence against famines.

Finally, it is important to note that despite the gigantic size of excess mortality in the Chinese famine, the extra mortality in India from regular deprivation in normal times vastly overshadows the former. Comparing India's death rate of 12 per thousand with China's of 7 per thousand, and applying that difference to the Indian population of 781 million in 1986, we get an estimate of excess normal mortality in India of 3.9 million per year. This implies that every eight years or so more people die in India because of its higher regular death rate than died in China in the gigantic famine of 1958–61.[19] India seems to manage to fill its cupboard with more skeletons every eight years than China put there in its years of shame.

[18] On this see Sen (1982, 1983, 1984) and Ram (1986).

[19] This is so with the highest of the estimated mortality figures, viz. 29.5 million (due to Ashton *et al.* 1984). If instead we take, say, Peng's figure of 23 million, then every *six* years there is more extra mortality in India than in the Chinese famine of 1958–61.

Against the Current?

This section is about what public action can do to eradicate hunger in the modern world. A question that would occur to many people is this. Is this not a hopeless time to write in defence of public action? The world has, in recent years, moved decisively towards an unhesitating admiration of private enterprise and towards eulogizing and advocating reliance on the market mechanism. Socialist economies—from China to the USSR and East Europe—are busy de-socializing. Capitalist economies with a tradition of 'welfare state' policies—from the UK and the USA to Australia—have been absorbed in 'rolling back the frontiers of the state', with a good bit of privatization of public enterprise. The 'heroes' at this moment are the private ownership economies with high growth rates—not only old successes such as Japan, but also the new 'trail blazers'—South Korea, Hong Kong, Singapore. What chance is there of getting much of a hearing at this time for an argument in favour of *more* public action? And, more importantly, how can we possibly *defend* such a case, given the empirical regularities that are taken to have emerged in the recent decades?

Public action is not, of course, just a question of public delivery and state initiative. It is also, in a very big way, a matter of participation by the public in the process of social change. As we have discussed, public participation can have powerful positive roles in both 'collaborative' and 'adversarial' ways vis-à-vis governmental policy. The collaboration of the public is an indispensable ingredient of public health campaigns, literacy drives, land reforms, famine relief operations, and other endeavours that call for cooperative efforts for their successful completion. On the other hand, for the initiation of these endeavours and for the government to act appropriately, adversarial pressures from the public *demanding* such action can be quite crucial. For this adversarial function, major contributions can be made by political activism, journalistic pressures, and informed public criticism. Both types of public participation—collaborative and adversarial—are important for the conquest of famines and endemic deprivation.

To emphasize the vital role of public action in eliminating hunger in the modern world must not be taken as a general denial of the importance of incentives, nor indeed of the particular role played by the specific incentives provided by the market mechanism. Incentives are, in fact, central to the logic of public action. But the incentives that must be considered are not only those that offer profits in the market, but also those that motivate governments to implement well-planned public policies, induce families to reject intrahousehold discrimination, encourage political parties and the news media to make reasoned demands, and inspire the public at large to cooperate, criticize, and coordinate.[20] This complex set of social incentives can hardly be reduced to the narrow—though often important—role of markets and profits.[21]

This *is* indeed a good time to keep in view the crucial role that public action—in various forms—can play in eradicating hunger in the modern world. The empirical experiences of different countries point to certain systematic connections, and it is important not to lose sight of them in the scramble to be more 'private'—more exclusively 'market-based'—than the next country. We have to recognize the functions of public action and the rewards they can bring. The cost of overlooking them can be very high—in terms of unnecessary misery, morbidity, and mortality.

References

Aird, J. (1982), 'Population Studies and Population Policy in China', *Population and Development Review*, vol. 8.

Ashton, B., K. Hill, A. Piazza, and R. Zeitz (1984), 'Famine in China, 1958–61', *Population and Development Review*, vol. 10.

Bernstein, T.P. (1983), 'Starving to Death in China', *New York Review of Books*, vol. 30.

——— (1984), 'Stalinism, Famine, and Chinese Peasants', *Theory and Society*, vol. 13.

[20] See Drèze and Sen (1989), chapters 4, 5–8, 10–12.

[21] We have also discussed the importance of combining and connecting state action and market response in strategies to combat hunger (see particularly Drèze and Sen (1989), chapters 6 and 7).

Coale, A. (1981), 'Population Trends, Population Policy and Population Studies in China', *Population and Development Review*, vol. 7.

Drèze, Jean and Amartya Sen (1989), *Hunger and Public Action*. Delhi: Oxford University Press.

Harvard School of Public Health (1985), *Hunger in America: The Growing Epidemic*. Cambridge, MA: Harvard University.

——— (1987), *Hunger Reaches Blue Collar America*. Cambridge, MA: Harvard University.

Jowett, A.J. (1988), 'Famine in the People's Republic of China', Occasional Paper No. 21, Geography Department, Glasgow University.

Mansergh, N. (ed.) (1973), *The Transfer of Power 1942–7*. London: HMSO, vol. iv.

Mao Zedong (Tse-Tung) (1974), *Mao Tse-Tung Unrehearsed, Talks and Letters: 1956–71*. London: Penguin Books.

Peng, X. (1987), 'Demographic Consequences of the Great Leap Forward in China's Provinces', *Population and Development Review*, vol. 13.

Platteau, J.P. (1988), 'Traditional Systems of Social Security and Hunger Insurance', paper presented at a Workshop on Social Security in Developing Countries held at the London School of Economics, 4–5 July; published in S.E. Ahmad *et al.* (eds) (1988), *Social Security in Developing Countries*. Oxford: Oxford University Press.

Ram, N. (1986), 'An Independent Press and Anti-hunger Strategies: The Indian Experience', paper presented at a Conference on Food Strategies held at WIDER, Helsinki, 21–5 July. Published in Drèze, J.P. and A.K. Sen (eds) (1986), *The Political Economy of Hunger*. Delhi: Oxford University Press.

Riskin, C. (1986), 'Feeding China: The Experience Since 1949', paper presented at a Conference on Food Strategies held at WIDER, Helsinki, 21–5 July; Working Paper No. 27, WIDER, 1987; published in Drèze J.P. and A.K. Sen (eds) (1986), *The Political Economy of Hunger*. Delhi: Oxford University Press.

——— (1987), *China's Political Economy: The Quest for Development since 1949*. Oxford: Oxford University Press.

Sen, A.K. (1981), *Poverty and Famines*. Oxford: Clarendon.

——— (1982), 'How is India Doing?', *New York Review of Books*, vol. 29.

——— (1983), 'Development: Which Way Now?', *Economic Journal*, vol. 93.

——— (1984), *Resources, Values and Development*. Oxford: Basil Blackwell.

Townsend, P. and N. Davidson (eds) (1982), *Inequalities in Health*. Harmondsworth: Penguin.

11

The Puzzle of Indian Democracy: A Consociational Interpretation[+]*

Arend Lijphart

India has long been a puzzle for students of comparative democratic politics. Its success in maintaining democratic rule since independence in 1947 (excluding the brief authoritarian interlude of the 1975–7 Emergency) in the world's largest and most heterogenous democracy runs counter to John Stuart Mill's (1958: 230)

+ *American Political Science Review*, vol. 90, no. 2, June 1996.

* Earlier versions of these articles were presented as seminar or conference papers at the Centre for the Study of Developing Societies, Delhi, on 3 December, 1993; the Department of Political Science at Delhi University, South Campus, on 8 December 1993; 'Regime Transformation and Democratization in Comparative Perspective', University of California, Los Angeles, 20–1 May 1994; and the Department of Political Science, University of California, Santa Barbara, 15 May 1995. A preliminary version was published as an occasional paper by the Rajiv Gandhi Institute for Contemporary Studies in New Delhi (RGICS Paper No. 18, 1994). It is part of a collaborative and comparative US–Indian research project, directed by K.S. Bajpai and supported by the Ford Foundation and the Rajiv Gandhi Foundation. I would like to acknowledge the valuable assistance of the Centre for Policy Research in New Delhi and its director, V.A. Pai Panandiker, and of the Library of the India International Centre, New Delhi. For helpful comments on earlier drafts, I am grateful to Kanti Bajpai, Paul R. Brass, Pradeep K. Chibber, Jyotirindra Das Gupta, Henry W. Ehrmann, Dipak K. Gupta, Thomas A. Koelble, Victor V. Magagna, G. Bingham Powell, Jr, V. Ramachandran, Varun Sahni, Ashutosh Varshney, and three anonymous referees.

proposition that democracy is 'next to impossible' in multi-ethnic societies and completely impossible in linguistically divided countries.[1] And it confounds Selig S. Harrison's prediction (1960: 338), in line with Mill's argument of India's democratic failure and/or territorial disintegration: 'The odds are almost wholly against the survival of freedom and...the issue is, in fact, whether any Indian state can survive at all.' The Indian puzzle is even more troublesome for consociational (power-sharing) theory. In contrast with Mill's and Harrison's thinking, power-sharing theory holds that democracy is possible in deeply divided societies but only if their type of democracy is consociational, that is, characterized by (1) grand coalition governments that include representatives of all major linguistic and religious groups, (2) cultural autonomy for these groups, (3) proportionality in political representation and civil service appointments, and (4) a minority veto with regard to vital minority rights and autonomy. In contrast, under majoritarian winner-take-all democracy—characterized by the concentration of power in bare-majority one-party governments, centralized power, a disproportional electoral system, and absolute majority rule—consociational theory regards stable democracy in deeply divided societies as highly unlikely. In other words, consociational theory maintains that power sharing is a necessary (although not a sufficient) condition for democracy in deeply divided countries.

Consociational theory has had a strong influence on comparative politics, and it has spawned a vast literature. Soon after it was formulated, Daalder (1974: 609) spoke of 'an incipient school' of consociationalism, and, a few years later, Powell (1979: 295) proclaimed the theory 'among the most influential contributions to comparative politics'. It has become a widely accepted paradigm for the analysis of democracies that can be regarded as the

1 Two other puzzles are posed by Indian democracy. The first is its survival despite widespread poverty and illiteracy (Dahl 1989: 253), which casts grave doubts on the hypothesized link between the level of socio-economic development and stable democracy, further weakened by the fact that several other Third World democracies have by now established stable democratic rule (e.g., Barbados, Botswana, Costa Rica, Jamaica, Malta, Mauritius, and Papua New Guinea). The second, which I shall discuss later, is Myron Weiner's (1989: 9) 'Indian paradox', that is, 'the far more puzzling contradiction between India's high level of political violence and its success at sustaining a democratic political system'.

prototypes of power sharing, such as the Netherlands (Daalder and Irwin 1989; Mair 1994), Belgium (Huyse 1987; Zolberg 1977), Austria (Powell 1970; Luther and Müller 1992), Switzerland (Lehmbruch 1993; Linder 1994; Steiner 1990), Lebanon (Dekmejian 1978; Messarra 1994), Malaysia (Von Vorys 1975; Zakaria 1989), and Colombia (Dix 1980; Hartlyn 1988). And it has been used for the interpretation of many other political systems, from tiny Liechtenstein (Batliner 1981) to the European Union (Chryssochoou 1994; Gabel 1994; Hix 1994; Lindberg 1974); in all parts of the world, for instance, Canada (Cannon 1982), Venezuela (Levine 1973), Suriname (Dew 1994), Italy (Graziano 1980), Nigeria (Chinwuba 1980), Gambia (Hughes 1982), Kenya (Berg-Schlosser 1985), and Sri Lanka (Chehabi 1980); and not only democracies but also such non-democratic states as the former Yugoslavia (Goldman 1985; Vasovic 1992) and the former Soviet Union (Van den Berghe 1981: 190–1). Furthermore, consociational democracy has been proposed as a normative model for many ethnically divided countries, and it had a decisive influence in the shaping of South Africa's 1994 power-sharing constitution (Huntington 1988; Lijphart 1994; Worrall 1981). Given its prominent status, consociational theory has received a commensurate amount of criticism (for example, Barry 1975; Halpern 1986; Horowitz 1985; Taylor 1992), but it has successfully held its own, partly by rebutting its critics and partly by incorporating many of the critics' concerns (Lehmbruch 1993; Lijphart 1985: 83–117; Steiner and Dorff 1980).

Nevertheless, consociational theory has remained vulnerable on one major count: the glaring exception of India to its otherwise unblemished empirical validity. Indian democracy has worked despite the fact that, according to the usual interpretation (Pathak 1993: 36; Weiner 1989: 78), the Indian political system devised by the founding fathers was patterned after the majoritarian and adversarial Westminster model. B.K. Nehru (1986: 74) writes that the Indian mind was 'completely conditioned to believing that whatever was British was best' and calls it no wonder that the Indian Constitution is but an 'amended version' of the 1935 Government of India Act. And Paul R. Brass (1991: 342) states that 'the consociationalists... consistently ignore the experience of India, the largest, most culturally diverse society in the world that has... functioned with a highly competitive and distinctly adversarial system of politics'. A theory with only one disconfirming case comes close to perfect validity, of course,[2] but one cannot simply shrug off a deviant case that looms as large as India's huge democracy, with its 900 million inhabitants.

In the admittedly rare attempts to come to terms with the Indian exception, consociational scholars have conceded that India's democracy is, in line with the usual interpretation, mainly majoritarian because of the frequency of one-party majority cabinets, the highly centralized federal system that K.C. Wheare (1964: 28) considers only 'quasi-federal' and a highly disproportional electoral system that has regularly enabled the Congress Party to win parliamentary majorities without ever winning a majority of the popular vote. Yet, they have claimed that India is not completely majoritarian, citing Rajni Kothari's (1970: 421) description of the Indian political system as a 'coalitional arena', akin to a grand coalition, and the autonomy for the major linguistic groups provided by the coinciding linguistic and state boundaries of India's federal design, and they have equivocated between calling India nonconsociational (Lijphart 1977: 181, 225) and semi-consociational (Lijphart 1979: 513; Powell 1982: 215). In other words, the argument was that, while India remained a deviant case, its negative significance for consociational theory was relatively mild.

This argument can be taken much further, however, on the basis of a more thorough examination of the Indian case. The evidence clearly shows that India has always had a power-sharing system of democracy, especially strongly and unmistakably during

[2] Three other counter-examples mentioned by Powell (1979: 296) are Sri Lanka, Trinidad, and the Philippines, but the first two are cases of majority 'control' instead of genuinely democratic majority rule with alternating majorities, in Ian Lustick's (1979) sense of the term. Lustick argues that power sharing is not the only method that can maintain stability in divided societies; the alternative is a system of control in which a dominant group uses its superior power to keep the other group or groups subordinate. In control democracies, power is almost permanently in the hands of the majority group (Sinhalese in Sri Lanka, Africans in Trinidad, and, until 1972, Protestants in Northern Ireland), and the minorities are excluded from power and often discriminated against. In the case of the Philippines, it is doubtful that we can speak of a true deeply divided society, and, in any case, democracy broke down in 1972 and was not restored for many years (see Lijphart 1985: 103).

its first two decades of independence, from 1947 to 1967, but continuing, albeit in somewhat attenuated form, after about 1967. As Indian democracy has become less firmly consociational, intergroup tensions and violence have increased. If this reinterpretation is correct, as I shall try to demonstrate, then India is no longer a deviant case for consociational theory and, in fact, becomes an impressive confirming case.[3]

The Four Elements of Power Sharing in India

Indian democracy has clearly exhibited all four of the defining characteristics of power sharing also found in the other prominent examples of consociational systems: Canada from 1840 to 1867 (strictly speaking, a consociational *pre*democracy), the Netherlands from 1917 to 1967, Lebanon from 1943 to 1975 and again after the 1989 Taif Accord, Switzerland since 1943, Austria from 1945 to 1966, Malaysia since 1955 with a temporary breakdown from 1969 to 1971, Colombia from 1958 to 1974, Cyprus from 1960 to 1963, Belgium since 1970, Czecho-Slovakia from 1989 until the 1993 partition of the country, and South Africa according to its 1994 interim constitution (Lijphart 1977, 1992, 1994; Olson 1994).

Grand Coalition

Government by grand coalition can take many different forms. The modal form is an inclusive cabinet coalition of ethnic, linguistic, or religious parties, as in the Austrian, Malaysian, and South African power-sharing systems, but there are many other possibilities. One entails the formation of grand governing coalitions in sites other than the cabinet, such as the Dutch pattern of permanent or ad hoc 'grand' councils or committees with much greater influence than their formal advisory role. Another entails grand coalitions in cabinets, defined not in partisan terms but more broadly in terms of the representation of linguistic or other groups in a predetermined ratio; for instance, Belgian cabinets have rarely been coalitions of all significant parties, but they have been ethnically 'grand' because of the constitutional rule that

3 India obviously remains deviant in terms of Mill's and Harrison's non-consociational thinking, mentioned earlier.

cabinets must consist of equal numbers of Dutch-speakers and French-speakers. Yet another option entails neither cabinets nor parties: the allocation of top governmental offices—such as the presidency, prime ministership, and assembly speakership in Lebanon, and the presidency and vice-presidency in Cyprus—to specified ethnic or religious groups.

The Indian case adds even greater variety. Its main vehicle for grand coalition is the cabinet, which is not an exceptional form, but the unique aspect in India is that cabinets are produced by the broadly representative and inclusive nature of a single, dominant party, the Congress party. In a seminal article, originally published in 1964, Kothari (1989: 21–35) tried to analyse the Indian party system from the comparative perspective of the distinction between one-, two-, and multi-party systems. He found that the intermediate category of one-party dominance provides a reasonably good fit but that Indian one-party dominance is still quite different from the authoritarian type in a country like Ghana. The Congress party's location in the centre means that minor parties surround it on all sides. These, in turn, which Kothari (ibid: pp. 22–3) calls 'parties of pressure', perform the role of preventing the ruling 'party of consensus' from straying too far from 'the balance of effective public opinion'. Hence, he assigns a separate conceptual category to India's party system, uniquely occupied by the Indian case: the 'Congress system'.[4] One important conclusion that emerges from this classificatory exercise is to highlight the vast differences between the Congress system, with virtually permanent rule by a centrist party, and the Westminster-style two-party system, with alternation in office by right-wing and left-wing parties.

The second major conclusion is that the Congress system has served as the foundation for a consociational grand coalition. Despite never winning a majority of the popular vote in parliamentary elections, the Congress party has been balanced in the political centre and has encompassed 'all the major sections and interests of society' (Kothari 1989: 27). Prior to independence the

4 A further comparison with Japan, not yet so obvious in the early 1960s, reveals the additional contrast between India's centrist Congress party and Japan's right-of-centre Liberal Democrats. Mexico's Institutional Revolutionary Party (PRI) is probably the closest parallel to the centrist Congress party, except that it does not operate in a fully competitive democratic setting.

Congress was already an internally federal organization with a high degree of intraparty democracy and a strong penchant for consensus. This 'historical consensus' Kothari (ibid: 23, 51) writes, was successfully transformed into a 'consensus of the present', and he comes close to using consociational terminology in describing Indian democracy as a 'consensus system which operates through the institution of a party of consensus', namely, the Congress party. Crawford Young (1976: 314) makes the same point in explicitly consociational language: 'Lijphart's theory of consociational democracy has application to the Indian pattern of integration.... At the summit is a national political elite who are committed to reconciling differences through bargaining amongst themselves.' The combination of the Congress party's inclusive nature and political dominance has generated grand coalition cabinets with ministers belonging to all the main religious, linguistic, and regional groups.

Cultural Autonomy

Cultural autonomy for religious and linguistic groups has taken three main forms in power-sharing democracies: (1) federal arrangements in which state and linguistic boundaries largely coincide, thus providing a high degree of linguistic autonomy, as in Switzerland, Belgium, and Czecho-Slovakia; (2) the right of religious and linguistic minorities to establish and administer their own autonomous schools, fully supported by public funds, as in Belgium and the Netherlands; and (3) separate 'personal laws'—concerning marriage, divorce, custody and adoption of children, and inheritance—for religious minorities, as in Lebanon and Cyprus. Indian democracy has had all these three forms, the last two from the very beginning, and linguistic federalism since the 1950s.

The British colonial rulers of India drew the administrative divisions of the country without much regard for linguistic or cultural cohesion. The Congress movement was opposed to this policy and committed itself to a thorough redrawing of the boundaries along linguistic lines; from 1921 on, it also based its own organization on linguistically homogeneous units, the so-called Pradesh Committees. Jawaharlal Nehru and other Congress leaders had second thoughts, however, and the Constituent Assembly, following the advice of its Linguistic Provinces Commission, decided not to incorporate the linguistic principle into the new Constitution. Pressures from below forced a complete change of policy in the 1950s. After the State of Madras was divided into the separate Tamil-speaking and Telugu-speaking states of Tamil Nadu and Andhra Pradesh in 1953, the States Reorganization Commission embraced the linguistic principle and recommended drastic revisions in state boundaries along linguistic lines in 1955. These were quickly implemented in 1956, followed by the creation of several additional states in later years.

Linguistic federalism has not fully satisfied the minorities' desire for autonomy and security. The balance of power in the Indian federal system was asymmetrical in favour of the central government from the beginning, and further centralization has occurred from the late 1960s on, a subject to which I shall return below. As a result, many states have been demanding greater autonomy. The special autonomous status constitutionally granted to Kashmir, the one Muslim-majority state, was in practice also soon undermined, and smaller linguistic minorities without statehood have agitated for the creation of new states. But the leadership's initial fears that linguistic federalism would strengthen fissiparous tendencies have not been realized, and, in retrospect, the policy is regarded as a success by most observers. As consociational theory would have predicted, the 'rationalizing [of] the political map of India' has made language 'a cementing and integrating influence' instead of a 'force for division' (Kothari 1970: 115; see also Banerjee 1992).

The crucial feature of educational autonomy is not just the minorities' right to set up and run their own schools but the ability to make this right effective through full government financial support of these schools. Dutch and Belgian religious minorities had to fight hard to obtain this right, and, while full educational autonomy was granted in the Netherlands in 1917, it was not instituted in Belgium until 1958. In India, however, the constitution provided this right from the outset. Article 30 states that 'all minorities, whether based on religion or language, shall have the right to establish and administer educational institutions of their choice' and, more important, that 'the State shall not, in granting aid to educational institutions, discriminate against any educational institution on the ground that it is under the management of a minority, whether based on religion or language'.

Separate personal laws for Hindus, Muslims, and smaller religious minorities already existed under British rule, and they were carried forward and sometimes amended or replaced by similar new laws in independent India. Examples are the 1955 Hindu Marriages Act, the 1956 Hindu Succession (that is, inheritance) Act, the 1937 Muslim Personal Law (Shariat) Application Act, the 1939 Dissolution of Muslim Marriages Act, and the 1872 Indian Christian Marriage Act (Fyzee 1964; Engineer 1987). These statutes were enacted by parliamentary majorities but, when intended for one of the minorities, were drafted in conformity with the minority's wishes. For instance, after the controversial 1985 Shah Bano decision by the Supreme Court (involving the right of a divorced Muslim woman to financial support from her former husband), a new Muslim Women (Protection of Right on Divorce) Act was adopted in 1986, largely in line with the wishes of the Muslim Personal Law Board. And the new 1993 Christian Marriage Act was proposed by the government after extensive consultations with and the final approval of all Christian churches, albeit only after a reluctant endorsement by the Roman Catholic Church.

The Constituent Assembly explicitly considered the question of whether separate personal laws ought to be continued in independent, democratic India. An amendment to the draft constitution was proposed that would have ended this form of religious autonomy: 'The Union or the State shall not undertake any legislation or pass any law...applicable to some particular community or communities and no other' (cited in Luthera 1964: 83). Significantly, such a clause was *not* included in the constitution. A year later, Law Minister B.R. Ambedkar, replying to accusations of discrimination on the ground of religion during a parliamentary debate, again emphatically endorsed the principle of minority personal laws: 'The Constitution permits us to treat different communities differently and if we treat them differently, nobody can charge the Government with practising discrimination' (cited in Luthera 1964: 86).

Proportionality

In accordance with the principle of proportionality, the normal electoral system in power-sharing democracies is proportional representation (PR). The plurality (first-past-the-post) and other majoritarian methods have the tendency to over-represent majorities and large parties and to discriminate against smaller minority parties, as well as the corollary tendency to create artificial parliamentary majorities for parties that fall considerably short of winning popular vote majorities, what Rae (1967: 74–7) has called 'manufactured majorities'. It is not impossible, however, for power-sharing systems to circumvent these disproportional effects. For instance, despite Malaysia's plurality elections, the interethnic coalition has succeeded in guaranteeing a nearly proportional share of parliamentary seats to the minority Chinese and Indian parties by giving them the coalition's exclusive nomination in a number of districts.

In India, too, power sharing has managed to coexist with the plurality electoral system inherited from the British. One reason is that plurality does not disfavour geographically concentrated minorities, and India's linguistic minorities are regionally based. Another is that the Congress party's repeated manufactured majorities have not come at the expense of India's many minorities due to its special status as the 'party of consensus', which has been deliberately protective of the various religious and linguistic minorities. Indian cabinets, which have been mainly Congress cabinets, also have accorded shares of ministerships remarkably close to proportional, especially given the constraint of only about twenty positions usually available, to the Muslim minority of about 12 per cent and even the much smaller Sikh minority (roughly 2 per cent), as well as to the different linguistic groups, states, and regions of the country (Pai Panandiker and Mehra 1996). In addition, a special feature of the electoral law guarantees the so-called Scheduled Castes (untouchables) and Scheduled Tribes (aboriginals) proportional shares of parliamentary representation by means of 'reserved seats', that is, seats for which only members of these groups are allowed to be candidates. Finally, these scheduled groups and the so-called Other Backward Classes have benefited from other quotas—so-called reservations—with regard to public service employment and university admissions (Mehta 1991; Prasad 1991; Srinivasavaradan 1992: 105–33).[5]

5 Clearly, the consociational interpretation does not fit India's caste conflict as well as it fits the linguistic and religious divisions. In the early years,

Minority Veto

The minority veto in power-sharing democracies usually consists of merely an informal understanding that minorities can effectively protect their autonomy by blocking any attempts to eliminate or reduce it. The major exception is countries in which one or a few minorities face a solid majority (such as Belgium, Cyprus, and the former Czecho-Slovakia), and the minority veto is formally entrenched in the constitution. India has a numerical Hindu majority of about 83 per cent, but the Hindus are so thoroughly divided by language, caste, and sect that they do not form a political majority. A good example of the informal veto in Indian politics is the 1965 agreement by the central government that Hindi would not be made the exclusive official language without the concurrent approval of the major non-Hindi speaking regions, in effect giving a veto to the southern states, which had opposed dropping English as a language of administration. The provision works best if the minority veto does not have to be used very often in order to protect minority rights and autonomy, and this has been the case in India. No attempts have been made to reverse linguistic federalism, and, while opposition to educational autonomy has been increasing, no governmental actions to weaken or abolish it have been undertaken. The one clear instance of the actual use of the minority veto occurred in the mid-1980s in connection with the separate personal laws: the Muslim minority saw the Supreme Court decision in the Shah Bano case as an attack on Muslim personal law, and it succeeded in vetoing this decision by persuading the government to propose, and parliament to enact, a law reversing the court's judgement.

The one respect in which India does seem to differ from the other consociational democracies is that power sharing was not instituted by a deliberate and comprehensive agreement, such as the 1917 Pacification in the Netherlands, the 1943 National Pact

---

an accommodation with the Scheduled Castes was reached, but further accommodation with the backward castes came about only later and mainly in parts of southern India. Especially in northern India, where there has been little intercaste accommodation, caste conflict is the most serious (see Frankel 1988).

in Lebanon, the 1945 Grand Coalition accord in Austria, and the Malayan Alliance of the early 1950s. But not all consociational democracies have been established by a compact of this kind of comprehensiveness and intentionality; in Belgium and Switzerland, for instance, power sharing developed in a slow step-by-step fashion over more than a century, and Daalder (1974) has argued that even the Dutch Pacification should be seen as merely one step in a long incremental process. This means that India's incremental and sometimes haphazard development of power sharing is somewhat unusual among consociational democracies but not at all unique.

In the face of overwhelming evidence concerning the consociational character of India's democratic system, how can we explain the explicit and complete rejection by Brass (1991: 342–3) of the applicability of consociational theory to India? Brass claims that India is not at all a consociational democracy and, on the contrary, has 'functioned with a highly competitive and distinctly adversarial system of politics'. One explanation is that he defines power sharing in much too narrow terms. His main point is that India has had a variety of interethnic and intercommunal as well as monoethnic parties and sometimes coalitions among these. The implication is that only cabinet coalitions of monoreligious and monoethnic political parties deserve to be regarded as grand coalitions, which is obviously incorrect in view of the great variety of forms that grand coalitions can assume. Moreover, by focusing exclusively on parties and coalitions, Brass completely ignores the evidence with regard to autonomy, proportionality, and the minority veto.

Brass (1991: 343) concedes that India 'has adopted many consociational devices, some permanently, some temporarily', but he fails to see that *together* these devices add up to a fully consociational system. Compared to India, the other consociational democracies do not have any additional or stronger methods of power sharing. The final explanation of Brass's disagreement with my interpretation may be that he focuses on India's more recent democratic experience, when its consociational character has not been as strong as in the first two decades, a subject that I shall treat at greater length later. But even in more recent decades India has remained basically consociational rather than 'not consociational at all'.

India's Power-sharing System: How Much of a Surprise?

Categorizing India as one of the consociational democracies, completely on par with the other well-known cases, is a novel interpretation, although several scholars have identified particular instances of power sharing in India (Brass 1991; Kothari 1989; Young 1976; see also Hardgrave 1993; Weiner 1969). What needs to be emphasized, however, is that, from the perspective of consociational theory, the adoption of power sharing by India and its maintenance for nearly half a century is not at all unexpected or surprising. For one thing, consociational theory places great emphasis on the contribution of prudent and constructive leadership in the development of successful power-sharing systems. Jawaharlal Nehru is an almost perfect example of such leadership. He was prime minister from 1947 until his death in 1964, during the heyday of Indian power sharing. Kothari (1976: 15–16) comments that in India 'it is essential that the institutional system provides for widespread diffusion of power. That this happened to a significant degree under Nehru, and that this trend even appeared to grow stronger in the later part of his career, is a tribute [mainly] to the democratic values, vision, and self-confidence of one man'. That Nehru was not a fully convinced consociational thinker is shown by his initial opposition to the principle of linguistic federalism. But his leadership combined firmness and self-confidence with flexibility and tolerance, and he unfailingly respected and promoted the internally democratic and federal nature of the Congress party. Even on the issue of linguistic federalism, he turned out in the end to be a consociational practitioner. In Kothari's (1970: 157) words once again, 'Nehru's understanding of the consensus framework represented by the Congress was better than that of most of his contemporaries', although he operated 'more on the intuition of a pragmatic politician than on any intellectual grasp of the logic of the system'.

Furthermore, consociational theory tries to explain the probability that power sharing will be instituted and maintained in divided societies in terms of nine background factors that may favour or hinder it. Since most of these conditions are favourable in India, it is again not very surprising that consociational democracy was established and has worked quite well. The following brief review of the nine factors rates India on each of them; the two most important factors are listed first.

(1) The most serious obstacle to power sharing in divided societies is the presence of a solid majority that, understandably, prefers pure majority rule to consociationalism; this factor was mainly responsible for the 1963 failure of the Cypriot consociational system, for instance. As indicated earlier, India's numerical Hindu majority is internally divided to such an extent that the country consists of minorities only.

(2) The second major factor is the absence or presence of large socio-economic differences among the groups of a divided society. In India, there are disparities of this kind among regions and, hence, among linguistic groups, as well as and more importantly between Hindus and Muslims. But even the latter difference is not as great as is often assumed. In a country such as India, where illiteracy is still quite high, literacy rates are good indicators of different levels of socio-economic development. In rural areas—and India is still mainly rural—there is very little difference in the literacy rates of Hindus and Muslims; in urban areas, about two-thirds of Hindus are literate compared with one-half of Muslims (Sharif 1993). Linguistic-regional variations in socio-economic development are mitigated by the fact that the poorer Hindi-speaking areas have historically exercised more power in the central government than the rest of the country, similar to the trade-off between the economically dominant Chinese and the politically dominant Malays in consociational Malaysia (Esman 1972: 25). Finally, socio-economic differences within religious and linguistic groups are so much larger that they overshadow intergroup disparities.

(3) If there are too many groups, then negotiations among them will be too difficult and complex. India, with its extremely large number of groups, including fourteen major languages, receives an unfavourable rating on this factor.

(4) If the groups are of roughly the same size, then there is a balance of power among them. India's division into very many minorities, without any clearly predominant groups, achieves such a rough balance.

(5) If the total population is relatively small, then the decision-making process is less complex (Dahl and Tufte 1973: 40). Since

India is the world's second most populous country, there appears to be no doubt that its score on this factor should be negative. Weiner (1989: 35–6) suggests, however, that India's success in sustaining democracy despite growing tensions and violence can be explained, first, in terms of its federal system (essentially a consociational explanation, because India's linguistic federalism is a key element of its power-sharing system) and, second, in terms of the size of the country, which means that much of the conflict remains localized and does not directly endanger the central authority. Weiner's second argument is also highly plausible and suggests that the relationship between size and the chances for power sharing is curvilinear instead of linear; as size increases, conditions for power sharing worsen initially, but beyond a certain critical point the tendency is reversed.

(6) External dangers promote internal unity. The long struggle against British colonial rule was such a unifying factor in India, as was the 1962 war with China. The wars with Pakistan had the potential of inflaming internal Hindu–Muslim tensions but did not produce this negative effect.

(7) Overarching loyalties reduce the strength of particularistic loyalties. Indian nationalism, powerfully stimulated by the Indian National Congress in the period before independence, has been such a unifying force (Khilnani 1992; Masselos 1985; Suntharalingam 1983). The only serious challenge came from the Muslim League, which claimed that India's Muslims constituted a separate 'nation', but this challenge was effectively removed by the 1947 partition.

(8) If groups are geographically concentrated, then federalism can be used to promote group autonomy. Although India's religious groups are territorially intermixed, the geographical concentration of linguistic groups has made India's highly successful linguistic federalism possible. Hence, on balance, a positive rating is justified.

(9) Traditions of compromise and accommodation foster consociationalism. The Indian National Congress was a movement based on consensus before it became the party of consensus in 1947. More generally, too, as Austin (1966: 315) writes, 'consensus has deep roots in India. Village panchayats traditionally reached decisions in this way.... Indians prefer lengthy discussions of problems to moving quickly to arbitrary decisions'.

In sum, India rates favourably on seven of the nine conditions for power sharing, or on eight if we accept Weiner's reasoning. These include the two most important factors. Among the other consociational democracies, such a favourable predisposition is matched only by Switzerland and the Netherlands. Perhaps it would have been more surprising if India had *not* adopted and maintained a power-sharing system!

The Weakening of Power-sharing after the Late 1960s

Indian power sharing from independence to the present can be divided into two periods: the two decades after 1947, when consociationalism was full-fledged and complete, and the period beginning in the late 1960s, when power sharing continued but in slightly weaker form. How can we account for this shift? Generally speaking, the main reason for the decline (and sometimes failure) of power-sharing systems is an inherent, deep-seated tension. Political leaders have to perform a difficult balancing act between compromises with rivals and maintaining the support of their own followers, both activists and voters. Pleasing other elites will tend to displease their own supporters, and vice versa, and the search for compromise is a time-consuming task that may lead to a degree of immobilism, which is also likely to discontent supporters, who expect and demand effective and decisive government action.[6] It is therefore easier for political elites to share power successfully if their followers are relatively passive and deferential, as shown in particular by the Dutch case (Lijphart 1968: 139–77). This also means that strong pressures from below will increase the elites' tendencies to concentrate and centralize power rather than to share it.

The weakening of power sharing in India after the late 1960s fits this explanatory framework very well. As many scholars have

6 Other possible causes of the decline of power sharing are the emergence of new and unforeseen problems, such as the international crisis that can explain much of the collapse of Lebanese power sharing in the 1970s (Lijphart 1985: 91–2), and the improvement in intergroup relations by successful power sharing to such an extent that full-fledged power sharing becomes superfluous, as in the Austrian and Dutch cases after 1966 and 1967, respectively.

pointed out, the 1960s marked the beginning of mounting democratic activism by previously quiet groups, especially the middle peasants (Brass 1990; Frankel 1988; Kohli 1990; Rudolph and Rudolph 1987). The resulting pressures for more decisive and less consensual government action have prompted greater concentration and centralization of power, especially in the Congress party and the federal system. Four factors contributed to this weakening.

First, under the leadership of Indira Gandhi, who became prime minister in 1966 (after the brief interregnum of Lal Bahadur Shastri, who succeeded Nehru after his death in 1964), the Congress Party was transformed from an internally democratic, federal, and consensual organization to a centralized and hierarchical party. According to Varshney (1993a: 243), 'Nehru had used his charisma to promote intraparty democracy, not to undermine it, strengthening the organization in the process. Indira Gandhi used her charisma to make the party utterly dependent on her, suspending intraparty democracy and debate, and weakening the organization as a result'. In very similar terms, Das Gupta (1989: 71) describes the new Congress party as 'less a national institution of interest reconciliation than a central organization for mobilizing endorsement for the leadership and its hierarchical apparatus'. It has remained a broadly inclusive party, but less by means of *representation* from the bottom up than by *representativeness* from the top down.

Second, the federal system, never highly decentralized, was centralized even more. One instrument was the increasingly frequent use of so-called President's Rule for partisan purposes. The founding fathers had given the central government the right to dismiss state governments and to replace them with direct rule from the centre for the purpose of dealing with grave emergencies, not foreseeing that the central government 'would resort to devices intended to safeguard unity and cohesion for undermining democratically elected [state] governments and seeking to diminish their role and importance' (Arora and Mukarji 1992: 8). President's Rule was invoked ten times before the end of 1967 and 66 times in the only slightly longer period from 1968 to early 1989 (Kathuria 1990: 339). Like the centralization of the Congress Party, the similar trend in the federal system is often attributed to Indira Gandhi. It would be wrong, however, to interpret these trends primarily in terms of the—admittedly starkly contrasting—leadership propensities of Nehru and his daughter. For one thing, they can be explained more convincingly in terms of the structural tensions inherent in power sharing. For another, Indira Gandhi's two main successors reverted to a less confrontational and more consensual style of leadership (Rajiv Gandhi intermittently and P.V. Narasimha Rao more consistently) without, however, undoing either the party's or the federation's centralization.

The third source of weakness is that the pressures from below have specifically included calls for the abolition of crucial consociational rules put in place by power-sharing compromises: separate personal laws, minority educational autonomy, and Kashmir's constitutionally privileged (although no longer actually implemented) autonomous status. Not all the criticism of the 1986 Muslim Women (Protection of Right on Divorce) Act necessarily entailed a wholesale condemnation of personal law; many critics objected mainly to the specific provisions of the new law, calling it 'a primitive anti-woman bill' (Iyer 1987: xvi). But the Supreme Court judgement in the Shah Bano case explicitly called for the elimination of separate personal laws and their replacement by a 'uniform civil code', arguing in a clearly anti-consociational vein that 'a common civil code will help the cause of national integration by removing disparate loyalties to laws which have conflicting ideologies' (cited in Engineer 1987: 33). The reversal of the court's decision gave new ammunition to the foes of separate personal laws.

In an examination of the claim that minorities enjoy more rights than the Hindu majority, Sharma (1993: 102, 106) argues that it is valid as far as the minorities, educational autonomy is concerned: their schools are not 'subject to governmental control in the way similar institutions run by the majority community are. The minorities in this respect do in fact enjoy rights not available to the majority community'. He concludes that 'this in effect means that the majority community subsidizes the educational system of the minority communities'. Sharma captures the growing criticism of minority educational autonomy very well, including the tendentious argument that it is the 'majority', instead of society as a whole, that does the subsidizing. One way to solve the problem would be to make educational autonomy available to any group, regardless of its majority or minority status and regardless of whether it is a religious, linguistic, or any other kind of group, such as a group of people espousing a particular educational philosophy like Montessori. Instead of such an improvement of the system along consociational lines, as in the Netherlands, for instance, the prevailing tendency among the critics is the anti-consociational one of abolition.

The Bharatiya Janata Party (BJP) has made itself the main mouthpiece against the government's alleged pandering to minorities, what its leader L.K. Advani calls 'minorityism' (Varshney 1993a: 252). The BJP, usually described as a 'Hindu nationalist party', is clearly anti-consociational, and its growing strength represents a major potential danger to power sharing in India.[7] The 1991 state elections brought the BJP to power in India's largest state, Uttar Pradesh, with one-sixth of the country's population, as well as in Madhya Pradesh, Rajasthan, and Himachal Pradesh. After the imposition of President's Rule and new elections in November 1993, the BJP retained control only in Rajasthan, but it also won the election in the union territory (and capital city) of Delhi. In the February 1995 state elections, it extended its influence from the northern Hindi-speaking heartland to the western part of the country by winning elections in Gujarat and, allied with the Hindu fundamentalist party Shiv Sena, in Maharashtra.

The fourth and final source of weakness derives from a combination of the inherent tensions of power sharing and the unique Indian form of grand coalition, based on the predominance of a broadly representative party. All the pressures from below make it especially difficult to maintain broad support for a party explicitly committed to power sharing and minority rights. The Congress party has never won a majority of the popular vote, and in 1967 its plurality fell to only slightly more than 40 per cent. It lost the 1977 and 1989 elections outright, and because it gained a mere plurality of seats in 1991 it could only form a minority cabinet. In fact, the 1989 and 1991 election results show that India has shifted from a dominant- to a multi-party system. The shift in the effective number of parliamentary parties—the number of

7 The BJP also can be called a majority-control party in the sense that Lustick (1979) uses the term *control*: see fn. 2.

parties in parliament weighted by their size (Taagepera and Shugart 1989: 77–91)—is instructive in this respect: the eight elections from 1951 to 1984 yielded eight manufactured majorities (seat majorities won without vote majorities) and an average effective number of 22 parties, typical of either a two-party or dominant-party system; the elections in 1989 and 1991 failed to produce a majority party, and the average effective number of parties increased to 3.8, clearly a multi-party system.

These weaknesses do not signify that power sharing has ended or is ending in India. Congress party cabinets have continued to be broadly representative, and non-Congress cabinets have been only marginally less so during their two brief periods in power. Federalism has weakened but is far from dead, and the principle of linguistic federalism is very much alive. Minority educational autonomy and separate personal laws are under attack, but they have so far survived, along with the minority veto and the proportionality principle.

The above description of continued, although weakened, power sharing in India fits consociational theory in two other respects. The theory states that power sharing is a necessary condition for the survival of democracy in divided societies; indeed, Harrison's (1960: 338) dire prediction of India's democratic failure, quoted at the beginning of this article, is not shared by any knowledgeable observer of Indian politics today (see especially Varshney 1995). At the same time, while Indian democracy is quite stable in this fundamental sense, the weakening of power sharing should be expected to be accompanied by increases in intergroup tensions and violence, which clearly has been the case in India. The official figures, which tend to be on the conservative side, on Hindu–Muslim violence in the 1954–85 period presented in P.R. Rajgopal's (1987: 16–17) study show an alarming trend. When the first five years (1954–8) are compared with the last five years (1981–5), the number of violent incidents rose from 339 to 2290, the number of persons killed from 112 to 2350, and the number of persons injured from 2229 to 17,791. This trend, Rajgopal observes, 'shows no signs of being reversed'. Indeed, in the aftermath of the destruction of the mosque at Ayodhya in December 1992, rioting in many parts of India led to about 1200 deaths in one month, and more than 600 people were killed in anti–Muslim rioting in Bombay in January 1993 (Hardgrave 1993: 64–5).

The causal link between the weakening of power sharing and these problems of governance has also been noted by scholars not explicitly belonging to the consociational school. For instance, Weiner (1989: 11) writes that 'conflict management has become more difficult with the decline of the Congress party organization and the weakening of the federal structure'. Varshney (1993b: 17–18) finds it 'not surprising that the attempt by the post-Nehru leadership of the Congress party to centralize an essentially diverse and federal polity has co-existed with some of the worst stresses that the polity has experienced, including the insurgenc[ies] in Punjab and Kashmir'.

A Return to Full-fledged Power Sharing?

A final piece of evidence about the close fit between the Indian case and consociational theory is provided by the proposals for political and constitutional reform. If the consociational interpretation of India's democracy is correct, that is, if the survival of Indian democracy can be explained by its power-sharing character and if its increasing turbulence after the 1960s can be explained in terms of the weakening of power sharing, we should expect these proposals to have two characteristics. First, all or most of them should be aimed at strengthening the consociational aspects of the political system. Second, given the growth in intergroup tensions and violence and the growing opposition to the very principle of power sharing, they can be expected to call for far-reaching reform with a sense of urgency.

Both expectations are correct. Although there is no vigorous public debate about or widespread demand for political change, Indians who do call for reform have in mind drastic measures, indeed. For instance, Abid Hussain (1993: 11) asserts that India's 'deformed polity' is 'in need of drastic surgery'. In a volume entitled *Reforming the Constitution*, others have called for 'fundamental changes' (Reddy 1992) and 'major amendments' (Vira 1992) to the constitution, or even for the election of a new constituent assembly (Malaviya 1992) that should draft an entirely 'new constitution' (Rao 1992) as the foundation for a 'Second Republic' (Jaisingh 1992). Significantly, the substantive thrust of all but one of the major reform plans is in the direction of stronger power sharing. The one exception, which is only a partial exception, is the frequently voiced suggestion that India should adopt an American-style or French-style presidential system (Pathak 1993; Rao 1992; Sathe 1991: 37–8; Trehan 1993; see also Noorani 1989). From the consociational perspective, the problem with presidentialism is its concentration of executive power in the hands of one person, who, in a divided society, is inevitably a member of one particular group; power sharing requires joint rule by the representatives of all major groups in a collegial decision-making body, ideally provided by cabinets in parliamentary systems. The most prominent and detailed presidentialist proposal for India, however, put forward by B.K. Nehru, explicitly recognizes this disadvantage and tries to compensate for it by recommending a special form of presidentialism, used in Nigeria and also recommended by Horowitz (1985: 635–8) for ethnically heterogeneous societies elsewhere. Nehru's (1992: 138) proposal is to 'divide the country into four zones—east, west, south, and north—and require a successful candidate for the Presidency not only to get an overall majority of the votes cast throughout the country but also a specific, relatively small, percentage of votes in all the zones, before he can be declared elected'. This would ensure that the winning candidate has at least a minimum of support in regions other than his or her own.[8]

The other major reform proposals, entailing the strengthening of the federal system and the adoption of a proportional representation (PR) election system, are all fully consonant with power sharing. There appears to be almost universal agreement that India's federal system should be decentralized; this is the tenor of the 1988 report of the Sarkaria Commission on Union–State Relations, which Mukarji and Mathew (1992: 280) call 'conservative but constructive', since they and other reformers

[8] A serious drawback of the Nigerian system, used in 1979 and 1983 (in which the winner needs a nationwide plurality plus at least 25 per cent of the vote in no fewer than two-thirds of the states) is that it can easily result in none of the candidates being elected. This is not a problem in Nehru's (1992: 137) plan because he proposes the indirect election of the president—by an electoral college of national, state, and local legislators—in which repeated ballots can be conducted until a winner emerges. Of course, consociationalists would still prefer a broadly *representative* collegial executive to a broadly *supported* presidency.

would prefer to go much farther. An especially interesting proposal by Mukarji and Arora (1992: 270) is to establish a three-level federalism, with each state becoming a federation, or even a more radical multilevel federalism. They call such a system a 'cascading federalism: a federation of federations'. One reason this kind of reform is so attractive is that the Indian states are inordinately large; not counting the seven union territories, the *average* population of the 25 states is about 35 million, larger than California, the most populous state in the United States.

Another and more straightforward solution to the problem of unwieldy state size would be to increase the number of states. Kothari (1976: 81) suggests about 40, and a detailed proposal by Khan (1992: 108–22) specifies 58, six of which would be carved out of the huge state of Uttar Pradesh, with a population of almost 150 million. Similarly, Kashyap (1992: 32–3) recommends the creation of '50 to 60 states of almost equal size'. A considerable increase in the number of states also offers an opportunity for further fine-tuning of linguistic homogeneity.

Finally, many reformers have proposed the adoption of PR for parliamentary elections (Bhambhri 1971; Nehru 1992). The German system, which combines first-past-the-post elections for half the parliamentary seats with overall proportionality for all seats by means of list PR, is the most frequently mentioned specific suggestion (Hegde 1986: 107; Seth 1971; Singh 1986: 120; see also Vanhanen 1987). PR is based on the consociational principle of proportionality, and, as comparative studies of democratic systems show, it is conducive to multi-party systems, which in turn are conducive to broad multiparty cabinets (Lijphart 1984), although there is no guarantee, of course, that coalitions larger than a bare majority will be formed. In the case of India, even a narrow coalition of parties elected by PR is likely to be based on at least a popular majority, which means that it would be more broadly based than any Indian cabinet so far.

One reform that PR almost certainly would preclude, is a return to the 'Congress system', which Kothari (1989: 304–6) appears to favour and which, it should be noted, is also consociational in orientation, with either the Congress party itself or another party becoming the new party of consensus. Without a majority-manufacturing electoral system, it would be difficult for such a party to develop. But it is unlikely anyway that a new party of consensus could form without the advantage of the unique historical circumstances of 1947, when the ruling party emerged from an enormously effective and successful national liberation movement, and without Jawaharlal Nehru's unusually high quality of leadership. Moreover, instead of helping the moderate and centrist Congress party, first-past-the-post might well bring an anti-consociational party like the BJP to power with a manufactured majority.

Conclusion

The big puzzle of Indian democracy—its survival despite the country's deep ethnic and communal divisions—is solved by the consociational interpretation presented in this chapter. India has had a power-sharing system of democracy during its almost fifty years of independence, and an especially full and thorough form of it during its first two decades, displaying all four of the essential elements of power sharing as clearly as Austria, the Netherlands, Switzerland, Lebanon, Malaysia, and the other well-known examples of consociational democracy. That newly independent India embraced power sharing and has maintained it ever since is not even very surprising, because most of the conditions found to be conducive to it in these other countries are also favourable in the Indian case. After the late 1960s, as a result of greater mass mobilization and activation, power sharing became less strong and pervasive, evidenced by the centralization of the Congress party and the federal system, the decline of the Congress party's electoral strength, the attack on minority rights, and the rise of the BJP. As consociational theory would have predicted, Indian democracy has remained basically stable, but the weakening of power sharing has been accompanied by an increase in intergroup hostility and violence. Concern about these trends is reflected in the consociational thrust of the major proposals for political and constitutional change by reform-minded Indians.

The consociational interpretation of India strengthens our understanding of the Indian case by providing a theoretically coherent explanation of the main patterns and trends in its political development. Furthermore, it strengthens consociational theory by removing the one allegedly deviant case and by showing that, instead, the crucial case of India is unmistakably a confirming case.

References

Arora, Balveer and Nirmal Mukarji (1992), 'Introduction: The Basic Issues' in Nirmal Mukarji and Balveer Arora (eds), *Federalism in India: Origins and Development.* New Delhi: Vikas.

Austin, Granville (1996), *The Indian Constitution: Cornerstone of a Nation.* Bombay: Oxford University Press.

Banerjee, Ashis (1992), 'Federalism and Nationalism: An Attempt at Historical Interpretation' in Nirmal Mukarji and Balveer Arora (eds), *Federalism in India: Origins and Development.* New Delhi: Vikas.

Barry, Brian (1975), 'Political Accommodation and Consociational Democracy', *British Journal of Political Science*, vol. 5, October, pp. 477–505.

Batliner, Gerard (1981), *Zur heutigen Lage des liechtensteinischen Parlaments.* Vaduz: Veriag der Liechtensteinischen Akademischen Gesell-schaft.

Berg-Schlosser, Dirk (1985), 'Elements of Consociational Democracy in Kenya', *European Journal of Political Research*, vol. 13, March pp. 95–109.

Bhambhri, C.P. (1971), 'Electoral Reform and Party System in India: A Plea for Proportional Representation' in Subhash C. Kashyap (ed.), *Elections and Electoral Reform in India.* New Delhi: Institute for Constitutional and Parliamentary Studies.

Brass, Paul R. (1990), *The Politics of India Since Independence.* Cambridge: Cambridge University Press.

——— (1991), *Ethnicity and Nationalism: Theory and Comparison.* New Delhi: Sage Publications.

Cannon, Gordon E. (1982), 'Consociationalism vs. Control: Canada as a Case Study', *Western Political Quarterly*, vol. 35, March, pp. 50–64.

Chehabi, H.E. (1980), 'The Absence of Consociationalism in Sri Lanka', *Plural Societies*, vol. 11 Winter, pp. 55–65.

Chinwuba, Felix Aneze (1980), 'Consociationalism as an Approach to Political Integration: The Case of the Federal Republic of Nigeria'. Ph.D. dissertation, Tulane University.

Chryssochoou, Dimitris N. (1994), 'Democracy and Symbiosis in the

European Union: Towards a Confederal Consociation?', *West European Politics*, vol. 17, October, pp. 1–14.

Daalder, Hans (1974), 'The Consociational Democracy Theme', *World Politics*, vol. 26, July, pp. 604–21.

Daalder, Hans and Galen A. Edwards (eds) (1989), Special Issue on 'Politics in the Netherlands: How Much Change?', *West European Politics*, vol. 12, January, pp. 1–85.

Dahl, Robert A. (1989), *Democracy and Its Critics*. New Haven: Yale University Press.

Dahl, Robert A. and Edward R. Tufte (1973), *Size and Democracy*. Stanford: Stanford University Press.

Das Gupta, Jyotirindra (1989), 'India: Democratic Becoming and Combined Development' in Larry Diamond, Juan J. Linz, and Seymour Martin Lipset (eds), *Democracy in Developing Countries*. Boulder, CO: Lynne Rienner.

Dekmejian, Richard Hrair (1978), 'Consociational Democracy in Crisis: The Case of Lebanon', *Comparative Politics*, vol. 10, January, pp. 251–65.

Dew, Edward M. (1994), *The Trouble in Suriname, 1975–1993*. Westport, CT: Praeger.

Dix, Robert H. (1980), 'Consociational Democracy: The Case of Colombia', *Comparative Politics*, vol. 12, April, pp. 303–21.

Engineer, Asghar Ali (ed.) (1987), *The Shah Bano Controversy*. Hyderabad: Orient Longman.

Esman, Milton J. (1972), *Administration and Development in Malaysia: Institution-Building and Reform in a Plural Society*. Ithaca, NY: Cornell University Press.

Frankel, Francine R. (1988), 'Middle Classes and Castes in India's Politics: Prospects for Political Accommodation' in Atul Kohli (ed.), *India's Democracy: An Analysis of Changing State–Society Relations*. Princeton: Princeton University Press.

Fyzee, Asaf A.A. (1964), *Outlines of Muhammadan Law*, 3rd edition. London: Oxford University Press.

Gabel, Mathew J. (1994), 'Balancing Democracy and Stability: Considering the Democratic Deficit in the EU from a Consociational Perspective', paper presented at the Joint Sessions of Workshops of the European Consortium for Political Research, Madrid.

Goldman, Joseph Richard (1985), 'Consociational Authoritarian Politics and the 1974 Yugoslav Constitution: A Preliminary Note', *East European Quarterly*, vol. 19, June, pp. 241–9.

Graziano, Luigi (1980), 'The Historic Compromise and Consociational Democracy: "Toward a New Democracy"?', *International Political Science Review*, vol. 1, no. 3, pp. 345–68.

Halpern, Sue M. (1986), 'The Disorderly Universe of Consociational Democracy', *West European Politics*, vol. 9, April, pp. 181–97.

Hardgrave, Robert L., Jr (1993), 'India: The Dilemmas of Diversity', *Journal of Democracy*, vol. 4, October, pp. 54–68.

Harrison, Selig S. (1960), *India: The Most Dangerous Decades*. Princeton: Princeton University Press.

Hartlyn, Jonathan (1988), *The Politics of Coalition Rule in Colombia*. Cambridge: Cambridge University Press.

Hegde, Ramakrishna (1986), *Electoral Reforms: Lack of Political Will*. Bangalore: Karnataka State Janata Party.

Hix, Simon (1994), 'Approaches to the Study of the EC: The Challenge to Comparative Politics', *West European Politics*, vol. 17, January, pp. 1–30.

Horowitz, Donald L. (1985), *Ethnic Groups in Conflict*. Berkeley: University of California Press.

Hughes, Arnold (1982), 'The Limits of "Consociational Democracy" in the Gambia', *Civilisations*, vol. 32, no. 2, pp. 65–92.

Huntington, Samuel P. (1988), 'One Soul at a Time: Political Science and Political Reform', *American Political Science Review*, vol. 82, March, pp. 3–10.

Hussain, Abid (1993), *India: Challenges and Changes*. New Delhi: Rajiv Gandhi Institute for Contemporary Studies.

Huyse, Luc (1987), *De verzuiling voorbij*. Louvain: Kritak.

Iyer, V.R. Krishna (1987), *The Muslim Women (Protection of Rights on Divorce) Act, 1986*. Lucknow: Eastern Book Company.

Jaisingh, Hari (1992), 'Time for a Second Republic' in Subhash C. Kashyap (ed.), *Reforming the Constitution*. New Delhi: UBSPD.

Kashyap, Subhash C. (1992), 'Constitution: Its Working and Need for Reforms' in Subhash C. Kashyap (ed.), *Reforming the Constitution*. New Delhi: UBSPD.

Kathuria, Harbir Singh (1990), *President's Rule in India, 1967–89*. New Delhi: Uppal.

Khan, Rasheeduddin (1992), *Federal India: A Design for Change*. New Delhi: Vikas.

Khilnani, Sunil (1992), 'India's Democratic Career' in John Dunn (ed.), *Democracy: The Unfinished Journey, 508 BC to AD 1993*. Oxford: Oxford University Press.

Kohli, Atul (1990), *Democracy and Discontent: India's Growing Crisis of Governability*. Cambridge: Cambridge University Press.

Kothari, Rajni (1970), *Politics in India*. Boston: Little Brown.

——— (1976), *Democratic Polity and Social Change in India: Crisis and Opportunities*. Bombay: Allied.

——— (1989), *Politics and the People: In Search of a Humane India*. Delhi: Ajanta.

Lehmbruch, Gerhard (1993), 'Consociational Democracy and Corporatism in Switzerland', *Publius*, vol. 23, Spring, pp. 43–63.

Levine, Daniel II (1973), *Conflict and Political Change in Venezuela*. Princeton: Princeton University Press.

Lijphart, Arend (1968), *The Politics of Accommodation: Pluralism and Democracy in the Netherlands*. Berkeley: University of California Press.

——— (1977), *Democracy in Plural Societies: A Comparative Exploration*. New Haven: Yale University Press.

——— (1979), 'Consociation and Federation: Conceptual and Empirical Links', *Canadian Journal of Political Science*, vol. 12, September, pp. 499–515.

——— (1984), *Democracies: Majoritarian and Consensus Patterns of Government in Twenty-One Countries*. New Haven: Yale University Press.

——— (1985), *Power-Sharing in South Africa*. Berkeley: Institute of International Studies, University of California.

——— (1992), 'Democratization and Constitutional Choices in Czechoslovakia, Hungary, and Poland', *Journal of Theoretical Politics*, vol. 4, April, pp. 207–33.

——— (1994), 'Prospects for Power-Sharing in the New South Africa', in Andrew Reynolds (ed.), *Election 94 South Africa: The Campaigns, Results and Future Prospects*. New York: St Martin's Press.

Lindberg, Leon N. (1994), 'The Political System of the European Community' in Martin O. Heisler (ed.), *Politics in Europe: Structures and Processes in Some Postindustrial Democracies*. New York: David McKay.

Linder, Wolf (1994), *Swiss Democracy: Possible Solutions to Conflict in Multicultural Societies*. New York: St Martin's Press.

Lustick, Ian. (1979), 'Stability in Deeply Divided Societies', *World Politics*, vol. 31, April, pp. 325–44.

Luther, Kurt Richard and Wolfgang Müller (eds) (1992), Special Issue on 'Politics in Austria: Still a Case of Consociationalism?', *West European Politics*, vol. 15, January, pp. 1–226.

Luthera, Ved Prakash (1964), *The Concept of the Secular State and India.* London: Oxford University Press.

Mair, Peter (1994), 'The Correlates of Consensus Democracy and the Puzzle of Dutch Politics', *West European Politics,* vol. 17, October, pp. 97–123.

Malaviya, S.P. (1992), 'Case for a Constituent Assembly' in Subhash C. Kashyap (ed.), *Reforming the Constitution.* New Delhi: UBSPD.

Masselos, Jim (1985), *Indian Nationalism: An History.* New Delhi: Sterling.

Mehta, Piarey Lal (1991), *Constitutional Protection to Scheduled Tribes in India: In Retrospect and Prospects.* Delhi: H.K. Publishers.

Messarra, Antoine Nasri (1994), *Théorie générale du système politique libanais.* Paris: Cariscript.

Mill, John Stuart (1958) [1861], *Consideration on Representative Government.* New York: Liberal Arts Press.

Mukarji, Nirmal and Balveer Arora (1992), 'Conclusion: Restructuring Federal Democracy' in Nirmal Mukarji and Balveer Arora (eds), *Federalism in India: Origins and Development.* New Delhi: Vikas.

Mukarji, Nirmal and George Mathew (1992), 'Epilogue: Federal Issues, 1988–1990' in Nirmal Mukarji and Balveer Arora (eds), *Federalism in India: Origins and Development.* New Delhi: Vikas.

Nehru, B.K. (1986), *Thoughts on Our Present Discontents.* New Delhi: Allied.

——— (1992), 'A Fresh Look at the Constitution' in Subhash C. Kashyap (ed.), *Reforming the Constitution.* New Delhi: UBSPD.

Noorani, A.G. (1989), *The Presidential System: The Indian Debate.* New Delhi: Sage Publications.

Olson, David M. (1994), 'The Sundered State: Federalism and Parliament in Czechoslovakia' in Thomas F. Remington (ed.), *Parliaments in Transition: The New Legislative Politics in the Former USSR and Eastern Europe.* Boulder: Westview Press.

Pai Panandiker, V.A. and Ajay Mehra (1996), *The Indian Cabinet and Governance of India.* New Delhi: Konark.

Pathak, Bindeshwar (1994), 'Facets of the System: Presidential vs. Parliamentary' in Subhash S. Kashyap (ed.), *Perspectives on the Constitution.* Delhi: Shipra.

Powell, G. Bingham, Jr (1970), *Social Fragmentation and Political Hostility: An Austrian Case Study.* Stanford: Stanford University Press.

——— (1979), 'Book Review of Arend Lijphart's, *Democracy in Plural Societies*', *American Political Science Review,* vol. 73, March, pp. 295–97.

——— (1982), *Contemporary Democracies: Participation, Stability, and Violence.* Cambridge: Harvard University Press.

Prasad, Anirudh (1991), *Reservation Policy and Practice in India: A Means to an End.* New Delhi: Deep & Deep Publications.

Rae, Douglas W. (1967), *The Political Consequences of Electoral Laws.* New Haven: Yale University Press.

Rajgopal, P.R. (1987), *Communal Violence in India.* New Delhi: Uppal.

Rao, S. Ramachandra (1992), 'Plea for a New Constitution' in Subhash C. Kashyap (ed.), *Reforming the Constitution.* New Delhi: UBSPD.

Reddy, K. Brahmananda (1992), 'Case for Fundamental Changes' in Subhash C. Kashyap (ed.), *Reforming the Constitution.* New Delhi: UBSPD.

Rudolph, Lloyd I. and Susanne Hoeber Rudolph (1987), *In Pursuit of Lakshmi: The Political Economy of the Indian State.* Chicago: University of Chicago Press.

Sathe, Vasant (1991), *National Government: Agenda for a New India.* New Delhi: UBS.

Sheth, J.D. (1971), 'Towards a New Electoral Law' in Subhash C. Kashyap (ed.), *Elections and Electoral Reforms in India.* New Delhi: Institute of Constitutional and Parliamentary Studies.

Sharif, Abu Saleh (1993), *Some Socio-Economic and Demographic Aspects of Population According to Religion in India.* Bombay: Centre for the Study of Society and Secularism.

Sharma, Arvind (1993), 'Minority vs. Majority Rights' in Subhash C. Kashyap (ed.), *Perspectives on the Constitution.* Delhi: Shipra.

Singh, L.P. (1986), *Electoral Reform: Problems and Suggested Solutions.* New Delhi: Uppal.

Srinivasavaradan, T.C.A. (1992), *Federal Concept: The Indian Experience.* New Delhi: Allied.

Steiner, Jürg (1990), 'Power-Sharing: Another Swiss "Export Product"?' in V. Joseph Montville (ed.), *Conflict and Peacemaking in Multiethnic Societies.* Lexington, MA: Lexington Books.

Steiner, Jürg and Robert H. Dorff (1980), *A Theory of Political Decision Modes: Intraparty Decision Making in Switzerland.* Chapel Hill: University of North Carolina Press.

Suntharalingam, R. (1983), *Indian Nationalism: An Historical Analysis*. New Delhi: Vikas.

Taagepera, Rein and Matthew Soberg Shugart (1989), *Seats and Votes: The Effects and Determinants of Electoral Systems*. New Haven: Yale University Press.

Taylor, Rupert (1992), 'South Africa: A Consociational Path to Peace?', *Transformation*, vol. 17, pp. 1–11.

Trehan, Virender M. (1993), 'Need for Change' in Subhash C. Kashyap (ed.), *Perspectives on the Constitution*. Delhi: Shipra.

Van den Berghe, L. Pierre (1981), *The Ethnic Phenomenon*. New York: Elsevier.

Vanhanen, Tatu (1987), 'What Kind of Electoral System for Plural Societies? India as an Example' in Manfred J. Holler (ed.), *The Logic of Multiparty Systems*. Dordrecht, Netherlands: Kluwer.

Varshney, Ashutosh (1993a), 'Contested Meanings: India's National Identity, Hindu Nationalism, and the Politics of Anxiety', *Daedalus*, vol. 122, Summer, pp. 227–61.

———— (1993b), 'India's Democratic Exceptionalism and Its Troubled Trajectory'. Revised version of paper presented at the 1990 annual meeting of the American Political Science Association, San Francisco.

———— (1995), 'The Self-Correcting Mechanisms of Indian Democracy', *Seminar* (Delhi), vol. 425, January, pp. 38–41.

Vasovic, Vucina (1992), 'A Plea for Consociational Pluralism' in Jim Seroka and Vukasin Pavlovic (eds), *The Tragedy of Yugoslavia: The Failure of Democratic Transformation*. Armonk, NY: M.E. Sharpe.

Vira, Dharma (1992), 'Inadequacy and Impracticability of the Present Constitution: Case for Major Amendments' in Subhash C. Kashyap (ed.), *Reforming the Constitution*. New Delhi: UBSPD.

Von Vorys, Karl (1975), *Democracy Without Consensus: Communalism and Political Stability in Malaysia*. Princeton: Princeton University Press.

Weiner, Myron (1969), *Party Building in a New Nation: The Indian National Congress*. Chicago: University of Chicago Press.

———— (1989), *The Indian Paradox: Essays in Indian Politics*. New Delhi: Sage Publications.

Wheare, K.C. (1964), *Federal Government*, 4th edition. New York: Oxford University Press.

Worrall, Denis (1981), 'The Constitutional Committee of the President's Council', *Politikon*, vol. 8, December, pp. 27–34.

Young, Crawford (1976), *The Politics of Cultural Pluralism.* Madison: University of Wisconsin Press.

Zakaria, Haji Ahmad (1989), 'Malaysia: Quasi Democracy in a Divided Society' in Larry Diamond, Juan J. Linz, and Seymour Martin Lipset (eds), *Democracy in Developing Countries: Asia.* Boulder, CO: Lynne Rienner.

Zolberg, Aristide R. (1977), 'Splitting the Difference: Federalization Without Federalism in Belgium' in Milton J. Esman (ed.), *Ethnic Conflict in the Western World.* Ithaca, NY: Cornell University Press.

IV

Democracy and Development

In the Introduction to this volume, we discussed the scholarly debate on democracy and development in a comparative context, showing that the evidence on whether democracy inhibited or encouraged development was inconclusive. Indeed, from the point of view of the Indian experience, the debate was found to be somewhat misconceived. This section presents two arguments from the Indian perspective, both by economists. Deepak Nayyar's article argues that there is a tension between the economics of markets (which exclude people, especially the poor) and the more inclusive politics of democracy. He divides the history of independent India into three phases, and delineates the interaction between economic development and political democracy in each of these. In the first phase (1947–66), the state's role in economic development was not merely pre-eminent, it was also founded on a national political consensus. However, though the politics of accommodation were ostensibly practised, the poor did not benefit from the processes of economic development. In the second phase (1967–90), the erosion of this consensus became apparent, as did the ability of the state to mediate between conflicting interests. This explains the political efforts to co-opt the rich peasantry, as well as the politics of competitive populism. Nevertheless, this was the phase which saw an increase in the growth rate of the Indian economy, and a decline in poverty. In the third phase (1991–7), the external debt crisis forced the state to accept measures of fiscal adjustment and structural reform, leading to the opening up of economy. Correspondingly, the role of the state was reduced, with its ability to mediate conflicts between economic development and political democracy at its lowest.

The paper by Pranab Bardhan is the Epilogue to his well-known book *The Political Economy of Development in India* (1984). In that work, Bardhan had famously identified the three proprietary classes—the industrial capitalist class, the rich farmers, and the professionals in the public sector—who comprised the dominant proprietary coalition. He had pointed out that there are significant conflicts of interest between these classes, which belong to the top two deciles of the population, and are therefore separated by a wide gulf from the bottom half of the abjectly poor Indian population. The conflicts within the dominant coalition, Bardhan had argued, were exacerbated by the 'turmoil from below', which suggested a shift from hierarchical and deferential norms to more assertive forms of political expression. In the Epilogue reproduced here, Bardhan discusses the political economy and the political sociology of the reforms process in India. He argues that the recent drift of political power from the Centre to the states is paralleled by a shift of power towards the backward and lower castes. Though this is a sign of democratic progress in an unequal society, it also entails the erosion of earlier practices by which decision-making on economic management and public administration were institutionally insulated. The concern for group equity and group (rather than individual) rights represent, he argues, an anti-market streak in Indian political culture, and therefore a less than hospitable environment for the reforms.

12

Economic Development and Political Democracy: Interaction of Economics and Politics in Independent India[+*]

Deepak Nayyar

I

Introduction

There is a vast literature on the theme of economic development in India over the past fifty years. The literature on the subject of political democracy in India since independence is just as extensive. Both are rich in terms of range and depth. But they

+ *Economic and Political Weekly*, 5 December 1998, pp. 3121–31.

* An earlier version of this paper was presented at a conference on 'Nationalism, Democracy and Development' at the University of Bologna from 27–29 November 1997. This text was the basis of my lecture in the Golden Jubilee Series at the National Council of Applied Economic Research, New Delhi, on 11 September 1998. This was first published in *Economic and Political Weekly* and is to be also published in a volume that puts together the lectures in the series at the NCAER.

I am indebted to Amit Bhaduri, Arvind Das, Satish Jain, and Srirang Shukla for helpful discussion on some of the ideas developed here. I would also like to thank Partha Chatterjee, Ashok Mitra, and Achin Vanaik for valuable comments on a preliminary draft and Arjun Sengupta for helpful comments on the lecture text. I am particularly grateful to Rajni Kothari for searching questions and constructive suggestions, following the lecture, which have persuaded me to think further about the subject.

constitute two different worlds, divided into the disciplines of economics and political science. The intersections are few and far between. This essay makes a modest attempt to reflect on the inter-connections. It situates the process of economic development in the wider context of political democracy to explore the interaction between economics and politics in independent India. Section II sets out an analytical framework. It explains why markets and democracy provide no magic wand, to suggest that the real issue is the tension between the economics of markets and the politics of democracy. The problem, it argues, is compounded because markets exclude people, particularly the poor. The five decades are then divided into three phases. Any such periodization is obviously arbitrary but it serves an analytical purpose. Section III examines the first phase, 1947–66, in which the strategy of development was shaped by a political consensus and characterized by a long-term perspective. The spirit of nationalism meant that there was less need to manage conflict, but there was a conscious effort to accommodate the poor even if it was long on words and short on substance. Section IV analyses the second phase, 1967–90, which witnessed a qualitative change in the interaction of economics and politics. Economic policies and economic development were strongly influenced by the compulsions of political democracy. Those with a political voice made economic claims on the state. But the process of mediation and reconciliation had long-term economic and political consequences. Section V discusses the third phase, from 1991, characterized by an absence of consensus and a presence of short-termism, in which the economics of liberalization and the politics of empowerment seem to be moving the economy and the polity in opposite directions. The need for conflict resolution is greater than ever before. But the task has become more difficult. And, strangely enough, the effort is much less.

II

Democracy and Markets

As the twentieth century draws to a close and we approach a new millennium, *market economy* and *political democracy* are buzz words: not only in turbulent Eastern Europe attempting a transition to capitalism, but also across a wide spectrum of countries in the developing world from Latin America through Africa to Asia. This is partly a consequence of the collapse of planned economies and excessive or inappropriate state intervention in market economies. And it is partly attributable to a concern about authoritarian regimes, particularly in countries where there has been no improvement in living conditions of the common people, but even in countries where economic development has been impressive despite which there is no movement towards a democratic polity. Consequently, the mood of the moment is such that markets and democracy are perceived as both virtue and necessity. In this process, some countries are in search of new models of development, while others are attempting to adapt their erstwhile models of development. For the new orthodoxy believes that, insofar as democracy is about political freedom for individuals and markets are about economic freedom for individuals, the two together must serve the interests of the people. However, there is little basis for this inference either in theory or in practice.

For one, democracies function on the principle of majority rule or some variant thereof. This is clearly preferable to monarchies or oligarchies associated with the rule of an individual or of a few. But democracy can lead to the *tyranny of majorities.*[1] What is more, in countries characterized by social and economic inequalities that run deep, it is not clear how adult franchise alone can create political equality. We must not forget that universal suffrage is a twentieth-century phenomenon even in Europe. Indeed, we would do well to remember that it was property rights, rather than equality, which were at the foundation of liberalism. And, for a long time, it was property that endowed people with a right to vote so that access to political democracy was the privilege of a few and not the right of everyone.

For another, the proposition that markets create equal opportunities for all depends on the critical assumption that the initial distribution of property rights is equal. Thus, any defence of the market on the premise that it is good in terms of actual outcomes

[1] The principle that the will of the majority should always prevail in a democracy has been a matter of debate for a long time. John Stuart Mill, for example, argued that 'the government of the whole by a mere majority of the people', the principle of majority rule, is undemocratic. This was, then, developed into an argument for proportional representation (Mill 1859 and 1861).

must rest on a defence of the initial distribution of property rights. The argument that markets protect the interests of individuals or minorities, which even democracies cannot, is limited,[2] for such individuals or minorities are not guaranteed access to the market as buyers if they have no incomes or sellers if they have nothing to sell. It is important to recognize that while democracy may be about the *tyranny of majorities*, markets are inevitably about the *tyranny of minorities.*[3]

In practice, we know that the combination of democracy and markets is neither necessary nor sufficient to bring about an improvement in the living conditions of the majority of the people in a society. Consider egalitarian development, which brings about material well-being of people together with some equality of economic opportunities. We have seen such egalitarian development in planned economies without political democracy, as in the erstwhile socialist countries of Eastern Europe, and in market economies without political democracy, as in some East Asian and South-East Asian countries. In sharp contrast, markets and democracy together, where these institutions are not sufficiently developed and have not evolved over a long period of time, as in countries of Eastern Europe, have only produced chaos. The outcome is prosperity for a few and misery for the many. Clearly, there are no magic wands. Democracy and markets are both institutions. The outcome depends on how they are used.

The real issue, in my view, is somewhat different. The essence of the tension between the economics of markets and the politics of democracy must be recognized. In an economic democracy, people vote with their money in the market place. But a political democracy works on the basis of one-person-one-vote. The distribution of votes, unlike the distribution of incomes or assets, is equal. One adult has one vote in politics, even though a rich man

2 The argument is that even when a minority group is treated with hostility by the majority (say a group of people with extremist political views who wish to produce a newspaper), the market system offers the minority significant protection (say buying newsprint and employing journalists). Friedman (1962) provides a historical example, when he suggests that Jewish people were able to survive the hostile environment in medieval Europe largely because they were engaged in commerce and trade. And the economic (self) interest of the population prevailed over religious discrimination.

3 I owe this formulation to my colleague Satish Jain.

has more votes than a poor man, in terms of purchasing power, in the market. Governments are elected by the people. Even where they are not, the state needs legitimation from the people (most of whom are not rich or are poor). Markets, on the other hand, are driven by demand and not need. For this important reason, among others, successive generations of economic thinkers and social philosophers have stressed the role of the state in bringing the ideals of political democracy and economic democracy closer together. The state may or may not succeed in this task. It is clear, however, that in reconciling economic and political democracy, a sensible compromise must be reached between the economic directions which the market sets on the basis of purchasing power and the priorities which a political system sets on the basis of one-person-one-vote.[4]

This is easier said than done. Markets may, in fact, exclude a significant proportion of the people, particularly the poor, from the process of development. Joan Robinson once said: 'There is only one thing that is worse than being exploited by capitalists. And that is not being exploited by capitalists.' The same goes for participation in markets. For there is an *exclusion* in the process. Markets may exclude people as consumers or producers or both.

Markets exclude people as consumers or buyers if they do not have any incomes, or sufficient incomes, which can be translated into purchasing power. This exclusion is attributable to a lack of *entitlements.*[5] Such people are excluded from the consumption of goods and services which are sold in the market.

Markets exclude people as producers or sellers if they have neither *assets* nor *capabilities.*[6] People experience such exclusion if

4 For a discussion of this problem in the Indian context, see Bhaduri and Nayyar (1996). For a discussion of the complex relationship between democracy and development, with reference to theory and reality, see Bagchi (1995).

5 This term was first used by Sen (1981) in his work on poverty and famines.

6 In this paper, I use the word *capabilities* to characterize the mix of natural talents, skills acquired through training, learning from experience and abilities or expertise based on education, embodied in a person, that enable him or her to use these (capabilities as a producer or a worker) for which there is not only a price but also a demand in the market. It follows that even persons with capabilities may be excluded from employment if there is no demand for their capabilities in the (labour) market. It is essential to note that the same word, *capabilities*, has been used in a very different sense by Amartya Sen,

they do not have assets, physical or financial, which can be used (or sold) to yield an income in the form of rent, interest, or profits. The prime example of this for the rural poor in the developing world is exclusion from land. Even those without assets could enter the market as producers or sellers, using their labour, if they have some capabilities. Such capabilities which are acquired through education, training, or experience are different from abilities which are endowed. But the distribution of capabilities may be just as unequal if not more so. It is these capabilities which can, in turn, yield an income in the form of wages. Hence, people without capabilities, the poor, who cannot find employment are excluded. It must be recognized that even people with capabilities may be excluded from employment if there is no demand for their capabilities in the (labour) market.

Markets exclude people both as consumers and producers or as buyers and sellers if they do not accept, or conform to, the *values* of a market system. The most obvious example of such exclusion is tribal populations or forest communities in market economies. The same can be said, perhaps, for pockets of pre-capitalist formations in what are essentially capitalist systems. Such exclusion may also take other forms. There may be people who are unable or unwilling to sell their assets: for instance, a person may be unable or unwilling to sell an ancestral house in the market. Or, there may be people who are unable or unwilling to sell their capabilities: for instance, a person may be unable or unwilling to charge fees as an astrologer or a musician because of a belief system that such talents cannot and should not be sold. In other words, people who are excluded because of their set of norms can find some kind of inclusion in the market once they accept a different set of norms. In general, the terms of such inclusion are such that it intensifies insecurity and exploitation at least for some time.

---

who argues that the well-being of a person depends on what the person succeeds in *doing* with the commodities (and their characteristics) at his command. For example, food can provide nutrition to a healthy person but not to a person with a parasitic disease; or, a bicycle can provide transportation to an able-bodied person but not to a disabled person. Thus, for Sen (1985), *capabilities* characterize the combination of functionings a person can achieve, given his personal features (conversion of characteristics into functioning) and his command over commodities (entitlements).

As a concept, exclusion may describe a situation or characterize a process.[7] In describing a situation, whether it refers to a point in time or to a permanent state, the concept of exclusion is much the same as the concept of poverty. The object is to identify the excluded and the poor respectively. In characterizing a process, the concept of exclusion goes further to focus on how the operation of economic and social forces recreates or accentuates exclusion over time. This may be attributable to the logic of markets, which give to those who have and take away from those who have not, as the process of cumulative causation leads to market-driven virtuous circles and vicious circles. This may be the outcome of patterns of development where economic growth is uneven between regions and the distribution of its benefits is unequal between people, so that there is growing affluence for some combined with persistent poverty for many. This may be the consequence of strategies of development, as a similar economic performance in the aggregate could lead to egalitarian development in one situation, and growth which bypasses the majority of the people in another situation. It is clear that institutional arrangements which mediate between economic development on the one hand and social development on the other are critical. For these institutional mechanisms may accentuate exclusion or foster inclusion, just as they may limit the gains to an affluent minority or spread the gains to the poor majority. The initial distribution of assets and the subsequent distribution of incomes are important determinants of whether the vulnerable sections of the population are marginalized and excluded or are uplifted and included.

7 The term *exclusion* has become a part of the lexicon of economists recently, although it has been in the jargon of sociology and the vocabulary of politics in Europe for somewhat longer. The European Commission, for example, uses the phrase *social exclusion* to describe a situation, as also to focus on a process, which excludes individuals or groups from livelihoods and rights, thus depriving them of sources of well-being that have been assumed, if not taken for granted, in industrialized countries. The essential point is that economic stratification is inevitable in market economies and societies, which systematically integrate some and marginalize others to distribute the benefits of economic growth in ways which include some and exclude others. For an extensive discussion on social exclusion, ranging from conceptual issues through country studies to policy issues, see Rodgers, Gore, and Figueiredo (1995).

It is only to be expected that there is an interaction between exclusion from the market in the economic sphere and the non-economic dimensions of exclusion in the social, political, and cultural spheres. The social manifestations of exclusion can be powerful. This is best illustrated with an example where the underprivileged in society, such as the scheduled castes or the lower castes in India, are poor because they have little in the form of entitlements, assets, or capabilities. But, even where they are better endowed in terms of these attributes, their exclusion from markets, particularly from the market for land and labour in rural India, persists for social rather than economic reasons. At the same time, economic exclusion accentuates social exclusion. The marketization of economies has meant a roll-back of the state which has diluted social security provisions made available by governments, just as it has meant a weakening of the community and the extended family as institutions which were safety nets provided by society. In the sphere of politics, an economic exclusion from livelihood often creates or accentuates a political exclusion from rights. Thus, for the poor in India, the right to vote may exist in principle, but in practice it may be taken away by coercion or coaxed away by material incentives at the time of elections. Sometimes, the underprivileged or the poor are not allowed to vote. At other times, their votes may be cast by someone else. And, in some situations, their votes are purchased. This reality does not conform to the principle of one-person-one-vote. It also suggests that people do not vote with their money in the market place alone. Similarly, the very poor are vulnerable to exploitation and oppression because their civil rights or equality before the law exist in principle but are difficult to protect or preserve in practice. The reason is simple. They do not have the resources to claim or the power to assert their rights. Similarly, cultural exclusion such as that of immigrant groups, minority communities, or ethnic groups interacts with economic exclusion from the market. In all of this, there is an asymmetry that is worth noting. Economic exclusion exacerbates other forms of exclusion, but economic participation does not eliminate other forms of exclusion which have social, political, or cultural roots.

The preceding discussion may suggest that exclusion is bad and inclusion is good. But it is not meant to. It must be said that the nature of inclusion or exclusion matters. Inclusion is not always good. Coercive inclusion by markets, whether child labour, tribal populations, or immigrant workers can be exploitative. The employment of women as wage labour on terms inferior to those of men, or the employment of migrants from rural areas in the unorganized urban sector at wages lower than those of workers in the organized sector, provide other examples. The basic point is that inclusion which is coercive or on inferior terms is not desirable. For similar reasons, exclusion is not always bad. To those who do not accept the values of the market system, any voluntary exclusion from markets, on the part of individuals or groups, should be perfectly acceptable.

III

Nationalism and Development: 1947–66

The conception and the birth of political democracy in independent India was unique in its wider historical context. For democracy did not follow but preceded capitalist industrialization and development. What is more, democracy came to India neither as a response to an absolutist state nor as the realization of an individualist conception of society. In each of these attributes, it provided a sharp contrast with the experience elsewhere particularly in Europe.[8] In fact, it was not even an obvious outcome of the nationalist movement. The struggle for independence was much more about autonomous space for the nation than about freedom for the individual. Indeed, the Gandhian notion of a just state was premised on the idea that the collective interest must take precedence over individual interests.[9] And the legacy of nationalism was such that the end of colonialism may have imparted a sense of pride and hope to the people, but independence meant freedom and sovereignty for the nation as a collective of people rather than for individuals who together made up the people. Yet, the constitution adopted by independent India created

8 This argument is developed by Kaviraj (1995). See also, Bagchi (1995).

9 Cf. Kaviraj (1995). For a perceptive analysis of the ideological forms and substance of Indian nationalism, see Chatterjee (1993).

a democratic republic and pledged to secure justice, liberty, equality and fraternity for all its citizens. Universal adult franchise was provided at one stroke. The republicanism of the Western world was perhaps the role model. This was, in a sense, India invented.[10] A liberal democracy was constructed by an enlightened elite in accordance with its conception of a modern nation-state. It was democracy from above provided to the people.[11] And not democracy from below claimed by the people. This is perhaps an oversimplified view. The reality was, obviously, more complex. For the nationalist movement meant a dialectical relationship between the provision from above and the claim from below. All the same, democracy in independent India was unique insofar as it introduced universal suffrage in a predominantly agrarian society with an inadequate crystallization of class forces. In this construct, the state was the essential mediator. It had to perform a critical role in reconciling the conflict between political democracy and economic democracy as also in mediating between economic development and social needs. Thus, if the logic of markets meant exclusion of a significant proportion of people, particularly the poor, it was necessary for the state to ensure inclusion of such people in the economic sphere.

In this milieu, the strategy of economic development was shaped by the colonial past and the nationalist present. For one, there was a conscious attempt to limit the degree of openness and of integration with the world economy, in pursuit of a more autonomous, if not self-reliant, development. For another, the state was assigned a strategic role in development because the market, by itself, was not perceived as sufficient to meet the aspirations of a latecomer to industrialization. Both represented points of departure from the colonial era which was characterized by open economies and unregulated markets. But this approach also represented a consensus in thinking about the most appropriate strategy for industrialization. It was, in fact, the development consensus at the time.

The objectives were clear enough: to catch up with the industrialized world and to improve the living conditions of the

10 The phrase 'India Invented' is, in fact, the title of, as also an important theme in, a book by Das (1994).

11 This view is articulated by Kaviraj (1995) as also by Khilnani (1997).

people. So were the perceived constraints.[12] The scarcity of capital was seen as the fundamental constraint on growth but the low capacity to save limited the rate of capital accumulation, and even if savings could be raised there were structural constraints on transforming savings into investment. It was believed that primacy of the market mechanism would lead to excess consumption by the rich and under-investment in sectors critical for development. At the same time, it was assumed that agriculture was subject to diminishing returns whereas industrialization promised not only increasing returns but also productive employment for surplus labour from the rural sector. These perceptions shaped the contours of economic policies: the lead role of public investment, industrialization based on import substitution, the emphasis on the capital goods sector, industrial licensing to guide the allocation of investible resources in the private sector, or even the relative neglect of agriculture. And state intervention was meant to create the conditions for the development of industrial capitalism.[13] It did so. Large doses of public investment created a physical infrastructure and set up intermediate goods industries, which reduced the cost of inputs used by the private sector and increased the demand for goods produced by the private sector. Import substitution, implemented through protection, not only guaranteed existing markets for domestic capitalists but also ensured a future insofar as the excess demand attributable to import restrictions would continue to provide markets. This *modus operandi* of fostering industrialization, a state-led capitalism, was no different from state capitalism elsewhere in the world.[14]

At this juncture in independent India, industrialization was thought of as synonymous with development while it was presumed that national interest and the people's interest were the same. There was not only a consensus about the strategy of economic development that was adopted. There was also a political consensus on what was attempted. This was attributable in part to the legacy of nationalism which emphasized unity in diversity and in part to the nature of the Congress Party which represented

12 For a discussion on how such structural constraints shaped the strategy of development, see Chakravarty (1987). See also Bettelheim (1968).

13 Cf. Nayyar (1978). See also Gough and Sharma (1973).

14 See Bettelheim (1968) and Kothari (1970).

a composite coalition of interests. It was not as if there was no conflict of economic interests. There was. And it was recognized. Some steps were debated but ruled out. It was decided, for example, not to expropriate foreign capitalists or local landlords. Similarly, even though economic inequalities posed a problem, a redistribution of assets was not seen as desirable because it would be detrimental to savings while a redistribution of incomes was not seen as feasible because India could only redistribute its poverty. Other steps were taken in a half-hearted manner. Land reform legislations were passed. However, these were either replete with loopholes or simply not implemented.[15] The abolition of absentee landlordism was a significant outcome.[16] But these reforms did not give land to the cultivators. Instead, they forced owners to turn into cultivators. Some steps were devised to address the exclusion of the poor and the exploited. The community development programme was introduced to create an infrastructure in rural India. A system of *panchayats* was created to facilitate institutional change at the village level. Social legislation, which introduced reservations in educational institutions and government employment for the scheduled castes and scheduled tribes, made for affirmative action.

The consensus of the time meant that there was less need for conflict resolution. Yet, there was a conscious attempt by the state to reconcile economic policies with the compulsions of the political process, to minimize the conflicts in the interaction of economics and politics. But this was possible only within limits. For the state was substantively an alliance of the industrial capitalist class, the landowning class, and the educated elite.[17] There were, also, the people of India whose interests could not be set aside altogether, or forgotten, in a democracy. The solution was found in a politics of accommodation among the dominant economic and social classes, the rulers, on the one hand, and with

15 See Frankel (1978).

16 The origins, the nature and the consequences of land reforms in India are discussed, at some length, by Joshi (1975).

17 See Bardhan (1984) and Rudolph and Rudolph (1987). The complex but mutually profitable alliances of interest, combined with an interlocking system of patronage, which characterized the interaction of politics and economics in India was noted much earlier by Kothari (1970).

the multitude of people, the ruled, on the other. The accommodation among the rulers was a complex process because there were conflicts and tensions, particularly between the rural oligarchy and the industrial bourgeoisie, which were resolved through mediation by the state in the form of mutually acceptable trade-offs in the economy or in the polity.[18] This was inevitably based on a sharing of the spoils. The accommodation of the poor, who were the ruled, however, was long on words and short on substance. The strategy of economic development was given a statist orientation, epitomized in the phrases 'commanding heights of the economy' and 'socialistic pattern of society'. The building of industrial capitalism was combined with the radical rhetoric of a political democracy as a means of reconciling economics and politics. It was no surprise, then, that the language of political discourse in this phase came to be strongly influenced by 'a virus of socialism without substance' across the ideological spectrum of political parties.[19]

All the same, it must be recognized that this strategy of development was characterized by a long-term perspective. In this phase, there was a vision, however imperfect, about the future of economy, polity and society. In the economy, the object was to eradicate poverty of the people and put the country on the road to industrialization. In the polity, it was believed that democracy was an alternative to revolutionary class struggle in equalizing society. For political democracy would, ultimately, endow the poor with the strength to exert strong pressures on the ruling classes for moving towards economic democracy.[20] It is

18 Mitra (1977) put forward a perceptive and clear hypothesis. The exercise of political authority and state power in India represented an arrangement between the rural oligarchy on the one hand and the industrial bourgeoisie on the other. While the bourgeoisie controlled the industrial sector and dominated the working class, they also needed the rural oligarchy, which could deliver the votes from the countryside and help maintain them in power. This alliance of convenience survived on the basis of mutual trade-offs, for even though political interests often coincided, economic contradictions abounded.

19 See Bagchi (1995: xxxv). Kaviraj (1995: 104) suggests that, at the time, political language did not provide any identification of social interests thereby 'creating a socialist night in which all parties were black'.

20 Cf. Frankel (1978). For a discussion on politics in India during this phase, see Kothari (1970) and Morris-Jones (1971).

worth noting that this perception reversed the sequence observed elsewhere, as economic development mounted pressures on the ruling classes for moving towards political democracy. In the society, it was hoped that affirmative action would make caste wither away, secularism would dispense with religious identities and modernization would reduce the significance of linguistic differences.

The reality, as it turned out, belied these expectations. Yet, at the beginning of this period, in the early 1950s, India was a role model. And the optimism extended beyond those who had a dream about India. For some, its mixed economy was an answer to the challenge posed by communism in China. For others, its strategy represented a non-capitalist path to development. For yet others, who recognized the problems of industrial capitalism, India was on the road to their ideal of a social democracy and a welfare state. It is another matter that, towards the end of this period, by the mid-1960s, there was a drastic change in perceptions. India ceased to be a role model in the outside world.

IV

Development and Democracy: 1967–90

The economic consequences and the political implications of the development process over the two decades that followed independence also surfaced at about the same time inside India.

The economic reality that unfolded did not conform to the expectations and the promises. The benefits of economic growth accrued mostly to the rich, while the process of development largely bypassed the poor. Indeed, available evidence suggests that there was a sharp increase in the incidence of poverty during the 1960s as both the number of the poor and the proportion of the population below the poverty line registered a substantial rise.[21]

21 There is an extensive literature and an intensive debate on estimates of poverty in India. Much of it, however, suggests a substantial increase in the incidence of poverty during the 1960s. Nayyar (1991), for example, estimates that, in rural India, the proportion of the population living below the poverty line (based on a norm of 2200 calories per day) increased from 34 per cent in 1960–1 to 57 per cent in 1970–1. The trend was not significantly different for urban India.

This was in keeping with the logic of markets which excluded people without entitlements, assets and capabilities. And, matters were brought to a head by the crisis in the economy in the mid-1960s. Successive droughts which necessitated large-scale imports of food from the United States under PL-480 created images of a 'basket-case'. The devaluation of the rupee, in June 1966, made a dent on autonomy in economic decisions as the government came under the influence of foreign donors. The industrial sector was caught in a persistent recession. Savings and investment rates dropped. Economic planning was suspended for an interregnum of three years.

The political scenario that emerged was characterized by two discernible changes. First, the ideology of nationalism had begun to wane. This was partly a consequence of the passage of time as the second generation came to the fore in the Congress Party. It was also related to the regionalization of politics that surfaced because the central leadership, after Nehru, was weaker. At the same time, politics in India witnessed the first revolts of the young, manifest in the Naxalite Movement and the stirring among the *dalits*. Second, there was a slow but steady erosion of the political consensus. The heritage of nationalism began to fade from memories and the compulsions of political democracy came home to roost. It became clear that governments were elected by the people and the mandate to rule had to be renewed at election time. But winning elections depended on the votes from the poor who constituted the vast majority of the people. The general elections of 1967 established that electoral outcomes could no longer be taken for granted and that the Congress Party could no longer assume the support of the people.[22]

The rise of the rich peasantry, sometimes described as capitalist farmers, provides a powerful illustration of the economic and political changes set in motion by the process of development.[23]

22 See Kaviraj (1995) and Vanaik (1990). The political consequence was a sharp erosion in the cohesion of the Congress Party as dissent and discord led to its split in 1969. It was, however, the decline of the Congress Party that explained the rise of Indira Gandhi and not the other way around (Vanaik 1990).

23 There is a rich literature on the economic origins and the political consequences of the rise of the rich peasantry. See, for example, Mitra (1977), Brass (1980), Byres (1988) and Vanaik (1990).

Semi-feudal landowners lost their economic strength and social dominance in the countryside. This power was captured by a class of farmers who cultivated their land, reinvested their surpluses in agriculture and engaged wage labour. It was this rich peasantry which captured the benefits of the land reform legislation, the community development programme, the *panchayati raj* system and the network of co-operatives. As a new entrant, it began to place demands on the ruling political coalition. Unsatisfied by what the ruling elite was willing and able to do for it, this rich peasantry deserted the Congress Party to join or to create coalitions of opposition parties. It was this that led to the defeat of the Congress Party, in almost every North Indian state, in the general elections of 1967.

It must be said that 1967 represented a watershed in an evolving situation and a continuum of developments. In retrospect, however, it is possible to discern a qualitative change in the interaction of economics and politics in independent India which surfaced around that time. It is difficult to understand, let alone analyse, the complexities of the development process in India over the next two decades or so. For an understanding, it is perhaps necessary to distinguish between two periods in this phase: the first from 1967 to 1980, and the second from 1980 to 1990. Such periodization is, in a sense, arbitrary but serves an analytical purpose.

Co-option and Mediation: 1967–80

The crisis in the economy and the political setback to the Congress Party, at the very beginning of the first period in this phase, led to rethinking in economics and politics. There was a recognition of two realities. For one, the rich peasantry had emerged as a new force demanding its due share in benefits derived from economic policies and seeking an upward mobility in the political process. For another, the poor, who had not seen any improvement in their living conditions, did exercise their right to vote in a political democracy. The system responded in accordance with its perceptions of this reality. This response can be characterized as a politics of co-option.

In the sphere of economics, the response was twofold. First, there was a strong, new, emphasis on agriculture. The new strategy for agricultural development, which culminated in the Green Revolution, was motivated by the imperative of increasing the output of foodgrains. This quest for food security was driven, in part, by a concern that the nation could not continue its 'ship-to-mouth' existence and, in part, by a concern that if there was a shortage of food it was the poor who went without. The end shaped the means. The better endowed farmers and regions were provided extensive support to increase their marketable surplus of food. This came in a variety of forms: mostly as lower (subsidized) prices of inputs whether fertilizers, seeds, water, power or credit, but also as higher prices of output through a system of procurement prices for producers and a manipulation of the inter-sectoral terms of trade in favour of agriculture.[24] Economic benefits of this regime of subsidies, explicit and implicit, accrued to the rich peasantry. It was not without political purpose. Second, poverty alleviation programmes began life in independent India, albeit on a modest scale. The Crash Scheme for Rural Employment, the Drought-Prone Areas Programme, the Small Farmers Development Agency, and the Marginal Farmers and Agricultural Labourers Development Agency were among the first to be introduced. These were followed, some years later, by the Employment Guarantee Scheme in Maharashtra and the Food for Work Programme in other states. Most of these programmes sought to create employment for the poor while a few sought to provide them with assets for self-employment.[25] The poor were thus provided with entitlements or assets to combat their exclusion.

In the realm of politics, the response had three dimensions. First, there was a conscious effort to co-opt the rich peasantry into the ruling coalition and, wherever possible, the Congress Party. Second, the dissent and the regionalism in the Congress Party was met by a strategy of 'divide-and-rule', where one faction was pitted against another to be neutralized and then vanquished. Third, populist rhetoric was born in an endeavour to woo the

24 This argument is developed, at some length, by Mitra (1977), who argues that the steady increase in the relative prices of food and raw materials sold by the surplus farmers was a principal manifestation of the trade-off principle (referred to above). See also Frankel (1971).

25 For a discussion on, and evaluation of, these poverty alleviation programmes, see Nayyar (1991).

people. The slogan of *garibi hatao*, even if it was mere words, captured the popular imagination. But the rhetoric went further to the nationalization of banks and the abolition of privy purses. It was these steps which gave Indira Gandhi, who dominated politics in this period through the democratic, populist and authoritarian phases of her rule, a stranglehold on the political process.[26]

These responses led to some expected outcomes in the economy and some unexpected outcomes in the polity. In the economy, rapid growth in the agricultural sector ensured food security. A surge in savings and investment boosted growth. The balance of payments situation surmounted the oil shock. Industrial growth revived. In the polity, the rich peasantry returned to the fold, the Congress Party won a decisive mandate in the general elections of 1971, and Indira Gandhi consolidated her control over both the party and the government by reaching out directly to the people. As it turned out, the economic bliss and the political equilibrium did not last long. Crises in the economy led to agitations in the polity. An erosion of the political mandate strengthened the opposition both inside and outside the Congress Party. In response, Indira Gandhi sought to control and curb the political opposition, to establish herself as an undisputed leader in the mode of Caesar. The majoritarianism soon turned into an authoritarianism. But this was not consistent with the checks and balances needed in a political democracy. And, it was this, rather than an economic crisis, which led to the Emergency.[27] However, the authoritarian regime did not last even two years. Democracy reasserted itself. There were two reasons. For one, the suppression of dissent and opposition was ultimately not sustainable because political democracy was, by then, embedded in the system. For another, the mediation between the constituents of the ruling elite that sustained the coalition of class interests required an institutional mechanism which had, until then, been provided by political democracy. Thus, it needs to be said that the Janata

26 Cf. Kaviraj (1995). For a perceptive analysis of this phase of politics in India, see also Vanaik (1990) and Brass (1992).

27 The factors underlying the imposition and the collapse of the Emergency are examined, among others, by Chatterjee (1977: 58–66). See also Vanaik (1990) and Kaviraj (1995).

government was the beneficiary rather than the cause of the return of democracy in India. In most respects, it was much like the Congress government before 1975. But, towards the end of its regime, the second oil shock and an inept management of the economy led to unprecedented inflation. The management of the polity was not even functional as the coalition failed to provide governance. The people were hurt by inflation and tired of squabbling among political leaders of the Janata regime. And, in 1980, the electorate voted a largely unrepentant Indira Gandhi back to power.

Populism and Patronage: 1980–90

The next period in this phase, the 1980s, was in a sense more of the same but not quite. The compulsions of political democracy exercised an even stronger influence on economic policies and economic development. It turned out to be the age of populism in both economics and politics.

In the sphere of economics, this led to some important changes in policies. First, there was a proliferation of subsidies. Some, such as the subsidies on food, fertilizers and exports, were explicit. These meant expenditure disbursed.[28] Others were implicit in underpriced services of public utilities such as irrigation, electricity and road transport, or in underpriced goods produced in the public sector such as steel and coal. These meant revenue foregone. There was something for everybody.[29] The rich peasantry, of course, continued to benefit from implicit and explicit subsidies. But the industrial capitalist class was not far behind. The public sector provided them with cheap inputs and carried

28 The explicit subsidies provided by the central government alone increased from 8.3 per cent of its total expenditure and the equivalent of 1.4 per cent of GDP in 1980–1 to 11.4 per cent of its total expenditure and the equivalent of 2.4 per cent of GDP in 1989–90 (*Economic and Functional Classification of the Central Government Budget*, annual issues). The corresponding proportions would be much larger if we could add the implicit subsidies and include the state governments.

29 The situation in the early 1980s, which was just the beginning of this phase, is described by Bardhan (1984: 70) as follows: '...a patron-client regime fostered by a flabby and heterogeneous dominant coalition preoccupied in a spree of anarchical grabbing of public resources...'.

the losses. The nationalized banks extended loans which turned into non-performing assets. And, in effect, *loan waivers* for big firms, the industrial sector, quietly came into existence much before they were announced for small farmers in the agricultural sector. *Loan melas*, which began life then, were just a more explicit example of such directed lending as patronage. The government took over sick firms from the private sector which privatized the benefits and socialized the costs. Second, beyond these subsidies, there was a rapid increase in public consumption expenditure, which provided a sharp contrast with the expansion in public investment expenditure during the first phase.[30] Some of it supported an increase in social consumption and, thus, contributed to an inclusion of the poor. However, a lot of such public expenditure, particularly that on salaries of those employed in the government and in the public sector, supported increases in private consumption. All of it contributed to an increase in aggregate demand and, to the extent that supply constraints were not dominant, an increase in output. Third, there was a massive expansion in poverty alleviation programmes. The National Rural Employment Programme and the Rural Landless Employment Guarantee Programme were launched in 1980. The object was to create employment and provide incomes to the poor. These programmes were extended, modified, or renamed in subsequent years but remained the same in substance. The Integrated Rural Development Programme, on the other hand, attempted to provide assets or training to the poor as a sustainable source of income through self-employment. This was a systematic attempt at creating a safety net for the poor, who experienced exclusion, by providing them with entitlements, assets, or capabilities. It needs to be said that this effort at the inclusion of the poor was far more extensive and substantive than it had been in the 1970s. Yet, it must be recognized that economic development did not create social opportunities for people at large. There were

30 The total expenditure of the central government increased from 16 per cent of GDP in 1980–1 to 20 per cent of GDP in 1985–6 and stayed above that level through the second half of the 1980s. Much of this was attributable to the increase in consumption expenditure and transfer payments, as the share of gross capital formation in total expenditure dropped from more than 40 per cent in 1980–1 to about 33 per cent in 1989–90. See Nayyar (1996).

transfer payments to sustain minimum levels of consumption. But the provision of basic education, health care and social security was simply inadequate.[31]

In the realm of politics, there were two discernible changes. For one, electoral compulsions, which required the support of the people through their votes, unleashed a competitive politics of populism. Political parties and political leaders across-the-board sought to woo the people with sops. In this quest, no group with a political voice was left unsolicited or untouched. And there was not much difference between the centre, where one party ruled for most of the time, and the states, where different parties ruled at different times. The number of promises made multiplied but the number of promises kept dwindled. For another, a state that was increasingly unable to mediate between conflicting interests and competing demands resorted more and more to a politics of patronage. This patronage, which came to be extended in a bewildering variety of ways, was a means of sharing the spoils among the constituents of the ruling elite.

These changes led to some visible, as also some invisible, economic and political consequences. The rate of growth of the economy during the 1980s was unprecedented. In real terms, national income increased at a rate of more than 5 per cent per annum and per capita income increased at a rate of more than 3 per cent per annum. At the same time, there was a substantial reduction in the incidence of poverty. The proportion of the population living below the poverty line dropped from 51.3 per cent in 1977–8 to 38.9 per cent in 1987–8. And, even with the rapid growth in population, the number of the poor declined a little from 329 million in 1977–8 to 307 million in 1987–8.[32] In economics this was attributable to rapid growth, moderate inflation and the spread of anti-poverty programmes. In politics, this was attributable to the compulsions of democracy for, after a time, elections could no longer be won by slogans alone. But there was also the other side of the coin. The seeds of the fiscal

31 This is the theme of an excellent book by Drèze and Sen (1985). For a detailed discussion of the poverty alleviation programmes during the 1980s, see Planning Commission (1985: 49–63) and Planning Commission (1992: 27–35). For an evaluation, see also Nayyar (1991).

32 The evidence on the proportion and the number of the poor, cited in this paragraph, is from Planning Commission (1993).

crisis and the debt crisis were also sown during this period.[33] There were no obvious dividends in politics, except that this period represented a concerted attempt at reconciling the distribution of gains from economic growth with the context of political democracy. There was, however, a visible consequence in the political process.[34] The arena of conflict shifted from the rich versus the poor to the centre versus the states. Dissent in democracy took the form of regional movements which turned to militancy and terrorism in Punjab, Assam and Kashmir. There was also an invisible political consequence in the consolidation of the subaltern classes who recognized that their political identity made their right to vote that much more potent.

The Solution as a Problem

In retrospect, it is clear that in the second phase as a whole, from 1967 to 1990, conflicts of interests were that much sharper and the need for resolution that much greater. This was attributable partly to the eroding consensus and partly to the development process. It was also inevitable given the essential tension between the economics of markets and the politics of democracy. The exclusion of the poor by market had to be reconciled with the inclusion of the poor by democracy. There was, indeed, a conscious attempt by the state to reconcile the process of economic development with the compulsions of political democracy. That the mediation did not lead to a resolution is another matter.

During the first period of this phase, from 1967 to 1980, the intervention was purposive. There was an attempt to build new coalitions in terms of economic interests and sustain them through a consolidation of political power. This process was laced with a dose of electoral populism. But the economics remained within the limits of prudence. The macro-management of the economy by the government was conservative. Inflation remained within limits of economic and political tolerance. The balance of payments situation was not allowed to get out of hand. It is not

33 The origins of the fiscal crisis and the debt crisis are analysed elsewhere by the author (Nayyar 1996). See also Bhaduri and Nayyar (1996).

34 For different perspectives on political developments in India during the 1980s, see Kothari (1988), Kohli (1990), Vanaik (1990), Das (1994), Kaviraj (1995), Chatterjee (1997) and Khilnani (1997).

as if there were no hiccups. There were. But the system had the ability to cope with shocks, whether the oil price increases in the economy or the Emergency in the polity. In other words, the economy and the polity both had a resilience.

The solutions, however, became a part of the problem. The management of the political process in this period had profound consequences with long-term implications. First, even though the government became stronger, the centralization of authority and power at the apex weakened the institutional base of the pyramid, so that the ability of the government to mediate between conflicting interests was much reduced.[35] Second, the same culture spread rapidly to institutions and structures in the political process so that there was no room for dissent or debate within political parties. In this situation, the choice was to stay but accept authority without question or to leave the mainstream and strike out on your own. Third, the politics of co-option meant inclusion for some but, at the same time, exclusion for others. This did lead to a *tyranny of majorities* which is always a possible danger in a democracy. It needs to be said that each of these changes in the political process was to have a lasting impact.

There was, also, an interaction between economics and politics which, slowly but surely, transformed the solution into a problem. It surfaced at the beginning of the first period in this phase, gathered momentum through the 1970s, and was established practice by the end of the second period in this phase. It was also to have a lasting impact, as the role of money extended beyond the economics of markets to exercise a profound influence on the politics of democracy. To begin with, votes were purchased at election time, not everywhere but in close contests or important constituencies. The practice spread. Those with money progressively acquired an advantage, over those without money, in the battle of the ballot. This created barriers to entry in politics, which are, by now, formidable. The process did not quite stop there. It was soon realized that, after elections, even legislators could be bought and sold. If the price was right, a legislator conveniently forgot the mandate on which he was elected and crossed over to support a programme, a party or a government in direct conflict with the interests of those who elected him in

35 Cf. Kaviraj (1995) and Chatterjee (1997). See also Kohli (1990).

the first place. It did not take very long for such practices to spread from legislators to parliamentarians.

The consequences are no surprise and are observable in the reality of contemporary India. Election season is about mobilizing gigantic vote banks. This is often based on money power. There are, of course, vote banks mobilized on the basis of caste, religion or ethnicity, but these can also be swayed in this or that direction, at critical moments, by the lure of money. Similarly, the scenario after elections, if there is no decisive mandate, is predictable as 'money-bags' descend upon state capitals, or even the national capital, to make or unmake coalition governments. It needs to be said that these attributes now almost characterize the political system in India. And, it should be clear that once profit maximization becomes an important motive for political acts or deeds, the conflict between the economics of markets and the politics of democracy is neither reconciled nor resolved. It is side-stepped or circumvented.

During the second period of this phase, from 1980 to 1990, the politics of co-option relied almost entirely on a politics of patronage. It was neither supported nor supplemented by an effective political mediation. The co-option during the first period of this phase, from 1967 to 1980, was based on an understanding, even if imperfect, of the interaction between economics and politics. It had a clear objective. The drift to an overwhelming reliance on patronage in the 1980s, however, simply represented a path of least resistance and a strategy of survival in state power. It was a means of buying time. This populist politics and cynical economics, taken together, translated into soft options, which had the most serious consequences for the economy. It was possible for the government and the country to live beyond its means, on borrowed money, for some time, but it was not possible to postpone the day of reckoning for ever. The inevitable crunch did come at the end of this phase.

V

Liberalization and Empowerment: 1991–

The external debt crisis, which surfaced in early 1991, brought India close to default in meeting its international payments obligations. The balance of payments situation was almost unmanageable. The fear of an acceleration in the rate of inflation loomed large. The underlying fiscal crisis was acute. This juxtaposition was neither an accident nor a coincidence. It was a consequence of the cavalier macro-management of the economy during the 1980s. The balance of payments crisis was man-made and policy-induced. The export performance remained modest, remittances from migrants tapered off and import substitution in the petroleum sector slowed down. The liberalization in the regime of trade policies and industrial policies created incentives for import-intensive industrialization. There was also a surge in defence imports. This was sustained by borrowing abroad which led to a continuous rise in external debt. The fiscal crisis was attributable to inadequate resource mobilization and a profligate increase in public expenditure. Direct taxes were progressively reduced while indirect taxes, which already contributed the bulk of tax revenues, could not be raised any further because such a step could be inflationary or regressive or both. At the same time, transfer payments on subsidies and government consumption expenditure proliferated, driven in part by the competitive politics of populism and in part by the cynical economics of soft options. Such a fiscal regime, which borrowed to support expenditure that did not yield any returns to the exchequer, was simply not sustainable for long.[36]

In response to the crisis situation, the government set in motion a process of macro-economic stabilization combined with fiscal adjustment and structural reform. This strategy was nothing new. In conformity with the orthodoxy of the IMF and the World Bank, it replicated broadly the response of several developing countries in Latin America and sub-Saharan Africa to the debt crisis in the 1980s. But it constituted a fundamental departure from the past in independent India.[37] First, economic growth combined with economic efficiency became the objective function. The object of bringing about a reduction in poverty and inequality was not set aside but such concerns about equity were subsumed

36 The factors underlying the fiscal crisis and the debt crisis are analysed, at some length, in Nayyar (1996) and Bhaduri and Nayyar (1996). See also Joshi and Little (1994).

37 Cf. Nayyar (1996). For an analysis and an evaluation of India's development experience, from the early 1950s to the late 1980s, see Byres (1994).

in the pursuit of growth on the premise that it is both necessary and sufficient for an improvement in the living conditions of the people. Second, there was a conscious decision to substantively reduce the role of the state in the process of economic development and rely far more on the market. Public investment, seen as a catalyst if not a leader until then, it was argued, pre-empts scarce resources at the expense of private investment and leads to inefficient resource utilization which constitutes a drain on the exchequer. Third, the degree of openness of the economy was increased significantly and at a rapid pace. The object was not simply to enforce a cost-discipline on the supply side through international competition, but also to narrow the difference between domestic and world prices. Foreign capital and foreign technology were assigned a lead role in the process. Every aspect of this quest for integration with the world economy provided a striking contrast with the development consensus four decades earlier. In sum, India moved from a quest for state-led capitalism to a world of market-driven capitalism.

It is clear that economic liberalization in India began on a dramatic note with sudden and fundamental changes in the strategy of development. In the context of a democracy, it is essential to understand the political foundations of such economic change. There are two obvious questions which arise.[38] First, why did a relatively minor crisis in the economy evoke this response while decades of persistent poverty had so little impact? Second, how were such far-reaching changes introduced by what was then a minority government while predecessor governments with overwhelming majorities were unable to do so? These complex political questions seem to have a relatively simple economic answer. The change was dictated by the immediate economic compulsions of crisis management. The external debt crisis which erupted in 1991 meant that the fear of default hung as the Sword of Damocles. There was a sudden realization that governments can and do become insolvent even if countries do not go bankrupt. The problem was accentuated by a change in the international context at about the same time. The collapse of communism meant that competing ideologies gave way to a dominant ideology, while

38 For a more detailed discussion on these questions, see Bhaduri and Nayyar (1996).

the collapse of the erstwhile USSR removed the countervailing force, an important prop for India in the past, from the international system. It is not as if there were no other underlying factors. The emerging concerns about efficiency and productivity—even if not about poverty and inequality—had led to a debate and some rethinking in India about development strategy through the 1980s. This had permeated vaguely through the political system inasmuch as the manifesto of every political party for the 1991 elections, across the ideological spectrum, talked about the need for restructuring the economy. In sum, it was a combination of the reality in the national context and the conjuncture in the international context which provided the impetus for sudden change. But there can be no doubt that the response was driven, even dictated, by the crisis. It was not planned.

It would seem that 1991 was a watershed much more for the economy than for the polity. The economic liberalization introduced as a big bang was crisis-driven, and not strategy-based. Yet, it was superimposed on a process of economic development and political democracy that had evolved in independent India over a period spanning four decades. It was, therefore, bound to influence the interaction of economics and politics.

Given the complexity of India's economic development experience, it would be idle to pretend that everything it did was right but it would be naive to suggest that everything it did was wrong. A discussion of this issue would mean too much of a digression. Suffice it to say that there were both successes and failures.[39] In a long-term perspective, the most important success was the significant step-up in savings, investment and growth, which provided a sharp contrast with the near-stagnation in the colonial era, particularly during the first half of the twentieth century. This was combined with the development of a diversified industrial sector, although the declining productivity of investment and the lack of international competitiveness emerged as problems that required a reformulation of policies and a restructuring of the economy. There was also a sustained expansion in the agricultural output which ensured food security, even if it did not lead to a significant reduction in absolute poverty. But there is the other side of the balance sheet. The most important failure, situated

39 Cf. Nayyar (1996).

in a long-term perspective, was that this process of development did not improve the living conditions, or the quality of life, for the common people. Persistent poverty and absolute deprivation remained the reality for a large proportion of the population.[40] So much so that, after more than 40 years of freedom from colonial rule, India was unable to meet the basic needs of more than 300 million people who lived in poverty. And the poor do not even have enough food and clothing, let alone shelter, health care and education. It needs to be said that, despite the significant reduction in the incidence of poverty during the 1980s, the number of the poor *circa* 1990 was larger than the total population of India at the time of independence. In retrospect, it is clear that the objectives of eradicating poverty of the people and placing the country on the path of sustained industrialization were not quite realized. Economic liberalization, however, is no panacea. It is limited in both conception and design.[41] At one level, it is concerned with the economic problems of the government such as the balance of payments situation, the rate of inflation and the fiscal crisis. At another level, it is concerned with the efficiency of industrialization. But it is not concerned with the economic priorities of the people, such as employment and poverty, agriculture and the rural sector, or physical and social infrastructure. Long-term development objectives, such as education and human resource development or the acquisition of technological and managerial capabilities, are simply neglected. What is more, the reform process stresses the need to eliminate weaknesses or what went wrong but neglects the possibilities of building on strengths or what turned out right.[42] This, too, is a serious shortcoming.

The story of the evolution of political democracy in India, spanning the first four decades of the republic, is as complex but somewhat more positive. The real achievement is that democracy has taken roots at the level of the people. There is a political consciousness among voters who judge political parties and their

40 For a lucid assessment and a perceptive analysis of India's failure to eliminate basic deprivation in the decades since independence, see Drèze and Sen (1995).

41 For an articulation of this view and critical perspectives on liberalization, see Drèze and Sen (1995) and Bhaduri and Nayyar (1996).

42 For further discussion, see Nayyar (1996).

performance. It is also possible to discern an increasing, almost silent, participation in the political process, combined with an emerging mobilization on some issues. In this respect, the expectations of the founding fathers of the republic have been more than realized. For one, there is an absolute institutionalization of adult franchise which is irreversible. For another, democracy which was provided largely from above is now being claimed increasingly from below by the people. Taken together, these two attributes reflect an increasing empowerment of the people in the political process. In other respects, however, the expected did not happen. Polity did not transform society. Caste did not wither away. In fact, reservations ultimately led to a politicization of caste. Secularism did not dispense with religious identities. If anything, religion became an increasingly important factor in politics. The significance of linguistic or cultural differences did not diminish. It persisted as ethnic identities and regional movements became an important form of dissent in politics. If the main vocabulary of politics turned out to be caste and religion, or other forms of social identity, rather than class, democracy did, in a sense, bring politics to the people. The irony is that, although democracy struck roots among the people, it was not so embedded in political parties. Indeed, intra-party democracy diminished slowly but surely with the passage of time. Thus, dissent did not lead to debates or factions within parties. It led to splinters. In this world, politics in political parties became more and more personalized so that ideology was less and less a point of reference. The economic liberalization which was introduced in 1991, and gathered momentum thereafter, was simply not related to the institutional framework of political democracy. It was, therefore, neither shaped by political processes nor rooted in social formations, which could have provided constituencies in polity and society.

It is always difficult to analyse the present without the benefit of distance in time. It is, however, plausible to suggest that the 1990s have witnessed an accentuation of conflict both in economic interests and in political interests. The former is implicit while the latter is explicit. This is bound to make the interaction of economics and politics even more complex.

The retreat of the state, which is almost a corollary of economic liberalization, hurts the poor in a material sense. And India is no different. The soft options in fiscal adjustment lead to cuts in public expenditure in social sectors, as the resources allocated for poverty alleviation, health care, education and welfare programmes decrease, or do not increase as much as they should, in real terms, so that there is a squeeze on social consumption. Cuts in subsidies are often at the expense of the poor. So are many of the increases in user charges for public utilities. The story does not end there as the state withdraws from investment in infrastructure. It is the poor who go without. But that is not all. Markets and globalization have a logic of their own, which leads to inclusion for some and exclusion for others or affluence for some and poverty for others. There are some winners. There are many losers. It is perhaps necessary to identify, in broad categories, the winners and the losers. If we think of people, asset-owners, profit-earners, rentiers, the educated, the mobile, and those with professional, managerial, or technical skills are the winners, whereas asset-less, wage-earners, debtors, the uneducated, the immobile and the semi-skilled or the unskilled are the losers. Globalization has introduced a new dimension to the exclusion of people from consumption possibilities. Exclusion is no longer simply about the inability to satisfy the most basic human needs in terms of food, clothing and shelter for large numbers of people. It is much more complicated. For, the consumption patterns and the lifestyles of the rich associated with globalization have powerful demonstration effects. People everywhere, even the poor and the excluded, are exposed to these consumption possibility frontiers because the electronic media has spread the consumerist message far and wide. This creates expectations and aspirations. But the simple fact of life is that those who do not have incomes cannot buy goods and services in the market. Thus, when the paradise of consumerism is unrealizable or unattainable, which is the case for the common people, it only creates frustration or alienation.

This process is juxtaposed with a politics of segmentation arising out of conflicts in the political process. For one, religion has become a major factor in political mobilization, reflected primarily in the rise of the Bharatiya Janata Party. For another, caste identities are now crucial in political parties and the electoral process, reflected not only in dalit mobilization by the Bahujan Samaj Party but also in the co-option of backward castes into most political parties, sometimes referred to as the 'Mandalization' of politics. At the same time, the decline of national political parties is leading to a regionalization of politics, reflected in the fact that regional parties now rule a large proportion of the states in India. This politics of segmentation means that there is no dominant political party and no stable coalition. The reality is constantly shifting coalitions or unstable governments. Yet, there is a functional stability in political democracy because each of these segments has a stake in the system and aspires to a share in state power. It is not about empowerment alone. There are the material spoils of office, with or without corruption.

These tensions are compounded by conflicts between the sphere of economics and the realm of politics. The people who are excluded by the economics of markets are included by the politics of democracy. Hence, inclusion and exclusion are asymmetrical in politics and economics. The distribution of capabilities is also uneven in the economic and political spheres. The rich dominate the economy now more than earlier, but the poor have a strong voice in the polity now more than earlier. And there is a mismatch.

It is, then, plausible to suggest that this third phase in independent India is characterized by an intensification of conflict in the economy, in the polity, and in the interaction between economy and polity. There can be little doubt that the need for conflict resolution is much greater than ever before. But the task has become more difficult. And the effort is much less.

It is more difficult to mediate in the conflicts between economic development and political democracy for two reasons. First, there is no consensus. In the sphere of economics, the old consensus has broken down while a new consensus has not emerged. The oft-stated view that there is a political consensus on economic reforms in India is not quite correct because such a consensus exists only among the rich, the literati, and the influential. It extends to most political leaders, whose discourse on the economy has come to be strongly influenced by a 'virus of liberalization without understanding', although not to the rank and file of most political parties. But it does not have an acceptance at the level of the people, most of whom are poor or silent and, thus, unheard. In the realm of politics, too, the old consensus has turned into a new dissensus, as divisive issues such as caste, religion, language and regionalism have multiplied. Second, a short-termism has replaced the long-term perspective of yesteryears. In the sphere of economics, the preoccupation with stabilization in the short term and adjustment or reform in the medium term, which is natural for the IMF and the World Bank respectively, leads to confusion between tactics and strategies or means and ends in the minds of governments. In the realm of politics, where governments are no longer sure about their tenure, a visible myopia has crept in. In this milieu, political parties and political leaders can think only about the next month or the next year or, at most, the next election. The next quinquennium or the next decade are simply irrelevant. Such short-termism leads to a neglect of long-term development objectives. There are two reasons for this. First, such objectives cannot be defined in terms of performance criteria in the sphere of economics laid down by the multilateral financial institutions. Second, such objectives do not bring tangible gains in the realm of politics which can be exploited by governments within one term as they seek to renew their mandate in the next election. This short-termism may also lead to 'hysteresis'—the effects of short-term policies or actions which persist over time to influence outcomes in the long term—in both the economy and the polity.[43] The past influences the present, just as the present shapes the future, if economic policies or political actions have consequences which are irreversible after a time lag.

The effort to mediate in conflicts between economic development and political democracy is also much less. Curiously enough,

[43] The experience in independent India, especially over the past twenty-five years, provides some powerful illustrations of such 'hysteresis' effects. In the polity, the centralization of authority and power at the apex, which began with Indira Gandhi in the early 1970s, weakened the institutional base of the pyramid, so that the ability of the state to mediate between conflicting interests was much reduced. We live with its consequences even now. In the economy, the populism of the 1980s translated into soft options where the solutions conceived for the short run turned into problems in the longer run. The fiscal crisis and the debt crisis, which surfaced in early 1991, were the consequences. Similarly, it is possible that the economic liberalization of the 1990s, in particular the trade liberalization and the financial liberalization, may have an adverse effect on the performance of the economy in the long term through 'hysteresis'. This argument about the long-term consequences of short-termism, in the context of public policies and economic development, is developed at some length elsewhere by the author; see Nayyar (1998).

the willingness and the ability of the state to mediate is not quite there. Its willingness to mediate is dampened by the use of money power to influence, or to use, the state apparatus for particular purposes. In most democracies, governments can be sectarian in their actions as they seek to protect or promote the interests of classes, or groups, whom they represent. The apparatus of governments is often used deliberately to promote the interests of the ruling elite. This does not surprise anyone. In India, however, the governmental system is increasingly being used to further, sometimes crudely and openly, the interests of powerful individuals through corruption and nepotism. In this milieu, people with money lobby hard and exercise influence in pursuit of their interests.[44] But people without money do not have the voice or the resources to support their cause. Thus, the desire of the state to mediate surfaces only in the election season. Its ability to mediate is constrained by the spread of markets and the march of globalization. This process is not only eroding the autonomy of the nation-state in the international context, but is also creating a situation where the political process is losing control over the economy in the national context. The credibility of the state as an institution has eroded and the government, it appears, is abdicating its role in reconciling economic and political democracy.

In sum, the economics of liberalization and the politics of empowerment represent an unstable, if not volatile, mix. Ultimately, empowerment is a more potent force than liberalization. At present, however, it would seem that these forces are moving the economy and the polity, for the first time in independent India, in opposite directions, without any concerted attempt at a reconciliation or a mediation. This is fraught with risk. And, if the state cannot perform this role, the mediation would have to come through citizens and civil society.

44 In extreme situations, the state may be used almost as private property. There is some cumulative causation here. Politics is about the seizure of power. And, power is a source of gathering income and accumulating wealth which, in turn, facilitates the capture of political power. In this milieu, the political freedom provided by democracy is curbed by the uneven spread of money power, just as the economic freedom provided by the market is vitiated by the unequal distribution of income and wealth.

References

Bagchi, Amiya K. (1995), 'Introduction: Democracy and Development: Heritage, Aspirations and Reality' in Amiya K. Bagchi (ed.), *Democracy and Development*. London: Macmillan.

Bardhan, Pranab (1984), *The Political Economy of Development in India*. Oxford: Basil Blackwell.

Bettelheim, Charles (1968), *India Independent*. New York: Monthly Review Press.

Bhaduri, Amit and Deepak Nayyar (1996), *The Intelligent Person's Guide to Liberalization*. New Delhi: Penguin Books.

Brass, Paul R. (1980), 'The Politicisation of the Peasantry in a North Indian State', *Journal of Peasant Studies,* vol. 7, no. 4, pp. 395–426 and vol. 8, no. 1, pp. 3–36.

——— (1992), *The Politics of India Since Independence*. Cambridge: Cambridge University Press.

Byres, Terence J. (1988), 'Charan Singh: 1902–1987: An Assessment', *Journal of Peasant Studies,* vol. 15, no. 2, pp. 139–89.

——— (ed.) (1994), *The State and Development Planning in India*. Delhi: Oxford University Press.

Chakravarty, Sukhamoy (1987), *Development Planning: The Indian Experience*. Oxford: Clarendon Press.

Chatterjee, Partha (1993), *The Nation and Its Fragments: Colonial and Postcolonial Histories*. Princeton: Princeton University Press.

——— (1997), *A Possible India: Essays in Political Criticism*. Delhi: Oxford University Press.

Das, Arvind N. (1994), *India Invented: A Nation in the Making*. New Delhi: Manohar.

Drèze, Jean and Amartya Sen (1995), *India: Economic Development and Social Opportunity*. Delhi: Oxford University Press.

Frankel, Francine R. (1971), *India's Green Revolution: Economic Gains and Political Costs*. Princeton: Princeton University Press.

——— (1978), *India's Political Economy, 1947–1977: The Gradual Revolution*. Princeton: Princeton University Press.

Friedman, Milton (1962), *Capitalism and Freedom*. Chicago: University of Chicago Press.

Gough, K. and H. Sharma (eds) (1973), *Imperialism and Revolution in South Asia*. New York: Monthly Review Press.

Joshi, P.C. (1975), *Land Reforms in India*. Bombay: Allied Publishers.

Joshi, Vijay and Ian Little (1994), *India: Macroeconomics and Political Economy: 1964–1991*. Delhi: Oxford University Press.

Kaviraj, Sudipta (1995), 'Democracy and Development in India' in A.K. Bagchi (ed.), *Democracy and Development*. London: Macmillan.

Khilnani, Sunil (1997), *The Idea of India*. London: Hamish Hamilton.

Kohli, Atul (1990), *Democracy and Discontent: India's Growing Crisis of Governability*. Cambridge: Cambridge University Press.

Kothari, Rajni (1970), *Politics in India*. Boston: Little, Brown.

———— (1988), *State Against Democracy*. Delhi: Ajanta Books.

Mill, John Stuart (1859), *On Liberty* and (1861), *Considerations on Representative Government*, with an introduction by R.D. McCallum. Oxford: Oxford University Press, 1946.

Mitra, Ashok (1977), *Terms of Trade and Class Relations*. London: Frank Cass.

Morris-Jones, W.H. (1971), *The Government and Politics of India*. London: Hutchinson.

Nayyar, Deepak (1978), 'Industrial Development in India: Some Reflections on Growth and Stagnation', *Economic and Political Weekly*, vol. XIII, nos 31–3, pp. 1265–78.

———— (1996), *Economic Liberalization in India: Analytics, Experience and Lessons*. R.C. Dutt Lectures on Political Economy. Calcutta: Orient Longman.

———— (1998), 'Short-termism, Public Policies and Economic Development', *Economies et Societies*, vol. XXXII, no. 1, pp. 107–18.

Nayyar, Rohini (1991), *Rural Poverty in India: An Analysis of Inter-State Differences*. Delhi: Oxford University Press.

Planning Commission (1985), *Seventh Five-Year Plan*, vol. II. New Delhi: Government of India.

———— (1992), *Eighth Five-Year Plan*, vol. II. New Delhi: Government of India.

———— (1993), *Report of the Expert Group on Estimation of Proportion and Number of Poor*. New Delhi: Government of India.

Rodgers, G., C. Gore and J.B. Figueiredo (eds) (1995), *Social Exclusion: Rhetoric, Reality, Responses*. Geneva: International Labour Organisation.

Rudolph, L.I. and S.H. Rudolph (1987), *In Pursuit of Lakshmi: The Political Economy of the Indian State*. Chicago: University of Chicago Press.

Sen, Amartya (1981), *Poverty and Famines: An Essay on Entitlement and Deprivation*. Oxford: Clarendon Press.
——— (1985), *Commodities and Capabilities*. Amesterdam: North-Holland.
Vanaik, Achin (1990), *The Painful Transition: Bourgeois Democracy in India*. London: Verso.

13

The Political Economy of Reform in India+

Pranab Bardhan

The reformer has enemies in all those who profit by the old order, and only lukewarm defenders in all those who would profit by the new.

Niccolo Machiavelli, in *The Prince* (1513), chapter VI

I

In the last few years I have often been asked if my thinking on the low-level equilibrium has changed in view of the on-going economic reform. Starting in the mid-1980s, but accelerating since the external payments crisis in mid-1991, India's industrial licensing and regulatory policies, trade, tax, investment, and fiscal policies have undergone substantial changes. In this chapter I shall briefly discuss the political economy of reform in India. I shall comment less on what should or should not have been done, and more on the socio-political background of what has been done: less on what is desirable and more on what is feasible. In doing this I shall have to necessarily move beyond economics, and at times dabble in political sociology. My comments are also confined to broad long- or medium-run patterns, and not to the ups and downs of the economy in short-run.

I have noticed in the recent literature two opposed general positions on the pace and prospect of reforms. One of these

+ *The Political Economy of Development in India (Expanded Edition)* (Delhi: Oxford University Press, 1998), pp. 119–38.

takes the rosy view that dramatic changes in policy have taken place since 1991, and that more could be done but for the messy politics that occasionally slow down reforms—for example, those relating to the insurance sector or industrial labour—but the reform process is now essentially irreversible, and most political leaders give assurances to this effect to business, despite rhetorical deviations in some of their public speeches. The other view is more pessimistic: only the easier reforms have been handled so far (given that the nightmarish extent to which the system of licenses and permits was stretched in the earlier regime was unacceptable to most people) while many difficult reforms have been stalled and are likely to remain so, given the path of rag-tag coalition politics that the country seems to be inevitably taking.

My own position in this respect is somewhere in between these two opposed general views. But I would like to differentiate my view from another intermediate position, taken, for example, by Jenkins (1997). This position is essentially about reform by stealth: that a great deal of substantial reforms has been accomplished, avoiding major headlines or political confrontations; a process of slow but steady creeping reform has set in, according to this view, and is likely to continue. In my judgement this intermediate position has considerable plausibility. I shall therefore discuss this position at some length, and point out where I agree and where I do not.

But first we need to look at some aggregative statistics on growth and investment, to give us an indication about the quantum of these changes in terms of macroeconomic outcome. Next we shall discuss some methodological points to help us interpret this data. Finally we will move into issues concering political economy.

For the macro data we shall draw upon the careful analysis of the National Accounts Statistics for the period of 1980–1 to 1995–6 made by Nagaraj (1997). One advantage of these statistics is that they allow for a relatively long time-series, and one does not have to depend on simple year-to-year variations in growth rates. On the basis of the time-series one can say that overall Gross Domestic Product (GDP), as well as sectoral GDP in primary and tertiary sectors, roughly maintained its earlier (that is, of the 1980s) growth rates in the 1990s. There have been no dramatic changes in these rates. In fact there is a small but statistically significant decline in the secondary sector (including manufacturing) in the

1990s compared to the 1980s (the addition of the last two years, 1996–7 and 1997–8, when data are available, is unlikely to change this as on all indications the growth rates in the industrial sector have slowed down in these two years).

Within the manufacturing sector one expects some decline in import-substitute industries with trade liberalization.[1] This has happened sharply in the capital goods industries. One indicator of the increased competition in these industries is the fall in prices of machinery and equipment relative to the GDP deflator since the late 1980s. Some consumer goods, particularly durables, experienced growth, fuelled by a rise in effective protection (due to devaluation as well as a fall in the relative price of inputs). Contrary to the usual expectation of the effect of trade liberalization, there has, however, not been much of an increase in the growth of traded, labour-intensive goods. In fact the growth rate in the unregistered manufacturing sector (which employs nearly half the total labour in manufacturing) declined from an average of 7.6 per cent in 1986–91 to 5.7 per cent in 1992–6. There has also been a marked decline in the growth rate of total employment in the organized sector as a whole in the 1990s compared to the 1980s. Again, contrary to expectation, some of the non-traded, tertiary sectors recorded a significant increase in growth. Much of the large rise in the growth rate in private corporate gross fixed capital formation has gone into the tertiary sector (most likely into finance and real estate). The share of infrastructure in total gross fixed capital formation in the economy declined from 37 per cent in 1986–7 to 26 per cent in 1995–6. This was associated with the decline in the public sector gross capital formation as percentage of GDP.[2] It is now agreed on all counts that India's creaking infrastructure (power, railways, roads, ports, etc.) is the major bottleneck on industrial growth.

In interpreting the decline in the manufacturing growth rate in the 1990s it is important to keep in mind one methodological

1 On the other hand, with imperfect competition trade liberalization may increase the perceived elasticity of demand facing each firm, lower its mark-up, and increase output. The domestic market for Indian firms is, however, often regionally segmented, reducing the impact of national-level competition.

2 Capital expenditure of the central and state governments taken together as a proportion of GDP declined from 8.3 per cent in 1990–1 to 5.7 per cent in 1995–6.

point: the effects of liberalization should be carefully distinguished from those of macroeconomic stabilization. Some of the adverse effects of the credit crunch in the first half of the 1990s or the fiscal squeeze necessitated by the past and present profligacy in our public fisc should not be attributed to liberalization *per se*, even in cases where one could think of better ways of carrying out the corrective fiscal and financial policies. For example, the sharp decline in growth of the unregistered manufacturing sector noted above may have much to do with the difficulty of getting credit that this sector faced.[3] It is also to be noted that the growth rate in the 1980s, financed to some extent by large external borrowings, may not have been macroeconomically sustainable for long, and thus any comparison with the growth rate of the 1980s has to be qualified to that extent. It is also possible that it is as yet too soon for the effects of the structural changes that have taken place since 1991 to show up in the aggregative growth statistics. In scattered parts of the economy (including in some public enterprises),[4] increased competition and restructuring may have improved total factor productivity, but hard evidence for this on a sustained basis and an adequately large scale is not yet available.

The other methodological point to note in discussing the effects of policy changes is that some reforms came not by design but more as unintended consequences of bankruptcy. This is particularly the case at the state level. Some reforms have generated a chain reaction creating a demand for pushing the reforms further than what was originally intended. We shall come back to this point when we discuss the issues of creeping reforms.

II

Next we discuss the politics of reforms. Politics is about distributive conflicts, about winners and losers, and how they get organized

[3] A Report of Internal Group on Small Scale Industries in the Planning Commission in 1997 observes that capacity utilization in this sector is only around 50 per cent, and one of the main factors responsible for this underutilization is the inadequacy of credit.

[4] Nagaraj (1997) refers to the significant rise in profitability (gross profit as percentage of capital employed) of central government public sector enterprises in the 1990s in general, and in the plant load factor of thermal power plants in particular.

about it or fail to. Who are the losers from reforms so far? The most vocal group in opposition is organized labour. Of course, not many jobs have been lost in government service (the part of the Fifth Pay Commission Report which recommended a streamlining and reducing of the future size of government did not have any takers, in contrast to the part about pay revisions), although there is a fear of potential job loss from privatization. In contrast to the white-collar labour unions, the labour movement for the manual or blue-collar workers is actually highly fragmented, an issue we shall take up later. The other vocal group, ignoring the occasional vandalism against Kentucky Fried Chicken or Cargill Seed Farm by organized farmers, is that of Indian business houses. Some of them have been clamouring for a 'level playing field', after they perceived their traditional family control to be threatened by foreign multinationals.[5] Patriotism is, of course, the first refuge of laggards in competition.[6] Yet all major political parties (the Left parties, BJP, the Janata Party, and even the Congress) have played the 'swadeshi' tune on this issue at election time.

The actual, as opposed to potential, losers in the 1990s may have been many small-scale enterprises. They were hit hard by the credit crunch, which was part of the macro stabilization policy. It may, of course, be claimed that even within the broad framework of stabilization some government policies, for example, those inducing transfer of savings to the equity markets, may have made access to finance more difficult for small enterprises compared to large companies. With the freeing of bank lending rates and the fiscal concessions for deductibility of interest costs that the corporate sector enjoys, the interest-rate structure has become more regressive, to the disadvantage of the unorganized sector.

5 The threat as yet is largely exaggerated for the corporate sector as a whole—a comparison of the *Business India* 100 in 1995 with the listing in 1978 suggests that the predominance of Indian business houses remains about the same. This is particularly the case in asset holdings. Foreign firms' share in fixed asset formation in the corporate sector remains at about 10 per cent in the 1990s, as can be seen from the estimates of the Centre for Monitoring the Indian Economy (CMIE).

6 For example, a company like Bajaj (whose chairman is one of the most vocal in demanding restrictions on foreign investment) has been losing market share largely because it does not use its own R&D, while its competitors have their own design and development units.

In general there has not been much of a political backlash against reforms, and no serious pitched battles (as opposed to occasional rhetorical skirmishes) have been fought on the issue of liberalization. Many state-level political leaders, irrespective of which party they belong to, have supported liberalization. If not for any other reason, simply because it has been associated with a more open-door policy for foreign investment, providing a way out of fiscal bankruptcy. The lack of serious opposition to reforms has sometimes been interpreted as evidence of a lack of substantive reforms, because reforms are not supposed to be painless. This view is not quite correct. A more plausible view, as exposited, for example, by Jenkins (1997), is that there has been a great deal of piecemeal reform, through a political process of diffusing resistance on part of the vested interests in various ways, without causing massive political confrontations. Like the stealth bomber, reform in India has largely avoided the political radar screen.

This process of diffusion of resistance may be illustrated by referring to the three major forms it has taken. Firstly, while some large business houses have lost on account of increased competition from new (often medium-sized) business groups, particularly at the regional level (providing a new constituency of reforms),[7] the large business houses have gained elsewhere as restrictions to entry in some sectors (formerly reserved only for public enterprises) have been eased. Thus, the potential opposition from large business houses has been muffled. Secondly, there has been a diffusion of resistance through regional fragmentation. As power has shifted more to the regions (indicated not just by the prominence of regional parties in power-brokering, but also by the increasing effective autonomy of the regional wings of national parties from the directives of the central party leadership), some regional governments, backed as they increasingly are by regional capital, have looked the other way when pre-existing restrictive rules have been breached or not effectively enforced. The opposition to non-implementation of existing laws has thus been splintered. This has happened, for example, in the case of opposition by labour unions to lockouts by owners of industrial firms or the non-enforcement of Section 25 of the Industrial

[7] In any case the regional business groups knew that the major beneficiaries of the old licensing system were the national big business houses.

Disputes Act, under which government permission is needed to sack workers. These are instances of a kind of reform by default.

Third is the case of reform by stealth or creeping reforms, as in the case of a slow chipping away at restrictions without causing much of a political splash. For example, in December 1997 the asset limit for small industries was multiplied fivefold (from Rs 6 million to Rs 30 million in terms of the value of plant and machinery), even though the number of products exclusively reserved for these small industries did not decline very much. Similarly, in some states the rules of acquisition and conversion of land for private industrial projects were allowed to be manipulated (evading the restrictive urban land-ceiling laws), in the process generating a great deal of illicit income for politicians and promoters. The monopoly power of the large public sector companies has been chipped away by backdoor privatization on a small scale or by allowing industrial firms to have captive power plants or coal mines (or allowing them to import if the domestic public enterprise fails in its supply commitments).

Reform by stealth has been especially important in the case of labour laws. These laws, particularly those relating to job security and automatic promotion, are on paper among the most stringent in the world. Several attempts to change these laws have faced enormous opposition, difficulty, and delay, much to the despair of reformers. Yet, in practice employers have often got away with many changes:

(i) many workers have been pushed out under the so-called voluntary retirement scheme with or without legal compensation, and very few of them have been retrained or redeployed;

(ii) there has been widespread use of contract or casual labour, substituting for regular employees, sometimes through job or task redefintion;

(iii) many unviable units have actually been closed through various subterfuges (in fact the average number of days lost due to lockout now far exceeds those due to strikes);

(iv) there have been many cases of subcontracting work out to small-scale units or backward areas, where the degree of enforcement of the existing laws is also backward.

While there are large elements of truth in the position thus taken by Jenkins (1997) and others, I happen to disagree with this position on some major points. Diffusion of resistance through regional fragmentation is limited on important issues of restructuring at the national policy level, where vested interests are nationally organized—for example, in the case of restructuring the management of large public enterprises at the centre and giving them *real* autonomy (not just the 'smoke and mirrors' of Memoranda of Understanding [MOUs] in the past or the 'navaratna' or 'mini-navaratna' status proposed currently); or in breaking the unholy nexus between the public-enterprises hierarchy, their private clients, and the criminal underworld and their political patrons; or in restructuring the insurance sector; or in the internal organization of public financial institutions;[8] or in reducing family control over large private-sector enterprises. Similarly, the practice of looking the other way while labour laws get diluted, may not be enough to attract foreign investors who may insist on more tangible guarantees. In general, reforms, if they remain clandestine, may strain credibility in the medium and long run.

The staggering burden of government subsidies, placating different powerful interest groups, shows how many crucial political-economy issues remain unresolved. A detailed study by the National Institute of Public Finance and Policy, reported in Srivastava and Sen (1997), provides a fairly comprehensive estimate of the explicit and implicit budget-based subsidies.[9]

[8] There have, however, been significant, though slow and halting, financial sector reforms. These include the deregulation of interest rates, more competition in the financial sector, insistence on capital adequacy norms in most public sector banks, etc. The 'non-performing assets' as a proportion of their total advances has now been brought down to below 20 per cent.

[9] This includes, apart from explicit cash subsidies (e.g. on food, fertilizer, and export), interest or credit subsidies (i.e. loans given at below market rates), tax subsidies (e.g. tax exemption of medical expenses, deduction of mortgage interest payment from taxable income, etc.), in-kind subsidies (e.g. provision of free medical services), equity subsidies (investment in equity in State enterprises yielding low dividends), procurement subsidies (say in government purchase of food grains) and regulatory subsidies (administered pricing). The estimate, by its method of computation, includes the effects of cost overruns, wastages, and inefficiencies on capital projects, and thus goes beyond the usual meaning of subsidies.

According to this estimate, the budget-based[10] subsidies of the central and state governments taken together amounted to about Rs 1.4 trillion, which is 14.4 per cent of GDP (or about twice the size of the aggregate fiscal deficit) in 1994–5. This study computes subsidies as the excess of providing a service over the recoveries from that service (excluding defence and general administration). If one also excludes expenditure items like primary education, public health and sanitation, flood control and drainage, roads and bridges, soil and water conservation, agricultural and various scientific research, and many social welfare schemes, and concentrates on what the study (not quite accurately) calls 'non-merit goods and services' (a large part of which go to the non-poor), the total estimate of such subsidies alone amounts to Rs 1.04 trillion, or 10.9 per cent of GDP in 1994–5.

Then there is the colossal public debt, servicing which takes up a large and increasing part of budgetary funds, moving inexorably towards an internal debt trap, and keeps the interest rates high, choking private investment.[11] The interest payments of the central government on the public debt as a proportion of GDP rose from about 3 per cent in the mid-1980s to 4 per cent in 1990–1, and then to about 5 per cent in the mid-1990s. While the fiscal deficit of the consolidated public sector (including the central and state governments and non-financial public enterprises) as a proportion of GDP declined slightly from about 12 per cent in 1990–1 to about 10 per cent in 1995–6, a large part of this was the revenue deficit (used primarily for government consumption), which as a proportion of GDP does not show any decline. This deficit steadily increased over the 1980s, and then, after a decline in the first two years of 'adjustment' (1991–3) went up significantly. It is likely to go up again after the hefty upward revision of wage and salary scales of government employees at all levels. This revision is to be shortly implemented following

10 This estimate excludes an off-budget subsidy like petroleum subsidy, which in 1994–5 was about Rs 66 billion (by 1997 the 'oil pool deficit' climbed to more than three times that amount).

11 Recently the finance ministry had a formal agreement with the Reserve Bank giving the latter a great deal of autonomy in the matter of monetization of the public debt. This illustrates that the Indian state is more sensitive to the short-run political dangers of inflation than to the long-run costs of choking investment.

upon (and exceeding) the recommendations of the Fifth Pay Commission (and its usual chain reactions for other public services at the central and state levels); at the mere hint of a strike by the central government employees, the government capitulated.

The budgetary problems are severe, particularly at the state level, where the governments, exposed as they are more closely to some of the particularistic interest groups, are practically bankrupt in many cases.[12] The revenue deficit of the states has trebled over the 1990s. In some cases 'development grants' for capital projects authorized by the Planning Commission are being used by the states largely to pay salaries to public officials. An increasingly larger share of the central loan to the states is utilized to repay earlier loans, and the states' aggregate outstanding loan to the centre was nearly Rs 1.5 trillion by the end of the financial year 1996–7. Circumventing the constitutional ceiling on market borrowings by state governments, the state-owned enterprises are issuing bonds with state government guarantees (generating large contingent liabilities); the outstanding level nearly quadrupled over the first half of the 1990s.

Yet, a chief minister celebrated his recent election victory by announcing that the farmers, a large and powerful lobby in his state, do not have to pay for irrigation water or electricity. In most other states as well, water and electricity are provided at throw-away prices (as are higher education and urban transport), much below even the operational and maintenance costs of the facilities, not to speak of the capital cost. In 1994–5 the gross electricity subsidy of all states for the agricultural sector alone exceeded Rs 100 billion. In 1996–7 the annual commercial losses (excluding subsidies) of the State Electricity Boards were more than six times what they were in 1985–6, and their combined rate of return is now estimated to be a negative 16.5 per cent.

There is a growing sense in some quarters that bankruptcy and the diminishing transfers from the Centre[13] will eventually make the states awaken to the hard reality and the pressing need for

[12] In Uttar Pradesh, for example, debt servicing is now more than the tax revenue of the state.

[13] The total net transfers from the central to the state governments, (i.e. the states' share of central taxes, and loans and grants to the states less interest and amortization of loans) fell from more than 6 per cent of GDP in 1990–1 to 4.7 per cent in 1995–6.

reform. Attempts are afoot, for example, to restructure the operations of the State Electricity Boards in a few states (like Orissa and Andhra Pradesh). As states are increasingly asked to fend for themselves and as inter-state competition to lure private investment heats up, this game is clearly to the advantage of the infrastructurally already better-off states. What is less clear, however, is how the Indian federal system will resolve the tension between the demands of the better-off states for more competition, and those of other states (which a weaker Centre can ill afford to ignore politically) for redistributive transfers through constitutional bodies like the Finance Commission or extra-constitutional agencies like the Planning Commission. Can, for example, a shaky coalition government at the Centre, dependent on MPs from infrastructurally weak states like Bihar, Uttar Pradesh, or Madhya Pradesh, ignore their redistributive demands to compensate them for losing out in the inter-state competition for private investment? Such bail-outs are likely to give wrong incentives in resource mobilization efforts by these states.

On the whole one should not exaggerate the extent of shift in the basic political equilibrium inspite of all the impressive changes that have taken place in economic policy. About fifteen years ago I had described a system of political gridlock in India, originating in the collective action problems of large, heterogeneous coalition of dominant interest groups with multiple veto powers, and with no interest group powerful enough to hijack the state by itself; the system thus settled for short-run particularistic compromises in the form of sharing the spoils through an elaborate network of subsidies and patronage distribution, to the detriment of long-run investment and economic growth. Since then there has certainly been an increase in the diversity, fluidity, and fragmentation in the coalition of dominant interest groups. The industrial scene is less dominated today by a few big business houses, with the rise of medium-sized and regional business groups (particularly in textiles, sugar, cement, steel, chemicals, and fertilizers in western and southern India) providing competition and conflict.[14] The rich farmer families are

14 The composition of the list of top twenty business houses has changed substantially in the last twenty-five years, with the entry of many new business houses and the exit of some old ones. Some of the regional business groups

diversifying their investments and often branching out into private trade and commerce, real estate, transport, and small industry (particularly in sugar and rice mills, food processing, etc.), and as such are not averse to the expansion of opportunities and the easing of government regulations in the urban sector. There is also a discernible change in the mindset of large sections of the elite regarding the limits of the role of the state.

There is a slow, and at times grudging, acceptance within the bureaucracy that the Indian state has overextended itself in the economy, far beyond the limits of its administrative capacity. Some of the new entrepreneurs, belonging as they do to the families of senior bureaucrats, army officers, and other members of the professional classes, or sharing ties through education in elite engineering and business schools, have forged new links between the bureaucracy and private capital. Regional governments have much stronger links with regional capital now. Furthermore, most members of the dominant coalition, families in the industrial and professional classes in particular but also some rich farmer and trader families, have now some close or distant relatives among non-resident Indians; a larger interaction and communication with foreign countries has helped thaw some of the antiquated, hard, autarchic attitudes. Meanwhile, the ideological props for pervasiveness of state control and regulations that the left intellectual community used to provide have been crumbling with the precipitous decline of state socialism in different parts of the world.

All these changes and realignments in the composition and attitudes of the dominant coalition have made some of the deregulatory reforms more acceptable than before. But, as we have mentioned in the preceding paragraphs, one should not underestimate the enormity and tenacity of vested interests in the preservation of the old political equilibrium of subsidies and patronage distribution. Matters are further complicated by evolving democratic forces, unleashed in an extremely hierarchical and heterogeneous society. This political sociology of reforms and its implications are discussed in the next section.

---

are now quite influential in business lobbies like the Confederation of Indian Industries (CII) at the national level.

III

Along with political power drifting from the Centre to the regions, there is an associated drift towards the backward and lower castes. This is clearly a sign of democratic progress in an unequal society. The numerical strength and increased assertiveness of some of the historically subordinate groups have compelled the upper classes and castes to form downward alliances and brought to the fore political actors from backward communities and regions. These players may be uninitiated in the etiquette of parliamentary democracy and in the social graces of modernity, but are quite astute in pursuing the interests of their constituencies (and, of course, their own self-interest). This victorious march of democracy in India with all its banality and gaudiness would have impressed Alexis de Tocqueville (1835) who had described the turmoil in nineteenth-century Europe generated by rising democratic aspirations in a highly unequal society.

What is disturbing, however, is that the diminishing hold of elite control and the unfolding of populist democracy to reach the lower rungs of the social hierarchy have been associated with a loosening of the earlier administrative protocols and a steady erosion of the institutional insulation of the decision-making process in public administration and economic management. It is now common practice for a low-caste chief minister in a state to proceed, immediately upon assuming office, to transfer civil servants belonging to upper castes and get pliant bureaucrats from his or her own caste. Many members of the supposedly independent civil service now try to curry favour with politicians to avoid transfers to undesirable jobs and locations. Administrative appointments outside the main civil service, like those to the boards of public sector corporations, particularly those under state governments, are often used as political sinecures to keep the clamouring factions happy. What all this does to the institutional independence of economic decision-taking bodies or the credibility of commitment to long-run developmental policies is anybody's guess.

There is certain nonchalance in the rampant corruption among politicians in the newly emergent groups. Lower-caste leaders, when they come to power, are sometimes quite unapologetic about being corrupt. They say that the upper castes in control of the state have been corrupt for decades, and now it is their turn.[15] Corruption is thus seen as a collective entitlement in an amoral game of group equity.

No major political party in India is opposed to the strong movements demanding large caste quotas in public sector jobs and higher education for backward castes, in addition to those stipulated in the Constitution for Scheduled Castes and Tribes. As the expansion of the public sector over the years created more opportunities for secure jobs and, not infrequently, for the associated extra, illicit income if the job was regulatory in nature, more and more mobilized groups in the democratic process have started using their low-caste status for staking a claim to the loot.

All this points to a major disjuncture between politics and economics in India so far as market reform is concerned. On the one hand, we are told that in recent years the era of market reform has arrived in India, and that there is a measure of political consensus that it is inexorable and irreversible. On the other hand, some of the major political events in the last decade or so that have captured public imagination constitute a phenomenon that is essentially anti-market: the propagation of group equity and caste rights, the carving of markets for new jobs in the public sector in protected niches, special dispensations and patronage for newly emergent groups, rampant caste-based violations of the institutional insulation of economic governance—all amounting to a drowning of considerations of efficiency in the name of inter-group equity.[16]

15 For a similar observation see Visvanathan (1997).

16 It is arguable that inter-group equity may sometimes serve the cause of dynamic efficiency. To the extent special preferential policies for groups are supposed to cope with a historical handicap, their economic rationale may be akin to that behind the age-old argument for infant-industry protection in early stages of industrialization. Some disadvantaged groups may need temporary protection against competition so that they can participate in learning by doing and on-the-job skill formation before catching up with the others. Some of the standard arguments *against* infant-industry protection are then equally applicable to job reservation policies. For example, the 'infant', once protected, sometimes refuses to grow up; reservations, once adopted, are extremely difficult to reverse. Another argument against infant-industry protection is that even when the goal is justifiable, it may be achieved more efficiently through other policies. For example, a disadvantaged group may be helped by preferential loans, scholarships, job training programmes, and

Cynics may even argue that the retreat of the state, implied by economic reform, is now more acceptable to the upper classes and castes, not only because the regulatory and interventionist state has become too burdensome for the Indian economy, but also because these classes are now losing their control over state power in the face of the emerging hordes of lower castes, and thus opting for greener pastures in the private sector (and abroad). This is a rather extreme, though interesting, hypothesis. It is certainly consistent with the fact that very few substantive reforms have yet been attempted in the agricultural sector[17]—a sector where appropriate reforms would have benefited the backward and lowly castes in massive numbers.[18] It is also consistent with the

---

extension services for its members, instead of job quotas that bar qualified candidates coming from advanced groups (in other words, equality of opportunity may be more justifiable than insistence on equality of outcome). Such indirect policies of helping out backward groups are also less likely to generate political resentment (particularly because in this case the burden may be shared more evenly, whereas in the case of job quotas the redistributive burden falls on a small subset of the people in advanced communities).

17 The major reason for this is, however, the inflation-sensitivity of the Indian polity. Substantial agricultural reforms will involve removal of controls on trade, which is likely to raise the price of major food grains that domestic consumers pay and the price of some raw materials (like cotton). Politicians of all parties are worried about the immediate consequences of such price rises, whatever their long-run benefits for producers may be. Indian farm lobbies (with the exception of some sections, e.g. those under leaders like Bhupinder Singh Mann or Sharad Joshi) are also not yet very active in demanding such reforms; they may be worried that the dismantling of the existing structure of food, fertilizer, water, and electricity subsidies in exchange of receiving international agricultural prices may be too complex and politically risky a deal. In any case, since 1991, the 'disprotection' of the agricultural sector, in terms of relative inter-sectoral prices, has gone down considerably.

18 The question has also been raised why, as the backward and lower castes are coming to acquire more political power, one does not see a major reallocation of public expenditure on projects like health, education, housing, drinking water, and other development projects from which they would gain the most. Instead their leaders are often preoccupied with symbolic victories—like littering the countryside with Ambedkar statues, or, as anecdotes have it, keeping upper-caste officers standing while the low-caste chief minister remains seated in the only chair kept in the office. To this one may respond and say that this probably is just a matter of time. These social and political

fact that public enthusiasm for reforms is largely confined to the upper classes and the English media—say, the top decile or so in the income structure, which for some reason is called the 'middle class' in India—and even the most avid reformist politicians find it necessary to tone down their reform rhetoric at election time, when they have to face the unwashed masses.

There may be larger political–philosophical issues involved here. Many economists assume that market liberalism and competition is the natural order of things, and its unfolding in India has been blocked all these years only by our intellectual elites' socialist infatuation. It is not usually appreciated that Indian political culture may have a dominant anti-market streak that will not easily disappear, even if that supposedly imported infatuation fades away. Our collective passion for group equity, for group rather than individual rights, and the deep suspicion of competition in which the larger economic interests are given an opportunity to gobble up the small, work against the forces of market and allocational efficiency. This is not surprising in a country where the self-assertion of newly mobilized groups in an extremely hierarchical society takes the form of long-suppressed, group-specific expression and of clamouring for protected group-niches, where small people (small and middle peasants, self-employed artisans and shopkeepers, bazaar merchants and petty middlemen, clerks, school teachers, and service workers) constitute an overwhelming majority of the population and their ranks are swelled by the inexorable demographic pressure

---

changes have come to north India rather late; in south India, where such changes have taken place several decades back, it may not be a coincidence that there has been a lot more effective performance in the matter of social expenditure. This reflects the fact that in south India there has been a long history of social movement against exclusion of the lower castes from the public sphere, against their educational deprivation, etc. in a way more sustained and broad-based than in north India. One should also not lose sight of the fact that the upper-caste opposition to social transformation is somewhat stronger in north India, as demographically upper castes constitute a much larger percentage of the population (for example, in UP and Bihar) than has been the case in most parts of south India. So new political victories of lower castes in north India get celebrated in the form of defiant symbols of social redemption and recognition aimed at solidifying the victories, rather than in committed attempts at changing the economic structure of deprivation.

and by the traditional inheritance practices involving subdivision of property. Gandhiji had given sensitive and eloquent expression to this anti-market, anti-big capital, small-is-beautiful populism and mobilized it in the freedom movement against the British. Some other strands that grew out of our freedom movement, whether it is the ideas of Savarkar on the right (emphasizing community pride) or, on the left, those of Lohia (stressing lower-caste self-assertion against the westernized upper castes) or the Communists focusing on class mobilization—none of these ideas are overly concerned with individual rights[19]—also put a premium on group equity and dignity rather than individualist liberalism in the public sphere (even though the Indian vision of spirituality is often deeply individualistic). In recent decades, those bearing the legacy of the Gandhian moral critique of market expansion and competition have joined forces with those espousing the left critique of capitalist exploitation of workers, peasants, and other small people and their rights over resources in building active grassroots movements all over the country for the protection of the environment, of women's rights, and of the traditional livelihood of the indigenous people. In this growing movement 'development' or 'market' has almost become a dirty word, synonymous with dispossession of the little people and with despoliation of the environment. Major strands in the Indian political culture thus provide a none-too-hospitable climate for market reforms, and, contrary to the wishful thinking of many economists and journalists of the Indian 'pink press', the process of economic reforms is not likely to be smooth sailing for quite some time to come. The prospects for more reforms are not bleak, but one should not underestimate the scale and nature of opposition.

References

Jenkins, R.S. (1997), 'Democratic Adjustment: Explaining the Political Sustainability of Economic Reform in India'. D. Phil. Thesis, University of Sussex.

19 The leader who carried in him the tension between individual and group rights was B.R. Ambedkar, a constitutional lawyer who was also a major spokesman of an oppressed group.

Nagaraj, R. (1997), 'What Has Happened since 1991? Assessment of India's Economic Reforms', *Economic and Political Weekly*, 18 November.

Srivastava, D.K. and T.K. Sen (1997), *Government Subsidies in India.* New Delhi: National Institute of Public Finance and Policy.

Tendulkar, S.D., K. Sundaram, and L.R. Jain (1996), *Macroeconomic Policies and Poverty in India: 1966–67 to 1993–94.* Report submitted to the South Asia Multidisciplinary Advisory Team. New Delhi: International Labour Organization.

Tocqueville, A. de (1954) [1835], *Democracy in America.* New York: Vintage Books.

Visvanathan, S. (1997), 'Gujral's Red Fort Doctrine', *Economic and Political Weekly*, 20 September.

V

Democracy, Locality, and Region

We are accustomed to thinking about democracy as a macro-phenomenon, experienced in broadly similar ways across the nation. What, however, are the dynamics of democracy at the local level? Do members of the polity experience democratic citizenship differently depending on where they are located? Do voters respond differently to elections to parliament, the state legislative assemblies, or local bodies like *panchayats*? In recent years, it has often been argued that people vote according to different registers even when they vote almost simultaneously for both the state assembly and parliament. Thus, local and regional issues are believed to influence the one, and the performance of the party (or parties) in government at the Centre the other. The experiment in democratic decentralization, inaugurated by the 73rd and 74th Constitutional amendments, is adding new dimensions to this debate, especially because institutions of local democracy now provide for 33 per cent reservation for women, in addition to quotas for Scheduled Castes and Tribes. These issues have attracted relatively little academic attention, apart from studies of regional or state-level politics in terms of ethnicity, political mobilization, and the party system.

The two essays in this section are almost two decades apart in terms of their time of writing. They are also instructively dissimilar in terms of the methodologies used. Thus, Subrata Mitra's study of the 1977 elections in a village in Dhenkanal district of Orissa may be described as an exercise in political anthropology. Richard Crook and James Manor's account of democracy and decentralization in two districts of Karnataka (in the late 1980s) is part of a larger comparative study, and is investigated through a rigorous application of quantitative as well as qualitative research methods, ranging from semi-structured elite interviews and observation to surveys.

Subrata Mitra's article demonstrates how, by 1977, the electoral process was no longer an alien imposition on rural society. Instead, universal adult franchise, as the vehicle of the diffusion of new egalitarian norms, had become the latest addition to the catalogue of power resources in the village. Indeed, elections added a qualitatively new dimension to the traditional ways of allocating authority and according legitimacy. As such, the competition for political power through elections became a major instrument of social change, enmeshed with local and regional struggles for power. These struggles were, of course, largely couched in terms of caste dominance, and political power was increasingly associated with control over resources for welfare and development. The 1977 election in Kashipur village, Mitra argues, divided the village, partly through intra-elite conflict, and partly through a new polarization between the upper castes, on the one hand, and *adivasis* and *dalits*, on the other. The distribution of political power within the village was thus substantially transformed.

Crook and Manor's study of *panchayats* in Karnataka examines two related issues: the first, changing patterns of political participation by individuals and groups following democratic decentralization; and the second, the impact of citizens' participation on policy as an indicator of the responsiveness and effectiveness of government institutions. The authors found high levels of electoral participation, including by vulnerable groups such as members of the Scheduled Castes and Tribes. However, the impact of these vulnerable groups, including women, on District Councils was found to be minimal, and on Mandal Councils (closer to the village level) next to none. The greater the proximity to local society, it appeared, the greater was the domination of landowning castes.

Nevertheless, Crook and Manor found that District Councils in Karnataka were most effective in terms of their output of development projects, and also more responsive to local needs than was the case before decentralization. Not only were projects implemented, the priorities reflected in the budgetary outlays closely reflected local perceptions of what was required, and this translated to a shift towards micro-projects such as wells, roads, health clinics, and schools. A free press and a competitive party system in Karnataka also fostered a culture of accountability.

14

Ballot Box and Local Power: Elections in an Indian Village[+]

Subrata K. Mitra

While differing in their concern and approach, election studies in India have consistently assumed the existence and continuity of the parliamentary form of government with free, competitive elections as an integral feature of the Indian political system. By creating a break in the working of these institutions, the national Emergency of 1975–7 for the first time brought the urgent importance of examining the stability of the representative political order, and the electoral process on which it is based, to the fore.

In this study of the parliamentary and assembly elections of 1977 in an Indian village, I intend to show that the electoral process is no longer an alien and unfamiliar institution, imposed from outside on the intimate and face-to-face society of rural India. Rather, electoral competition for power has become enmeshed with local and regional struggles for power, and elections—to a large variety of voluntary, semi-official, and political bodies at the local, regional, and national levels—have become a major instrument of political change. In India's plural (not dichotomous) society where groups and coalitions are always being formed and re-formed, elections are used as instruments by various sections of the society to convert their political resources and power into authority. This is what makes elections an essential feature of

[+] This article was first published under the title 'Ballot Box and Local Power: Electoral Politics in an Indian Village' in the *Journal of Commonwealth and Comparative Politics*, vol. 17, no. 3, 1979, pp. 282–99 by Frank Cass & Co. Ltd., 900 Eastern Avenue, Essex, England.

the bargaining political culture[1] that has developed during the last few decades since independence. Furthermore, elections are indispensable for the functioning of the political system because, in the absence of a serious alternative, they are the only available institution that can maintain a continuous flow of authority; their abrupt suppression can lead to a political void.

Social Structure in Kashipur

The role of elections can only be understood through an analysis of the social groups in village India. There is no avoiding the complexities which this involves. Kashipur, which is the name by which the study village would be known in this chapter, is a large village, which at the time of the 1977 parliamentary elections had 361 households. It is located about eight kilometres from Dhenkanal town, headquarters of the district of the same name in Orissa. People of twenty different castes live in the fifteen different *sahis* (clusters) of this village. These settlements can be classified into three groups: the 'inner village' which is inhabited largely by Hindu upper and intermediate castes, and the 'peripheral' and the 'outlying' areas which have large concentrations of Scheduled Castes ('Harijans' or former untouchables) and Scheduled Tribes (adivasis) (Table14.1).

The main street of Kashipur runs through the inner village and joins it with the national highway. Until very recently the peripheral and outlying areas had no direct link with the national highway and could be approached only through the inner village. Even now most of the outlying areas are connected with the outside world only by footpaths that become lost in the paddy fields after the first rains.

Khandayats are the largest single caste in Kashipur. Together with Dalua Paikas, who are ranked next to them in terms of ritual status, they constitute the dominant caste of the village. Both castes claim to be of Kshatriya origin. Traditionally soldier–farmers (Paikas)[2] by occupation, they were settled in this area by the Rajah

1 For a detailed discussion of the concept of bargaining political culture and its evolution in India, see Rajni Kothari, *Politics in India* (Boston: Little Brown, 1970), pp. 90–1, 218, 263–4, 277–8.

2 The word Paika originates from *padatika* which means a foot soldier. The Paikas provided recruits for the King's army and were endowed with *jagir* land according to the rank they held in the army.

of Dhenkanal during the princely era. British rule, by taking away from the Rajah his military and eventually most of the police functions, eroded the power and influence which the Paikas used to enjoy as the local instruments of royal authority.

Table 14.1: Pattern of Settlement by Neighbourhood and Caste (including Tribes)

	Scheduled Castes[a]	Scheduled Tribes[b]	Hindu Intermediate Castes[c]	Hindu Upper Castes[d]	Total
Inner village	1 (3)	0 (0)	95 (283)	79 (265)	175 (551)
Peripheral areas	33 (112)	35 (142)	1 (1)	5 (14)	74 (269)
Outlying areas	48 (125)	64 (119)	0 (0)	0 (0)	112 (244)
	82 (240)	99 (261)	96 (284)	84 (279)	361 (1064)

Note: Figures in brackets are electors, others families.

[a] Consist of Hadi, Dama, and Pana castes.

[b] Consist of Juanga, Sabara, and Kamara tribes.

[c] Consist of Barika (barber), Keuta (fisherman), Dhoba (washerman), Teli (oilman), Sundhi (distiller), Tanti (weaver), Kumbhara (potter), Mali (priests and priests' assistants), Gudia (confectioners), and Gopala (cowherds) castes.

[d] Consist of Khandayats, Dalua Paika, Karana (writer caste), and Brahmin castes.

The main social rivals of the Khandayats are the Karanas[3]—the 'writer caste' of Orissa. The epithet seems to have originated from the fact that the Karanas took to English education in a big way before the other castes did. Many of them served in the lower bureaucracy during the British days. During the 1930s when the Rajah of Dhenkanal started reorganizing his bureaucracy, many Karanas managed to find places in it. Karana ascendance coincided with the erosion of Khandayat authority—a fact much resented by the Khandayats of Kashipur.

[3] In ritual status they are the equivalent of Kayasthas in Bengal and Bihar.

The Hindu upper-caste households (mainly Brahmins, Karanas, Khandayats, and Dalua Paikas) are usually referred to as *bhadralok*[4] by others. Among themselves the *bhadralok* households, who constitute about 21 per cent of the village, own nearly half of the total agricultural land and nearly all of the double crop land (see Table 14.2). Most *bhadralok* households engage one or more *halias* (farm servants working on annual contracts) who are recruited mostly from the tribal population. As farm servants, tribals are considered to be docile and are preferred to the Scheduled Castes, among whom Panas are the largest and the most influential community. The Scheduled Castes mostly work as day labourers and agricultural workers.

Table 14.2: Distribution of Land

Size of Holding in Standard Acres	Scheduled Castes	Scheduled Tribes	Hindu Intermediate Castes	Hindu Upper Castes
Landless	24	61	18	8
0–1	29	20	28	12
1 acre to 2.5 acres	22	14	22	27
2.5 acres to 5 acres	6	4	23	20
5 acres and more	1	0	5	17
Average landholding by caste (in acres)	1.0	0.4	1.9	3.0
Percentage of total village land owned by caste	15.0	7.1	31.8	46.1

The artisans among the Hindu intermediate castes have fallen on lean days. Their traditional crafts have been wiped out by the invasion of mass-produced household goods from outside. The only exception are the potters who have taken to making tiles, a non-traditional item. Otherwise, the artisans have generally taken to agriculture, increasing the pressure on land, and leading to

4 Or, approximately, 'gentry'. The concept should not be confused with Broomfield's *Bhadralok*. It connotes prestige and social status more than wealth and power though they are often found together. But unlike Broomfield's *Bhadralok* they are manager farmers more than rentiers. See J.H. Broomfield, *Elite Conflict in a Plural Society: Twentieth Century Bengal* (Berkeley: University of California Press, 1968), pp. 5–6.

extreme fragmentation. Some people of the distiller caste are engaged in seasonal trade in paddy. This and the tile 'factory' are the only elements of 'trade and industry' in Kashipur.

In terms of local power structure, the Khandayats and Karanas together with the Dalua Paikas constitute the elites. Being divided into various factions, however, they rarely work as a group. The main opposition to the elites in local politics comes from the adivasi–Harijans (Scheduled Tribes and Castes), with the Hindu intermediate castes generally siding with the *bhadralok*. The adivasis and Harijans do not present a solid oppositional phalanx to the dominant role that the *bhadralok* play in the politics of Kashipur, though a first glance at village politics may lead one to that interpretation. Although these communities as a whole share certain interests in common, they are divided by complex factional alignments. Some of the sources of conflict are traditional, such as the unequal ritual status of various groups and family feuds.[5]

The Changing Power Structure in Kashipur

In the early 1950s, the political arena in Kashipur was dominated by the Khandayats. A leading Khandayat was the *sarpanch* (council chairman)[6] through the 1950s and 1960s, besides being president of the high school committee. A first cousin of his was the secretary of the *panchayat* and of the *grain gola* (the agricultural service cooperative dealing mostly in food grains and agricultural loans).

5 But the more important sources of conflict and group rivalry are the result of the extension of conflict at the upper echelons of the village society into the lower level. Extension of political involvement of this kind, brought about through various dependency relations, appears to be the natural outcome of the competitive political process.

6 Kashipur used to have a traditional *panchayat* (local government with limited functions) during pre-independence days. In the mid-1950s, when regular elected panchayats were set up on the basis of the recommendations of the Balwant Rai Mehta Committee, the Khandayat leader became the sarpanch in the new structure. The official *panchayat* has not taken over all the functions of the traditional structure. For social and religious matters as well as the residual category of important subjects on which the whole village needs to make 'a decision' (e.g., an election) the traditional *panchayat* is still convened. The results of its deliberations are, however, not as effective as they used to be.

Another cousin was the president of the service cooperative of the village and the youth association. In his capacity as a contractor, he was also the main executor of *panchayat* activities in the village. A sister-in-law of the *sarpanch* was president of the Mahila Samiti (a state-aided women's organization). There was little room at the top for the Karanas, the social rivals of the Khandayats, or for anybody else. At the apex of the power scale stood the richer Khandayat families followed by their less prosperous brethren, with the non-Khandayats occupying the lower ends of the scale. The Panas were the more organized and politically active group among the non-elites, while the destitute tribals had the least influence in affairs of the village.

The political system and the distribution of power were supported by a consensus in social decision-making and the concept of village unity. Both were evolved and utilized by the old Khandayat *sarpanch*. The assembly and parliamentary constituencies were, during the same period (the 1950s and 1960s), controlled by the Ganatantra Parishad (which later merged with the Swatantra Party) that drew its leaders from the local leaders who were mobilized into politics during the State People's Movement of the 1940s.[7]

The *panchayat* elections of 1970 precipitated a change in the power structure of Kashipur. For the first time a prominent Karana leader contested the elections, with the explicit aim of challenging the political supremacy of the Khandayats. In this election there were three important candidates. The two candidates from Kashipur were the leading members of the Khandayat and the Karana communities. The third came from a neighbouring village and belonged to the caste of Dalua Paikas. The Khandayat candidate won the election by a wide margin but the defeat was not taken lightly by the Karanas.

The strong 'Congress wave' of 1971 provided the lift that the Karanas needed. Contacts were established between the Congress leadership of the district and the Karana leaders of Kashipur.

7 In Orissa the freedom movement under the leadership of the Congress party was most active in the districts of the coastal plains, while the State People's Movement was effective in some princely states including Dhenkanal. The partisans of the movement in Dhenkanal were aided in many ways by Congressmen, but the movement in Dhenkanal was not a direct extension of the coastal movement. The old *sarpanch*, while owing public allegiance to the ruler, was secretly in league with the State People's Movement.

After the elections to the state assembly in 1971 in which the Congress party won the seats from the local constituency, the Karanas set out with vigour to build a coalition with the defeated Dalua Paika candidate from the neighbouring village. They even succeeded in causing defections from the Khandayat community by taking advantage of an internal feud. As a result, several important Khandayats came over to the Dalua–Karana coalition. In the keenly contested *sarpanch* election of 1973, the Dalua Paika candidate defeated the old *sarpanch* by a narrow margin with the help of the newly emergent coalition.

During the months following this election, the winning coalition of Daluas and Karanas worked hard at consolidating its electoral gains. Members of the coalition lent enthusiastic support to the Congress candidate in the 1974 assembly elections which resulted in the victory of the Congress party over the Swatantra Party. Later on, a Karana leader, a graduate who had taken to modern farming, became a leader of the Youth Congress (the youth organization of the Indian National Congress) of the area. After his defeat the old *sarpanch* retired from politics. Some of the Khandayat defectors went back to their own fold, and an implicit compromise was reached whereby leaders of the Dalua–Karana coalition appropriated for themselves the right to be the sole representatives of the village for purposes of meeting officials and aid-givers from outside, while leaving the Khandayats the prerogatives of managing internal, social affairs such as village festivals. This was clearly an ad hoc working compromise, because, while ostensibly exclusive in theory, the respective areas were not so in practice. The overlap was bound to remain a potential source of discord between the Dalua–Karanas and the Khandayats.

On the face of it, no noticeable structural changes occurred in the 'configuration of power' (that is, the ranking of the various social groups in terms of influence) in Kashipur in the 1970s, except that the rise and fall of electoral fortunes led to some reorderings in the relative ranks of the groups at the top. As a whole, the age-old supremacy of the Khandayats was broken and the Dalua–Karana coalition appeared on the scene as strong contenders for the top position. But there were other forces at work that were to have a far greater impact on the configuration of power than the mutual rivalry of sections of the elite. Two major developments had come about in the meantime that together were to cause significant structural changes in the configuration of power. The first was the availability of resources for both development and welfare purposes and a growing understanding that their allocation was related to political power. This intensified the quest for power among new groups as well as within existing groups, thus increasing the amount of political conflict in the village and the number of competing factions. In this process, the concept of 'village unity' lost its legitimacy. The second major development was the polarization of *bhadralok* and adivasi–Harijan interests and their political mobilization. The adivasi–Harijan communities, especially the more aggressive Panas, now started questioning the privileges that the *bhadralok* enjoyed such as a more-than-equal share of controlled sugar, or more prominent positions in the celebration of major village festivals. This cleavage, as we shall see later, became quite visible during the electoral campaign in the village. However, instead of leading to the development of a class-based organization, this simply led to an increase in the number of factions among both *bhadralok* and adivasi–Harijans.

During the assembly election of 1974, the Panas of Kashipur took the initiative in setting up an association of Harijans, adivasis, and poor *sabarnas* (that is, caste-Hindus) mostly belonging to the intermediate castes. Word had spread, thanks to the electoral campaign of the Congress party, that land would be made available to the landless. Some among the adivasi–Harijans decided to set up their own organization rather than work through the existing *bhadralok*-dominated village institutions. Nearly a hundred people paid a rupee each to become members. The committee which was set up for getting the association registered met several times. It was led by a few prominent Panas of the village. However, in the new atmosphere where the equation between power and individual gain was firmly established, the older Pana leadership lost its customary legitimacy and became suspect. Therefore, not too long after the association was launched and when no immediate tangible group rewards were coming in, people started talking about misappropriation of the association funds. Factionalism among the adivasi–Harijans now became more virulent. When the *sarpanch*, taking advantage of the Emergency, asked the leaders of the association to disband it, there was not a murmur of protest against the *sarpanch*; criticism was directed mainly against the Pana leadership which stood discredited.

Political Mobilization in the Parliamentary Elections, 1977

The political situation, from the perspective of the leaders of Kashipur, was not adversely affected by the declaration of Emergency. Some adivasis in the village were provided with houses along with title deeds to the sites. The family planning operation was carried out vigorously but primarily through monetary incentives. No substantive measures were undertaken that would adversely affect powerful interests.

This situation was radically altered when Mrs Nandini Satpathy (who hails from the district) was ousted from her position as chief minister of the state through the initiatives of politicians operating at the federal level. Though it did not affect them directly, the removal of Mrs Satpathy, who for the politicians of Kashipur served as a symbol of their access to power, was seen as showing how easily their power and privileges could be taken away through 'an arbitrary fiat from above'. The authoritarianism of the Emergency regime thus loomed large as a denial of the legitimate exercise of local power. The change in the equation of power at the higher levels gradually manifested itself in the form of retribution against some local politicians closely identified with Mrs Satpathy by the followers of the new leadership of the Congress party at the state level. This led to sullen resignation on the part of politicians and Kashipur; when, in 1977, the elections were announced, the leaders of the Dalua–Karana coalition moved *en bloc* to the Congress For Democracy (CFD), the party formed by Jagjivan Ram, Nandini Satpathy, and some others.

The first phase of campaigning in the village reached its peak with a meeting of the members of the three *panchayat*s in the area, including Kashipur, which had coordinated their electoral strategies in the election of 1974. Their last experience had shown them the benefits of making a deal whereby they pooled votes and then shared out resources. This time, however, the meeting was not held exactly to decide who to vote for. The decision to support the candidate of the Janata–CFD was already taken by the *sarpanch* and the Karana leader who had been till recently the local leader of the Youth Congress. The meeting, quite well attended, unanimously accepted the political line suggested by them. This was the high point of influence of the Dalua–Karana coalition. The meeting set off a process of mobilization by various groups in the village leading to substantial changes in the configuration of power in the village. This was reflected in the changes in the tone and style of the electoral campaign.

As the persons in charge of the Janata–CFD campaign in the village, the leaders, especially the former Youth Congress leader and Karana progressive farmer and the sarpanch, were commonly believed to have received a 'huge sum' for electoral expenses. No one was sure about the amount received but everyone felt that the money should be divided 'equitably'. Old factional lines were resurrected on this issue. Some new factions also came up to assert their right to a share of the funds.

The main body of the Khandayats as well as those that had defected to the Dalua–Karana coalition had so far acquiesced in the new order of things, though they had all along resented the growing power and prominence of the leaders of the Dalua–Karana coalition. Jealousies were aroused by the power and prosperity of the Karanas, and some Khandayat defectors who had broken off socially from their Khandayat brethren now went back to the fold. But there were no overt conflicts within the upper socio-economic strata. Instead, their energies were diverted towards the best exploitation of the opportunities thrown up by elections. After the meeting, however, a feeling grew in the Khandayat circles that the Karana leader and the *sarpanch* were monopolizing the power and the contacts and material rewards that it brought. Resentment quickly spread over the whole of the Khandayat community which now started taking an ominously neutral position in the election.

A second challenge to the power of the Karana–Dalua coalition came from the Panas. The articulate and organized Panas have long dominated the rest of the adivasi–Harijan population of Kashipur. The general challenge to the traditional configuration of power was a challenge both to the overall power of the Khandayats and to the 'relative' power of the leading Pana families. The bond between Khandayats and Panas—exploitative in social and economic terms but symbiotic in terms of power—had continued through the last *sarpanch* election where the leading Pana families supported the old *sarpanch*. Gradually, as the Khandayats made a working compromise with Karana power and the adivasi–Harijans tried to set up an association of their own, the two groups had drawn apart from each other. However resentful the Panas were towards the *bhadralok* in general, they were specifically distrustful of the newly gained power of the Karanas.

In the meeting of the three *panchayat*s of the area it was decided that the responsibility for door-to-door campaigning should be given to the Pana ward member from Kashipur. This person had represented the Harijans in the formal and informal political forums of the village for the last three decades and had, by virtue of this, acquired the stature of a village leader. In making him responsible for door-to-door canvassing, the village leadership had assumed that he would be able to deliver the votes of the adivasi–Harijan *sahi*s to the Janata–CFD. They could not have been more mistaken. The Pana ward leader had felt increasingly challenged by the younger sections of the Panas who found him too 'moderate and ineffectual'. Among the 'dissident' leaders was a young and educated Pana who worked as a technical assistant in a college not too far from the village. He and his brother had tried, unsuccessfully so far, to organize the Harijans and adivasis of the area into a powerful political force.[8] The dissident young Panas now demanded a more efficient and aggressive leadership and therefore rejected the traditional leadership.

The father of these two young Panas used to be an employee of the former Rajah of Dhenkanal who, as the Congress candidate, was contesting against the husband of Mrs Nandini Satpathy. The Congress candidate had contacted dissident Panas early in the campaign. Soon after the meeting of the three *panchayat*s the dissident Panas secretly met and denounced the traditional Pana ward leader and the *bhadralok* leadership of the village. What added to their resentment was the alleged receipt of money by the leaders for 'delivering the adivasi–Harijan votes' to the Janata–CFD.

The father of the two dissident Panas now joined forces with the young men to mobilize support for the Congress candidate. It was rumoured that the Congress party was concentrating its efforts on the adivasi–Harijan voters and that its resources would soon be made available to these communities.

8 The political ambition of these young Panas spills over the boundaries of the village. In their search for power, they have turned to their brethren in nearby villages and tried to take advantage of the intra-elite conflict in the village itself.

A week before the polls, the adivasi–Harijan communities of Kashipur split into several factions. Propaganda and token distribution of agricultural and homestead land during the Congress regime had built a favourable image of the Congress party in general and Mrs Nandini Satpathy in particular among the adivasi–Harijan sections. The Kamaras, a section of the adivasis who were recipients of homestead lands and houses as gifts from the government (or from 'Nandini' as they saw it), were steadfast in their loyalty to her and, through her, to the Janata–CFD. The bulk of the community, especially the dissident Panas, however, felt that Mrs Satpathy, without the backing of the Congress party, could not do very much for them. The Congress for them continued to be the fountainhead of resources and, even more, a vehicle to defeat the power and dominance of the *bhadralok*. A third faction, through the traditional Pana leader, took the line of 'village unity' and continued to support the village leaders and, through them, the Janata–CFD.

This was a low point in the power and influence of the Dalua–Karana leadership. Their attempts to mobilize the village in favour of the Janata–CFD were thwarted by the resistance of substantial sections of the *bhadralok* on the one hand, and large numbers of adivasi and Harijan voters led by the Pana youth, on the other. During the last week of the campaign, they set out to win back some of the lost support by appealing to the disaffected groups directly rather than through political propaganda aimed at the whole village. They contacted their former ally, the Khandayat turncoat (who had previously defected to the Dalua–Karana coalition and had since gone back to his own community) and a compromise was reached between the two factions. The Khandayat leader became the Janata–CFD polling agent, and then went around the *bhadralok sahi*s along with the *sarpanch* and the Karana leader to solicit support directly from the Khandayat households. The young Pana dissident was contacted and persuaded to become a Janata–CFD worker. At a streetcorner meeting organized by the village leaders in the Harijan neighbourhood he spoke out in support of the Janata–CFD. This strategy was only partly successful because it further split the dissident Panas and intensified the campaign for counter-mobilization. The bulk of the dissident Panas came to distrust the young Pana leader and remained with the Congress. Indeed, his brother became the Congress polling agent. The extent of success achieved by the Dalua–Karana leadership in mobilizing the village can be seen from the following estimates of partisan support a week before and immediately after the polling (see Table 14.3).

Table 14.3: Estimates of Partisan Support in Kashipur a Week Before and Immediately After the Parliamentary Elections

	Size of Electorate[a]	% of Votes Polled	% Support a Week Before			% Support Post-election	
			Janata	Congress	Undecided	Janata	Congress
The inner village	551	62	74	24	2	93	7
The peripheral areas	269	70	65	26	9	66	34
Outlying areas	226	42	54	41	5	83	17

[a] The size of the electorate does not add up to 1064, since Morangapal *sahi* has been deleted.

The estimates (which were made immediately after polling so as to prevent the possibility of over-reporting in favour of the winner, once results are known)[9] show the differential impact of mobilization attempts to gain support for the Janata–CFD during the last week of the campaign. The campaign was quite successful in the *sahi*s inhabited predominantly by the *bhadralok*, where support for Janata went up from 74 per cent to 93 per cent, and in the outlying areas, where estimated support went up from 54 per cent to 83 per cent. The success of counter-mobilization by the dissident Panas is evident from the increase in the Congress vote in the peripheral area from 26 per cent to 34 per cent, though the greater part of the adivasi–Harijans was estimated to have supported the Janata–CFD. The others do not show any clear pattern except for sections of adivasis who supported Janata–CFD and showed an increase in their support.

9 These estimates were obtained from informants (from the fifteen *sahi*s). Their accounts (of partisan support in their respective *sahi*s) were later aggregated to obtain estimates for the inner village, peripheral areas, and outlying areas.

The 'success' of the Dalua–Karana leadership had a cost attached to it. By staying aloof and neutral, the Khandayats succeeded in forcing the Dalua–Karana leadership to share with them some of the influence that contacts with external political authority had brought to them. Similarly, the dissident Panas, forced to mobilize support independently of their own traditional leadership and of the village leaders, gained a measure of confidence. Both these factors caused some changes in the configuration of power in the village. The effects of the change were clearly visible in electoral mobilization during the assembly elections a few months later.

Political Realignment in the Assembly Elections of 1977

The parliamentary elections left a trail of bitterness in the village, especially among the Khandayats and more so in the adivasi–Harijan sections. The resentment can be traced primarily to the pre-eminent role the Dalua–Karana leadership played in the campaign and to the electoral funds they were alleged to have misappropriated. At the same time events during the last week of the campaign gave a new sense of power to the Khandayats, who aspired to regain the leadership of the village, and to the Harijans, particularly the Panas, who now thought of independent political mobilization.

The lines of intra-elite conflict were somewhat sharpened in a village feud that occurred during the interval between the two elections. A folk opera was organized by a person close to the Dalua–Karana leadership. A controversy started when the demand of a young Khandayat to be seated close to the platform was denied. While the incident stopped short of causing general disorder, feelings ran high among the Khandayats. Shortly afterwards, a Khandayat-dominated youth association set out to 'bring back the leadership to the middle of the village'. This had an obvious reference to the fact that most of the members of the Dalua–Karana leadership were located at one end of the village and the *sarpanch* came from a neighbouring village whereas the Khandayats were concentrated in the middle of the village.

The first part of the campaign saw hectic activity by the Janata and Congress candidates to win over the dominant leaders of the village. The Janata candidate had the initial advantage of the general pro-Janata attitude of the bhadralok. He had assiduously cultivated the support of the newly mobilized Khandayat youth and reactivated old contacts in the village. The campaign of the Congress candidate to gain the support of the bhadralok sections suffered from the cumulative impact of his lack of experience (and, hence, old contacts in the village) and from the fact that Mrs Nandini Satpathy, the symbol of economic progress and development of the area, was in the opposite camp. Having failed to gain support in the inner village, he concentrated his efforts on the adivasi–Harijan neighbourhoods of the village.

That the Kashipur *bhadralok* favoured Janata was quite evident from the beginning of the campaign. But power relations had changed since the previous election. More people were now consulted in important decisions concerning the village and the interval ranking of the dominant political elite had changed somewhat in favour once again of the Khandayats. This was evident from the traditional meeting of the 'village elders' (from which adivasi–Harijans were now excluded) to settle on the candidate to vote for, which took place in the middle of the campaign. The proposal of the Karana leader to support the Janata candidate was contested by an elderly villager, belonging to the oilman caste, who was a close associate of the old Khandayat *sarpanch*. The Dalua–Karana coalition was now being challenged by the resurgence of Khandayat power. A second important feature of the meeting was the exclusion of the adivasi–Harijan communities who were present in the previous meeting during the parliamentary elections. Their absence in this meeting eloquently demonstrated the polarization of the village arena into different political camps.

A larger meeting of the village (or rather the inner village, since no adivasi–Harijans were present) convened next evening to mobilize support for the Janata candidate revealed the composition of the new power configuration. Seated with the candidate on the platform were the Khandayat leaders of the village, while the Karana leader who was at the centre in the last election meeting sat on the floor with the audience. No other leading member of the Dalua–Karana leadership, not even the *sarpanch*, was present.

The lines of electoral mobilization of the village became fairly clear after the meeting. To the social distance between the *bhadralok* and the adivasi–Harijans was now added separate political mobilization—a process that was completed by the exclusion of adivasi–Harijans from the meeting. Their identification with the Congress—resulting from a combination of symbolic defiance of political control by the upper, socio-economic strata and an earlier identification with the cow and calf (the electoral symbol of the Congress) as the fountainhead of welfare—was quite clear and no serious attempts were made by Janata workers (who were mostly young Khandayat members of the youth association) to mobilize them.

During the second half of the campaign, once the partisan preferences had become clear, the intensity of public canvassing became quite low. No other political meetings were held in the village. The representatives of the adivasi–Harijans, however, attended a meeting of their own communities of the area which was convened by the Congress candidate. But the candidate did not provide them with any organizational support or resources to conduct the campaign in Kashipur.

The level of participation[10] in the assembly elections (see Table 14.4) declined from the relatively high figure of 59 per cent in the parliamentary elections to the lower figure of about 34 per cent, but this drop is much more pronounced in the case of the adivasi–Harijans. Considering the large numbers in which they participated in the parliamentary elections, the low turn-out of the adivasi–Harijans in the assembly elections cannot be attributed merely to traditional apathy. Compared to the parliamentary elections, the preferred candidate of the adivasi–Harijans in the assembly elections was much weaker. This must have contributed to the weakening of the position of those among the adivasi–Harijans who wanted to break off completely from the village leadership and mobilize themselves separately. On the other hand, the Janata candidate, favoured by the *bhadralok*, was in a much stronger position and so was his campaign in the village. Thus, with a weak candidate and divided leadership, it is not surprising that adivasi–Harijan participation fell off from the high figure of 54.4 per cent to 20.6 per cent. In view of these factors the low participation of the adivasi–Harijans appeared more like

10 Data on participation was collected by putting an identification mark on the voters' list against the names of electors who actually voted. These were later cross-tabulated against their place of residence and caste/tribe.

Table 14.4: Aggregate Voting Figures by Caste and Sex

	Caste-Hindu[a]			Harijan[b]			Adivasi[c]			Total
	Men	Women	Total	Men	Women	Total	Men	Women	Total	
	299	264	563	110	130	240	131	130	261	1064
Parliamentary	68	59	64	75	38	55	54	54	54	60
Assembly	59	32	46	25	9	16	30	30	25	34

[a] 'Caste-Hindu' includes the rest of the electors of Kashipur.

[b] Harijan includes the Hadi, Dama, and Pana castes.

[c] Adivasi includes the tribes of Juanga, Sabara, and Kamara.

well-reasoned abstention than merely a manifestation of traditional apathy towards elections.

Elections and Institutionalization of Power

Elections, as I have tried to show in the preceding discussion, play an instrumental role in the power struggle which goes on at all levels of the political system. Furthermore, electoral outcomes (except for cases of large-scale rigging) also provide a quiet legitimacy to the new configuration of power in society. The rules of universal adult franchise are a comparatively new addition to the various sources of power that play a significant role in the village arena. In the context of Kashipur, we saw the process of political change from the exclusive dominance of the Khandayats (whose decline came as a natural consequence of the end of the princely order in Dhenkanal) to the control of Kashipur politics by the Dalua–Karana coalition. However, the Khandayats, who adapted to the rules of the new order, were able successfully to challenge the dominance of the Dalua–Karana combination in the assembly election. More remarkable was the way in which the lower strata for the first time succeeded in mobilizing itself independently of the *bhadralok*. This by itself was no mean achievement when considered against the background of centuries of political subjugation and lack of any political identity except that of being adjuncts to the *bhadralok*.[11]

11 The growing power and organization of the Panas of Kashipur has not yet resulted in any spectacular achievements such as their capturing of an elected office of real importance or manipulation of those in power to gain any tangible material rewards such as communal facilities and agricultural and homestead land. Location of the authority (in this case, the state government) that is competent to make these decisions is still too remote for the adivasi–Harijans of Kashipur. In any case, as illustrated by the successful land reforms of Karnataka and some other states, organization on a much larger scale than we have seen in Kashipur or in the rest of Orissa is necessary to generate the requisite political pressure. But in local matters that fall under the jurisdiction of the *panchayat* (though these are very few indeed), such as public distribution of controlled sugar or mid-day meals for children, a programme started by CARE that is administered by the *panchayat*, the interests of the adivasi–Harijan can no longer be treated as easily dispensable. This is a net gain for the lower strata.

The pattern of land distribution described in Table 14.2 has not changed very much over the years. The upper landowning castes have continued to have near total control on the best lands in the village. Of course, land has changed hands in keeping with the rise and fall of family fortunes, but the process has not led to further concentration of landownership and consequent increased proletarianization. Migration and the cultivable waste around the village have provided a cushion against outright impoverishment. Increase in population has caused more and more marginal land to be brought into cultivation. Land being the major source of wealth in this village, the distribution of wealth between the landowning upper castes and the lower strata of the society has remained largely static.

The distribution of political power in the village, however, has remained far from static. Thanks to the competitive political process, the size and level of organization of the community has emerged as an important source of power, and the lower strata, traditionally underprivileged, have learnt to use these new levers to stake their claims. This and the other institutional changes have induced a larger process of social transformation. This is the political polarization of the *bhadralok* and the adivasi–Harijan that is as yet at the nascent stage. The new egalitarian ethos has given rise to new institutions for its expression and furtherance. Thus, instead of the traditional *panchayat* and village festivals[12] that

12 Village festivals within the traditional order performed the function of social allocation of prestige and legitimation of influence. Of course, this was limited to the upper and intermediate castes, the lower strata being ritually excluded from participating in the religious parts of the festivals. The decline of communal celebration of Dussera, the major village festival, demonstrates the comprehensive reach of the new egalitarian ethos and the natural limits to the flexibility of the hierarchical social order to adjust to change. This can be illustrated by some details from the episode of the Dussera of 1976. Dussera is considered by the Paikas to have originated from Lord Rama's invocation of Goddess Durga at the time of his war with Ravana and, therefore, seen as an exclusively Kshatriya (and hence Paika) festival; only Paikas used to raise the funds for the festival from among themselves, each making a contribution in keeping with his status. The formal beginning of the festival was marked by a ritual called *Gahana*—a ceremonial procession of Paika heads of families to the accompaniment of beating of drums by Hadis (the lowest caste in Kashipur). In the Dussera of 1976 the village elders decided that rather than

exclusively took care of allocation of prestige and the legitimation of influence, we now have the official *panchayat* and elections based on universal adult franchise that supplement the traditional institutions in the allocation of authority to competing groups in society.

The new sense of power and participation in the lower strata in Kashipur has not resulted in what can be called political polarization along class lines to convert political power into economic gain. One immediate reason is the absence of a major economic enterprise where the interests of individual participants are complementary. In any economy of small individual holdings accompanied by scarcity of inputs such as water, interests are strictly competitive. This is probably one reason why the structure of group competition has moved from domination by the landowning groups to that of free-floating alliances and unstable coalition-building. This is the structure that has become an enduring feature of Kashipur as well as much of the countryside.

---

the Paikas alone contributing money for the celebration (especially in view of hardships caused by drought), the village should sell its sugar quota for the month in the black-market and use the profits for the festival. Formal consent of all the ward members of the *panchayat* (which has the responsibility of distributing controlled sugar) including those of the adivasi–Harijan members was obtained. The festival had barely started when it was discovered that the Pana leaders had not yet come. On enquiry it was found out that the Panas would come only if they were invited the way the Paikas were, even if a token of only one drum was sent to invite them. 'After all', the Pana leader asserted, 'the sugar that was sold to pay for the festival was ours, too.' Though this was a direct affront to Khandayat social dominance, in the prevalent mood of bargaining Khandayat leaders chose to reason with the Panas rather than resorting to outright violence. The suggestion of the village elders that some members of the *bhadralok* would go to invite the Panas was acceptable to them, but it turned out that the emissaries were not the *bhadralok* elite but simply ward members of the village *panchayat.* This was not acceptable to the Panas who wanted the Khandayat elite to come to their sahi to invite them and in this they had the tacit moral approval of a section of the Karanas. So the matter was left there. In this turmoil, the festivities came to a halt, leaving a trail of bitterness between the *bhadralok* and the Panas. This was the last occasion when the village tried to celebrate Dussera collectively. Dola, the festival of colour which came next, was celebrated separately by the different communities. In 1977 the Harijans celebrated Dussera in their own neighbourhood.

The Emergency of 1975–7 did not adversely affect any significant social groups in Kashipur. There was no forced sterilization; no unionized workers that would have been affected by the curtailing of bonus; no marginal migrant population from the village that could have carried back the horror of demolition and forced evacuation from the cities. Instead, the symbolic values of the welfare programmes and development resources to the village won over the lower strata as well as the elites to the regime, which probably accounts for the absence of significant resistance to the Emergency in Kashipur. However, from the perspective of Kashipur as of the bulk of the country, the situation was again far from having reached equilibrium. The suppression of the adivasi–Harijan association during the Emergency did not lead to any significant resistance from the community because it lacked a coherent leadership. But the group was being steadily mobilized, and before long the mediating role of the Emergency regime would have been put to the test by its demands for real power at the local level. Similarly, it was the summary dismissal of Mrs Satpathy that brought home to the leadership of Kashipur the fact of their powerlessness and vulnerability to arbitrary dictates from above. Again, there was no overt act of resistance, but it alienated these early supporters from the Emergency regime—alienation which was effectively mobilized for the restoration of the bargaining political culture that had been superseded by the Emergency.[13]

In conclusion, thousands of little political systems like Kashipur together constitute the political entity of the India we know. Decades of national struggle for independence and various other movements connected with it, and three decades of post-independence politics, have familiarized the people with the electoral process in large parts of the country as an integral part of the power

13 We are now in a position to answer the question raised by Professor Morris-Jones: 'why would a creeping but uneasy authoritarianism order elections in the first place?' Granted that the regime could not have had foreknowledge of shape of things to come, elections were still (as they are for any party in power) a calculated risk. And judging from the enormous cost of failure, one can surely see that the value of success in securing a popular mandate must have been seen as very high indeed to justify the gamble, and this was so in spite of the Emergency. See William H. Morris-Jones 'Creeping but Uneasy Authoritarianism: India 1975–6', *Government and Opposition*, vol. 12, no. 1, 1997, pp. 39–41.

struggle at all levels of the system. By and large, diffusion of the norms of legal equality and the egalitarian ethos, and the steady expansion of government into areas of village life that were for centuries immune to political manipulation from outside, have provided the lower strata of the rural society with the institutional means with which to confront the power of the upper strata. As such, elections—to local bodies as well as to the central and state legislatures—and, perhaps more, the electoral spirit that is in the process of pervading the whole range of group activities in rural life, have been a major factor in the devolution of power. As a medium of power struggle at local and regional levels, the instrumental role of elections is already recognized by a wide cross-section of the society.

When consensus-building is posed as a prime concern (and indeed it has been the dominant norm of Indian politics), the existence and availability of the electoral option acts as an incentive to the parties to concede, coalesce, compromise, and come to a consensus. It is the pursuit of power canalized through the political system that has provided the parties to the struggle with the incentives to extend the boundaries to the arena in which they are placed to search for allies. This is the dynamics behind the political integration of the country and the larger involvement of the citizenry in its politics. In the Indian context the latter factor is probably the most important source of support for the competitive political system based on parliamentary democracy.

15

Democracy and Decentralization in Karnataka (India)+

Richard C. Crook and James Manor

The Background

The Structure of Decentralization

At an election in 1983, the Janata party won control of the government in the Indian state of Karnataka at a time when the Congress party held power at the national level. To revive their party's fortunes nationally, Janata leaders wanted to demonstrate that they were more imaginative and radically democratic than their Congress rivals. They also had next to no party organization in the state, and they believed that a new system of elected councils at the district level and below would provide a framework for party-building. They therefore undertook a programme of decentralization which gave elected councillors control of more than half of the state's bureaucrats and responsibility for nearly every field of development.

Elected councils were created at two levels—the district and the lower, Mandal level. The small size of the Mandals, in relation to the much larger and far more powerful District Councils (*Zilla Parishad*), made them the less important of the two elements in the system. This was apparent from the power of the District Council to approve the annual budget estimates of the Mandals,

+ Excerpts from chapter 2 of *Democracy and Decentralisation in South Asia and West Africa* (Cambridge, UK: Cambridge University Press, 1998).

to investigate their annual accounts and administration reports, to intervene in the event of irregularities, and to appoint and control their administrative staff.

District councillors elected a president and vice-president. The latter had the status of a deputy minister in the state government. The former had the status of a junior minister and since he headed a council that controlled nearly all government agencies in the district, his actual power matched his status. He supervised and largely controlled a formidable staff of senior administrators deputed from line ministries, which was headed by a chief secretary drawn from the elite, generalist Indian Administrative Service (IAS). The result was usually a system characterized both by managerial competence and by the ascendancy of elected representatives. In an indication of the power of the District Council, the chief secretary was senior to another IAS officer who served as the deputy commissioner—the figure who for over a century had dominated district administration, but who now dealt only with non-developmental activities.[1] In Indian terms, this represented a radical devolution of power on to elected councils.

To ensure adequate influence for less powerful groups, 25 per cent of the seats on all councils were reserved for women, and a minimum of 18 per cent for members of the Scheduled Castes (ex-untouchables) and Tribes. Provision was also made for the 'Backward Classes'—the groups standing above the Scheduled Castes, but below the higher castes in the traditional hierarchy.

The Karnataka experiment lasted only for the first five-year term of the councils, from January 1987 when the Councils were first elected until the end of 1991, when a Congress state government hostile to decentralization abandoned the system.

Our field research concentrated mainly on two districts in the state of Karnataka—Dharwar and Mysore. We paid particular attention to two sub-districts (taluks) within each.[2]

Participation

The first section ('Popular Participation') below deals with changes in patterns of political participation by individuals and

1 Ray (1991), p. 24.

2 In Dharwar District, these were Hubli and Kundagol, while in Mysore District, they were Heggadedevankote and Hunsur.

groups as a result of democratic decentralization. The second section ('Representation and Institutional Accountability') extends the discussion beyond that. If 'inputs' from those at the grassroots are to have an impact on government institutions, they must be transmitted through elected representatives to civil servants who execute policy. If that does not occur, citizens' participation can increase without having any tangible effect. So the second section assesses relations between elected politicians and bureaucrats, and the performance or non-performance of institutions as transmitters of information and influence from below.

Popular Participation

ELECTORAL PARTICIPATION

Elections to the District and Mandal Councils were held on separate days in January 1987. Local elections had been something of a rarity in Karnatka,[3] but civil servants there had abundant experience at conducting free and fair legislative and parliamentary elections. That tradition was maintained on these occasions. Turnout was high—60 per cent for the District Councils and 75 per cent for the Mandal Councils.

The overwhelming majority of successful candidates stood as representatives of one of the two parties which then predominated in the state, Congress and Janata. This extended the already well-advanced process by which factional rivalries at the local level were given a party political character. Conflict among rival groups in rural areas intensified as a consequence and a modest amount of violence occurred at and after elections, but this did not pervert the results. Our survey of villagers found that fully 95.4 per cent saw these elections as 'completely fair'; 3.6 per cent regarded them as 'fair with some problems'; and only 1 per cent stated that they were 'very unfair'.

VILLAGE MEETINGS (*GRAM SABHAS*)

Each Mandal Council in Karnataka was legally required to hold

3 They had only occurred on three previous occasions, in 1960, 1968, and 1978. State governments had preferred to allow local councils to expire after their terms of office ended, and to do without them for periods of several years before holding fresh elections.

twice-yearly meetings in every village within its boundaries, to which all residents were welcome. These gatherings, or *Gram Sabhas,* were the main device to ensure councils' accountability to citizens between elections and had two main purposes. They allowed people to seek information and air their views on the work of the Council, and they were to identify the most deserving recipients of assistance from anti-poverty programmes.

Neither of these things appealed to Mandal councillors. Villagers demanded explanations for unfulfilled election promises, and councillors' answers often produced heated reactions. Popular pressure sometimes forced politicians to abandon private arrangements with clients. In one such case, villagers demanded genuinely open competition for the sale of fishing rights in a local tank, and this resulted in an increase in council revenue from Rs 12,000 to 75,000.[4] As one observer put it, 'People got the power in their hands and they said whatever they liked—earlier the system was not like that.'[5] Most chairmen resented what they saw as the Gram Sabha's usurpation of their 'right' to allocate benefits from government programmes.

As a result, councillors in most places abandoned Gram Sabha meetings after the first year or two.[6] Some resorted to subterfuge—holding unannounced meetings at times when most villagers were away at work or at market, or staging Gram Sabha 'meetings' in the Mandal office. Many did not even bother with such charades. This spared them painful encounters with constituents and allowed chairmen and councillors to draw up lists of beneficiaries—including their clients' names at the expense of the deserving poor.

How and to what extent did people participate in the political process which developed round the new councils? We investigated opportunities which elected politicians provided for participation in two ways. We first asked respondents how often, and by what means, councillors had consulted them about development projects in their localities. Table 15.1 summarizes their answers.

4 Hegde (1994), p. 22.

5 Interview with an activist from the India Development Service, a local non-governmental organization, Dharwar, 6 April 1993.

6 See in this connection, for example, *The Times of India,* 4 and 6 September 1990.

Table 15.1: Consultations with Villagers about Projects

	Percentage of projects with consultation
At a public meeting	18.3
At a small group meeting	0.7
Our leader was consulted	0.9
Unspecified consultations	20.0
None	61.1

We asked respondents whether they had taken the initiative to contact a member of the District or Mandal Council about a matter of personal concern to them. Their replies are set out in Table 15.2. To have nearly a quarter of our sample engaged in contacting is quite impressive.

We then asked them whether they had ever contacted public employees. Their answers are aggregated in Table 15.3. These figures are less striking, but we were often told that villagers understood that under the decentralized system, councillors possessed the leverage to persuade bureaucrats to act. After four decades of representative government, they also understood that elected councillors had an obligation to constituents—and they believed that councillors knew this too (as indeed they did). Citizens therefore proceeded straight to the person who was most likely to be helpful.

Table 15.2: Contacting of Councillors (in per cent)

Yes, District Councillor	6.0
Yes, Mandal Councillor	15.6
Yes, unspecified	3.0
No	75.4

Table 15.3: Contacting of Bureaucrats (in per cent)

Yes	17.7
No	83.2

PARTICIPATION BY DISADVANTAGED GROUPS

We address the issue of disadvantaged groups' participation in two ways. First, we analyse *all* of those who participated in three types of political activity to see how large a role various disadvantaged groups played in each. The main categories which may be regarded as 'disadvantaged' are women and those with no education. The latter serves well as a proxy for poor people. Second, we consider in more detail the range of activities which were engaged in by women and, more especially, Scheduled Castes—ex-untouchables (15.1 per cent of the state population).

When we examine the composition of all participators, we see that men predominated heavily among those who contacted councillors and those who attended group meetings and spoke there, but that more than one-third of those present at such meetings were women—a reasonably high figure.

More crucially, people with no education (and those with only primary education) were remarkably active in contacting councillors. More of those without education engaged in contacting than those with secondary education, and uneducated people were only slightly outnumbered by those with secondary education in the overall attendance at meetings—although the latter were much more inclined to speak there. This indicates that in Karnataka, disadvantaged groups were far less inhibited participators than we might have expected. Better educated—which is to say more prosperous and high-status groups—clearly did not dominate participation in this system.

We arrive at a more ambiguous but broadly similar conclusion when we consider political awareness and the *range* of participatory activities in which the Scheduled Castes and women engaged. Our survey of villagers found that in all types of elections, Scheduled Caste respondents had voted in only slightly fewer numbers than members of other groups.

Scheduled Caste respondents believed that elections were fair: 14.8 per cent ventured no opinion on fairness, but 100 per cent of the rest stated that elections were 'completely fair'. They had slightly more faith in elections than did our total sample, of which 95.4 per cent took that view.

Members of the Scheduled Castes were nearly as active in associations as were people in other groups. Precisely half of those members of Scheduled Castes who were active in organizations had joined them since decentralization in 1987. This suggests that decentralization galvanized associational activity, even among the most disadvantaged groups.

To what extent did they engage in proactive forms of participation? The Scheduled Castes were more active than the generality of villagers at petitioning. Our evidence indicates that this usually entailed efforts to obtain legal entitlements. However, these efforts seldom bore fruit.

The other form of proactive participation in which they engaged at a relatively high level was election campaigning. Local politicians needed their votes and thus had good reason for systematically encouraging them to participate—in contrast to other times when they were discouraging. Scheduled Caste campaigners usually operated separately from campaigners from other castes, in the spatially distinct sections of villages where their caste fellows lived. The other types of participation entailed Scheduled Castes mixing with others—which the others discouraged. It is thus not surprising that participation rates among the Scheduled Castes should be so low. Their total exclusion from meetings organized by non-officials in the villages is especially striking.

These groups may be poor, ill-educated, and subject to severe discrimination, but they are neither ignorant nor inert politically. This sets up a cruel irony, since—as we shall see later—they gained little from democratic decentralization.

The law required that a minimum of 18 per cent of seats in every district be reserved for Scheduled Caste and Scheduled Tribe candidates, but that more be provided when they constituted a greater share of the population. Statewide, they held 20.4 per cent of all seats.[7]

7 The two locally dominant landowning caste groups, the Lingayats and Vokkaligas (who constitute 27 per cent of the state's population) were also over-represented. They held 50.61 per cent of seats (Institute of Social Sciences 1989: 17–28).

The reservation of seats for Scheduled Caste representatives was done, as it has been in state and national elections in India for decades, by declaring that certain constituencies could elect only members of Scheduled Castes to the council. The voters in such constituencies come from all sections of society, but only Scheduled Caste candidates may stand for office.

It should be noted that well-connected local politicians were able to exploit their links with legislators, prior to the election of the District Councils, to ensure that the District Council constituencies where they wished to stand for election were not reserved for Scheduled Caste candidates. This tended to result in disadvantages for the Scheduled Castes, since it brought members into District Councils who were less sympathetic to them.

This did not mean, however, that Scheduled Caste District councillors achieved much—individually or collectively. An energetic individual from a disadvantaged group could make a modest difference. In meetings of the Dharwar District Council, a forceful woman from a Scheduled Tribe often tackled bureaucrats and the district president in a rustic manner about inadequate help to poor groups. Her interventions were so unvarnished and entertaining to most councillors that she often got her way. In Gulbarga District, a Scheduled Caste councillor with Communist cadre training and long experience as a health worker at the sub-district level was less ostentatious but similarly effective. But such people were extreme rarities.

Nor did they undertake much collective action on District Councils. The Scheduled Castes (and other poor groups) never constituted an effective lobby. They almost never received assistance from other disadvantaged groups.

In one district, Hassan, a Scheduled Caste man was elected president of the District Council. But he could accomplish little for his caste because his election was arranged by a powerful dominant caste politician—elected Karnataka's chief minister in late 1994—whose son sat on the council and ensured that resources went mainly to that dominant group. This was in one sense an admirable attempt by the Janata Party to signal its empathy with the Scheduled Castes, but in practice, it amounted to tokenism.

What of the lower-level Mandal Councils? These stood so close to the village level, where the traditionally dominant castes still exercise overwhelming power, that it was virtually impossible for Scheduled Caste representatives to influence events. Other poor groups, who lacked reserved seats on Mandal Councils, were poorly represented there. Scheduled Caste members of Mandal Councils seldom had much education and often their election was due to a dominant caste patron. Since the Mandal Councils played a decisive role both in implementing many district programmes and in selecting beneficiaries, they often prevented poorer groups from gaining even from enlightened District Councils.

The whole cultural milieu in those local arenas weighed against assertiveness from low-status groups. On several occasions, chairmen of Mandal Councils told us how they had prevented Scheduled Caste councillors from influencing decisions and obtaining resources earmarked for the Scheduled Castes. Others stated that Scheduled Caste representatives 'obviously' could not question decisions by other councillors or make suggestions. They were, in the main, utterly passive. The most that could be expected were occasional requests that their caste fellows receive the percentage of funds due to them under law.[8]

As we shall see below in the section 'Institutional Performance', most Mandal Councils systematically prevented such funds from reaching the Scheduled Castes and discriminated against them in other ways. So decentralization to Councils located so close to the grassroots where landed castes dominate meant that power was being taken from higher levels where Scheduled Castes gain a little justice, and injected into arenas where that is almost impossible. It is thus naive to expect the devolution of power on to councils at such localized levels to serve the causes of poverty alleviation or social reform, whatever its other virtues.

What of participation by women and other disadvantaged groups? Our survey of rural dwellers found that in council elections, as in parliamentary elections, women probably turned out in slightly lower numbers than men.

When women contacted councillors, they tended far more strongly than men to confine themselves to Mandal councillors who lived locally. Men spoke much more often at officially organized meetings—52.8 per cent of men who had attended such meetings, as opposed to 20 per cent of women. Overall, these findings indicate a modest but significant level of proactive participation by women villagers.

Women had 25 per cent of the seats reserved for them. No woman candidate won a seat in an unreserved District Council constituency.[9] A tiny number won unreserved seats in Mandal elections, but nearly all of them appear to have been closely related to influential men. The same can be said of the handful of women elected to chair Mandal Councils, but some of the small number of women who were chosen as vice-presidents of District Councils were formidable, respected figures in their own right.

8 The comments in this entire section are based on extensive interviews with Scheduled Caste and other councillors, and with knowledgeable outsiders like local journalists and community leaders in six districts (especially in Mysore and Dharwar Districts), March–April 1993.

9 Institute of Social Sciences (1989: 6).

Since reservations for women were an innovation—unlike reservations for the Scheduled Castes, the norm in legislative elections since 1952—they caused greater controversy than the latter. Similarly, it had long been common for Scheduled Caste issues and grievances to be addressed in legislatures and public discussions more generally, but women's grievances arose far less often.

On most District Councils, women spoke less often than the Scheduled Castes, and when they spoke they tended to address matters of concern to all constituents rather than to women—unlike the latter who often raised caste questions. They also managed some modest achievements in districts where women councillors held nearly all of the seats on the Standing Committee for Women's and Child Welfare. But in general, women district councillors performed more timidly and ineffectually than male councillors from the Scheduled Castes.[10]

Representation and Institutional Accountability

This section deals with the extent to which information and influence from the grassroots were transmitted through institutions, especially elected councils, to those exercising power and implementing policy. The record of Karnataka's decentralized system here was mixed, but often quite positive.

RELATIONS BETWEEN BUREAUCRATS AND POLITICIANS

If good working relationships exist between politicians and civil servants, institutional performance (including 'outputs' from government) should be enhanced. But if bureaucrats are genuinely accountable to elected representatives, it means that the 'inputs' will often be transmitted from participating citizens, through elected councillors to bureaucrats executing policy.

It was bound to be difficult for elected councillors and bureaucrats to develop a constructive working relationship under the new system. Each group regarded the other with suspicion after

10 The comments in the preceding paragraphs are based on extensive interviews with women and men councillors and with other knowledgeable observers in six districts (especially Mysore and Dharwar Districts), March–April 1993.

many years in which civil servants had operated at the district level and below with considerable autonomy. The patterns which gradually emerged were variegated and ambiguous, but in general, the two sides eventually adjusted uncomfortably but tolerably well.

District Council meetings, particularly in the early years, were often marked by councillors' strident criticisms of bureaucrats. In one case, criticism grew so fierce that bureaucrats boycotted council meetings in protest.[11]

The logic which led to these scenes changed over time. In the early years, they were often inspired by councillors' naive over-estimates of their powers over bureaucrats. Later, when councillors grasped that more senior civil servants could only be disciplined by state-level ministries which were disinclined to intervene, they seized upon the sole avenue left to them—public embarrassment of allegedly errant officials. But in either case, life was often distinctly unpleasant for bureaucrats.

One perceptive chief secretary who had served as a deputy commissioner (senior district-level official) before decentralization said that in that previous period, the deputy commissioner's 'control' over line ministry personnel was only 'notional'. They were 'practically independent' within the budget and enjoyed 'huge discretion'. 'Real accountability was to their state department heads', but the distances which separated most of them from the state capital meant that they were beyond effective control from there as well.[12] They therefore operated with something like a free hand.

A forestry officer in a sub-district, for example, would decide what sorts of projects should be implemented and (often) where they should be located. He would then inform the generalist development officer in charge of the sub-district who seldom disagreed, and they would inform the generalist deputy commissioner at the district level. These proposals would be discussed at a monthly district-level meeting of these officers with legislators, but the latter were so sketchily informed that they tended to

11 This owed much to bungling by the chief secretary and to 'virulent attacks' on councils by the Congress party's Minister of Panchayati Raj. *The Times of India*, 24, 26, 28, and 30 July 1991.

12 Interview with the official in question, Bangalore, 21 April 1993.

approve anything as long as their constituencies got a reasonable share of resources. This allowed most line ministry officials an untroubled life.

Decentralization changed things dramatically for these people. It brought many more elected representatives into the process, and Mandal councillors demanded fair distribution of resources on a far more disaggregated basis. They then closely monitored the quantity and quality of work actually done, and reported problems early and often to higher authorities. Line ministry officials faced relentless enquiries and pressure to work harder, longer, and more scrupulously. They found it far more difficult to get away with corrupt acts or to falsify records on the amount of time spent in the field.

One result of this, which enhanced the effectiveness of government institutions, was a distinct improvement in the coordination of civil servants working for different government departments at and below the district level.

Within every district, bureaucrats at all levels were made considerably more accountable to elected politicians than they had ever been before. Bureaucrats—many of whom had earlier been almost 'totally non-functioning'—became far more energetic and amenable to councillors.[13]

A small minority of the bureaucrats working for line ministries in the districts eventually came to like the new system. This was particularly true of senior figures in some development departments who found that if they cooperated with councillors on the district standing committee which oversaw their work, the latter would lobby on their behalf in the District Council for resources. Some found that councillors' links to citizens could be exploited to explain to villagers why certain projects—inoculations and other forms of preventive medicine, for example—were being undertaken, so that the uptake improved. This also helped to defuse popular resentment at the temporary inconvenience caused by certain construction projects. It helped to acquaint people with the limitations on what government departments could achieve, minimizing unrealistic expectations. It also drew

13 These comments are based on discussions with a wide range of politicians, bureaucrats, and informed non-officials. The quotation comes from a highly knowledgeable journalist, Mysore, 19 April 1993.

villagers into projects at crucial stages—for instance, into watch and ward arrangements to protect newly planted saplings from destructive animals.[14]

But most line ministry officials were traumatized by the changes and, as one chief secretary stated, 'never came out of it fully'. They adjusted grudgingly, under duress. Most eventually developed an uneasy *modus vivendi* with councillors.

For most chief secretaries, it was a very different story. The adjustment to the new role was difficult, but in time, the majority of them became advocates and even ardent enthusiasts for decentralization. When they were initially appointed, nearly all felt trepidation and frustration. There was, for example, the question of status. In theory, the chief secretary was senior to the deputy commissioner—the long-standing senior figure in the district who continued to handle law and order, revenue collection, and some other tasks. But in practice, this was far from clear. The deputy commissioner continued to receive the traditional deference paid to him while the chief secretary had to operate in roughly equal partnership with an elected district president who was often less polished and educated than any senior civil servant. Many chief secretaries also faced rustic, truculent councillors with an inflated sense of their own importance. A large minority of chief secretaries performed impressively and eventually became passionate advocates for decentralization. They took risks in career terms by bargaining aggressively with state-level officials and by encouraging councils to be assertive.

Conflicts between civil servants and Mandal councillors were less serious. Mandal Councils employed just one bureaucrat, a secretary who was very junior and highly subservient. Mandal chairmen found some of these officials corrupt or inefficient, but they often got help from their representative on the District Council to deal with this.

DECENTRALIZED PLANNING

In Karnataka, decentralization was supposed to foster planning from below to enable citizens' views to shape official policy.[15] It was, however, largely unsuccessful.

14 This is based on numerous interviews with department heads in Dharwar, Mysore, and Bangalore Districts.

15 See in this connection Hegde (1994: 19–28).

District officials' main job had always been implementing policies handed down from above. After decentralization, they still had to do that, but they were also asked to absorb from below ideas which might go into a plan. They needed to collect other data on local facilities and problems, which were in short supply given the virtual absence of a district planning tradition. They found both of these tasks difficult, since they had little experience of either.

Once such information had been amassed, bureaucrats had to consider the feasibility of various projects, seek to balance requests from various areas, form judgements about how disparate inputs might be coordinated, and finally distil variegated proposals into a coherent whole. These tasks would have been taxing even if they had done this before, but for these people, they were well nigh impossible. Elected councillors were supposed to assist, but their main preoccupation was—understandably—to maximize resources for their constituencies. So, far from easing the bureaucrats' problems, they compounded them and left most civil servants 'at a loss'.[16]

The main elements of district plans were selected because councillors favoured them for political rather than developmental reasons. That was inevitable and in some ways healthy, but many plans became fragmented lists of pet schemes rather than integrated sets of mutually reinforcing proposals. Nor did councillors pay much attention to existing local resources or to ways of building plans around them. This doomed many projects to failure. For example, a councillor pressing for a dairy might not recognize the need to reinforce it with inputs like fodder provision and arrangements for outputs like a butter- and ghee-making facility. Without this, a dairy on its own was unlikely to succeed. Such poorly conceived plans gave bureaucrats at the state level an excuse to disregard district plans, which many of them were happy to do.[17]

They were assisted in this by the practice of earmarking a huge proportion of the funds passed down to the councils from above

16 I am especially grateful to V.K. Nataraj of the Institute of Development Studies, Mysore, for insight into these problems.

17 The preceding two paragraphs are derived from conversations with Abdul Aziz of the Institute of Social and Economic Change, Bangalore, who has researched the subject thoroughly (Aziz 1993).

for specific programmes. The rules had to be adhered to quite closely. This left councils with just two options. They could, to a limited degree, interpret or bend the rules in ways that enabled them to accomplish a little of what they preferred. Or their president and chief secretary could lobby the state government to allow them greater freedom. This latter tactic produced modest benefits, but neither rescued decentralized planning from the constraints of earmarking.

EARLY WARNINGS OF DISASTERS

Perhaps the most crucial service which elected representatives can perform for their constituents is to transmit urgent messages to government agencies about problems which might develop into disasters—droughts, floods, outbreaks of disease, or shortages of food, drinking water, or other essentials. Scholars have rightly stressed the role which India's free press plays in providing early warnings of such disasters.[18] But decentralization in Karnataka provided a far more effective system of early warnings than the press could.

This point was made most forcefully by journalists in northern Karnataka who, before decentralization, had raised the alarm when disasters loomed. They insisted that their conditions of employment make them an undependable source of warnings. Most reporters in that drought-prone area are stringers for newspapers in the state capital. This is necessarily a part-time job. Since most use a motor scooter for transport and receive no allowance for hiring other vehicles, their ability to roam widely within their districts (some of which are huge) is further limited. This seriously undermines their effectiveness at discovering and investigating emerging calamities.

They also seldom look beyond the boundaries of their districts, since this means trespassing on the bailiwick of a colleague on the same newspaper. And yet the full seriousness of a drought or outbreak of disease may only become apparent when borders are crossed.

Even when district-level bureaucrats are directly informed by citizens of impending calamities, they often fail to respond. To

[18] See for example Drèze and Sen (1989), chapter 5; and Drèze and Sen (1990), especially chapters 2 and 3, by Drèze.

ensure that such messages trigger prompt action, some means must exist to put political pressure on civil servants. District and Mandal Councils provided the means.

We might expect state legislators to play a role in raising the alarm and pressing for action. But most spend too much time politicking in the state capital or elsewhere to do this effectively. There was a time, long ago, when the Congress party organization in the districts was sufficiently strong and penetrative to help with this. But it has decayed severely.

Before decentralization, legislators and bureaucrats from each district conferred every three months. Information at these meetings mainly flowed in one direction, from the deputy commissioner to legislators. The latter mostly asked questions about what was being done at the grassroots and received what reporters call 'cursory' answers. Most legislators were too ill-informed to see how inadequate these were. As a result, the drought relief programme remained mainly on paper.

Decentralization changed things dramatically. Coming from much smaller constituencies, district councillors were extremely well-versed on conditions in the villages. The law gave them sufficient powers and status to make them assertive in monthly council meetings, which were always well attended.

In these circumstances, civil servants and representatives of statewide newspapers learned early and in great detail about water shortages, outbreaks of disease, and flooding in rural areas. Councillors' formidable powers gave them the clout to force prompt action from bureaucrats. If a council president was slow to respond to reports of distress, the presence of opposition councillors guaranteed that he would be forced to act. It is not surprising, then, that journalists regarded District and Mandal Councils both as a virtually foolproof source of early warnings, and an effective means of ensuring that warnings were heeded.

Institutional Performance

We now turn to the other main concern of this study: the changes produced by decentralization in the performance of government institutions. We first assess the 'effectiveness' of institutions, and then discuss 'responsiveness' and changes in the political and administrative 'process'.

Effectiveness

THE AUTONOMY, POWERS, AND RESOURCES OF THE COUNCILS

The state government spent roughly the same amounts after decentralization as before. But it gave elected councils substantial control over these funds and over a huge array of subjects including agriculture, animal husbandry, fisheries, rural development, primary and secondary education, health and family welfare, the welfare of Scheduled Castes and Tribes, rural employment schemes, sericulture (an important subject in this state), village and small industries, and civil supplies.[19]

This gave councils charge of nearly all state development funds—including those to pay salaries of development ministry employees at the district level and below (a relatively small proportion of the total outlay[20]) and those used for goods and services. Thus, they received roughly 40 per cent of the state budget, a huge concession. And since they also had considerable control over personnel from the line ministries, this represented a genuinely radical devolution of authority and resources.

We found very little discontentment among members of District and Mandal Councils, either with the amount of resources available or with the manner in which they were distributed among various councils and councillors' constituencies. District Council leaders sometimes expressed regret that they (unlike Mandal Councils) lacked tax-raising powers,[21] but this was not a major concern. District councillors knew that to impose fresh taxes was to risk unpopularity (a major reason why Mandal Councils seldom made full use of their limited taxation powers).

19 They did not gain control of law and order, revenue collection, public works, irrigation, horticulture, or forests. Cooperatives, which were initially given to them, were subsequently withdrawn (Karnataka 1989: 8).

20 The chief minister who presided over the creation of the system has given the example of one district where 16 per cent of the funds went on establishment costs while the rest went on development (Hegde 1994: 22). The share going to establishment costs was greater in many other districts, but not vastly so.

21 They had the power to charge licence fees, collect rents from property and, with the approval of the state government, raise loans (Karnataka 1989: 11–12; and Karnataka 1983: chapters 1, 19, 33, and 35).

In the first two years of the councils' existence, the District Councils had control over very substantial resources for two major national programmes to provide rural employment. In 1989, however, Prime Minister Rajiv Gandhi integrated these and other initiatives into a programme called the Jawahar Rozgar Yojana (JRY). Under this heading, massive funds were channelled from New Delhi directly to institutions at or near the village level. When more than one tier of decentralized government existed, the lion's share of JRY resources was to go to those closest to the grassroots. Thus in Karnataka, the Mandal Councils received 80 per cent of these funds, while the District Councils—which had previously controlled all of them—retained only 20 per cent. This represented a huge increase in resources at the Mandal level.

The Mandal Council also has great freedom to decide how to spend this money. Officially, councils were free to decide how to spend only 20 per cent of JRY funds. But in practice, they did what they liked with most of it and nearly always got away with it.

Decentralized systems in which most resources are provided from above are often condemned by analysts for giving councils no autonomy. The same analysts often presume that this also gives higher levels of government control over the councils and wrecks democratic decentralization. The evidence from Karnataka shows these complaints to be baseless.

MANDAL COUNCILS' PROBLEMS AND RELATIONS WITH DISTRICT COUNCILS

The Mandal Councils, which stood only slightly above the village level, were the main agencies responsible for implementing development projects and mobilizing local resources. Very little was accomplished on that latter front, since councillors found that levying taxes and pressing people for voluntary contributions made them unpopular.[22] They concentrated instead on spending the substantial funds received from above on projects. The District Councils' tasks were to oversee and coordinate them, to provide staff to assist them in project implementation, and to link the Mandals with the state government.

22 Our findings are at variance with comments in Karnataka (1989: 12).

The Mandal Councils had such limited staff resources that there was 'a gross mismatch' between their developmental duties and their capabilities.[23] At best, a Mandal Council possessed only a single, poorly trained secretary to keep records and accounts. And since these bodies were created anew in 1987, long delays occurred before many of them acquired even one functionary. This left them far too dependent on District Councils for staff to help with implementation, and the latter had too many Mandal Councils to serve to respond adequately.

The decision by Karnataka's decentralizers to establish elected councils at only these two widely separated levels—with no elected body in between[24]—made it difficult for District Councils to assist, communicate with, monitor, or coordinate the doings of Mandal Councils, or to be informed and lobbied by them. These problems were exacerbated by the failure to arrange regular meetings between Mandal Chairman and key district officials.[25] These districts are huge, with an average population in 1991 of 2.4 million. Distances between the district headquarters and many Mandals were enormous, and the sheer numbers of Mandal Councils per district (130 on average) meant that this was one of the few serious flaws in this system.

Knowledgeable observers argue convincingly that the only way to integrate the two levels was to obtain sustained help from the sub-district level in between, where the key figure was a bureaucrat, the block development officer (BDO). It was difficult, however, to mobilize BDOs, for two reasons. First, they and the level at which they worked had lost status and power when decentralization was introduced. They went from being the main focus of rural development efforts to a marginal role, as levels above and below were empowered.

23 Ibid., p. 22.

24 The decision to adopt this approach owed much to the preference of the Janata Party's state government (which instituted the system) for the model of decentralization that had been devised by the Ashok Mehta Committee, appointed by the Janata government in New Delhi during the 1970s (India 1978). This preference was not merely the result of partisan feeling, however, since by adopting the Mehta model, the state government avoided the time-consuming business of establishing their own committee to conduct a prolonged investigation into decentralization.

25 Karnataka (1989: 34).

Second, the BDOs were closely associated with state legislators who were the other major losers from decentralization. The state government had created bodies at the sub-district level as 'an ego-satisfying institution' for the legislators who headed them.[26] But these had so little power that many legislators took this as an affront. Their antagonism to the new councils reinforced that of the BDOs who were thus unenthusiastic link-men between district and Mandal levels. So Mandal Councils were never effectively integrated with the district level.

This gave them immense autonomy[27] which was sometimes put to beneficial effect. But it also meant that Mandal leaders often got away with violations of laws and regulations—see the discussion below of their failure to meet obligations to the Scheduled Castes. Mandal leaders either concealed these omissions by creative accounting or they openly admitted them on the usually safe assumption that no punitive action would follow. Mandal Councils' misdeeds were also supposed to be checked by mass meetings (Gram Sabhas). But we have seen that Mandal leaders soon abandoned these.

District Councils gained a little influence over certain Mandals by providing administrative support for development projects.

[26] These words were attributed to Ramakrishna Hegde, the chief minister who presided over decentralization, who uttered them in the presence of a District Council chief secretary, interviewed in Bangalore, 19 April 1993.

[27] Mandal Councils' autonomy was derived partly from the informal practicabilities of politics outlined in the text, and partly from formal provisions. For example, they received their main block grants on the basis of population within the Mandal, so that neither the state government nor the District Council could influence them much via discretionary payments. Their resources were rather limited until 1989, when the Rajiv Gandhi government created the Jawahar Rozgar Yojana programme that delivered 80 per cent of central development funds directly from New Delhi to the lowest tier of local government. Mandal Councils then gained immense new resources at the expense of District Councils which retained only 20 per cent.

They had to obtain District Council approval for projects on which this money was spent, but the worst problem that they usually experienced on that front was a delay of one to two months. They also had to gain approval of lists of beneficiaries for various projects, but they were usually able to arrange the lists in ways that prevented the overburdened and under-informed district authorities from undermining their decisions. (Interviews with numerous Mandal chairmen in four districts, March and April 1993).

But in the main, they felt unable to maintain contact with most of them, 'like postmen' whose main task was merely to pass funds down to the Mandals.[28] They sometimes acted as spoilers, preventing Mandal Councils from operating effectively. But in general little influence, oversight, or coordination was exercised by the District Councils.[29]

ABSENTEEISM AND WORK-RATE AMONG GOVERNMENT EMPLOYEES

The effectiveness of institutions is undermined if government employees absent themselves from work while taking their salaries, or do little when they turn up. The Karnataka government sees this as a significant problem.[30] Advocates of decentralization there have argued that absenteeism declined radically after the creation of elected councils—by as much as 91 per cent.[31] Our research indicates that such figures exaggerate the change somewhat, but that considerable progress was made nonetheless.

The creation of elected councils vastly expanded the number of people in authority to whom citizens could complain about government employees. Villagers had 'many masters to ask', as one councillor put it.[32] Members and chairmen of Mandal Councils could also see these things with their own eyes. They often took action themselves, by pressuring workers in the local school or medical dispensary. If they needed additional leverage, they could contact their representative on the District Council.

Our village surveys and elite interviews indicate that the main result was not less absenteeism—it declined 'remarkably' in certain

28 Interview with a former District councillor, Mysore, 18 April 1993.

29 These remarks are based on a large number of interviews with journalists, bureaucrats, and District and Mandal councillors in three districts (Dharwar, Mysore, and Mandya) in March and April 1993.

30 *The Times of India*, 10 November 1993.

31 This figure, which refers to primary school teachers and health workers, was cited by L.C. Jain in a Ford Foundation symposium (Ford Foundation 1992: 35). For unquantified comments in a similar vein, see Karnataka (1989: 9–10 and 24–5) and the statement by Abdul Nazir Sab, the Minister concerned (*Deccan Herald*, 8 July 1987).

32 Interview with D.R. Patil, opposition leader of the Dharwar District Council, Hubli, 4 April 1993.

areas,[33] but usually only moderately—but more assiduous, more responsive, and less corrupt behaviour by those who were on the job. Many were compelled to work longer hours. They also faced pressure to bend bureaucratic rules—usually to enhance service delivery rather than to facilitate corruption.

District Councils also reduced urban bias in the administration, not least because they were elected almost entirely by rural dwellers. In several districts, new routines were introduced to get officials out of the larger towns and cities. For example, one District president decreed that officials working out of his office had to spend twenty days per month on tour, and required them to keep diaries which were randomly checked.[34]

It was also common for District Councils to transfer significant numbers of employees—especially teachers—from urban to rural areas.[35] Such transfers were not always altruistic. Employees have long proffered payments to politicians to ensure good postings, and councillors sometimes accepted bribes after threatening transfers. But across most of the state, there was nevertheless at least a modest shift of personnel from urban to rural areas as a result of decentralization—despite state government resistance.

Taken overall, these changes produced a limited but still significant enhancement of the effectiveness and responsiveness of government institutions—at no extra cost to the taxpayer or the state exchequer. It is also widely believed—with good reason—that if decentralized institutions had been allowed to survive, further improvements of this kind would have occurred.

DECLINING CORRUPTION AND ITS IMPACT ON EFFECTIVENESS

Where corruption is a serious problem, the effectiveness of government institutions is impaired. If politicians and/or bureaucrats steal money from development programmes, citizens receive fewer benefits. If they demand bribes before delivering goods and services, citizens gain less. It is therefore appropriate in a discussion of institutional effectiveness to consider the changes which decentralization wrought in patterns of corruption.

33 Interview in Bangalore with a former Chief Secretary in a southern district, 19 April 1993.

34 Interview with K.N. Puttubuddhi, Mysore, 13 April 1993.

35 See for example, *Star of Mysore*, 16 February 1991, on the transfer of 500 teachers at once.

Decentralization in Karnataka yielded paradoxical results. The number of people involved in corrupt acts increased significantly. But the overall amount of money stolen almost certainly decreased—at least modestly.

The growth in the numbers of people engaged in malfeasance was inevitable. This should be understood wherever democratic decentralization is contemplated. When power was dispersed into the hands of (on average) nearly 3000 elected councillors in every district, the number of people with influence to peddle naturally rose. Little more than a score of legislators, bureaucrats and others in each district had previously had access to state power. Therefore the villagers who told us that the creation of District and Mandal Councils entailed 'a decentralization of corruption' were correct.[36] But those (and there were many) who then drew the further conclusion that decentralization entailed an increase in the overall amount of money illegally diverted were mistaken.

Decentralization made the political process much more transparent, and the theft of funds and the sale of influence far more visible. A lively two-party system ensured that it was not left to citizens to detect and protest against corrupt acts. Opposition parties seized every opportunity to sound the alarm, even on flimsy evidence.

Our argument about the decline in the overall amount of corruption rests on an understanding of the logic of corruption before decentralization. Consider first the state level under the old system where ministers and legislators exercised immense influence over the flow of development funds. Their ability to conceal how those funds were managed, and the spectacular levels of corruption which prevailed at that level after 1972, ensured that a large (but unknowable) proportion of development resources was siphoned off before it reached lower levels. When the new councils were given control of development programmes, this became immensely more difficult.[37]

Consider next the 'taluk' or sub-district level which stands between the district and Mandal levels. The key institution here

36 They made similar observations to an Institute of Social Sciences team headed by Anand Inbanathan. Interview with him, Bangalore, 9 April 1993.

37 Interviews with E. Raghavan, Bangalore, 10 April 1993, and with numerous senior bureaucrats in development departments.

in former days[38] had been the Taluk Development Board. It consisted of directly elected members, but it was far weaker than the District and Mandal Councils, and its members had far less information about the influence over development programmes. This lack of information was central to the old system of corruption. Taluk Board members never knew how much money passed from New Delhi and the state capital down to their level in any given year. Only four or five persons had access to this information: the chairman of the board, the taluk's state legislator (who sat on the board), the block development officer (chief developmental bureaucrat), the chief engineer, and sometimes an accounting officer. The first four of these people had such tight control over development funds, and operated in such secrecy, that they could divert large amounts to themselves, their friends, and clients without being found out. It is impossible to say how much was stolen under the old system. But when old Taluk board members got elected to the new Councils in 1987, they were amazed at the amounts of funds provided to district and Mandal levels. When they learned that the government had not increased such provisions, they saw immediately that substantial amounts must have gone astray under the earlier system.

Many new councillors stole funds and took bribes. But the new system was so open that a large number of people—councillors, journalists, senior and junior bureaucrats, informed citizens—knew how much money was available. Party competition made councillors eager to pounce on the misdeeds of opponents. Pounce they did, and journalists seized avidly on the merest sign of scandal. *Serious* cases of corruption could only occur when bureaucrats and councillors colluded or when one side acquiesced in the

38 In the period after 1960, the reluctance of most state-level leaders to permit decentralized councils to exercise influence caused them to hold elections to the Taluk Development Boards rather irregularly. This meant that when the Boards' official term (four and then five years) ended, their functions were turned over to the bureaucrats. As a result, these Boards actually existed only about half of the time between their creation in 1960 and the election of District and Mandal Councils under the new system in 1987. When the boards did not exist, a taluk's legislator and one or two civil servants exercised virtually complete and highly secretive control over the funds which came to the Board. Even when they did exist, elected members of the Board were unable to learn how much money was available for various programmes.

other's misdeeds. But the social distance between these two groups severely limited the number of such cases.

At the Mandal level, inadequate remuneration—nothing for councillors, Rs 300 per month for chairmen, Rs 150 for vice-chairmen—encouraged profiteering.[39] Corruption there mainly entailed sharing percentages skimmed off of construction projects. But the high visibility of corruption at the Mandal level imposed restraints upon it. As one knowledgeable bureaucrat said, 'The veil of secrecy, almost a steel curtain, that had hidden things before the councils had now been removed.' In villages, we and others found that 'everyone was talking about corruption',[40] usually in a well-informed manner. Many Mandal councillors said that villagers learned about virtually every underhand deal, and that this checked corruption. Citizens routinely protested against it at periodic village meetings. When councillors stopped holding these, they were angrily assailed at public celebrations. It was virtually impossible for them to budget for a project and then not build it. When they used sub-standard materials, they often encountered trouble. One group of villagers who spotted a bridge builder using inferior quality cement levelled the structure to the ground. All of this meant that, after decentralization, it was extremely difficult for people at this level to steal much.

What of corruption at the district level? Knowledgeable sources believe that nearly all efforts at profiteering there were uncovered. Allegations usually triggered investigations by councils, so that press reports are full of accounts of probes into the non-payment of workers in a forestry project, the diversion of wood from a housing scheme, and so on. If the district president delayed or refused an investigation, major ructions followed.[41]

When it was discovered, as it almost always was, that a district president was conspiring with bureaucrats to divert development funds, a bipartisan uproar would ensue. In one district, for example, it was shown that borewells which had supposedly been dug were non-existent and that the president was involved. Councillors from both parties threatened his removal and prevented the theft.[42]

39 Karnataka (1989: 31).

40 The quotation comes from a conversation with B.S. Bhargava who has studied the Mandal level very extensively.

41 See for example, *The Times of India*, 4 January 1988.

42 Interview with a former District councillor, Mysore, 13 April 1993.

Some corruption went unpunished. There were two main reasons for this. First, the security of tenure which IAS officers enjoy—to insulate them from unwarranted political intrusions—impeded anything more than transfers of errant members. Second, after November 1990, when the Congress party changed its chief minister, Karnataka suffered its most flagrantly corrupt government. With bureaucrats being pressed to assist state-level politicians in looting the exchequer, it was immensely difficult to discipline wayward district officials. But such cases were rare enough that the overall level of corruption almost certainly declined as a result of decentralization.

One unexpected check on corruption deserves attention. Every civil servant, male councillor, and journalist that we interviewed—many of whom were hard-eyed realists—stated that they knew of no instance when a woman councillor indulged in corrupt acts. Since they held 25 per cent of the seats, this had an impact on the incidence of corruption.

The actual levels of corruption in Karnataka varied from district to district and from time to time. The arrival in a district of a new chief secretary who lacked the skill and determination to curb malfeasance among bureaucrats, or a change of council president (a much rarer occurrence) which ushered in a man who was dishonest or inept at tackling councillors' misdeeds, would allow the level to rise. Problems were less serious in districts which (i) had effective voluntary associations, (ii) had a strong local press, and—less crucially—(iii) were nearer the state capital. In such districts (roughly half the state), it is reliably estimated that corruption consumed only 5–10 per cent of council funds.

Since the councils lapsed in late 1991, corruption is reliably reported to have soared. Tens of millions have been stolen by one means alone—persons filing bills for work that was not done, something that was exceedingly difficult while the councils existed.[43]

OUTPUTS

How many and what sort of tangible benefits, in the form of development projects or 'outputs', did the councils deliver? Our

[43] This is based on interviews with two skilled investigative journalists and two well-informed and perceptive former District Council chief secretaries.

survey of villagers yielded information on several hundred local-level projects.

Only 10.8 per cent of the projects identified to us had been implemented by the government prior to decentralization in 1987, as against 73.4 per cent which had been wholly or partially funded by the councils. Although council projects were fresher in respondents' minds, the evidence clearly indicates a marked increase in micro-level development 'outputs' as a result of decentralization.

Often and without prompting, villagers stated that more development had taken place during the councils' five years than in the forty years before that. This view is clearly inaccurate, but it is a revealing misperception. It highlights four important things.

First, the decentralization of decision-making about development heightened citizens' awareness and, therefore, made development projects more visible—even though opportunities for villagers to participate in decisions did not increase dramatically. Second, the bias of successive state and national governments before decentralization had caused micro-level development to suffer far greater neglect than most politicians and bureaucrats realized.

The third point emerges from the councillors' strong bias towards the construction of physical facilities. It is that more micro-level, infrastructural projects were completed than were intended by the state and central governments that earmarked funds passed to the councils. Earmarking was often ignored, especially by the Mandal Councils. As a result, the provision of services suffered, although this was somewhat counterbalanced by a reduction in absenteeism and an increase in hours worked and work rates among bureaucrats.

Finally, this increase in micro-level projects occurred even though spending on development did not increase with decentralization. This is partly explained by the bias of councillors for such projects, but the increase was so marked that it also owed something to the decrease in corruption. Development funds that had earlier been stolen now found their way into actual projects.

Responsiveness

Democratic decentralization plainly enhanced the responsiveness of government institutions in Karnataka. Virtually all of our sources agreed that the speed of response increased enormously.

Nearly all agreed that significant improvements occurred in both the quantity and the quality of responses. That is, institutions responded far more often than before, and their responses were deemed to be more satisfactory and to have conformed more closely to the felt needs of villagers. Let us consider each of these changes.

THE SPEED OF RESPONSES

The increased speed at which responses emerged is partly explained by an acceleration in the rate at which felt needs were communicated to people in authority. Councillors were quick to pass requests for official action to key government offices at and below the district level. Since district councillors had substantial influence over what went on in those offices, civil servants tended to be prompt both in their replies and in reporting problems to elected officials. Things would have worked even better had Mandal Council chairmen been able to meet District Council personnel on a regular basis, but this fault in the system[44] did not prevent a significant acceleration of responses.

The autonomy of the councils provides the rest of the explanation for this. Officials at the district and sub-district levels no longer needed approval from the state capital for development projects. In former days this usually delayed things by weeks, even when urgent action was needed.[45]

THE QUANTITY AND QUALITY OF RESPONSES

We asked villagers to name the sources of funding for the various development projects which they recalled in their localities (see Table 15.4). These answers probably overstate somewhat the number of projects funded by the Mandal Council to the detriment of the District Council, since the former usually implemented the decisions of the latter. Some projects credited to the government

44 Karnataka (1989: 34).

45 Under the decentralized system, non-urgent projects proposed by Mandal Councils which were to be funded by money which the Government of India provided under the Jawahar Rozgar Yojana programme were subject to approval by the District Council. Mandal chairmen estimate that this usually entailed a delay of one to two months. Projects funded by other programmes did not require such approval from the district level.

since decentralization may also have been the work of councils. But even if we take the figures as they stand, 73.4 per cent of projects were seen to have received at least partial financial support from the councils—a mightily impressive total.

Table 15.4: Funding of Development Projects (in per cent)

Government before decentralization	10.8
Government since decentralization	4.0
District Councils	3.0
Mandal Councils	58.7
District and Mandal Councils	2.6
Mandal Council and NGOs	1.7
District Council and NGOs	0.3
Government and Mandal Councils	5.1
Self-help	0.2
Government and self-help	0.2
NGOs	9.3
Government and NGOs	0.3
Mandal Council and NGOs	1.7
District Council and NGOs	0.3
Others	0.1
Don't know	1.7

We asked for information on the status of development projects which they identified. They indicated that 79.7 per cent of all projects had been completed, while 7.5 per cent had been abandoned unfinished, and 12.8 per cent were still in progress. This evidence demonstrates Councils' strong inclination to see projects through.

Let us now compare Council projects mentioned by villages in our survey with villagers' comments on their communities' needs. In no case did councils implement significant numbers of projects of a type that villagers did not regard as genuinely needed. Councils tended to see direct aid to social groups or associations as lying outside their remit. The interest in houses and house sites arose because earlier government programmes had promised these, but such schemes had been largely discontinued and councils thus felt unable to move on that front. Beneficiaries of those programmes had mainly been poor families, and the inaction of councils here is partly explained by their disinclination to provide assistance to poorer groups. Villagers were somewhat unfair to councils here, since some projects identified by them under other headings were targeted on vulnerable groups.

Our survey found that villagers were, with some reservations, reasonably satisfied with the projects implemented by councils. A total of 16.8 per cent of comments registered dissatisfaction, but the councils were clearly substantially successful.

How and why did these changes in responsiveness occur? The relative lack of responsiveness before decentralization resulted from hauteur and procrastination among some bureaucrats, state legislators, and ministers, the predominance of development programmes designed at national and state levels, etc. But that is only part of the story. Many politicians and civil servants in the state capital and district headquarters genuinely wanted to respond to the grassroots, but had been impeded by an inadequate flow of information from below. It is clear from their comments, however, that until decentralization, they were unaware of how poorly informed they had been. It was only when the new system massively increased the flow of information that they grasped the limitations of the old system.

Before decentralization, the immense psychological distance between villagers and the deputy commissioner made it hard for him to break through their deference, even when they were exasperated with a problem. So news of problems often reached him only after they had simmered for extended periods.

All of this changed after decentralization. Visits to villages produced greater information than before, partly because the presence of Mandal councillors (about whom villagers often complained) eroded the psychological distance between this senior official and common folk, and partly because decentralization yielded much more information to villagers about government projects.

The chief secretary's problem was thus not too little information but too much. He was now expected, and often pressured, to respond.[46]

46 Interview with M.R. Sreenivasa Murthy, Bangalore, 2 April 1993. The supplementary comment was provided by A. Ramaswamy, New Delhi, 27 March 1993. The material in these paragraphs is consistent with that provided by many other former chief secretaries. Numerous sources indicated that touring by civil servants at and below the district level—especially Block

And respond they often did. District presidents frequently set deadlines for responses by various departments—in Mysore district, seven days for borewell repairs, three for pipes bearing tap water, etc. District councillors toured rural areas to monitor work by departments under their standing committees (health, education, social justice, etc.). If they found bureaucrats falling short, they often told them to mend their ways within a specified period. If they did not comply, it went to the district authorities. These injunctions did not always produce results, but it happened often enough to transform the old, ossified system.

Two other qualitative gains were often stressed by informants. First, the suitability of technical work improved considerably, because elected representatives closely tied to villagers frequently advised on design and implementation. Prior to decentralization, this kind of input had only rarely come from state legislators. After decentralization, councillors who nearly all lived locally were able to achieve far more. Second, and for the same reason, decisions about locating projects were much more fully informed by local knowledge and dialogues with villagers than before.

Mandal Council chairmen stressed that there was greater equity in geographical terms. Before decentralization, if a legislator took a dislike to a set of villages, they could be starved of resources from government. Once councils were created, any semi-assiduous Mandal chairman could ensure that this area was not excluded. Even with an ineffectual chairman, a Mandal received substantial resources commensurate with its population, as a matter of right.

The district authorities heard pleas from remote villages that had seldom received development projects, and their responses clearly undercut urban bias. They also heard from disadvantaged groups that had seldom had assistance (though rural elites dominated the system) concerning problems that had arisen. Subsidized fertilizer and farm implements occasionally went to poor farmers in remote villages as well as to prosperous cultivators. A fisherfolk sub-caste within a low-status caste cluster that had never received much funding, because other groups in the cluster lobbied only for help to agriculture, gained access to village ponds and aid from the fisheries department. And so it went on.

Development Officers at the sub-district or taluk level—also increased markedly.

Given the radical increase in the amount of information and appeals for assistance that poured forth from the state's lively civil society, and given that 'local grievances which had been hidden all those years were now vented',[47] the new councils inevitably failed to do enough to satisfy many people. Popular exasperation was especially evident over a few issues on which the councils were impeded by the state government. Nowhere was this more apparent than in the government's refusal (for financial reasons) to permit District Councils to hire more primary school teachers—to which villagers everywhere attached high priority. But enough was accomplished on most fronts to earn the system high marks for responsiveness.

RESPONSIVENESS TO WHOM?—VULNERABLE GROUPS

We must also consider which groups received responses. Elites made gains, but democratic decentralization in Karnataka did little to benefit vulnerable groups—poor people, Scheduled Castes (ex-untouchables), and women. Indeed, its net effect—particularly at the lower Mandal level—was to enhance the share of resources going to prosperous groups at the expense of the poor. It placed the Scheduled Castes in a less advantageous position than previously, even though it was supposed to help them. We should therefore not expect democratic decentralization in India to assist in poverty alleviation over the short to medium term, unless the decentralized system is dominated by a leftist party, and that seems possible only in the state of West Bengal.

The Karnataka government's efforts to assist vulnerable groups unwittingly caused problems for them in two ways. First, its guidelines stated that the Scheduled Castes were to receive 18 per cent of Council resources, but it was unclear whether this meant 18 per cent of plan funds, total development funds, projects, or whatever. This played into the hands of those who preferred not to assist the Scheduled Castes. Second, the state government was supposed to monitor the District Council's management of anti-poverty programmes, but it largely failed to do so. This left things to the Councils, and actual performance varies.

We saw earlier that elected Scheduled Caste members of District Councils seldom asserted themselves. This did not, however,

47 Interview with M. Ahiraj, correspondent of *The Times of India*, Hubli, 6 April 1993.

destroy any chance that they might gain something from these councils. In a small number of cases, where one landowning caste group[48] had influence and where it was led by persons unsympathetic to the poor, vulnerable groups had little hope of concessions. In many cases, however, district-level politicians had internalized enough of the state-level penchant for bargaining between rich and poor groups to permit some accommodation. In a small number of districts, enlightened politicians from the dominant castes led the fight on behalf of low-status groups.[49] Karnataka's two-party system also helped, since opposition councillors often complained about inadequate help to the poor and Scheduled Castes. They did so mainly to embarrass the ruling party, but this still produced modest benefits.

It is widely believed—within and beyond India—that bureaucrats are more committed to the poor than are elected politicians from elite backgrounds. In Karnataka, however, this was often untrue. In Dharwar District, civil servants were reliably reported to be especially inclined to pilfer funds intended for the Scheduled Castes or to leave such money unspent. This 'played havoc with schemes to help the needy'. In Mysore District, reliable sources argued that 'the key' to ensuring that programmes for Scheduled Castes worked was the control of corruption and inaction among bureaucrats.[50]

Legal requirements that Scheduled Castes be assisted were, however, widely flouted by Mandal Councils. They tended to spend money intended for the Scheduled Castes in ways that mainly or wholly benefited prosperous groups while claiming that it went to Scheduled Castes. Numerous Mandal chairmen

48 It is more precise to say not 'caste group', but '*jati*-cluster'. A jati is an endogamous caste group. Each of the so-called 'dominant castes' of Karnataka—the Lingayats and the Vokkaligas—in fact consists of a cluster of jatis. The two clusters tend to occupy distinct parts of the state, although there is some overlap. See Manor (1977 and 1989).

In some districts, where one jati-cluster is found almost exclusively, it is easier for it to exercise great influence.

49 This was true, for example, of one leading Congress politician in Dharwar District who was a Lingayat. Interview with M. Madan Mohan, Hubli, 5 April 1993.

50 Interview with M. Ahiraj and M. Madan Mohan, Hubli, 6 April 1993, and with M.V. Maramkal and V. Nagaraj, Mysore, 13 April 1993.

explained to us how this was done. A council would, for example, mount a project to provide electricity and lighting to an entire village. This might extend into the Scheduled Caste quarter, but even if it did, 90 per cent of the benefit would go to others. But the entire sum spent was listed among the 18 per cent of funds devoted to Scheduled Caste uplift. Projects for village road repair, water supplies, etc., were handled similarly. Such deception was practised systematically in every part of the state, and next to nothing was done to curtail it.

We also saw earlier that women District councillors largely failed to assert themselves. This did not mean, however, that nothing was done at that level to assist women. Bureaucrats whose task was to implement programmes for women's and child welfare indicated that service delivery sometimes improved as a result of decentralization. The existence of women councillors gave these civil servants useful links to women at the grassroots and made it easier for them to understand women's needs. Responses from the district level occurred more quickly than before. The most significant gains were when the (often mainly female) bureaucrats in these government departments persuaded elected councillors (of both genders) to publicize opportunities for immunization, family planning, etc. But these changes seldom occurred on the initiative of women representatives. Rather they were the result of general improvements in services and communication with citizens.[51]

Apart from this, only very limited tangible benefits for women materialized. The best that women's leaders in the districts could say was that by the end of the councils' five-year-term, a greater willingness had developed among prominent women to fight future council elections.[52]

It has been argued that, in time, vulnerable groups will become more confident, assertive, and impatient in councils such as these, and that councils' failure to respond adequately to such groups will therefore be a temporary problem,[53] but the evidence from the Mandal level raises doubts.

51 This is based on interviews with bureaucrats working in this field in Dharwar, Mysore, and Bangalore Rural Districts.

52 This was the consensus view that emerged from interviews with numerous women councillors and women's leaders in Karnataka, March and April 1993.

53 Blair (1988).

It is not naive to expect such things at the district level where the state-level culture of power-sharing between elites and disadvantaged groups was in evidence. But when elected bodies are created at or just above the village level—as in the case of Mandal Councils—it is very difficult to break down the dominance (in both gender and caste terms) of conservative men from landowning castes. Women councillors who press their claims at that level risk embarrassment and intimidation, and the Scheduled Castes risk harassment and violence.

Nor can low-caste voters be confident about remaining anonymous when they vote in such a localized council election—as they can when they and thousands of others elect a legislator. In a constituency with only 400 voters, if the Scheduled Castes combine to defeat a candidate who is the favourite of dominant groups, their action will be apparent and violent retribution may follow. We therefore remain concerned that, despite its many virtues, democratic decentralization to very localized levels empowers arenas where social justice is much harder to achieve than at higher levels. And this may not change much any time soon.

Process

How did decentralization in Karnataka affect the processes through which government and society interacted, and the popular perception of these processes?

Elections were extremely fair, but since that had long been true here, it produced little change in citizens' views. The political process became much more transparent than before. However, this did not earn the system the popular appreciation it deserved because people could more clearly see the shortcomings of government as well as its achievements. In Karnataka, ironically, although corruption declined as a result of decentralization, most people believed that it had increased because it was now more apparent than under the old, opaque system.

The increased speed of government responses was clearly perceived and welcomed by ordinary folk, as was the marked increase in the number of those responses. They also regarded the quality of most projects as good, and the types of projects implemented conformed quite closely to their felt needs. All of these things facilitated creative interactions between the state and local society, and made the political process appear more congenial and worthwhile.

Decentralization also created a huge number of opportunities for would-be politicians, and eased frustration among them. However, the introduction of inter-party competition into local arenas tended to embitter local rivalries further—a cause of some popular dismay. And the failure of the councils to meet their legal responsibilities to the Scheduled Castes caused resentment among some. But in most respects, this more open, effective, and responsive system made government appear more tractable and legitimate to most villagers.

Generalizing from the Karnataka Case

Democratic decentralization in Karnataka achieved considerable success. But we must be cautious about inferring from this that decentralization can produce similar benefits elsewhere. Many of the gains here resulted from things external to the experiment, from socio-political conditions which are often absent elsewhere.

Karnataka had a reasonably lively civil society. The resilience of caste and other social institutions meant that society was not dependent upon or structured by groups' access to the state, since organized interests had had decades of experience with democracy, their leaders and activists possessed many of the bargaining, organizing, and lobbying skills necessary to make open, decentralized politics work creatively. Karnataka was largely free of extreme socio-economic inequalities which can generate oppression, desperation, and vicious conflicts that make it difficult for liberal institutions to function.

Social forces here were also accustomed to working through political parties. Competition between parties was lively but moderate in character, thanks in part to one thing that was internal to the system of decentralization—the requirement that most resources be distributed among councils according to population. That prevented politicians at higher levels from starving opposition-controlled councils. It was quite common for councillors from both parties to unite when confronting corruption or serious mismanagement, or when a council's interests were threatened.[54]

Both main parties were strongly enough represented on District Councils to ensure spirited interplay between them. This contributed to greater transparency—to revelations that unearthed and impeded corruption, to investigations into budgets, policies, and project implementation, and to early warnings of potential disasters. Party competition yielded similar benefits on many Mandal Councils too. Party connection tenuously integrated many Mandal Councils with higher levels in the political system in ways that proved creative, especially since the formal institutional links between the Mandals and higher levels were inadequate.

Karnataka also enjoyed the advantages of a free and assertive press, and a bureaucracy which was used to working under elected politicians and which tended to comply both with politicians' wishes and with the law. It is unusual to find so many of these factors robustly present elsewhere in Asia, Africa, Latin America, or Eastern Europe.

References

Aziz, A. (1993), *Decentralised Planning: The Karnataka Experiment.* New Delhi: Sage Publications.

Blair, H.W. (1988), 'Success or Failure in Rural Development: A Comparison of Maharashtra, Bihar and Bangladesh'. Paper presented at the Association of Asian Studies.

Drèze, J. and A. Sen(1989), *Hunger and Public Action.* Oxford: Oxford University Press.

———— (1990), *The Political Economy of Hunger, Volume Two: Famine Prevention.* Oxford: Oxford University Press.

Ford Foundation (1992), *Perspectives on India's Development in the 1990s: Overview.* New Delhi: Ford Foundation.

Hegde, R. (1994), 'Local Self-Government in Karnataka: Planning from Below' in M.S. Adiseshiah *et al.* (eds), *Decentralised Planning and Panchayati Raj.* New Delhi: Institute of Social Sciences.

54 Examples of this are plentiful. See for example, *The Hindu*, 14 August 1989, and 7 March 1990; and *The Times of India*, 10 April and 6 November 1987, 12 January 1988, 11 June 1989, 11 and 30 April 1990, and 1, 12, and 13 January and 24, 25, and 30 July 1991.

India, Government of (1978), *Report of the Committee on Panchayati Raj Institutions*. New Delhi.

Institute of Social Sciences (1989), *Social Background of Zila Parishad Members in Karnataka*. New Delhi: Institute of Social Sciences.

Karnataka, Government of (1974), *Statistics for Planning*. Bangalore.

——— (1983), *The Karnataka Zilla Parishads, Taluk Panchayat Samithis, Mandal Panchayats and Nyaya Panchayats Act, 1983 and Various Rules Framed under the...Act*. Bangalore.

———(1989), *Report of the Zilla Parishad and Mandal Panchayat Evaluation Committee*. Bangalore.

Manor, J. (1977), 'The Evolution of Political Arenas and Units of Social Organisation' in M.N. Srinivas *et al.* (eds), *Dimensions of Social Change in India*. Bombay: Allied Publishers, pp. 169–87.

——— (1989), 'Karnataka: Caste, Class, Dominance and Politics in a Cohesive Society', in F. Frankel and M.S.A. Rao (eds), *Dominance and State Power in Modern India: Decline of a Social Order*, vol. 1. Delhi: Oxford University Press, pp. 322–61.

Ray, A. (1991), *Political Participation, Rural Development and Local Government Reforms in India*. Tokyo: Pinter.

VI

The Future of Indian Democracy

Where is Indian democracy headed? Some have argued that the proliferation of political parties (even if these are caste-based) is indicative of greater democratization, and even of the fact that democracy is striking deeper roots in Indian society. Others believe that this is a double-edged process, such that even as the democratic principle is universalized, the idea of citizenship is compartmentalized, as caste and other primordial identities are entrenched.

It is arguable that among the many challenges facing Indian democracy today, two are pre-eminent. One is the challenge of *dalit* identity, the symbolic importance of which cannot be underestimated. For the first time in five thousand years, the most oppressed sections of Indian society are finding a voice in the polity. Arguably also for the first time in as many years, the multicultural ethos of India is under attack from the hegemonizing cultural project of Hindutva. These two challenges are the subject of the essays in this section. In the first of these essays, Gail Omvedt traces the evolution of *dalit* politics, from Phule through Ambedkar to the Bahujan Samaj Party and other contemporary articulations of *dalit* identity. She reflects also on the ideological ambiguities that remain, in terms of the analysis of the chief sources of exploitation, and the ways of overcoming it. The *dalit* movement, Omvedt argues, remains oblivious to environmental and alternative development issues as well as to the question of the exploitation of the subsistence labour of women and peasants. Until these issues are also linked to the project of *dalit* emancipation, the transformation of Indian politics will remain unaccomplished.

Finally, Christophe Jaffrelot's article provides an account of the Hindu nationalist conception of democracy whose anti-individualism led it, even in the 1950s, to oppose the Westminster parliamentary system as an alien model. Its group-based conception of democracy bears some resemblance to the corporatist state, but also draws upon elements of the Gandhian vision of decentralized village-level democracy. Nevertheless, Hindu nationalists have, since before independence, favoured democracy because it guaranteed majority rule in a society where Hindus constituted a demographic majority. There remains however some tension between this endorsement of democracy and the contrary pull of the Hindu tradition of *raj guru* (king's guru), a role for which many RSS *pracharak*s have seen themselves as ideally suited. Within the party and the constituents of the sangh parivar, inner democracy is conspicuous by its absence. In recent years, the BJP leadership has expressed its sympathies for a presidential system, ostensibly because this would guarantee a stronger Centre, but also, Jaffrelot argues, because of the opportunities this affords for the personalization and concentration of power. The increasing democratization of the polity, as evidenced by backward caste politics, has also had an impact on the BJP, traditionally a party of the upper castes (*brahmin*s and *baniya*s).

16

The Anti-caste Movement and the Discourse of Power[+]

Gail Omvedt

We do not want a little place in Brahman Alley. We want the rule of the whole country. Change of heart, liberal education will not end our state of exploitation. When we gather a revolutionary mass, rouse the people, out of the struggle of this giant mass will come the tidal wave of revolution... . To eradicate the injustice against Dalits, they themselves must become rulers. This is the people's democracy.

Dalit Panther, 1973

The events of 1990–1 placed the issue of caste squarely at the centre of Indian politics, with a newly solidified 'left and democratic front' (the National Front–Left Front alliance) taking as its principal identifying programme, under the name of 'social justice', a major demand of the Dalit and non-Brahman movements from the time of their origin: reservations in education and public service. It began when a minority Janata Dal (JD)–National Front (NF) government was elected to power in 1989; its manifesto had included implementation of the Mandal Commission (MC) Report, which promised reservations for 'backward classes' [the mainly Shudra castes, estimated (by the MC) at 52 per cent of the population] in addition to those already existing for Scheduled Castes (SCs) and Scheduled Tribes (STs). Even then, 'anticipatory'

[+] T.V. Sathymurthy (ed.), *Social Change and Political Discourse in India: Structure of Power, Movements of Resistance, Volume 3: Region, Relation, Caste, Gender and Culture in Contemporary India* (Delhi: Oxford University Press, 1996).

riots broke out in northern cities. Then in August, in the context of a growing confrontation with Devi Lal, the deputy prime minister and self-proclaimed spokesperson of the peasants, who was also at the centre of a series of corruption charges, V.P. Singh announced the implementation of the Commission's recommendations.

This unleashed a storm of protest, with upper-caste youth throughout northern Indian cities demonstrating and rioting; then, a wave of 'self-immolations' followed, spurred by tremendous newspaper publicity and intellectual support, and by the desperation of many lower-middle class, upper-caste youth who had seen their future in terms of government jobs. There was a chorus in the press against V.P. Singh, talk of the 'Mandalization of India', and respectable social scientists who had made their careers analysing the reality of caste in India now rediscovered the economic factor and threatened a 'brain drain' of high-caste talent abroad. The Bharatiya Janata Party (BJP), whose 'Hindu unity' was most threatened by the unleashing of contradictions between Dalits/Other Backward Castes (OBCs), on the one hand, and the upper castes, on the other, then unleashed its forces in a massive onslaught to build a temple to Rama at Ayodhya, and when this was halted by the police forces of the state, withdrew its support from the government.

The minority NF government fell; but V.P. Singh, far from withdrawing his backing, began a tour of the country, drawing huge crowds not only in the north, to which his own mass appeal had been limited in 1989, but also in the south and west. The events established his personal hegemony over the Janata Dal, and whereas earlier he had identified himself with various toiling sections, speaking of participation in management for workers and remunerative prices for farmers, now he began leaving aside all concrete issues and centring on the single issue of the MC and reservations for the Shudra caste groups. He was, in the words of an article in *Sunday*, turning the Janata Dal into an 'up-market Bahujan Samaj party', and though there had been numerous JD leaders and activists unenthusiastic about reservations, there was little they could do about it. And he had been using the language of power to justify his stand. As he stressed in a *Frontline* (16 February–1 March 1991)[1] interview, 'the greater debate is not

[1] 'We are the Forces of Change' (interview with V.P. Singh by N. Ram).

about government jobs.... The point is of share in the decision-making and power structure'.

In doing so, in rendering Dalit parties like the Bahujan Samaj Party (BSP) irrelevant, and forcing the Left into the position of simply rallying around him without an ability to devise any alternative programme (that the Left has no relevant programme today is another matter), V.P. Singh, the politician, had learned what most Marxists did not, namely that:

(1) the abolition of caste was a core question of any democratic or revolutionary movement in India;

(2) it was not a question simply of a Dalit movement but of an anti-caste movement in which Dalits must play a leading role, while forging a Dalit–Shudra (OBC/non-Brahman) alliance;

(3) that the central term of its discourse is not jobs, ending atrocities, and certainly not 'uplifting the oppressed', but that of power.

The outcome of the election (in which Congress-I emerged as the largest, but not majority, party and BJP became the largest single opposition party) had been heralded in many quarters as a setback for the National Front and 'Mandal'; certainly large sections of the bourgeoisie and bureaucracy as a whole, and a major section of the intelligentsia breathed a sigh of relief. Yet, it is worth stressing that the NF–Left alliance won 127 Lok Sabha seats, making it the largest opposition force—in spite of extreme lack of funding in the comparison to the other fronts, lack of party organization, and the sympathy factor after Rajiv Gandhi's death which played a significant role especially in the southern states. What the events of 1990–1 and the stress on 'social justice' accomplished was to create, for the first time in Indian political history, a stable national political platform of democratic and Left parties, with no section of Socialist/Communist forces able to ally with the Congress or the BJP under the rubric of 'opposition unity'. This alliance should not be overrated; it was centred on a 'one–point' programme of caste justice without any effective economic programme to give this a base, any new vision of socialism capable of overcoming the crises of the period, or any ability to really draw in other new social movements and the constituencies they represent.

But it was an important step forward, and it was accomplished by taking up one of the basic issues of the anti-caste movement, in the context of forging an alliance of non-Brahmans (OBCs) and Dalits (Shudras and *ati*-Shudras) which had been a concern of this movement from the beginning. And it had adopted a central theme of this movement's discourse, that of power. Throughout its history, the anti-caste movement has engaged in dialogue with the Marxist Left, but it has its own history, analysis, and discourse. This chapter will briefly examine some of the moments of that history.

The Nineteenth-Century: Jotirao Phule

Jotirao Phule, the Maharashtrian middle-caste social revolutionary whose death centenary was celebrated in 1989–90, is regarded by both Dalits and radical non-Brahmans alike as their forerunner. In Maharashtra, the peasant movement and the women's movement also look upon him as a founder. Indeed, he inaugurated a new discourse, a new understanding of Indian history from the viewpoint of the Shudra and *ati*-Shudra (Dalit) peasantry which continues to be relevant today (Phule 1986; Omvedt 1976; O'Hanlon 1985).

Phule took up the 'Aryan theory' which the Brahmanic and nationalist elite at the time was using to justify its ascendancy and equivalence with Europeans, and turned it around to celebrate the middle and low castes as descendants of an original non-Aryan peasant community, which had had its traditions of equality and prosperity until it was conquered by the cruel invading Aryans. For Phule, the history of caste in India was a history of violence, *force majeure*, and subjugation. The holding of state power, and the use of religious deception in order to consolidate their position, was the hallmark of Brahman–Aryan rule, or the *bhatshahi*. The British were but another set of conquerors in this line, after the Aryans and the Muslims; only Phule sees their conquest (that of both the British and the Muslims as having certain liberatory aspects because their religion, unlike the caste system imposed by the Aryans, was egalitarian. Under the British too, though, exploitation of the Shudra peasantry was primarily a function of Brahman control of the state bureaucracy, which extracted taxes and bribes, whilst at the same time cheating the peasants in the courts, backed up by Brahmanic cunning and religious justification: Brahmans were the money-lenders who ensnared the peasant in debt, and the priest who cheated him on his very deathbed.

The central figure of this new ideology-mythology for Phule was that of Bali Raja. To the Brahmanic myths, Bali is a *rakshasa* or demon-king, and the boy Waman who sends him down beneath the earth is an incarnation of Vishnu. To peasants in Maharashtra, though equally so in south India, Bali is the symbol of an ideal king and an era of happiness, and Phule celebrated him as such, weaving into his reinterpretation the names of the various Maharashtrian peasant and nomadic gods (Vithoba, Khandoba, Jotiiba) as his lieutenants. From Waman through Parashuram and all the *avatar*s, history was thus one of conquest and deception. Phule also added that of the non-Aryans who fought against this conquest, who were all Kshatriyas as well as peasants, the bravest of these were the Mahars and Mangs (the untouchable castes of Maharashtra) who, in return for their heroism, were thrown down into the lowest position in the system.

For Phule, the crucial preconditions for the defeat of the exploitative bhatshahi were the rejection of the inegalitarian Brahmanic religion and the unity of the Shudras and *ati*-shudras. He very often lists these, including *kunbi*s, *mali*s, *koli*s, *dhangar*s... down to *bhik*s, *mahar*s, and *mang*s; in the process denying the *kunbi*s the more status-claiming title of 'Maratha', and normally laying special emphasis on the (Dalit) *mahar*s and *mang*s. He also explicitly opposed the Indian National Congress (INC), then in the days of its first formation, as Brahman-dominated, and raised the point that India can become a 'nation' only when caste is overcome and the masses of Shudras and *ati*-Shudras are able to come forward.

These themes—the need for Dalit–Shudra unity: the need for a new religion to transcend Brahmanism;[2] and characterization of the Congress as a party of Brahmanism (and later, also of capitalism)—was subsequently adopted by all anti-caste movements.

In addition, in analysing Phule's ideas, a useful comparison can be made between his stress on violence, conquest, and state power in the history of exploitation, and Marx's emphasis on the role of primitive accumulation prior to and outside the sphere of factory production, the arena in which most of the Third World peasantry finds itself, where 'violence is the midwife of history'.

2 Phule was to formulate what he called a *sarvajanik satya dharm*; Periyar was to choose atheism, Ambedkar Buddhism, and so forth.

Ambedkar: Dalits and Non-Brahmans during the Independence Movement

After 1917, non-Brahman and Dalit movements arose as separate movements, though interlinked, and drawing on common ideological themes. Non-Brahman movements were strongest in Maharashtra, in Madras Presidency (Tamil Nadu and coastal Andhra), and in Mysore with differing impact.[3] Dalit movements were actually wider in spread if weaker in resources, including not only south and west India, but also movements such as the Ad-Dharm in Punjab, Adi-Hindus in western UP, and Namashudras in Bengal (Omvedt 1976; Omvedt 1994; Juergensmeyer 1982; Irschick 1970).

Let us look at the common fate of anti-caste movements from the viewpoint of the Dalit movements. These arose separately and always expressed their autonomy because of the obvious contradictions with the middle castes. Yet they shared common traditions with the non-Brahman movements, stressed common themes, used a common language, and nearly always looked to alliances. Ambedkar, the towering figure of the Dalit movement, at times even spoke of himself as a part of the 'non-Brahman movement' and consistently argued for alliance with the non-Brahman leaders of Maharashtra. A common theme of the Dalit movement was the *adi* theme, drawn from Phule; that of being original non-Aryan inhabitants, oppressed through conquest and subjugation.

Nearly all of the regionally diverse Dalit movements had both an economic and a social thrust: they tried to get land for Dalits (normally forest and 'waste' lands), freedom from *vethbegar* or the caste-enforced, caste-specific imposed labour; and became involved in organizing the working class where Dalits were employed as wage labour in the mills in cities such as Nagpur and Bombay. They also fought for education and tried to generate internal social reform, including marriage between sub-castes and the ending of customs such as the *devadasi*-type prostitution.

But power was the key. Ambedkar's statement, 'we must become a ruling community', has become one of the most famous sayings of the movement. At the 1930 Round Table Conference, Ambedkar made his position clear with regard to independence in

[3] The south Indian movement had a large base amongst landlords; the Mysore movement was more popular among the educated urban section; the Maharashtra movement had a base among the peasantry.

precisely these terms, arguing that Untouchables, more than any other section, needed freedom from British rule, because only under Swaraj would they have an opportunity of garnering power, and that was the key to their liberation (Ambedkar 1981).

But how was power to be achieved? Ambedkar took political strategy very seriously, and he was clear about two aspects of the prevailing political situation: first, that the Congress was irrevocably a party of the Brahmans and the bourgeoisie, and that Dalits should remain independent of and from it. And second, that the struggle of the Dalits could not be waged by the Dalit party alone, but as part (and hopefully the leading part) of a political party uniting peasants and workers, Dalits and the *bahujan samaj* (middle castes).

His first and most vigorous political effort consisted of the formation of the Independent Labour Party (ILP) during the 1930s, and its campaigns against the *mahar watan*, against the *khoti* landlord system in the Konkan spearheaded by activists in that region from 1930 onwards, and against the anti-working class 'black bill' of 1938. The anti-*khoti* struggle united both Mahars and Kunbi tenants, and produced one of the biggest peasant marches of its time to the Legislative Council in Bombay in 1938.[4] The massive textile workers' strike in 1938 was initiated by Ambedkar's party and carried out in alliance with Communists and moderate trade union leaders.

Throughout this period, Ambedkar continually urged Maharashtrian non-Brahman leaders (for example, Jedhe) not to join the Congress; and continually sought for allies among similar forces throughout India—for example, with Periyar, making an effort to revive the Justice Party, and with Swami Shahajanand, leader of Bihar's militant peasant movement. Ambedkar's effort to forge fraternal links with Swami Shahajanand produced an almost paradigmatic meeting between the two. It was at a time (1938) when Jagjivan Ram, a Congress protégé, was both trying to wean Dalits away from Ambedkar by forming a 'Depressed Classes League' and to split agricultural labourers from the Bihar peasantry with his Khetmajoor Sabha.

But Ambedkar ignored Jagjivan Ram. His paper had been praising the militancy of the Kisan Sabha, which was becoming

[4] This struggle has been neglected by Left historians, perhaps because it was outside the framework of the Kisan Sabha of the time.

autonomous and moving away from 'Gandhism'; but he urged that it should also move away from Congress and that 'peasants and workers must have their own political party'. When the two leaders met in Bombay, Ambedkar reiterated these points. The Swami argued that Congress was an 'anti-imperialist united front', and that the leadership could be changed; Ambedkar argued that it was simply a party of Brahmans and the bourgeoisie, and was not even truly 'anti-imperialist'. The alliance failed on this point of political strategy—and not on 'class or 'caste' differences between Dalits and non-Brahmans, agricultural labourers, and peasants (See *Janata* 1937–8).

Throughout this period also, Dalits in various parts of the country, and Ambedkar, were carrying out a fight against 'atrocities' in which it was normal for them to confront directly the non-Brahman middle peasant castes such as the *kunbis*. Nevertheless, both Ambedkar and other Dalit leaders of the time followed a policy of alliance with non-Brahmans and peasants and workers as a matter of political strategy. Thus, Punjabi Ad-Dharm leaders joined forces with the Unionist party in the 1930s, and the Bengali Namashudras with the Muslim Krishak Praja Party. All these parties and groups realized that unity among them was a pre-condition for winning power. Ambedkar's ILP, with its strong rhetoric of 'worker-peasant' struggle, can also be seen as constituting a practical application of what the Communists had proposed in the 1920s but never carried through, namely, 'worker–peasant parties'.

The demand for reservations also saw Dalits and non-Brahmans by and large acting together, in spite of considerable tensions. Ambedkar himself has, in his writings, referred to himself as a 'Shudra' and part of the non-Brahman movement; and his eloquent defence of reservations referred to both the Dalits and the non-Brahmans—and, strikingly, used the language of power and self-determination:

Now, one would like to ask those who deny the justice of the case of the Backward Classes for entry into the Public Services is whether it is not open to the Backward Classes to allege against the Brahmans and allied classes all that was alleged by the late Mr. Gokhale on behalf of Indian people against the foreign agency? Is it not open...to say that by their exclusion from the Public Services a kind of dwarfing or stunting is going on? Can they not complain that as a result of their exclusion they are obliged to live all the days of their lives in an atmosphere of inferiority?... Can they not lament that the moral elevation which every self-governing people feels cannot be felt by them and that their administrative talents must gradually disappear owing to sheer disuse till at last their lot as hewers of wood and drawers of water in their own country is stereotyped. [Quoted in Omvedt 1976: p. 211]

However, Ambedkar's radical strategy of a united struggle against brahmanism and capitalism in the 1930s did not succeed. His political activities and much of his theoretical writing during the 1940s must be seen in the light of this failure. Instead of a revolutionary democratic political movement of workers and peasants, Dalits and Shudras, the Congress strategy won hegemony, for a time succeeding in co-opting elements from all sections, from 'Harijans' to many of the non-Brahman peasantry. It should also be noted that the post-independence Congress political strategy (which has basically consisted of uniting 'Harijans, Adivasis and minorities' with the upper castes against the middle castes, or agricultural labourers with the bourgeoisie against the peasantry) had its first glimmerings in the organizing tasks that it had carried out during the 1930s and the promotion of leaders such as Jagjivan Ram.

Against the background of this failure, Ambedkar also took a step backward and formed the Scheduled Castes Federation (SCF) as a party exclusively consisting of Dalits, in order to gain whatever concessions and benefits that could be won out of India's inevitable independence under Congress Raj. Instead of workers' and peasants' struggles and attempts to unite Dalits and middle castes, its activities focused on demands for reservations and separate village settlements. In other words, the overall radical liberatory strategy was given up for one of constituting Dalits as simply an 'interest group' in an otherwise pluralistic system. The whole period of the drafting of the Constitution has to be seen in this light, as well as Ambedkar's very pessimistic conclusions about unity. Thus, in his unpublished writings he could state that

[i]t is obvious that these three classes [Dalits, Shudras, and Tribals] are naturally allies. There is every ground for them to combine for the destruction of the Hindu social order. But they have not...the result is that there is nobody to join the untouchable in his struggle. He is completely isolated. Not only is he isolated he is opposed by

the very classes who ought to be his natural allies. [Ambedkar 1989: pp. 115–16]

Ambedkar did not fully give up the effort; his 1951 election manifesto for the SCF stated that it might 'dissolve itself' into a 'Backward Caste Federation' if this seemed viable: before his death he recommended the transformation of the SCF into a Republican Party whose declared intention (which was, however, unrealized in practice) was to become a broader party of all oppressed sections; and one of his last actions was to join the Samyukta Maharashtra (SM) movement (the first real Left–democratic front in Maharashtra) in spite of the fear of the 'dominance of Marathas' in a united Maharashtra state.

Nevertheless, Independence occurred against a backdrop of failure of unity attempts, in a process controlled by the Brahman/bourgeoisie-dominated Congress party which had begun a process of co-opting and integrating lower-caste representatives and of speaking in the name of 'agricultural labourers' and the 'rural poor', but without giving these sections any real power. It was an independence dominated by capital and a large-scale bureaucracy—controlled, predictably, by Bania castes and an aristocratic Brahman elite—in which the Nehru model of heavy industrialization based on a public sector and planning was to structure an unbalanced, inegalitarian, and environmentally destructive and unsound course of development.

The 1970s: Dalit Panthers Proclaim Revolution

The formation of the Dalit Panthers in 1972 took place against a background of such oppressive developments—namely, the repeated failure of the Republican Party to fulfil any of the hopes of the Dalits, of rising tensions in the countryside, and of the revolutionary inspiration provided by the Naxalbari insurrection which was crushed by the state. It was a year of the beginning of all kinds of new movements—the year of the formation of the All Assam Students' Union (AASU), of the Jharkhand Mukti Morcha (JMM), of the new farmers' organizations in Punjab and Tamil Nadu; it was also the year of the rise of the Chipko movement and of the beginnings of the women's movement with the establishment of the Self-Employed Women's Association (SEWA), and the year in which the Anandpursahib Resolution was drafted. In this ferment, Dalit youth in Bombay set out to organize revolution.

In spite of their proclamation of the goal of power in the manifesto, however, the Dalit Panthers did not really have a political strategy. Instead, they fought battles on two fronts and against two enemies: at the symbolic level, against Brahmanism; and at the concrete level, against the caste Hindu peasants and artisans who were directly responsible for numerous atrocities committed against *ati*-Shudras. Indeed, the 1970s were a decade in which the 'principal contradiction' seemed to be shifting, due to the development of agricultural capitalism and the coming forward of '*kulak*s' belonging to 'backward castes', to one between Dalit agricultural labourers/poor peasants and a middle-caste, non-Brahman rich peasant/landlord section. Most Left intellectuals at the time (which includes me) believed this to be the case, and stressed that the 'rich peasants' were becoming the main enemy, and that a 'non-Brahman movement' or movement of middle castes—as opposed to the Dalit movement—had exhausted its historically progressive role. The massive rioting that spread throughout Marathwada in 1978, when Maratha-*kunbi*s attacked and assaulted Dalits over the issue of renaming Marathwada University after Ambedkar clearly appeared to be a confirmation of the validity of such a view.

Statistics (and even village level experience) fail to show a real increase in differentiation; the growing numbers of agricultural labourers represented not a true proletariat but an 'immiserated' section, a large proportion of which was 'landless', thrown back on agriculture due to lack of employment opportunities elsewhere. The real growing differentiation appeared to be between agriculture and industry/services, and the unorganized and organized sectors (see Tables 16.1, 16.3 and 16.8). Yet, Left activists and intellectuals spoke about the tremendously increasing number of 'landless agricultural labourers', of 'rich peasants' (or even 'rich and middle peasants') as the rising rural ruling class, and of 'caste Hindus' as the enemies of Dalits. Thus, not only was the movement of peasants for higher crop prices attacked as being in the interest of '*kulak*s', but reservations for 'backward classes' were said to be nothing but a 'class' strategem of the same sections, of the 'rich and affluent OBCs' responsible for the principal atrocities on Dalits.

Table 16.1: Income of Organized and Unorganized Sector Workers, 1981

	Workforce (thousands)	Income (Rs crores*)	Average annual income per worker (Rs)
1. Wage and salary earners	965	43,121	4468
A. Organized sector	229	24,850	10,851
(Public)	155	16,495	10,643
(Private)	74	8354	11,289
B. Unorganized sector	736	18,271	2482
(Agricultural workers)	555	9454	1703
(Non-agricultural workers)	181	8817	4871
2. Self-employed	1260	24,719	3549
A. Cultivators	925	27,754	3000
B. Non-cultivators	335	16,971	5066

* 1 crore = 10 million

Source: Centre for Monitoring the Indian Economy, 1985, Table 10.1.

Table 16.2: National Income by Sectors of Industrial Orgin (Percentage Distribution)

	1950–1	1970–1	1984–5
Agriculture and allied activities	54.04	49.19	37.91
Manufacturing, construction, and mining	17.14	20.62	22.17
Tertiary activities (of which) defence and public administration	24.81	31.19	39.91

Source: Mitra, 1988, p. 4.

Table 16.3: Occupational Classification of Workers by Sector (Percentage Distribution)

	1901	1951	1961	1971	1981*
Agriculture and allied activities	71.7	72.1	71.8	72.2	68.8
Manufacturing, mining etc.	12.6	10.7	12.2	11.2	13.5
Tertiary: trade, commerce transport, other services	15.7	17.2	16.0	16.7	17.7

* excludes Assam

Source: Centre for Monitoring the Indian Economy, 1987, Table 9.1-B.

Table 16.4: Caste and Rural Class: Distribution of Caste-groups among Hindu Rural Households (Late 1950s)

	Scheduled Caste	Lower Caste	Middle Caste	Upper Caste	Total
Agriculture:					
Farmers	0.18	1.69	0.93	1.09	3.89
	(6.95)	(6.95)	(7.57)	(24.38)	(7.35)
Cultivators	3.19	10.20	6.52	1.96	21.87
	(27.05)	(41.79)	(53.30)	(43.91)	(41.35)
Sharecroppers	1.00	1.51	3.76	0.17	3.44
	(8.50)	(6.17)	(6.18)	(3.91)	(6.50)
Agricultural Labourers	4.27	4.11	1.46	0.05	9.89
	(36.19)	(16.85)	(11.91)	(1.09)	(18.70)
Forestry, fishing, livestock	0.28	0.81	0.17	0.02	1.28
	(2.38)	(3.31)	(1.39)	(0.62)	(2.42)
Others	2.87	6.09	2.39	1.17	12.52
	(24.34)	(24.93)	(19.65)	(26.09)	(23.47)
Total	11.79	24.41	12.23	4.46	52.89
	(100.0)	(100.0)	(100.0)	(100.0)	(100.0)

Note: Definitions:
farmers=those cultivating mainly with hired labourers;
cultivators=mainly cutivating owned or rented land, etc.;
upper castes=those who use sacred thread by custom;
middle castes=those from whom Brahmans take water by tradition;
lower castes=other castes who were not scheduled.

Source: P.C. Joshi, 1979, p. 363.

The effect of this analysis and the strategy that it implied was to throw the largest section of toiling people into the ranks of the class enemy and to propagate the notion that Dalit-*bahujan* unity would be impossible to achieve. One of the results of such a reading of the political horizon was to make it easier for Dalit leaders to justify their alliance with the Congress, which continually claimed to speak in the name of the 'rural poor'. Most Dalit Panther leaders have, in fact, taken this route sooner or later. But several aspects of the developing situation went unnoticed. Thus, many failed to realize that the success of Congress strategy in dividing Dalits and 'other backwards' was making unity difficult. The constant reiteration of propaganda to the effect that 'reservations' were for Dalits and that they were responsible for the unemployment and

Table 16.5: Changes in Size and Distribution of Operational Holdings

	Marginal (less than 1 ha)	Small (1 to<2 ha)	Semi-medium (2 to<4 ha)	Medium (4 to<10 ha)	Large (10 ha & above)	All
Number of holdings (in millions)						
1970–1	36.2	13.4	10.7	7.9	2.8	71.8
1980–1	50.1	16.1	12.4	8.1	2.2	88.9
1990–1	62.1	20.0	13.9	7.6	1.7	105.3
Operated area (in million hectares)						
1970–1	14.6	19.3	30.0	48.2	50.1	162.1
1980–1	19.7	23.2	24.6	48.5	37.7	163.8
1990–1	24.6	28.7	38.3	45.0	28.9	165.6
Average size of operational holdings (hectare)						
1970–1	0.40	1.44	2.81	6.08	18.1	2.28
1980–1	0.39	1.44	1.98	6.02	17.4	1.84
1990–1	0.40	1.44	2.76	5.90	17.3	1.57
Distribution of the holdings in size categories (per cent)						
1970–1	51.0	15.9	15.0	11.2	3.9	100
1980–1	56.4	18.1	14.0	9.1	2.4	100
1990–1	59.0	19.0	13.2	7.2	1.6	100
Distribution of operated areas in size categories (per cent)						
1970–1	9.0	11.9	18.5	29.7	30.9	100
1980–1	12.1	14.1	21.2	29.6	23.0	100
1990–1	14.9	17.3	23.2	27.2	17.4	100

Source: All India Agricultural Censuses, as cited by Nadkarni, 1996, A-69.

Table 16.6: Changes in Distribution of Owned Holdings

	Marginal (less than 1 ha)	Small (1 to<2 ha)	Semi-medium (2 to<4 ha)	Medium (4 to<10 ha)	Large (10 ha & above)	All
Percentage of holdings						
1960–1	60.06	15.16	12.86	9.07	2.85	100.00
1970–1	62.62	15.49	11.40	7.83	2.12	99.46
1981–2	66.64	14.70	10.78	6.45	1.42	99.99
1991–2	69.38	21.75	5.08	2.84	0.96	100.01
Percentage of area						
1960–1	7.59	12.40	20.54	31.23	28.24	100.00
1970–1	9.78	14.68	21.92	30.75	22.91	100.04
1981–2	12.22	16.49	23.38	29.83	18.07	99.99
1991–2	16.93	33.97	17.63	17.64	13.83	100.00

Source: NSS Reports cited in Rao and Hanumappa, 1999, A–135.

misery of other low-caste poor was effective. But precisely this situation was becoming transformed by the Mandal Commission proposals to extend reservations to various Shudra sections—proposals that provoked violent and widespread opposition from higher castes, including higher-caste intellectuals who continued to emphasize that the 'backwards' were the principal enemies of the Dalits.

Table 16.7: Agricultural Labourer Households as a Percentage of Rural Households

	1956–7	1964–5	1974–5	1977–8
Total	24.5	21.8	25.9	29.9
With land	12.2	9.6	12.8	14.5
Without land	12.3	12.2	13.2	15.3
Scheduled Castes				
With land		40.5*	40.3*	34.3*
Without land		40.7*	41.9*	39.1*
Scheduled Tribes				
With land		9.8*	10.4*	12.9*
Without land		9.3*	9.5*	12.2*

* Percentage of all agricultural labourer households in the category.

Sources: My rearrangement of tables contained in Government of India, 1954, 1965, 1975; Government of India 1978, 1978a.

The Mandal Commission, appointed in 1978 by the first opposition (Janata) government at the Centre, was in part a culmination of attempts of certain state (including a few Congress) governments, since 1971, to extend reservations to 'backward classes'. It was also, in part, an outgrowth of the tradition harking back to Ram Manohar Lohia's interventions in Indian politics, as well as an upsurge of Dalits and OBCs in north India. It is worth noting that the Commission also located the reservation issue in the context of power:

> In a democratic set-up every individual and community has a legitimate right and aspiration to participate in ruling this country. Any situation which results in a near-denial of this right to nearly 52 per cent of the country's population needs to be urgently rectified. [Government of India, 1980: vol. 1, p. 57]

The Marathwada riots were the last of their kind to range the middle castes and the Dalits against each other on a mass scale. The Gujarat reservation riots of 1981 and 1985 have sometimes been placed in the same category, but in fact they represent a different phenomenon. In Gujarat, Dalits were attacked not by the middle castes but by the upper castes, which blamed the former for the state government's proposals to extend reservations to the OBCs. While this seems ironical, it illustrates the degree to which reservations are seen as a Dalit issue (and in which ending reservations for Dalits remains the principal goal of any anti-reservation movement, despite disclaimers), whilst the Shudra castes for whom reservation is intended have been normally less aware of their implications than the Dalits.

Thus, in the first riots, the backward castes themselves apparently remained passive, but gradually OBC and Dalit organizations began to work together. In the second round of rioting, however, a significant change was observable. The OBCs attacked upper castes, although this was to some extent distorted by the fact that the police force which attacked the press and the upper-caste neighbourhoods was primarily composed of recruits drawn from the OBCs. Finally, the Dalit-OBC/upper caste conflict was given a communal twist with the engineering of Hindu-Muslim riots. The text and the subtext became inversions of each other. This was a clear indication of the shape of things to come at the start of the 1990s. After the events in Gujarat, the upper castes would never again dare to attack the Dalits and OBCs directly, but rather would push the ideology of 'Hindu unity' in order to maintain their power.

Kanshi Ram and the Dalit Movement in the 1980s

'We have a one-point programme—take power.' This statement, by the office secretary of the Bahujan Samaj Party (BSP), illustrates the principal thrust of the strongest Dalit organization to emerge in the 1980s. And, indeed, the BSP, under Kanshi Ram's leadership, was envisaged precisely as a party of Dalits and backwards and minorities, with Dalits playing a vanguard role; and from the outset, it has been projected as an organization based on practical politics and not on sentiment. Power was within its grasp precisely because the Dalits and Shudras together constituted a majority.

Table 16.8: Scheduled Caste and Scheduled Tribe Occupations, 1981

	Scheduled Caste Lakh*	%	Scheduled Tribe Lakh	%	Others Lakh	%	Total Lakh	%
1. Agricultural Sector (a+b)	289 (19.5)	(76.4)	192 (13.0)	(87.1)	999 (67.5)	(61.4)	1480 (100.0)	(66.5)
a. Cultivators	107 (11.6)	(28.2) (13.0)	120	(54.4) (75.4)	698	(42.9) (100.0)	925	(41.5)
b. Agricultural Labourers	182 (33.8)	(48.2)	72 (13.0)	(32.7)	301 (53.2)	(18.5)	555 (100.0)	(24.9)
2. Non-Agricultural Sector	89 (12.0)	(23.6)	8 (3.8)	(12.9)	628 (84.2)	(38.6)	745 (100.0)	(33.5)
Total (1+2)	378 (17.0)	(100)	220 (10.0)	(100)	1627 (73.0)	(100)	2225 (100.0)	(100)

* 1 lakh=100,000

Source: Centre for Monitoring the Indian Economy, 1985, Table 1.8c.

'We are 85 per cent—we don't need to make any alliances; we can rule on our own'. This statement echoes the view which Arun Kamble (one of the few of those who eventually joined the Janata Dal!) had propagated as a leader of the Dalit Panthers—namely, that 'Dalits and backwards and minorities together, we are 85 per cent. We are the majority. We don't want a separate Dalitisthan—India should become Dalitisthan'. But the BSP went further than other Dalit organizations of the time by projecting itself not as a 'Dalit' party but as a 'Bahujan' party, using the terminology of the non-Brahman movement of the 1920s in order to project itself as a party of Dalits and non-Brahmans—and minorities. And, with a solid base among north Indian *Chamars*, it also succeeded in attracting significant backing from OBCs and minority communities.

The 1980s was, in fact, the decade in which Dalit–Shudra unity gradually came to be constructed. The need for it was forcefully proclaimed not only by Kanshi Ram and Kamble, but also by Rajshekar of *Dalit Voice*, by Sharad Patil of the Satyashodhak Communist Party, by the Dalit Sangarsh Samiti (DSS) of Karnataka as it examined the issue of reservations and its relations to the Ryotu Sangh, asserting the need for the two movements to come together even though the latter was dominated by the 'main enemies of Dalits at the village level'. Rajshekhar put this strongly in one of his early booklets:

> Dalits are born Marxists. Because we have not understood the law of contradictions, we get confused and therefore come to the wrong conclusion.... As Dalits, we become the natural leaders of the Indian Revolution, and therefore it is our responsibility not to commit any mistakes.... We have to convince the OBCs that fighting Brahmanism is as much their duty as freeing themselves from Shudra slavery. The enemies of OBCs are not Dalits.... Similarly, every Dalit organization is pointing out that Dalits are victims of Brahmanism.... Hence, the contradiction between Dalits and OBCs is non-antagonistic. [Rajshekar 1989: 10–21]

Dalits, throughout this period, were in the process of articulating strategies of alliance; rather than simply fall in line behind the middle-caste Shudras, they wanted to pursue specific goals germane to their struggle. 'We support reservations for Jats', stated a Backward and Minority Classes Employees Federation (BAMCEF) activist of the anti-Kanshi Ram group, 'provided they stop acting like Thakurs'. Or, in Arun Kamble's terms, 'There should be a Kunbi-ization of Marathas.'[5] Or, as the DSS argued in relation to the Ryotu Sangh, they must stop being 'economistic'. Generally, such demands amount to urging the middle castes to de-Sanskritize themselves, as Guru (1991: 12) has pointed out in a paper on Phule and reservations:

> Mandal Commission might forge the unity of all the exploited non-Brahman castes as against those exploiting castes...this process, instead of consolidating the caste structure, would devour it from within. Moreover, the introduction of Mandal Commission would radically undermine the process of Sanskritization which had helped in maintaining the hierarchized structure like pure Marathas (*shannavkuli*) versus impure Marathas.... The whole development is making Phule's category of absorbing the 'local great tradition' representing so-called Maratha into 'little tradition' representing the vast Bahujan Samaj masses....

For some time, it was the BSP which was most successful in capturing the new anti-caste upsurge. A look at the 'discourse' of Kanshi Ram's principal slogans illustrates BSP's appeal: *brahman bania thakur chor/baki sab DS-4*[6] in fact contains a formulation of the alliance strategy, identifying the 'main enemy' and the 'allies'; *mat hamara raj tumara nahi chalega nahi chalega*[7] is a clear statement of the thrust to political power, while the more recent *vote se lenge PM/CM, arakshan se SP/DM*[8] illustrates the limited nature of the drive to power.

'Politics' in the end was the undoing of the BSP's success, as Kanshi Ram's support of Devi Lal and Chandra Shekhar lost him

5 This is almost what, in fact, happened with the Mandal Commission's classification. In Maharashtra, this includes 'Kunbis' but not 'Marathas'. Maratha opposition to reservations has, as a consequence, been effectively silenced. One of the significant reasons for the lack of anti-reservation riots in Maharashtra stems from this irony.

6 Meaning, colloquially, 'Brahmans, Banias and Thakurs are thieves, the rest are with us'. DS-4 refers to the Dalit Shoshit Samaj Sangarsh Samiti, (DSSSS), a front organization under Kanshi Ram's leadership, prior to the formation of the BSP.

7 Meaning, 'No longer "We vote—you rule".'

8 'We shall take the posts of PM and CM through the vote; we shall take the posts of DM and SP through reservation.'

PM=Prime Minister, CM=Chief Minister, SP=Superintendent of Police; DM=District Magistrate.

much of the prestige he had won earlier in the Dalit community. Though the BSP still remains a party to be reckoned with in UP and Haryana, in the rest of the country V.P. Singh emerged as the effective spokesperson of the Dalit and low-caste aspiration to power through reservations. The responses at a massive rally in Pune (28 November 1990) were significant:

> Dondiba, a backward-caste farmer from Sangli who had waited in the blazing sun for four hours to hear V.P. speak...angrily told this correspondent, 'For centuries we have been dehumanized and oppressed.... When V.P. Singh announced one little step in our favour it could not be tolerated by the Brahmanical parties which have never stood for the Dalits. V.P. Singh has sacrificed his gaddi for our sake, now we must stand by him'. 75 year old Savitribai of Pune was attending the meeting.... Why had she, despite failing vision, ill health and arthritis made it a point to come? Savitribai answered, 'I have come to see and hear V.P. Singh. He belongs to the same caste as me.... I am a Dalit and I consider V.P. Singh as a man of my caste because he has stood up for us, spoken of social justice for us'. [*Sunday Observer*, 2 December 1990]

The 1991 Threshold

A major transformation had taken place in Indian politics. Congress hegemony had apparently vanished for good—not in the sense of a major decline in the share of the popular vote, but in the sense that it could no longer parley a 30–45 per cent share of the popular vote into 60–70 per cent Lok Sabha seats, and also, in the sense that its ideology, derived from Nehru's time in power, stood thoroughly discredited. No longer could the Congress-I convincingly appear as the party of the toiling masses; at best, it could promote 'stability', the only alternative to Hindu fundamentalism; it was, more clearly than before, the party of the more secular bourgeoisie and Brahman-dominated bureaucracy.

And this happened in a context in which a Left–democratic political alliance focused on anti-caste issues and brought together the uncomfortable allies: Dalits and OBCs.[9] Yet the lack of a full programme remained a serious problem. The question of an

9 It has to be added that this alliance is also taking a regional-national form, with even the Janata Dal and the CPI(M) becoming almost de facto regional parties.

alternative socialist vision stood, and just as revolutionary communists for decades had been describing the parliamentary communists as 'reformists', so the peasants and other sections of labourers involved in the 'new social movements'—the women's movement, the farmers' movement, and the environmental struggles—had been to see the National Front/Left coalition as essentially representing yet another betrayal of their interests. This was a crisis for the movements: the crisis of how they would obtain political representation; and it was crisis for the democratic and left parties of winning a solid mass base.

In part it was specifically a crisis of the anti-caste movement which had been partly embodied in the NF/Left alliance—for this movement never took reservations as its sole goal; it always saw economic issues (land, wages, relief from exploitation by the bureaucracy, etc.) as central. Yet, from Phule to Ambedkar, there has been a history of uncertainty and ambiguity as to the root causes of exploitation and the path to overcome it. Ambedkar's argument for 'state socialism' (which assumed only private property as the root of exploitation, and overlooked the question made so poignant in the crisis of state–socialist societies today), as much as the Mandal Report's statement that 'exploitative relations of production' had to be dealt with even as it stressed only exploitation within agriculture and not within industry or between agriculture and industry—reflects these problems of analysis. These movements left out environmental issues, questions of the exploitation of peasant and women's subsistence labour, and indeed the entire question of 'alternative development' which was raised so strongly later on.

These issues will have to be dealt with. Until then, there can be no transformation of Indian politics; there will only be a prolonged impasse.

Dalits: The Path to Power (2000)[10]

In the 1990s, the drive towards Dalit political expression has continued, not only with the ongoing growth of the Bahujan Samaj Party (BSP), but also with the formation of new parties and political fronts. However, the hoped-for 'third front' alternative,

10 This section has been written in 2000, especially for this volume.

based on Left and anti-caste forces, has not emerged; instead in the face of a continuing decline of Congress, the BJP has become the strongest national political force and has proved able to establish a governing alliance of supporting parties, including some important regional and caste-based parties.

The BSP remains the largest Dalit-based party. With a share of 4.7 per cent of the national vote in 1998 and 4.2 per cent in 1999, it is now significantly ahead of the CPI (1.5%) and closing in on the CPM (5.4%). However it has not established itself as a national party; after a brief upsurge in the southern states of Andhra and Maharashtra in the early 1990s it lost this base when it compromised with the BJP in UP. It remains strongly based in the northern states of UP, Haryana, and Punjab, mainly upon the Chamars though with a significant appeal to lower OBCs and some Muslims. It can play the role of a spoiler and a bargainer; and has some ability to make a play for power in the large state of UP—but it is not a serious road to empowerment for Dalits in the rest of India.

Elsewhere, the Republican Party of India (RPI) continues to be the main political expression of the Buddhist-Mahars in Maharashtra, undergoing splits and 'unity efforts' and splits again, exercising some influence as a pressure group able to claim a share of seats and a role in ministries by bargaining with the Congress party. Other new parties have come up, most notably in Tamilnadu. After a long period of violence in the southern part of the state between the Dalit jati formerly known as Pallars (now calling themselves Devendra Kulam Vanniyars or DKVs) and the OBC Thevar community, the DKVs formed a party under their leader Dr Krishnasami, the Puthiya Thamizhagam (PT). More recently, in 1999, a militant 'Dalit Panther' movement based on the Paraiyas in the northern part of the state has also moved into electoral politics. Both tried a 'third front' alliance with the Tamil Manila Congress in the 1999 elections; this having failed, both are not tentatively discussing with the DMK which itself is now allied with the BJP.

Other political parties can be identified as expressions of OBC political assertion. The Pattali Makkal Katchi (PMK) in Tamilnadu led by Dr Ramdoss is founded basically on the farming community of Vanniyars, and also emerged after a militant and sometimes violent struggle. It is also allied with the DMK. In north India, in many ways both Mulayam Singh Yadav's Samajwadi Party (SP) and Laloo Prasad Yadav's Rashtriya Janata Dal (RJD) are parties based on Yadavs but with a broader appeal to other low-caste and minority communities, also expressing anti-caste sentiment and some ideology. Laloo's party emerged out of several splits within the Janata Dal, and in spite of the charges of corruption against him, it has maintained its strength among the frustrated voters of Bihar. In addition, some of the 'regional' parties have disproportionate bases among some specific castes, for instance, the Dravida Munnetra Khazagham (DMK) among Vanniyars, and the Telugu Desam Party (TDP) among Kammas in Andhra.

Though all these parties represent an expression of Dalit–Bahujan political aspiration, they have not led to a transformation of Indian politics. Some have become 'spoilers' and been able to exert important influence in alliances, but with the partial exception of the BSP in Uttar Pradesh, none has been in a dominant position. They have not exercised a transformative perspective on the alliances; rather theirs has been the politics of pressure groups.

For the general picture of Indian politics, the years 1990–1 did indeed prove to be a turning point but the path that was rather hopefully delineated ten years earlier in this article was not taken. An enduring alliance of the Left and the anti-caste movement was not formed. Instead, with the Left faltering, the Congress caught in doldrums, and the political forces based on Dalits and OBCs unable to come up with any all-around programme of their own, the BJP has moved into the vacuum. Today it is more securely in power than ever at the centre itself, having proved flexible enough to put some restraint on its RSS core and fashion a soft, flexible face as a 'party of governance'. The most contentious parts of its agenda, in particular the rebuilding of the 'Ram Mandir', the common civil code directed against the Muslims, and the resolve to take away the little autonomy Kashmir has, have been temporarily shelved in favour of a 'national agenda' which served as common ground to unite with it a whole array of regionally based parties. It has also fairly successfully sidelined the 'Swadeshi' RSS-based hard core to fashion a rather determined process of liberalization. This does not mean that its Hindu chauvinism has disappeared; vicious attacks on Christian missionaries and on Adivasi Christian converts, the takeover of political-scholarly bodies, rewriting of textbooks, and the continuing assault on the secular tradition in education all indicate this.

The other stark fact of Indian politics is the ongoing and apparently irrevocable decline of the Congress, with not even the fading glow of the dynasty able to save it. At the same time, the Left has failed to offer any real alternative and no 'third force' has been able to maintain itself, let alone grow. Part of the problem appears to be programmatic. The economic reforms initiated in 1991 by then Prime Minister P.V. Narasimha Rao provided a handy focus for any opposition; but there proved to be little difference between the opposition by the Left and that by the Hindutva forces—and especially the more hard-core RSS elements within it, which was the fountainhead of the swadeshi lobby. For many years the nation was treated to the spectacle of all the non-Congress forces coming together in opposition to 'globalization, liberalization, and privatization' when out of power, without much distinction between the 'Swadeshi' RSS and the Left in rhetoric, and when in power, turning around to implement even if in a half-hearted way various proposals of reforms. There seemed to be no independent ground from which the Left could find to oppose the elite-led reforms; in fact it found itself defending in practice each and every aspect of the 'Nehru model' which was coming under challenge. There was hardly even a recognition of the way the failures of this model had led to the crisis. In some ways, the 'fall of socialism' has seemed to fix the Left in a defensive and gloomy posture that foreclosed creativity.

Dalits may not mourn the decline of the Congress. Dalits and other sections of the anti-caste movement have continually argued that there is no fundamental difference between Nehruvian nationalism and the more openly Hindu parties. From their point of view—articulated by numerous anti-caste intellectuals throughout the nineteenth and twentieth centuries—the Congress' 'secular and socialist' version of elite nationalism had never really challenged the 'Hinduistic' modernization of an Aryan, Vedic-centred identity; rather it had offered a Gandhian version of an all-encompassing 'Hinduism' rather than a Savarkarite version. Bringing 'Hindus' and 'Muslims' together assumed a 'Hindu' identity encompassing Dalits and the former Shudras. Thus militant Dalits have refused to see any radical difference between 'hard Hindutva' and 'soft Hinduism'—or 'sacred Brahmans' versus 'socialist Brahmans' in the language of the polemicist Rajshekar. And thus also the Dalit-based parties have been ready to make alliances with or support or take the support of BJP as against the Congress or other parties.

This is perhaps only a temporary situation. Dalits and other 'low' castes have been taking their first steps towards political power. Though initially the fight may be defensive—to gain and hold political office, to resist atrocities, to maintain reservations—long-term empowerment is much more. It requires an ability to lead a cultural revolution, and to formulate and push a programme for economic change, for a sustainable and poor-oriented development. It implies the transformation of society. The great Dalit and Bahujan intellectual tradition, beginning the nineteenth century, from Phule, Iyothee Thass, Aiyappan, Acchutanand and many others and leading to Ambedkar and Periyar, embodied an all-around political, economic, and cultural perspective dedicated to this. Such a Dalit perspective has been slow to develop in post-independence India for many reasons. Part of the problem has been the slow development of mass education, one of the most important unachieved aspect of the anti-caste programme and continued upper-caste monopoly of communications and culture. In any case, the result is that the Dalit drive for political empowerment is still in its early stages, dependent for programme and political direction on mainstream parties.

References

Ambedkar, B.R. (1979–91), *B.R. Ambedkar: Writings and Speeches*, 7 vols. Edited by Vasant Moon (vol. 2 published in 1981; vol. 5 in 1989.) Bombay: Government of Maharashtra.

Centre for Monitoring the Indian Economy (CMIE) (1985), *Basic Statistics on the Indian Economy 1985, Volume 1: All India, 1985.* Bombay: CMIE.

——— (1987), *Basic Statistics on the Indian Economy 1987, Volume 1: All India, 1987.* Bombay: CMIE.

Dalit Panther (1973), *Manifesto* Translated (from Marathi) by G. Omvedt (n.d.). Bombay: Model Art Printing.

Government of India (1954), *Agricultural Labour Enquiry (1953–1954).* New Delhi: Ministry of Labour, GOI.

——— (1965), *Rural Labour Enquiry (1964–1965).* Ministry of Labour, GOI.

——— (1975), *Rural Labour Enquiry (1974–1975).* Ministry of Labour, GOI.

———— (1978), *Rural Labour Enquiry (1977–1978).* Chandigarh: Labour Bureau, Ministry of Labour, GOI.

———— (1978a), *Final Report on Indebtedness among Rural Labour Households.* Delhi: GOI.

———— (1980), *Report of the Backward Classes Commission (Mandal Commission Report) (7 vols in 2 parts).* New Delhi: Backward Classes Commission, GOI.

———— (1989), *Basic Statistics Relating to the Indian Economy, 1989.* New Delhi: Central Statistical Organization, GOI.

Guru, G. (1991), 'Mahatma Jotirao Phule and Reservations', Mimeograph, Centre for Social Studies Surat.

Irschick, E.F. (1970), *Politics and Social Conflict in South India: The Non-Brahmin Movement and Tamil Separatism.* Berkeley: Center for South and Southeast Asia Studies.

Janata (1930–46), A Marathi Weekly published by Dr B.R. Ambedkar partial set available in the Vasant Moon collection, Nagpur.

Joshi B. (1986), *Untouchable! Voices of the Dalit Liberation Movement.* London: Zed Press.

Joshi P.C. (1979), 'Perspectives on Poverty and Social Change: The Emergence of the Poor as a Class', *Economic and Political Weekly*, vol. 14, nos 7–8, February, pp. 355–6.

Juergensmeyer, M. (1982), *Religion and Social Vision: The Movement Against Untouchability in 20th Century Punjab.* Berkeley: University of California Press.

Mitra, A. (1988), 'Disproportionality and the Service Sector', *Social Scientist*, vol. 4, no. 179, 16 April, pp. 3–8.

O'Hanlon, R. (1985), *Caste, Conflict and Ideology: Mahatma Jotirao Phule and Low-Caste Social Protest in Nineteenth Century Western India.* Cambridge: Cambridge University Press.

Omvedt, G. (1976), *Cultural Revolt in a Colonial Society: The Non-Brahman Movement in Western India: 1910–1930.* Pune: Scientific Socialist Education Trust.

———— (1988), 'The New Peasant Movement in India', *Bulletin of Concerned Asian Scholars*, vol. 20, no. 2, April, pp. 14–23.

———— (1990), *Report on the History of Dalit Movement in Maharashtra, Andhra and Karnataka.* Indian Council of Social Science Research, Mimeograph, New Delhi.

———— (1994), *Dalits and the Democratic Revolution.* Delhi: Sage.

Patil, S. (1980 and 1990), *Dasa–Shudra Slavery*, 2 vols. Delhi: Allied Publishers.

Phule, J. (1986), *Samagrah Wangmay* (in Marathi). Bombay: Government of Maharashtra.

Rajshekar, V.T. (1989), *Dilemma of the Class and Caste in India.* Bangalore: Dalit Sahitya Academy.

Ram Kanshi (1987), *The Chamcha Age.* Delhi: n.p.

17

Hindu Nationalism and Democracy[+]

Christophe Jaffrelot

No wing of the Hindu nationalist movement, whether the militant youth of the Bajrang Dal or political parties like the Jana Sangh or its successor, the Bharatiya Janata Party (BJP), has ever been really attracted by the fascist, putschist strategy. The Rashtriya Swayamsewak Sangh (RSS) and its offshoots probably never promoted a *coup d'état* because they did not regard state power as the most important object of conquest—they preferred to work at the grassroots level with a long-term perspective.[1] They could have stayed out of the institutional framework or even the political domain, as many RSS leaders argued they should in the late 1940s to early 1950s. However, the Jana Sangh and the BJP, and before them the Hindu Mahasabha, have always played the game of electoral politics. The Jana Sangh distanced itself somewhat from the elections in the 1970s, when A.B. Vajpayee considered that it was 'becoming increasingly difficult to dislodge the Congress by the ballot-box since elections proved to be an unequal battle, since the Congress has money power'.[2] But this stand was not uncommon then—as the JP (Jayaprakash Narayan) movement was to testify—and, in any case, the Jana Sangh continued to contest elections.

+ Francine R. Frankel, Zoya Hasan, Rajeev Bhargava, Balveer Arora (eds), *Transforming India: Social and Political Dynamics of Democracy* (Delhi: Oxford University Press, 2000) chapter 13, pp. 353–78.

1 I have developed this point in the first chapter of my book, *The Hindu Nationalist Movement and Indian Politics, 1925–1990s* (New Delhi: Viking, 1996).

2 *The Hindu*, 16 September 1974.

Does this rejection of putschist strategies mean that Hindu nationalism fully adheres to democracy? This chapter proposes to give some answers to this question by analysing how the Sangh Parivar and the Hindu Mahasabha have approached this political system even before Independence, by studying the kind of democracy they tended to favour, and by highlighting the limits of their democratic credentials.

The Hindu Nationalist Ideology of Democracy

India, A Democracy from Time Immemorial

Even before Hindu nationalism crystallized in the inter-war period, Hindu revivalists were not averse to the notion of democracy. On the contrary, they argued that democracy was not alien to India. Aurobindo even claimed that democracy was born in India; it was merely returning via the British after a long journey. All that was needed was to free it from the foreign elements which were now affecting it.[3] This discourse naturally reflected a nationalist strategy: the British prided themselves on being democrats, and members of the Indian intelligentsia (and among them, Hindu revivalists) did not want to see their country lagging behind. The Hindu nationalists inherited this conception from the revivalists in the 1920s and 1930s.

As did many others,[4] the first Hindu nationalist ideologues emphasized the existence of a democratic precedent in India. This they generally situated in Buddhist institutions, the village, and the ancient 'republics'. Radha Kumud Mookerji, a professor of history at Lucknow University in the inter-war period, was one of the intellectuals of the Hindu Mahasabha who advocated such ideas.[5] In *Hindu Civilization*, the first edition of which came out in 1936, he explains that the monarchy of Vedic times was far from

3 Sri Aurobindo, *Collected Works*, vol. 1, 'Bande Mataram', (article dated 20 March 1908) (Pondichery: Shri Aurobindo Ashram Trust, 1970), pp. 767–9.

4 See, for instance, K.P. Jaiswal, *Hindu Polity: A Constitutional History of India in Hindu Times* (Calcutta: Butterworth, 1924); and even Beni Prasad, *The State in Ancient India* (Allahabad: The Indian Press, 1928), p. 170.

5 R.K. Mookerji belonged to the Bengal Hindu Sabha and was one of the opponents of the Communal Award in 1932. See J. Chatterji, *Bengal Divided: Hindu Communalism and Partition, 1932–1947* (Cambridge: Cambridge University Press, 1994), pp. 26–7.

absolute: 'Within the framework of autocracy, there were operative certain democratic elements, the significance of which should not be missed.'[6] For instance, Mookerji found that 'the *Atharvaveda* has several passages indicative of the people choosing their king'.[7] But the republics were naturally seen by the author as the main embodiments of democracy in ancient India:

> The growth of republics as a feature of Indian political evolution implied that of the necessary democratic procedure by which their working was regulated and governed. It is a remarkable testimony to the popular republican instincts and traditions of the times that democratic procedure was applied in every sphere of life, political, economic and even religious. The Pali texts furnish interesting information on the working of the Buddhist Samghas in strict and minute conformity with genuine democratic principles. The essence of democracy is government by decision based on discussion in public meetings or assemblies. The Pali texts describe the meetings of religious assemblies or Samghas in all their stages.[8]

Mookerji emphasizes the role of voting in the making of decisions within the Buddhist Samgha.[9] So-called democratic procedures typical of a *religious* body, the Buddhist community, were used to substantiate the claim that ancient India knew *political* democracy.

This kind of discourse was not confined to the Hindu Mahasabha. Hindu traditionalist Congressmen made assiduous use of it, as the 1946–50 Constituent Assembly debates testify. When the question of regime type arose in the Assembly, many of them declared that India could choose only democracy, because that is what she had always known (before she was conquered by 'foreigners'). To substantiate this claim, soon after the opening session of the Constituent Assembly, Purushottam Das Tandon, well known for his Hindu traditionalist leanings,[10] established a parallel between this Assembly and an illustrious Buddhist precedent:

6 R.K. Mookerji, *Hindu Civilization: From the Earliest Time up to the Establishment of the Maurya Empire* (Bombay: Bharatiya Vidya Bhavan, 1950), p. 99.

7 Ibid.

8 Ibid., p. 209.

9 Ibid., p. 214.

10 In the late 1940s, he was closely associated with Hindu nationalist leaders (such as Shyama Prasad Mookherjee), for his fight on behalf of Hindi and the refugees from East Bengal.

After centuries, such a meeting has once more been convened in our country. It recalls to our mind our glorious past when we were free and when assemblies were held at which the Pundits met to discuss important affairs of the country. It reminds us of the Assemblies of the age of Asoka (the third Emperor of the Maurya dynasty who lived and ruled till 232 BC).[11]

The assemblies presented here as the precursors of the Constituent Assembly were in no way political: the pundits evoked by Tandon were Brahmins versed in Sanskrit scriptures who could have debated questions of theology or ritual, but even for these purposes, they were not representatives of society. As far as the assemblies convened by Asoka are concerned, they also undoubtedly had a religious vocation: the Emperor, it seems, had indeed convened the third Buddhist Council and thus contributed to the building of the canon of the religion to which he had been converted.

Like many Congressmen, and especially Hindu traditionalists such as Tandon, Hindu nationalist ideologues were not hostile to democracy insofar as it appeared to be rooted in Indian soil and culture. To that extent, it was a prestigious feature adding to the country's glory.

An Anti-individualistic Conception of Democracy

Even though Hindu nationalists have generally praised democracy and appreciated its advent in India, they have tended to distinguish their conception of democracy from the Westminster model borrowed from Britain in the 1950 Constitution. This argument was made clear during the 1975 Emergency. At that time, the RSS and its affiliates projected themselves as being at the forefront of the fight against Indira Gandhi, but this claim needs to be qualified. First, the RSS fought less for democracy than for regaining a right to legal existence. (The then RSS chief, Balasaheb Deoras, proposed to Indira Gandhi that she accept its collaboration. The RSS launched its anti-Emergency agitation *after* she refused.[12]) Second, Hindu nationalists suggested that the democracy for which they fought was not necessarily that of the parliamentary system. For

11 *Constituent Assembly Debates* (New Delhi: Lok Sabha Secretariat, 1989), vol. 1, p. 65.

12 For more details, see C. Jaffrelot, *The Hindu Nationalist Movement*, op. cit., p. 273.

instance, D. Thengadi, who was one of the main RSS leaders underground, declared:

The Constituent Assembly imposed British-type institutions on the people. India too has had a democratic tradition, a tradition of thousands of years, and the temperament of the Indian people can be easily moulded accordingly. But the Indian democratic system has been different. Its nature is different from that of the British democratic system.[13]

Thengadi does not explain here what the differences are, but he is more explicit in other writings, borrowing heavily from the organicist worldview of his mentor, Golwalkar.

In Defence of Social Organicism

Golwalkar's favourite political arrangement combined territorial representation (election by constituencies) with functional representation, where each corporate body nominates delegates at the request of both its local branches and the central organization. This mechanism was described as merely giving concrete shape to what was already practised in ancient India, where each of the *varnas* chose its representative for its village council (*gram panchayat*) and thence to the royal council.[14] Golwalkar did not hesitate to demand, if necessary, a revision of the Constitution to put this plan into action.

This programme looks like an Indian variant of the corporatist state, since the group, not the individual, is regarded as the relevant unit; this group can be the family, the village, the varna, but also the 'industry'. Indeed, Thengadi, who was the founder of the Bharatiya Mazdoor Sangh in 1955, proposed a parallel system from the trade unionist point of view:

Bharatiya culture believes that the 'Nation', and not the 'class', is the basic unit of human society. Horizontal division of the world is a fiction. Vertical arrangement of it is a fact.... [In ancient India] like a family, the community had its life based upon mutual love and confidence, and consequently, its horizontal division could not even be dreamt of.

13 D.P. Thengadi, 'Lamp at the Threshold', preface to P.G. Sahasrabuddhe and M.C. Vajpayee, *The People versus Emergency: A Saga of Struggle* (New Delhi: Suruchi Prakashan, 1991), p. 45.

14 M.S. Golwalkar, *Bunch of Thoughts* (Bangalore: Jagrana Prakashan, 1966), pp. 37–8.

It was further realized that the various communities are but different limbs of the same organism, i.e., the Bharatiya Nation. The Bharatiya social order thus implied the industry-wise arrangement and not class-wise arrangement.[15]

Thengadi not only dealt with 'economic democracy', he also criticized the foreign inspiration of parliamentary democracy, in comparison with the Indian version of democracy, because 'Unlike the western form of democracy, which is more intellectual, the Indian alternative—the dharmic system—is based on human values.'[16] Thengadi even suggested constitutional reform because 'checks and balances provided by the Constitution and our legal systems can be effective only if they are supplemented by checks and balances in human, social mind as a result of appropriate *samskaras*[17] of dharma'.[18] Thengadi's discourse bears testimony to the latent hostility of Hindu nationalists towards a secular form of democracy, a political system separated from religious notions such as the most all-embracing one, dharma, which also underlies social organicism.

Thus, Hindu nationalist leaders disapprove of parliamentary democracy because it is alien to religious (*dharmic*) notions and does not fit into their non-individualistic view of society. Today, these conceptions are propagated not only by old-timers or more or less sidelined leaders such as Thengadi, but also by mainstream ideologues. In the BJP, K.N. Govindacharya, for instance, has adopted the same perspective in a recent assessment of India after fifty years of independence.

The Constitution is not the product of our soil; a minimum addition is required to make it more responsive. Consensus, instead of majority–minority concept, suits the country better. Occupational representation (participation of various social groups based on their occupation) in the system will deliver the goods. Such a system will be in conformity with our traditions and ethos....

15 *Organiser*, 24 October 1955, p. 6 and p. 12.

16 'Adhivakta Parishad wants checks and balances through Dharma in Constitution', *Organiser*, 5 January 1995.

17 Here, the notion of *samskaras* does not refer to 'rites of passage' but, as often in the RSS's discourse, to all the good influences which can be exerted on the formation of character (for more details, see C. Jaffrelot, *The Hindu Nationalist Movement*, op. cit., p. 48).

18 Ibid.

It is clear the system has to be rooted in our soil. Public and political education are essential ingredients for our evolution. M.K. Gandhi, Aurobindo Ghosh and M.N. Roy had reservations about the system right since its inception. There was skepticism about the efficacy of adopting the parliamentary system of democracy. Dr B.R. Ambedkar emphasized the need of having an Indian Union—a true reflection of our ethos—instead of federation. Jaya Prakash Narayan favoured party-less democracy. RSS founder M.S. Golwalkar considered 'unanimity' as the mode of elections, with an added component of functional representation as the best model of governance.

I feel Golwalkar's view is best suited for our society. In the process of evolution, the system is bound to tend towards this goal. As of now, I am not pessimistic about the survival of our system. We need improvement, not change in the system.[19]

Like his predecessors, Golwalkar and Thengadi, Govindacharya does not reject democracy, but shows a strong inclination for a reformed version of parliamentary democracy. Interestingly, he does not draw his inspiration from Golwalkar alone but also from Gandhian views. Indeed, this variant of the Hindu nationalist conception of democracy overlaps with ideas propagated by Gandhi and his disciples.

Does Hindu Nationalism Echo Gandhian Views?

It is well known that Gandhi's first and only book, *Hind Swaraj* (1908), is not only an indictment of western, modern materialistic civilization, but also of parliamentary democracy:

> The condition of England at present is pitiable. I pray to God that India may never be in that plight. That which you consider to be the Mother of Parliaments is like a sterile woman and prostitute. Both these are harsh terms, but exactly fit the case. That Parliament has not yet of its own accord done a single good thing, hence I have compared it to a sterile woman. The natural condition of that Parliament is such that, without outside pressure, it can do nothing. It is like a prostitute because it is under the control of ministers who change from time to time.[20]

Gandhi agrees with one of the main ideas of the opponents of parliamentary democracy, namely that deputies are too corrupt to

19 'Agenda', *The Pioneer*, 6 April 1997.

20 M.K. Gandhi, *Indian Home Rule* (Madras: Ganesh and Co., 1922), 5th edition, p. 26.

represent the voters, that they waste their time in useless debates, and that they stick to their parties' programme without thinking for themselves. The Mahatma, then, preferred the reign of 'a few good men'.[21] This stand reflected a strong distrust of the people who allegedly are not able to make up their minds; they live under the influence of the press and populist leaders.

In a book professing to be a reflection on 'democratic values', Vinoba Bhave opposed *raj-niti* (power politics) to *lok-niti* (democratic ethics). This view implied the dissolution of parties and the relinquishing of any electoral system aimed at reaching a consensus. Bhave's anti-individualism encompassed a germ of authoritarianism. He wrote that social harmony would reign if everyone fulfilled his or her duty in the social order: 'if every limb were to function smoothly, the whole body would function properly'.[22]

The main work of Jayaprakash Narayan (JP) (another Gandhian leader mentioned by Govindacharya), *A Plea for Reconstruction of Indian Polity*, is also an indictment of parliamentary democracy which, as he saw it, implied excessive centralization of power and systematically betrayed the wishes of the people. In parliamentary democracy, the electors are 'manipulated by powerful, centrally controlled parties, with the aid of high finance and diabolically clever methods and super media'.[23] In setting forth his political ideal, JP also claimed he drew upon models from ancient India, and particularly from the interpretation of these models provided by Aurobindo who, like Gandhi, was one of his sources of inspiration. Going back to the thesis of this author about a century later, JP maintained that the political order of ancient India was based 'on the system of the self-governing village community', which only British colonization was able to destroy.[24] Ancient India, therefore, held the key to 'an organically self-determining communal life', and for JP, the challenge at hand was just 'a question of an ancient country finding its lost soul again'.[25]

21 Ibid., p. 27.

22 Cited in D. Dalton, 'The Concept of Politics and Power in India's Ideological Tradition', in A. Jeyaratnam Wilson and Dennis Dalton (eds), *The States of South Asia: Problems of National Integration* (London: Hurst, 1982), p. 186.

23 Jayaprakash Narayan, *A Plea for Reconstruction of Indian Polity* (Kashi: Akhil Bharat Sarva Seva Sangh, 1959), p. 66.

24 Ibid., p. 22.

25 Ibid., p. 26.

Obviously, JP opposed parliamentary democracy because he wanted a democracy expressed through a truly decentralized system of governance. Gandhi's political ideal was already a network of independent villages, drawing its inspiration from the orientalist stereotype of the 'village republics':

My idea of Village Swaraj is that it is a complete republic, independent of its neighbours for its vital wants, and yet interdependent for many others in which dependence is a necessity.... The government of the village will be conducted by the Panchayat of five persons, annually elected by the adult villagers, male and female, possessing minimum prescribed qualifications. These will have all the authority and jurisdiction required. Since there will be no system of punishments in the accepted sense, this Panchayat will be the legislature, judiciary and executive combined to operate for its year of office.[26]

The RSS and its offshoots were also in favour of a decentralized state. As early as the 1950s, the Jana Sangh proposed in its election manifestos to divide the Indian territory into about one hundred large districts, or *janapadas*. These would be much smaller than the states and would, it was argued, promote village autonomy. In its 1954 election manifesto, the party committed itself to make the village councils, or *panchayats*, 'the foundation of administration', granting them an increase in financial resources and (re)establishing the so-called traditional rule that their members would be elected unanimously.[27] However, the Hindu nationalists' emphasis on the unity of Indian society led them to advocate a unitary rather than a federal state, a move which reflected their basic difference with the Gandhians, that is, their rejection of diversity. While the latter have always stressed pluralism, Hindu nationalists cannot accommodate the notion of a plural society.

The Limits of the Hindu Nationalists' Commitment to Democracy

Democracy, the Most Convenient Regime for a Majority

Hindu nationalists favoured democracy before Independence not

26 M.K. Gandhi, 'The Kingdom of Rama', in K. Satchidananda Murty (ed.), *Readings in Indian History, Politics and Philosophy* (London: George Allen and Unwin, 1967), p. 186.

27 'Manifesto-1954', in Bharatiya Jana Sangh, *Party Documents*, vol. 1 (New Delhi: BJS, 1973), p. 62.

only because of the prestige they could draw from the claim that India had been a democracy since its antiquity; they also espoused it as early as the 1930s because this regime relied on the notion of majority rule. Hindu nationalists were increasingly obsessed by demographic figures from the late nineteenth century onwards, when the first censuses showed a limited but steady erosion in the proportion of Hindus in the population of India. This sensitivity led them to overemphasize the fact that Hindus formed a majority in India, and that it was their nation for this reason. In addition, they could claim to be its first inhabitants. Democracy has suited them more than any other regime because it relies on the principle of 'one man, one vote'.

This first became clear in the speeches of Veer Savarkar after he took over as chief of the Hindu Mahasabha. In the presidential address he delivered at the 1937 session of the party he declared, 'Though we form an overwhelming majority in the land we do not want any privileges of our Hindudom'.[28] In fact, Savarkar did not want any privileges for any community *because* the Hindus were in a majority. From this perspective, he added:

> Let all citizens of Indian States be treated according to their individual worth, irrespective of their religious or racial percentage in the general population. Let their language and script be the national language and script of the Indian State which is understood by an overwhelming majority of the people, as happens in every other State in the world. Let no religious bias be allowed to tamper with that language and script. Let 'one man, one vote' be the general rule irrespective of caste, creed, race or religion.[29]

Savarkar was favourably inclined towards democratic principles, because they guarantee the domination of the 'overwhelming majority', that is, the Hindus—a logic which would enable Hindi to become the national language. The universalistic discourse of democracy was evidently hijacked in order to promote communal interests.[30] The Hindu Mahasabha leaders seem to have been deeply

28 *The Indian Annual Register*, vol. 1, 1938, p. 420.

29 Ibid.

30 Savarkar reiterated this stand in even more explicit terms in his 1938 presidential address: 'The Hindu Sannathanist Party aims to base the future Constitution of Hindusthan on the broad principle that all citizens should have equal rights and obligations irrespective of caste or creed, race or religion,

convinced that they could make their point through the use of universalistic values, so much so that the party's working committee decided to refer the Hindu–Muslim question to the League of Nations in 1940.[31]

This discourse heralded the present-day propaganda of the RSS and its offshoots in favour of the disbanding of the Minorities Commission. Even though this Commission was established by the Janata Party, of which the former Jana Sangh was a component, the Hindu nationalist movement quickly criticized it as an institution responsible for the 'division of the nation'. The BJP, the Jana Sangh's successor, proposed to replace it with a Human Rights Commission,[32] which would have enabled it once again to use the language of universalism for particularistic ends. The aim was to remove some of the protections granted to the minorities because of their vulnerability and, in effect, to assert the strength of the Hindu majority.

The BJP shaped the notion of 'minorityism' in the same perspective. The term was first used by L.K. Advani after he took over as BJP president in 1986. In January 1987, in an address to the BJP's National Council, he referred to the 'dangers of minorityism' in an obvious allusion to the Congress government's concern to protect certain interests of the Muslims, as exemplified in the Shah Bano controversy.[33] Advani had specifically condemned the Muslim Women's (Protection of Rights in Divorce) Bill on behalf of modern, universalistic values. Addressing the plenary session of the BJP as the party's incoming president, he stated in 1986 that in the Shah Bano affair some Muslim leaders had acted as 'obscurantists' and 'fanatics' because they disregarded the rights of their community's wives.[34]

---

provided they avow and owe an exclusive and devoted allegiance to the Hindusthani State.... No attitude can be more National, even in the territorial sense than this and it is an attitude in general which is expressed by the curt formula "one man, one vote",' *The Indian Annual Register*, vol. 2, 1939, p. 325.

31 *The Indian Annual Register*, vol. 1, 1940, p. 10.

32 See, for instance, the Party's election manifesto in 1996. Bharatiya Janata Party, *For a Strong and Prosperous India: Election Manifesto 1996* (New Delhi: 1996).

33 L.K. Advani, Presidential Address, 9th National Council Session, 2–4 January 1987, pp. 8–9.

34 L.K. Advani, Presidential Address, BJP Plenary Session, 9 May 1986, p. 465.

Hindu nationalism has thus become adept at promoting the interests of the majority community in the guise of universalistic values that are pillars of liberal democracy. In reality, Hindu nationalists appreciate the majority rule of democracy because it means that Hindus can never lose power, provided they vote *en bloc*, which is indeed their chief objective. As Sudipta Kaviraj has suggested, the main enemies of democracy in India are those who would like to merge democracy and 'majoritarianism', as if both things would mean the same. They do not oppose democracy openly; on the contrary, 'they are in fact the greatest supporters of majority rule. But they do not want democratic government to be a complex arrangement in which majority rule is counterbalanced by a system of secure enjoyment of minority rights'.[35]

This analysis can be applied to different categories, including the Other Backward Classes (OBCs) and the Hindi-speaking population, but, of course, it is especially relevant in the case of Hindu nationalism. Savarkar's reaction to the abolition of separate electorates by the Constituent Assembly is very significant in this respect. In May 1949, soon after Sardar Patel made this decision known, Savarkar sent him the following telegram:

> I heartily congratulate you and the Constituent Assembly on leading and adopting the resolutions doing away with separate electorates, reservations and weightages based on invidious racial or religious distinctions and on having thus vindicated the genuinely national character of our Bharateeya state.[36]

Savarkar did not reject a religion-based state to promote an individualistic civil space; he opposed separate electorates and reservations because they hindered his efforts to equate democracy and majoritarianism, that is the pursuance of 'a permanent unbeatable majority which would place [large groups] in power for ever'.[37] But in a true democracy, 'Large majorities are bearable only if there is a random element in them, if individuals and

35 S. Kaviraj, 'Democracy and Development in India', in A.K. Bagchi (ed.), *Democracy and Development* (London: Macmillan, 1994), p. 123

36 S.S. Savarkar and G.M. Joshi (eds), *Historic Statements: V.D. Savarkar* (Bombay: Popular Prakashan, 1967), p. 224.

37 S. Kaviraj, 'Democracy and Development in India', op. cit., p. 124.

groups are sometimes in the winning and sometimes in the losing group'.[38]

Thus, while the Hindu nationalists look at democracy as something that is not alien to India, and furthermore, as an element of its historical prestige, they have promoted a non-individualistic version of it, and they have been especially interested in this political system because it is a convenient way to establish the domination of the majority community.

The Sangh Parivar and Democratic Procedure

Since Independence, the RSS has not been able to claim to represent the people because it did not contest elections, but its democratic credentials have been affected by its desire to influence those in power. In his attempts to transform the RSS into a kind of adviser to the government, Golwalkar drew his inspiration from the classic connection between temporal power and spiritual authority:

> The political rulers were never the standard-bearers of our society. They were never taken as the props of our national life. Saints and sages who had risen above the mundane temptations of self and power and had dedicated themselves wholly for establishing a happy, virtuous and integrated state of society, were its constant torch-bearers. They represented the *dharmasatta* [religious authority]. The king was only an ardent follower of that higher moral authorty.[39]

Golwalkar was invoking the Hindu tradition of the king's guru (*raj guru*) and, because of the RSS's emulation of the values of renunciation—the *pracharaks* are known for their ascetic life-style—he proposed for his organization the traditional function of 'dharmic' counsellor to state power:

> We aspire to become the radiating centre of all the age-old cherished ideals of our society—just as the indescribable power which radiates through the sun. Then the political power which draws its life from that source of society, will have no other [goal but] to reflect the same radiance.[40]

Golwalkar's successor, Deoras, tried to play the role of the *raj guru* during the Janata phase when he met Morarji Desai, Charan Singh,

38 Ibid., p. 124.

39 M.S. Golwalkar, *Bunch of Thoughts*, op. cit., pp. 92–3.

40 Ibid., p. 103.

and Jayaprakash Narayan in order to influence power from outside. This activity, as noticed by D.R. Goyal, tended to turn the RSS into a 'supra party' and 'extra-constitutional authority'[41] that was incompatible with the logic of democracy, simply because this centre of power was not subject to the verdict of the polls.

The problem became even more acute after the BJP came to power in 1998. Even though the new prime minister, Atal Behari Vajpayee, was known for not being as close to the RSS as, for instance, Lal Krishna Advani, the then BJP president, he had been trained in this organization and still regarded it as his 'family'.[42] He praised the 'RSS ethos' in general and the way it 'change[d]...the collective mind'. While in power, the BJP enabled the RSS to exert a stronger influence over Indian politics. Sangh leaders regularly met the prime minister and key ministers such as Advani. In July 1998, two meetings were convened by RSS chief, Rajendra Singh, for interacting with the 180-odd BJP MPs. Vajpayee and Advani attended parts of this event. Such meetings had been organized previously, but this time the BJP MPs were the pillars of the ruling coalition.[43] More importantly, in Uttar Pradesh, Rajendra Singh was allowed to address a group of about fifty-five top bureaucrats, including the chief secretary and the director general of police, on 'how they could emerge as ideals before the public'.[44] The meeting took place in the presence of ministers of Kalyan Singh's government; bureaucrats could hardly miss Rajendra Singh's message since their political bosses were obviously supporting what he said.

The RSS and its offshoots have traditionally been apprehensive about elections, which they never really regarded as the legitimate procedure for filling posts of responsibility. The Jana Sangh and then the BJP have professed that they were more democratic than other parties. For one thing, they limited the number of terms of the party chief (as in the BJP today, where the term of the president can only be renewed once); for another, they held party elections often. Through these elections local committees designate state

41 D.R. Goyal, *Rashtriya Swayamsevak Sangh* (New Delhi: Radha Krishna Prakashan, 1978), p. 196.

42 Interview with A.B. Vajpayee, 'Sangh is My Soul', *Organiser*, May 1995, reprinted in *Communalism Combat*, February 1998, pp. 28–9.

43 *The Hindustan Times*, 21 July 1998.

44 Ibid., 27 July 1998.

units, which then nominate delegates to an all-India council, which in tun elects the party president. The Jana Sangh and the BJP have certainly held party elections more often than other parties, but in contrast with what has happened in the latter, there have been very few *contested* elections. Most of the time, there has been one candidate per post, because the very notion of contested elections is rejected as divisive.[45]

Inner democracy is not very evident in any other Indian political party or organization. During the 1920s, the Congress had been given a more representative All India Congress Committee (AICC) by Gandhi; even so, it suffered from the Mahatma's interference—as testified by the 'dismissal' of Subhas Chandra Bose in 1939. After independence, Nehru forced P. Tandon to resign and, more importantly, there were no party elections for the twenty years between 1972 and 1992. However, this was largely due to factionalism which was a form of pluralism that is rejected by the BJP today. When the BJP itself was affected by groupism and factionalism as a result of its coming to power in several states in the early 1990s, it preferred not to conduct party elections in several regional party branches, such as Madhya Pradesh.

The limited role of elections in the functioning of the Jana Sangh and the BJP is well in tune with what happens in their mother organization, the RSS. The latter was obliged to draft a constitution after its ban in the wake of Gandhi's assassination. This document required local branches of the RSS to elect provincial assemblies whose members would nominate the delegates to the Akhil Bharatiya Pratinidhi Sabha (ABPS—All India Delegate Assembly). This body was empowered to elect the general secretary, who in turn appointed the executive committee. In practice, there have never been more candidates than posts to be filled, and the general secretary has more or less been free to nominate, transfer, or even suspend the pracharaks. Similarly, the *Sarsanghchalak*, the RSS chief who embodies supreme authority, cannot be voted out. He remains at the helm until his death or until he resigns. He is not elected, but designated by his predecessor, as in 1940 and 1973, when Hedgewar and Golwalkar, respectively, designated their successors.

45 For more details, see C. Jaffrelot, *The Hindu Nationalist Movement*, op. cit., p. 149 ff.

The taste for personalizing power that is evident in the structure of the RSS and its offshoots partly explains the interest of the Hindu nationalists in the presidential system. Whereas members of a parliamentary cabinet are responsible to parliament, in the presidential system members of the executive are any persons chosen by the president, and are responsible to the president alone.

Parliamentary Democracy or Presidential System?

The BJP reaffirmed its faith in a presidential form of government in 1991, as a means to guarantee a stronger Centre.[46] Several of its top leaders elaborated on this point while assessing the achievements of India after fifty years of independence. A.B. Vajpayee went into this question more deeply than any other BJP leader. In the 13th Desraj Chowdhary Annual Memorial Lecture which he delivered on 11 November 1996, he declared that 'the *present* system of parliamentary democracy has failed to deliver the goods and that the time has come to introduce deep-going changes in our structure of governance'.[47] Among the 'ills of the present system of parliamentary democracy...fashioned after the British model nearly five decades ago',[48] Vajpayee highlighted the incapacity of parliament to satisfactorily exert its legislative function and to launch serious debates. As a remedy, he envisaged, first, the presidential system; or second, proportional representation (PR); or third, the strengthening of democracy within the political parties. While everybody will agree with the third proposal, the first two are debatable; they seem to be contradictory, since the presidential system is intended to concentrate the authority of the state, while the main asset of the electoral system known as PR lies in its capacity to represent different opinions.

46 *The Statesman* (Delhi), 16 January and 2 February 1991.

47 A.B. Vajpayee, 'Challenges to Democracy in India', *Organiser*, 24 November 1996, p. 4.

48 Vajpayee reiterated his attacks on the foreign origin of parliamentary democracy on several occasions. Delivering the M.S. Golwalkar Memorial Lecture organized by the Deendayal Research Institute on 22 February 1997, he considered that the low level of the socio-economic development in India resulted from 'the present system of parliamentary democracy, which we borrowed blindly from the British'. ('Vajpayee Advocates a Change in Our System of Governance', *Organiser*, 9 March 1997.

However, the strengthening of the president's role is obviously favoured by Vajpayee, and a subsequent interview suggests that this process would have authoritarian implications:

> It's 50 years since Independence and time we reviewed the functioning of our institutions. I have made a few suggestions. For example, I feel that where political parties are unable to form a government at the Centre, the President should carry on the administration with the help of advisers.[49]

Such a schema, which amounts to extending a kind of president's rule to the Centre, has clear anti-democratic consequences. First, the president would acquire significant prerogatives even though he would not be elected by the people, but by members of Parliament and of the legislative assemblies. Second, it would be very difficult to assess 'where political parties are unable to form a government'—the president could interpret the situation according to his personal inclinations. Third, the president would be free to choose his advisers, and not necessarily from among elected politicians whose legitimacy derives from universal suffrage. Vajpayee's formula reflects a certain fascination for strong, personalized power, which is well in tune with the middle-class craving for the replacement of politicians by bureaucrats and technicians.

After the 1998 elections, the BJP and its coalition partners evolved a National Agenda for Governance, in which one of the items read: 'We will appoint a Commission to review the Constitution of India in light of the experience of the past 50 years and to make suitable recommendations.'[50] In April 1998, L.K. Advani, the home minister, virtually spelt out the terms of reference of such a commission: whether the political system needed to be decentralized, whether to continue with the parliamentary system, and whether the electoral system needed to be reformed.[51] A few days later, during the BJP National Council session, he explained that the proposed commission would go into the 'merits and demerits' of the parliamentary system and the

49 *India Today*, 15 May 1997.

50 Digvijay Singh, the chief minister of Madhya Pradesh, for instance, recently advocated a presidential form of government (*National Mail*, 21 October 1996).

51 'National Agenda for Governance', *Organiser—Varsha Pratipada Special*, 29 March 1998, p. 29.

presidential system to make recommendations, but he pointed out that parliamentary democracy was not among the basic features of the Constitution which could not be changed.[52]

The presidential system is not necessarily opposed to democracy, even though it reflects an inclination towards concentration (even personalization) of power. In fact, the growing attention that is paid to this system is not limited to the Hindu nationalist milieu. Several Congressmen, for instance, have been toying with this idea for some time,[53] and it is even referred to by many politicians who are concerned with the need to reform the state. Yet, the form that presidentialization of the regime would take under the auspices of the BJP appears to be more threatening than it would under other parties, because of the BJP's ideological background and the way in which the RSS and its offshoots function.

The Sangh Parivar: Stronghold of Social Status Quo?

The BJP: Still the Party of an Elite

One of the major changes on the Indian political scene since the late 1980s has been the rise of the OBCs and the *dalits.* The share of the former among the MPs of the Hindi belt—where the BJP won most of its seats and where social change was much slower than in the South—has increased from less than 5 per cent in the 1950s to about 25 per cent in the 1990s. For the first time, the Lok Sabha harbours a large proportion of agriculturists (many of them from the lower castes), whereas it used to be a stronghold for lawyers and other professionals. In many respects, this trend represents a democratization of Indian democracy. However, the BJP, until recently, did not participate in this process.

Classifying Lok Sabha members according to their profession is difficult because of the large number of those who declare agriculture as their profession, even though they may have some land but do not cultivate it themselves. In Table 17.1 which analyses Uttar Pradesh, Bihar, Madhya Pradesh, Rajasthan,

52 *The Hindu,* 27 April 1998.
53 Ibid., 5 May 1998.

Table 17.1: Occupational Distribution of Hindi-belt MPs of the Three Main Parties

Occupation	1989 BJP	1989 Cong	1989 JD	1991 BJP	1991 Cong	1991 JD	1996 BJP	1996 Cong	1996 JD
1	2	3	4	5	6	7	8	9	10
Agriculturalist	14	13	34	16	23	19	35	10	10
	21.8%	37.1%	32.3%	18.6%	38%	35.8%	28.8%	29%	40%
Lawyer	15	5	20	9	12	8	18	6	1
	23.4%	14.2%	19%	10.4%	20%	15%	14.8%	17.6%	4%
Trader	5	2	3	12	3	1	19	2	1
	7.8%	5.7%	2.8%	13.9%	5%	1.8%	15.7%	5.8%	4%
Industrialist	2	0	0	6	0	1	5	0	0
	3.1%			6.9%		1.8%	4.1%		
Ex-civil servant	2	0	0	2	0	0	4	0	0
	3.1%			2.3%			3.3%		
Ex-army	1	0	1	5	2	1	4	1	1
	1.5%		0.9%	5.8%	3.3%	1.8%	3.3%	2.9%	4%
Policeman/Pilot	1	1	0	0	1	0	0	1	0
	1.5%	2.8%			1.6%			2.9%	
Journalist	2	0	6	1	1	2	1	1	0
	3.1%		5.7%	1.1%	1.6%	3.7%	0.8%	2.9%	
Writer & artist	0	0	2	1	0	0	2	2	3
			1.9%	1.1%			1.6%	5.8%	12%
Teacher	5	3	9	5	5	6	9	2	3
	7.8%	8.6%	8.6%	5.8%	8.3%	11.3%	7.4%	5.8%	12%

(Contd.)

(contd.)

1	2	3	4	5	6	7	8	9	10
Doctor	4 6.25%	0	2 1.9%	6 6.9%	0	0	7 5.7%	1 2.9%	0
Engineer	0	0	2 1.9%	1 1.1%	0	3 5.6%	0	2 5.8%	3 12%
Trade unionist	0	2 5.7%	1 0.9%	0	0	2 3.7%	0	0	1 4%
Social worker	4 6.25%	2 5.7%	3 2.8%	6 6.9%	0	3 5.6%	10 8.2%	2 5.8%	2 8%
Political worker	5 7.8%	5 14.2%	19 18%	3 3.4%	10 11.6%	5 9.4%	1 0.8%	1 8%	0
Former ruler	2 3.1%	1 2.8%	0	2 2.3%	1 1.2%	0	2 1.6%	2 5.8%	0
Religious figure	2 3.1%	0	2 1.9%	8 9.3%	0	1 1.8%	3 2.4%	0	0
Sportsman	0	0	0	2 2.3%	2 3.3%	1 1.8%	0	0	0
Other, not known	–	1 2.8%	1 0.9%	1 1.1%	0	0	1 0.8%	1 2.9%	0
Total	64 100%	35 100%	105 100%	86 100%	60 100%	53 100%	121 100%	34 100%	25 100%

Source: All India Agricultural Censuses, as cited by Nadkarni, 1996, A-69.

Haryana, Himachal Pradesh, Chandigarh, and Delhi, the MPs who, in *Who's Who in Lok Sabha*, have given agriculture as their profession but hold an LLB, have been classified as lawyers. Nonetheless, the 'agriculturalists' category remains very heterogeneous, since it encompasses landlords as well as tenants. In spite of these caveats, it is noteworthy that the share of the agriculturalists among the BJP MPs has tended to increase, while that of the lawyers has been on the decline. However, the group composed of traders and industrialists represents about one-fourth the total number of BJP MPs in the 1990s—compared to less than 4 per cent for the Janata Dal and 6 per cent for Congress—a clear indication that in parliament the BJP still represents the business community to a greater extent than do other parties.

The proportional over-representation of upper-caste MPs among the BJP members elected from the Hindu belt and Gujarat, where the party won most of its seats, was evident from 1989 (see Table 17.2). Their percentage declined in the 1996 election, but remains prominent and much more important than in the Congress and the Janata Dal (see Table 17.3). Interestingly, in 1996 the erosion of the upper castes' share benefits the MPs from the Scheduled Castes (SCs), who are largely elected by non-SC voters, as much as those from the OBCs. In fact, very few Dalits vote for the BJP, as testified by the exit poll made by the Centre for the Study of Developing Societies in 1996. This poll also shows that the upper castes are still over-represented among the BJP electorate, while the Scheduled Tribes are significantly under-represented. The OBCs are also under-represented, but to a lesser extent.

The forward castes' votes polarize in favour of the BJP in Maharashtra, Uttar Pradesh, and Bihar, where respectively 50, 64, and 67 per cent of the upper castes preferred this party. The BJP also remains a predominantly urban party. Thirty-two per cent of the urban dwellers voted for it, as against 19 per cent of the people living in rural constituencies. As for the upper-caste graduates living in towns and cities, 52 per cent of this category opted for the BJP in 1996.

The Upper-caste Middle Class and the BJP

The upper-caste middle class has always been over-represented within the Hindu nationalist movement, to such an extent that the

Table 17.2: Caste and Community Background of the Hindi-belt and Gujarat MPs (Party-wise) (in per cent)

Castes and Communities	BJP 1989	Cong 1989	JD 1989	BJP 1991	Cong 1991	JD 1991	BJP 1996	Cong 1996	JD 1996	BJP 1998	Cong 1998	JD +SP +RJD 1998
1	2	3	4	5	6	7	8	9	10	11	12	13
Upper castes	46.67	34.21	28.45	51.40	27.69	16.99	42.75	27.27	14.28	43.26	22.22	15.22
Brahmin	17.33	15.79	6.90	24.30	10.77	1.89	19.57	15.91	4.76	18.44	6.67	–
Rajput	16.0	7.89	14.66	17.76	6.15	13.21	13.77	4.55	7.14	12.77	2.22	15.22
Bhumihar	–	2.63	1.72	–	3.08	1.89	1.45	–	–	1.42	2.22	–
Baniya/Jain	6.67	5.26	1.72	3.74	3.08	–	5.07	4.55	–	4.96	6.67	–
Kayasth	2.67	–	2.59	1.87	3.08	–	2.17	–	2.38	2.13	2.22	–
Other*	4.0	2.63	0.86	3.74	1.54	–	0.72	2.27	–	2.13	2.22	–
Intermediate castes	8.0	7.89	15.52	9.35	13.85	1.89	7.97	20.45	–	8.51	22.22	–
Jat	–	2.63	11.21	2.80	10.77	1.89	4.35	13.64	–	4.26	11.11	–
Maratha	1.33	2.63	–	0.93	1.54	–	0.72	2.27	–	0.71	2.22	–
Patidar	6.67	–	4.31	5.61	1.54	–	2.90	4.55	–	3.55	4.44	–
Bishnoi	–	2.63	–	–	–	–	–	–	–	–	4.44	–

(Contd.)

(contd.)

1	2	3	4	5	6	7	8	9	10	11	12	13
OBC	16.0	5.26	26.72	14.02	13.85	39.62	18.1	11.36	54.76	17.02	8.89	50.0
Yadav	1.33	–	14.66	–	1.54	22.64	1.45	–	33.33	1.42	2.22	21.74
Kurmi	5.33	5.26	4.31	7.48	4.62	9.43	5.80	–	4.76	7.09	–	10.87
Lodhi	2.67	–	0.86	2.80	–	–	2.90	–	–	2.13	–	–
Other	6.67	–	6.90	3.74	7.69	7.55	7.97	11.36	16.67	4.26	6.67	17.39
SC	16.0	18.42	18.10	16.82	15.38	24.53	21.01	11.36	14.29	15.60	11.11	17.39
ST	9.33	23.68	3.45	4.67	21.54	–	7.97	22.73	–	6.38	26.67	–
Muslim	1.33	5.26	6.9	–	4.62	13.2	–	4.55	14.29	0.71	4.44	13.04
Sikh	1.33	–	–	0.93	–	–	0.72	–	–	0.71	–	–
Christian	–	2.63	–	–	–	1.89	–	–	2.38	–	–	2.17
Sadhu	–	–	–	1.87	–	–	–	–	–	–	–	–
Unidentified	1.33	2.63	0.86	0.93	3.08	1.89	1.45	2.27	–	7.80	4.44	2.17
Total	100 N=75	100 N=38	100 N=166	100 N=107	100 N=65	100 N=53	100 N=138	100 N=44	100 N=42	100 N=141	100 N=45	100 N=46

*Khattri, Amil, Tyagi.

Table 17.3: Caste Background of the Parties' Electorates

	Cong(I)	*BJP*	*NF/LF*	*BSP*	*State Parties*	*Others*
Forward	29	33	17	1	10	10
OBC	25	23	25	2	18	7
SC	31	11	21	16	14	7
ST	47	17	15	2	7	12

Source: *India Today*, 31 May 1996, p. 27.

Jana Sangh was known as a 'Brahmin-baniya' party. The Sangh Parivar held some attraction for these milieus for two main reasons. One was its sanskritized style and defence of social hierarchy; the other was its economic liberalism and defence of the 'middle world', a world, according to Bruce Graham, composed of 'the provincial professions, small industry, and country trading and banking'.[54] The affinity between Hindu nationalism and these categories was particularly noticeable in the towns of the Hindi belt. Since the late 1980s, however, the BJP has benefited from the growth of a new middle class that has emerged largely as a result of economic liberalization. The system of values of this rising social category is based, in theory at least, on merit gained through hard work. Its members thus show little concern for the poor[55] and disapprove of reservation systems in principle. These views overlap with those of the BJP. The party advocates a more vigorous liberalization of the domestic economy. It also expresses apprehensions about caste-based reservations, though publicly it has to moderate its stand so as not to alienate the OBC voters. In fact, the Mandal affair was probably as important as the Ayodhya movement in rallying upper-caste middle-class support around the BJP in the early 1990s.

This middle class not only shares the BJP's concern about the rise of new groups (the OBCs and the dalits)—that is, its apprehension regarding the social dimension of democracy—they also have in common with it a growing questioning of parliamentary

54 B. Graham, *Hindu Nationalism and Indian Politics* (Cambridge: Cambridge University Press, 1990), p. 158.

55 See R. Kothari, 'Class and Communalism in India', *Economic and Political Weekly*, 3 December 1988.

government. In 1993, an opinion poll conducted in Bombay, Delhi, Calcutta, Madras, and Bangalore revealed that 58 per cent of interviewees agreed with the following proposition: 'If the country is to progress, it needs a dictator.'[56] The anti-parliament attitude underlying this stand reflects the opprobrium affecting politicians. The survey conducted by the Centre for the Study of Developing Societies during the 1996 elections showed that only 22 per cent of the interviewees thought that their MP cared for the people (as against 27 per cent in 1971).[57] The authoritarian option, however, seems to be considered by the urban middle class alone. Among the interviewees of the 1993 survey, 68 per cent declared that they belonged to the 'middle class' (as against 8 per cent to the 'lower-middle class', 9 per cent to the 'upper-middle class', and 10 per cent to the working class'). Indeed, the masses continue to regard the act of voting as useful, as testified by the fact that ordinary people vote more than the elite groups.[58]

The urban middle class obviously aspires to a more orderly day-to-day life and a kind of discipline that is regarded as a precondition for economic progress. This is one of the reasons for the attraction the BJP holds for this group, since it is known for its RSS background. The urban middle class also approves of the BJP's crusade against corruption, a theme that it has cashed in on despite allegations that some of its leaders had been involved in corruption. The common assumption is that parliamentary democracy not only needs to be disciplined; it also needs to be purified.

Conclusion

Historically, the Hindu nationalists have supported democracy largely because, in contrast to today's advocates of 'Asian values' in South East and East Asia, for whom democracy is an import from the West, they have regarded it as a *national* regime. According to them, India was always a democracy—before foreign

56 *The Times of India*, 28 December 1993, pp. 1 and 11.

57 *India Today*, 31 August 1996, p. 31.

58 Among those who voted more, one finds the 'very poor' people (+2.9 points above the average turnout), the Scheduled Castes (+1.9 point), and the villagers (+1.1. point). Among those whose turnout is below the average, one finds the upper castes (–1.6 point), urban dwellers (–3 points), and graduates and post-graduates (–4.5 points) (Ibid., pp. 30–9).

invasions—and to say so was a good means for regaining one's self-esteem in front of the British. This 'traditional' democracy, however, does not meet the criteria of parliamentary or liberal democracy, since Hindu nationalists have tended to be favourably inclined towards an organicist arrangement. This approach is not fundamentally different from the Gandhian view of democracy.

The democratic credentials of Hindu nationalists can be questioned for other reasons. First, they supported democracy as the most convenient regime for establishing a permanent Hindu domination, since Hindus were a majority. Second, the RSS has been keen to exert some influence on the political domain even though it has not contested elections itself. Third, even though the BJP holds internal elections more often than most other organizations and parties, the RSS and its offshoots are not ruled by democratic procedures, since there is often only one candidate for one post and the personalization of power, as well as the repression of any dissent, are commonplace. Today, these authoritarian leanings find expression in a more or less openly declared interest in a presidential system of governance.

The fourth factor affecting the credibility of the Hindu nationalist commitment to democracy lies in its sociological composition: the movement is still identified with the upper castes, since a large number of its leaders, militants, and voters belong to this milieu. Though the BJP is gradually promoting low-caste cadres within the party apparatus, it still does not contribute to the present-day (social) democratization of Indian (political) democracy.

Annotated Bibliography

Democratic Theory

The theoretical literature on democracy is vast and varied. Anthony Arblaster's *Democracy* (Milton Keynes: Open University Press, 1987) is a good introduction to the historical development, and the fundamental ideas, of democracy. Russell A. Hanson's essay 'Democracy' in Terence Ball, James Farr and Russell A. Hanson (eds), *Political Innovation and Conceptual Change* (Cambridge: Cambridge University Press, 1989) provides a nuanced historical argument on democracy, focusing on America where, he argues, the popularization of democracy contributed to the degradation of its meaning. More complex theoretical issues relating to democracy are discussed in a series of papers in David Copp, Jean Hampton and John E. Roemer (eds), *The Idea of Democracy* (Cambridge: Cambridge University Press, 1993), while a variety of theoretical disputes—such as feminism, direct democracy, and cultural particularity—are addressed in David Held (ed.), *Prospects for Democracy: North, South, East, West* (Cambridge: Polity Press, 1993). David Held's own *Models* of *Democracy* (Cambridge: Polity Press, 1987) provides a useful classification of types of democracy. Philip Green (ed.), *Democracy* (in the Key Concepts in Critical Theory series, New Jersey: Humanities Press, 1993) is a collection of readings on many aspects of democracy, presenting a selection of the best writings not only from the classics of political philosophy, but also from contemporary theorists. Helena Catt, *Democracy in Practice* (London: Routledge, 1999) provides a comprehensive discussion of the institutional aspects of democracy, which is sensitive to the diversity of democratic practice. Problems of measuring democracy are discussed in a collection of essays, David Beetham (ed.), *Defining and Measuring Democracy* (London: Sage Publications, 1994), and in Axel Hadenius, *Democracy and*

Development (Cambridge: Cambridge University Press, 1992). Probably the most interesting contemporary discussion of the political and intellectual challenges to democracy in Eastern Europe and the nations of the South is Adam Przeworski with Pranab Bardhan, *et al.*, *Sustainable Democracy* (Cambridge: Cambridge University Press, 1995). Desmond King and Gerry Stoker (eds), *Rethinking Local Democracy* (London: Macmillan, 1996) has several essays on the normative aspects of local democracy, including the attraction of the local for feminists and environmentalists.

The literature on democratization is quite large, but a sensible introduction which provides a historical account as well as a comparative survey of the present is David Potter, David Goldblatt, Margaret Kiloh and Paul Lewis (eds), *Democratization* (Cambridge: Polity Press, in association with The Open University, 1997). Geraint Parry and Michael Moran (eds), *Democracy and Democratization* (London: Routledge, 1994) has some theoretical essays, as well as a few case-studies. At least two journals, the *Journal of Democracy* (from the Johns Hopkins University Press, USA) and *Democratization* (from Frank Cass, UK) are exclusively devoted to the discussion of questions of democracy.

Indian Democracy Prefigured

Apart from the article by James Chiriyankandath, which is reproduced in this volume as chapter 1, there are a handful of readings which provide a glimpse of the evolution of democratic ideas and institutions in India. Granville Austin's *The Indian Constitution: Cornerstone of a Nation* (Delhi: Oxford University Press, first published in 1966, and reprinted in 1999) is indispensable for an account of discussions in the Constituent Assembly. Tapan Raychaudhuri's 'Constitutionalism and the Nationalist Discourse: The Indian Experience', in Douglas Greenberg, Stanley N. Katz, M.B. Oliviero and S.C. Wheatley (eds), *Constitutionalism and Democracy: Transitions in the Contemporary World* (New York: Oxford University Press, 1993) discusses the troubled relationship between Indian nationalism and constitutionalism. Farzana Shaikh's book *Community and Consensus in Islam: Muslim Representation in Colonial India, 1860–1947* (Bombay: Orient Longman, 1991) is a fascinating historical discussion of the Muslim response to liberal ideas of representative democracy. A shorter version is available in her article 'Muslims and Political Representation in Colonial India: The Making of Pakistan', *Modern Asian Studies,* vol. 20, no. 3, 1986, more recently reprinted in Mushirul Hasan (ed.), *India's Partition: Process, Strategy and Mobilisation* (Delhi: Oxford University Press, 1993).

Two essays which look at Indian democracy both before and after 1947 are Sunil Khilnani's 'India's Democratic Career' in John Dunn (ed.), *Democracy: The Unfinished Journey* (Oxford: Oxford University Press, 1992), which accounts for the emergence and survival of representative democracy in India, and Ravinder Kumar's 'The Historical Roots of Democracy in India' in his *The Making of a Nation: Essays in Indian History and Politics* (Delhi: Manohar Publications, 1989), which locates the strength of India's democratic polity in the historical tradition of 'popular' participation in politics as also the character of the struggle for freedom. The best and perhaps only article to examine Indian democracy in the first phase after independence is James Manor's 'How and Why Liberal and Representative Politics Emerged in India', published in *Political Studies* (vol. 38, 1990, pp. 20–38). In *The Short Oxford History of the World* series, Judith Brown's *Modern India: The Origins of an Asian Democracy* (Delhi: Oxford University Press, 1984) is a survey of two centuries of Indian history, with an epilogue mapping, in broad brush-strokes, the successes and failures of Indian democracy, especially the economic and social forces that have prevented the democratic political system from responding creatively to some of the country's major problems.

Democracy and the State

The earliest writings on Indian democracy were embedded in the institutional studies of government and politics, in which context democracy essentially connoted the party system, party politics, and elections. Norman D. Palmer's *The Indian Political System* (London: George Allen and Unwin Ltd., 1961) is a general overview of this type. Hugh Tinker's *India and Pakistan: A Short Political Guide* (London: Pall Mall Press, 1962) is similar, except that it has a chapter on local democracy, arguing the importance of the Gram Panchayats. Possibly the most perceptive work in this genre was W.H. Morris-Jones's *The Government and Politics of India* (London: Hutchinson University Library, 1971, 3rd edition), which noted the role of the dominant Congress Party in undermining the federal structure of government, and diminishing both parliamentary independence as well as the institutionalization of the party system.

The best introduction to various dimensions of the subject is Atul Kohli (ed.), *India's Democracy: An Analysis of Changing State–Society Relations* (Delhi: Orient Longman, 1991). Among the most useful contemporary overviews of Indian politics is Paul Brass, 'The Politics of India since Independence', vol. IV.1, in *The New Cambridge History of India* (Delhi: Foundation Books, 1992), though his explanation for India's crisis depends a trifle too heavily on an argument about the centralizing tendencies of the political leadership. Brass's rejection of structural factors is challenged by the argument of Achin Vanaik's *The Painful Transition: India's Bourgeois Democracy* (London: Verso, 1990), which is also the best Marxist analysis of Indian democracy. More recently, Ayesha Jalal's *Democracy and Authoritarianism in South Asia* (Cambridge: University Press, 1995) seeks to examine why a common colonial legacy has resulted in different patterns of political development in India, Pakistan, and Bangladesh. She argues the case for seeing democracy and authoritarianism, not as neatly opposed categories, but as processes which co-exist with, and inform, each other.

The sociology of India's democratic structures is discussed by Satish Saberwal in his essay 'Democratic Political Structures', in T.V. Sathyamurthy (ed.), *State and Nation in the Context of Social Change,* which is the first in the four volume series on *Social Change and Political Discourse in India: Structures of Power, Movements of Resistance* (Delhi: Oxford University Press, 1994). The relationship of India's democratic structures with society was also the subject of much scholarly writing in the 1970s. Lloyd I. Rudolph and Susanne Hoeber Rudolph, *The Modernity of Tradition* (Chicago: University of Chicago Press, 1967) and Rajni Kothari (ed.), *Caste in Indian Politics* (Delhi: Orient Longman, 1970) are the best examples of this genre. Kothari's *Politics in India* (Delhi: Orient Longman, 1970), adopting the then influential structural–functional mode of analysis, also interpreted the process of modernization in India in terms of the politicization of a fragmented social structure. Harold A. Gould's *Grassroots Politics in India: A Century of Political Evolution in Faizabad District* (Delhi: Oxford and IBH Publishing

Company, 1994) argued that the complex cultural pluralism of India yielded a unique democratic polity, in which the centralized power at the top was counterbalanced by semi-autonomous political institutions at the grassroots level. Among the more wide-ranging recent contributions to this body of literature is the two-volume *Dominance and State Power in Modern India*, edited by Francine Frankel and M.S.A. Rao (Delhi: Oxford University Press, 1989 and 1990). These volumes examine the interaction, in several states, of state power with the social dominance of caste, class, and ethnicity. Also useful is Subrata K. Mitra, 'Caste and the Politics of Identity: Beyond the Orientalist Discourse' in his *Culture and Rationality: The Politics of Social Change in Post-colonial India* (New Delhi: Sage Publications, 1999).

Though much writing on Indian democracy has been preoccupied with its impact on a traditional society, the more formal facets of India's democracy, ranging from electoral politics to the party system and factionalism, have also been written about. Myron Weiner's early work on interest groups in Indian democracy, *The Politics of Scarcity: Public Pressure and Political Response in India* (Chicago: University of Chicago Press, 1962) and his *Party-Building in a New Nation: The Indian National Congress* (Chicago: University of Chicago Press, 1967) belong to this phase of writing on Indian politics, as does Stanley Kochanek, *The Congress Party of India: The Dynamics of One-Party Democracy* (Princeton: Princeton University Press, 1968). The most influential essay on the Indian political system in the years of Congress dominance is unarguably Rajni Kothari's 'The Congress "System" in India', *Asian Survey*, vol. 4, no. 2, 1964.

This was also the phase when explanations of Indian politics relied heavily on the category of 'faction'. Thus, in *Caste, Faction and Party in Indian Politics*, 2 volumes (Delhi: Chanakya Publications, 1984), Paul Brass attributed governmental instability to the absence of organization and party institutionalization which he saw as positively, rather than negatively, associated with high levels of political participation and mobilization. Inner party factionalism and leadership conflicts were, he argued, important in promoting instability and change in Indian politics. The second volume carried forward the argument through an analysis of class, caste, and party, in Uttar Pradesh (UP) (1972–84). David Hardiman's essay 'The Indian "Faction": A Political Theory Examined', in

Ranajit Guha (ed.), *Subaltern Studies I: Writings on South Asian History and Society* (Delhi: Oxford University Press, 1982) is a critical review of faction-based analysis.

Paul Brass, *Language, Religion and Politics in North India* (Cambridge: Cambridge University Press, 1974) was one of the earliest studies of the political mobilization of identity. This study of the Maithili movement in north Bihar, Muslim separatist politics in Uttar Pradesh and Bihar, and the politics of language and religion in Punjab, emphasized the symbolic aspects of group identity as well as the role of political elites in the construction of nationalist myths. More recently, some case studies of the state confronting democratic challenges in the form of identity conflicts in India have been brought together in Atul Kohli and Amrita Basu (eds), *Community Conflicts and the State in India* (Delhi: Oxford University Press, 1998); see especially Kohli's own paper 'Can Democracies Accommodate Ethnic Nationalism? The Rise and Decline of Self-Determination Movements in India'.

The standard account of ethnic conflict as transacted between the state and ethnic elites is sought to be corrected in accounts of how ethnic parties transact with social groups. Zoya Hasan's *Quest for Power: Oppositional Movements and Post-Congress Politics in Uttar Pradesh* (Delhi: Oxford University Press, 1998) documents the decline of the Congress in UP, and explores the tension between the politics of empowerment (with the increase in the political participation of formerly excluded groups) and the politics of difference (in the form of communal politics). Narendra Subramanian's *Ethnicity and Populist Mobilization: Political Parties, Citizens and Democracy in South India* (Delhi: Oxford University Press, 1999), a study of Dravidian politics, shows how the populist politics of Dravidian parties effectively contained the potential for violent ethnic conflict and actually helped to reinforce stability in a pluralist democracy.

Recent work on the party system marks a break with the earlier studies, which focused on one particular party (like the studies on the Congress party or the Bharatiya Janata Party), and attempt a more overarching view of the changed and changing party system in India. Kanchan Chandra's argument regarding the ethnification of the party system in her article 'Post-Congress Politics in Uttar Pradesh: The Ethnification of the Party System and its Consequences' in Ramashray Roy and Paul Wallace (eds), *Indian Politics and the 1998 Election: Regionalism, Hindutva and State Politics* (New Delhi: Sage Publications, 1999), is a case in point, as is her 'The Transformation of Ethnic Politics in India: The Decline of Congress and the Rise of the Bahujan Samaj Party in Hoshiarpur', in the *Journal of Asian Studies*, vol. 59, no. 1, February 2000, pp. 26–61. In *Democracy Without Associations: transformation of the Party System and Social Cleavages in India* (New Delhi: Vistaar Publications, 1999), Pradeep K. Chhibber emphasizes the role of the state and weak associational life to explain why political parties that draw support from particular caste and religious groups have come to dominate the electoral landscape in the 1990s, and why catch-all parties have declined.

The most authoritative work on the Bharatiya Janata Party (BJP) is Christophe Jaffrelot's *Hindu Nationalism and Indian Politics* (Delhi: Viking Books, 1996). Its early history is analysed in Bruce Graham's *Hindu Nationalism and Indian Politics: The Origins and Development of the Bharatiya Jana Sangh* (Cambridge: Cambridge University Press, 1993) which takes the story up to 1967. The ideology of Hindutva, and the cultural politics of the BJP's affiliate organizations are discussed in Tapan Basu *et al.*, *Khaki Shorts and Saffron Flags: A Critique of the Hindu Right* (Delhi: Orient Longman, 1993). The view that the BJP should not be seen as a national monolith, but as a party which is penetrated by the specific configurations of caste politics and factionalism in the states, is advanced in Thomas Blom Hansen and Christophe Jaffrelot (eds), *The BJP and the Compulsions of Politics in India* (Delhi: Oxford University Press, 1998). Of particular interest is Hansen's article in the same volume, 'The Ethics of Hindutva and the Spirit of Capitalism'. On communalism as ideology, see S. Gopal (ed.), *Anatomy of a Confrontation: The Ramjanmabhoomi–Babri Masjid Dispute* (Delhi: Penguin India, 1991), Gyanendra Pandey (ed.), *Hindus and Others: The Question of Identity in India* (Delhi: Viking, 1993), and a wide-ranging collection of essays in K.N. Panikkar (ed.), *The Concerned Indian's Guide to Communalism* (Delhi: Penguin, 1999).

There is surprisingly little scholarly writing on the darkest period in the history of Indian democracy, the Emergency. From a Marxist point of view, see Sudipta Kaviraj's 'Indira Gandhi and Indian Politics', in the *Economic and Political Weekly*, vol. 21, nos 38–9, 1986. Rajni Kothari has three essays on the Emergency in his *State Against Democracy: In Search of Humane Governance* (London: Aspect Publications Ltd., 1990). Among the few books on the subject are Henry C. Hart (ed.), *Indira Gandhi's India: A Political System Reappraised* (Boulder, Colorado: Westview Press, 1976), and David Selbourne's *An Eye to India: The Unmasking of a Tyranny* (Harmondsworth: Penguin Books, 1977). Myron Weiner's *India at the Polls: The Parliamentary Elections of 1977* (Washington, DC: American Enterprise Institute for Public Policy Research, 1978) tells the story of the election which brought the Emergency to an end, from the campaign to the formation of a new government. In a somewhat different genre is P.N. Dhar's revealing 'insider' account, *Indira Gandhi, the 'Emergency' and Indian Democracy* (Delhi: Oxford University Press, 2000).

The writings on elections have been of broadly three types: compendia of data; survey research; and thematic case studies. Of the first type, which are excellent sources of primary data on elections, David Butler, Ashok Lahiri and Prannoy Roy, *India Decides: Elections 1952–1995* (Delhi: Books and Things, 1995) contains not merely constituency-wise and state-wise Lok Sabha results, but also provides state census data and a comprehensive introductory section on vote–seat relationships, political parties, and psephology. Another useful compilation of data on the Lok Sabha elections, with the all-India picture, as well as state and constituency level results, is V.B. Singh and Shankar Bose, *Elections in India: Data Handbook on Lok Sabha Elections 1952–85* (Delhi: Sate Publications, 1986), followed by a second volume covering the period 1986–91 (New Delhi: Sage Publications, 1994). V.B. Singh and Shankar Bose have also edited the five-volume *State Elections in India: Data Handbook on Vidhan Sabha Elections 1952–85* (Delhi: Sage Publications, 1987–8).

One of the earliest election studies based on survey research was Samuel J. Eldersveld and Bashiruddin Ahmed's *Citizens and Politics: Mass Political Behaviour in India* (Chicago: University of Chicago Press, 1978) which surveyed over two thousand citizens in the 1967 general elections, to explore themes like party identification and political involvement, and their consequences for the party system, social conflict, and policy decisions. More recent survey research is reported in Subrata Mitra and V.B. Singh, *Democracy and Social Change in India: A Cross-Sectional Analysis of the National Electorate* (New Delhi: Sage Publications, 1999). Based upon the post-poll National Election Study 1996, conducted by the Centre for the Study of Developing Societies, this book presents empirical findings on a variety of themes: from a cohort analysis of the electorate to economic policy and regionalism. For an interpretation of state elections, see Yogendra Yadav's article 'Reconfiguration in Indian Politics: State Assembly Elections 1993–1995', in *Economic and Political Weekly,* vol. 31, nos 2 and 3, 13–20 January 1996, reproduced in Partha Chatterjee (ed.), *State and Politics in India* (Delhi: Oxford University Press, 1997). The same issue of the *Economic and Political Weekly* also has a number of articles on individual states. Yogendra Yadav's 'Understanding the Second Democratic Upsurge: Trends of Bahujan Participation in Electoral Politics in the 1990s', in Francine Frankel, Zoya Hasan, Rajeev Bhargava and Balveer Arora (eds), *Transforming India: Social and Political Dynamics of Democracy* (Delhi: Oxford University Press, 2000) carefully weighs the evidence (from survey data) to comprehend the new 'bahujan' upsurge in Indian democracy, and to question some of the received wisdom about political participation in Indian elections.

In the case study genre, one of the earliest, and most ambitious, election studies was contained in the volumes that emerged out of a Massachussetts Institute of Technology project studying elections between 1952 and 1972. Myron Weiner and John Osgood Field were the general editors of the five-volume *Electoral Politics in the Indian States* (Delhi: Manohar Publications, 1974–7) though the individual studies examining electoral politics in relation to women, tribals, communist politics, migration, agrarian modernization, ethnic cleavages, and much else, were authored by many well-known, mostly American, political scientists. More recent examples of the case study approach include the essays in Harold A. Gould and Sumit Ganguly (eds), *India Votes: Alliance Politics and Minority Governments in the Ninth and Tenth General Elections* (Boulder, Colorado: Westview Press, 1993). This volume deals with patterns of political mobilization in the 1989 elections, which was the first time after the Emergency that the Congress was voted out of power at the Centre, and the 1990 elections, held in the shadow of events which were to prove decisive in shaping recent Indian political history, including Mandal, the Mandir, and Dalit politics. Ramashray Roy and Paul Wallace (eds), *Indian Politics and the 1998 Election: Regionalism, Hindutva and State*

Politics (New Delhi: Sage Publications, 1999) examines, through a series of state-level case studies, three major strands in the parliamentary election of 1998, viz. Hindutva, the importance of regional parties, and the decision of the BJP to engage in nuclear tests within days of assuming power.

More recent works on India's democracy have assumed a broader focus. Many of these have also focused on the role of the state. Atul Kohli's book *The State and Poverty in India: The Politics of Reform* (Cambridge: Cambridge University Press, and Delhi: Orient Longman, 1987) explains the differences in the performance, on redistributive and welfare policies, of state governments in Uttar Pradesh, Karnataka, and West Bengal, by the nature of parties and political regimes. Kohli's *Democracy and Discontent: India's Growing Crisis of Governability* (Cambridge: Cambridge University Press, 1990) explains the problems of governability in terms of the overpoliticization encouraged by Indian democracy.

In their *In Pursuit of Lakshmi: The Political Economy of the Indian State* (Bombay: Orient Longman, 1987), Lloyd I. Rudolph and Susanne Hoeber Rudolph argued the centrality of the state as the determinant of India's political economy. The political economy of rural society is characterized by the pluralist politics of community and caste rather than class politics, and though rising levels of mobilization have weakened the capacity and autonomy of the state, they have nevertheless resulted in a more equitable distribution of economic benefits and political power, in turn enhancing the legitimacy of the state. This important book was discussed through a symposium of reviews in the *Journal of Commonwealth and Comparative Politics*, vol. 26, no. 3, November 1988.

Rajni Kothari's *State Against Democracy: In Search of Humane Governance* (Delhi: Ajanta Publications, 1990) brings together his writings on the Indian state, democracy, and authoritarianism. It contains his critique of the centralized state and associated structures of governance, as also his concern for the erosion of democratic norms in India. Kothari's *Politics and The People: In Search of a Humane India*, 2 volumes (Delhi: Ajanta Publications, 1989), a collection of his essays on Indian politics before and after the Emergency, documents the shift from his earlier 'functionalist' view of the Indian political system, and his later concerns about people's movements, human rights, ecology, ethnicity, and the interrogation of the dominant model of development.

There has been rather little reflection on the discourses of democracy. See, for instance, the wide-ranging essay by Sudipta Kaviraj, 'On State, Society and Discourse in India', in James Manor (ed.), *Rethinking Third World Politics* (London: Longman, 1991). Arguably the most elegant elaboration of how the democratic idea has taken hold of the political imagination is chapter 1 of Sunil Khilnani's *The Idea of India* (London: Hamish Hamilton, 1997).

Democracy and Civil Society

Among the earliest volumes to appear on social movements was M.S.A. Rao (ed.), *Social Movements in India* (Delhi: Manohar, 1978–9). The first volume dealt with the movements of peasants and backward classes, while the second focused on sectarian, tribal, and women's movements. Later, Ghanshyam Shah's *Social Movements in India: A Review of the Literature* (New Delhi: Sage Publications, 1990) surveyed the theoretical literature on social movements and also that on particular types of movements, such as dalit, backward caste, tribal, and women's movements. M.S.A. Rao's *Social Movements and Social Transformation: A Study of Two Backward Class Movements in India* (Delhi: Macmillan, 1979) and Ghanshyam Shah's *Protest Movements in Two Indian States: A Study of the Gujarat and Bihar Movements* (Delhi: Ajanta Publications, 1977) belong to the period before the change in the vocabulary of studies of social movements.

Gail Omvedt's *Reinventing Revolution: New Social Movements and the Socialist Tradition in India* (New York: M.E. Sharpe, 1993) examines the women's, peasant's, tribal's, and environmental movements, to suggest that the conventional ways of looking at these movements in 'class' terms has to be rethought. This is because, though these groups are engaged in economic struggles, it is not class struggle in the narrow Marxist sense, provoking us to widen the analysis of relations of production and exploitation. Amrita Basu's *Two Faces of Protest: Contrasting Modes of Women's Activism in India* (Delhi: Oxford University Press, 1993) compares two forms of left-wing political activity in India through the lens of women's experience. This is a study in contrast of parliamentary communism under the leadership of the CPI(M) in West Bengal and the grassroots activism of the Shramik Sanghatana in Maharashtra. Leslie J. Calman's *Protest in Democratic India: Authority's Response to Challenge* Boulder, Colorado: Westview Press, 1985) argues that democratic government has failed to provide economic growth and political power for India's poor, and that the actions of government elites have contributed to the development of disequilibriums, providing fertile soil for the growth of these movements. She examines three movements of poor tribals—one revolutionary Naxalite movement in Andhra Pradesh, and two in Maharashtra which use the more traditional tactics of non-violent direct action.

Smitu Kothari's 'Social Movements and the Redefinition of Democracy' in Philip Oldenburg (ed.), *India Briefing 1993* (Boulder, Colorado: Westview Press, 1993) provides a synoptic view of social movements. Harsh Sethi's 'Micro-Struggles, NGOs and the State', in Manoranjan Mohanty, Partha Nath Mukherji and Olle Tornquist (eds), *People's Rights: Social Movements and the State in the Third World* (New Delhi: Sage Publications, 1998) reflects on a fairly neglected area in the literature, namely the role of non-governmental organizations (NGOs). T.V. Sathyamurthy (ed.), *Region, Religion, Caste, Gender and Culture in Contemporary India* (Delhi: Oxford University Press, 1996, the third volume in the series mentioned earlier) provides a fairly comprehensive coverage of many kinds of identity politics.

Jyotirindra Das Gupta's *Language Conflict and National Development: Group Politics and National Language Policy in India* (Berkeley: University of California Press, 1970) and D.L. Sheth's 'The Great Language Debate: Politics of Metropolitan versus Vernacular India' in Upendra Baxi and Bhikhu Parekh (eds), *Crisis and Change in Contemporary India* (New Delhi: Sage Publications, 1995) deal with language politics. The definitive—though pre-Mandal—work on 'compensatory discrimination' for the Scheduled Castes, Scheduled Tribes and Other Backward Classes is Marc Galanter's *Competing Equalities: Law and the Backward Classes in India* (Delhi: Oxford University Press, 1984). Also useful, as a backdrop to the later politics of reservations, are the essays by D.L. Sheth, 'Reservations Policy Revisited', in *Economic and Political Weekly*, vol. 22, no. 46, 1987, Myron Weiner's 'The Political Consequences of Preferential Policies', in his *The Indian Paradox: Essays in Indian Politics* (New Delhi: Sage Publications, 1989), and Subrata K. Mitra's 'The Perils of Promoting Equality: The Latent Significance of the Anti-Reservation Movement in India', in his *Culture and Rationality: The Politics of Social Change in Post-colonial India* (New Delhi: Sage Publications, 1999). The ideological and historical complexities of the *dalit* movement are discussed in Gail Omvedt's *Dalits and the Democratic Revolution: Dr Ambedkar and the Dalit Movement in Colonial India* (New Delhi: Sage Publications, 1994). Mushirul Hasan's *Legacy of a Divided Nation: India's Muslims since Independence* (Delhi: Oxford University Press, 1997) is a panoramic survey of Indian Muslims—mainly from Uttar Pradesh—from Partition to the demolition of the Babri Masjid in 1992. 'Ecological Conflicts and the Environmental Movement in India', by Madhav Gadgil and Ramachandra Guha in *Development and Change*, vol. 25, no. 1, January 1994, provides an excellent and fairly comprehensive introduction to environmental movements in India. Harsh Sethi's 'Survival and Democracy: Ecological Struggles in India', in Ponna Wignaraja (ed.), *New Social Movements in the South: Empowering the People* (New Delhi: Vistaar Publications, 1993), is a plea for level-headedness in classifying ecological struggles, not to be confused with conflicts which have ecological ramifications. While there is a vast literature on gender and politics, little of it engages directly with the idea of democracy. An unusually interesting essay is Wendy Singer, 'Women's Politics and Land Control in an Indian Election: Lasting Influences of the Freedom Movement in North Bihar', in Gould and Ganguly (eds), *India Votes* cited above.

Democracy and Development

Francine Frankel's *India's Political Economy 1947–1977: The Gradual Revolution* (Delhi: Oxford University Press, 1984) is the definitive work on the political economy of development in the first three decades of Indian independence. Frankel shows how accommodative politics, and especially the power of the propertied classes in India, inhibited the implementation of social and economic reform. Pranab Bardhan's *The Political Economy of Development in India* (Delhi: Oxford University Press, 1984)—the latest postscript to which is reproduced in this volume—also provides an account of the political and economic constraints on development in India. The impact of a democratic polity on the growth of the economy is discussed in terms of the conflicting pressures on the state for subsidies and patronage by the 'dominant proprietary classes' (the industrial capitalists, rich farmers, and the professionals).

Sudipta Kaviraj has two articles on democracy and development in the Indian context. The first, 'Dilemmas of Democratic Development in India', is in Adrian Leftwich (ed.), *Democracy and Development* (Cambridge: Polity Press, 1995), while the second, 'Democracy and Development in India', is in Amiya Kumar Bagchi (ed.), *Democracy and Development* (London: Macmillan/St. Martin's Press in association with the International Economic Association, 1995). This volume also includes a well-known paper by Adam Przeworski and Fernando Limongi called 'Political Regimes and Economic Growth', and some case studies of the workings of different political regimes around the world.

Partha Chatterjee, 'Development Planning and the Indian State', in T.J. Byres (ed.), *The State and Development Planning in India* (Delhi: Oxford University Press, 1994) and reproduced in Partha Chatterjee (ed.), *State and Politics in India* (Delhi: Oxford University Press, 1997), is a fine philosophical analysis of the politics and discourses of Indian planning. In the four-volume series, edited by T.V. Sathyamurthy, and titled *Social Change and Political Discourse in India: Structures of Power, Movements of Resistance* (Delhi: Oxford University Press) see vol. 2 (*Industry and Agriculture since Independence*, 1995) and vol. 4 (*Class Formation and Political Transformation in Post-colonial India*, 1996). These volumes provide a wide-ranging view of India's political economy in the early 1990s, that covers land reform, poverty reform, liberalization, regional imbalances in development, and movements of resistance in industry, agriculture, and the environment.

Shalendra D. Sharma, *Development and Democracy in India* (Boulder: Lynne Rienner Publishers, 1999) examines India's development strategy from the Nehru era to the present, with a concluding chapter comparing post-liberalization India with post-authoritarian Chile. Ashutosh Varshney, *Democracy, Development and the Countryside: Urban–Rural Struggles in India* (Cambridge: Cambridge University Press, 1995) analyses the costs to the economy of rural collective action on prices and subsidies. Some aspects of the relationship between democracy and development are also addressed in works such as John Echeverri-Gent, *The State and the Poor: Public Policy and Political Development in India and the United States* (Berkeley: University of California Press, 1993), and Atul Kohli, *The State and Poverty in India: The Politics of Reform* (Delhi: Orient Longman, 1987). G.K. Lieten's *Development,*

Devolution and Democracy: Village Discourse in West Bengal (New Delhi: Sage Publications, 1996) examines the ability of *panchayats* to mediate between an interventionist state and the need for empowerment at the grassroots. Despite its title, the overriding theme in Sugata Bose and Ayesha Jalal (eds), *Nationalism, Democracy and Development: State and Politics in India* (Delhi: Oxford University Press, 1997) remains nationalism.

In a now well-known argument, Amartya Sen interprets development in terms of the enlargement of human capabilities, a wide-ranging theoretical elaboration of which is available in his *Development as Freedom* (Delhi: Oxford University Press, 2000). Jean Drèze and Amartya Sen, *India: Economic Development and Social Opportunity* (Delhi: Oxford University Press, 1995) assesses India's failure to eliminate basic human deprivation in these terms.

Democracy, Locality, and Region

State politics have acquired increasing importance relatively recently, which probably accounts for their absence from earlier scholarship. Two early volumes on state politics were Iqbal Narain (ed.), *State Politics in India* (Meerut: Meenakshi Prakashan, 1976), and Myron Weiner (ed.), *State Politics in India* (Princeton: Princeton University Press, 1968). More recently, essays in John R. Wood (ed.), *State Politics in Contemporary India: Crisis or Continuity?* (Boulder: Westview Press, 1984) focused on Uttar Pradesh, Bihar, Bengal, Kerala, Karnataka, Maharashtra, and Gujarat to discuss whether Indian democracy was in crisis, as a result of social and political change, the rise of previously disadvantaged groups in politics, and the changing nature of Centre–State relations. The volumes edited by Frankel and Rao argue forcefully for regional specificity in analysis, while those edited by Gould and Ganguly, and by Roy and Wallace, (all cited above), explore the regional dimension in the context of elections. A largely neglected area of state politics is addressed in James Manor's essay 'Chief Ministers and the Problem of Governability' in Philip Oldenburg (ed.), *India Briefing 1995* (Boulder, Colorado: Westview Press, 1995).

On local democracy, Anne Phillips 'Why does Local Democracy Matter' in Lawrence Pratchett and David Wilson (eds), *Local Democracy and Local Government* (London: Macmillan, 1996) is the best introduction to the theoretical aspects of the question. In the

Asian context, see the lucid Introduction to Abdul Aziz and David D. Arnold (eds), *Decentralised Governance in Asian Countries* (New Delhi: Sage Publications, 1996). George Matthew's *Panchayati Raj: From Legislation to Movement* (New Delhi: Concept, 1994) is a useful, though somewhat dated, survey of local democracy. On the experience of the new Panchayati Raj system, see George Matthew and Ramesh C. Nayak, 'Panchayats at Work: What it Means for the Oppressed', *Economic and Political Weekly,* vol. 30, no. 22, 3 June 1996. Kumud Sharma's 'Transformative Politics: Dimensions of Women's Participation in Panchayati Raj', in *The Indian Journal of Gender Studies,* vol. 5, no. 1, January–June 1998, is a good overview of women's participation in the panchayats.

Name Index

Subject Index